Reading the
Old Testament

An Introduction

by

Lawrence Boadt

PAULIST PRESS
New York, N.Y./Mahwah, N.J.

Book design by Theresa M. Sparacio.

The publisher gratefully acknowledges the use of selected excerpts from James B. Pritchard, ed., *Ancient Near Eastern Texts: Relating to the Old Testament,* 3rd edn. with Supplement. Copyright © 1969 by Princeton University Press.

Cover art and design by Gloria Claudia Ortiz.

Illustrations by Frank Sabatte, C.S.P.

Discussion Questions and Index prepared by Michael Kerrigan, C.S.P.

Copyright © 1984
The Missionary Society
of St. Paul the Apostle
in the State of New York

The Library of Congress has cataloged the first printing of this title as follows:

Boadt, Lawrence.
    Reading the Old Testament: an introduction/by Lawrence Boadt: [illustra-tions by Frank Sabatte; discussion questions and index prepared by Michael Kerrigan].—New York, N.Y.: Paulist Press, c1984.
    569 p., [1] p. of plates: ill., maps, plans; 23 cm.
    Bibliography: p. 554-560.
    Includes indexes.
    ISBN 0-8091-2631-1 (pbk.): $7.95

    1. Bible. O.T.—Introductions. I. Title.
BS1140.2.B63 1984   221.6'1—dc19   84-60723
                            AACR 2 MARC

Published by Paulist Press
997 Macarthur Boulevard
Mahwah, New Jersey 07430

Printed and bound in the
United States of America

*To the students of the
Washington Theological Union,
from whom I have learned
most of the questions and many
of the answers suggested in
the following pages*

OUTLINE OF
READING THE OLD TESTAMENT

4   CONTENTS

Chapter 1

INTRODUCING THE OLD TESTAMENT

What Is the Bible?

The English word "Bible" comes from the Greek *ta biblia* which means "The Books," a name well-chosen since the Bible is a collection of many individual works, and not the product of a single person. In the New Testament there are twenty-seven books, and in the Old Testament, either thirty-nine (in Protestant and Jewish editions) or forty-six (in Catholic editions). Year after year, the Bible remains the world's largest selling book, averaging thirty million copies a year—perhaps one hundred and fifty billion in all since Gutenberg invented the printing press in 1453 and made the Bible his first project. As best sellers go, the Bible would seem to have everything against it—it is a collection without a great deal of unity; its size is overwhelming (1,461 pages in one *New American Bible* edition, 2,045 pages in a *Jerusalem Bible*); the names and places are often strange and hard to pronounce; the ideas belong to a world that has long since passed away.

If the task of reading the Bible is so difficult, why should it be considered so worthwhile by so many? Over the centuries many reasons have been put forward to explain the value of Bible study. Some of these are: (1) it is a treasure chest of the wisdom and inspiration that guided the generations before us; (2) it contains some of the most profound insights into the meaning of human life; (3) it is the single most important source for our Western culture, especially the expressions and words we use; (4) it has had the most profound influence on modern religious thought; (5) it is the most complete history of the ancient past that we possess. It is all of these, but more as well. For millions of people around the world today, the

Bible is above all God's *revelation*. For Jews and Christians, and to a lesser extent Moslems, all or part of the Bible contains a source and record of God's self-communication to the world he created—and that alone makes it of absolute importance to their lives.

Divine Revelation

All religion in some fashion or another seeks to make known divine communication to humans. This "knowledge" can come through the discovery of God in nature or through actual divine words and decrees. The Old Testament knows both. Compare Psalm 104:24:

How your works are multiplied, O Lord;
    you have fashioned them all in wisdom.
The earth is full of your creatures.

and Psalm 119:129–130:

Wonderful are your decrees;
    therefore I guard them with all my life.
The revealing of your words gives light,
    giving the simple understanding.

The constant use of the second person, "*your* works ... *your* creatures ... *your* decrees," indicates how personal is the Old Testament idea of revelation. It is not primarily a body of truths, but God himself, who makes known his love for his people. This God, in Israel's tradition, made himself known in numerous ways, including in nature, but above all in certain "mighty acts" when he saved Israel as a people—in their exodus from Egypt, in the conquest of Palestine, in the selection of David as king, etc.—and in words, such as the covenant given on Mount Sinai with its Torah, or Law, which outlines the response and way of life to be followed. Each type of literature in the Old Testament witnesses these various ways of revelation in its own manner. Thus the Pentateuch contains the mighty deeds and the Law; the prophets stress the covenant and the Law; the Wisdom writings often add beautiful reflections on God's manifestation in nature.

This whole understanding of the communal faith lived and witnessed and passed on in different ways warns us at the start of our study never to read only one book of the Bible as though it contains the whole revelation. Each book must be read in the context of the whole collection of sacred writings, and be seen as part of an ever-growing faith. The *Decree on Revelation* of Vatican II sums up this understanding:

> To this people which he had acquired for himself, he so manifested himself through words and deeds as the one true and living God that Israel came to know by experience the ways of God with men (n. 11).

A STATEMENT ON BIBLICAL INTERPRETATION

The following represents a recognition of the importance of critical method for the study of the Bible by an official Church body.

What is the literal sense of a passage is not always as obvious in the speeches and writings of the ancient authors of the East as it is in our own times. For what they wished to express is not to be determined by the rules of grammar and philology alone, nor solely by the context. The interpreter must go back wholly in spirit to those remote centuries of the East and with the aid of history, archaeology, ethnology and other sciences, accurately determine what modes of writing the authors of that period would be likely to use, and in fact did use.

For the ancient peoples of the East, in order to express their ideas, did not always employ those forms or kinds of speech which we use today; but rather those used by the men of their time and centuries. What those exactly were, the commentator cannot determine, as it were, in advance, but only after a careful examination of the ancient literature of the East. The investigation carried out on this point during the past forty or fifty years with greater diligence and care than ever before, has more clearly shown what forms of expression were used in those far-off times, whether in poetic description or in the formulation of laws and rules of life or in recording the facts and events of history.

Pope Pius XII's Encyclical **Divino Afflante Spiritu**
on biblical studies, issued in 1943, paragraphs 35–36

To understand the Bible as God's revelation, we must not think of it merely as a book for people living two thousand years or more in the past. The Bible still speaks to modern people. When we read about the experience of Israel, we discern a living God who still speaks to us. By looking into their history, we can learn about the values of our own history and our goals. In the most important aspects of our lives, the discovery of who we are and what we believe in, the Bible offers a great wealth of insight, both negatively and positively. Negatively, it reveals what destroys and breaks up a people by showing the results of sin and unbelief. Positively, it offers a way of life based on discovering and obeying a loving God.

The Nature of the Old Testament

For Christians, this book of revelation contains both the Old and the New Testament, while for Jews it contains only the Old Testament. Since the New Testament proclaims the life and message of Jesus Christ as "good news" for all peoples, and sees in Jesus the continuation and fulfillment of the Old Testament hopes of a Savior and Messiah, it is faith in this Jesus that makes the crucial difference between Jews and Christians. Both share a conviction born from the Old Testament that God has revealed himself to his people Israel. Jews, however, do not see in Jesus a binding revelation from God. Christians do. It is customary in writing about the Bible to keep the difference between the two Testaments clear so that we do not mistake the meaning of faith in the one as the same as in the other.

Because this is an introduction only to the Old Testament, and aimed at Christian readers, its special task is to open up the riches and meaning of God's word found there. It must give Christians an appreciation of how much common faith they share with their Jewish neighbors. Above all, it must avoid confusing study of the New Testament with that of the Old, so that the reader may come to understand the Old Testament first on its own terms. Then and then only will the believing Christian have a faithful insight into the relationship of God's earliest revelation to Israel with the further revelation in Christ.

Thus it makes sense to begin the study of the Bible through the Old Testament. But we run the risk that for Christians it may appear only as a long-past and nearly dead history. To prevent this loss of a living sense of the Old Testament, it helps Christians to experience first-hand the biblical faith of modern Jews. Judaism is much more than a relic of biblical times, of course; it has had its own long development of faith through the centuries since the Old Testament was completed. But they are the first heirs of the Old Testament, and it not only gives them a keen sense of their religious and ethnic roots, but forms a guide to living for today. Christians, who are often woefully ignorant of the Jewish roots of their own Christian faith, and only vaguely aware of any Jewish practices, could gain some feeling for the Old Testament by attending a Friday night sabbath service at a local temple or synagogue. Seeing a Jewish community at worship will reveal the deep and inspiring faith which Judaism keeps alive today.

The Books of the Old Testament

There are forty-six books in the Old Testament, and such a large number requires some way of dividing them into groups for easier study and organization. Jewish tradition recognizes three divisions: "The Law, the Prophets and the Writings." From the initial letters of this threefold division in Hebrew (*Torah, Nebi'im, Ketubim*) an acronym, or abbreviation, is formed, written *TaNaK*, by which Jews often refer to the Scriptures. But when discussing the Bible with Christians, Jews frequently replace *Tanak* by the phrase "Hebrew Scriptures" to distinguish their canonical books from the New Testament. This triple division occurs at least as early as the prologue to the Book of Jesus ben Sirach (also called Ecclesiasticus) about 130 B.C. The Gospel of Matthew knows this usage when it refers to the Scriptures as the "Law and the Prophets" in Matthew 5:17 and 7:12. This simple division of Law and Prophets and Writings can be confusing, however, since the Jewish canon groups the Books of Joshua, Judges, Samuel and Kings with the "Prophets" even though they recount the historical deeds of the conquest of Palestine and the reign of Israel's kings.

For this reason, Christian Bibles have made four divisions by adding a category for the historical books separate from the prophets. This follows the usage of the ancient Greek translation of the Old Testament, the Septuagint—so called because of the legend that the Jewish colony living in Alexandria, Egypt needed a Greek translation of the Law and got it from seventy scholars who all worked completely alone yet produced seventy exactly identical translations. Its four divisions are (1) the Pentateuch (Greek for "five books"), (2) the Historical Books, (3) the Wisdom Writings, and (4) the Prophets.

The accompanying list of the Old Testament books illustrates the breakdown of each division. It is easy to note that the Pentateuch and the Jewish Torah both signify the same group—the first five books of the Bible, traditionally given by Moses himself and containing the revelation given on Mount Sinai after the exodus from Egypt. In Jewish understanding, these five books form the most sacred center of Scripture, with the Prophets and Writings only offering further commentary and reflection upon it. At this stage, too, it would be valuable to look at the contents page of the Bible that you use and become familiar with the order and names of each book of the Old Testament. Knowing where to find Isaiah and Deuteronomy removes half the barrier to reading them.

The Canon and Deutero-Canonical Books

Why are these forty-six books and not other ancient writings considered sacred? Churches call this the "canonical question" after the Hebrew word for a reed which was used as a measuring stick (*qaneh*). A canon includes the official writings "measured" by a church or religious group and recognized to contain divine revelation. The need for a canon naturally arises when so many writings have been handed on that deciding which are normative and essential and which are not becomes difficult. Setting up a canon gives a rule for acting and provides a fundamental source for knowing the faith. The canon becomes like the constitution of the nation—an expression of the basic principles by which a religious community understands itself.

For the Old Testament, the final decision as to which books make up the complete canon, and to which no further books may be added, came only slowly through a long period of time. Nor has it been an easy question to deal with, because Protestants, Jews and Catholics disagree on what should be included. The Jewish canon, later taken over by the Protestants, contains only thirty-nine books, all written in Hebrew or Aramaic languages, and all discussed and accepted by the rabbis, the Jewish religious leaders, in the first century A.D. or shortly after. On the other hand, for the Catholic Bible the canon contains forty-six books, seven beyond the thirty-nine in Hebrew. These forty-six books were first listed as the canon by local church councils in North Africa in the fourth century: at

THE CANON OF THE OLD TESTAMENT
(39 books in Hebrew/Protestant Bibles; 46 in Catholic Bibles)

PENTATEUCH: ("TORAH")	GENESIS EXODUS LEVITICUS NUMBERS DEUTERONOMY	
HISTORICAL BOOKS:		
"Deuteronomic History"	JOSHUA JUDGES 1 & 2 SAMUEL 1 & 2 KINGS	In Greek Bible = 1 & 2 Kings In Greek Bible = 3 & 4 Kings
"Chronicler's History"	1 & 2 CHRONICLES EZRA NEHEMIAH	In Greek Bible = "Paralipomenon"
	RUTH ESTHER LAMENTATIONS	
Apocrypha/ Deuterocanon*	JUDITH TOBIT BARUCH 1 & 2 MACCABEES	Only included in the Greek Septuagint and part of the Catholic Bible
WISDOM WRITINGS:	JOB PSALMS PROVERBS ECCLESIASTES SONG OF SONGS	 ="Qoheleth" ="Canticle of Canticles"
Apocrypha/ Deuterocanon*	ECCLESIASTICUS WISDOM OF SOLOMON	="Sirach" or "Jesus ben Sira"
PROPHETS:		
Major Prophets:	ISAIAH JEREMIAH EZEKIEL (DANIEL)	 In Hebrew, Daniel is not a prophet
Minor Prophets: ("The Twelve")	HOSEA NAHUM JOEL HABAKKUK AMOS ZEPHANIAH OBADIAH HAGGAI JONAH ZECHARIAH MICAH MALACHI	

*Books that are underlined are found only in Catholic Bibles

Hippo in 393, and at Carthage in 397 and 417 A.D. But they were not given solemn approval by the Church until the Council of Trent in April of 1546, although they had been accepted as binding in practice from the time of the fourth century decisions.

The difference of seven books between the two canons stems from the fact that the Greek translation of the Old Testament, the Septuagint, had more books in it than were generally accepted in Palestine by the Hebrew and Aramaic speaking Jews. These extra seven books, listed in the chart above in italics, are all written in Greek, although we know that at least one, Sirach, was originally in Hebrew. These works we call "deuterocanonical" (i.e., a "second canon" of inspired books besides the Hebrew ones) to indicate that the Jews do not accept them into the canon. But for Christians at the time of Christ and in the early Church, the common book of the Scriptures was not the Hebrew Bible at all but the Septuagint Greek Bible. It had much wider use in the Roman world because most Jews lived far from Palestine in Greek cities, and because most Christians were Greek-speaking Gentiles and not Jews at all. Thus the Greek Bible, although mostly a translation of the Hebrew books, had almost as exalted a status as the Hebrew itself did. Sometimes scholars even speak of an "Alexandrian canon" of forty-six books that was parallel and equivalent to the "Palestinian canon" of only thirty-nine books.

All seven of the deuterocanonical books, 1 and 2 Maccabees, Judith, Tobit, Baruch, Sirach and The Wisdom of Solomon, are known and referred to by authors in the New Testament, but then so are some other writings that did not become accepted as "Scripture" such as Enoch and The Assumption of Moses. We can at least say that the question of exactly how many books made up the canon of inspired Scriptures was still open at the end of the Old Testament period, and that, after a time, Jewish tradition went one way and Christian tradition another. It was not until the reformers in the sixteenth century demanded a return to the Hebrew canon that Christians fought over two distinct canons.

Protestant terminology has often referred to these seven books (and some additional passages in the Books of Daniel and Esther) as the apocrypha ("hidden" books). This sense should be avoided, however, since Catholics have long applied the term apocrypha not just to the disputed seven books, but also to works like Enoch and The Assumption of Moses and many others besides. Protestants ordinarily refer to such totally non-canonical books as the pseud-epigrapha, "false writings," because most were written claiming the name of some great religious hero of old, such as Moses or Enoch, as the author. Such confusion! In this book the term "deuterocanonical" will be used for those seven books in the Catholic canon which are not found in the Hebrew and Protestant canons, and "apocryphal" will be reserved for works which are not considered inspired in anybody's modern canon.

The Term "Old" Testament

Throughout this book we refer to the Old Testament rather than to *Tanak* or Hebrew Scriptures. The main reason is that for Christians this has been the traditional name used through the centuries, and in a beginning Introduction it would only confuse the reader to develop a new vocabulary. But there are other reasons why the phrase "Hebrew Scriptures" does not fully express the Catholic viewpoint. First of all, the deuterocanonical books are not written in Hebrew nor are they part of the accepted Bible of Protestants and Jews, yet they are an essential part of the Catholic Scriptures. Second, the idea of "Hebrew Scriptures" versus, presumably, "Greek" Scriptures suggests a strong division between them which is foreign to a Christian faith commitment to the *continuity* of both Testaments. "Testament" was the Latin word chosen to translate the biblical idea of "covenant." But, unfortunately, "testament" was also a word used in a person's will leaving his possessions and final words to his heirs, and so misses the living sense of a covenant as an agreement between two people or two parties. Because it is so tied to the idea of death and a final statement, "testament" makes the new covenant of Jesus seem even more "new" and different than it should.

Jewish people in particular express some fears about the Christian use of "old" in the Old Testament—and with good reason in the light of history. Many times, Christians, in the name of the Gospel of Jesus, have labeled the Jews as rejected by God and part of an old and replaced religious faith, as people who refused to accept Christ and therefore have no place or rights in the Kingdom of God which has now been taken from them and offered to the Gentiles instead. This is based on an over-zealous stretching of the New Testament itself, and in practice has led not to *Christian* actions, but to terrible injustice against Jews. This occurred throughout the Middle Ages, and even in our own time. Although Hitler was not Christian, many of his supporters were, and many kept silent during his genocide because of an anti-semitism based on a belief that it was willed by God. In light of all this, Christians must be very careful how they understand the Scriptures.

The term "Old Testament" cannot be used if we see it as a word that puts down the Jewish faith. But it becomes valuable when we realize that it roots all that we say about Christ in the proper and original soil of Israel's faith. Christians believe that God has spoken through Christ a new and a fuller word than the *Old Testament alone* contains. But this is so only because it adds a fuller dimension to the *primary word* that God had already spoken to Israel when he made them his people and his witnesses. Isaiah speaks of Immanuel as "God with us." God cannot be with us if he rejected or refused his own. Anti-semitism is ruled out for Christians who place their faith in Jesus, since he himself was only a Jew and never a Christian! He fulfilled the heart and essence of the Law and the prophets (Mt 5:17). We may believe that Christianity sees a larger role for the divine covenant, but it often does not see as deeply into parts of the mystery. Christians therefore need the spiritual insights of the Jewish faith. Vatican Council II's *Declaration on Non-Christian Religions* (n. 4) declares that we cannot forget that the Church "draws sustenance from the root of that good olive tree onto which have been grafted the wild olive branches of the Gentiles (Rom 11:17–24)." It is "Old Testament" in the wonderful sense of a parent to our new, young faith in Christ.

Brief Survey of the Total Picture of the Old Testament

(1) The Old Testament fittingly begins with the five books of the Pentateuch. Genesis describes a pre-history of God's call and preparation of a people in creation and the patriarchs. Exodus portrays the mighty deeds of the deliverance of Israel from Egypt and the giving of the covenant. Leviticus describes the obligations of that covenant, while Numbers adds more laws, and continues the story of Israel's time in the desert. Deuteronomy, written as a speech of Moses, serves to deepen and sum up the meaning of the covenant for Israel later on in her history.

(2) The Historical Books explore the living out of the covenant in the promised land of Palestine. Joshua describes its conquest, Judges the settlement and struggle for survival, 1 and 2 Samuel the growing need for, and coming of, its first kings in Saul and David. 1 and 2 Kings traces the history of religious fidelity in the kings that

followed David down to the end of the monarchy about 586 B.C. Since all six of these books have a style and message similar to Deuteronomy, they are known as the "Deuteronomic History." They teach one consistent lesson that points out Israel's infidelity to the covenant and warns of coming destruction. In Jewish tradition, these same six books are called "The Former Prophets," because they have a strong prophetic tone of moral judgment. Many of the lessons are put into the mouths of various prophets.

(3) After the destruction and exile of 586 B.C., 1 and 2 Chronicles again looked at Israel's history from the perspective of a priestly writer, and its account was carried forward to the end of the fifth century B.C. in the Books of Ezra and Nehemiah. This later period after the exile also saw many smaller works. Ruth tells the story of a faithful Israelite woman from the time of the Judges. Esther tells of a faithful Jewish queen in the Persian court of the fifth century. Judith relates how a heroine at the time of exile saved her people. Tobit describes a faithful Israelite from among the people exiled in 722 B.C. to Assyria. All of these are moralistic tales emphasizing the best qualities of Jewish piety, and were both edifying and entertaining. They helped to communicate a sense of Jewish pride after the exilic period. The original incidents may have been based on historical persons or deeds, but these were long forgotten or are past our ability to recover them. Thus they are best called "edifying tales."

Finally, the post-exilic period is brought to a close by the two Books of Maccabees which tell the story of the Jewish revolt for independence against the Greek government of Syria in 168 to 164 B.C. They contain excellent history, but also many edifying stories, especially 2 Maccabees, so that history and homily get mixed up.

(4) The next section, the Writings, contains many profound and beautiful examples of Israelite reflections on their faith. The Book of Psalms gives us the prayers and hymns of both personal and public worship. Job wrestles with the question of suffering and God's goodness. Proverbs, Qoheleth, Sirach and The Wisdom of Solomon offer the proverbial statements and insights of the wise men. The Song of Songs is a series of love poems treasured as an analogy of God's love for his bride Israel.

(5) The Prophetic Books are divided into two major parts by our modern Bibles: the major prophets and the minor prophets. The main reason for the division is size. The major prophets are all long books—Isaiah, Jeremiah, and Ezekiel. Daniel, in line with the Septuagint, is included here, but strictly speaking it belongs with the Writings as an inspirational work. It forms the first of a biblical type

A BRIEF HISTORY OF THE OLD TESTAMENT.

3000   Growth of Semitic civilization in Mesopotamia (Sumer, Akkad, Babylon, Assyria) and in Syria-Palestine (Mari, Ebla) provides the cultural backdrop for the beginning of biblical traditions.
↓
2000

1900   The Patriarchal Period (Genesis 12–50) in which migration of peoples and life of mixed nomadic and village settlement are the setting for the earliest traditions of God's revelation to Israel's ancestors as the "God of their Fathers." The later half of this period was spent by several of the tribes living in northern
↓
1300   Egypt.

1300   The Exodus and march to Canaan of the tribes in Egypt. The most likely time for Moses and the Exodus events is during the reign of pharaoh Ramesses II (1290–1235). The experience of God and the giving of the Covenant at Mt. Sinai was the central event in forming the idea of a "Chosen People" Israel and was the real beginning of the Twelve Tribes as one nation
↓
1250   (Exodus, Numbers, Joshua).

1250   The Period of the Judges. The invasion of Canaan by the tribes under Joshua did not lead to immediate conquest. It began a two hundred year period of fighting, internal upheavals, peaceful penetration and tribal alliances that gradually formed Israel into a
↓
1020   single nation (see Judges and 1 Samuel).

1020   The United Monarchy of David and Solomon was the high point of Israel's power and prestige as a nation. In just one hundred years, they moved from a tribal federation to an empire with its own highly developed culture. This led to tensions between the values of the tribal past and the secular ambitions of the new
↓
930   kings (see 2 Samuel and 1 Kings 1–12).

930   The Empire of David and Solomon splits into a northern kingdom (Israel) and a southern (Judah). The two areas develop different interpretations of Israel's past traditions that will both be reflected in later ideas in the Bible. The two also fight one another as well as
↓   the small states to the East: Damascus, Edom, Moab.

722 — The great Assyrian empire begins its rise in the East, and efforts to fight them off, leads northern Israel to total defeat and exile in 722/721 B.C. (1 Kings 13–2 Kings 17).

722 – 586 — Judah survives as the only independent part of Israel. It is a period of submission to Assyria's power. Some kings resist (Hezekiah and Josiah), others give in totally (Manasseh). Eventually, despite religious reform under Josiah (640–609), Judah's kings resist the new Babylonian empire of Nebuchadnezzar, which overthrows Assyrian rule, and Judah is destroyed in two invasions in 598 and 587 (2 Kings 18–25, Jeremiah).

585 – 539 — A period of exile in Babylon for all the leading people of Judah. It is ended with the victory of the Persian king Cyrus the Great who allows the Jews to return home.

539 – 332 — The Post-exilic period. Judah remains a very small state of the lands immediately around Jerusalem and no longer has any independence but is ruled by Persian governors and guided religiously by the High Priests of the Temple. Ezra (458–390) and Nehemiah (445–420) begin the religious reform that leads to the canonization of the Scriptures and the religious practices much like those of modern Judaism.

332 – 175 — Alexander the Great conquers the Near East and begins the hellenistic period of Greek culture and rule. The Jews still have no independence but are governed first by the Greeks in Egypt (Ptolemies) and then by the Greeks in Syria (Seleucids).

175 – 1 B.C. — The Maccabees fight for independence and win a limited freedom for Judah in the period from 175 to 63 B.C. Much infighting takes place among the Jewish groups themselves and leads to the rise of the major Jewish factions of the First Century: Pharisees, Sadducees, and Essenes. Pompey, the Roman General, enters the area in 63 and establishes Roman rule. Eventually, the Romans give power to a local ruler, Herod the Great, who controls Palestine for the Romans down to the birth of Christ.

of *apocalyptic* literature, with which we may be familiar from the Book of Revelation (or Apocalypse) found at the end of the New Testament. The minor prophets are called "The Twelve" in the Jewish canon, probably because they were all copied down, one after another, on the same scroll in order to save space. These prophets range from Amos, the first prophet in the eighth century, down to Joel and Malachi in the fifth century or even the fourth century B.C.

This then is the Old Testament. It spans a great sweep of time from perhaps 2000 B.C. down to the century before Christ. It tells the story of one people and their relationship to their God. If this book were a movie, it would make a Cecil B. DeMille epic drama. But in noting this large span of time, we must beware of thinking that the books in the Old Testament are arranged in chronological order from the beginning down to the end. They are not. Written at many different times, they are found mixed throughout the Bible. Because of this, we will consider them as part of Israel's history as a people so that we can grasp their development. This is as it should be. For to read the Old Testament through from cover to cover would soon tire us and we would lose its direction and be put off by its lack of logical order. The Old Testament is a great storehouse of experience, but we must become familiar with each book and each prophet as an individual so that we can choose to read one or another section as we have need, or as our own mood demands at the proper moments of our lives. No part is useless or worth passing over altogether—if we wish to know Israel, or the roots of modern Judaism, or even the New Testament. A book like Leviticus often seems boring to a Christian because much of its material is no longer observed. Yet we will never understand in what ways a Christian differs from a Jew, or why Paul's letters make such sharp statements about the Law, unless we have tried to appreciate the teaching of Leviticus by a sympathetic reading.

In short, we must seek out each book of the Old Testament for its own time, and then we must create some kind of order in our minds so that the picture of a people who lived and changed their ideas emerges for us. We need to identify and understand the central *moments* of Israel's faith so that we can tell religiously vital points from merely popular ideas about science and the workings of nature that are not essential to God's revelation. These can be, and often have been, discarded for newer and better ways of expression within the Old Testament itself.

In order to proceed to the study of individual books of the Old

Testament, we need to know some background of Israel, the land they lived in, and the people and places they knew. Chapter Two thus provides a summary of the ancient world that was Israel's stage in history. But first a word should be said on *how* to go about reading and studying the biblical text.

How To Use This Textbook

An Introduction to the Old Testament cannot substitute for reading the Bible itself. It helps the readers identify the background and setting in which to place their own personal study of the biblical text. It also points to the major questions and problems to be faced. And hopefully it stimulates an excitement and interest in the Bible which will carry the students to undertake further investigation and reading by themselves.

For these reasons, each chapter of this Introduction includes a suggested number of passages in the Old Testament that should be read to get the most out of the subject of the chapter. These readings are found at the beginning of the chapter, and include both the Old Testament books that will be treated in the chapter, and a few suggested passages which highlight the main points discussed. At the end of each chapter, some discussion questions are proposed to help the reader focus on the significant ideas and to probe deeper into the meaning of the ideas in that chapter. Finally, at the end of the book there is a list of books and audio-visual aids which will prove helpful to further study or to supplement the textbook.

Because the main point is to help people to begin reading the Bible itself, the choice of a translation can be a most important starting point. At the present time, many good translations are available in English (as well as in French, German or Spanish for those who prefer another language). Almost all maintain high standards of accuracy in the choice of words and proper meaning, but differ a great deal in the style of writing they use. Some like the *Revised Standard Version* try to be serious and yet very literal in their translation. Others, like the *New English Bible*, write in a much more literary and much less literal manner. The *New American Bible* attempts to capture the spirit of the ordinary language used in the United States today. The *Good News Bible* keeps to a very simple level of vocabulary and yet maintains an easy reading style so that even the poor reader can enjoy the Scriptures. The

Jerusalem Bible achieves a lively and almost poetic flair. The choice of Bible text should be made on the grounds of which translation gets *you* to read more of the Bible and understand it better.

The best course of action for anyone who seriously reads the Bible for study or prayer is to have more than one translation and vary them when we read, for passages we know well often leap out at us afresh when we see them in a different translation. The only texts I do not recommend are ones that paraphrase the Bible itself rather than letting you face the text. These are such school Bibles as *The Way* or *The Reader's Digest Bible*. They serve a useful purpose among younger schoolage readers, but they leave out important parts, especially the difficult ones. This prevents the serious reader from facing the less interesting passages and more difficult problems in the Old Testament and coming to grips with how and why they too are part of biblical revelation.

Finally, the way to read the Old Testament is meditatively and prayerfully. We should take the time to think about the message. We should also be prepared to look into things we don't understand or can't picture in our minds. For this, the notes and diagrams in a good commentary on the books of the Bible will be very useful. In the bibliography at the back of this volume, several series of commentaries on the individual books of the Old Testament are mentioned. Just as helpful are maps. A good atlas of the Bible, or even constant reference to maps placed at the back of some ordinary Bibles, can give us an easy way of following many of the descriptions, journeys, battles, and place-names that fill the biblical books.

STUDY QUESTIONS

1. What does the term "Bible" mean?
2. What are some reasons one may give to justify the value of studying the Bible?
3. Explain "Divine Revelation". How did God make Himself known to Israel?
4. Explain how one should read and make use of the Bible.
5. What is the primary difference between the Jewish and Christian understanding of the Old Testament?
6. How many books are contained in the Old Testament? What are the main divisions according to the Jewish tradition? Why do Christian Bibles have a different division?

7. Define the following terms: Canon, Septuagint, Deuterocanonical, Apocrypha, Pseudepigrapha, Testament.

8. Historically, Jews, Protestants, and Catholics disagree on the number of books which comprise the complete canon of the Old Testament. Explain why this occurred.

9. How should one use and understand the term "Old Testament"?

10. Give a brief overview of the Old Testament; discuss the principal divisions, books, history, and composition.

Chapter 2

THE PEOPLE AND LANDS
OF THE OLD TESTAMENT

A. THE IMPORTANCE OF "HISTORY" AND "GEOGRAPHY"

The Study of History

Although the Old Testament continues to speak to millions of people in our own time, we cannot fully understand its message unless we are able to understand the people of the ancient world. Nobody thinks or writes without being part of a culture that has its own ideas and ways of doing things. To be heard, or at least listened to, a speaker must use words that everyone recognizes; otherwise the listeners will be bored or confused. Good speakers and writers always address today's scene in a lively and up-to-date manner. No modern religious leader could speak the English that Chaucer wrote in his *Canterbury Tales:* "Now preye I to hem alle that herkne this lital tretis or rede, that if ther be any thing in it that lyketh hem ..." Shakespeare was a great dramatist, but as every student knows, he is more than difficult to translate into everyday language. In the same way, when we read the Old Testament, we cannot forget that each and every phrase was originally written for a "modern" audience two or three thousand years ago. In most respects those people lived, worked, and thought much differently than we do. They had none of our scientific knowledge, they traveled little or not at all, they rarely met a foreigner, they had no hint at all of the coming of Christ, and most never read or wrote a word in their whole lives.

It is a period of time that stretches back as far before Christ as we live after him. Imagine Cicero or St. Peter transported to the modern world. Not only their clothes would be different! So, too, the world of Abraham was far different from the world of the prophet Jeremiah a thousand years later, or from that of Jesus ben Sirach, the wisdom writer, some five hundred years still further down the line.

An honest effort to understand ancient ways of thinking will give us a fresh sense of the personality and the times of the people we study—the wise and careful Abraham, the shrewd and plotting King David, the fiery prophet Amos. It will also help us to sort out what is important and lasting in the message of the Bible and what is just part of the social customs and habits of a given moment in history.

Reading the Old Testament becomes an adventure, an exciting story of a people who were sometimes even a fairly important nation, but always a real people. They lived long ago, dealt with nations and powers now long gone, and in general went about things much differently than we do. This is history, but it is also a detective story that traces the ups and downs of one people from only a few clues; and it is a jigsaw puzzle, in which bits and pieces from geography, old objects of stone and metal, broken tablets of writing, and those few complete books that we call the Bible must all be fitted together.

Organizing Ancient Times

In reading about the Old Testament as history, with so many names and places and dates, some order of time is essential. We must be willing to pay attention to dates, especially the big ones, or else what we read becomes a jumble of facts with little or no connection among them.

Scholars usually divide ancient history into three major periods that get their names from the type of tools used: the Stone Age, the Bronze Age, and the Iron Age. Early man first discovered that stones can be sharpened into crude tools and weapons. By chipping and flaking one stone against another, these ancestors developed some very fine and specialized instruments before the discovery of how to smelt copper into bronze made the stone axe or knife as rare as a horse-drawn buggy on a modern superhighway. The Stone Age lasted from pre-historic times down to the period about 3500 B.C.

The Bronze Age which followed lasted until about 1200-1100 B.C. when metal-workers learned to forge and produce the much better and harder metal iron in usable amounts. Iron dominated from 1200 on, but we normally don't refer to events as part of the Iron Age after the rise of the great empires in the Near East. Dates are more accurately pinpointed as part of the "Assyrian" or "Persian" or "Greek" period, etc.

Strictly speaking, Old Testament history lies only in the later part of the Bronze Age and the Iron Age. But many of the Ancient Near East's most important ideas and cultural patterns were already being set in the last centuries of the Stone Age as the human family moved from a nomadic and hunting life-style to settled town and agricultural life. As far as present knowledge goes, this change first took root in the very area of the "Bible lands," stretching from the Mediterranean seacoast of Palestine and Turkey eastward to modern Iran. This was a profound change—and its effect forced people together and to learn how to cooperate with one another. It was the beginning of civilization, and it took place in the period between about 9000 B.C. and the beginning of the Bronze Age about 3500 B.C.

MAJOR ARCHAEOLOGICAL TIME PERIODS IN THE ANCIENT NEAR EAST

100,000 to 12,000 B.C.	Paleolithic (Old Stone Age)
12,000 to 7,500 B.C.	Mesolithic (Middle Stone Age)
7,500 to 4,000 B.C.	Neolithic (New Stone Age)
4,000 to 3,150 B.C.	Chalcolithic (Copper-Stone period)
3,150 to 2,200 B.C.	Early Bronze Age
2,200 to 1,550 B.C.	Middle Bronze Age
1,550 to 1,200 B.C.	Late Bronze Age
1,200 to 586 B.C.	Iron Age
586 to 332 B.C.	Persian Period
332 to 37 B.C.	Hellenistic Period
37 to 324 A.D.	Roman Period

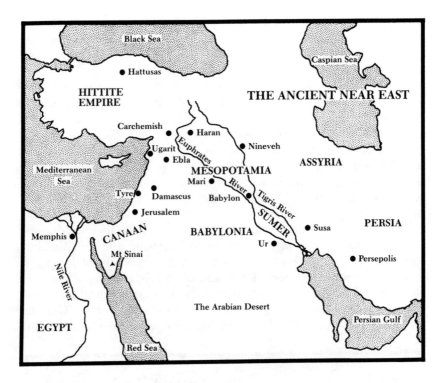

The map shows THE ANCIENT NEAR EAST with the following labels: Black Sea, Caspian Sea, Hattusas, HITTITE EMPIRE, Carchemish, Haran, Nineveh, Ugarit, Euphrates, Ebla, ASSYRIA, Mediterranean Sea, MESOPOTAMIA, Mari, River, Tyre, Damascus, Babylon, Tigris River, SUMER, Jerusalem, BABYLONIA, Susa, PERSIA, Memphis, CANAAN, Ur, Persepolis, Mt Sinai, The Arabian Desert, Persian Gulf, Nile River, EGYPT, Red Sea.

The Extent of the Ancient Near East

When we speak of the Ancient Near East, we limit ourselves to a certain area whose inhabitants shared much the same culture and kept up political and economic ties with one another. Yet many languages were spoken, many different ethnic groups lived as neighbors, and many hatreds and rivalries existed among them. Our task will be to distinguish the common from the different so we can make sense out of the whole.

First, in extent, the term "Ancient Near East" covers more territory than our modern terms "Near East" or "Middle East." It always includes the country of Egypt, all of Palestine and Syria along the eastern coast of the Mediterranean Sea, Mesopotamia between the Tigris and Euphrates Rivers in modern day Iraq, Persia (the modern state of Iran), and Turkey, which was the homeland of a number of peoples and states. By right it should also include all of Arabia, even though little mention was made of it in the Old

Testament, and we cannot exclude totally the tribes and peoples who frequently raided or moved down into the Near East from the lands still farther north in southern Russia. A developing civilization along the Indus River in northern India, which had much in common with the world of the Ancient Near East, also flourished in the early period before 1500 B.C. and traded with the West, especially in spices and herbs.

Different ethnic groups often lived side by side. The largest number belonged to what we call the Semitic family, a classification based mostly on the type of language they spoke. These Semitic peoples were the Akkadians (Babylonians and Assyrians), Arabs, Arameans, Canaanites, Moabites, Edomites, Ammonites, and Hebrews. Other people were not Semitic. The earliest city-state rulers in the Near East, the Sumerians, are of a language family quite distinct from any known today, while Hurrians and Hittites and Persians are all related to the Indo-European family of language from which our own Greek, Latin and Germanic tongues come. It is possible to locate some groups mostly in one geographical territory, e.g., the Sumerians in lower Mesopotamia near the Persian Gulf, or the Hittites in the high plateau of Anatolia of modern Turkey. But

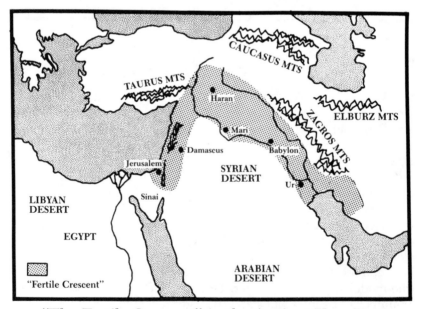

"The Fertile Crescent" in the Ancient Near East

many ethnic groups were forced to move by war or need for better land, and others were nomadic and did not settle down in any one place for long. Thus we find Hittites mentioned in the Bible living in Palestine, as well as Hurrians from the most northern part of Mesopotamia.

These groups spoke many types of languages: Egyptian differed from Indo-European, which differed from Sumerian, which differed from Semitic. And within each major language division were many smaller groupings. For Old Testament study, the most important family is Semitic, because the language of the Old Testament is mostly Hebrew with only a little Aramaic in the Books of Ezra and Daniel, and Greek in the six deuterocanonical books. Hebrew was closely related to the language of the Canaanites who lived in Palestine and Syria. All three areas were part of the Northwest Semitic language family. Tablets found in the Syrian ruins of Ebla, in the Palestine coastal city of Ugarit and in Israel itself have proved to be as close together as Spanish and Portuguese and Italian are. As for Israel's small neighbors, Edom, Moab and Ammon, their languages are not much more than dialects of Hebrew.

Geography of the Near East

Just as the people differ, so do the lands they live in. Egypt and Mesopotamia, home of the first great civilizations, were both river valleys. Between them lay mostly desert in Syria and Arabia. To the north and east high mountain ranges divided one nation from another. Deserts could also serve as barriers. Egypt felt secure through most of its history from outside forces because of the African deserts which surrounded it on all sides. Above all, fertile land for farming was at a premium. Because so much of the Near East was desert, population was concentrated in a wide arc of agricultural land that extended from the Nile river valley in Egypt, up along the sea coast of Palestine, across northern Syria, and then down the great river system of Mesopotamia to the Persian Gulf. Frequently this is called the "fertile crescent" because of its shape. But besides this important belt of workable farm land, mountain areas, especially in Turkey and Iran, often had small pockets, and sometimes even extensive valleys, that were good for agriculture. However, the rich fields and villages of the fertile crescent constantly attracted wild mountain tribes to invade and try to capture some of the land for themselves.

The Geography of Palestine

The natural geography of Palestine divides the land into a series of long, north-south zones with very few easy means of getting across the country from west to east. The four major zones are:

1. The *coastal plain* with sandy or marshy soil that stretches from a narrow belt in the north to broad areas in the south.

2. The *hill country* or *shephelah*, a series of low hills and valleys up from the coastal plain, often good for sheep-herding and orchards, and well-settled in ancient times.

3. The *central mountain range* which runs like a spine down the eastern part of the country, often reaching two thousand feet in height and sparsely settled in early times. Jerusalem sits on this range.

4. The *Jordan Valley* which is the lowest area on earth and stretches down the whole eastern border. It is broken twice by water: the *Lake of Galilee* in the north (684 feet below sea level) and the *Dead Sea* in the middle (1,290 feet below sea level). The two lakes are connected by the *Jordan River*, which takes two hundred miles to go the sixty miles between them as it wanders in loops. Below the Dead Sea, no river flows, but the valley continues for another one hundred and eighty-five miles to the Red Sea. This section is called the Arabah.

These north-south zones are broken only by the *Esdraelon Valley* stretching across the middle of the country just above Mount Carmel. It is the most fertile farming area and was heavily populated at all times. *Mount Carmel* itself sticks out into the Mediterranean, breaking the easy journey up the coastal plain and forcing people to pass through near Megiddo. This narrow pass became the center of many battles for the land of Palestine and has become popularly known in English as *Armageddon*.

The land can also be divided by four major regions that stretch across its length from east to west. These are:

1. *Galilee* is a mountainous region north of the Esdraelon Valley which goes up to the high mountains of Lebanon.

2. *Samaria* is the middle of the country, and its hilly nature is bordered on the north by the Esdraelon Valley. It formed the heart of the northern kingdom after the time of Solomon.

3. *Judah* is a mixture of the high mountains and dry, wilderness area to the east, but on its west it is the country of the rolling hills and wide plains that produced much of the fruits and vegetables of the land.

4. *The Negev* is a desert area stretching across the whole southern part of the land and making up more than half of the total area of Palestine. It gradually becomes the Sinai desert dividing Palestine from Egypt. Few settlements were made in the Negev.

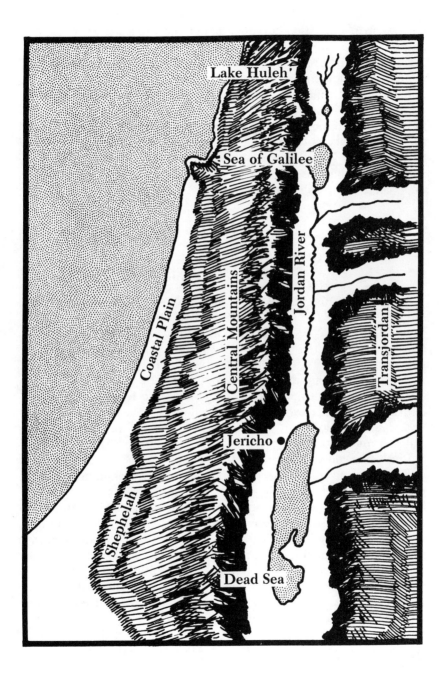

Lake Huleh'

Sea of Galilee

Coastal Plain

Central Mountains

Jordan River

Transjordan

Jericho

Shephelah

Dead Sea

Palestine itself had little natural protection since it was only a narrow strip of settled territory along the seacoast. It formed a natural highway for merchants, visitors, pilgrims, and invaders moving between the great city-states in Mesopotamia and Egypt. Being mountainous for the most part, it could support only a modest population which could not hope to compete with the massive numbers that could be summoned from Egypt to Mesopotamia. Being an international crossroads probably led directly, however, to the high literary culture found in the Old Testament. Biblical authors seem to have known well the beliefs and writings of other nations, but they also produced a quality of writing and thought unequaled in the ancient world.

B. EGYPT

"The Gift of the Nile"

Egypt's history is the story of the Nile and the desert. The Greek historian Herodotus, in the fifth century B.C., called Egypt "the gift of the Nile." Rainfall was almost unknown, and all life revolved around the waters of the river. It provided drink and irrigation, a highway of communication for its towns, and a cheap means of transportation for goods and trade.

In ancient times, as they still do today, the Egyptians lived on and farmed a narrow band of land along the last thousand mile stretch of the Nile River, which flowed northward for four thousand miles from central Africa to the Mediterranean. The ribbon of cultivated green is never more than twelve miles across except for its last hundred miles when it widens into a lush delta area nearly one hundred and sixty miles wide. Vast sand deserts surround this little sliver of life, and beyond the river valley only a few oases exist to support any settled population. In this harsh and seemingly hostile world, one of the greatest of ancient civilizations arose, prospered, and maintained its way of life almost unbroken for twenty-five hundred years, from 3000 B.C. until 500 B.C. Each fall the river, swollen by melting snow from Kenya, rose rapidly over its banks and flooded the soil with a new layer of silt and fertility for another year. The rhythm of the river divided the year into two parts, the growing season when the people worked the fields, and the waiting season, while the land was flooded. In this latter period, most of the farmers were idle, and the pharaohs would use them for their massive building projects. Everything depended on the river; in fact, it was so central to their thinking that Egyptians regularly described northern countries which depended on rainstorms as "lands watered by a Nile that flows in the sky."

But the desert too was important. It sealed Egypt off from all around her. It created a great sense of self-importance and contentment that often led Egyptian scribes to bemoan the poor foreigners who were not blessed by being Egyptian. High desert ridges formed parallel walls along the Nile valley, and so Egyptians thought in terms of north and south more than of east and west. It also brought home the difference between those who lived in the wide and more open Delta area, and those who lived along the narrow banks up the river. From the beginning, Egypt was the "Two Lands," Upper and Lower Egypt. Around 3000 B.C., a king of Upper Egypt, Menes, conquered the Delta people, and joined Lower and Upper Egypt into one nation. But from that time on, the pharaohs always used two titles, wore two separate crowns, governed two regions.

Although African in race, Egyptians were Semitic in outlook, directed more to the rich lands of Lebanon and Palestine for trade and new ideas than to their southern neighbors. Ships and caravans regularly journeyed between the Delta and Asia Minor, bringing wood, horses, dyed wool and other elegant clothes to Egypt and carrying back ivory, paper, finished chariots and other woodwork.

Two Thousand Years of History

Egyptian history from 3000 B.C. down to the time of King David of Israel, about 1000 B.C., is traditionally divided into three major periods, which are called the Old Kingdom (2800–2200 B.C.), the Middle Kingdom (2000–1750 B.C.), and the New Kingdom (1550–1150 B.C.). Between each of these was a period of chaos. From 2200 down to 2000 B.C., rival regions fought for power among themselves; from 1750 to 1550, foreign invaders from Asia, the Hyksos, dominated the country.

Since the time of Manetho, a Greek writer of the third century B.C., the history of Egypt has been divided into thirty dynasties, although there is a lot of confusion in this system, and its accuracy is not very high for many periods. But it provides a convenient framework to outline the most important events in Egyptian history.

Dynasties 1–2 last from 3000 to 2800 and represent the period when the state was developing its unique system in which the pharaoh was a god-man and owned all the land.

Dynasties 3–6 last from 2800 to about 2200, and make up the Old Kingdom, an age of great prosperity and peace. It is the time of the great pyramids, built as monuments to the cult of the dead pharaoh. The artwork fills the museums of the world with serene and confident statues of scribes, administrators, princes and their families, all aware of their importance, poised and optimistic about life. It was the golden age of Egyptian life.

Dynasties 7–9 are almost unknown and fall in the time of the First Intermediate Period when the unrest and breakdown of central leadership led to a discovery of pessimism which left a mark on Egyptian character from that moment on. Never again would Egypt completely recover the confident air of the Old Kingdom.

Dynasties 10–12 cover the years 2000 to 1750 B.C. and represent the Middle Kingdom, when the rulers of Thebes, a city far up the Nile, managed to gain power over the country and established a new period of peace and wealth. It extended its power to the south into Sudan and set up a major sea trade with the Phoenician cities in Asia Minor.

Dynasties 13–17 mark the Second Intermediate Period, when Asiatic tribes and peoples moved down into the Delta and part of the Nile Valley, and overthrew the Egyptian princes. Called in Egyptian the Hyksos ("Foreign Kings"), these Semitic conquerors held all the rival Egyptian princes in check for one hundred and fifty years or more, until a new dynasty in Thebes slowly gained power and drove them back in battle after battle.

Dynasty 18. The founder of the 18th dynasty, Ahmose I, reunited Egypt as a single nation again about 1550. Under a series of brilliant kings, this dynasty pushed Egyptian borders deep into the Near East, and controlled all of Palestine, Lebanon and most of Syria. It set up naval bases along the coasts of Asia, put armed garrisons and Egyptian governors in important fort cities, and made regular marches of the full army through the territory to "show the colors." Because of the excellent communications set up across the Sinai desert, the pharaohs were able to control the Asiatic states for at least one hundred and fifty years. The greatest of the 18th dynasty pharaohs was Thutmoses III (1490–1436); under his rule Egypt reached the greatest power it had ever attained. This was despite the fact that he had to contend with an older relative, Hatshepsut, who usurped the title of king for eighteen years

(1486–1468)—even though she was a woman! It was also the dynasty of Amenhotep IV, the "heretic king," who began a radical reform of religion in 1378 B.C. by attempting to replace the hundreds of Egyptian gods with a single deity, worshiped as the sun-disc visible in the sky, the "Aton." He even changed his name to Akhenaton, "The Beloved of Aton," and devoted all his energies to internal problems at home, including setting up a new capital city at El Amarna. The Asiatic empire began to slip away, and the people's reaction to the new faith was violent in rejection. His young nephew and successor, Tutankhamen, only a boy king, was forced to restore the old faith.

Dynasty 19 rose to power about the year 1300 under Sethi I and Ramesses II, two dynamic kings. They reasserted Egypt's power in Asia Minor and set up a new capital city right on the border of the Sinai desert in the Delta area to be nearer their armies in the field. Most scholars identify this move as the background to Exodus 1, in which Israel is reduced to slavery and forced to labor on the building of this new Delta fortress. Thus it has become widely accepted that Sethi I was the pharaoh who enslaved Israel, and Ramesses II was the pharaoh during the actual Exodus.

20th Dynasty and beyond stretched from 1200 B.C. down to the Greek conquest of Egypt under Alexander the Great about 330 B.C. After the thirteenth century, Egypt declined rapidly in power and barely had enough energy to repulse the massive invasions of the "Sea Peoples," groups of Indo-European race who were migrating down through Turkey, Greece and the Mediterranean islands of Crete and Cyprus. Most of the ones who failed to conquer Egypt finally settled along the coast of Palestine and became known as Philistines. These attacks would have begun about the middle of the twelfth century while Ramesses III was the pharaoh.

From the year 1000 down to the end of the biblical period, an occasional pharaoh managed to get enough power to lead an army against Palestine. But most often the best they could do was raid and take booty. None were able to hold onto an empire there. Sheshonq is mentioned in 1 Kings 14 as conducting such a raid about 930 B.C., shortly after the death of King Solomon. Piankhi, an Ethiopian who had seized the Egyptian throne, tried to fight the Assyrians in 700 B.C., and Necho tried to stop the Babylonian armies in 609 and 605 and 601 B.C. None were successful. Assyria attacked and ruled in Egypt for a few years after 663 B.C., and the Persians swept over Egypt and made it a province in 525 B.C., while the Greek armies of Alexander conquered the land in 332

B.C., and Alexander named himself the pharaoh. In Roman times, Egypt became the major agricultural and cultural center of the eastern part of the empire.

C. A SURVEY OF THE SEMITIC PEOPLES

Sumer

The beginning of the Bronze Age about 3500 B.C. also saw the rise of the first great civilization in the world when the Sumerians suddenly appear in lower Mesopotamia on the marshes and fields between the Tigris and Euphrates Rivers. Their origins are unknown, but many of their traditions lead us to believe they came from the north, possibly from the mountain country of Iran. They built cities and began large irrigation projects to drain the southern swamps and to channel river water to the dry but workable fields that stretch across the plains of Mesopotamia. Important centers of power and religion developed in the cities of Eridu, Uruk, Nippur and Ur. The need for large work forces to keep the irrigation system going led to more and more social organization. As the towns grew, so did the tools of civilization. The Sumerians invented writing about 3200 B.C. as well as an advanced mathematics based on a system founded on the number 6 (rather than on 10 as we now use). They seemed to have developed the cart wheel and its counterpart, the potter's wheel, as well as the first systematic law books, the idea of collections of proverbs and wisdom sayings, and formal schools. Thousands of Sumerian tablets with writing on them have been found in ruined cities, and many contain stories of great value, including religious myths and historical epics about legendary heroes. From clues scattered in such writings, it appears that the Sumerians originally governed their city-states by an assembly of free citizens drawn from different classes: elders, nobles, priests, etc. There were also slaves, usually prisoners of war. As the city-state, which included a large town and all its surrounding farmland and villages, became greater and more powerful in the period from 3000 B.C. to 2400, the local assembly gave way to the idea of divinely-appointed kings who ruled as the god's regent or deputy. No doubt this shift was made necessary by the constant warfare between cities which required strong leaders.

Above all their other accomplishments, however, it is the quality of their art that still stands out fresh and alive today. The beauty

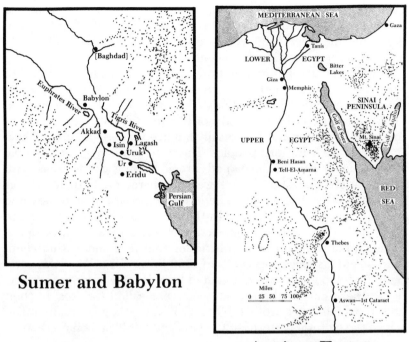

Sumer and Babylon

Ancient Egypt

and careful work of their metalwork in gold and silver can still be seen in the wonderful collection of Sumerian objects gathered in the British Museum from the royal tombs at Ur, dating to the twenty-seventh or twenty-sixth century B.C. These treasures have been reproduced in numerous art books for the student of the ancient world, and are well worth searching for.

The Akkadians

The Sumerian civilization was established in the midst of an older population of Semitic peoples who dwelt not only in Mesopotamia but also farther westward into Arabia, Syria and Palestine. About 2400 B.C., Sargon of Akkad became the first great Semitic ruler to break the power of Sumer. Akkad was a town in the middle of Mesopotamia, and from there Sargon and his grandson built an empire that extended westward even into Syria. Except for its Semitic language, the Akkadian empire owed most of its cultural ideas to the Sumerians before them. For a brief period from 2050 to

1950 B.C. the Sumerians did regain leadership under the rulers of the city of Ur, but otherwise the Semitic people controlled Mesopotamia for the next 1800 years—until Cyrus the Great of Persia created his empire in the sixth century B.C.

After the fall of Sumerian power and the short-lived empire of Sargon from Akkad, northern and southern Mesopotamia gradually developed in different directions. The southern half, usually called "Babylonia" after the chief city of the region, Babylon, remained the cultural center and universally admired model of true civilization for all Near Eastern peoples. The northern half, called Assyria, after its chief power, developed strong trading connections with other nations and also a more warlike character. Both territories were settled by closely related Semitic peoples and shared the same language and general culture. In the long years between 2000 and 1000 B.C., Assyria never reached the status of a world empire, although Babylon had two centuries of greatness under King Hammurabi and his successors (1750 to 1550 B.C.). For most of this early period, Mesopotamia was dominated by a dynasty of kings from the far southern part of the region, who were called Kassites. In their empire which lasted from 1500 to 1150 B.C., they generally maintained the cultural patterns of Babylon and left little behind them in the way of new contributions.

In the first millennium, at least from 1000 to 500 B.C., the two nations of Babylon and Assyria had quite different histories.

Babylon

Although Babylon had reached world power under Hammurabi, it did not again achieve true independence until the reign of King Nabopolassar and his son Nebuchadnezzar from 625 to 562 B.C. But as the seat of the Sumerian and Akkadian heritage, it was always looked to and revered for its art, literature and science. The Babylonian language was used all over the Near East as the common diplomatic language between nations. Even Egypt's pharaoh used it to write the cities of Palestine! Copies of its literary masterpieces such as the Gilgamesh epic have been found not only in Egypt and Palestine but even in the Hittite capital of Hattusas in northern Turkey.

Besides the undenied influence of Babylonian literature in the stories of Genesis 1–11, most of the biblical references to Babylon center on the period from 700 to 540 B.C. A Babylonian leader,

Merodach Baladan, convinced King Hezekiah of Judah to support him in a revolt against the Assyrians in 721 and again in 704 B.C. This effort was unsuccessful and Judah paid the price of being besieged and ravaged by the armies of Sennacherib. But after 625, as Assyrian power fell, the Babylonians quickly took advantage of the situation and formed a new empire from the remnants of the Assyrian conquests. King Josiah gave his life trying to stop Egypt from assisting the Assyrians, and his hopes that Judah would find independence under Babylonia were dashed when Nebuchadnez-zar marched west and demanded tribute and subjection much as had the Assyrians before him. Judah's attempts to revolt in 597 and 586 led to the end of the Israelite kingship, the total destruction of Jerusalem, and the exile, which lasted from 586 until 539 when the Persian armies of Cyrus the Great defeated the Babylonians and made their old empire part of a new Persian one. Cyrus graciously allowed captured peoples, including the Jews, to return to their native homes.

Assyria

Assyria became a world power in the tenth century B.C. when it began to expand to the north and west and to form an empire based on a threefold policy of (1) deportation of peoples, (2) threats of brutal retaliation, and (3) a tightly-controlled province system for conquered lands. In the ninth century, two Assyrian kings, Asshur-nasirpal II (888–859) and his son Shalmaneser III (858–824), were able to extend their power over most of Syria and thus approach the borders of the northern kingdom of Israel. Both kings bragged of reaching the Mediterranean in their military campaigns, and Shal-maneser has left behind a monument, the famous "black obelisk," on which he pictured Jehu, the king of Israel from 842–815, bowing down and offering tribute as a vassal king.

From 800 to 750 B.C., Assyria was unable to maintain its hold on the Syrian states of Damascus, Hamath and Calno, due to inter-nal revolts and weak kings. But in 745, a new king, Tiglath-Pileser III, took the throne and began a reorganization of the empire and revitalized his army. In order to better hold conquered peoples in line, he introduced the policy of mass deportations of whole cities after they were taken. It became the standard Assyrian policy from that time on. Under a series of strong rulers, Assyria formed an empire that included as conquered provinces all of Babylon, Urartu to the north, Syria, and northern Israel, and, as subject states with their own kings, all of Lebanon, the Philistines, Judah and the small kingdoms across the Jordan of Edom, Moab and Ammon.

From Tiglath-Pileser in 745 down to the fall of Nineveh in 612 which ended Assyrian power forever, every ruler in Israel and Judah and every prophet was concerned with the question of Assyrian relations. Crucial moments include the rebellion of the northern kingdom and its total destruction by Shalmaneser V and Sargon II in 722 B.C., the invasion of Judah by Sennacherib in 701 B.C., and the revolt of Josiah in 628–622 B.C.

Assyrian documents record many events pertaining to the Bible, including mention of the Israelite kings Jehu, Omri, Ahab, Pekah and Hoshea, and of the Judean kings Hezekiah and Manasseh. Perhaps the most valuable and intriguing monument is the complete pictorial account of the taking of the Judean fortress city of Lachish from King Hezekiah by the Assyrian King Sennacherib in 701. It once adorned a public room in Nineveh and can be found today reconstructed in the British Museum in London.

The last great king of Assyria was Ashurbanipal (669–632), who left a large library of ancient literary works, many in Sumerian, which he had gathered to preserve Akkadian culture. After his death the empire quickly collapsed before the unrest of its conquered subjects and the rising power of Babylon to the south and of the fearsome Medes to the east. By 609, the Assyrian nation was no more, fallen to a coalition of Babylonians and Medes.

Syria

The history of ancient Syria has been largely unknown until recently. Sandwiched between Egypt and Mesopotamia, most scholars thought Syria had little original culture of its own. The discoveries at Ugarit in 1929, in which thousands of tablets from before 1200 B.C. were found, and from Ebla, a nearby city, from which nearly sixteen thousand tablets from 2400 B.C. or earlier have been found, have opened up to us a whole new view of the rich cultural achievements of the Western Semitic peoples. They were called Amorites in Babylonian and Assyrian tablets but little was known of their culture. Many of the epics and cultural patterns found in Mesopotamia may really have developed first in the Syrian states. Certainly the documents written in Ugaritic reveal a religious and social life that matches the picture painted by biblical books about the native Canaanites of Palestine. We are now certain that the religious ideas which the Israelites met when they entered Palestine were much closer to the thought of the peoples of Syria and Phoenicia (modern Lebanon) than they were to the thoughts and ideas of the Akkadian peoples in Mesopotamia.

Ugarit itself was a flourishing seaport and trading center. Perhaps its most important contribution to biblical study is the significant number of religious epics and rituals that reveal the religious ideas of the Canaanites in their own words. For the first time, we do not have to attempt to understand what Canaanite religion was all about by getting behind the strong and condemnatory attacks of the prophets. Ugarit was destroyed for good about 1200 by an invasion from the sea. In its last years it was a vassal state of the Hittite empire.

Aram represents a later group of Syrian city-states formed by the gradual consolidation and settlement of desert tribal groups in Syria after 1300 B.C. Assyrian armies battled against these tribes continually. In the ninth century Damascus became an important kingdom under Ben Hadad and Hazael. It was able to hold its own against Israel (see 1 Kgs 20–2Kgs 8), and was only kept from attacking Palestine successfully by the constant threat from the Assyrians behind them. The control of these Aramean states became the chief aim of Assyrian expansion under Tiglath-Pileser III in the eighth century.

Finally, the Phoenicians occupied the coastal cities of Byblos, Tyre, Sidon and Beirut. They created a remarkable cultural center, built on shipping. It gave a home to craftsmen and artists who blended the best of Egyptian, Greek and Mesopotamian arts in metal and ivory works. It developed a worldwide sea-trade in every kind of goods, and founded trading colonies as far west as Spain and Sardinia. They developed the alphabet, a major advance over the awkward cuneiform writing of the Babylonians which required hundreds of signs in order to read or write. Their simple system of vowels and consonants was borrowed by the Greeks about 1000 B.C. and thus came down to us today as the basis of our written language. The heyday of Phoenician culture and commercial success was in the tenth and ninth centuries. But it was still a power in commerce as late as the sixth century B.C., as we can discover in the prophet Ezekiel's dramatic condemnations of Tyre and Sidon found in Ezekiel 26–28.

The Philistines

The Philistines are first recorded in the land of Palestine (which was later named for them!) about the same time as Israel began its conquest—that is, around 1200 B.C. The Egyptians recorded attacks by a group called the "Sea Peoples" in the early twelfth century, and one of these groups had a name similar to the later Philistines. They represent a wave of invaders who were not Semitic but came through Greece, western Turkey, the island of Crete and on to Palestine. Their origins were in the area of southern Russia. Some tribes had already served as soldiers of fortune in the Egyptian army before the major waves of invasion began.

In Palestine, the Philistine invaders settled along the southern coastal area and formed a tight alliance of five city-states—Ekron, Ashdod, Ashkelon, Gaza and Gath. This happened about the time that Israelite tradition places the conquest of Joshua and Israel's fight under the judges for control of the mountain country. For a while they lived in peace, but near the end of the period of the judges, about 1050 B.C. or so, a major expansion of the Philistines into the hills where Israel had settled took place. Israel suffered several major defeats, including the loss of the ark of the covenant at the battle of Ebenezer. Philistine settlers moved into the major agricultural region of the Esdraelon Valley and into the hill country of Judah. The crisis caused by these attacks led to the call for a king over Israel at the time of Samuel. The story of Saul and David in the Books of 1 and 2 Samuel is closely tied up with the task of repelling the Philistines.

One reason for the success of such a relatively small group of people was their knowledge of iron-making. The use of iron for weapons was far superior to the soft copper spears and swords employed by the other Canaanite dwellers, and the "Sea Peoples" had brought this knowledge with them as a closely guarded secret. They had learned it from the Hittites of Turkey, who had first discovered how to work iron ore on a large scale in the fourteenth century. But gradually the knowledge spread even to Israel.

King David was able to make the Philistine cities his subjects, but after the death of Solomon in 930 B.C. they regained their independence and existed independently until the Assyrian invasions of the eighth century B.C., although they were never again strong enough to threaten Judah or Israel.

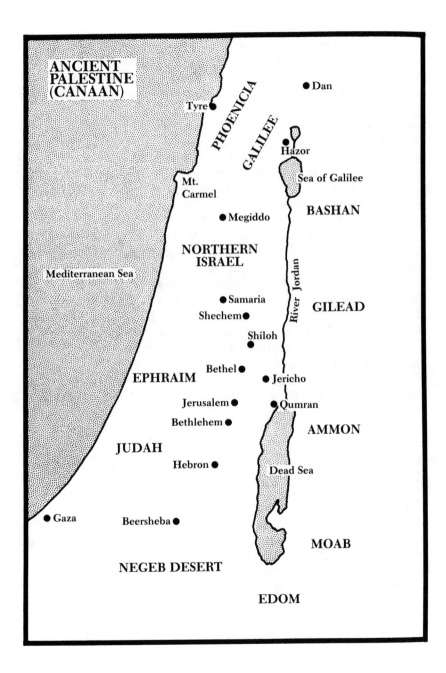

ANCIENT
PALESTINE
(CANAAN)

Dan

Tyre

PHOENICIA

GALILEE

Hazor

Sea of Galilee

Mt.
Carmel

Megiddo

BASHAN

NORTHERN
ISRAEL

Mediterranean Sea

River Jordan

Samaria

Shechem

GILEAD

Shiloh

EPHRAIM

Bethel

Jericho

Jerusalem

Qumran

Bethlehem

AMMON

JUDAH

Hebron

Dead Sea

Gaza

Beersheba

MOAB

NEGEB DESERT

EDOM

The Small States Across the Jordan

The Transjordanian area was not heavily settled in the second millennium B.C. Many nomadic groups wandered its area, and the Book of Deuteronomy in chapter 2 still preserved some memory of these early tribes. But about the same time as Israel's exodus from Egypt, new groups began to settle the east bank territory of the Jordan. We hear of the Amorite kingdoms of Sihon and Og which Israel destroyed in Numbers 21, as well as kingdoms of Edom, Moab and Ammon, which they carefully avoided.

Edom was settled by tribal groups closely related to the Arabs. The story of Jacob and Esau in the Bible makes Esau the father of Edom and thus identifies Edomites as blood-brothers with the Israelites. The territory of Edom stretches from the Dead Sea south along the valley that leads to the Red Sea, called the Arabah. Despite the traditional relationship between Esau and Jacob, conflict with Edom was continuous in the period of the kings. Saul, David, Solomon, Amaziah and Azariah all fought and dominated the Edomites, but several other passages suggest that often the tables were turned (cf. the prophecies of Obadiah, Jeremiah 49 and Ezekiel 35). Psalm 137 is so impassioned with hatred against the Edomites that we must assume that Israel and Edom considered themselves major enemies.

Moab lay north of Edom, across the Dead Sea up to the Arnon river valley. It was settled in the same period as Edom by a semitic nation who worshiped the god Chemosh. King David conquered it early in his reign and it was part of Solomon's empire. A hundred years later we know from the important find of a chronicle of its King Mesha, the so-called "Moabite Stone," that it was still being ruled by the kings of northern Israel. Mesha won freedom for Moab but the conflicts with the Israelite kingdoms continued. Moab regularly laid claim to the lands of Gilead and Heshbon north of the Arnon River, which were also traditionally the lands claimed by the Israelite tribes. Because of this and because of Israelite opposition to Moabite religious rites in honor of Chemosh, including child sacrifice (see an especially horrible example in 2 Kings 3:4–27), the prophets denounce Moab fiercely. See Isaiah 15 or Jeremiah 48 or Amos 2.

Ammon lay above Moab between the Arnon and the Jabbok Rivers on the far side of the Jordan. Its capital was Rabbat-Ammon, the same as present day Amman, the capital of modern Jordan. The

Ammonites, or, as they are more frequently called in the Old Testament, the "Sons of Ammon," were an Aramean tribe that settled the land in the twelfth century B.C., and, like their neighbors, had a long history of conflict with the Israelites across the Jordan River. Several well-known stories were remembered in the Bible about these wars. The Book of Judges tells how Ehud saved the tribes from the rule of Eglon, king of Moab and his Ammonite allies (Jgs 3:12–30). Saul routed the Ammonites in battle at Jabesh Gilead (1 Sam 11:1–11), and David nearly wiped out the country to avenge the mockery and humiliation the Ammonites showed toward his goodwill ambassadors (2 Sam 10 and 12). The Assyrians reduced Ammon, as well as Edom and Moab, to vassals, but when Judah was weakened under the Babylonian attacks of 598 B.C., Ammonites took advantage of the situation to raid Israelite territory.

D. DISTANT NON-SEMITIC NEIGHBORS

The Hittites

The Hittites were a non-Semitic people who built up an extensive empire in the area of Modern Turkey in the period from 1500 to 1200 B.C. Its capital was near modern Ankara, and named Hattusas (modern Boghazkale). The empire fell apart at the same period as Israel's judges flourished, possibly under pressure from invaders from the north, among whom would have been the same tribes known in Egypt and Palestine as the "Sea Peoples." Extensive remains of Hittite cities can still be visited in Turkey, and an extensive body of myths and religious writings have been found that bear very close resemblance to the ancient Greek myths of Zeus and the gods, suggesting that the Hittites were an Aryan, i.e., Indo-European, people like the Greeks. Because of their conquests in Syria and even once into Babylon (about 1550 B.C.), they borrowed heavily from the cultures of Mesopotamia and Canaan-Syria for art and religious epics. Several times the Bible notes the Hittites among the peoples of Canaan (Ex 3:8; 23:23; Jos 9:1). These were most likely small groups that had moved south as exiles when Hittite cities in northern Syria were conquered by Arameans or other invaders.

Persia

The modern nation of Iran, east of Mesopotamia, was the homeland of two powerful national groups, the Medes in the north and the Persians in the south. Evidence of a highly developed pottery art and metalwork date back well into the third millennium B.C., but the influence of these two nations was not felt by Israel until the time of the exile in the late sixth century. The Medes allied themselves with Babylon to overthrow the Assyrians from 614 to 609 B.C., but their power lasted only a brief time as they soon fell victim to the victory of their own subject king, Cyrus of Persia, about 550.

Cyrus not only went on to conquer Babylon but was able to create an empire stretching from India to the borders of Greece. Unlike the terror tactics used by Assyria and Babylon to control small states, he organized his empire into satrapies, or giant provinces, with local leaders sharing power with Persian officers. He followed a policy of letting each subject people follow their own customs and religion, but built an elaborate system of highways and communications to link the different regions to his three capitals at Susa, Persepolis and Ecbatana in Iran.

Persian religion was founded by Zoroaster, in the early sixth century B.C. It was a combination of the worship of a single deity, Ahura Mazda, and belief in a huge system of good and evil forces that affected human life. Many of the more important ideas of Zoroastrian faith influenced later beliefs. Mithra, the chief of the forces of good, became a favorite god in Roman paganism, and the ideas of heaven, hell, angels, a last judgment, and other Jewish-Christian doctrines were colored by similar descriptions in Persian thought.

The two centuries of Persian rule from 539 to 333 B.C. were a period of relative quiet and stability in the West, and thus left little impression in the Old Testament writings. In fact, the later years of Persian control from 450 to 330 B.C. are some of the least known years in biblical history!

Greece

Alexander the Great was able to gain control of the Greek cities about 336 B.C. and in three years put together an army with mobility, using the new phalanx technique, and created zeal enough to take on the vast armies of the Persian satrapies. In the short space of ten years, from 332–323, Alexander conquered the entire Persian kingdom up to the Ganges River in India. He settled colonies of Greeks throughout the Near East to begin the process of forcing Greek customs and values on the East. After his early death at the age of thirty-three in 323, his generals divided his empire and continued this process of Hellenizing the East. Later biblical writings show the deep inroads that Greek culture made in this period. By the second century B.C., Greek was the universal language between nations throughout the Near East, and no nation had escaped its influence in art, politics, religion and philosophy.

STUDY QUESTIONS

1. "History and geography are very important in reading and understanding any literary text." Prove or refute this statement by examples and illustrations.
2. What are the three major periods in ancient history? How do they relate to Old Testament history?
3. Define the following terms: "Ancient Near East", Semitic, Sumerians, "fertile crescent", "the Gift of the Nile", Hyksos, Philistines.
4. Describe some of the distinctive features of the geography of the Near East.
5. What are the three major divisions in Egyptian history? What years comprise each major division?
6. Give some major highlights and contributions of the Egyptian dynasties.
7. Describe some of the major accomplishments of the following Semitic civilizations: Sumer, Akkadians, Babylon, Assyria, Syria, Philistines, Edom, Moab, Ammon.
8. Identify the following: Hittites, Persia, Cyrus, satrapies, Zoroaster, Alexander the Great.

Chapter 3

ARCHAEOLOGY AND THE OLD TESTAMENT

What Is Archaeology?

The study of the Old Testament primarily means the study of the biblical books themselves as a religious heritage. Yet what we have written there is not enough to fully understand the historical situation of Israel. Besides knowing the Scriptures, we must familiarize ourselves to some extent with the world in which the Israelites lived, their neighboring peoples and common culture. When the nineteenth century began, our libraries contained little information on Babylon and Assyria beyond the references in the Bible and some descriptions in Herodotus, the Greek historian, and absolutely no one knew of the Sumerians at all. One hundred and fifty years later, our museums and universities bulge with artifacts, diagrams and scholarly studies about these peoples, and their storerooms are filled with tablets and literary works dug from the ruins of the ancient cities of the Near East. Most of this advance is due to the work of archaeologists and linguists, scholars who have sought the records of the past and deciphered them.

Archaeology literally means "the study of beginnings." As an organized and systematic science of humanity's past, it is relatively young, born of the curiosity of the last century. Western civilization has always been fascinated with the records of its own past, but much of what passed for knowledge, even in the Middle Ages, was mostly fanciful and legendary. This began to change dramatically in the fifteenth century Renaissance, with its rediscovery of the classical cultures of Greece and Rome, its serious investigation of languages, and its passionate search for ancient written sources. At the same time, wealthy patrons began collecting antique objects of interest and value. The eighteenth century Enlightenment accelerated the concern for history, and free-lance explorers began to comb the lands of Greece and Egypt for treasures to sell to princes and other sponsors.

Napoleon's invasion of Egypt in 1798 brought with it teams of scientists and linguists, and began a rage for Egyptian culture that led every great museum in Europe to gather vast collections of Egyptian statuary and monuments. At the same time, the discovery of the famous Rosetta Stone, with its text written in three languages—Greek, Demotic (a late form of Egyptian), and ancient hieroglyphics ("picture writing")—led the French scholar Jean-Francois Champollion to a major breakthrough in 1821: the deciphering of the ancient Egyptian hieroglyphic language by comparison to the Greek. The vast number of tombs and temples that dotted Egypt were covered with such hieroglyphic inscriptions, but had until then remained silent and unyielding. Soon, other adventuresome men, such as Paul Emile Botta of France and Henry Rawlinson of England, discovered the ancient cities of Assyria by digging into the great mounds that dotted the plains of Iraq. Finely carved reliefs of heroes, gods and battle scenes were brought back to London, Paris and Berlin and excited popular interest still further. The deciphering of the Babylonian cuneiform ("wedge-shaped") writing quickly followed the archaeological finds. European governments competed against one another to gain the right to dig the important sites in the Near East from the Turkish Ottoman Empire. Between 1890 and the beginning of the First World War in 1914, over twenty-five major expeditions were mounted by French, British, American and German teams.

The field of biblical archaeology was given life in 1871 by the electrifying announcement of George Smith, a young curator at the British Museum, that he had been able to read a Babylonian tablet on which he had found a flood story like that of Noah, but hundreds, perhaps a thousand, years older! The rush to explore the lands of the Bible was on. Every new object or tablet uncovered led to claims and counter-claims and often even wild new guesses about the background of biblical stories. The researchers into Babylonian culture were so sure that they had mastered ancient history that Franz Delitzsch, a German scholar, could announce in his little book *Babel und Bibel* (1904) that Near Eastern culture was now so well known that further study was unnecessary. Babylonian thought could explain most of the religious thought in the Bible, and scholars should now turn their attention elsewhere.

Naturally, as with all sweeping claims about the Bible, Delitzsch was far from the mark. Many of his own ideas and conclusions now appear ridiculously naive and oversimplified. Yet from this rash, headstrong period of youth, the discipline of archaeology has grown more mature through the years, refined its methods, and often changed its interpretations, and it still continues to provide new and important information for the study of the Bible in its ancient setting.

The Method of Archaeology

Archaeology as a science studies the physical remains of the human past. It examines the remains of walls, roads, pieces of pottery, artwork. It investigates plant seeds, animal bones and human skeletons (although each of these is now its own highly specialized field: paleobotany, paleontology, etc.). Above all, the archaeologist prizes the discovery of clay tablets and papyri rolls covered with writing, for these are the primary sources of what our ancestors thought, although, as writings become more numerous, the archaeologist yields to the historian for interpretation. Archaeology focuses on the *human* remains and especially the highly civilized and densely populated ruins of towns and cities where people lived over long periods and where the interaction of different groups can be studied more intensely.

To understand what archaeology can tell us, we must understand its method. To gain results, the archaeologist must know in advance where to dig, what to look for, what kind of excavation will yield the best information for this site. For ancient sites, in particular, the two most important aspects of method are stratigraphy and pottery typology, and so preparations must be made for their use. Much more effort will go into preparation and later analysis of finds than into digging time itself.

The archaeological team must first select the site for the "dig," as an expedition is popularly known. This may include large, easily visible monuments known to all, such as the pyramids of Egypt, or the famous temple of Baalbeck in Lebanon. Or it may be, as is more often the case, a large mound or hill that stands alone in a plain and shows signs of long habitation in the past from such telltale clues as broken pieces of pottery of different styles and ages, exposed walls,

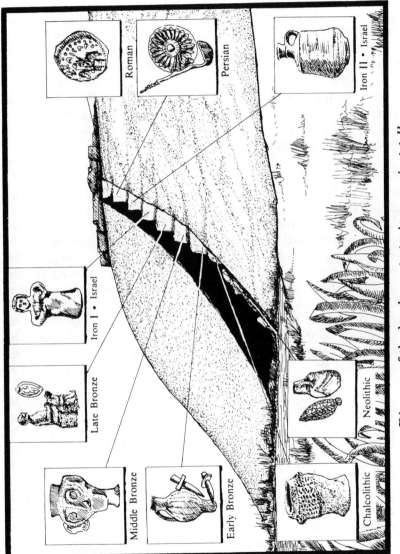

Roman

Persian

Iron II • Israel

Iron I • Israel

Late Bronze

Middle Bronze

Early Bronze

Neolithic

Chalcolithic

Diagram of the levels, or strata, in an ancient *tell*.

or other signs of settlement. Such mounds are known as "tells,"
from the Arabic (and Hebrew) word for a ruin. They are, in effect,
artificial mountains made up of the accumulated layers of mudbrick
and refuse left by successive levels of occupation. Usually picking an
important spring or ford in a river, the ancients built up a town of
mud bricks, which through rain and time and the destruction of war
decayed and had to be pushed down flat so new mud bricks could
be laid over the old layer. With each new rebuilding or resettle-
ment, the height of the town grew. Many biblical towns were
occupied for thousands of years and have left very high mounds.
The tell of Megiddo in Palestine, for example, stands seventy feet
high. Lachish, known in ancient documents for over two thousand
years, achieved a height of one hundred feet and covered eighteen
acres. Even the biblical authors recognized these tells as ancient
cities. The Book of Joshua records how the Israelites took the Canaanite town of Ai and destroyed it completely: "So Joshua burned
Ai, and made it into a tell, which it is to this day" (Jos 8:28).

Selecting which tell to dig at depends on numerous factors. A
reading of historical accounts in the Old Testament often gives the
excavator a clue that this is the probable location of some famous
town. Sometimes even the modern name of a town helps, such as
that of the Arabic village of el Jib, which led archaeologists to
suppose that its nearby tell was ancient Gibeon, mentioned in
Joshua 5–6. This educated guess was strikingly verified when the
excavations revealed a number of jar handles with "Gibeon"
stamped on them. Other factors may also play a decisive role in
choice of a dig: money available, a water supply close by for the
staff, ability to bring in heavy equipment, local living accommoda-
tions, climate and the like. Such considerations may make a team
decide against a particularly difficult, though otherwise promising,
tell.

Stratigraphy is the primary concern of the actual digging. It is
literally noting and mapping the strata, or levels, of civilization and
settlement on this particular mound. But this is no easy task. It
requires trained and patient eyes that can detect slight changes in
soil color or texture and recognize even fragmentary remains, slight
as they may be, of ancient plaster or packed mud flooring. It takes
skill to notice shapes in the dirt that outline where an ancient piece
of wood or cloth had lain and long since decayed, leaving only its
form, filled with dirt, to signal its presence. Stratigraphy works on
the conviction that each layer was deposited after the one below it,
so that as one digs down through a mound from top to bottom, he

reaches earlier and earlier levels of occupation. By comparing the remains of structures, wall designs, style of objects and pottery found at each level, a picture of the different customs and artifacts used by each group becomes possible over a period of time. If the levels are clearly marked off and recorded precisely, they can be compared with similar levels in other tells throughout Palestine and a comparative picture drawn for each similar level and time frame. Thus, if at the twelfth level down at Lachish we find a certain style of wall building and a distinctive type of pottery which are also known at the ninth level of Samaria, we may infer that these were probably contemporary cities, and that Lachish was subsequently rebuilt eleven more times, but Samaria only eight times.

Finding the exact date of such levels presents more problems. Style and similarities do not tell us when objects were used. More is needed. Sometimes, with luck, an inscription giving the name of a king who is well known may be found in a level, and for some sites we have outside information from ancient literature. This is the case for Samaria. The book of 1 Kings tells us how King Omri "bought the hill of Samaria from Shemer for two talents of silver, built on the hill, and called the name of the city he built by the name of Shemer . . ." (1 Kgs 16:24). We can pinpoint the date of Omri to about 875–870 B.C. and know that the bottom-most level of the mound likely represents this first town.

By crosschecking each and every site excavated, patterns emerge which can be charted for different centuries, and sometimes even down to separate decades, in the thousand years before Christ; these in turn aid in identifying levels found at new sites that are excavated.

The remains of living beings, bones or plant seeds or cloth, can be measured separately to find their age by checking the radioactive carbon that all living creatures accumulate, and which begins to decay when the creature dies. This method, called Carbon-14 Dating from the fact that it measures an unusually heavy carbon molecule of atomic weight 14, can date objects to within a general period. Since the test is repeated several times it gives a figure based on the average of all the samples of radioactive carbon 14 remaining in an object. These will vary somewhat, and the results are listed within a range on the scale. That is why a skeleton or piece of garment is listed for example at 3415 years old plus or minus 245 years. This means that the age of the sample probably falls within the range of 3660 down to 3170 years old. The older the object examined, the greater become the margins, so that carbon-14

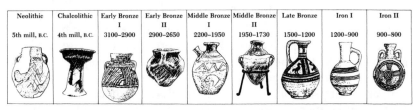

Neolithic	Chalcolithic	Early Bronze I	Early Bronze II	Middle Bronze I	Middle Bronze II	Late Bronze	Iron I	Iron II
5th mill., B.C.	4th mill., B.C.	3100–2900	2900–2650	2200–1950	1950–1730	1500–1200	1200–900	900–800

A "Pottery Clock" shows the approximate date of ancient pottery
finds by the changes in style and design from one period to the next.

dating is highly accurate only for objects not too old. And even at
best, the scientists will only claim that there is a 2 to 1 chance that
the dates fall within the listed margins. But in many cases, it has
proved a great help when no other criteria are available. However,
newer methods are being developed all the time. The use of argon
and potassium instead of carbon should improve accuracy greatly.

By far the best method for obtaining a sequence of dating styles
for ancient cities and cultures is through pottery typology. Pottery
was used by all ancient peoples for containers. Once the clay is
fired, it will not disintegrate and becomes virtually indestructible,
yet in the form of a pot it is extremely fragile. Best of all it is cheap,
so that when a pot cracks, the pieces may be discarded easily.
Around and on every ancient mound lie innumerable broken potsherds which leave a lasting record of settlement there.

Since Sir William Flinders Petrie first developed pottery typing
in the 1890's, both in Egypt and at Tell Hesi in Palestine, it has
gradually been perfected into the chief tool for identification of
periods within Near Eastern archaeology. An enormous body of
pottery shapes and styles has been gathered, catalogued and arranged in proper sequence from past excavations so that by now
archaeologists almost possess a complete "time-clock" of pottery
designs and materials that stretches from nearly 5000 B.C. until the
Islamic period after 600 A.D. A trained archaeologist who knows his
pottery "clock" can walk over the surface of a tell which has not yet
been dug, collect the loose *sherds* washed free by rain and time, and
give a reasonably accurate estimate of exactly the periods in ancient
history when this site had been occupied. This ability can often
prove crucial in the decision whether a mound is worth excavating
or not.

Because the archaeologist must evaluate coins, artwork, archi-
tectural remains, tablets and inscriptions, geological and botanical
information, pottery typology, and several other highly specialized

areas of expertise, the dig is never a one-man operation. The archaeologist who directs the dig must be himself an expert in the history and culture of the Ancient Near East, and must gather a team of specialists in the different fields needed. Identification of the site dug and interpretation of the finds requires the use of a whole range of modern scientific advances. Many times an even wider consultation becomes necessary, for sites often reveal objects or pottery imported from elsewhere, e.g., from Greece or Iran, each with its own pottery clock sequence.

Some Major Archaeological Excavations in Palestine

When the Palestine Exploration Fund in 1890 asked Sir Flinders Petrie to excavate the mound of Tell el Hesi in the Negev desert of Judah as its first Palestinian dig, many important explorations had already been made in the Near East. Emile Botta had found Nineveh and Khorsabad, Austen Henry Layard had uncovered the Assyrian city of Nimrud, Heinrich Schliemann had revealed both Mycenae and Troy, and Petrie himself had spent ten years digging at the great pyramids of Giza. And although off to a late start, archaeological interest in Palestine benefited far more than other areas from the connections to the Bible. Money and talent were available from religious organizations all over America and Europe, so that rapid progress has been made in the intervening ninety years.

Some of the most important sites that have been discovered in Israel include the following:

Arad. Known in the Bible as a Canaanite stronghold that prevented Moses from invading from the Sinai (Num 21:1–3), and finally taken by Joshua (Jos 12:14), Arad was a very large (twenty-five acres) Early Bronze Age city from about 3000 B.C. and an unusual Israelite fortress with a possible temple to Yahweh from the ninth century B.C. Most valuable for biblical studies has been the discovery of a number of ostraca (potsherds with writing in ink on them) with commercial and political accounts dating from about 700 B.C.

Gezer. One of the most important fortress cities of Judah, Gezer was continuously settled for over four thousand years, from about 3500 B.C. to 500 A.D. Held by the Canaanites, Philistines and Egyptians, it came into Solomon's possession in the tenth century B.C.

Hazor. Situated above the Sea of Galilee in the north, Hazor is the largest tell in Palestine, measuring one hundred and eighty-three acres. It was the capital of the northern coalition of Canaanites against Joshua (Jos 11:10), and became a royal fortress of Solomon's kingdom. With twenty-one levels of occupation, Hazor stretches from 2700 B.C. down to the Greek period.

Jericho. Made famous by the story of Joshua 2 in which the walls came tumbling down before Israel, this city near the Dead Sea has an even more important distinction: it is the oldest known town in the world with towers and walls dating to at least 7000 B.C. The general site has been continuously occupied ever since, two of its more famous visitors being Elijah (2 Kgs 2:4–5) and Jesus (Lk 19:1–9).

Jerusalem. According to 2 Samuel 5:6–10, David took Jerusalem from the Jebusites, a Canaanite tribe, and made it his capital. Already well known in Egyptian inscriptions a thousand years earlier, the city has had four thousand years of continuous occupation, and has been the scene of many archaeological digs, most notably the work in the 1970's on the temple mount and the Old City of David, called today the Ophel.

Lachish. After Jerusalem, Lachish was the second city in southern Palestine. It guarded the highway into the mountains from invasion by peoples along the coast. It was the scene of archaeological exploration from 1932–1938, in which many important ostraca were found that shed light on the invasion of King Nebuchadnezzar of Babylon in 598. More helpful still, it is the subject of a whole series of Assyrian reliefs from Nineveh showing Sennacherib's attack on Judah in 701 (2 Kgs 18–19), which are now on display in the British Museum in London.

Megiddo. Perhaps the most famous city in Palestine, Megiddo played a major role in all periods of Near Eastern history. It stood on its mound commanding the only major pass on the road between Egypt and Mesopotamia through Mount Carmel. 1 Kings 9:15f tells us it was one of Solomon's chariot cities, and it was here that King Josiah died in 609 B.C. trying to stop the Egyptian army. In Revelation 16:16, it becomes Armageddon, site of the final cosmic battle.

Samaria. Founded by King Omri of northern Israel in the first half of the ninth century B.C., Samaria was the capital of the northern kingdom until the Assyrians captured the land and destroyed the city in 722 B.C. After the return of the Israelites from captivity in 539 B.C., Samaria formed the capital of a separate Persian province, and a gradual religious split developed between

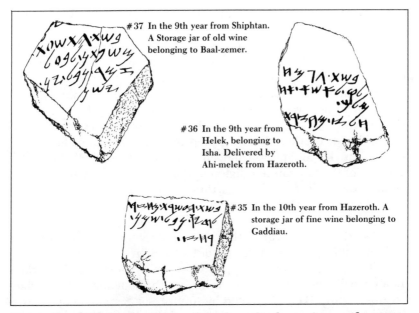

#37 In the 9th year from Shiphtan. A Storage jar of old wine belonging to Baal-zemer.

#36 In the 9th year from Helek, belonging to Isha. Delivered by Ahi-melek from Hazeroth.

#35 In the 10th year from Hazeroth. A storage jar of fine wine belonging to Gaddiau.

Examples of Hebrew writing found on broken pieces of pottery recovered from the ruins of the ancient capital city of Samaria. They are receipts for shipments of wine and can be dated to about 750 B.C.

Samaritans and Jews which was prominent in the time of the Gospel and lasts even until today.

Shechem. Shechem plays a major role in biblical history. It was a town prominently connected to stories of Abraham and Jacob in Genesis, became the place where Joshua had the covenant renewed in Joshua 24, and was well-settled during the Israelite period. Archaeological remains of its massive walls and gates indicate that Shechem may have had an even more glorious splendor in the Middle Bronze Age from 1900 to 1550 B.C.

Major Literary Finds in Syria

All archaeologists and historians dream of the excavation that uncovers a huge library from an ancient city. In the last century, the discovery of the library of Assurbanipal at Nineveh in Assyria, and a treasure of over twenty thousand tablets in Nippur in southern Iraq, opened up for historians the civilizations of Assyria and Sumeria. In our own century, we have been just as fortunate, with three major finds since 1929: Ugarit, Mari, and Ebla.

Ugarit is a coastal city in northern Syria just across the sea from the pointed tip of Cyprus. Here an important Canaanite city was destroyed about the year 1200 B.C. by invading Sea Peoples, and never rebuilt. Left buried in the debris was an entire library from the royal palace which has provided us with hundreds of texts in a dialect very close to ancient Hebrew. Many are economic and political texts of life at the time, and there is an invaluable body of religious myths and liturgical documents which provide a first-hand account of the Canaanite religion just at the moment that Israel was coming up against it a little farther south. What had been known only through Israel's prophets, who fought against its pagan practices tooth and nail, was now revealed in writings by its own believers. Discovered in 1929, the study of Ugaritic documents has become an important handmaid of Old Testament research.

Mari is located at the opposite end of Syria on the Euphrates River border with Iraq. Here a major city flourished in the eighteenth century B.C., populated by Amorites, a Semitic people closely related to the Canaanite culture of the West. In 1933, Andre Parrot excavated the palace of King Zimri Lim to find two hundred and fifty rooms and twenty thousand tablets, mostly bearing on political questions of the time. Already material from this library, written in Akkadian, the language of Mesopotamia, has thrown light on prophecy in the Bible, the nature of the Israelite tribes, and the movement of peoples westward.

Ebla, also called by its modern name Tell Mardikh, lies inland from Ugarit some fifty miles. Italian archaeologists began digging in 1964, and were able to identify the name of the city in 1968 from a piece of a statue with a twenty-six-line inscription which named the donor as a ruler of Ebla, a city well known from Sumerian and Akkadian records. A greater bonanza was struck in 1974, when part of a library was uncovered from a level dating to somewhere between 2500 and 2400 B.C. Since then, over sixteen thousand tablets and fragments have been unearthed, many written in ancient Sumerian, but some in the oldest form of Canaanite that has ever been found. This Canaanite dialect has been named "Eblaite" and shows a continuity from the third millennium to Ugaritic in the second millennium to Hebrew in the first. Before Ebla historical information about the peoples of Syria had been very sparse. Now, Syria will prove to be a whole new cultural link between the Akkadians of Mesopotamia and the Canaanites of the Mediterranean coastline.

MAJOR ARCHAEOLOGICAL FINDS OUTSIDE OF ISRAEL

Enuma Elish The Babylonian Creation Epic which records a great battle between the forces of Order and those of chaos among the gods and has many parallels to Genesis 1.

Gilgamesh Epic The Babylonian story of an ancient king, Gilgamesh, who sought immortality but failed to find it. In the process he hears the story of the great primeval flood from Utnapishtim, who built an ark and was saved by the gods. Many parallels are found between this story and Genesis 6–9, Noah and his Ark.

Hammurabi's Law Code The most famous and complete of ancient law codes was inscribed on a pillar by the great Babylonian king in the 18th century, B.C. The laws in Exodus 21 to 23 show very close parallels to Hammurabi.

Amarna Tablets From 1400 to 1375 B.C., the kings of the small city states of Palestine wrote letters to the pharaoh of Egypt asking help against the hapiru, who seemed to be raiders and lawless groups. These letters tell us much about the land just before the Hebrew Exodus and even the word Hebrew and hapiru may be related!

Merneptah Stele The first mention of Israel in any ancient text is found on an inscription of pharaoh Merneptah about 1225 B.C., claiming he wiped out "Israel" in his attack on Palestine during that year.

Sheshonq Inscription This pharaoh attacked and devastated both Israel and Judah in 918. The attack is recorded in 1 Kings 14:25–26 and by the pharaoh himself on the walls of the temple of Karnak in Thebes.

The Black Obelisk King Shalmaneser III of Assyria left a memorial column on which he pictures king Jehu of Israel (842–815) bowing down before him submitting to Assyrian rule. Jehu's career is recorded in 2 Kings 9–10, but this event is not mentioned in the biblical account.

Sennacherib's Prism 1 Kings 18–19 tells the story of how king Sennacherib of Assyria attacked Jerusalem and suddenly the city was spared by divine help after an oracle by Isaiah the prophet. Sennacherib himself left a detailed account of this battle which does not admit defeat but hints that he failed to take Jerusalem.

Above all, no longer will the Bible stand alone as a witness to life in Canaan. We now have both Ugaritic and Eblaite literature to help us understand the world of the Old Testament.

Major Non-Biblical Literary Finds in Palestine

Significant finds of inscriptions and literary works in Palestine proper have been far fewer than in the drier desert climates of Syria and Iraq. Most of the important objects with writing on them take the form of seals on pottery jars, rings, and tomb inscriptions. Apparently, clay tablets never were common in Palestine; far greater use was made of Egyptian papyrus which unfortunately decays rapidly in moist climates. But a few outstanding examples have come to light.

The Gezer Calendar. A seven-line exercise of a schoolboy, perhaps, this small tablet lists the months and seasons of the year in the tenth century B.C.:

Two months olive harvest, two months sowing,
two months late planting, one month hoeing,
one month grain harvest, one month festivals,
two months vine-tending, one month summer fruits.

The Moabite Stone. Carved for King Mesha of Moab to commemorate his war for freedom against the rule of the Israelite kings in the ninth century B.C., this stone reveals much about Moabite writing, the worship of its national god, Chemosh, and its relation to Israel. It names Omri as the Israelite king who subjugated the land before Mesha was able to free it:

Omri, king of Israel, humbled Moab many days for Chemosh
was angry at his land.... But Chemosh restored it in my
days.... And Chemosh said to me, "Go, take Nebo from
Israel," and I went by night and fought against it from
the break of dawn until noon, taking and slaying all,
seven thousand men, boys, women, girls, and even maid-
servants, for I had devoted them to destruction for the
god Ishtar-Chemosh....

The Samaria Ostraca. Dating from the later period of the northern kingdom of Israel, these few potsherds have written on them

THE MOABITE STONE

The date of this inscription from a king of Moab can be dated to about 830 B.C. It is important because of its mention of Israel and the killing of a whole village as a herem to the god Chemosh, as in Joshua. See 2 Kings 3:4.

I (am) Mesha, son of Chemosh (. . .), king of Moab, the Dibonite—my father (had) reigned over Moab thirty years, and I reigned after my father,—(who) made this high place for Chemosh in Qarhoh (. . .) because he saved me from all the kings and caused me to triumph over all my adversaries. As for Omri, (5) king of Israel, he humbled Moab many years (lit., days), for Chemosh was angry at his land. And his son followed him and he also said, "I will humble Moab." In my time, he spoke (thus), but I have triumphed over him and over his house, while Israel hath perished for ever! (Now) Omri had occupied the land of Medeba, and (Israel) had dwelt there in his time and half the time of his son (Ahab), forty years; but Chemosh dwelt there in my time.

And I built Baal-meon, making a reservoir in it, and I built (10) Qaryaten. Now the men of Gad had always dwelt in the land of Ataroth, and the king of Israel had built Ataroth for them; but I fought against the town and took it and slew all the people of the town as satiation (intoxication) for Chemosh and Moab. And I brought back from there Arel (or Oriel), its chieftain, dragging him before Chemosh in Kerioth, and I settled there men of Sharon and men of Maharith. And Chemosh said to me, "Go, take Nebo from Israel!" (15) So I went by night and fought against it from the break of dawn until noon, taking it and slaying all, seven thousand men, boys, women, girls and maid-servants, for I had devoted them to destruction for (the god) Ashtar-Chemosh. And I took from there the (. . .) of Yahweh, dragging them before Chemosh. And the king of Israel had built Jahaz, and he dwelt there while he was fighting against me, but Chemosh drove him out before me.

notations about the delivery of fine olive oil or wine, perhaps from the royal warehouses of Jeroboam II (789–748) or Menahem (748–737).

The Siloam Inscription. Found just inside a long water tunnel built under the old Davidic city of Jerusalem during the time of King Hezekiah of Judah in 715–689 B.C., this inscription describes in detail how two work parties, beginning from opposite ends, met successfully in the middle of the tunnel. Now in the museum in Istanbul, the inscription was probably carved as part of the preparations for the siege of Sennacherib of Assyria in 701 B.C., as reported in 2 Kings 20:20 and 2 Chronicles 32:30. It reads in part:

> While there were still three cubits to be cut, there was heard the voice of a man calling to his fellow.... And when the tunnel was driven through, the workers hewed the rock, man to man, axe against axe, and the water gushed from the spring toward the reservoir twelve hundred cubits away....

The Lachish Ostraca. Found in the ruins of Lachish at the level destroyed by the attack of Nebuchadnezzar of Babylon against Judah in 597 B.C., these few small military reports give us a vivid picture of the last days of independent Judah from the vantage point of a commander of a small outlying fort about to be attacked:

> And let my lord know that we are watching for the signals of Lachish, according to all the directions my lord has given, but we cannot see Azekah.

Already Azekah had fallen before the advancing enemy. Another letter mentions a message from "the prophet" to beware. Several commentators have seen in it a possible reference to Jeremiah, who repeatedly opposed armed resistance to Babylon.

All of these provide glimpses into the life of the Old Testament, although none are as long nor as detailed as we would wish for. Besides the examples above, we have seals with the names of Ahaz, Jotham, Shebna and Eliakim on them, all kings or high officials of Israelite times, and there are important ostraca from Tell Arad in the seventh century and from Yavneh Yam giving glimpses into daily life. A broken tomb inscription from the late eighth century Jerusalem area may refer to Shebna, the steward of King Hezekiah, mentioned in Isaiah 22:15f: "Go to the steward Shebna, the steward, who is over the house, and say to him, '... you who would have hewn a tomb on the heights, and carved a house for yourself in the rocks....'" The actual tomb inscription begins similarly: "This is the sepulchre of ... *yahu*, who is over the house...." His name is incomplete, but in Hebrew, Shebna ends with a "-yahu" when correctly spelled: Shebanyahu. This clearly suggests a connection to the saying in Isaiah 22:15–16.

Qumran finds are more properly treated in a New Testament Introduction. A community, probably of Essenes, a Jewish sect, lived by the shores of the Dead Sea at the time of Christ. They hid their precious biblical and sectarian scrolls in caves when the Romans attacked them during the First Jewish Revolt of 66–70 A.D. Found accidentally by a shepherd boy in 1947, they have provided a new perspective on the diversity of religious practice in Judaism in the first century, and show some striking similarities to New Testament situations and ideas. For Old Testament study, the presence of the oldest copies of the Hebrew books of the Bible yet to be uncovered anywhere makes this a find of vital importance for questions of textual accuracy.

The Value and Limit of Archaeology

Archaeology does not, and cannot, claim to know all about the place it excavates, nor the people who lived there. The nature of the finds, scattered, broken, and accidentally preserved by the fortunes of time and weather or the oversight of ancient plunderers, requires us to interpret them as pieces in a large jigsaw puzzle, of which most of the missing pieces are lost for good. Through careful detective work, by suggesting models and testing them against the evidence, much can be suggested about the shape of ancient life. Writings in particular allow us to look in on the thoughts of the peoples whose charred and buried cities have been found. But in no case do we have the full story. Evidence from one ancient site often seems to contradict the information gleaned from another. The task of dating objects of stone or clay, even written tablets, is tricky and as much an art as a science.

Archaeology *does not* prove the Bible to be "true" or "false." It *does* provide, at times, strikingly helpful evidence for customs and practices mentioned in the Bible of which we had no previous examples. It can support the accuracy of Old Testament writers as observers of the daily life of their times. Pagan gods and goddesses, known before only through the Old Testament polemics, have been revealed as part and parcel of Canaanite worship through excavations at Megiddo, Hazor, Ugarit and elsewhere. But the literary and religious affirmations of Old Testament faith are not open to being believed because archaeology can support them. Never shall we find the truth about Abraham and Jacob from archaeological remains. Their lives were individual and particular, while archaeology only confirms the general pattern. We have learned much about practices and customs, objects and buildings, that gives us a clearer picture of how and when such men might have lived, how they would have traveled, where they would have settled, and the names of people, rulers, divinities that might have been known to them. But in ninety percent of cases, it will not tell us if the individuals of the biblical stories *actually* lived, rather than just being literary creations of some ancient storyteller or fiction writer. Nor will archaeology tell us if they really experienced the recorded events the way the Old Testament presents them. These questions can only be answered as historical problems when archaeology cooperates with the historian, the literary critic and the theologian. For our primary knowledge of what the Old Testament says, we are thrown back upon the text itself.

STUDY QUESTIONS

1. What is archaeology? What have been some significant historical developments in archaeology?
2. Describe the method of archaeology. What is the importance of "the dig", stratigraphy, pottery typology, carbon-14 dating?
3. Which is the best method for obtaining a sequence of dating styles for ancient cities and cultures? Why?
4. What were the results of some major archaeological excavations in Israel? How do these results relate with biblical stories; do they concur, contradict, facilitate understanding, show errors, are insignificant?
5. What were some of the major literary discoveries in Ugarit, Mari, and Ebla?
6. Describe some of the major non-biblical finds in Palestine.
7. What is the significance of Qumran?
8. "Archaeology can absolutely and unquestionably prove the Bible to be true or false." Do you agree or disagree with this statement? Why? State the reasons for your position.

Chapter 4

LITERARY TOOLS FOR OLD TESTAMENT STUDY

The Bible Is a *Written* Document!

The Scriptures, divinely inspired though they may be, still appear on paper in human words. They were passed on and saved for future generations by being hand-copied time and again when older copies became worn out and faded. Even when the printing press was invented and made the reproduction of the Bible easier, human effort was needed to check the copy to be printed, and human mistakes were made. Unfortunately the scribes of old ran even more risks of error when they hand-copied manuscripts. They were not saved from making mistakes by divine help, and so a whole science has grown up within the study of the Bible in order to judge the accuracy and quality of the ancient texts that have come down to us.

The science of detecting what is wrong with the text and either looking for a better and more accurate manuscript, or suggesting a better reading by means of trained guesswork, is called "textual criticism." Earlier scholars referred to it as "lower criticism" to distinguish this task from the next step up, the interpretation of the corrected text, which they termed "higher criticism." If anything, however, lower criticism forms the more rigorous and exacting chore. Of course, we should not be fooled by the fact that the Bibles we read in translation make sense everywhere. All translators attempt to give sensible meaning to every line in the Bible, even if the Hebrew text is a mess. They listen to the text critics and decide on a good reading that will appear in our Bibles. The only clue that there may be a problem will be the tiny footnote that says "The Hebrew of this passage reads . . ." or "Some authorities say . . ."

Pope Pius XII, in his encyclical letter *Divino afflante spiritu* (1943), boldly endorsed the statement of St. Augustine that the main responsibility of biblical scholars is to produce a corrected text. The Pope called on the scholars to insure that the "text be restored as perfectly as possible, be purified from the corruptions due to the carelessness of the copyists and be freed, as far as may be done, from glosses and omissions" (n. 17).

Since an exact understanding of the Bible requires an ability to do both lower and higher criticism, as well as to have a working knowledge of the original language or languages in which the texts were written, most readers of the Old Testament depend on the scholarship of others. But everyone can draw on the results of good scholarship through a number of ways.

(1) Modern translations are available in a variety of styles and layout, but are generally all quite accurate.

(2) The notes that accompany a translation at the bottom of the text give very valuable background information, point out problems with the original text, and explain difficult terms. It is worth getting a Bible that has footnotes—sometimes these are called Annotated Bibles.

(3) There are many commentaries on individual books of the Old Testament available for deeper study. Anyone who begins to read the Bible regularly will want to find a commentary that not only explains the biblical author's way of thinking but also offers some theological insights into the meaning of the text for Christians and Jews.

Textual Criticism

The first responsibility of biblical scholars is to make sure that the text handed down to us from ancient times is the best and most accurate possible. But they do not have an easy task. First of all, ancient Hebrew was written in consonants only, leaving out the vowels. In English, we could easily read many sentences which lacked vowels, as "Kng Dvd klld tht wckd prsn, th Phlstn Glth." But if the sentence had "Kng Dvd klld th mn," should we read "man" or "men"? If we see "Kng Dvd lvd," does it mean "lived" or "loved"? Many Hebrew texts include similar difficulties.

A second problem developed because the ancients possessed no printing presses. All literature was hand-copied, and there were no proofreaders to check the spelling before the book was published. A scribe usually sat and copied from an older manuscript, and if he got tired or distracted, he could either omit part of his text, or copy it twice. As all who do typing or copy work know, the eye often leaps ahead to a second example of a word farther down the page if we look up for a moment, and we start again there, leaving out several lines of our text. Or the opposite can happen. We can glance down at an earlier occurrence of the word we had stopped at, and repeat a whole section twice. This is called dittography, or "writing twice," and was a common error in copying the Bible. Take the famous case of 2 Kings 18:17. The present Hebrew Bible reads strangely enough:

> The king of Assyria sent the commander to Hezekiah with
> a great army up to *Jerusalem,* and they went up and ar-
> rived at *Jerusalem* and they went up and arrived and stood
> at the channel of the upper pool.

Fooled by the two occurrences of "Jerusalem," the scribe looked back down and began copying from the first one a second time, thus repeating himself.

Sometimes scribes copied by dictation as someone read to them. Then words that sounded alike occasionally got confused. Just as, in English, people sometimes write "their" for "there," so in the Bible we find the preposition *'al,* "upon," often confused for *'el,* "to, for."

A fourth common mistake stems from sloppy handwriting (yes, even then). Many letters in Hebrew script look alike, and scribes often must have been tired or in a hurry, for confusion between *y* and *w, r* and *d* are very common. This may affect the meaning of the word, just as, when we fail to close the loop on our "g" in English, it looks like "y." Then "bog" becomes "boy" and "tog" becomes "toy."

A few Old Testament passages that seem to be clumsy have been cleared up by discovering another kind of mistake—scribes sometimes ran words together and made a new word with a differ-ent meaning. Thus in Jeremiah 46:15, the Hebrew text has the consonants *nshp* which can mean "it was swept away." This makes a certain amount of sense: "Why was it swept away, why did not your bull stand?" But since Jeremiah addresses the question to Egypt, scholars have seen a much clearer meaning if the word is divided into two: *ns hp.* "Why has the Apis-bull fled?" Jeremiah issues a strong condemnation of idolatry through worship of the sacred bull, a well-known practice from ancient Egyptian history.

In the opposite way, words that were originally one can be divided into two. In Proverbs 26:23, older Bibles read: "Like silver dross over a clay pot are smooth lips with an evil heart." This makes sense if we can somehow imagine the rejected muddy slag left over from the process of smelting silver as something valuable. But the sense has greatly improved since scholars discovered that the two words for "dross of silver" probably were originally a single word, meaning "glaze." Now, a smooth tongue hiding an evil heart really is like the glaze that covers a poor earthen jar.

A final difficulty is caused not by mistakes so much as by *intentional additions.* Books were expensive when hand-copied, and readers often put important comments and critiques directly in the margins of a manuscript, or, if they themselves found a copy error from the past, they would write the correct words above the line. Since in ancient times, books did not have pages with wide margins, but were written in columns on a long scroll, the space was very cramped and added words often touched against the original text. Later copyists sometimes added the marginal comments right into their new text, either by mistake, or because they honestly believed that earlier scribes had accidentally left them out of their document while copying, and had put them in the margin at a later time.

Text scholars face two major tasks in dealing with these problems. They must compare many ancient manuscripts of a given book in order to establish the best reading from the oldest sources possible. And secondly, if this proves impossible because the text seems corrupted as far back as copies exist, they must suggest possible changes which they think reflect the more original text. Text critics do not just guess, but use their best professional judgment. They compare ancient translations, such as the Greek or Syriac, to see if the ancient translators used a better manuscript than we now possess. They look for parallel expressions and ways of expressing the same thought in other passages from the Bible which might give clues to the meaning in the problem phrase. This can often be helpful since ancient peoples were highly traditional in their use of language. Study of other ancient Semitic languages, such as Aramaic, Ugaritic, Babylonian and even modern Arabic, can help find words which parallel the meaning needed for the Hebrew word that is not understood and reveal a new sense for an uncertain sentence. Rather than being errors, such unknown words suddenly become long-lost members in good standing of the Hebrew vocabulary. Such attention to the neighboring tongues can prevent the textual scholar from changing or removing a word unnecessarily.

In technical terms, the decision of a critic to make a change in the Hebrew text of the Bible in order to improve the reading is called emendation. It should be the last resort, not the first. Caution should guide changing any ancient literary work, for we are not Hebrews of old, and what we think religious ideas "should be" for our day may not always be how they thought. In the twentieth century, too many scholars have been led by their own philosophy or particular dogmatic creed to decide that difficult biblical texts "had" to say one thing or another.

If interpreters read their own ideas into a text, or use the text all twisted around to defend some modern meaning, we say that they do "eisegesis," that is, they "read into the text" what they wish to see. It differs widely from proper interpretation of the text, which we call "exegesis," or "reading from" the text itself, and which is discussed below.

Text Traditions

There were quite a variety of copies of the Hebrew Old Testament available by the time of Jesus. Since copying had gone on for a long time already, many different editions circulated, some longer with sections added in, some shorter with sections omitted. All had some change or error in them. Since a scribe in one area often copied from a local text, the same error or change often appeared regularly in one place, say, Babylon, but not in texts copied in Egypt. Thus, at the time of Christ, three major "families" or groupings of text types could be found: the Babylonian, the Palestinian, and the Egyptian. The Babylonian Jews, for example, treasured their texts which had a very short, tightly-knit edition of the Pentateuch, while Egyptian Jews used a richer and more expanded text. Only at the end of the first century A.D. did the rabbis decide to end the confusion and select one text, the best they could find, for each part of the Bible. In the Pentateuch they chose the Babylonian tradition, but in other books, such as the prophets Jeremiah and Isaiah, they followed the Palestinian-type text.

These first century rabbis also inaugurated a method of guarding the text from any more glosses and additions, though not completely from copying errors. They counted words, syllables, and sections, and wrote the totals at the end of each book of the Old Testament. These could be checked in later copies to see if the numbers corresponded exactly. The system worked marvelously, helping preserve a good text for the last eighteen hundred years, and paving the way for the addition of vowels to the text—a need that was becoming very acute as fewer and fewer readers were familiar with the Hebrew language.

Versions

The standard Hebrew text that resulted from the decisions of these early rabbis has become known as the "Masoretic text," named after a later group of Jewish scholars of the eighth to eleventh centuries A.D., the *masoretes,* or "interpreters," who put vowels into the text, and thus "fixed" the words in a definitive form. No longer could a reader be confused by whether the word *qtl* in the text meant *qotel,* "the killer," or *qatal,* "he killed." The masoretes worked carefully from the best available tradition of textual interpretation and made the task of later readers much easier. Any scholar will admit the great debt he owes these Jewish experts. But, at times, having such a fixed text raises more problems than it solves. After all, the masoretes themselves lived a thousand years or more after the major writing of the Hebrew Scriptures, and many words had changed their meaning and grammatical shape over the centuries. Such later generations simply did not understand the proper meaning of a passage. That is why the task of the textual critic still goes on today.

Besides the use of the scientific tools mentioned above, text critics can glean much help from other ancient translations of the Hebrew into Greek, Syriac, Latin and Aramaic. The most important of these are:

1. *Septuagint:* the Greek translation of the entire Hebrew Scriptures and all of the deuterocanonical books, made from the third century B.C. on and often revised by later Greek translators. It was widely used by the Jews outside of Palestine, and especially by the New Testament writers and early Christians. Because of its age, it offers valuable help in clearing up confused passages in Hebrew. By assuming that the Greek translator faithfully put into Greek what he saw in his Hebrew copy of the Bible, scholars can work back from the choice of Greek words to what the Hebrew original must have been. The Jews have looked with disfavor on the Septua-

gint and especially on the deuterocanonical books because Christians have claimed so much from them about Christ.

2. *Peshitta:* the Syriac translation made by Christians in Syria. It may date in part back to the second century A.D. but was at least completed by the fourth or fifth centuries. It has readings that sometimes support the Hebrew text and sometimes support the Septuagint. Experts use these differences to help get past difficulties. *Peshitta,* or also *peshitto,* means "simple" or "common" and represents the daily-use Bible of the people.

3. *Vulgate:* the name of St. Jerome's careful Latin translation made in the fifth century A.D. He followed the Hebrew text as far as possible. Jerome had help from Jews in Palestine and often explained why he chose a particular translation. It is a help to textual studies, but more than for that reason, the Vulgate gained a position of honor because it became the common ("vulgate") Bible of the whole Middle Ages in the Western Church.

4. *Targum:* since many Jews at the time of Christ no longer spoke Hebrew, but Aramaic, there was need for Aramaic translations to understand what was read in the synagogues. The *targum* ("translation" or "interpretation" in Aramaic) developed as a loose paraphrase to be read alongside the Scriptures in the services. It was not usually a very strict translation and had many additions in order to make a passage easier to understand.

The Bible as Literature and Story

The Bible is much more than a "text" to be restored to its original beauty; it is the literature of a living people. And because authors in every age and every culture express themselves differently, modern literary-theory must offer us ways of understanding ancient writers. There is, for example, the basic distinction between prose and poetry. Some thoughts are best expressed by poetry: love songs, hymns, intense pain of sorrow and loss. Others are better expressed in prose: biographies, historical records, and lists. Some human expression can take either form: describing the beauty of nature, heroic sagas of famous people or prophetic warnings of doom. What type an author selects is determined by how he feels that he can best communicate what he wants to say.

Even these categories may be easily broken down into more limited ones. Thus a list may be a "king list" giving the names and dates of all the rulers of a nation, or a genealogy list showing someone's ancestors, or a telephone directory, or a dictionary. Hymns may be hymns of joy, or laments, or songs of thanks, or of praise of God's creation such as Psalm 148, which is almost a list. A sermon may be an impassioned plea, a persuasive appeal or a thoughtful explanation. In every case, the identification of what *type* we are dealing with will help us know much about the author's purpose in writing it, for whom it is intended, and from what situation it developed.

Thus when the second-grade librarian read to us "The Little Shepherd Boy" from *Grimm's Fairy Tales*, beginning "Once upon a time there was a little shepherd boy who was famed far and wide for the wise answers he gave to every question . . ." we *knew* from the opening words, "Once upon a time . . ." to expect wonderful things and not a dry recital of the multiplication tables. So, too, the ancient listener who heard the prophet begin "Thus says the Lord . . ." knew that he was going to receive a warning of hard judgment and not a comment on the weather. We expect certain types of information by the choice of words and the form in which they are expressed. Even today the student cringes with fear if he or she has not done the homework and the teacher announces, "Now we shall recite . . ."

Another important aspect in appreciation of a story is familiarity. Small children love to hear the same old favorites over and over again. Indeed, more than that, children often demand that the story be told just the way it was last time, and if daddy makes any important changes, they are likely to correct him. Usually, children's stories, such as nursery rhymes, have a simple structure, much repetition, and rhyme or other helps for the memory. Even now most of us remember:

> Hot cross buns! Hot cross buns!
> One a penny, two a penny, hot cross buns!
> If your daughter doesn't like them,
> Give them to your sons.

Even adults prefer repetition to identify their favorite programs or book plots. The theme song for the Lone Ranger was never so well loved when it was merely the overture to Rossini's opera *William Tell.* Today it is identified by thousands with the masked rider, his horse Silver, and his friend Tonto. In the early cowboy movies, the good guys wore white hats and bad guys wore black hats. And how many science fiction thrillers use the same props, because audiences expect them: ray guns, interplanetary space ships, robots, and evil machines gone wild! How many modern novels focus on problems of self-identity and rebellion against parents because our society is concerned with these as *the* problems today! Totally new ideas and totally new story plots, like totally new types of music, usually find stiff resistance from the audience.

Oral Tradition

The problem of introducing totally new information was even more acute in the ancient world when culture was much more traditional than now. People depended much less on looking up information for themselves in books than in listening to and mastering the passed-down wisdom of the ancestors. Communication in the ancient world was mostly oral, and societies that rely on oral tradition look at knowledge and history far differently than do peoples accustomed to reading.

First of all, their memories were generally much better than ours. We are lazy about memorizing things because we can look them up. Nevertheless, even they did not in our sense "memorize" every word. They did not hold vast amounts of exact texts in their heads like the heroes of the Ray Bradbury science fiction tale *Fahrenheit 451* who thwarted a tyrant who was trying to destroy all the world's past literature. Each one memorized word for word one great classic and preserved it for the next generation. Rather, the ancient people often heard stories and events told in a communal setting, either on special feast days when religious leaders would recite the ancient traditions, or in schools where masters gave and interpreted the laws with vivid examples, or in gatherings for entertainment. Very rarely were any of these simply recited by rote memory. Traditions were constantly updated and enlivened by new examples. Oral style demanded that the storyteller stick to the well-known plot or the basic outline of the facts, but he often varied the details and the order of minor incidents, or even added in extra episodes if the celebration were a big one. He worked to create the most pleasing effect and the best presentation for the occasion on which he was asked to recite.

Studies have been done on the techniques of oral folk singers of Yugoslavia in the 1930's, and on the nature of the great epics of Homer, the *Iliad* and the *Odyssey* (both written before 700 B.C.). This research has shown that oral folksingers in all ages combine a variety of set phrases and traditional expressions of different lengths to create musical lines. Thus, let us suppose that each line of an epic must be twelve syllables long. If we want to say "the hero fought the dragon," that involves seven syllables, and we still need five more syllables for the line. We can add the well-known epithets, "who breathes fiery darts," or "terrible of claw" after the word dragon to get a complete line. Either will do. The audience loves them both. And the singer may one time use the one, another time the other. But as audiences respond more favorably to one recital than to another, the artist will tend to favor the version that gets the best response. It was probably in exactly this way that the singers of ancient Greece repeated those wonderful and marvelous expressions of Homer over and over until they became known to every schoolboy: "rosy-fingered dawn," "the wine-dark sea," "grey-eyed Athena."

A second factor about oral cultures in the ancient Near East was their almost positive *dislike* for exact facts and specific dates. The common religious belief was that salvation and wholeness were found in a return to that first moment of creation when all things had been originally perfect. Between the day of creation and their day, the history of the world had been one of sin, trouble, and failure. If history could only be overcome, and a leap made back past all the intervening events to the ideal *beginning time,* humanity could be healed and begin anew. Religion was centered on sacred times of the year when the people could reach back and touch that primeval creation—for example, celebrating in temples, cut off from the everyday world, the great New Year's feast, when nature renewed its beginning like the first beginning. In this world view, remembering the deeds and events of the past year could be a block to achieving union with the moment of divine creation. It does not mean that Babylonians or Assyrians had no sense of their own history; they surely did, but they expressed it and gave it meaning for themselves by using themes from the great myths about creation, or through reference to the heroic deeds and lives of the great primeval gods, heroes, and kings. The actual details of historical events were far less important to an ordinary man of ancient times than was the *pattern* by which it was explained and the essential primeval event to which it was compared.

Such a world of thought might appear far removed from modern ideas on science and history, but many of the same elements remain hidden in our own Western traditions. Mircea Eliade, the anthropologist, tells the story of how a researcher came upon a

A COMPARISON OF ANCIENT AND MODERN METHODS OF RECORDING HISTORICAL EVENTS

Ancient Israelite Historian	Modern Scientific Historian
Records the traditions of the tribe or nation as they interpret them.	Attempts to reconstruct past events objectively and accurately.
Uses oral sources with a few written records or lists.	Relies on documents and written records almost exclusively.
Often includes several parallel versions of the same story.	Sorts out the conflicting accounts in order to find the single original one.
Does not have much exact information of dates and places, and so gives rough approximations.	Carefully searches out the correct chronology of events.
Relies strongly on fixed types of literary descriptions or motifs that can be applied to all similar situations.	Seeks to get behind literary genres and narrative modes to find out what really happened.
Uses a common-sense approach to describing human behavior and does not guarantee every fact.	Uses all the critical tools and means of information to check sources and their claims.
Use past history to explain convictions for the present time or for a particular point of view.	Writes history without special bias or undue emphasis towards only one side of the picture.

Romanian village where people told the tragic story of how a young suitor had been bewitched by a fairy. Driven with jealousy, the demon threw the youth off a cliff to his death on the eve of his marriage. The researcher was told it had happened "long ago." But checking further, he discovered it had happened only forty years earlier, and the boy's fiancée was still living. When asked about the sad event, she told of a tragic, but very ordinary, accident. One evening her lover had slipped and fallen off the mountain path. He was badly injured, but his cries were heard and rescuers brought him to the village where he soon died. Yet, despite the living witness of the fiancée and others, only a few years were enough to "forget" the historical details and transform the story into a legend of the mountain fairy. From the villagers' point of view, a mere death by falling was not enough to explain the true inner meaning of such a terrible fate for two lovers. The tragedy only made sense when identified with the well-known mythical category of the supra-human, magical, dangerous, and often spiteful powers of the fairy world.

In the Old Testament we shall run into quite a number of "wonders" and strange tales, such as the strength of Samson deriving from his hair (Jgs 14–16), or the power of the prophet Elisha to lift a heavy axe from the bottom of a lake (2 Kgs 2), that may have taken on some of the color of the heroic and legendary in their retelling over the years. In these we expect to find some "mythic" elements, because through them the story-teller preserved the real meaning: that God gave these men supernatural help. Moreover, human memory does not recall *exact* details for long—perhaps a generation or two. Any story that lasts must be retold through one of the traditional models that everyone knows. No doubt, this explains why so many heroes through the ages have been noted as dragon-slayers like St. George. Don't all great heroes best a dragon if they are really of top stature? If a medieval knight is said to slay such a dragon, it tells us very little about the existence of dragons in thirteenth century England, but much about the purity and great deeds that characterize this new St. George.

Higher Criticism

Once we recognize the great variety that old traditions take when passed down in an ancient culture, we will understand better the need to develop tools that can identify the types of literature found in different books of the Bible. Even more importantly, there must be tools to trace how the types changed as they were passed down, what happened when they were put into writing, how many versions of the same stories existed, and a host of other questions. Literary analysis is needed to sort out the many layers of religious thought over hundreds of years that are found in the Old Testament. Not all biblical books were written at the same time, and there are many older as well as newer levels in them. This supports the declaration of the author of the Letter to the Hebrews in the New Testament that "God, in many and various ways, has spoken to our ancestors by the prophets, but now, in this final time, has spoken to us through his Son."

Even though all the books of the Bible are now joined together as one canon that traces the shape our faith has taken from the beginning of the world until the time of the apostles, a serious student of the Old Testament must get behind the present unity to discover how Israel grew and changed and deepened its faith. This process of getting behind the finished Bible to the older layers of thought is done by use of three literary tools: source criticism, form criticism and tradition history criticism.

Source Criticism

Source criticism is sometimes referred to as "literary criticism," but this can be a source of great confusion. As we have seen above, "literary criticism" is used by most students of literature to refer to the artistic and stylistic merits of the Bible as a literary masterpiece. Source criticism studies the specific problem of whether there are written *documents* behind our present text. As we shall see in more detail in the next chapter, this method has been developed over the last three centuries, mainly to answer the problems of repetitions and inconsistencies in the Pentateuch. The use of two distinct names for God in Genesis led eighteenth century researchers such as Jean Astruc (1753) to conclude that Moses must have used two or more different *written* sources when he composed the books of Genesis, Exodus, Leviticus and Numbers. Other differences were soon noted. Source critics showed the contradictory styles of writing that appeared side by side in a single book, for example, calling the covenant mountain Sinai in one line and Horeb in the next. More telling, they pointed to the repetition of whole incidents a few chapters apart. The most famous case is the strange tale of how a patriarch lies in telling a foreign king that his wife is really his sister. It occurs three times in Genesis 12, 20 and 26, twice involving Abraham and once involving Isaac. Even the beginning reader might question how such a unique event could happen to Abraham without his learning a lesson, yet he seems to have forgotten everything when the second time arises.

Discussions on these and other questions flew hot and heavy

A DOUBLE TRADITION OF SARAH IN THE HAREM

Genesis 12:10–20

Then famine struck the land and so Abram went down to Egypt to live, for the famine was severe in his own land. [11] When he came to Egypt he said to Sarai his wife, "I know that you are a beautiful woman to look at, [12] and when the Egyptians behold you they will say 'She is his wife'; so they will kill me, but let you live. [13] Tell them you are my sister so that it will be treated well on your account." [14] When Abram entered Egypt, the Egyptians did see that the woman was very beautiful. [15] Pharaoh's princes saw her and praised her to pharaoh, and the woman was taken into the pharaoh's house. [16] He treated Abram well because of her so that he received sheep, cattle, he-asses, menservants, maidservants, she-asses and camels. [17] But the Lord struck Pharaoh and his household with great plagues on account of Sarai, the wife of Abram. [18] Then the pharaoh summoned Abram and said, "Why have you done this to me? Why did not you tell me she was your wife? [19] Why did you say, 'She is my sister,' so that I took her as my wife? Here is your wife; take her and depart now." [20] Then Pharaoh gave his men orders concerning Abram, and they sent him away with his wife and all his belongings.

Genesis 20:1–18

Abraham travelled on from there to the land of the Negev, and settled between Kadesh and Shur, living in Gerar. [2] And Abraham said of his wife Sarah, "She is my sister." So Abimelech, the king of Gerar, sent for Sarah and took her. [3] But God came to Abimelech in a dream at night, and said to him, "You will die because of the woman you have taken, for she is another man's wife." [4] Abimelech had not yet approached her, so he said, "Lord, do you slay the innocent? [5] Didn't he himself say to me, 'She is my sister'? and did not she say, 'He is my brother'? I have done this with a sincere heart and clean hands." [6] Then God said to him in the dream, "I know that you have acted with a sincere heart. It was I who kept you from sinning against me; I did not allow you to touch her..... [10] And Abimelech said to Abraham, "What were you thinking about in doing such a thing?" [11] Abraham said, "I thought that there was certainly no fear of God in this place, so that they will kill me because of my wife. [12] Besides, she is truly my sister, the daughter of my father, but not of my mother. Now she has become my wife. [13] When God caused me to leave my father's house, I said to her, 'You must do this favor for me: in every place to which we go, tell them that I am your brother.'" [14] Then Abimelech took sheep and cattle, male and female slaves, and gave them to Abraham, and he restored Sarah his wife to him.

In these two stories, the place names have been changed, and the name of the king, perhaps indicating that the same story was passed down in two different locations, one near the Negev town of Gerar, the other farther up where the highway to Egypt met the main areas of Judah. What is most noticeable, however, is that the authors of the second account, are much more worried about the moral implications of Abraham's acts and create an extended apology for his actions. This account is usually attributed to the Elohist source, while chapter 12 with its emphasis only on God's help to Abraham, is assigned to the Yahwist source.

among German and English scholars of the eighteenth and nineteenth centuries until the results reached a now-classical formulation in the work of Julius Wellhausen. In his *Prolegomena to the History of Ancient Israel* (1872), he identified four clear written sources in the first five books of the Bible. They are discussed in detail in Chapter 5 below.

For Wellhausen and his co-workers, the identification of early sources always meant *written* sources. He largely left aside the question of even earlier oral traditions. He was concerned to identify accurately and date the diverse theological documents which had been written, gathered together and edited in several stages until the final Pentateuch as we have it today emerged. Wellhausen doubted that many old traditions had survived. He believed that almost all the present Pentateuch material grew up after King David.

Of course source criticism does not confine itself to the Pentateuch. Scholars provide continual studies detailing written sources behind the codes of law in the Bible, earlier collections of prophetic writings, and original small groupings of the Psalms. In the last, for example, many authorities see a unity in Psalms 42–83 which they call the "Elohist Psalter" because God is called *Elohim* (Hebrew for "God") where almost all other Psalms refer to him by his proper name Yahweh. Behind the Book of Job, we can detect some stages of how it came together. Notice that chapters 1–2 and the final chapter 42:7–17 are written as a prose folk-tale, while the rest of the book is in poetry. There is another inconsistency in the plot where Job and three friends have completed their dialogue with each other and Job has called for God to come, but suddenly a fourth person, Elihu, appears. Elihu speaks in a monologue for four chapters, 33–37; when he finishes, God appears and speaks to Job and the three friends but seems not to know Elihu ever existed. Scholars thus believe that the Elihu section was an afterthought tacked on. Many commentaries now divide the development of Job into four steps, combined at different times:

1.	The Prose Tale	chs. 1–2, ch. 42:7–17
2.	The Poetic Dialogue	chs. 3–27, 29–31, 38–42:6
3.	The Elihu Speech	chs. 33–37
4.	The Wisdom Poem	ch. 28

Although the results in the Book of Job may prove helpful in showing how its parts all fit together, some source critics went to an extreme in their work on other books. They tore the text apart to find earlier documents. Within the Book of Judges, for instance, the German scholar Karl Budde identified at least nine writers and editors—and editors of editors—so that it almost seemed as if an evil genius had intentionally tried to create a monster by piecing together a jigsaw puzzle out of scissors and paste.

Form Criticism

Form criticism was born in the dismay over the excesses of some source critics. In 1901, Hermann Gunkel used the insights of the Brothers Grimm about German folktales to ask if biblical traditions had not also often developed from oral traditions. Unlike Wellhausen, Gunkel understood the diversity and inconsistencies in the Pentateuchal narratives as signs of typical *oral* style. Behind the narrative prose of Genesis, he detected earlier poetic originals. He opposed the general belief of his time that all we could hope to know were the late documents from the times of Israel's kings. Fundamental to his understanding was the conviction that oral tradition was not carried on by brilliant individual authors but by the *community*, which had to listen, remember and carry on the tradition. The literary "forms" we spoke of earlier were the building blocks of an oral society.

Each *type* of story, tradition, or communication belongs to a very concrete *setting in life*. Thus if we can identify a funeral lament, we know it was spoken at the time of a death; joyful marriage songs were sung at weddings, etc. If the scholar can only identify the earliest form that each type took in the ancient Israelite culture, he gains a very good clue to the kind of situation and the period of history in which this unit of traditional material originated. From this point, he can detect a history of additions and growths to the original, and watch the way its form developed and changed through the centuries all the way up to and including the time when it was finally written down and kept as a document.

The form critic always asks: Who is speaking? Who is the audience? What is being said? Where is it said? What is the purpose? It may seem a simple procedure, but it can become very difficult when one must ask the question of every stage of development along the way. The critic must ask not only who spoke originally, but who was the one who added the additions, and who was the editor who wrote it down, and who revised that edition, and on and on. And of course he must then also ask the where and when and why for each of these. Moveover, to make useful suggestions in this area demands that the form critic have a good sense of ancient history and its different cultures so that he can recognize possible answers to his questions.

One fundamental aspect of the form-critical method is a belief that oral tradition *does not change* its forms rapidly. These are truly "traditional" and tend to keep the same wording and favorite formulas frozen over long periods of time. Besides this, community memory for details is not nearly so accurate as is its preservation of the different "forms" themselves. As we saw above in the case of the Romanian peasants, historical events rapidly find themselves clothed in one special form or another, whether hero saga, sorrowful lament story, or whatever.

A very simple and popular way of describing the work of form criticism is to list the following four steps:

(1) *Defining the unit.* In order to identify the form of a piece of literature, the form critic must have the whole piece, nothing more and nothing less, or he may confuse different types together. Our modern Bibles often mark off different units by paragraphs or bold-type headings.

(2) *Naming the form used.* Is the unit a lament? A letter? A saga? This is often referred to as naming the literary *genre* of the unit. If we miss the proper kind of genre or form, we may never find out how it came to be used where it is.

(3) *Describing its setting in life* (the German word *Sitz-im-Leben*). After knowing what form the piece has, we try to identify its original *social* context, and, further, to ask what kind of thinking gave rise to such expression. Can we know something about the people from the way they spoke?

(4) *Identifying its purpose.* The final step seeks what function or purpose this piece served in the original oral stage, and what purpose does it now serve in the larger written work of which it is a part. Can we trace what changes took place in the people of Israel by knowing how these two uses differ?

All this may seem quite a game that scholars play, but it serves a very serious end: to reach back and understand history the way Israel saw it, which was far different from our modern scientific outlook. To simply read the Bible all on one level as though no changes had taken place in biblical thought over the centuries is to miss the living spirit of Israel's growing faith. Form criticism seeks to capture that actual growth.

Tradition History

Form criticism by its nature includes tracing a text through all levels from the most primitive oral saying up to the finished product. But many biblical scholars became so enthused over the search for the original, simplest oral forms behind the biblical text that they almost forgot the written and edited stages that we know much more about. In recent years, experts have been turning back from too much emphasis on the oral stages of tradition, and have become more concerned with the total process of growth. They are looking hard at the various *times* when the biblical texts were edited, and the different circles from which the editors came. The positive role of editing, or *redaction,* as it is often called, is now appreciated more. No longer do scholars see the redactors as un-imaginative bureaucrats pasting together older texts, but as men (and women possibly) passionately involved in the problems and needs of their time, who are updating and re-expressing the traditions so that they can speak to a new generation.

In tradition history, the scholar studies the circles of scribes, wise men, priests, or prophets and how they responded to new situations. There is concern about the cult and the legal professions, and an effort to pinpoint the diverse interests of each region of Palestine in order to better understand the moments of decisive importance and change when the traditions had to be reworked to meet new needs. One such period may have been the coming of the kingship of David and Solomon when old tribal ideas had to be adapted to a more advanced and complex urban style of life. Anoth-er important moment may well have been the loss of the kingship and the massive exile of 586 B.C. when all the older supports of Israel's religion were taken away: king, temple, and independence. Certainly there were many others as well.

The specific task of tradition history (or transmission history, as it is sometimes called) is to trace the use and reuse of biblical materials from their earliest forms and settings in the life of Israel down through all the stages of being written and rewritten until it reached the final form as it is now found in our Bibles. Where form criticism alone stresses discovery of the earliest oral units, and source criticism alone stresses the earliest written sources, tradition history particularly concerns itself with the later adaptations and reworkings of the text.

The use of such modern historical-critical tools for interpreting and understanding the Bible was at first limited to Protestant bibli-cal scholars in Germany and England. Catholic scholars, along with the Jews, were mostly reluctant to abandon the ancient traditions of the Church and synagogue that Moses was the author of the Penta-teuch. Moreover, source criticism won wide popularity among the rationalists and anti-Church thinkers of the eighteenth and nine-teenth centuries because it directly challenged the naive beliefs of the faithful. Religious leaders thus saw these methods not as helps but as dangers to the faith of the churches. A second area of concern was the nineteenth century tendency to see the Scriptures as a record of Israel's growth from superstition under Moses and the judges to the enlightened insights of the prophets to a repressive reaction of Priestly doctrines. This was born from the Romantic movement with a nod to the philosophy of Hegel, and gained great strength as anthropologists discovered primitive Indian societies in South America and the Pacific Islands that supposedly still lived the way ancient Israel would have lived in its early days.

Many Catholic scholars were attracted to the possibilities of critical methods, but they did little with them until the 1940's because of the crisis of modernism. Pope Pius X condemned the modernists in 1907 because the push for a "modern" critical spirit about the Church had led many to question the existence of anything supernatural. Finally, in 1943, Pope Pius XII issued an encyclical letter, *Divino Afflante Spiritu,* that gave Catholic biblical scholars encouragement to examine the ancient sources and literary forms in order to deepen the understanding of the sacred texts. From that time on, Catholic scholars have pursued a sober use of source and form criticism as seriously as do most Protestant scholars and many Jewish ones.

Rhetorical Criticism

We can close this section with a brief word about a method that is growing in popularity—rhetorical criticism. Form criticism often leads to tearing the biblical passages down to their smallest units and thereby making it much more difficult for the reader to build them back up to the full story that has come down to us as God's revelation. By examination of the artistic and rhetorical elements used in the major Old Testament passages, the rhetorical critic accents the wholeness and unity of many chapters and books. The rhetorical critic shows that many repetitions or seemingly unusual features in fact add to the dramatic force or stylistic beauty of the work. Such an artistic analysis stresses the harmony and value of the final written passage as we find it today and thus serves the useful function of enriching our daily scriptural reading with a deeper appreciation rather than always raising more doubts about the text. At the same time, rhetorical criticism brings us closer to the goals of the literary critics who value reading the Bible as a masterpiece of world literature. It reminds us once again that despite all the scientific tools we use to understand the Bible, *imagination* is still the heart of real literary art. The inspired writers created with imaginative and carefully chosen phrases to stimulate a response of faith to God's merciful actions for his people. Modern scholars will constantly add new literary tools to help correct the limitations of the present ones, but always to better grasp the faith experience recorded in the Old Testament as a whole.

STUDY QUESTIONS

1. Define textual criticism. Describe the relationship between "Lower Criticism" and "Higher Criticism".
2. What is the significance of *Divino Afflante Spiritu?*
3. What are some of the problems and difficulties that one encounters in textual criticism?
4. Define the following terms: emendation, eisegesis, exegesis, "Masoretic Text", masoretes, source criticism, form criticism, redaction.
5. What were the three major "families" or groupings of text types at the time of Christ?
6. What are some other ancient translations of which text critics make use?
7. Explain the significance and importance of identifying the literary type. Give examples to illustrate this answer.
8. Describe oral tradition. What are some of its strengths and weaknesses?
9. Describe the contributions of the following scholars: Jean Astruc, Julius Wellhausen, Hermann Gunkel.
10. What are the steps in form criticism?
11. What is Tradition History?
12. What does Rhetorical Criticism attempt to do?

Chapter 5

THE PENTATEUCH

The Five Books of Moses

We begin where the Bible begins, with the books which were placed first, not only because they cover the oldest period of Israel's history, but because their traditional author was Moses, who has the place of honor in Jewish tradition.

Genesis opens with the "history" of creation and the earliest human societies told in mythological forms. It rapidly narrows its aim to God's choice of the patriarchs Abraham, Isaac, Jacob and Joseph who receive his promise, carry out his plans, and prepare for his great act of deliverance from Egypt and the giving of his covenant at Mount Sinai.

Exodus tells the story of how God chose Moses to deliver Israel from slavery in Egypt and lead them to accept a covenant so that he would be their God and they would be his people (Ex 6:7). The book closes with detailed descriptions for the building of the tent of meeting and the ark of the covenant, central signs of God's presence with Israel.

Leviticus contains the laws and commandments that God gave to his newly sanctified people to obey as their share in the covenant relationship. These regulations deal mostly with sacrifice, feasts, priesthood, and the ritual obligations of worthiness and holiness.

Numbers adds many more laws and regulations about the twelve tribes and their organization as a holy people on the march. Chapters 10–20 then continue the story of Israel's wanderings in the desert, complete with a forty-year punishment for constantly rebelling against God and Moses.

Deuteronomy (or "second law" in Greek) is a later book composed entirely as a reflective speech of Moses which sums up the meaning of the exodus event and the desert journey, and reaffirms the importance of the covenant law as a guide for Israel's life in the promised land. It is Moses' "farewell speech" and supposedly takes place just as the people are ready to invade the promised land.

The present structure of these five books has a definite shape. At the center stands the giving of the law on Mount Sinai in all its detail. Leading up to that moment are succeeding *periods of promise* in Israel's history: the age of creation in Genesis 1–11, the times of the patriarchal ancestors in Genesis 12–50, and the events of deliverance from Egypt in Exodus 1–18. Leading away from the central scene on Mount Sinai which stretches across the Books of Exodus, Leviticus and Numbers 1–10, Israel continues the march toward the promised land in Numbers 11–34, while Deuteronomy gives final guidance for the conquest and instructions on how Israel is to act in the land. This can be diagramed as follows:

The whole Pentateuch looks forward to the possession of the promised land. Life in the land of Israel will form the basic background for the rest of the Old Testament story. These other books can be divided among three groupings. The *history books* from Joshua to Kings tell of the days of the judges and kings; the *prophetic books* speak of the divine challenges to Israel's faithfulness; the *writings,* including wisdom books, psalms and later histories, relate religion in everyday life to theological reflection. The Pentateuch lays out the directions for this life, and becomes a *constitution* of Israel's existence in the promised land—or outside of it, as the situation later develops.

The covenant combines God's free offer of a special relationship and the people's willing response in faith by agreeing to take on the obligations to worship and obey only this God, Yahweh. It forms a fundamental event that creates Israel as a people who are essentially united more by faith than by blood ties. It is a binding moment and sets the Pentateuch which records it apart from the rest of the Old Testament. For the Jews it is the most sacred part of the Bible; it is "the teaching" (*Torah*) par excellence, and the remainder of the canonical writings are really only an enrichment of its message or a commentary on living it out more fully in history.

Moses as Author

At least from the post-exilic period (after 539 B.C.) Moses has been explicitly identified as the author of the Pentateuch. Several

THE STRUCTURE OF THE PENTATEUCH

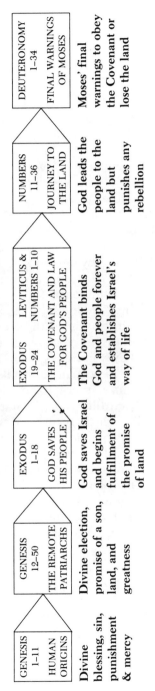

GENESIS 1–11 HUMAN ORIGINS	GENESIS 12–50 THE REMOTE PATRIARCHS	EXODUS 1–18 GOD SAVES HIS PEOPLE	EXODUS 19–24 LEVITICUS & NUMBERS 1–10 THE COVENANT AND LAW FOR GOD'S PEOPLE	NUMBERS 11–36 JOURNEY TO THE LAND	DEUTERONOMY 1–34 FINAL WARNINGS OF MOSES
Divine blessing, sin, punishment & mercy	Divine election, promise of a son, land, and greatness	God saves Israel and begins fulfillment of the promise of land	The Covenant binds God and people forever and establishes Israel's way of life	God leads the people to the land but punishes any rebellion	Moses' final warnings to obey the Covenant or lose the land

passages of Scripture point in this direction. Thus we read in Ezra 3:2 that Ezra read aloud from the "law of Moses, the man of God." The books of the Pentateuch frequently mention that Moses gave laws and instructions to the people, and the whole Book of Deuteronomy begins with the claim that it is the "words of Moses spoken beyond the Jordan" (Dt 1:1). By the fifth century B.C., the author of 2 Chronicles quotes a passage from Deuteronomy 24:16 as coming from the "book of Moses" (2 Chr 25:4). By the time of Christ, not only Jesus, but other well-known Jewish authors such as Josephus the historian and Philo the Jewish philosopher of Alexandria, Egypt, take for granted that Moses authored the five books of the Pentateuch.

The late Old Testament Books of Ezra and Nehemiah suggest that Ezra the priest reformed the lax practice of the faith among the Jews in post-exilic Palestine by demanding a commitment on their part to the *book of the law*. It appears very probable that this is nothing other than the Pentateuch as we know it. Whether Ezra was the final editor who combined the five books together or not, tradition definitely associates him with its establishment as a binding rule of life. There is therefore good reason to maintain that the Pentateuch did indeed exist in Ezra's lifetime between 460 and 400 B.C., and that he had an important role in its acceptance.

Even in ancient times there were those who doubted that Moses could have written the whole Pentateuch. Such passages as Deuteronomy 34:5–12, which records Moses' death, were often cited to show Moses certainly did not write all of it. It was commonly believed that his faithful follower Joshua had added that section. But with the exception of a few writers like St. Jerome, who was of the opinion that Ezra had written the Pentateuch from notes handed down from Moses himself, Christians and Jews never seriously doubted Mosaic authorship up until the time of the Protestant Reformation in the sixteenth century.

The Source Critics and the Pentateuch

The first scientific questions about the origins of the material in the Pentateuch came with observations by Richard Simon and Baruch Spinoza in the seventeenth century that these books were full of repetitions and contradictions and seemed to lack the style of a single author. In the next century, Jean Astruc was able to identify a very concrete case, when he pointed out that the creation story in

Genesis 1 used the Hebrew word "elohim" for God's name, while a second creation story in Genesis 2 and 3 regularly used "Yahweh elohim." Moreover the style of the first was dry and list-like, while the second was anthropomorphic and earthy. He proposed that Moses had combined two sources to produce these early chapters of Genesis. Thus source criticism was born. For the next two centuries it focused most of its attention on the problems of the Pentateuch, and it took two centuries to reach a consensus that there were four major written sources behind our present Pentateuch.

At first, scholars thought there were only two earlier documents, one called the Yahwist source, and the other the Elohist, based on the way each referred to God's name. But it soon became clear that the passages in Genesis and Exodus which used *elohim* represented two separate writers. One had a very priestly cast to it, with interest in genealogy lists, rituals, laws, and other liturgical matters. This became known as the Priestly source, and included the hymn-like creation account in Genesis 1. The other contained many old stories of Jacob and Moses and was concerned with historical traditions. This was allowed to keep the name Elohist for itself. Now there were three sources, and it didn't take long to identify a fourth. The unique style of the Book of Deuteronomy set it apart from the other three. Where the latter were filled with brief scenes and incidents, Deuteronomy loved long speeches and sermons. These four sources are often simply called by their first letters, *J, E, P, D*. The "*J*" instead of a "*Y*" comes from the German word *Jahve*, for it was German scholars who first proposed the abbreviations.

Many other characteristic elements and ways of thinking identify each of these sources. By examining the numerous cases of *repeated* stories and *duplicated* passages, they can be easily separated from one another. A few of the most important examples are (1) the three different accounts of the patriarch who lies about his wife as his sister in Genesis 12, 20 and 26; (2) the two creation stories in Genesis 1 and Genesis 2–3; (3) the two accounts of how Abraham sends out Hagar with her son Ishmael to the desert in Genesis 16 and 21; (4) the two calls of Moses to lead his people out of Egypt in Exodus 3 and 6.

But even within a single story, critics have been able to detect more than one source blended together by the change in particular words. Two clear cases of this type are the story of the flood (Gen 6–9) and of Joseph being sold into Egypt (Gen 37–48). In the flood story, Noah is told to take seven pairs of all clean animals and one pair of all unclean animals in Genesis 7:2, but in 7:9 and 15 it looks as though God told him to take just one pair of each animal species. In the Joseph story of Genesis 37, his ten brothers plot to kill Joseph, but Reuben pleads for the boy and they put him into a pit and later Midianites find him and sell him. Side by side with this account, we find a second in which Judah is the one who pleads for Joseph and so the brothers sell him to Ishmaelites instead. At other times we find two different words appearing again and again throughout the Pentateuch for the same object. Thus the mountain on which God gives the covenant is sometimes called Sinai, and sometimes Horeb. Or the people who live in Palestine are called sometimes Canaanites and sometimes Amorites.

All of these examples can be explained by themselves with some skill so that no real problem seems to exist, but when they are all examined and sorted out into columns the effect is much stronger. Four basic narratives appear, each with a certain style of its own that tells the story of Israel from a unique perspective.

Wellhausen's History of the Four Sources

It was Julius Wellhausen who worked out this schema in its complete form and published it in his *Prolegomena to the History of Israel* (1878). He gave this "Documentary Theory" added strength and made it convincing to most Protestant scholars by drawing up a history of how each source came to be. Now the biblical student not only could discover four different authors and their literary styles but could picture clearly the time and place from which each source came. A brief sketch based on Wellhausen's work will show the proposed development in which the early and mostly oral traditions of Israel were gradually written down, preserved in four written documents, and then combined to make one Pentateuch.

When David and Solomon united Israel as a kingdom, a new era of trained scribes and writers was made possible. Sometime during Solomon's reign, or soon after, in Jerusalem, an unknown author put together the Yahwist account from the viewpoint of the southern tribe of Judah, and to glorify the monarchy created by David and Solomon.

When Solomon died and the nation split into a northern kingdom, which called itself just plain Israel, and a southern kingdom, called Judah, the northerners needed a revised version of the traditions which would not glorify Jerusalem and the kings of Judah so much. They produced a second and revised account of the old traditions which used Elohim for God and place names that were more familiar to their part of the country. They also stressed the role of the covenant of Moses over the role of the king, and avoided much of the Yahwist's intimate language about God walking and talking with humans. They favored instead a more "spiritualized" and awesome sense of God's dealings with Israel. These two accounts existed side by side as long as the two kingdoms lasted. When the north fell to the Assyrian army in 722 B.C., the northerners who fled south carried their written Elohist source with them. The J and E documents were then combined as one during the following century for the people who lived now only in Judah.

At the same time, there arose a group of priests, levites and prophets who attempted to reform many bad practices of the faith in Judah. Out of their efforts came the Book of Deuteronomy (D source). This arose partly in reaction to "primitive" ideas in J's and E's theology of promise and blessing for the promised land. The Deuteronomist reformers collected covenant legal traditions and added to them sermons stressing obedience and faithfulness to the covenant if the people were to receive blessings in the promised land. Although put together out of the best of both northern and southern traditions during a long period from Hezekiah (715–688) through Josiah (640 B.C.), it was only "discovered" hidden away in the temple when Josiah began his reforms of 622. The king and people alike recognized its authority and genuine Mosaic flavor, and D was joined with J and E as part of the nation's sacred traditions.

Finally when the whole country went into exile under the Babylonians in 597 to 586, a school of priests seems to have gathered many of the cultic and legal traditions together. This included the lists of ancestors preserved in the temple, the isolated stories and traditions not found in the earlier works, and most of the great law collections in Leviticus and Numbers. This Priestly work (called P) thus formed a fourth source which made the earlier historical accounts more complete and at the same time set forth a whole way of life under the law that would allow Israel's covenant with God to be lived and to last even when there was no land or temple or king. According to Wellhausen, these four sources were finally edited by the Priestly school into the Pentateuch after the exile ended in 539 B.C. This then is the classical four-source theory followed by the majority of scholars in our own century. The accompanying chart shows its lines of development.

The underlying view behind this picture belongs really to the nineteenth century with its romantic view of how cultures develop

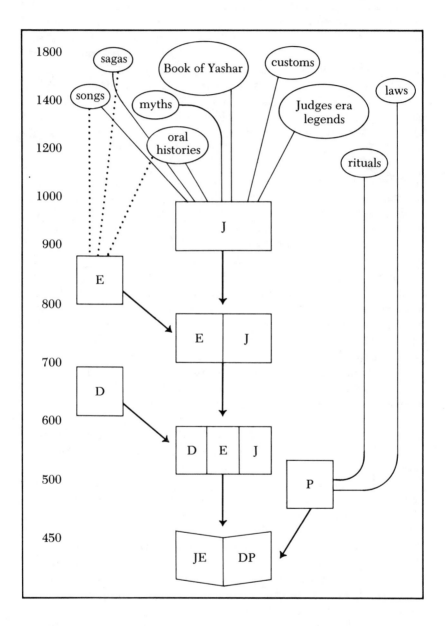

from primitive levels to more advanced ones. Thus the Yahwist represents such a primitive anthropomorphic view of God, still filled with magical appearances and mythical details. The Elohist shows a deeper awareness of God's distance, while the Deuteronomist reflects the later and more sensitive concern of the prophets to the ethical demands and oneness of God over the whole world. Finally, the Priestly source brings together the complex institutional, cultic, and legal aspects of Israelite faith that would support a life of fidelity to the covenant through exile and times of loss.

We can summarize these four strands or sources in a chart that lists their major characteristics:

Yahwist (J)	Elohist (E)	Priestly (P)	Deuteronomist (D)
God is Yahweh	God is Elohim	God is Elohim	God is Yahweh
God walks and talks with us	God speaks in dreams, etc.	cultic approach to God	moralistic approach
stress on blessing	stress on fear of the Lord	stress on law obeyed	stress on Mosaic obedience
earthy speech about God	refined speech about God	majestic speech about God	speech recalling God's work
stresses the leaders	stresses the prophetic	stresses the cultic	stresses fidelity to Jerusalem
narrative and stories	narrative and warnings	dry lists and schemata	long homiletic speeches
stress on Judah	stress on northern Israel	stress on Judah	stress on whole land of Israel
uses term "Sinai"	uses "Horeb"		
calls natives "Canaanites"	calls natives "Amorites"		
		uses genealogy lists	loves military imagery
			has many fixed phrases

Now follows a brief overview of the three major narrative sources in Genesis to Numbers. Deuteronomy will be treated separately in Chapter 17. The Priestly editing of the entire Pentateuch into one document will be expanded in Chapter 19.

The Yahwist Epic

The Yahwist forms the heart of the Pentateuchal structure, for all the various traditions are built around the basic "plot" first found in J. It consists of seven steps:

1. Stories of human origins
2. The promise of the patriarchs
3. The oppression in Egypt
4. The exodus from Egypt
5. The wandering in the wilderness
6. The covenant at Mount Sinai
7. On the edge of the promised land

This material covers only the Books of Genesis through Numbers. Deuteronomy as a separate source has no J material. The seven steps also show that the J author wrote a continuous story, and was not just a collector of individual events. Since form criticism has pointed out the many different settings and types of traditional units that existed in ancient Israel, we can be certain that J did not write from whole cloth. He brought together old poems, stories, and songs of the exodus that were alive in the cult, particularly favoring those from Judah. It is most likely that the Israelite tribes in Palestine had already worked out a general order of the main traditions according to an historical plan. The sequence of exodus, desert period, conquest, and period of the judges must have been known and celebrated very early. On the other hand, the order of the patriarchs Abraham, Isaac and Jacob may have differed in various areas of the country. Local tradition favored Abraham rather than Jacob, for example, at Hebron, where Abraham had lived. The stories of Genesis 1–11 on the world's beginnings had never been part of the older tradition but had come from liturgical or catechetical schools, and were unique in style and message from the historical remembrances. Part of the genius of J was his ability to put together a complete story of God's actions, not just back to the exodus, but all the way to the beginning of the world.

However J did not just write down facts and legends as he had received them. He was an artist as well as a theologian and used many devices to create his own style. He loved to put words and speeches into the mouths of famous people. Often they *foreshadow* what was later to happen. An excellent example occurs in Genesis 15:13–15 where God lays out for Abraham Israel's coming history right up to the time of King David as a preview of the fulfillment of the divine promise to the patriarch. The speech helps the listener know what God's plan is and how carefully God works everything out to fulfill his promises. The Yahwist especially enjoys putting the long speeches into God's own mouth. Yahweh dialogues with Adam in the Garden of Eden about the first sin; he carries on a monologue with himself over whether he should bring on a flood in Genesis 6; he discusses with Abraham the sin and destruction of Sodom in Genesis 18; he plays with Moses' request to see the divine face in Exodus 33.

The Yahwist also likes to point out important themes from folk tradition. The motif of *conflict between brothers* is central to the stories of Cain and Abel, Jacob and Esau, and Joseph and his eleven brothers. The *triumph of the younger brother over the older brother* forms an important element in each of these stories also. Still another theme centers on the *wife who cannot bear children.* Abraham's wife Sarah, Isaac's wife Rebecca, Jacob's wife Rachel—all are barren until God gives a special blessing to them.

The Yahwist epic also has a fine sense of *story-telling.* It becomes even more remarkable when compared to the other writings of the ancient world. Most of the Babylonian or Assyrian or Hittite works we know seem stilted and very formal, with very little dramatic sense of history. For a book written in the tenth century before Christ, the J epic has the quality of a modern historical novel.

J has to be traced to the great outburst of energy and talent that flowered in the new empire created by David and Solomon. Several other parts of the Bible come from this same period and share many of the artistic merits of the Yahwist. There is, for example, the wonderful story of the conflicts among David's sons for the right of succession to the throne that we find in 2 Samuel 9–20 and 1 Kings 1–2. It is a masterpiece of psychological insight into David the mighty ruler who was too soft on his own sons. A very similar talent for portraying the weakness and strengths of Saul can be found in the story of David's own rise to power in 1 Samuel 16–31. These both have been written in the style seen in J: vibrant, action-centered, full of psychological insight into the chief persons, and dramatically oriented toward the coming of some great hero to power. In the throne succession narrative, that hero is Solomon; in the conflict with Saul, it is David.

These connections to David and Solomon have led scholars to place the J epic in the heady days of David's new empire. Certainly its spirit of optimism that Israel would be a great nation and blessed by Yahweh (Gen 12), and the hints of nationalistic pride in Judah, the tribe from whom a king will arise (Gen 49), and the promise of power over the neighboring countries of Edom and Moab (Gen 27:39–40) all fit best the empire created by David and Solomon, and seem far removed from the struggling and weak state of the two kingdoms that existed after Solomon died. The real meaning of themes such as the triumph of the younger brother over the older would not be missed by an audience who knew that David was the last of eight brothers, or that Solomon was the last of even more. The climax of the Yahwist story comes in the final great vision of the prophet Balaam in Numbers 24 where the seer is paid to curse Israel but instead sees the glorious future:

> I see him but not now;
> I behold him but not near:
> A star will come forth from Jacob
> And a scepter from Israel will rise.
> It will crush the forehead of Moab
> And shatter the sons of Shet.
> Edom will be dispossessed
> And no survivor left in Seir,
> But Israel will act valiantly
> And Jacob will rule over his foes (Num 24:17–19).

Many biblical source critics think that the J epic ends right at this point. God has taken care of his chosen patriarchs and tribes, he has led them from danger and slavery in Egypt, he has promised them a land of blessing to come, and now the vision is before them. The Yahwist knows that everybody who hears this story in Solomon's time will immediately say: "Yes, God has truly fulfilled his promise in our own time, for we have become a great nation and blessed in power over our enemies."

Naturally, the coming of the empire had its strains and less honorable moments, as when David took Bathsheba and killed her husband (2 Sam 11), or when Solomon killed his own brother after taking the throne (1 Kgs 2). But the Yahwist understood those events as the dark side of Israel's response to God's gift of land. He expressed the reality of good and evil side by side pointing to the traditions of the patriarchs themselves, and even further back to age-old beliefs about creation itself. Abraham was portrayed as a faithful believer in Yahweh's promise despite the frequent blocks he placed in its way—blocks that included his willingness to hand over his wife to foreign kings (Gen 12:20) or his free-wheeling offer to let Lot take the promised land (Gen 13). Jacob kept the divine blessing even though he was often dishonest and shifty in his dealings with both Esau and Laban (Gen 27:29–31).

The theme of Adam's sin followed by punishment and a new start, or Cain's sin, punishment and new start, or all of humanity's evil, punishment by flood and new start under Noah, highlighted for the Yahwist an abiding conviction that human freedom to do evil will always play a part even in the midst of God's most generous bountiful blessings to Israel, and to the world as a whole. He pushes his "history" back to the beginnings to illustrate the divine planning and lordship over all of creation. Israel only plays one role, although a special role, in the much greater plan of God for all human beings. And God can use Israel, or any other nation, and David, or any other king, with their sins and weaknesses as well as their strengths, to accomplish his will.

The Yahwist created more than a *story* of Israel's past; he created a theology and a purpose that explained the religious faith and special spirit of the nation. It became the foundation for Israel's future meditation upon Yahweh's love.

The Elohist Source

The second major source of the Pentateuchal tradition is the Elohist reworking of the basic Yahwist account. Generally it is believed that this was done in the northern kingdom after it became established as an independent state at Solomon's death. It does not include as much material as does the J story, and what it does cover tends to favor *northern ideas.* For example it pays much less attention to Abraham than to Jacob, a patriarch who lived in the area of Shechem, Bethel and other northern cities. It puts much less stress on the role of Moses and the elders in the giving of the covenant than does J, and accepts a much larger role for all the people giving their assent to the covenant. This reflects the difference between the J concern for proper leadership and E's suspicion of authorities which claim too much power. Also in line with northern respect for the role of prophets such as Elijah in speaking on national policy, E refers somewhat oddly to Abraham as a prophet (Gen 20:7). E takes a strong stand against foreign gods because of the ever-present threat of the religion of Baal in the north (see Gen 35:2). E never speaks of God walking and talking with humans in the garden or on the road as does J. God keeps his divine distance and majesty and communicates through messengers or dreams (Gen 20:3). E shows its opposition to the dynastic claims of David's house by recalling God's warning to Moses not to start a dynasty (Ex 18). It reflects problems with the shrines to Yahweh at Dan and Bethel where the first King Jeroboam had put up golden calves when it points out the problems with a golden calf in the time of Moses and Aaron (Ex 32).

Perhaps the major religious insight of the Elohist source is the importance of the "fear of God" among the people. It is the theme of submission to the divine power and willingness to accept God's will even in a time of testing and hardship. When asked to sacrifice his son Isaac, Abraham obeys out of fear of God (Gen 22:12); Joseph spares his brothers from death when they are at his mercy because he fears God (Gen 42:24); Israel prospers in the midst of Pharaoh's persecution because the midwives fear God (Ex 1:15–17); Moses fears God (Ex 3:6), and the elders fear God (Ex 18:21); finally all the people fear God and accept his covenant at Sinai (Ex 20:18–20). The difference between J and E in this respect can be seen most clearly by contrasting the two stories of how Abraham passed Sarah off as his sister to a powerful king in order to save his own life. The J version in Genesis 12:10–20 does not condemn Abraham's foolish conduct but tells how God punished only Pharaoh. This reflects J's interest in Abraham as the perfect model of a leader very much like King David. E, on the other hand gives a version in Genesis 20:1–17 in which both Abraham and the king realize that Abraham has done a great wrong by lying, but explains Abraham's mistake by excusing his lack of trust with the words: "I said to myself, 'Surely there is no fear of God in this place and so they will kill me because of my wife'" (Gen 20:11).

These examples reveal a spirit in the E document that is much more concerned about *ethical and moral questions* than is J. This falls in line with the great prophetic campaigns in the north by Elijah and other zealots for Yahweh who had to fight tooth and nail against the sexual license and lax standards of pagan fertility cults. Where J reflected many of the ideals of David's kingdom and the hopes of Judah for a lasting and intimate relationship of Yahweh to his temple in Jerusalem, E favors the ideals of the covenant in the desert, where the tribes endured difficulties and temptations until they finally won through to their new home in Palestine.

E is not as large as J, and it was written to supplement or correct certain royalist leanings in J, so naturally it seems a bit thin to modern readers. Perhaps it was never an independent book in its own right at all, but only a series of additions to the basic J story. And even where it may be present in our books, sometimes there is no way of telling J from E since they would both cover the same material. An example of this is Genesis 15, the great covenant with Abraham. Almost all scholars simply throw up their hands at deciding this passage and call it a combined JE. The same is true of the sacrifice of Isaac in Genesis 22. Often the easiest way to tell them apart is from the use of the names for God, Elohim or Yahweh. But this only works up to Exodus 3, where God tells his name to Moses for the first time. After that moment, E and P both call God Yahweh just as J has done all along.

But if we cannot always tell E from J in one passage, we can see over the whole story in Genesis to Numbers that there are clearly two views mixed which correspond to the differences between Judah and the northern ten tribes in the period from David (1000 B.C.) to the fall of Samaria and the North (722 B.C.). It is from this period that both J and E come.

The Priestly Source

The P source was the last great narrative source to be put together. It clearly intended to supplement what J and E said about the historical traditions of Israel with special materials on worship, observance of the covenant in day to day life, and social structures of Israelite community. J and E traced the promise of God up to the covenant on Sinai and the taking of the land of Canaan as a gift. This was adequate to Israel while it had full possession of the land and a king or kings to protect their religious practice from pagan threats. But P shows many signs that it was written in the time of the exile when the land and the king had both been taken away. One piece of evidence is found in the comparison of the prophet Ezekiel's message during the exile with the thought of P in Leviticus 17–26. They show such similarities that it seems certain that P knew Ezekiel's writings. To help people maintain their faith in Yahweh even when everything seemed to have been lost, P set out all the aspects of Israel's faith that were still valid. It includes in its story the reasons for keeping the sabbath (Gen 1), the origins of circumcision (Gen 17), the divine command to obey all the cultic and religious laws (Lev 1–27, Num 1–10, 25–36), and the important role of the high priest next to Moses himself (Ex 4:28; Num 1, etc.). The center of the tradition for the P source was not the promise of land but the time in the desert at Sinai where the law was given and the tent and ark were built for Yahweh. P's treatment of these themes takes up more space than the entire J and E narratives put together.

Everything that P treats offers the possibility of practicing one's faith despite conditions of hardship or even loss of the land. This is explained in greater detail in Chapter 19 as part of the new outlook on faith that took place in the exile. But at the same time, P was very concerned to give Israel a sense of trust in Yahweh's goodness and fidelity so that they would not lose faith in their God. To this end, P structured many details of the old tradition into new patterns that put the emphasis on continuity. Some of these can be listed:

(1) *The use of genealogies.* There is nothing like tracing one's roots back many generations to give a sense of stability and strength to a family. Thus P inserted genealogies between many of the key scenes in the JE narrative. Thus he showed the continuing care of God over his human creatures by adding Genesis 5 and 11 to link Adam to Noah and Noah to Abraham. He adds further lists of Ishmael's family (Gen 25), Esau's family (Gen 36) and Jacob's family (Gen 46).

(2) *Place names.* Just as genealogies traced human history up to Abraham and then away from him, so P lists the place names of all the camping sites where Israel stayed while in the exodus and desert years. Six lead up to Mount Sinai and six take them from Mount Sinai to the promised land (Ex 12:37; 13:20; 14:1; 15:22; 16:1; 17:1; 19:2; Num 10:12; 20:1; 20:22; 21:10; 22:1).

(3) *Establishing laws for future generations.* The decrees on sabbath observance in Genesis 2:3, on not eating bloody meat in Genesis 9:4, on circumcision in Genesis 17:9–11, and the regulations of Sinai in Leviticus 1 through Numbers 10 are aimed not at those who lived in the past but at those who will come much later. Thus the Israelite will read the ancient traditions as really speaking to the present day.

(4) *Emphasis on the divine presence in Israel's midst.* P gives a great deal of attention to the building of the tent and the ark which represent a promise of the temple to come (cf. the descriptions in Exodus 25–40 with the plan of the temple of Solomon in 1 Kings 6–7). The regulations of Moses also describe in detail the role of sacrifices and feasts, and appoint priests, levites and other cultic personnel. Above all God makes himself known to his people in his "glory" which fills the tent and goes with the people through the

desert (Ex 40). These are all elements that any Israelite would and did experience in the temple at Jerusalem. What had been true in the days of Moses was still true in the centuries after: God was close to his people when they worshiped and listened to his voice.

(5) *God's word is primary.* Whenever there is an important moment in Israel's history, the divine word creates it: Genesis 1 and the creation of the world; Genesis 6:13–21 and God's command about the flood; Genesis 17 and the covenant to Abraham; Exodus 6 and the promise of exodus and land; Exodus 25 and the instruction for a permanent resting place for Yahweh. Events may go one way or another, but the word of God is proclaimed and heard in every age.

(6) *The importance of blessing.* Where J and E so often brought in the failures of people as part of God's plan, P overlooks these in favor of God's enduring promise of blessing upon the world. The P story of creation in Genesis 1 records how God blessed the first humans, and Genesis 9 repeats that blessing after the flood. God creates and recreates, and each time he is prepared to bless humanity anew. This was an important message for an Israel suffering exile. It gave the people grounds for continued hope.

When all of these are considered together, it is easy to see that P moves the story of salvation along as a single historical lesson for future generations. One stage always leads to the next, and at each stage God acts in a deeper or fuller way without losing what was earlier. P has actually woven the themes of blessing, promise, covenant, the revelation of the divine name, and human response to God around the stories of the major patriarchal figures before Moses. The pattern falls into four stages, each with its special characteristics:

Patriarch	Blessing	Signs of Promise	Name of God	Obligation on us
Adam	fertility, dominion	sabbath rest	Elohim	eat only plants, rest for land
Noah	renewed fertility, dominion	rainbow	Elohim	sacrifice, no blood in meat
Abraham	promise of land	buys cave at Machpelah (Gen 23)	Shaddai	circumcision

Patriarch	Blessing	Signs of Promise	Name of God	Obligation on us
Moses	Sinai covenant ("I will be your God; you shall be my people")	the glory of Yahweh	Yahweh	obedience to the law

Form Critics and the Pentateuch

By 1900, many biblical scholars were convinced that Wellhausen had basically solved all the major problems involved in the growth of the first five books of the Bible. But suddenly the area of major interest shifted to form criticism and its interest in the *typical* ways of primitive folk culture, especially the factors involved in oral transmission of stories and information.

The form critics, such as Hermann Gunkel, reacted against many of the conclusions of the so-called documentary thesis, pointing out that the source critics often overlooked the oral poetry and the primitive forms still present in the Pentateuch. They asked some hard questions of the four-source theory. They objected to the idea that editors would paste together a brilliant new work by cutting up four older ones. They asked why they did not manage to eliminate so many contradictions and repetitions—poor editors they seemed to be! Many denied that the Elohist source was ever a written source at all—it simply did not have enough substance. They suggested instead that the Elohist represented a reworking of the Yahwist using oral traditions known only to the northern kingdom. In the same way they challenged the belief that P was a complete narrative story. It, too, seemed to be a collection of laws, temple records, and a few special stories (the creation account in Genesis 1, the covenant with Abraham in Genesis 17) that were probably used in liturgy or religious instruction. In short, the form critics have opened up the possibility that everything not in the original J account was handed on piece by piece—by the judges and legal offices, by temple liturgists, by folksingers in the north, by prophets, by the wise men in the court of the king. Over the centuries these were gradually added to the J account. In this scheme, the Yahwist represents the common tradition known in tenth century Israel, and it grew in several stages through the following centuries until a truly brilliant final editing by Priestly circles sometime before Ezra in the fifth century gave it the final form we know today. The Pentateuch is understood then as a complex of many types of traditions, ranging from some still close to their oral origins, as are the Song of Miriam in Exodus 15 or the Song of the Well in Numbers 21, up to some very highly developed law codes found in the Books of Leviticus and Deuteronomy which date only to the seventh or sixth centuries.

We can summarize the century of development from source criticism through form criticism by observing that *neither stands alone.* Writing and oral story-telling may have been used at the same time. Laws, for example, were written down as long ago as 1000 B.C., and a tradition that Moses gave the law on two stone tablets could easily rest on solid foundations. Yet at the same time, we have found no written laws in Egypt at all, and so we can just as rightly conclude that much of the law was decided by custom and principles handed down orally. The same may be said of the treaty form of the covenant with God at Mount Sinai. We know of many ancient Near Eastern treaties long before the Israelite kings appeared, and there is no reason to rule out that some legal-covenantal documents could have been kept by the tribes in Palestine before the time of David.

Moreover, the Bible itself records that many written sources were known in Israel. Numbers 21:14 quotes a "Book of the Wars of Yahweh," and Joshua 10:13 cites the "Book of Yashar." The two Books of Kings frequently mention the chronicles of the kings of Israel and the chronicles of the kings of Judah. Evidence from the practice of Babylon and Ugarit indicates that laws, lists of kings, and the texts of religious rituals to be read or proclaimed aloud in the temple were all stored in written forms.

The addition of form criticism to the study of the Pentateuch has prevented us from seeing only four complete books put together so tightly that the main task of Bible study is to untangle them. Now we can see that Genesis 1–11 is indeed a different type of literature—myth—and can be appreciated for what it is. We can see that the Abraham stories use many hero saga motifs and better understand how Abraham was remembered and known in early Israel. To return to the original question raised in this chapter— "Who really wrote the Pentateuch?"—modern criticism has come around almost full circle. Instead of Wellhausen's doubt that anything could be attributed to Moses, form criticism affirms that— while the Pentateuch was not actually written down by Moses—

many of its traditions, legal practices and covenant forms may actually date back to the time of Moses, and their central importance for Israel may even have originated with him, or at least with the community of the exodus and conquest. Chapters 6 through 9 will develop the contributions of the form critics in more detail.

STUDY QUESTIONS

1. Briefly describe each of the five books which comprise the Pentateuch.
2. "Undoubtedly, Moses is the sole author of the first five books of the Bible." Assess the validity of this statement.
3. Give a brief overview how source criticism began. What were the four sources identified in the Pentateuch?
4. Briefly describe some of the major characteristics of J, E, P, D.
5. What are the seven steps contained in the Yahwist source? In what books is this material found? What does the Yahwist source attempt to do? What are some major themes in the Yahwist source? How are they developed?
6. How does the Elohist source differ from the Yahwist? What is distinctive about the Elohist source? What are its major themes? How are they developed?
7. How does the Priestly source differ from the Yahwist and Elohist? What is distinctive about the Priestly source? What are its major themes? How are they developed?
8. Explain how source criticism and form criticism have contributed to understanding the Pentateuch.

Chapter 6

GENESIS 1–11:
THE PREFACE TO ISRAEL'S STORY

Suggested Scripture Reading:

Genesis 1–11

Genesis: The First Book of the Bible

The Book of Genesis covers a vast amount of time, stretching from the beginning of the world down to about 1500 B.C. According to geologists, the earth is at least four billion years old, and some anthropologists believe that we humans have been around at least two million of those years. The authors of Genesis did not know much about this long history, nor did they care. They wished to sketch instead a few highlights about human origins that had particular religious significance for Israel's view of life, and to record a few traditions about their own ancestors that would help them understand how they came to be a people and a nation. In fact, eighty percent of Genesis is dedicated to the few founding patriarchs, Abraham, Isaac and Jacob, and only twenty percent to the remaining story of creation and life through the first two million years.

We cannot speak of a true sense of national history in Israel until the time of the exodus. The events of liberation from Egypt and conquest of land, added to the unifying power of a new religious faith built around the covenant with Yahweh, created the Israel whose history is the subject of all subsequent biblical narrative. Anything earlier is a kind of pre-history, a collection of remembrances and theological reflections that help throw light on the

109

meaning of the exodus. Genesis can be understood somewhat like a special background briefing that government officials often give to newspaper reporters before a big event. Israel understood that God had begun something big in the exodus, but they also knew that God did not just begin to act on a whim. He had been involved in the world and in their story from the beginning. To indicate this concretely, they gathered early tribal traditions about great ancestors around a special theme of *promise*. Genesis 12–50 represents Israel's attempt to show that Yahweh had guided their ancestors in a way of promise up to the events of the exodus. For a fuller treatment of this theme, see the next chapter.

Finally, in the days of King David's new world empire, it seemed important to prepare a preface that would place God's saving actions for Israel in the light of his care for the whole world. Thus Genesis 1–11 began to take shape, and although it has the first place in the Bible, it is by no means the first part to be written. Rather it is the fruit of prolonged thought and reflection over several centuries. But it is the place to begin the biblical *story*. Its strong images and rich language explore the depths of human experience at its most mysterious—the awesome wonder of creation, the joys of life, the agony of sin, the fear of death, the terrible human capacity for evil, the existence of God and the questions about his patience and justice. In bold strokes it makes us understand what God's *salvation* meant to Israel.

Genesis 1–11 as Preface

The outline of this preface, or the Primeval History, as it is often called, can be broken into several stages:

1. Two creation accounts (Gen 1–2)
2. The fall of humanity into sin and punishment (Gen 3–4)
3. The list of ancient heroes from Adam to Noah (Gen 4:17–5:32)
4. The story of how giants were born due to sin (Gen 6:1–4)
5. The flood as punishment of that sin (Gen 6:5–9:29)
6. The new list of nations spread across the world (Gen 10)
7. The sin of the tower of Babel (Gen 11:1–9)
8. The list of patriarchs from Noah down to Abraham (Gen 11:10–32)

Source critics have shown that this outline in turn belongs to two basic sources, the Yahwist and the Priestly:

Yahwist (J)	Priestly (P)
	Creation of the world (Gen 1)
Creation of humans (Gen 2)	
Sin and loss of Eden (Gen 3)	
The sin of Cain (Gen 4)	First list of patriarchs (Gen 5)
The giants (Gen 6)	
A flood story (Gen 6–9)	A flood story (Gen 6–9)
Table of nations (Gen 10)	
Tower of Babel (Gen 11)	
	Second list of patriarchs (Gen 11)
Story of Abraham	Story of Abraham

The older of the two is of course J, who has joined together several old stories and myths and rewritten them to fit his religious message about Yahweh. Thus the original preface contained only those stories that are in the first column. They reflect Israel's thinking in the tenth century when it had become large enough as a nation to face other countries and their beliefs. It became important to discuss why God had chosen Israel over the nations, and why pagan beliefs, which seemed so attractive, were not faithful to God's will. Such a time of national confrontation and rethinking came under the great new empire of David and Solomon.

Examination of the J outline above shows that the original primeval history spoke mostly about how humans acted toward God and God's patient response. The J creation begins with humanity; other creatures are made for human use. All is rooted in goodness, but very soon sin enters into the picture and challenges God's rule through disobedience. For the Yahwist, early human history is continually a *four-part* story of *sin*, God's warning *punishments*, divine *mercy*, and then further *sin*. When Adam and Eve sin, God punishes them but promises future hope. Cain kills Abel (evil spreads more deeply), but God spares Cain's life even as he punishes. Soon humans multiply their wickedness and wanton behavior, even unnaturally as in the story of the giants, and God sends the flood, but he spares Noah and restores humanity. Despite the blessing to Noah and the great increase of nations seen in Genesis 10, the people again rebel in pride to challenge God's rule by building a tower to heaven. God punishes them by confusing human languages, but again gives promise for the future in choosing Abraham.

J's purpose in Genesis 1–11 is to underline how God remains *faithful* to his human race despite their hardness and frequent rejection of him. The author has taken ancient stories of various types and used them to show how God gave us dominion and responsibility for the world, the freedom to act on our own, and the gifts to achieve happiness. But through pride and a rebellious spirit, we have rejected this important task because we would not be subordinate to God. The sin in the human heart has unleashed on the world an evergrowing round of murder, war, and hatred, robbed us of life and brought frustration and pain to our labors. But over and over, the theme of God's mercy to a sinful world can be heard in the background. It finds its strongest expression in the great compassion of God to Noah, his one faithful servant in the midst of worldwide corruption, by sparing him from the flood. Thus for the Yahwist, a true perspective of faith always includes the promise of *blessing* for our fidelity to God even while we know and experience the effects of sin and evil in us and around us. The beautiful promise of Genesis 8:21–22 sums up this hope:

> Never again will I curse the ground because of humans,
>   however evil their inclinations from their youth. Never
>   again will I destroy all living creatures as I have just done.

> While the earth lasts
>   seedtime and harvest
>   cold and heat,
> Summer and winter,
>   day and night
>   shall never cease.

The citizens of the kingdom of David and Solomon would undoubtedly appreciate that the message was directed to them. God had indeed blessed them for the difficult years of the judges by giving them empire because they had faithfully fought in his name.

In contrast to J, the P source materials in Genesis 1–11 focus on a few crucial events: the creation of the world, the destruction of life by flood, the restoration of blessing to Noah, and the family history of Abraham. Because the P writers were also the final editors of Genesis, they simply took the earlier J preface and worked it into their outline. It is clear that the principal way they achieved the final union of the two was by arranging the concrete stories of sin and blessing in J within a series of *lists*. The P creation story in Genesis 1 lists God's works of creation; its treatment of the flood lists the ten patriarchs before Noah; it adds numerous dates to the original flood narrative in Genesis 6–9 which correspond to the solar calendar of three hundred and sixty-five days; it then follows J's table of nations with their own list of peoples in Genesis 11.

But on another level, P works out a wider theology built around the *goodness* of God's creation. P adds no more stories of sin to those already found in J, but concentrates on moments of blessing. Creation is entirely good and it reaches its peak in the blessing God bestows on Adam and Eve in Genesis 1:28:

> Be fruitful and multiply, fill the earth and subdue it; rule over the fish of the sea, the birds of the air, and over all living creatures moving upon the earth (NEB).

In Genesis 9, after the flood ceases, God restores this same blessing to Noah and his descendants, but adds to it a further gift—the right to eat meat (Gen 9:1–3). Later in the P narrative, the authors will extend other important moments of blessing to Abraham (Gen 17), to Jacob (Gen 28) and to Moses (Ex 6).

Much of the Priestly account shows definite signs of its origin with the priests and temple schools: (1) the account of creation in Genesis 1 has the refrains and solemn tones of a liturgical prayer, not unlike the singing of the *Exultet* at the Easter vigil in Catholic worship; (2) it emphasizes blessings and sacrifices as part of religious ceremonies; (3) it maintains an interest in precise genealogy lists, a task of ancient temple scribes who kept the birth, marriage, and death records, as well as most business contracts and debts; (4) it stresses the covenant that God makes with all humans at the time of Noah, and which is later extended in a special way to Abraham and his descendants, and finally to Moses and the whole people of Israel.

It is only in the combination of both J and P together that the full richness of Hebrew thought on human beginnings is revealed. The following description of the individual sections will help us appreciate how Israel's vision grew from the time of David and Solomon with its national optimism to the time of the Priestly writers in the exile or shortly after, when a more *universal* view of God's blessing was needed—one that was not tied so closely to the land and that did not make God quite so "human" and available as did J.

The Priestly Creation Story (Gen 1:1–2:4)

The P account of creation in seven days is a brilliant beginning to the Old Testament. It combines the best of Hebrew narrative style with the soaring refrains of a hymn. It does not waste a word, but uses a carefully worked out structure combined with repetition of key expressions to create a powerful effect on the reader or listener. As in a good drama or carefully told children's story, we experience the awe and majesty of God's creative power in the very telling of the event.

The creation itself unfolds in six days, carefully balanced into three days each:

1st Day	creation of light	4th Day	creation of bodies of light
2nd Day	creation of heavens and water	5th Day	creation of creatures of heaven and waters
3rd Day	creation of land and vegetation	6th Day	creation of life on land and its vegetable food, creation of humankind

On the first three days, God creates the physical world and separates each part into its place; on the last three days, God populates this world with living creatures and assigns them their proper roles. The climax of the creative process is the human being, whom God makes male and female, blesses, and appoints as his deputy to have dominion over his new creation.

The world which is thus described does not share the same scientific view that we have, in which the earth is one planet around one sun in a universe full of suns and planets. The ancient picture of the universe is more like that depicted, in which the earth is a disc surrounded by water not only on the sides, but underneath and above as well. A firm bowl (the "firma-ment") keeps the upper waters back but has gates to let the rain and snow through. The sun,

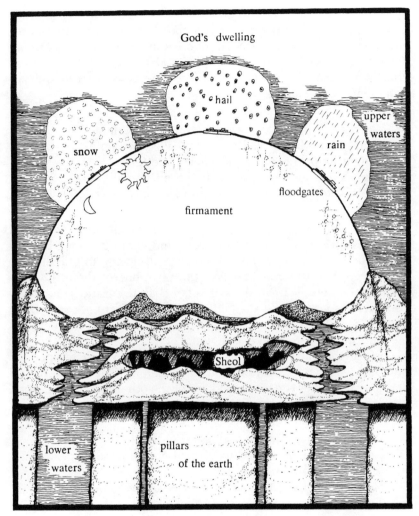

A reconstruction of Ancient Hebrew Cosmology

moon, and stars move in fixed tracks along the underside of this bowl. From below the disc, the waters break through as wells, rivers, and the ocean, but the earth stands firm on pillars sunk into the waters like the pilings of a pier. Deep below the earth is Sheol, the abode of the dead, which can be entered only through the grave.

In this picture, the Israelites were no different from other ancient people around them. Even the order of creation is very similar to the Babylonian account of creation, which we call *Enuma Elish*. In this story, known from at least 1700 B.C., long before the Priestly account, the world begins from the gods of fresh and salt water, Apsu and Tiamat:

> When on high the heavens had not been named,
> Firm ground below had not been called by name,
> Naught by primordial Apsu, their begetter,
> (And) Mummu-Tiamat, she who bore them all,
> Their waters commingling as a single body (ANET 60–61).

From the union of the primeval waters, all other gods and goddesses spring. Soon there is discord and fighting among them— and Apsu and Tiamat, deeply disappointed, decide to kill all their offspring. When the gods discover the plan, one of them, Ea, kills Apsu. Alone now, Tiamat, the symbol of chaotic darkness and disorder, declares war against the gods. The gods in fear choose a young warrior god, Marduk, to lead them against their own mother. But they must agree to make him king of the gods before he will undertake the battle. He wins by means of his storm weapons of thunder, wind and lightning, and slays Tiamat. Out of one half of her body he makes the earth, and out of the other half, the heavens. Marduk next proposes to create humans:

> Blood I will mass and cause bones to be.
> I will establish a savage, 'man' shall be his name.
> Verily, savage-man I will create.
> He shall be charged with the service of the gods
> That they might be at ease! (ANET 68).

Marduk has Ea, the wise god, fashion human beings from the blood of one of the defeated gods. Marduk also fixes the roles of all the gods, sets order to the world, and finally celebrates his kingship over gods and humans alike by a banquet.

The *Enuma Elish* has a number of similarities to the account of creation in Genesis 1. For example, Genesis 1:2 mentions the darkness and the waters of chaos. But the closest links between the two accounts are found in the order of creation that both follow:

Comparison of Genesis 1 and the Enuma Elish

Genesis	Enuma Elish (ANET 66–69)
Divine spirit creates by *word* all matter but is independent of it.	Divine spirits and cosmic matters coexist and are co-eternal.
Earth is desolate with darkness over the deep (*tehom*)	Primeval chaos; war of gods against *Tiamat*, the sea.
1st Day light created	Light emanates from the gods
2nd Day the sky dome created	creation of firmament (dome)
3rd Day creation of dry land	creation of dry land
4th Day creation of heavenly lights	creation of heavenly lights
6th Day creation of man	creation of man
7th Day God rests and sanctifies the sabbath	The gods rest and celebrate with a banquet.

While the Priestly authors obviously knew the Babylonian story, or one similar, and used its outline, they did not accept its theology. P makes no mention of a battle between Yahweh and the forces of chaos represented by the water: nor does it say that human beings are made up of the flesh of a god; nor does it claim that we have no purpose but to be slaves of the gods; nor is Yahweh portrayed as one among many competing, bickering and openly jealous divinities. Rather, in *direct opposition* to all that the Babylonians held about the origins of the universe, and in particular about the claims of their city god Marduk to be lord over all other gods, P solemnly affirmed the basic insights of Israel's faith:

(1) there is one God, without sexual gender, alone from the start,

(2) who created from his goodness and wise plan a world of order,

(3) in which matter is good and not the result of whim or magic,

(4) but God's *word* decrees what is to be and establishes limits;

(5) he gave humans a place of honor, made in his own image;

(6) they were to have responsibility over what was created,

(7) and share divine gifts of pro-creating life, sharing his sabbath rest and knowing God personally,

The entire picture that P presents of God's power, freedom and unchallenged control over the world he created is reinforced by the calm and deliberate repetition of the basic formula that is used:

God said: *Let there be . . .*
And it was so!   *God saw that it was good.*
And it was evening and morning   *on day (X).*

The scope of Genesis 1:1–2:4 contains an entire portrait of the nature of Yahweh, the God of Israel, over against all pagan claims. Such a profound statement was not the earliest, but rather is the *last part* to be added to the Pentateuch, a summary of what God can do, a guarantee that the story to follow makes sense. How close it comes to the wonder and praise expressed in Psalm 8:

> When I look up at the heavens, the work of your hands,
>   the moon and the stars you have set in their place,
> What is man that you should remember him,
>   mortal man that you should care for him?
> Yet you have made him little less than a god,
>   crowning him with glory and honor.
> You make him master over all your creatures,
>   you have put everything under his feet (Ps 8:3–6).

The Yahwist Creation Story (Gen 2:4–25)

After the solemn tones of the Priestly creation narrative, the reader notices a definite change in mood in the J story. Where the P account moves toward the creation of humanity as its climax, the J writer begins with God's creation of the man, and describes how subsequently God builds up a world for his new creature. In reality, J presents *two* stories. The first is the story of how God created one human being, but saw that he needed companions. God made a garden, but it was not enough; then he made the animals, and they did not prove enough; finally he made woman from man's flesh and human community was created, and it was enough. The second story tells how God gave humans care over the garden and made everything perfect for them. It sets the stage for the sin of the first human couple. The author speaks almost as in a fairy tale—God walks with his man and woman and talks to them, he thinks out loud, he works as a potter, fashioning people from mud and breathing life into them. There is a concrete sense of closeness to the earth about the story-teller's manner in J.

As in Genesis 1, many elements are drawn from common myths of the Ancient Near East. The tree of life is well known in Babylonian circles as a symbol of long life, or even immortality. The picture of a paradise garden in the East is known from Sumerian poems. The mystical power of the great rivers, the Tigris and the Euphrates, is praised in many Babylonian hymns. While no parallel to the tree of knowledge of good and evil has yet been discovered, the question of a human becoming like God in wisdom after eating food reserved for gods is treated in the *Legend of Adapa,* a Mesopotamian myth. It tells how the first man was allowed into the council of the gods where he was offered the bread and water of life to give him immortality and divine status. But he refused it, thinking it was a trick, and so lost the opportunity to be among the gods forever.

The theology of the J account uses all these elements from pagan myths to give a very Israelite message: Yahweh God begins creation with the human species and then fashions a world that they are to cultivate and tend, and makes animals for them to rule over, and then establishes marriage and human community of two sexes to complement one another.

Though the J account was quite different in style from that of P, the Priestly editors found no difficulty incorporating the two together. God's magnificent creation of the world in Genesis 1 set the stage for his intimate concern with man and woman in Genesis 2. What God did was awe-inspiring, but it was also very close to us.

The Sin in the Garden (Gen 3)

Genesis 2 ends with the peace and harmony of God's creation of man and woman expressed by their nakedness without shame. Genesis 3 begins with a play on words to show how quickly that reversed itself. Whereas they were naked (Hebrew *'arom*), the serpent was shrewd (Hebrew *'arum*). He presents the first couple with the temptation to be like god, wise and immortal. The Yahwist creates a masterpiece of psychological insight here, with the serpent hinting that great things are possible and playing upon Eve's vanity. Both man and woman fall readily, despite their clear recognition that God had forbidden them to eat of the tree of the knowledge of good and evil. They are not pictured as innocent babes in the woods, but as free adults, and so the sin is the greater. Once they have committed the act, they do indeed know something new: *shame* and *guilt*. It makes them hide their bodies, and, even more revealing, it leads them to hide from God himself. Naturally God finds them out, and the final scene explains how God permitted the pain and evil of the present life to be established as punishment for our own sin. In true artistic manner, J has Yahweh hear out the defense of each in turn, and then in reverse order address the serpent, the woman, and the man with the consequences of their acts. It is a dramatic scene which declares that the causes of sin and shame are rooted in human pride and disobedience, that humans are free to decide but must bear the consequences, and that we are not gods and must live now in a certain distance from God outside his garden. But God remains tenderly concerned to make them adequate clothes even as he expels them from their hopes of immortality.

We have seen how in the *Legend of Adapa* the hero loses his chance for immortality. The famous Babylonian story of Gilgamesh also explores this theme. The hero conquers all kinds of hurdles but

A possible reconstruction of the ziggurat (temple-tower) of Ur-Nammu of Ur (2100 B.C.)

A Babylonian statue of Gilgamesh

he cannot pass the final test needed for immortality: to simply stay awake. Although condemned to being mortal like the rest of humanity, Gilgamesh does receive a consolation prize, a twig from the plant of rejuvenation with which he will be able to renew his youth for as long as the plant lasts. But on his journey home, he takes off his clothes to go swimming and leaves the plant unguarded on the shore. Suddenly a snake smells its odor and swallows it, and as a result can shed its old skin again and again. Perhaps the J author was familiar with such stories. At any rate, he builds up his own explanation from many of the same mythical elements: the tree of life, the serpent, the search, the hopes for wisdom. But he carefully avoids the position so often assumed by the pagan myths—that the gods *purposely* kept humans from immortality so that there would be no threat against the divine order. J asserts that we *ourselves* are to blame. God offered the gift, and if it did not turn out to be so, the reason can be found in *human choice*.

The focus of this story is the tree of knowledge of good and evil. The phrase "to know good and evil" often meant sexual maturity in Hebrew. Taken together with the snake, which symbolized fertility, and the mention of their shame at being naked, it seems clear that the author was connecting the fundamental sin of pride and disobedience with the sexual excesses of pagan cults and the lustful side of human nature. But it would be a mistake to see the main point of the story as sexual. The most significant factor is the choice between obeying God or one's own desires. It is the human struggle from the first couple until now, and the Yahwist's use of this story does not so much teach an original sin, i.e., that Adam passed his guilt on to his descendants, as it stresses the common human tendency toward sinful desires, a weakness present from the beginning. We must wait until St. Paul and the Church theologians to find a strict doctrine of original sin developing.

Besides these important themes of immortality and human sin, J addresses a host of other interesting questions about human life that the ancients had. Genesis 2–3 explains why snakes crawl on the ground, why women have pain in childbirth, why people have to work for a living, why we wear clothes, why the sexes are different, why people are ashamed when naked, why we die, and why men and women feel sexual attraction to one another. We call these *etiological* stories because they explain the *reasons* for current names and customs. The ancient Israelite delighted in them as part of the tradition.

Cain and Abel (Gen 4)

No doubt in this story also, the Yahwist has made use of an older story or stories with mythological overtones. Quite simply, the biblical writer gives a dramatic example of how the alienation and sin of the garden spread to new levels of evil: not only murder, but murder of one's own brother.

Elements that have been borrowed include the traditional conflict between the farmer and the sheepherder—still a fighting issue in the American west of the last century. In line with his overall purpose, the Yahwist has only sketched the details briefly, but added a dialogue between Yahweh and Cain to underscore Israel's belief that human sin leads not only to God's punishment but also to his compassionate mercy.

The Genealogies of Genesis 4–5

After the story of Cain and Abel, the Yahwist added a list of Cain's descendants (Gen 4:17–26), emphasizing those who gave the world the civilized gifts of music and ironworking, and concluding with a small poem that showed how the evils of violence and revenge were increasing:

Adah and Zillah, hear my voice;
    wives of Lamech listen to my words:
I have killed a man for wounding me,
    a boy for hurting me.
If Cain was avenged sevenfold,
    surely Lamech will be seventy-sevenfold (Gen 4:23–24).

In Genesis 4:25, the Yahwist records how Adam had a new son, Seth, and how this marked a positive turning point. From that time on the human race began to call God by his name Yahweh (Gen 4:26).

At this point, the Priestly author inserts his own genealogy of the ten descendants of Adam down to Noah. Many of the names are similar to those in the J list of Genesis 4, and probably stem from an old tradition that had been passed down through the centuries in different forms:

Genesis 4:17–22 (J)		**Genesis 5:1–32 (P)**		
1.	Adam	1. Adam	lived	930 years
2.	Cain	2. Seth	lived	912 years
3.	Enoch	3. Enosh	lived	905 years
4.	Irad	4. Cainan	lived	910 years
5.	Muhajael	5. Mahaleel	lived	895 years
6.	Methusael	6. Jared	lived	962 years
7.	Lamech	7. Enoch	lived	365 years
8.	Jabel	8. Methusalah	lived	969 years
9.	Jubel	9. Lamech	lived	777 years
10.	Tubalcain	10. Noah	lived	950 years

The first seven names in the J list correspond closely to names in the P list: Adam—Adam, Cain—Cainan, Irad—Jared, Muhajael—Mahaleel, etc. But what has always interested readers is the long lifespan that P credits to his patriarchs. This was not intended as proof that humans lived to such ripe old ages in the first days of the world, but a device to show just how vast a distance separates our own world of experience from that of the story itself. The "myth" of enormous lifespans was commonly used in the ancient world to show the superiority of the *beginning times.* The Sumerian king list, only one of many such that we know from the Near East, lists the names and ages of the kings who lived before the flood:

1.	Alulim	28,800 years	5.	Dumuzi	36,000 years
2.	Alalgar	36,000 years	6.	Ensipazianna	28,800 years
3.	Enmenluanna	43,200 years	7.	Enmenduranna	21,000 years
4.	Enmengalanna	28,800 years	8.	Ubartutu	18,600 years

Some Hindu traditions are even more exaggerated. One Jain myth speaks of the perfect first age of the world when humans stood six miles high and lived 8,400,000 years! P's purposes are served by much more modest claims.

The Giants Born of Sin (Gen 6:1–4)

This story belongs in style and approach to the Yahwist. It forms the reason for the flood story to come. If humans killing one another had not been sin enough, the evil got worse when God's divine beings (lesser gods in early thought, angels in later theology) violated the limits set for humanity at creation. Originally the story explained why there had been giants in the old days—a widespread ancient belief as we can see from other references to giants in Deuteronomy 2:20 and 3:11. The Yahwist views the existence of these monsters as a sign of the gross abnormality caused by sin in the world. It fully merited the destruction and purification that flood water could bring.

Noah and the Flood (Gen 6–9)

The J and P stories of the flood are closely joined in one dramatic narrative. P has built on the older J tradition so that the disaster leads to a moment in Genesis 9 when God *renews* his blessing on humankind that matches the first blessing to Adam in Genesis 1:28. We can detect certain signs that there were two original accounts in the fact that God announces the flood twice (Gen 6:13; 7:4), and twice promises never to send a flood again (Gen 8:21; 9:15). Noah is told to take a pair of each kind of animal in some passages, but seven pairs of clean animals with one pair of unclean in others. There also seems to be two different numbering systems at work, one based on seven and forty day periods, the other on longer lengths that add up to a full year. A brief comparison illustrates the differences:

J and P share a single message, however. When God decides he must punish the world for its sin, he spares the one man who has been faithful to him by allowing Noah to ride out the flood on an ark. When the disaster is over, God restores his covenant with the world through this man. The climax for the J version comes in Genesis 8:20–22, in which God's forgiveness extends even to lifting the curse upon the earth for what humans have done in their hearts. People may still choose to sin, but the goodness of God and his everlasting mercy will be seen in the bounty and the regularity of nature's seasons:

> As long as the earth lasts, planting and harvest, cold and
> heat, summer and winter, day and night, will never cease.

P's climax comes in Genesis 9:1–17 where God renews the blessing of Genesis 1 on human beings. P even enlarges the covenant conditions so that now people may eat meat as well as plants, thus removing the last restrictions on their rule over the creatures

COMPARISON OF J AND P FLOOD ACCOUNTS

J Version	P Version
And the Lord said unto Noah, Come thou and all thy house into the ark; for thee have I seen righteous before me in this generation. Of every clean beast thou shalt take to thee seven and seven, the male and his female; and of the beasts that are not clean two, the male and his female;	And God said unto Noah, The end of all flesh is come before me; for the earth is filled with violence through them; and, behold, I will destroy them with the earth. Make thee an ark of gopher wood; rooms shalt thou make in the ark, and shalt pitch it within and without with pitch.
And it came to pass after the seven days, that the waters of the flood were upon the earth. . . . And the rain was upon the earth forty days and forty nights;	And of every living thing of all flesh, two of every sort shalt thou bring into the ark.
And it came to pass at the end of forty days, that Noah opened the window of the ark which he had made: and he sent forth a raven.	In the six hundredth year of Noah's life, in the second month, on the seventeenth day of the month, on the same day were all the fountains of the great deep broken up, and the windows of heaven were opened.
And he stayed yet another seven days; and again he sent forth the dove out of the ark;	And the waters prevailed upon the earth a hundred and fifty days.
Noah removed the covering of the ark, and looked, and, behold, the face of the ground was dried.	And God made a wind to pass over the earth, and the waters assuaged;
	And in the second month, on the seven and twentieth day of the month, was the earth dry.

of the world. But with it comes an increased obligation to respect human life:

> Whoever sheds the blood of a man,
>   by man shall his blood be shed;
> For in God's image
>   has God made man (Gen 9:6).

Ancient Israelites undoubtedly fully believed that a flood had once destroyed the earth. Indeed, almost every nation around them also believed that a major flood had occurred near the beginning of time. But Israel also understood that the story of Noah was not history in the ordinary sense. It was a religious lesson told in mythological language about how God's mercy and promise far exceeded any terrible disaster to human life.

The Epic of Gilgamesh and the Flood

Since 1872, the story of the flood has figured prominently in all discussion of the historical background to the Genesis accounts. In that year, the *Epic of Gilgamesh* was revealed to the world. This Babylonian myth has become one of the better-known works in world literature because it contains a flood story on the eleventh of its twelve tablets.

Copies have since been discovered all over the ancient world, so that we can be sure it was as influential and familiar in the period from 2000–1000 B.C. as Chaucer is to modern high school students today. Briefly, it tells how the hero king Gilgamesh is so much greater than his subjects that he tyrannizes them. To divert his attention, a goddess makes a companion for him nearly as strong as he is. They become fast friends and embark on a series of exploits, killing the giant Humbaba who guards the cedar forest of the gods, rejecting the love of the goddess Ishtar, and then slaying the bull of the god Anu. The gods decree that Enkidu must die, and this leads Gilgamesh on a frightened search for immortal life. He goes to the ends of the earth where he has heard that the hero of the original flood, Utnapishtim, had been given immortality by the gods. Utnapishtim tells Gilgamesh the story of the flood and how the gods had specially blessed him for his role in saving humanity. He does this in order to point out to Gilgamesh that *he cannot hope for personal immortality.* And although the details of the Babylonian flood are remarkably similar to those in Genesis, the point of the Babylonian version is always this lesson in the mortality of human beings. Gilgamesh himself is sent home disappointed but wiser. The story ends with his return to his capital city of Uruk. There his adventures end as he resumes his duties. The final episode contains a melancholy description of the underworld by the ghost of his friend Enkidu. This is to be man's fate, even for a Gilgamesh, because the gods reserve everlasting life to themselves.

COMPARISON OF THE BABYLONIAN AND
HEBREW FLOOD STORIES

Genesis 6–9	Gilgamesh Epic
Yahweh plans to destroy humanity because they are wicked	The gods plan to destroy humans because they have gone astray
Yahweh warns Noah to build an ark and cover it with pitch	The god Ea warns Utnapishtim to build a boat and use pitch
Every species of animal is to be brought on the ark and his immediate family.	Every species of animal and of skilled craftsmen are to be saved, as well as his family
The flood comes and destroys all life from the earth	The flood comes and destroys all life from the earth
The waters subside gradually and Noah sends out a raven and a dove	The waters subside slowly and Utnapishtim sends out a dove, swallow and raven
The ark comes to rest on the top of Mt. Ararat	The boat comes to rest on the top of Mt. Nisir
Noah builds an altar and sacrifices to Yahweh	Utnapishtim builds an altar and sacrifices to the gods
Yahweh smells the sweet odor	The gods smell the sweet odor
Yahweh removes the curse from the earth and promises bounty and no more floods	Enlil is reconciled with Utnapishtim and repents of his rash decision to destroy the earth
Yahweh blesses Noah and his sons to repopulate the earth	Enlil bleses Utnapishtim and his wife with immortality on the far western isles

Early models of the same story are known from about 2000 B.C. in Sumerian, and the setting is always somewhere in Mesopotamia, so that there is no question that the biblical account is a development or offshoot from the Babylonian. The differences in detail, such as the size of the ark, or the length of time that the water stayed on the land, or the types of birds, may argue that the biblical writers knew a slightly different version, perhaps one from an area closer to them, such as Syria. But it also suggests that Israel believed that a flood, like the giants, or the long life of the primal humans, or the struggle of the first humans to be like gods, was part of the way it was in the beginning, just as did their pagan neighbors. Where Israel's vision was unique was in its understanding of God. The

Babylonians believed in a mysterious tension between gods and humans which often broke out in divine anger or apparently wrathful actions because humanity annoyed the gods or disturbed their peace. They felt a great deal of uncertainty about what the gods wanted and what would please them. Israel, in contrast, affirms a god who is always the same, always faithful, always just and always loving toward the creatures he has made. He punishes only for clear moral evil and he is quick to forgive. Both versions struggle with how humans relate to god, but Israel rejects any sense of a moody, petulant god and describes a God whose will can be known and his way lived and his blessing fulfilled.

The List of the World's Nations (Gen 10)

The nations of the world are divided among the three sons of Noah: Shem, Ham and Japheth. These generally reflect the three major groupings of people in Hebrew world geography: Shem includes the Arameans, Assyrians and Arabs, all Semites to the east; Ham includes the Semitic peoples in the west: the Canaanites and the peoples of North Africa (Egyptians, Libyans and Sudanese); Japheth generally includes the non-Semitic peoples of the north and the Aegean: the Greeks, Hittites and peoples of Cyprus. As it stands, the seventy nations are a symbolic number representing all the nations of the earth. The Priestly editors have created this final form by adding (especially in Genesis 10:1–7) to an older list used by the Yahwist. Their purpose was to show how God's restored blessing after the flood led to even more fertility and success than was the case before the flood.

The Tower of Babel (Gen 11:1–9)

J ended his account of the beginning of the world with a story that makes the point that sin did not disappear with the flood. The human race still prided itself on its own glory and rebelled against God. The key symbol of this idolatrous faith for the Yahwist was the huge ziggurat, or temple tower, sometimes rising two hundred feet or more, that the Babylonians regularly raised to their gods. J delighted in showing God's punishment of such human pride. The nations are so scattered and so closed off by scrambled language that they will never even cooperate with one another, much less challenge God. One of the ironies in the story of Babel is that while people thought the tower was so grand, God found it so puny that he had to come down to earth just to make out what it was. To mock Babylon even more, the author makes a pun: the tower is *babel* (the Babylon of history), the divine punishment is *balal* (confusion of language).

The Genealogy of Abraham (Gen 11:10–32)

The final unit in Genesis 1–11 continues the genealogy list of the Priestly author from chapter 5. P bridges the final distance from mythical time to historical time by listing the generations from Noah down to the call of Abraham. Theologically, P makes the point that God had to give up on humanity as a whole after the tower of Babel incident and instead narrow his choice to one man and one nation who would learn obedience and devotion to God and eventually bring this knowledge and divine blessing to all other people. Thus with Abraham the Bible begins to deal with people and places actually known to exist. Interestingly, archaeology has revealed that many of the names listed in Genesis 11:27–32 as Abraham's close relatives were actually the names of towns near Haran in Mesopotamia: Nahor, Terah, Haran. It is a symbolic way of expressing Abraham's roots in that area. With this new beginning, we leave the stage of *myth* and *prologue* and enter the historical world of the second millennium before Christ, as dim, fragmented and uncertain as much of it may be for us still.

The Final Shape of Genesis 1–11 (Summary)

P has given Genesis 1–11 its final shape by incorporating the earlier J pattern of sin—punishment—mercy into a wider frame of God's blessing to creation. The final pattern then becomes:

(a) The goodness of creation and God's blessing of human life.
(b) The history of ever increasing sin: rebellion in the garden, murder in the first family, Lamech's excessive vengeance, corruption of human society by marriage with angels.
(c) God's major punishment of all humanity by the flood.
(d) Divine renewal of creation and blessing to Noah.
(e) Persistence of human sin and rebellion in tower of Babel.
(f) Choice of Abraham to bring the blessing to all.

Is Genesis 1–11 Myth or History?

The stories in Genesis 1–11 certainly disturb the modern historian. They have no particular "facts" that can be located in a given moment, no eyewitness reports, and no direct connections to other events that are known. If taken literally, the dates they do offer cannot be reconciled with the findings of geology about the age of the earth, nor do the lifespans of people conform to the ages of ancient human remains studied by anthropologists. They are much more like "model" stories of how things *should have been* at the beginning, and resemble the literary creations of other ancient peoples. In all of them the moment of creation was not like any subsequent period of time. In that time the gods spoke directly to people. To the ancient mind it was a golden age; it was primeval time before history began.

In ancient thought, such time was expressed by means of certain traditional themes or motifs that were different from everyday language and experience. This type of literature is known everywhere as *myth*. Myths are not all of one kind, nor do they only speak of creation. They also tell stories of the gods, or of legendary heroes of old, or of the origins of customs and ethnic groups. In many cases, the myth is tied closely to a ritual action in worship and forms the dramatic explanation for an actual celebration. In other cases, the myth is *etiological*, which means "explaining the causes" of something, such as why a holy place has its name, or why the gods made a certain creature, or why some tribe follows unusual customs. Myth allows us to speak of events of primal importance at the very beginning of time because it does not depend on knowing the scientific facts, but upon understanding the inner meaning of what happened and what purpose stands behind the event. It especially concerns itself with divine beings and their relation to the human world. It is not history in the strict sense, but it surely is not antihistorical either. It is at least profoundly historical in *outlook*, for all ancient peoples knew that gods acted according to their relation with humanity. Past events and experience formed the *grounds* for future *expectations* of divine acts. By understanding the past we can better direct our lives, our worship, our prayers, to the gods, and better know what choices to make in the present moment.

The common themes and motifs used in myths are the symbols cherished by all ancient civilizations. These include creation in or near water, a fight among the gods for order in the universe, the defeat of chaos by a hero god, the making of humans from mud or other lowly material, and a death and rebirth of the hero god parallel to the annual winter and spring cycle of nature. They explore the basic contrasts of nature: sun and earth, light and darkness, water and drought, male and female, gods and human creatures.

Genesis 1–11 incorporates many such elements into its stories, and many of its individual incidents find parallels in the myths of other ancient Near Eastern peoples, especially the Canaanites, Babylonians and Egyptians. Clearly, the biblical tradition did not hesitate to make use of these literary forms. But this does not mean that the biblical "myth" always has the same view of the world as does the original pagan story. So we must be careful to distinguish our use of the word "myth" on two levels.

On the first level, myth is a story using traditional motifs and themes. It is not scientific or historical in outlook as we would expect; it is more like folktale, but it does convey how the Israelites saw the shape of the world—it was their "science," so to speak. A very good example of this use of myth is the description of the Garden of Eden in Genesis 2: life originated in the East; there was a central source of water which split into the great rivers of the earth; the first man was made out of dust and the first woman out of a rib; God planted two special and unusual trees in the garden—the tree of life and the tree of good and evil; there was harmony between humans and animals in the beginning. These were all familiar parts of ancient descriptions of the world, and since Israel accepted them as true, we can say that the Bible contains many myths simply because ancient Israelites were not as sophisticated in their knowledge as we are.

On a second level, however, myth is a "theological" explanation of our relation to the gods, and often refers to ancient beliefs of a polytheistic nature in which natural powers were manifestations of the divine, where the gods were symbols of fertility and bound to the seasonal pattern of rainy and dry seasons, where each year the gods must reassert their power over the forces of chaos that threaten the world. When myth is used in this sense, we must be more careful about calling the biblical stories myths, for the authors of Genesis consciously intended to refute and contradict such a view of religion by reworking the traditional stories to *remove* any idea that there is more than one God, that the world is subject to chaos, that God is callous or uncaring, or that superstitious sexual practices are needed to renew nature. By telling the story of Genesis 1–11 as they did, stressing Yahweh's freedom and power versus human refusal of responsibility, the Israelites *demythologized* the myths—they destroyed the heart of pagan belief and reinterpreted the real meaning of the world in light of the one God who had revealed himself as Savior and Ruler to Moses.

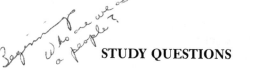

STUDY QUESTIONS

1. Briefly describe the Book of Genesis. What does it attempt to do? What is its scope?
2. Genesis 1–11 is generally considered as the preface to the story of Israel. Compare and contrast how the Yahwist and Priestly sources develop.
3. What are some signs which show that the Priestly account has its origins with priests and temple schools?
4. Briefly describe the major characteristics of the Priestly Creation Story (Genesis 1:1–2:4).
5. What is *Enuma Elish?* How does it compare with the creation story in Genesis?
6. What are the major differences in the creation story of the Yahwist and Priestly sources? Contrast the major characteristics and themes. How are they developed?
7. Define the following: "the Sin in the Garden", etiological stories, *Legend of Adapa*, Çain and Abel, genealogies, *Epic of Gilgamesh*, Shem, Ham, Japheth, ziggurat, Tower of Babel.
8. Compare and contrast the J and P accounts of Noah and the Flood.
9. Distinguish the two levels of the word "myth".
10. Is Genesis 1–11 a myth or history? Why? Give reasons to explain your position.

Chapter 7

GENESIS 12–50:
THE PATRIARCHS

Suggested Scripture Readings:

Genesis 12–15
Genesis 27–31
Genesis 39–45

The Patriarchs as "National" Heroes

After relating its lessons from human origins, the Book of Genesis focuses quickly on the history of one family that lived in northern Mesopotamia. Genesis 11:27–32 gives the family tree for Abraham in such a way that his grandfather, father and brothers are all named after towns that flourished in that area near the old caravan city of Haran. This was a device among ancient writers called "eponymous" writing, and it helped to fix for the reader or listener the exact roots of the hero. The *eponym* is the person from whom a tribe or nation gets its name. Thus we could say that Mother *America* had two daughters, *Virginia* and *Georgia*. Such a poetic way of expressing our historical past uses daily family terms to explain how both states are equals ("sisters"), yet stem from and are subordinate to the country as a whole (their "mother"). A fine biblical example occurs in Genesis 19:36–38:

(36) Thus both daughters of Lot came to be with child by their father.

(37) The first bore a son and named him Moab; he is the father of the Moabites to this day.

(38)   The younger also bore a son and named him Ben-ammi;
        he is the father of the Ammonites to this day.

The traditions in Genesis 12–50 dwell on four such heroic
ancestors: twelve chapters on Abraham, two on Isaac, nine on Jacob,
and ten on Joseph, although, most properly, Joseph should be understood as part of the history of Jacob.

The Setting of the Patriarchal Stories

The lifetimes of the patriarchs are clearly set *before* the period
in which Israel was in Egypt, and so can be dated no later than the
fourteenth century B.C. Although many elements in the tradition
have been rewritten and updated over the centuries, the sources
tried to preserve a description of the way people lived in the Middle
Bronze Age, i.e., in the period from the twenty-second century B.C.
down to the fifteenth. Although a growing minority of archaeologists and biblical scholars think that much of the actual material in
these chapters is fiction—in the sense that it is a romantic projection
back from later times of an ideal life of faith—the majority still
accept that there are genuine *remembrances* of this early period
that form the *core* of the tradition. Many of the details about travel,
semi-nomadic life, marriage customs and inheritance rights that are
supposed in the narratives were well known in this period. The
archives of Mari, a town on the Euphrates River in the eighteenth
century B.C., present several descriptions of nomadic life similar to
that in Genesis 12–50. The archives of Nuzi, a town in northern
Mesopotamia in the fourteenth century, also present some close
(but not exact!) parallels to customs mentioned in Genesis. The oral
will of Isaac on his deathbed in Genesis 27:2 was also an acceptable
legal practice in Nuzi, Esau's sale of his birthright (Gen 25:31–33) is
paralleled in a Nuzi contract, and the protected position of a slave
woman who bears her master a son in place of his barren wife (Gen
16) is known at both Nuzi and in the famous law code of Hammurabi (1700 B.C.).

There is evidence also of a strong westward movement of
Semitic peoples from Mesopotamia about 2100 B.C. or earlier.
These were known as Amorites ("Westerners"), and even if Abraham is not placed among them, it indicates the likelihood that such
travels as his were normal. There is some mixed archaeological
evidence that the Negev desert, which is the scene of much of the

Abraham and Isaac tradition, was settled in the era around 2000 B.C., but largely deserted in the centuries after. A good case could be made for a period of prosperity there between 2000 and 1800 B.C. under the secure rule of the strong pharaohs of the Middle Kingdom in Egypt. Trade and travel such as reported in Genesis 12:9 or 20:1 would be encouraged by such periods of stability. Moreover, the Bible itself remembers that Israel spent almost four hundred years in Egypt between the arrival of Jacob and the time of the exodus (Gen 15:13; Ex 12:40). This would place Abraham even earlier, near the beginning of the second millennium.

The general description of the lifestyles of Abraham, Isaac and Jacob suggests that they were the chiefs of wealthy clans whose livelihood depended mostly on raising small livestock such as sheep and goats. They seemed to have had semi-permanent roots near some large city, or at least within a definite area, but often moved with their flocks to new pastures according to the seasons of the year. Their life was not that of the city-dweller or villager, but they were never far from the major urban centers. Abraham settled near Hebron in the south, Isaac had connections to Beer-sheba in the same area, while Jacob dwelt in the area of Shechem and Bethel in the middle of Palestine. Among all the traditions, Abraham most appears to follow a semi-nomadic lifestyle, while Jacob seems the most settled. The story of how Joseph's brothers sold him to a caravan while they were pasturing their father's flocks far from home in Genesis 37 vividly illustrates this way of life. In good years, and in the mild winters, the clan stayed near the permanent settlement, but in the dry summer season or in years of drought, they might wander far abroad in search of grazing land and food.

The same incident in Genesis 37 hints at still another possible aspect of their life: *commerce* and *trade*. Their wide-ranging knowledge of the land, the safety of numbers in travel, and the likelihood that the clan had more members than herding required all support the suggestion that trade was an auxiliary part of their livelihood. Certain references to the longer journeys of Abraham especially make this an attractive idea. He moves between Haran, Damascus, Shechem, Hebron, and Egypt, all of which are on the caravan routes, all large cities or trading centers. A tomb painting from Beni Hasan in Egypt during the eighteenth century B.C. shows a Semitic clan of tinkers, metalsmiths and sellers of antelope meat visiting a local Egyptian prince to offer their goods and services. It could easily have been Abraham or Isaac.

The patriarchal story opens in Mesopotamia and northern Syr-

A tomb painting from Beni Hasan in Egypt, showing the visit of wandering Semites from Canaan to an Egyptian prince. They sell eye-paint, wild antelope and do metal work.

ia, and throughout Genesis the clans maintain their ties back to their original homeland. Both Isaac and Jacob go back to marry wives from among their relatives in Haran. Also many of the customs and practices in the Abraham narratives have parallels in documents from the ruins of fourteenth and fifteenth century Nuzi in upper Mesopotamia. This, too, is no doubt part of the original memory of Israel's ancestors.

The Story of Abraham (Gen 12–25)

The Abraham narratives take us from Genesis 12 to the middle of chapter 25 in a series of individual events that are often only very vaguely connected to one another by the editors. See, for example, the change between Genesis 12:9 and 12:10: "Abraham went on and traveled toward the Negev, *and* there came a famine in the land." There is no indication whether the famine began immediately or years later, or even if it was the next incident in order. Briefly, we can outline the major incidents in the following way with the *blessings* emphasized by being placed to the left in italics:

1. *12:1–9*   God calls and blesses Abraham and he moves west into Canaan.
2. 12:10–20   Abraham risks his blessing in Egypt by giving up Sarah.
3. 13:1 –18   Abraham and Lot divide their territory and Abraham receives Palestine.

4. 14:1 –24   Abraham shows himself a hero and blessed in warfare.
5. *15:1–20*   God renews his promises and makes a covenant with Abraham.
6. 16:1–16   Abraham risks the promise of a son by taking Hagar to bear Ishmael.
7. *17:1–27*   God renews his covenant and promise of a son, but commands Abraham to take on the sign of circumcision.
8. *18:1–15*   God renews his promise to give a son to Sarah and Abraham.
9. 18:16–33   Abraham shows his blessing by interceding for Sodom and Gomorrah.
10. 19:1 –38   Lot proves to be the only faithful person in Sodom; it is destroyed.
11. 20:1–18   Abraham risks the blessing to Sarah with the king of Gerar.
12. *21:1–21*   God gives the blessing of a son, Isaac, and sends Ishmael away.
13. 21:22–34   Abraham makes a treaty with Abimelech and his people.
14. 22:1 –24   Abraham sacrifices Isaac in obedience to God.
15. 23:1–20   Abraham lays claim to possession of the land by buying the cave of Macphelah to bury Sarah and himself.
16. 24:1–67   Abraham arranges a wife for Isaac to continue the blessing.
17. 25:1–18   Abraham's death and burial; Ishmael's descendants; the blessing passes to Isaac.

The person of Abraham emerges suddenly and dramatically from the long list of persons in Genesis 11 when God addresses him out of nowhere in Genesis 12:1, "Go out from your land and your clan and your father's house to a land that I will show you." This marks the start of a new development in God's plan. The world as a whole is no longer the stage of action, but one small corner of it. The biblical picture of Abraham is told as a *journey*—Abraham moves through Canaan, stopping at major places in the mountain country, Shechem, Hebron and Beer-sheba, moving down into the southern Negev desert area, traveling even to Egypt. He indeed appears with a large number of followers and many flocks and herds, and he

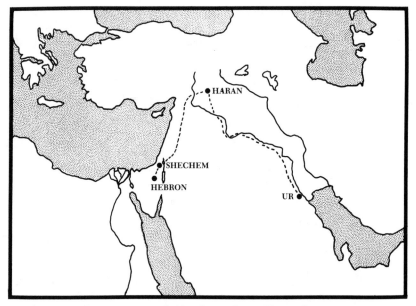

The Journey of Abraham from Ur to Canaan

occasionally does trade (Gen 15:2), but we really learn very little about any business dealings or even about his relationships with his Canaanite neighbors. The entire story of Abraham is presented to us in a way that stresses two major themes: (1) God made a *promise* to Abraham which will control all the events narrated in the Pentateuch, but which already begins to unfold in Abraham's own lifetime; (2) God *blessed* Abraham and made him his specially chosen friend because Abraham was faithful to God.

These two themes are found mixed together throughout the story. They reflect the original outline of the J source, but have been expanded by the additions from E and P.

Promise and Covenant

The Abraham cycle has connected the promise of land and a son to a series of covenants, or formal agreements, between Yahweh and Abraham. In Genesis 12 and 15, they are free gifts of God, very much like the royal grants of kings to favorite courtiers. In Genesis 17, it uses the language of mutual obligation treaties more typical of the Sinai covenant in Exodus 19–24. To emphasize the importance of this theme, God announces his promise in the very first scene (Gen 12:2–3):

> I will make of you a great nation; I will bless you and make your name great so that you will become a blessing. I will bless those who bless you, and curse those who curse you. And all the peoples of the earth shall bless themselves in you.

The sense of the promise in this passage is very broad. Abraham will become a great nation, implying great numbers and large territory, and other nations will be subject to this nation's fortunes so that they will pray for blessing as Abraham had been blessed. But it is made concrete and specific by later statements given by God:

Gen 12:7	"To your descendants I will give this land."
Gen 13:15	"All the land which you see I will give to you and your seed forever."
Gen 15:5	"Look at the heavens and count the stars if you can. So shall your descendants be."
Gen 17:4	"You shall be the father of a multitude of nations."
Gen 18:18	"Abraham shall surely become a great and powerful nation, and all the nations of the earth will be blessed through him."

All of these promises are given to Abraham in theophany, which means literally an "appearance of God," an overwhelming personal experience of God's presence that affects the entire direction and quality of a person's life. Let us look at two of these scenes in detail, one from the older J and E epic, and the second from P.

Genesis 15:1–21 contains many very primitive details, including the cutting of the animals in two and passing fire through them to consume them as an offering to God. There is a similar ceremony already in the Mari letters of the eighteenth century B.C. in Mesopotamia:

> I sent that message to Bina-Ishtar, and she replied as follows: "I have killed that ass with Qarni-Lim, and thus I spoke to Qarni-Lim under the oath of the gods: 'If you despise Zimri-Lim and his armies, I will turn to the side of your adversaries.' "

But the early part of Genesis 15 is heavily theological with its reflections on the promises made to Abraham. Source critics have detected the hand of J in the frequent use of the name Yahweh, but also of E in mention of the Amorites in verse 16, the theme of "Fear not" in verse 1 and the hints that Abraham is a *prophetic* figure in the use of the formula, "the word of the Lord came to Abraham," in verses 1 and 4. There are other signs that this is not just an old tradition handed down. Verse 13 actually refers to the full period of Israelite residence in Egypt as four hundred years, and so comes from the hands of the J or E editors themselves. In its present form, the chapter expands the promise from a hope for an heir to a further promise of land, and emphasizes the *total act* of faith that Abraham made in this promise that would not be fulfilled until centuries after his death. The detailed covenant scene confirms what God's word and Abraham's faith in that word have already sealed. Indeed the very words of God's promise in verses 5 and 18 are repeated by Moses to God on Mount Sinai in Exodus 32:13. Thus the whole of Genesis 15 becomes a *prediction* and *preparation* for the Sinai covenant. The words of God are not intended as a fake prophecy, but are basically due to the story-telling technique of J, which favors incidents that *foreshadow* the events of the exodus and after. By means of such hints, he ties the stories of Abraham, Isaac, Jacob and Joseph to the later traditions of the exodus, Sinai and life in the promised land.

The second major covenant scene comes from the hand of P in chapter 17. God appears once more and renews his covenant with Abraham. This time there are no colorful ceremonies, nor is there any dialogue between God and Abraham. God speaks solemnly as El Shaddai, the God of majesty, and echoes in verse 6 the theme of blessing from Genesis 1:

> I will make you a father of many nations. I will make you very fruitful; I will bring nations out of you, and kings shall descend from you. I will establish my covenant between you and me and your descendants after you for all genera- tions as an everlasting covenant to be your God and the God of your descendants after you (Gen 17:5-7).

The divine speech emphasizes that the covenant will last through the times of the kings and never leave Israel. This, too, is the view of P, who wrote with a long view of history. Living in the time of exile, P offers the reassurance that the covenant remains in effect despite changing fortunes and even loss of the land. The author goes on in the rest of chapter 17 to explain how the rite of circumcision will be a sign of the covenant. P is thus able to present a way of keeping the covenant which does not require an independent state to live in or even temple buildings to worship in. We know that the practice of circumcision was especially important to Judaism after the Babylonian exile of the sixth century as a sign of membership in the community. P in this chapter has thus managed to bring together the promise and covenant themes from a later perspective than J but one which stresses much the same message: what God did for Abraham was only a foretaste of what he would do even more completely later.

Abraham the Faithful

God freely offers Abraham the promise of an heir who will found a great nation and the promise of land, but God can only bring these about if Abraham and Sarah trust enough. This brings us to the second major theme of the Abraham stories: his *faithfulness* to God's promise. It is summed up in Genesis 15:6, "Abraham believed the Lord, who credited it to him as righteousness." But biblical tradition does not make Abraham a perfect person without any flaws. In chapters 12 and 20 he tries to save his own life by giving up his wife Sarah and thus risking the promise of a son. In chapter 16 he is uncertain enough to take a slave girl in order to gain a son. In chapter 17, he doubts the angel who tells him that Sarah will bear a child. But these are rare moments in a life that stands open to God's direction. For one thing, Abraham always worships Yahweh wherever he stops on his travels—at Bethel in chapter 12, at Hebron in chapter 13, at (Jeru)Salem in chapter 14. He always accepts God's command to move on, and frequently has face to face experiences of God (chapters 15, 17, 18). In a moment of great sorrow, he obeys God and sends off his son Ishmael to a new life in order to prevent any threat to Isaac (chapter 21).

In all things Abraham proves devoted to God's commands. But the ultimate test comes when God seems to demand that Abraham sacrifice Isaac back to him in chapter 22. This is the high point of the Abraham story, and the authors maintain a high sense of drama and artistic skill in narrating the horrifying moment. Abraham is weighed down so greatly that he cannot bear to tell Isaac the truth, and Isaac in turn is so trusting in his father that he never suspects

THE YAHWIST AUTHOR'S SCHEMA OF THE ABRAHAM SAGA

(Following the outline proposed by Peter Ellis,
The Yahwist, Fides Press, Notre Dame)

1. Abram receives God's Promise.   Gen 12:1–3

2. Abram endangers the promise but God   Gen 12:6–20
   overcomes Abram's lie about
   Sarah;
   foreshadows that Abram's children
   will receive the land (12:7).

3. Abram endangers the promise by allowing   Gen 13:1–18
   Lot to choose the promised land;
   foreshadows that all land will be to
   Abram's descendants (13:14–17).

4. Abram blessed by Melchisedek: Gen 14:1–24
   foreshadows Jerusalem as holy city.

5. The covenant with Abram seals the   Gen 15:1–4, 6–12, 17–21
   promise;
   foreshadows the promise of land
   and descendants (15:18)

6. Abram risks the promise by having a son   Gen 16:1–14
   by Hagar who is not the promised
   one;
   foreshadows a hard life for Ishmael
   (16:11–12).

7. God overcomes Sarah's old age as a block   Gen 18:1–15
   to the promise;
   foreshadows the son to come
   (18:14).

8. Abram proves a powerful intercessor but   Gen 18:16–19:29
   cannot save idolators;
   foreshadows all nations bless
   themselves through Abraham
   (18:18).

9. Origins of the Moabites and Ammonites in   Gen 19:20–38
   the evil of fertility cults;
   foreshadows that they are not the
   children of promise.

10. Isaac's sacrifice tests Abraham's faith in   Gen 22:1–19
    the promise;
    foreshadows God's further
    blessings of the promise (22:17–18)
    which sum up the full promise of
    Gen 12:1–3.

what is happening. The boy asks naturally curious questions, and the grieving Abraham can barely answer. He preserves the privacy of the terrible last moments by sending the servants off. Just when all seems lost, God stops his hand and provides an animal to sacrifice instead. This story often shocks modern readers. They wonder how God could ask a thing like that. Perhaps the biblical authors themselves believed that Abraham could never go through with the act. But they wanted to make a point for all later Israel. It was not uncommon in the ancient world for parents to sacrifice a son in times of great need or illness to try to appease the gods. The Bible records several examples, ranging from Jephthah in the Book of Judges (chapter 11) down to Manasseh in the seventh century (2 Kgs 21). All of these are looked upon with horror, and the story of Isaac certainly shows how Yahweh forbade any human sacrifice—he did not want human flesh but *would* accept animals as an offering instead, although he *most* wanted faith and trust.

This whole story sums up perfectly the character of Abraham as the man of faith. In Islamic traditions he is still called *khalil Allah,* "the friend of God." Even in the New Testament, St. Paul cites Abraham as a model of faith in Romans 4:1–25 and in Galatians 3:6–9. Abraham becomes the example for all Christians who believe in God's promise yet have never been part of the Jewish people. The Letter to the Hebrews, in chapter 11, says that Abraham believed in the promise without ever seeing it fulfilled so that Christians have become the receivers of the promise in Christ the true Son. Such New Testament passages, written in controversy against a Judaism that believed all of the essentials of faith were already revealed in the Torah, attempted to get beyond the law of Moses by holding that the true promise could *only be fulfilled* in the coming of Jesus. For the Christian, Abraham had faith without any aid of the law to guide him, and so his faith was greater than those under the law. Such opposition between Abraham and Moses would be offensive to any believing Jew and does not do justice to a full Christian understanding of the Old Testament. The patriarchal stories of Abraham were preserved by the Jews themselves as a true promise and prelude to the deeper covenant and promise of Mount Sinai, and can be read in no other way, certainly not as in opposition to Moses. What lies behind the New Testament's strong statements against the Torah as the way of justification before God is opposition to an attitude, found in some Jewish teachers of the first century, that legal observance can replace a personal faith and reliance on Yahweh's larger demands for love and obedience. But this same opposition to legalism pervades the prophets and psalms in the Old Testament and many Pharisees in Jesus' time. For prophet, Pharisee, and Christian, the true covenant is indeed typified by Abraham himself: a personal faith and trust in God above everything else in life.

The Story of Isaac and Jacob (Gen 24–36)

After the purchase of a piece of the promised land by contract in chapter 23, the history of the patriarchs passes rapidly on to the stories of Isaac and Jacob. Isaac barely stands out in his own right, and serves mostly as a bridge to the saga of Jacob. Two key Isaac stories are (1) his marriage to Rebecca from the home country, and (2) the birth of their sons Jacob and Esau. What few other incidents are recorded in chapter 26 seem to duplicate events in chapters 20–21 from the life of Abraham: the fear of King Abimelech that makes Isaac deny Rebecca is his wife, and the dispute over the wells of Negev. The drama turns immediately to Jacob, and chapters 25–36 can be divided into a series of short incidents from his life:

1. Gen 25:19–34   *The birth of the twins* Esau and Jacob and how Jacob wins Esau's birthright.
2. Gen 26:1–35   (Incidents from the life of Isaac)
3. Gen 27:1–45   *Jacob cheats Esau out* of the first-born's blessing.
4. Gen 27:46–28:9   *The blessing takes hold:* Jacob goes to Mesopotamia for a wife, but Esau marries the Canaanite woman.
5. Gen 28:10–22   *God gives the promise to Jacob* in a vision at Bethel.
6. Gen 29–30   *Jacob and Laban in contest:* Jacob's marriages, children and wealth at the expense of Laban.
7. Gen 31:1–55   *Jacob flees Laban's anger,* but finally they make a lasting covenant.
8. Gen 32:1–22   *Jacob has a vision* and makes overtures to Esau for peace.
9. Gen 32:23–34   *God fights with Jacob at Penuel.* Jacob's name changed to Israel.
10. Gen 33:1–17   *Jacob makes peace with Esau:* Esau takes the land of Edom; Jacob receives Palestine.

11. Gen 33:18–34:31 *Jacob at Shechem:* his sons conquer the city to avenge the rape of his daughter Dinah.

12. Gen 35:1–29 *Jacob settles at Bethel:* God renews the promises again to Jacob. Benjamin is born and Isaac dies. Final note is the death of Isaac.

13. Gen 36:1–43 (Genealogy of Esau)

Basically, there are three different types of Jacob stories that were collected, probably separately from one another. *First,* there are a number of stories about the conflict between Esau and Jacob, who are said to represent Edom and Israel in the prophecy of Genesis 25:23:

Two nations are in your womb
    and two peoples born of you shall be divided.
One shall be stronger than the other;
    the elder shall serve the younger.

No doubt these stories were first cherished by Israel as *heroic tales* of their own superiority and greater cleverness above their neighbor and rival across the Dead Sea in Jordan, Edom.

Second, a group of *sagas* grew up around Jacob's marriages and his adventures with Laban, his Aramean relative. The tricks and deceits of Jacob and Laban against one another gave delight to Israelite audiences who saw in this single combat between heroes a mirror of the battle between the nation Israel and the Arameans in later days (1 Kgs 20 and 22), in which Israel outfoxed Aram. Both the first and second group of stories, which pit Esau or Laban against Jacob, are really "eponymous," where the individuals stand for the whole nations.

A *third* group preserved a number of *theophanies* of God to Jacob at various important shrines: Bethel in chapter 28, Mahanaim in chapter 32, Penuel in chapter 32, and twice at Bethel again in chapter 35. Israel treasured these traditions because they not only detailed God's blessing on special sites within their land, but they also provided a framework of divine guidance for Jacob, and special moments in which God reaffirmed his promise, made first to Abraham, and renewed to Isaac in Genesis 26 and repeated now to Jacob.

In this collection of Jacob materials, the process of gathering the traditions together becomes easier to understand. We can trace the likely sequence of development from the oral state to the final written form. The three different types of stories were originally kept and transmitted for different reasons, sometimes by the same people, sometimes by others. The sagas of Jacob's conflict with Esau were *tribal stories* told about the times when the Jacob-tribe(s) first settled the land and had to fight for control. This "history" was remembered in the form of the personal struggle between Jacob

---

THE JACOB SAGA IN THE PATRIARCHAL NARRATIVES

1. **Earlier Sources**
   Scholars generally agree that the Jacob stories were first gathered together in cycles around three major themes, and can be traced back to oral traditions centered on tribal and cultic centers.

   The Conflict between Jacob and Esau
       Act 1 The twins struggle for first place in the womb (25:19–28);
       Act 2 they struggle for the birthright (25:29–34);
       Act 3 they struggle for Isaac's blessing (27:1–45);
       Act 4 they find reconciliation (32:3–21; 33:1–17).

   The Conflict between Jacob and Laban
       Act 1 Jacob must marry into Laban's family (27:46–28:9);
       Act 2 Jacob tricked by Laban but gains double family (29:1–30:24);
       Act 3 Jacob tricks Laban out of his flocks (30:25–43);
       Act 4 Jacob escapes with Laban's gods (31:1–24);
       Act 5 Jacob and Laban are reconciled (31:25–32:3).

   Theophanies
       Act 1 God appears to Jacob at Bethel to renew the promise
           (28:10–22);
       Act 2 God appears at Penuel and names Jacob "Israel" (32:22–32);
       Act 3 God renews the promise at Bethel (35:1–15).

2. **Saga Motifs**
   At the oral tradition level, many of the Jacob narratives are built around traditional folk motifs. Some of these are:
       a) the shepherd bests the hunter (Jacob over Esau);
       b) origins of famous place names (Bethel = "house of God");
       c) a night encounter with a mysterious god (Jacob versus the
          angel);
       d) puns on the name of an enemy (Esau is hairy and red, named
          for Israel's enemy Edom).

(Israel) and Esau (Edom), their chief rival for the land around the Dead Sea and the Jordan River. Single incidents may have been remembered by individual clans or villages, but gradually were collected into a larger body of stories for the whole nation, probably in the period of the judges, between 1200 and 1000 B.C. The second group of stories about Laban and the Mesopotamian roots of the Jacob tribes began as *family histories,* but as relations between Israelites and Arameans turned into battles, these tales developed into hero sagas about how Israel bested the Arameans in their contests.

The divine appearances to Jacob may have originated in *local shrines,* where some divine appearance was remembered and drew worshipers to the holy place. At the time of the Hebrew conquest the Israelites associated the shrines near the areas that Jacob had lived as places where God had shown blessing and guidance to Jacob their ancestor.

The growth of so many traditions probably took centuries to become organized into an heroic epic that followed Jacob from birth to death. The crucial element that united them was the religious theme of God's choice and guidance, so that each incident and story could be fitted to the others as part of God's blessing. This stage, perhaps still completely oral, would have been achieved only after the exodus and conquest when the tribes would have developed a sense that they all belonged together as one people, and combined their individual traditions into one.

Finally, they were carefully organized as a written history by J and then by E, and, still later, other versions were included or reworked by P. These sources can still be detected by the appearance of the same story in two different forms. In chapter 35 we note that Jacob arrives at Bethel twice—in verse 6 and again in verses 10–15; twice his name is changed from Jacob to Israel, once in chapter 32 and again in chapter 35.

By the last editing under the Priestly school at the time of the exile in the sixth century B.C., Genesis 12–36 has developed into a great epic of faith, including all the traditions from Abraham until the slavery in Egypt. But it still betrays its origins from the days when many of the stories were oral tales about the mighty exploits of a local leader over enemy tribes. Israel kept the whole tradition, warts and all, the way it had been passed down, because the people did not want to lose touch with their historical roots or with the way their ancestors remembered Yahweh, the God of history.

The Patriarchal Stories as Sagas

The patriarchal traditions of Abraham, Isaac and Jacob have often been called "legends," half-historical, half-entertaining stories of the past. Because "legend" in English often comes to mean simply fictitious, many scholars today have come to use the term "saga" borrowed from Icelandic family stories of the Middle Ages. Sagas are heroic tales about the ancestors of a well-known family. They give luster to the family or clan today by telling of the adventures of one or more of its great-great-grandfathers or grandmothers long ago. They often have legendary features, building up the fearless hero almost bigger than real life, and they share some of the characteristics of the epic style: long and very elaborate poems about great heroes who affected the whole course of the nation. Homer's *Iliad* and *Odyssey* and Virgil's *Aeneid* fall in this type of literature.

Sagas show signs of being repeated orally at first, sometimes with more than one version of each story in circulation. Each storyteller can adapt or add themes and local color to his retelling. By the time it is written down, the oral saga may have developed much beyond its earliest form, and two different versions may show quite striking changes from one another. The patriarch's stories of Genesis show signs of this. Compare the three cases of the patriarch's claiming that his wife was really his sister in order to save his life in Genesis 12, 20, and 26.

Gen 12:10–20	Gen 20:1–18	Gen 26:1–11
Hero: Abraham	*Hero:* Abraham	*Hero:* Isaac
King: Pharaoh	*King:* Abimelech of Gerar	*King:* Abimelech of Gerar
Pharaoh desires Sarah	Abimelech desires Sarah	Citizens desire Rebekah
God sends plagues on Pharaoh	God warns Abimelech in dream	------------------------------------
Pharaoh understands cause	God explains the cause	Abimelech finds out for himself
Pharaoh berates Abraham	Abimelech berates Abraham	Abimelech berates Isaac
Abraham is silent	Abraham explains reasons	Isaac explains

Gen 12:10–20	Gen 20:1–18	Gen 26:1–11
Pharaoh sends him packing	Abimelech gives Abraham gifts	Abimelech warns people to avoid Rebekah
	Abraham intercedes to heal Gerar women of barrenness	

When we look at these three stories, there would seem to be only one chance in a million that such a coincidence of events could happen three times in two generations, and that both Abraham and King Abimelech could have been so foolish as to fall into the same trap twice in their lives. Originally these three different stories were only *one* story. The same heroic tale about how a patriarch had almost lost his wife to a powerful king was possibly told in three separate cities or towns. One would be Beer-sheba, a city near Gerar associated with Isaac's life, and another would be Hebron, where the story was transferred to Abraham, who was the local hero there. Or else story-tellers in three different tribes each adapted the story to their local audience so that some tribe who lived near Gerar quickly identified the powerful king with Abimelech, while those farther south near the Egyptian border, made the king the Pharaoh of Egypt. In any case, three different versions arose. We cannot know just when and how this happened, but we do know that sagas are preserved and retold only within the group or groups for which they have meaning. Perhaps there was a special story-teller for each tribe which passed on its traditions to his successor. Or perhaps the stories were told at shrines where the priests would learn all the stories and preserve them. While no longer as vital as the oral method of handing on stories, historical legends are preserved in small towns in Europe through the local festivals in honor of a patron saint, now forgotten everywhere but in that village. Even the famous Passion Play of Oberammergau, produced every ten years by one small German village, is an example of how unique traditions are preserved in one special place.

The Story of Joseph (Gen 37–50)

The story of Jacob does not end in chapter 35. Although the following chapters, Genesis 37–48, focus on the person of one of his sons, Joseph, they remain only a sub-plot of the larger portrait of

Jacob and his twelve sons. In concluding, Genesis 48–50 return to the final days of Jacob. There is also room for other additions along the way. Genesis 38 breaks the Joseph section with an incident about his brother Judah, and Genesis 49 is an ancient poem about the characteristics of the twelve brothers, who are the founders of the twelve tribes that make up Israel as a nation. Indeed, Jacob is important to the authors of Genesis because the twelve tribes came from him, but the action must shift in the story of Joseph to the rivalry between the brothers. The stories are largely eponymous where each brother actually represents the tribe that goes by his name. Just as we could speak about how Virginia became a state before Georgia did, the Bible talks about Reuben as older than Gad to show that the traditions of one go back further than those of the other. In this perspective, Joseph would figure as an upstart tribe that became more important than his brother tribes. This may actually be historically true, since the two strongest tribes in northern Israel were Ephraim and Manasseh, and they are described as Joseph's "sons" in Genesis 48:1–22.

From one angle, the long story of Joseph is necessary in order to bring the tribes from Palestine of the old days down into Egypt and into captivity in order to prepare for the exodus. The biblical writers must, in effect, set the stage for the next act. Yet the long Joseph narrative is remarkable for another reason. It makes a *single complete dramatic plot,* carefully woven together and leading to the moment when the brothers are reconciled with Joseph. It is far different from the short, independent sagas about the earlier patriarchs. Many modern biblical scholars refer to it as a "novella," a short romantic novel. It delights in aspects completely ignored by the sagas: delighted descriptions of foreign customs, psychological insights, dramatic encounters, and detailed descriptions of Joseph's character—prudent, modest, gifted in dream analysis, well-spoken, and bred to nobility—in short, the perfect wise man of the world.

The plot is simple and yet a literary masterpiece. Joseph receives strange dreams in which he is more important than his brothers. This leads to their envy and Joseph finds himself in ever-deeper trouble. They sell him into slavery, he is falsely accused of adultery, and he ends in prison for life. Then with divine help the tide changes. He uses his dreams to help royal officials, then Pharaoh himself. He is made prime minister, and in the great famine that follows his brothers come into his power. But instead of doing to them what they had done to him, he forgives them and brings his father down to Egypt to live in peace and prosperity. The drama ends with the family reunited.

This is the kind of plot where nothing can be taken out as unnecessary. It is not just a collection of old incidents thrown together. But how did it become so different from the rest of the traditions in Genesis? The best solution understands that there must have been older saga stories about Joseph and about Israel's days in Egypt. But the Yahwist (or another) *rewrote* them into a novel about the time of Solomon, or even later, and it was included in the final form of the Book of Genesis.

There is some evidence for the early origin of many of the details. The coat of many colors (Gen 37:3) was the type worn by early Semites pictured on the eighteenth century B.C. tomb at Beni Hasan. The relations of the brothers are similar to tribal rivalries described in the Mari letters of the eighteenth century. The rise of a Semitic ruler to high position best fits the age of the Semitic Hyksos conquerors of Egypt in the eighteenth and seventeenth centuries. Various other incidents reflect a knowledge of Egyptian literature. Especially interesting is the similarity between Joseph's dealings with the wife of Potiphar and the *Tale of the Two Brothers,* in which the wife of the older brother tries to seduce the younger and when he resists, screams that he attacked her (ANET 23–25). Another Egyptian tale tells of seven years of plenty followed by seven years of famine that matches the descriptions in Genesis 41 (ANET 31).

But the discovery of a statue in the city of Alalakh in Syria of King Idri-mi, who ruled about 1400 B.C., provides the most remarkable similarity of all (ANET 557–558). The king inscribed on the statue how he quarreled with his brothers, escaped to a foreign land where he was exiled for many years, received a series of oracles, gathered an army, reconquered Alalakh, became king, and forgave his brothers. It is not the same event historically, nor even the same plot, but it does share many themes in common with the Joseph story, and lets us see how the biblical tradition borrowed a number of well-known topics about the *reversal of fortune* and used them to show how God took care of Joseph. Joseph himself expresses this central message when he says to his brothers in Genesis 45:7–8:

God sent me before you to preserve a remnant on earth, and to keep alive for you many survivors. So it was not you who sent me here, but God.

And again in Genesis 50:20 he says:

> As for you, you meant evil against me, but God meant it for
> good, to bring about that many people should be kept alive
> as they are today.

The Patriarchs and the "God of the Fathers"

The Joseph story expresses the major theme of the entire patriarchal history. Through ups and downs, successes and failures, God
has directed the course of events so that his promises will be
fulfilled. He overcomes all obstacles, whether it be the power of
kings, the threats from neighboring peoples, the curse of childless-
ness, the occasional lapses of an Abraham or the human craftiness of
a Jacob. For the Yahwist and Elohist, as well as for the later Priestly
editors, this God was the one God of Israel, Yahweh. Where the
Yahwist has announced in Genesis 4:26 that people called God by
his proper name "Yahweh" from the beginning, both the Elohist
and Priestly writers reserve the revelation of that sacred name until
Moses' meeting with God on Mount Sinai at the burning bush in
Exodus 3:14. Before that point in the Bible, they always call God by
the general word "Elohim" which means simply "God." In this they
are probably closer to the historical reality than is J's use of the
name so early. Exodus 3 clearly implies that Moses was the one who
first brought about the use of the name "Yahweh" for Israel's God.

Some of the earlier names used by different tribes and leaders
can still be discovered in the older parts of the Genesis traditions.
Thus Abraham addresses God as El-elyon, "God most high," in
Genesis 14:19–20, while Jacob prays to his God under the name
"The Fear of his father Isaac" in Genesis 31:53. In Genesis 35:11,
God identifies himself as El Shaddai, "God the Almighty," and it
occurs again in Genesis 49:25 in the blessing of Joseph. In the
previous verse, Genesis 49:24, God receives the archaic name "Bull
of Jacob." Different patriarchal traditions know of different ancient
names for the deity, but by far the most common designation is the
term "God of your father(s)." This comes up often: Genesis 26:24,
31:53, 46:1–3, and 49:25. This phrase is striking, especially since it is
the term by which God makes himself known to Moses at first in the
burning bush (Ex 3:6): "I am the God of your father, the God of
Abraham, the God of Isaac, and the God of Jacob."

In old Assyrian tablets from the time of Abraham, we also find the expression "god of the fathers" or "god of your fathers" used to refer to the *personal god* of someone. But here it is not the case of total loyalty to one deity, for the individual also worships all of the great gods. However, Asshur and Anu are so far away and so great that the Assyrians felt the need for a more intimate and more personal god, usually a less important divinity, who had special ties to their family. One statement sums it up perfectly: "Without the (personal) god, man eats no bread." Such personal gods served almost as a guardian angel would in Christian thinking.

The closest parallel to this unusual custom of identifying a god by referring to the worship of one's ancestors instead of giving the god a proper name can be found among the nomads in Arabia about the time of Christ. Hundreds of tribal hands have scratched on desert cliffs prayers to "the god of our fathers," or to "the god of our master," or to the "god of (the man) Aumou." The special nature of this type of prayer and worship is that the god is identified with the clan's leader, and is rarely ever attached to a specific place. The inscriptions reflect the personal devotion of members of a tribe or family who carry on the worship started long before by a famed forefather.

Understanding that "God of the fathers" was a term used for the worship of the special deity known only to *our* clan or tribe will help us explain how the patriarchal traditions were joined together as one story for all the tribes. Each tribe or clan perhaps worshiped God under a different name, but when the tribes were united, they realized that the "Fear of Isaac" or the "Bull of Jacob" or "God Most High" were all really the same God who had now revealed his proper name as Yahweh. The Bible tells us that Abraham, Isaac and Jacob were grandfather, father and son. But this is just a way of expressing that *these originally independent clans named after a great founder or leader were now united as one family.* Where they had worshiped their gods under different names, they now accepted a single God and a single national identity as Israel. This surely began under the leadership of Moses who drew the tribes together and taught them the worship of Yahweh. But it must have taken many years during the time of the judges for all the traditions to be combined into the present plan. The arrangement of the patriarchs into a family structure helped emphasize that all the tribes shared a real unity of roots since they had all worshiped the "God of their Fathers" and all claimed possession of some area of Palestine.

STUDY QUESTIONS

1. What is "eponymous" writing?
2. Briefly describe the setting of the patriarchal stories.
3. "The story of Abraham is told as a journey." Explain the meaning of this statement.
4. Briefly describe the promises and covenants made by God to Abraham.
5. "Abraham always showed himself as the man of faith." Assess the validity of this statement.
6. What are the three different types of Jacob stories?
7. Define the following: promise, covenant, theophany, legends, sagas, epic.
8. How can one explain the similarities of the three patriarch stories in Genesis 12:10–20, Genesis 20:1–18, and Genesis 26:1–11?
9. What is the purpose of the story of Joseph? How does it relate to the rest of Genesis?
10. Explain the meaning of the term "God of the Fathers."

Chapter 8

THE EXODUS FROM EGYPT

Suggested Scripture Readings:

Exodus 1–6

Exodus 14–18

The Exodus Event

The exodus marks the real beginning of the history of Israel as a people. Before this one experience of God's deliverance from slavery, whatever traditions there were centered on individual *clans* and *persons*. From now on, every text speaks of a *nation* unified by faithfulness to a God who chooses them for a special role. There now become two clear focal points: a single God and a single people bound together for better or for worse. The historical event itself, no matter how everyday and ordinary it might seem in our times, used to world wars and fearful of universal atomic destruction, was built up and described with all the images of divine power and miracle significant to ancient peoples.

Yet we cannot separate the escape from Egypt from what follows in the desert and in the conquest. This divine act of liberation was motive enough for a group to pledge itself to this God in a binding covenant. The exodus miracle had proven the love and power of Yahweh and shown that he was worth trusting. But at the same time, the escape was *not complete* in itself, but was tied to the conquest of the land of Palestine by a puny nation despite the overwhelming strength of the native pagans who lived there already. To be trapped in the desert would hardly be an escape to celebrate! Thus the tradition is threefold: (1) deliverance, (2) binding covenant, (3) conquest of a promised land. In turn, these events

155

make sense out of the numerous traditions about promised sons and land to patriarchs and clan groups. All those traditions can now be focused on this moment in history and become a source of union for many different tribes, who either had taken part in the exodus or who later asked to join the new people Israel. Knowing how traditions build, we can be sure that the course of events from exodus to conquest was slow and probably far from as simple as the Bible now paints it to be.

Egypt in the Period of the Exodus

The Book of Genesis ends with the Hebrews settled properously in the land of Goshen, a fertile section of the Nile Delta nearest to Palestine. Egyptian records tell of Asiatic settlers there in almost every century. But in the eighteenth century B.C., the flow of peoples from Asia Minor became more intense; possibly more warlike, they overwhelmed the weak Egyptian defenses. Later Egyptian writings remembered bitterly the next two hundred years of foreign rule by the Hyksos, literally, the "foreign chiefs." It seemed as though the gods had abandoned Egypt altogether. Hatshepsut, a ruler shortly after the final expulsion of those Hyksos, wrote:

> I have not slept forgetfully, (but) I have restored that which had been 'ruined. I have raised up that which had gone to pieces formerly, since the Asiatics were in the midst of Avaris of the Northland (their capital), and vagabonds were in the midst of them, overthrowing that which had been made. They ruled without Re (the sun god), and he did not act by divine command down to (the reign of) my (own) majesty (ANET 231).

While the story of Joseph gives us no inkling of the hatred of the native Egyptians for these foreign peoples, we can imagine the anger of the people toward a despised Semitic conqueror if the policies described in Genesis 47:13–26 were followed, in which people lost the ownership of their land and they became state slaves. Genesis 47 is an attempt to explain the Egyptian system of government to Hebrews. While the present story of Joseph reads like a novel, it still reflects many of the *actual historical* situations in the Hyksos period.

But a new age dawned for Egypt when she finally overthrew

the Hyksos under King Ahmose of Thebes about 1550 B.C. The princes of Thebes, far up the Nile from the Delta, had managed to stay nearly independent of the Hyksos, and gradually strengthened their position as the foreigners became weaker. Upon his final victory, Ahmose began a new dynasty, the 18th, which ushered in a glorious era of conquest in both Asia and Africa.

Under a skilled series of kings, all of them named either Thutmoses or Amenophis, Egypt expanded her empire to include the Sudan, Libya, Palestine and most of Syria. Wealth flowed to her from all over the known world, including Asiatic craftsmen, traders, ambassadors and prisoners in greater numbers than had been true under Hyksos rule. While Semites who had stayed on in the Delta area, and most newcomers, were no doubt subjected to rigorous supervision, and perhaps at times virtual slavery, there is no reason to believe that Egypt systematically tried to exclude foreigners from her soil. The evidence shows the opposite. Semitic influences in religion and culture increased enormously under the 18th dynasty (also called the *New Kingdom*).

This period of prosperity for Egypt was matched by equal success in Palestine and Syria. Archaeology reveals the growth of large cities: Jerusalem, Megiddo, Jericho, and Beth-shan all flourished. One such city, Hazor, north of the Sea of Galilee, had a population of perhaps thirty thousand people. Its fortified acropolis, or upper city, was larger than the total area of most ancient cities.

Egyptian rule was generally benevolent. The governor ruled from Byblos in Phoenicia and from Beth-shan in Palestine, and left most of the control to local princes and chiefs as long as taxes and goods continued to be delivered to the Egyptian overlords. The army ventured to war only in cases of civil war, rebellion, or attack from the northern kingdoms of the Hittites or Assyrians and Babylonians. Culture in Palestine reached new heights of beauty and delicacy in pottery design, and commerce flourished. This period, known to archaeology as the Late Bronze Age, saw wide contacts with the Minoan civilization on Crete and the Mycenean civilization in Greece. Excellent examples of the fine Mycenean pottery were carried to cities all over the Near East.

The strongest threat to Egyptian control came from a new rival far to the north, the growing empire of the Hittites in Anatolia, located in the central part of modern Turkey. Under a series of warlike kings, they expanded steadily southward into northern Syria until they were border to border with the Syrian possessions of Egypt.

Pharaoh Akhenaton and Monotheism

The most striking event of the New Kingdom was the decision of Pharaoh Amenophis IV (1375–1358) to change the religion of Egypt toward a simpler faith. Egyptians worshiped a great number of divine beings inherited from each town and district of the kingdom, all loosely organized under the headship of the god of the ruling city of Thebes, Amon (or Amun). The cults of these gods were very rooted in the nation, but traditionally a special place of supremacy had been accorded to Re, the sun god. When the city of Thebes became the capital under the pharaohs of the Middle and New Kingdoms, its god Amon replaced Re as the head of the gods. The priesthood of Amon's temples was a powerful and controlling force in Egyptian politics. In a revolutionary move, Amenophis (whose name means "Amon is satisfied") encouraged a new cult of the sun disc (the Aton) as the supreme and only divine principle. He began a persecution of the priests of Amon, had the name Amon erased from all monuments, and founded a new capital far from the old city of Thebes, which he named Akhetaton ("The horizon of Aton"), at the site we call today Tell el Amarna. Finally, he changed his own name to Akhenaton, "The Glory of Aton." Unfortunately, the pharaoh's reign was too short to bring his reform to success and the religion proved too cold and esoteric to be popular. It centered on the power of the sun disc and its life-giving rays, but in practice it focused on the cult of the pharaoh himself. He worshiped the Aton; the people were to worship him. Yet, though it eventually failed soon after Akhenaton's own death, it was to have lasting effects. The very attempt to destroy the name Amon, and to erase the plural word "gods" from any monuments on which it was found, shows the monotheistic direction of the new faith. Perhaps "true monotheism" is too strong a label to use. The Aton was often associated with the older sun god Re, and the practice of the new faith seemed to stress the divine role of the pharaoh as much as of the Aton, a practice much in line with the traditional faith in Amon and the general pantheon of gods.

We can guess that this short-lived attempt at monotheism must have affected the Egyptians profoundly. The priests of the temple of Amun and the rulers who succeeded Akhenaton wiped out every trace of the heretic religion that they could find. Their hatred shows what a threat it posed to Egypt's traditional way of life. Akhenaton's new movement had given rise to a new and very realistic style of art

The great pyramid of pharaoh Cheops at Giza. The sphinx stands nearby as part of the temple complex of the 2nd pyramid built by pharaoh Khephren (both 4th dynasty, before 2600 B.C.).

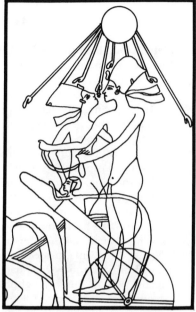

Pharaoh Akhenaton and his wife Nefertiti in the royal chariot with the rays of the Aton blesing them.

which emphasized even the king's physical deformities. This was a far cry from the normal Egyptian practice of showing all kings and important people as ideal persons in perfect health and with good looks. Akhenaton lived too early for Moses to have seen his faith in action, but it is possible that the heretic king's ideas continued to permeate people's thoughts, and in some small way helped even the Semitic settlers in the Delta to develop more deeply their own understanding of Yahweh as a God who stood alone against the claims of so many hundreds of competing divine beings.

The Amarna Letters

Luckily, archaeologists in 1887 discovered a large number of letters that date from the time of Akhenaton and his father, Amenophis III, between 1400 and 1350 B.C. Many of these were royal letters, written from the kings of small city-states in Palestine and Syria to the pharaoh, giving reports, carrying on international relations and asking for help. They were written on clay tablets and were stored in the royal library at Tell el Amarna. For this reason,

---

AMARNA LETTER

A letter from the prince of Jerusalem, Abdu-Heba, to pharaoh Akhenaton, complaining about the attacks of the Apiru (about 1375
B.C.)   (ANET 487)

To the king, my lord, my Sun-God, my pantheon, say: Thus
Shuwardata, thy servant, servant of the king (5) and the dirt (under)
his two feet, the ground (on) which thou dost tread! At the feet of the
king, my lord, the Sun-God from heaven, seven times, seven times I
fall, both (10) prone and supine.

Let the king, my lord, learn that the chief of the 'Apiru has risen
(in arms) against the lands which the god of the king, my lord, gave
me; (16) but I have smitten him. Also let the king, my lord, know that
all my brethren have abandoned me, and (20) it is I and 'Abdu-Heba
(who) fight against the chief of the 'Apiru. And Zurata, prince of
Accho, and Indaruta, prince of Achshaph, it was they (who) hastened
(25) with fifty chariots—for I had been robbed (by the 'Apiru)—to my
help; but behold, they are fighting against me, so let it be agreeable to
the king, my lord, and (30) let him send Yanhamu, and let us make
war in earnest, and let the lands of the king, my lord, be restored to
their (former) limits!

---

they have been named "The Amarna Letters." They have been
valuable for Old Testament study, because they reveal the conditions of the country at the time just before the exodus and conquest.
Numerous small towns, each with its own ruler, struggled against
one another for positions of power, grasping for more land or
defending themselves against another town's attack. All of them
had to face wandering bands of marauders called Apiru, made up of
people who were landless or exiled from their own territories.
Sometimes the Apiru included whole tribes or clans without loyalty
to any state. They were often employed by one king against another, so that at least part of their living was made as soldiers for hire. It
is not clear whether these Apiru were primarily nomadic groups,
seeking lands for themselves, or local peasants forced off their land
by economic pressures and taxes who turned to revolt. What does
seem clear is that many kings could not withstand their attacks
without outside help. Their letters plead with the pharaoh to send
troops quickly before all is lost. They assure the pharaoh of their
loyalty forever, while claiming that other rulers were plotting

against the Egyptian government and against the pharaoh's loyal
servant the king. Consider the pleas of Abdu-Heba, king of Jerusalem:

> To the king my lord, say: Thus Abdu-Heba, thy servant. At
> the two feet of my lord, the king, seven times and seven
> times I fall. What have I done to the king, my lord? They
> blame me before the king, my lord (saying): "Abdu-Heba
> has rebelled against the king, his lord" ... Why should I
> commit transgression against the king, my lord? ... Let the
> king turn his attention to the archers, and let the king, my
> lord, send out troops of archers (for) the king has no lands
> (left)! The Apiru plunder all the lands of the king.

Egypt, however, failed to send the strong military force needed to
keep order. Akhenaton's concerns centered on religious reform,
and he possessed little of the warlike spirit of earlier pharaohs. The
unrest continued and perhaps grew even worse. Thus about 1400
B.C., Palestine presents a picture of small walled city-states in the
valleys and coastal plains whose kings were constantly at war among
themselves and against rootless and landless bands who roamed the
countryside and hills, raiding where they could. It shows a weak
Egyptian army, bent more on plunder than protection, corrupt
officials, petty rivalries, and a generous amount of anarchy.

Many authors have pointed to Apiru as a possible form of the
word "Hebrew," often used in the Bible to identify the Israelites
(Gen 14:3; 40:15; Ex 1:15–19; 1 Sam 4:6–9, etc.). Not all scholars
agree with this identification, and in many ways the Apiru of the
Amarna letters do not match the description of the Israelites after
the exodus. But they do reveal how much social unrest was present
and how Palestine was ripe for a change in the balance of power.

Israel's Time in Egypt

Exodus 1:8 says only, "A new king came to power in Egypt who
did not know Joseph." The Israelites became persecuted and enslaved. But when did this begin? One possibility is at the time when
the foreign Hyksos were driven out in 1550 B.C. This could mean a
long period of hardship. But Exodus 1 seems to indicate a fairly
short period of actual persecution just before the actual escape.
Since experts do not agree on the meaning of the dates and events

mentioned in the exodus story, several quite different positions are argued for in books about the exodus. The two most common dates suggested are (1) between 1450–1350 B.C. and (2) between 1300–1250 B.C. The latter is the more favored today. Those who favor the earlier dates, however, point to the Amarna letters as evidence that groups of Apiru/Hebrews were already in Palestine by 1350. They also argue that the most likely time for a persecution of a Semitic tribe was shortly after the Egyptian defeat of the Hyksos and not much later. There is further evidence for Semitic slaves in the period between 1500 and 1400 at Serabit el Khadem, an Egyptian turquoise mine in the Sinai desert. The rocks nearby were covered with inscriptions written by Semitic workers in the mines. Finally, they point to the date suggested by 1 Kings 6:1 that Solomon dedicated the temple four hundred and eighty years after Israel left Egypt. If the temple is to be placed about 950 B.C., this would mean an exodus date about 1430 B.C.

Those who maintain a date between 1300 and 1250 also point to specific evidence inside and outside the Bible. Exodus 1:11 clearly states that the Israelites were forced to build the store cities of Ramses and Pithom. Although archaeology has not yet definitely located these sites, Egyptian records reveal that they were building projects started by the founders of the 19th dynasty, Seti I and his son Ramesses II, between 1310 and 1300. They moved the capital of Egypt from Thebes to the Delta's border with the Sinai desert in order to better direct military campaigns in Palestine and Syria. Moreover, proponents of the late date can point to the famous victory inscription of Pharaoh Merneptah, Ramesses II's son, which dates to 1212 or so, mentioning his victory over Israel:

> The princes are prostrate, saying: "Mercy!"
> Not one raises his head among the Nine Bows.
> Desolation is for Tehunu; Hatti is pacified;
> Plundered is the Canaan with every evil;
> Carried off is Ashkelon; seized upon is Gezer;
> Yanoam is made as that which does not exist;
> *Israel is laid waste, his seed is not;*
> Hurru has become a widow for Egypt! (ANET 378)

Since Israel is marked with the sign for a tribe or clan, and not for a city or land, scholars argue that this means the Israelites had not yet settled down fully by 1225–1220 B.C. The pharaoh exaggerates his great victory, of course, and we can be sure that his great "slaughter" was little more than a skirmish which drove the Israelites back into the hills. If this is the case, and the traditional forty years in the desert (Ex 14:33) is not just a symbolic number for one lifetime, it follows that the exodus took place before 1275.

A date for the exodus in the reign of Ramses II, sometime between 1300 and 1280, seems the most likely. It would fit the notice in Exodus 12:40 that Israel had been in Egypt four hundred and thirty years, i.e., since about 1700 B.C. when the Hyksos took control of the country. But the biblical story does not depend on the certainty of the exact date. The drama of a people or clan escaping into the Sinai desert was probably a common occurrence, and

---

EGYPTIAN ARMY CHASE AFTER RUNAWAY SLAVES

This was a letter written down about 1200 B.C. for schoolboys to imitate, but it could be much older. The situation is not much different from that experienced by Israel as it escaped Egypt (ANET 259).

The Chief of Bowmen of Tjeku, Ka-Kem-wer, to the Chief of Bowmen Ani and the Chief of Bowmen Baken-Ptah:

In life, prosperity, health! In the favor of Amon-Re, King of the Gods, and the ka of the King of Upper and Lower Egypt: User-kheperu-Re Setep-en-Re—life, prosperity, health!—our good lord—life, prosperity, health! I say (xix 5) the Re-Har-akhti: "Keep Pharaoh—life, prosperity, health!—our good lord—life, prosperity, health!—in health! Let him celebrate millions of jubilees, while we are in his favor daily!"

Another matter, to wit: I was sent forth from the broad-halls of the palace—life, prosperity, health!—in the 3rd month of the third season, day 9, at the time of evening, following after these two slaves. Now when I reached the enclosure-wall of Tjeku on the 3rd month of the third season, day 10, they told (me) they were saying to the south that they had passed by on the 3rd month of the third season, day 10. (XX I) (Now) when (I) reached the fortress, they told me that the scout had come from the desert (saying that) they had passed the walled place north of the Migdol of Seti Mer-ne-Ptah—life, prosperity, health!—Beloved like Seth.

When my letter reaches you, write to me about all that has happened to (them). Who found their tracks? Which watch found their tracks? What people are after them? Write to me about all that has happened to them and how many people you send out after them.

(May your health) be good!

several Egyptian documents actually mention attempts to stop such groups (ANET 259). We do not expect to ever find mention of Moses or the exodus in Egyptian records of either the fifteenth or fourteenth centuries. What set this escape off from all others like it was the religious encounter with God that it involved *for Israel.* Egypt probably did not even realize this aspect at all. However, Egypt had a profound influence on Israel—even many of the names of Hebrews in the Book of Exodus are Egyptian: Phineas, Hophni, Merari, and Moses himself (similar to Pharaohs Thut*moses* and Ah-*moses*)! The Israel that took part in the exodus, whether a small group or large, whether early or late, always defined herself *in contrast* to the ways of Egypt.

The Book of Exodus

The Book of Exodus is divided into several distinct episodes:

1. The childhood and call of Moses
2. The struggle to free Israel by plagues, climaxing in the passover
3. The escape and journey into the wilderness of Sinai
4. The giving of the covenant and its laws
5. The instructions for building the ark and the tent of meeting, and their execution

There is a dramatic element to this story that cannot be overlooked. We are asked to see the hopelessness of the Hebrew situation, the almost impossible struggle to change the pharaoh's mind, the power of Yahweh and his total mastery of events at the showdown at the Red Sea, the bitter disappointment and forgetfulness of Israel in the desert, and the final, compelling show of divine majesty and offer of a covenant at Sinai. All of this is told from the viewpoint of Moses the leader. And yet, although Moses is certainly the hero of the story, he never claims the credit. He always appears instead as an instrument of God. The drama and tension of the story center on whether God will act at this moment or not. We never doubt who runs the show, but only when he will choose to reveal his plan. At times we even despair over Moses and Aaron and the people for their hard-headed behavior, their faults and lack of insight into what is happening.

In short, Israel narrates the story of the exodus to glorify God who saves. To modern readers, much of the biblical story seems harsh and primitive and too violent and warlike. But in a world where the weak had little protection and fewer rights, a God who can fight for his people and defend them is the God who receives worship. The Israelite story frankly praises God as a warrior, as *the* warrior. His military prowess is miraculous; he leads, he defeats enemies, he even marches triumphantly to his own holy mountain and receives his people's obedience and praise there. It is summed up in the victory hymn of Miriam at the Red Sea (Ex 15:11–13):

> Sing to the Lord for he is gloriously triumphant,
>> horse and chariot he has cast into the sea.
>
> The Lord is my refuge and my defense,
>> he has proven himself my deliverer.
>
> He is my God, I will praise him;
>> the god of my fathers, I will glorify him.
>
> The Lord is a warrior. Lord is his name!

Moses and the Struggle for Freedom (Ex 1–4)

The exodus story begins with the enslavement of the Hebrews in Egypt, and how one child escaped this fate to grow up and lead his people to freedom. The name Moses is itself Egyptian and supports the biblical tradition that Moses' own background and training was Egyptian. The importance of the person Moses to the entire complex of exodus traditions is strengthened by the possibility that he grew up with first-hand knowledge of both Canaanite and Egyptian practices.

But already in the story of his birth (Ex 2:1–10) the biblical tradition adds borrowed themes of the heroic. The charming tale of how he was set adrift in a boat among the bulrushes and rescued by the princess of the pharaoh's own family is similar to many ancient folktales where a great leader as a baby is unwittingly saved from death by the very people he will later overthrow. The best known and closest parallel was already told for many centuries in a legend about the great Sargon, king of Akkad, about 2300 B.C.:

> Sargon the Mighty, king of Akkad am I
> My mother was a high priestess, my father I knew not . . .
> My mother, the high priestess, conceived me, in secret she
>> bore me.

> She set me in a basket of rushes, with bitumen she sealed my
> lid.
> She cast me into the river which rose not (over) me.
> The river bore me up and carried me to Akki, the drawer of
> water.
> Akki, the drawer of water (took me) as his son (and) reared
> me.
> While I was a gardener, Ishtar granted me (her) love,
> And for (?) years I exercised kingship (ANET 119).

The second stage of his life is remembered as one of exile in the Sinai for the justified killing of an Egyptian. Exodus 2 and 3 show years spent among the nomadic Midianite tribes, learning the desert and the ways of its people. It is here, in the story of the burning bush, that Moses first experienced the unique revelation of God. Whatever the picture of a burning bush meant to the ancient mind, the event bears all the marks of a great and awesome experience of God as a Holy One, the kind of moment of total conversion that has marked many great leaders, including another man of the desert centuries later, Mohammed. It was an experience no less revolutionary for Moses than was the conversion of St. Paul on the road to Damascus.

At the burning bush, God revealed to Moses both his *plan* to save Israel and his own personal *name*. In the powerful scene of Exodus 3:14–15, a confused and uncertain Moses questions God:

> "When I go to the Israelites and say to them, 'The God of
> your Fathers has sent me to you,' and they say to me, 'What
> is his name?' what shall I answer them?" And God said to
> Moses, "I am who I am; and thus you will say to the
> Israelites, I AM has sent me to you." And God spoke again
> to Moses, "Say this to the Israelites: Yahweh, the God of
> your fathers, the God of Abraham, the God of Isaac and the
> God of Jacob, has sent me to you. This is my name forever;
> this is my title generation after generation."

The name "Yahweh" by which God reveals himself can mean something like "He who is" or, better, "He who causes what is." It derives from the verb meaning "to be" (*hawah*). When the name is combined with the claim to be the same God that Moses' ancestors had known and worshiped, it is best understood to mean "The god who is always present (to Israel)." The name carries a sense of the mystery and numinous power of God, beyond the reach of Moses' question. He can be grasped as the God of the great ones of the past, the God who acted for them. In this small encounter, the theme of promise is highlighted. Not only are past promises to the fathers recalled, but a new promise of deliverance and land is made known.

The Book of Exodus presents the name Yahweh as *new* to Moses. But scholars have long speculated on the earlier origin of the name. Since Moses had close contact with the Midianites through his Midianite father-in-law Reuel (or Jethro) while in the Sinai (Ex 2:11–25), scholars think that Yahweh, who has many characteristics of a god of nomadic peoples, was *already worshiped at Sinai* by the Midianites. An inscription of Pharaoh Amenophis III (1408–1372), the father of Akhenaton, already mentioned "the land of the Shosu (bedouin), the tribes of Yhw' " for an area just east of the Sinai. But even if Moses owed much to his experience with the Midianites, little of a pagan, nomadic deity remained in Israel's idea of God. The unique events of the exodus, the covenant, and the conquest of Palestine molded a deeper understanding of the nature of God. Under the divinely inspired genius of a Moses, a startling new faith formed that was totally unlike any other ancient religion we know of.

The Plagues and the Passover of the Lord (Ex 5–12)

Exodus 5 begins the struggle between Moses, who works wonders in the name of Yahweh, and the pharaoh, who hardens his heart and refuses to listen. It involves ten plagues which have been built up from different sources. The J and E authors are responsible for eight plagues, and P has added two others. In the basic J and E account, Moses asks the pharaoh to let the people go, the pharaoh refuses, Moses causes a plague, the pharaoh begs him to stop it and the people can then go, but then the pharaoh hardens his heart again. The two from P, the gnats and boils (8:16–19 and 9:8–12), stress the role of Aaron the priest and the nature of each plague as a *sign* of God's power.

The first nine plagues all have a natural explanation in conditions found even today in Egypt. Minute organisms often turn the Nile red in the August flood time, plagues of frogs in September were recorded even in antiquity, and flies and gnats are endemic to the country, as every modern traveler knows first-hand! The "sign" and "wonder" to an Israelite was found *not in the plagues them-*

selves but in the control that God exercised over the whole series to
bring about his plan.

The tenth and final plague stands apart. Although it may seem
coldly brutal to us, Israel saw the death of Egypt's first-born as God's
clear choice on behalf of his people and his life-and-death concern
for their freedom. The pharaoh relents before this example of
divine intervention and the Israelites depart in haste, taking what
they can. They formed, as Exodus 12:38 says, a ragtag collection of
refugees. The flight into the Sinai gains extra drama as the pharaoh
changes his mind and sets out in pursuit, knowing the group has
little chance to escape.

But the drama is twice interrupted by the editors to include the
directions for the passover festival (chapter 12), and the rules for the
circumcision and consecration of the first-born sons of Israel (chapter 13). These descriptions reflect the peaceful celebrations of *later
times* when families gathered together in their new homeland to
remember and to rejoice. The rituals include eating certain foods,
the manner of dressing or standing, and the prayers chosen to
remind the people how their ancestors had suffered bitterly, fled in
haste, and acted in trust. The entire escape reads somewhat like a
Church liturgy, for every scene is heavy with meaning for believers.
The killing of the lamb in order to put its blood on the doorposts,
and the supper with its unleavened bread, bitter herbs and roast
lamb reflect two ancient feasts that predate the exodus and may
even go back long before the dawn of history: one is a sheepherder's
rite of killing a new-born lamb and using its blood to drive away evil
spirits as the tribe begins its springtime move from one pastureland
to another; the second is a farming village ceremony of ridding the
houses of the old yeast and old grain to celebrate the new spring
crops with a feast of dedication and rejoicing.

The Israelites took over these traditional feasts and transformed
them into a great celebration of the exodus events so that each
action and detail took on a new meaning as the original pagan ideas
were suppressed. The early Christians did much the same in setting
up Christmas on December 25. The New Testament never says
when Christ was born, but the Church took over the pagan feast of
the rebirth of the sun-god, which was celebrated in midwinter
when the sun had reached its lowest point on the horizon. What
better way, they reasoned, to show that the birth of Jesus was new
life, giving true light to the world, than to replace the feast of the
old sun god with that of the new Sun of Justice.

In the same way, passover becomes a new spring and a new beginning, whose every action has commemoration value. The modern Jewish passover seder service shows the power of the ancient symbols to make alive an event of the distant past for our own age. The passover narrative with its circumcision and consecration laws recalls God's salvation to all the people of Israel in every age. Christians, too, recall these events with thankful praise to God. Without the exodus, no one would have recognized the merciful and powerful God who saves and delivers anew that Jesus proclaimed in his ministry.

The Miracle at the Red Sea (Ex 13–15)

We possess two accounts of the crossing of the Red Sea, or, more properly in the Hebrew text, the *Reed Sea* (the term "Red Sea" dates only from the Greek Septuagint translation). There is a prose version in chapter 14 and one in poetry in chapter 15. They differ somewhat, with chapter 14 emphasizing the role of the pillars of cloud and fire, the east wind, and the Israelites passing dryshod through the waters which then close upon the pursuing Egyptians, while the poem in Exodus 15:1–18 mentions only the drowning of the Egyptians as the miracle. Both accounts agree that Israel passed through a section of wet land that had been made nearly dry by a withering east wind, and that when the Egyptians tried to follow, their chariots were caught in the mud or returning water, and the soldiers drowned. The tradition that this area was a shallow arm of the Red Sea is less likely than that it was located in a marshy area of Lake Timsah or Lake Sirbonis farther to the north near the present-day Suez Canal. Major Palmer, a nineteenth century English explorer, described a similar occurrence at Lake Sirbonis:

> Strong north-easterly gales, on reaching Suez, would, by its action on an ebb tide, make it abnormally low, and prevent while it lasted, at least for a time, the return of the usual flood tide. In this way a good passage across the channel might soon be laid bare and remain so for several hours. In the morning, a shift of wind to the south, probably of cyclonic nature, takes place. The pent-up flood tide, now freed from restraint, and urged on by the south gale, returns to its wonted flow.

Behind the greatly magnified accounts of the Lord's victory that we find in the present text stands an authentic memory of Israel. The doubts over the possibility of any miracle at all simply misses the point. Scientists will tell us quite readily that every plague, from the annual locust swarms to the virulent outbreaks of skin diseases, can be found naturally in northern Africa. The same is true of the phenomenon of the hot winds and the marshy waters. The miracle does not stand on any of these factors. In fact, ancient peoples, dependent on oral story-telling, who cherish traditions of a god acting in a special way and breaking in upon their normal way of life with astounding suddenness, almost always magnify the details and accent the heroic aspects. The miracle is only in the *timing* of such fortunate events, a timing that cannot be explained in any way except by design or because of prayer. A refugee band such as Israel just does not escape the power of the Egyptian army unless God chooses to protect and guide it. The very words the Old Testament uses for such miracles mean more properly "signs" or "wondrous, unexplainable things." They suggest that the event in question can only have divine direction because it is beyond human control. For the ancient Near East, there were no lucky chances or accidental happenings; all things were the result of the divine will. When the ordinary pattern changed dramatically, then it was a sign to be read and understood by all.

Nor must we forget that the prose and the poetic account differ in form and purpose. Exodus 14 continues the narrative drama begun in chapter 1. Exodus 15:1–18, on the other hand, is an ancient poem, perhaps the oldest in the Bible, that celebrates the victory of God at the sea, but continues its references even up to the conquest of Palestine. This poem has been placed after the prose story to act as a summary and hymn of thanksgiving for the saving deed of God at the Reed Sea. It does not pretend to give all the facts, nor does it limit itself to a sober telling of the event. It is a climax and it is praise, and glowing words and epic exaggeration are to be expected.

Desert Escape (Ex 15–18)

From this point on, the narrative moves quickly to the next great meeting with God at Mount Sinai. Exodus 15–18 sketches several incidents of God's care that were answered by Israel's murmuring and rebellion against the hardships of the desert. Many of the stories, such as the feeding with manna and quail, or the gift of water from the rock, or the complaints at Marah, are found again as part of the later desert traditions in the Book of Numbers, and will be treated in the next chapter. The repetition of similar stories reveals that two different sources were known, and both were used to doubly reinforce the point of God's continual care and the people's continual lack of appreciation and rebelliousness.

Exodus 12:38 tells us that the Israelites left with a motley group of followers, and despite the claim of six hundred thousand men, not including women and children, Israel was probably not large enough a group to attract much notice in Egyptian records. At best, too, even in a world power like Egypt, control of the lands far from major settlements and highways was spotty at best and usually

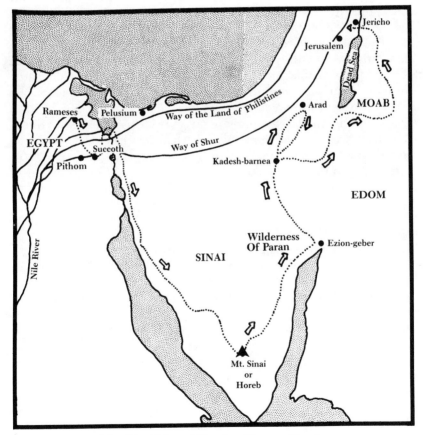

The Traditional Exodus Escape Route

exercised by a single annual military raid to keep the peace and collect tribute. The Israelites stayed far from the military garrisons (Ex 13:17) and probably would remain unbothered once they managed to reach the Sinai wilderness.

Many routes of escape have been proposed. Because of the notice in Exodus 13:17 that Israel avoided the way of the Philistines, the normal road to Palestine, few suggest the coastal route. Some would propose a trek through the desert in the northern part of Sinai straight to Kadesh Barnea (see the map), even though this has little support in tradition; others defend a more popular tradition (at least since early Christian times) of a route deep into southern Sinai, to the imposing range of mountains with the peak Jebel Musa (mountain of Moses). From there, Israel would have journeyed up the opposite side of the Sinai peninsula to Kadesh Barnea. Even today, the Greek Orthodox monastery of St. Catherine stands at the foot of Jebel Musa to welcome visitors.

The Sinai is hardly capable of supporting many people at a time, and even with quail and the manna, a dew-like secretion of certain desert plants and insects, the oases could not provide water for more than a few hundred individuals, if that. Later generations telling the story provided numbers more fitting to the days of King David and the monarchy, perhaps out of pride as much as anything. If indeed six hundred thousand men had left Egypt, no army on earth at the time could have withstood them—they could have had Egypt itself if they had wanted it!

STUDY QUESTIONS

1. What is the significance of the Exodus Event?
2. Briefly describe the historical circumstances and situation in Egypt.
3. Identify the following: Hyksos, Pharaoh, Akhenaton, monotheism, Apiru, the Amarna letters, Yahweh.
4. What are the two most common dates suggested for the incidents and events in the Exodus story? Briefly describe the evidence supporting both sets of dates. Which one would you favor as more probable? Why?
5. How is God depicted in the Exodus story?
6. Describe the role of Moses in the Exodus story.
7. Briefly describe and compare the prose and poetic account of the crossing of the Red Sea. How do they differ?

Chapter 9

THE COVENANT
AND JOURNEY TO CANAAN
(EXODUS 19 THROUGH NUMBERS)

Suggested Scripture Readings:

Exodus 19–24
Leviticus 16–19
Numbers 21–24

The Importance of the Sinai Covenant

The first part of the Book of Exodus moves *from* Israel's slavery *through* Moses' struggle against the pharaoh *to* freedom and the dangerous journey to the sacred mountain of Sinai in only eighteen chapters. The remaining twenty-two chapters of Exodus, all twenty-seven chapters of Leviticus, and the first ten chapters of Numbers describe a single stay at this mountain where God made a covenant with Israel. This covenant is thus the central event of the Pentateuch.

The older J and E traditions know of covenants made with Abraham (Gen 15), renewed with Isaac (Gen 26), renewed yet again with Jacob (Gen 28) and finally sealed with Moses and the people on Sinai (Ex 3 and 24). But it is the P source that emphasizes covenant most fully, seeing God's actions in the world as a series of blessings and promises that lead up to fulfillment at Sinai. These include:

(1) Gen 1:25–26   God blesses creation with Adam and Eve.
(2) Gen 9:1–7   God renews the blessing with Noah.

(3) Gen 17   God gives further promise to Abraham.
(4) Ex 6   God prepares a new covenant with Mo-
                     ses.

The Book of Deuteronomy is written in covenant language
from beginning to end, seeking a national renewal of fidelity to
Yahweh in the promised land. This theme is echoed in the covenant
scenes of Joshua 23–24 and the reform program of Josiah in 2 Kings
22–23. Among the prophets, Amos and Hosea echo many of the
covenant ideals without mentioning Moses or Sinai, but the later
prophets Jeremiah and Ezekiel make constant reference to the
covenant in the desert. Finally, the post-exilic reform of Ezra the
scribe (around 450–400 B.C.) is centered on a covenant renewal.

We should not, therefore, underestimate the importance of this
covenant in the biblical narrative. All of biblical history may be
called a theology of the covenant, if we are careful not to force
books such as the Psalms or Proverbs into the category of the
historical where they were never intended to belong. Covenant
theology not only applies to the moment on Mount Sinai, it provides
the framework for understanding God's earlier promises to Noah,
Abraham, Isaac and Jacob; it gives the whole Pentateuch its character as "torah" rather than "history"; it becomes the standard for
judging Israel's national success or failure for the period of the
conquest in Joshua and Judges; it serves as the measuring stick for
each king of Israel in the Books of Samuel and Kings; it forms the
background of the prophets' oracles of promise and judgment to
Israel from the tenth century until after the exile; it shapes the
thought of Deuteronomy in interpreting the entire story of Israel in
light of fidelity to the covenant of Sinai.

The Nature of a "Covenant"

What then is this term "covenant" that it should be so central to
Israelite faith? The Hebrew word *berit*, which is used most often to
express the idea of a covenant, originally meant a "shackle" or
"chain," but it came to be any form of binding agreement. It
expresses the solemn *contract* between Jacob and Laban in Genesis
31:44, or the *alliance* of friendship between David and Jonathan in
1 Samuel 18:3. It describes the *peace pact* made by Abraham with a
whole tribe of Amorites in Genesis 14:13, and the *bond of marriage*
in Proverbs 2:17 or Malachi 2:14. And it can be a solemn *treaty*

between kings, as is the case with Solomon and Hiram of Tyre in 1 Kings 5, or with Ahab and Benhadad of Syria in 1 Kings 20:34. But most often it is used of the special alliance between Yahweh and Israel.

Berit is a term so rich it captures the heart of Israel's religious beliefs: (1) they are bound to an unbreakable covenant-union with their God; (2) he has made known his love and his mercy to them; (3) he has given them commandments to guide their daily life; (4) they owe him worship, fidelity and obedience; (5) they are marked by the sign of that covenant-bond. The covenant created the unity of the nation Israel, based not on blood relationship but on submission to the divine will and the confession that he alone is God. In turn, God pledges himself to be Israel's personal protector and helper, not only against foreign enemies, but against sickness, disease, and chaos as well. Most of all, he will be present whether it is a time of prosperity or of failure, for he has laid claim to this people as his own. Yahweh is a personal God who demands personal loyalty. He gives no guarantee that his protective love and help always involves victory in battle, wealth in possessions, or increase of territory; it may at times include such gifts, but more often it describes the blessing that trust in the Lord will bring: freedom from fear in the promised land, the fruitfulness of children and crops, permanent peace and the joy of knowing God is near. In this vein, Jeremiah announces the good news of a renewed covenant:

> At that time, says the Lord, I will be the God of all the tribes
>   of Israel and they shall be my people.
> Thus says the Lord:
> A people who escaped the sword has found favor in the
>   desert.
> As Israel has traveled to seek rest, Yahweh appeared from afar
>   to her.
> With an everlasting love have I loved you, and so kept my
>   faithful kindness to you.
> I will again rebuild you and you will be rebuilt, O virgin Israel
>   (Jer 31:1–4).

Yahweh was a *personal* God who demanded personal loyalty. The sides were by no means equal. Israel recognized that the covenant was a gift from Yahweh and an honor for them and not the other way around. God freely chose to bind himself to this people, but not blindly no matter what they did in return. As the centuries went on, first the Yahwist, then the prophets, and finally the authors of Deuteronomy expressed the conviction that Israel's continual sin and rebellion would bring divine punishment that would lead to the end of the covenant blessings. Violations of the solemn agreement would bring consequences against God's people just as fidelity would bring divine favor. Both were aspects of the one covenant.

One of the richest expressions of Israel's understanding of what the covenant with Yahweh meant can be found in Exodus 34:6–7. It has been inserted by someone who summed up the best of J, E, and P, the prophetic traditions of Jeremiah and Ezekiel, and the thought of Deuteronomy. In a tense moment after God restores the ten commandments on new tablets after Moses has broken them, Moses asks to see God's face. God refuses but offers to pass by and solemnly intone his own divine name:

> Yahweh, a god of mercy and compassion, slow to anger, but rich in faithful kindness and fidelity, he who maintains his faithful kindness to thousands, forgives wickedness, rebellion and sin, who does not simply declare someone innocent but visits the wickedness of the fathers upon their sons and grandsons to the third and fourth generation (Ex 34:6–7).

Ancient Covenant Forms

We can learn much about Israel's covenant with Yahweh by comparing the Old Testament descriptions with actual examples of covenants from other ancient nations. We have two major passages about the covenant in the Pentateuch: Exodus 19–24 and the Book of Deuteronomy. Luckily we also have two major sources of ancient Near Eastern covenants: the Hittite treaties from the period 1400–1200 B.C. and a series of Assyrian treaties from the eighth and seventh centuries B.C. Since so much time divides the Hittite from the Assyrian examples, many differences can be found between the two groups. But we must also remember that nearly six hundred years separate the events in Exodus from the time of Deuteronomy (about 650 B.C.), and that we will find quite a number of differences in the biblical accounts as well.

Ancient treaties show two major types. One is a treaty between equal kings. This is generally called a *parity treaty*. We possess an excellent example of this kind of covenant in the peace treaty made between King Ramesses II of Egypt and the Hittite King Hattusilis to end their war in Syria about 1290 B.C. The second type is the *vassal treaty*, made between an overlord, a major power, and the small nations that were either conquered by him or were forced to cooperate lest he take them over. The two types of treaty differ in the kind of obligations that the parties take on. In the parity treaty, each side agrees to mutual responsibilities because they have equal status and neither can force the other to carry out their obligations. But in the vassal treaty, the overlord usually does not bind himself to any particular duties beyond being kindly and protective of the vassal, but he does spell out a series of demands for the vassal to faithfully perform. This second type is the more helpful in interpreting the Sinai covenant between Yahweh, the divine overlord, and Israel, the mere creatures whom he has chosen.

Let us look at a sample of an early Hittite treaty form. Since no treaty tablet has been completely preserved, the quoted illustrations are borrowed from different texts:

1. *The Preamble* in which the overlord, or great king, gives his name and title:
    "These are the words of the Sun Mursillis, the great king, the king of Hatti-land, the valiant, the favorite of the storm-god, the son of Suppiluliumas, the great king"(ANET 203).
2. *The Historical Prologue* in which the great king lists his past acts of kindness to the vassal as the reason for the vassal king's obligation to obey:
    "Aziras, your grandfather, and Du-Teshub, your father remained loyal to me as their lord. . . . Since your father had mentioned to me your name with great praise, I sought after you . . . and put you in the place of your father" (ANET 203–204).
3. *The Stipulations or Demands* that the overlord binds the vassal to keep:
    "If anyone utters a word unfriendly to the king or the Hatti-land before you, Duppi-Tessub, you shall not withhold his name from the king" (ANET 204).
4. *Deposit of the treaty in a temple and public readings at set times:*
    "A duplicate of this treaty has been deposited before the sun-goddess of Arinna. . . . In the Mitanni land, a duplicate has

been deposited before Teshub. . . . At regular intervals they shall read it in the presence of the king of the Mitanni land and in the presence of the sons of the Hurri land" (ANET 205).

5. *The list of witnesses* is important to any contract. But for a solemn state covenant, the witnesses are the gods of the two lands:

"We have called the gods to be present, to listen, and to serve as witnesses: the sun-goddess of Arinna . . . the sun-god, the lord of heaven, the storm-god, the lord of the Hatti-land . . . the mountains, the rivers, the Tigris and Euphrates, heaven and earth, the winds and clouds" (ANET 205–206).

6. *The Curses and Blessings* end the treaty. The divine beings are called on to maintain the treaty in the divine courtroom by imposing rewards and penalties:

"Should Duppi-Teshub not honor these words of the treaty and oath, may these gods of the oath destroy Duppi-Teshub together with his person, his wife, his son, his grandson, his house, his land. . . . But if he honors these words . . . may these gods of the oath protect him with his person, his wife, his son, his grandson, his house and his country" (ANET 205).

The later Assyrian treaties show many of the same parts, although they sometimes lack the elaborate preamble and prologue of the Hittite types, while the list of curses and exotic punishments increases dramatically, perhaps to serve as a scare tactic to make the vassal keep the treaty. A fine example of an Assyrian *vassal treaty* is the seventh century agreement that King Esarhaddon forced on the small nations subject to Assyria that they would swear support for his son Ashurbanipal as his successor, and not rebel when Esarhaddon died. It lists all of the gods who back up the oath first, and then contains literally hundreds of different obligations covering all possible threats against the crown prince and his right to become king. It can be found in ANET 534–541.

It would be very pleasant to discover that the early Hittite covenants matched the early Israelite covenant at Mount Sinai, and that the later description in Deuteronomy matched the Assyrian treaties of the same period. But it doesn't work out that way. The covenant described in Exodus 19–24 is pictured very generally and does not match detail for detail the exact format of either the Hittite or the Assyrian treaties, although there are some points of similarity with the Hittite structure:

(1) *Preamble* and *Prologue* in which God gives his reasons for the covenant are seen in Exodus 19:3–6 and 20:2.

(2) The *stipulations* or *demands* are reflected in the ten commandments (Ex 20:3–17) and in the following covenant law code (Ex 20:22—23:19).

EXAMPLE OF A HITTITE VASSAL TREATY BETWEEN MURSILIS OF THE HITTITES AND DUPPI-TESSUB OF AMURRU

Preamble: These are the words of the Sun Mursilis, the great king, the king of Hatti land, the valiant, the favorite of the storm god, the son of Suppiluliumas, the great king, the king of Hatti land.

Historical Prologue: Aziras, your grandfather, Duppi-Tessub, rebelled against my father, but submitted again to my father.... When my father became a god (i.e. died), and I seated myself on the throne of my father, Aziras behaved toward me just as he had toward my father. . . . when your father died, in accordance with your father's word. I did not drop you. . . .

Stipulations: With my friend you shall be a friend, and with my enemy you shall be enemy ... If you send a man to that enemy and inform him as follows: "An army and charioteers of the Hatti land are on their way, be on your guard!" you act in disregard of your oath.... If anyone utters words unfriendly to the king of Hatti land before you, Duppi-Tessub, you shall not withhold his name from the king ... If anyone of the deportees from the Nuhassi land or of the deportees from the country of Kinza whom my father removed and myself removed, escapes and comes to you, if you do not seize him and turn him back to the king of the Hatti land ... you act in disregard of your oath.

Witnesses of the gods: The sun-god of heaven, the sun-goddess of Arinna, the storm-god of Heaven ... Ishtar of Nineveh, Ishatar of Nineveh, Ishtar of Hattarina. . . . Ninlil, the mountains, the rivers, the springs, the clouds—let these be witnesses to this treaty and to the oath.

Curses and Blessings: The words of the treaty and the oath that are inscribed on this tablet—should Duppi-Tessub not honor them, may these gods of the oath destroy Duppi-Tessub together with his person, his wife, his son, his grandson, his house, his land and together with everything that he owns. But if Duppi-Tessub honors the words of the treaty and the oath that are inscribed on this tablet, may the gods of the oath protect him together with his person, his wife, his son, his grandson, his house, his country.

(3)   The *deposit of the treaty* and its public nature is understood in the use of stone tablets for a permanent record.

(4)   The *curses and blessings* and *divine witnesses* are naturally missing since Israel's faith made no room for other gods. But God himself backs up the obligation to obey this covenant by the signs of his powerful presence in thunder, lightning, and dark clouds (Ex 19:16–19; 20:18–20).

The Book of Deuteronomy reveals the covenant forms much more clearly. It is written so that it resembles a formal treaty between God and Israel through the speech of Moses. It has all the elements of the classical Hittite treaties and yet shows strong connections to the later interests of the Assyrian types as well in its stress on extended blessings and curses (Dt 27–28) and on the right of inheritance of the land by Israel.

Joshua 24, under the influence of Deuteronomy, describes a renewal of the Sinai covenant under Joshua which is the closest parallel to a Hittite covenant in the Old Testament. It even includes the people as witnesses against themselves (Jos 24:22) and a public writing and deposit of the agreement in a sanctuary (Jos 24:25–26). The only part missing is the list of curses and blessings.

From another angle, the entire Pentateuch must have been influenced by the covenant format. The "story" from Abraham to the escape through the Red Sea serves as a formal preamble and prologue listing the overlord's great deeds to the vassal before the giving of the law on Sinai.

Because there were no common courts of law to decide cases between nations, ancient treaties depended heavily on the power of the oath that each party took before the gods as witnesses, and on the conviction that the gods would in fact act to punish offenders. As a result, such a treaty demanded some form of ceremony in order to ratify it, a *ritual* that made the point clear. The most common form was cutting an animal in two. Thus in a Mari tablet from the eighteenth century we find a covenant sealed by cutting a donkey into two parts. Similarly, an eighth century treaty from Sefire in Syria records a number of animals cut into parts, with a curse attached to each: "As this calf is cut into two, may Mati'el be cut in two." Even Jeremiah refers to this custom when he condemns those who violated Yahweh's covenant:

The men who violated my covenant and did not observe
the terms of the agreement they made before me, I will

make like the calf which they cut into two, and between whose parts they passed (Jer 34:18–19).

Even the usual Hebrew expression for making a covenant employs this idea: *karat berith,* "to cut a covenant." Genesis 15 may make reference to this ceremony when Abraham cuts the animals in two and God passes through them in fire.

Other means were known, however, such as smearing the body with oil, or drinking water that is cursed so that the very power of the curse will enter into the bodies of the parties.

Exodus 19–24 and 32–34: The Giving of the Covenant

In the present narration, Exodus 19–24 describes a first presentation of the covenant, and Exodus 31–34 tells how it was given again after Moses broke the original tablets in anger at the people's apostasy with the golden calf. But behind this arrangement, there were originally two separate accounts of the same Sinai event, one from the E source (now in chapters 20–24) and one from the J source (now in chapters 33–34). To fit both accounts in, the editors have made two stages of one act. Chapter 19 combines the introductions to both versions. We can divide the two accounts to show the difference in outlook between the J and E sources:

Chapters 19, 33–34, "J"

24:1–2, 9–11 Moses joined by elders—all eat a sacrificial meal

34:10–26 God gives covenant laws, many of them rituals

34:27–28 God gives the ten commandments (again)

Chapters 19, 20–24, "E"

29:21–23 Moses alone without priests is to go to the mountain

20:1–17 God gives the ten commandments

20:18–23:33 The covenant law code sums up the major demands of justice

24:3–8 People all accept Moses' law and are anointed by blood

The J covenant stresses Moses as the mediator between Yahweh and the people, but also gives an honored place to the elders and priestly class. It highlights the cultic aspects of eating a meal to seal the covenant and the importance of following ritual laws in its covenant rules of chapter 34.

The E covenant separates Moses from all others, but accents that all the people together share the ratification in blood and accept the terms. It also stresses the ethical and moral rules, and in its commandments adds the warning notes typical of the prophets in later times.

The differences in the E account may well reflect the northern Israelite distaste for the Jerusalem temple ceremonies and the traditional power of priests and elders reflected in J's southern version. In a northern spirit, E also accentuates the position of Moses as a *prophet* and his direct involvement with all the tribes as equals.

Naturally, in being combined together, many aspects are made to fit smoothly together and not appear as contradictory, and the later Priestly editors have themselves added many notes about the glory of Yahweh on the mountain and the special instructions given to Moses; and it is P who brings Aaron, the first high priest, so strongly into the picture. Many details would also be affected by centuries of studying and retelling the covenant in liturgy and education. An example of liturgical influence is the blowing of the ram's horn to let the people approach the mountain in Exodus 19:13. It would be unnecessary on a mountain where God let his will be known in thunder, but would perfectly fit a Church liturgy where the ram's horn is blown to symbolize the sound of thunder.

Behind the mixed accounts of the making of the covenant, however, we can note the important elements of the Near Eastern treaty. God identifies himself and his blessings to the people in Exodus 20:2 as he gives his stipulations and laws. In chapter 24, Moses brings it down for formal reading and acceptance by the people. Missing are curses and the witness of other gods, but this is understandable when we realize that there was only one God for Israel. And although there are a few threats to punish those who do not keep the commandments (cf. Ex 20:5), curses seem rare in this early covenant, unlike the long lists in the later Book of Deuteronomy (chapters 26–27). This is similar to the difference between the early Hittite treaties with their few short lists of curses, and the later, greatly lengthened curses of the Assyrians. It argues that the tradition behind the story of Mount Sinai is very old.

Exodus 25–31 and 35–40:
The Ark of the Covenant and Tent of Meeting

Closely connected to the giving of the covenant is the building of the tent and the ark in Exodus 25–31 and 35–40. Both are considered in biblical tradition to be essential to the actual living out of the covenant in the desert years.

Most readers find the description of all the small details needed for the building of the ark and tent extremely boring. Chapters 35–40 repeat almost word for word the phrases and directions of chapters 25–31. This is the ancient way of giving emphasis to an important project. Not only does God instruct exactly how these two shrines are to be built, but in every detail of construction the builders follow his commands.

The ark resembled the small shrines for the symbols of the gods known among many of the pre-Islamic tribes of Arabia. Such shrines were portable and could be carried on a camel with the tribe as it moves. On occasion they could also be carried to war. We find both aspects present in the Israelite usage. It was portable and often went to war in important moments such as at the siege of Jericho in

A bas-relief portraying a portable tent shrine, from Palmyra (Roman period).

The famed stele of Hammurabi, king of Babylon (1728–1686) showing the king before the God of Justice, Shamash. Under them is inscribed the most complete law code known in the Ancient Near East.

the Book of Joshua and against the Philistines in the Book of Samuel. The ark may well have symbolized the presence of Yahweh with the people. But at the same time, another ancient tradition of a tent where Moses would go to meet God and where God would appear in his cloud of glory was present. Perhaps these were *two separate traditions* of how God made himself known in the early days, but at least by the time these traditions were written down, Israel combined them so that the ark would be placed *in* the tent in any permanent settlement place. Naturally, since most of our written descriptions were finished after the temple that Solomon built was already in existence with the ark inside its holy place, the description we get of the rich furnishings and instruments so unsuited to desert travel is a picture drawn from the temple of Jerusalem. The tent and the ark become the first models for the temple. To avoid any superstition or thought that the invisible and almighty God was actually living in a box or a tent, later expressions underline that it was the ark of the covenant to hold the tablets of the law, and not to hold God. The ark disappeared with the fall of Jerusalem and the burning of the temple in 586 B.C. by the Babylonians. The tent tradition apparently died when David and Solomon built the original temple to replace any temporary centers of worship.

The Pentateuch as Law

If the Jewish word "torah" means primarily "teaching," it still has the sense of *binding* teaching or legal demand. In Jewish tradition, the Talmud lists 613 separate laws in the five books of the Torah. Clearly, law is a primary element of the Pentateuch, taking up many parts of the Book of Exodus, all of Leviticus, Numbers 1–10 and 27–30, and Deuteronomy 1–30.

Scholars have sorted through the various bodies of law and isolated certain groups that belong together:

(1)   *The law of the covenant* in Exodus 21–23 is an early body of law reflecting rural life before the city-centered time of the kings.

(2)   The *ten commandments* are found in two versions, one in Exodus 20, the other in Deuteronomy 5. Both represent early covenant law.

(3)   The *cult commandments* of Exodus 34 reflect the period of the early kings or even the time of the judges. Some of the commands, such as Exodus 34:26 ("Do not boil a kid in its mother's milk"), reflect a reaction to pagan customs of the Canaanites.

(4)   *Leviticus 1–16* contains a series of laws on sacrifice and feast days. In their present form they reflect the large sacrifices made in the temple during the times of the kings. Probably they were put in final form only at the latest period before the exile, but have much earlier roots.

(5)   *Leviticus 17–26* is called the "Holiness Code" because it has a very moralistic and preachy style that sets it apart as a later Priestly tradition, close to the thought of the prophet Ezekiel (593–572 B.C.).

(6)   *The Deuteronomic laws* were written in a sermon style and aimed at economic and social conditions typical of the later monarchy, about 700–600 B.C.

Study of Israel's Laws reveals much about the daily life and customs of the people. Above all, we can distinguish between two large classes of law: *case law* and *apodictic law*. Case law (or casuistic law) follows the pattern of:

If someone does this thing, *then* he receives this punishment . . .

Such laws are common everywhere in the ancient world, based on the problems of everyday conflicts. For each possible offense or case of dispute, a proper penalty or fine is worked out.

On the other hand, the ten commandments and the cult laws of Exodus 34 give no conditions and no suggested penalties. They are strong, dramatic demands made upon the believer with an unstated, but threatening, hint that disobedience will be severely dealt with. In our own society, these kinds of laws are ones that a parent might give to a child, or a teacher to a student in grammar school. In ancient society, they may well reflect the commands of tribal leaders to all members of the clan. On the other hand, such direct proclamation of basic divine law is what would be expected during the celebration of the liturgy. In any case, the only expected answer is a firm "Amen" said in trust. Although these laws are not found only in Israelite tradition, they do reflect *the special character of covenant obedience*. They are not open to compromise or discussion as is case law, but must be solemnly accepted. The ten commandments stand out among such apodictic laws both by their solemn form and by their precise number, easily counted and remembered on the fingers.

Both case law and apodictic law have very old roots in the Near East, but we can be quite sure that we are close indeed to the original directives of Moses himself in the first two commands of the ten, for they are so distinctively Israelite: Yahweh alone is God, no other gods are to be worshiped; and no images are to be made of him or of any other gods.

Other Ancient Law Codes

Archaeology has uncovered no less than seven ancient codes of law from Israel's neighbors. They range from the Sumerian code of Ur Nammu in the twenty-second century B.C. down to Babylonian codes of the sixth century B.C. The most exciting discovery of all was the black stone monument of Hammurapi (or Hammurabi, as he has commonly been called), which was found in Susa, an Elamite city, in 1901. It had been dragged there after some Elamite king had won a victory over Babylon, and although broken in three pieces, it survived the centuries. Scholars had already known the fame of Hammurapi (1732–1680) as a lawgiver through other ancient writings, so that this was an exciting confirmation of their work.

Hammurapi's code consists of 282 laws engraved on a stone pillar with a scene at the top showing the king praying before the god of justice, Shamash. It covers many legal questions, but does not include every kind of case. Scholars have often tried to determine what purpose such a partial law code would serve. Since it was on a pillar in a public square, it could not have been a secret guide for judges, but may well have served to update older laws. It may have been just a sample of good laws to prove the king's concern for justice. In this sense, it was like a modern political campaign ad for the king: he was on the side of right!

Like many ancient law codes, it began with a lengthy prologue describing how the high gods had appointed Hammurapi king in order to "promote the welfare of the people . . . to cause justice to prevail in the land, to destroy the wicked and the evil that the strong might not oppress the weak" (ANET 164).

Then follows the list of laws, many of them very much like those found in the Pentateuch. Thus:

Hammurapi #196–197	Exodus 21:23–24
If a noble has destroyed the eye of another noble, they shall destroy his eye. If he has broken another noble's bone, they shall break his bone.	. . . If injury ensues (in a fight), you shall give life for life, eye for eye, hand for hand, foot for foot, burn for burn, wound for wound, stripe for stripe.

Sometimes, Israelite law is even more demanding than Babylonian. Thus, Hammurapi law #195 decrees, "If a son has struck his father, they shall cut off his hand," but Exodus 21:15 demands, "Whoever strikes his father or mother is to be put to death." This may seem harsh, but the Israelite law is humane compared to the even more drastic penalties commonly found in the Assyrian laws of the twelfth century B.C. And as a measure to end blood feuds between families and the power of the wealthy to force tenfold repayment of loans from the weak, it was a step forward. Generally speaking, the Babylonian laws often required money payments for injuries where the Israelite laws exacted physical punishment and had a rather higher percentage of death penalties. Unlike Babylon with its large economy and customary use of money to pay for everything, Israel's laws reflect the still vibrant and proud sense of strict justice inherited from a tribal background.

Nevertheless, Babylon and other ancient Near Eastern nations shared with Israel an *ideal of justice* for the nation, and especially for the ruler who is responsible for just government. Hammurapi brags at the end of his law code that he has written the precious words of the law "in order that the strong might not oppress the weak, that justice might be dealt the orphan (and) the widow" (ANET 178). Some centuries later to the West, a Canaanite text from Ugarit, criticizes King Keret because:

You have let your hand fall into mischief,
You fail to judge the case of the widow,
Nor decide the case of the wretched;
You drive not away those who prey on the poor,
Nor feed the orphan before you,
The widow behind your back.

Israel's psalms are filled with many similar expressions:

> Exult before him;
>> the father of orphans and the defender of widows
>> is God in his holy dwelling.
> God gives a home to the abandoned
>> and leads forth the captive to prosperity" (Ps 68:6–7).

Leviticus

The Book of Leviticus contains nothing but priestly legislation, yet it is not simply a jumble of laws. It has order to it—an order which reveals much about Israel's religious practices. One thing is certain—these are not the customs of the time in the desert, but rather an entire code of conduct for priests and levites who serve at the temple in Jerusalem. The sacrifices and offerings demanded for great feast days can only come from a farming people. The very size and types of sacrifices and festivals mentioned presuppose a large population raising many herds and crops in the promised land. However, since sacrifice and atonement rites were practiced even in Israel's earliest period, the sixth century Priestly editors of Leviticus could include them under the words of Moses as the natural and current expression of the divine commands he had first spoken.

The Book of Leviticus is a mixture of *narratives* and *legal* passages. A simple diagram gives an idea:

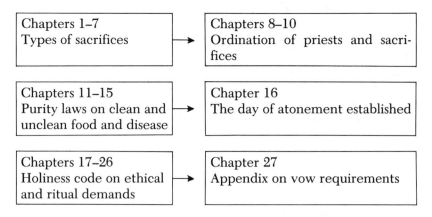

Chapters 1–7
Types of sacrifices → Chapters 8–10
Ordination of priests and sacrifices

Chapters 11–15
Purity laws on clean and unclean food and disease → Chapter 16
The day of atonement established

Chapters 17–26
Holiness code on ethical and ritual demands → Chapter 27
Appendix on vow requirements

Most of the material in Leviticus consists of rules on proper behavior in acts of divine worship. This includes extended discussion of several types of *sacrifice* that Israel is to offer for different reasons and on certain occasions. It also includes very detailed lists of religious taboos in the areas of food and disease. Each of these major bodies is followed by a *narrative story* telling how Moses set up the liturgical rituals themselves. So, for example, chapters 1–7 are followed by the ordination of the priests and the first actual sacrifices in chapters 8–10. The taboos in chapters 11–15 are followed by the liturgy for the day of atonement in chapter 16. This rite is the climax of the first part of Leviticus. It is reserved to the high priest to place all the sins of Israel on the head of a goat once a year and drive the goat into the desert to die. It symbolizes God's forgiving nature which always wipes the slate clean for his people. This is the origin of the idea of a "scapegoat."

The *taboo* laws on diet and sickness show that Israel's idea of proper worship was not limited to the temple. These restrictions apply to people in everyday life and make every moment fitting for the praise of God. Similar customs are found in other cultures throughout the world. Many of the individual taboos against animals are very ancient, and may be rooted in primitive experience with dangerous eating habits. Many experts believe that the risk of trichinosis from eating undercooked pork may have played a role in rejecting the pig. In the same way, the contagious nature of certain skin rashes and sores may have led to the practice of quarantining victims as described in chapters 13–14. Since the priests were the trained personnel in making such decisions, these originally medical problems gained religious status.

But such explanations are not enough to fully understand the thinking of Israel on the subject. The extensive list of animals contains many that would have been no health risk to the eater. In fact, a close look at the total division of the animals in chapter 11 reveals a pattern based on Genesis 1. God has given order to the world by establishing plants in the ground, birds in the air, fish swimming in the sea and animals that graze. All of the forbidden foods in Leviticus fall under failures to this order. Creatures living in the sea that have no fins or scales are taboo because they walk on the bottom as animals would on land; birds that do not fly are forbidden; animals that do not graze are to be avoided. *It teaches us that the basic outlook of Israel toward food was not just to gain nourishment but to reflect God's goodness in creation.* What one ate was highly symbolic of what one believed.

The last part of Leviticus consists of a special body of laws that are called together the "holiness code." It gets this name from the stress it places on God as holy, and the need for the levites to imitate God's holiness, and to keep themselves separate from merely profane behavior unworthy of their special calling. It includes rules on sex, marriage, touching blood, violating moral commandments, and upholding justice, and above all on the keeping of feast days and celebrations for Yahweh. It is one of the most advanced expressions of Israel's special relationship to its God.

The book ends with an appendix chapter on repayment of vows. It has been added to update older laws that demanded every vow be fulfilled no matter what (cf. Num 30 or Dt 23). With time, Israel needed to provide for money substitutions instead of handing over actual property where that would prove difficult or impossible. Chapter 27 sets a money value for different types of objects.

The Book of Numbers

The name "Numbers" comes from the Greek word *arithmoi*, which describes the census in chapter 1. The structure of Numbers marks a change from the laws of Leviticus. From this point on, all regulations and directives are aimed at a community on the move. While they show a continuity with the concerns of Leviticus, repeating or elaborating many of its instructions about levites, sacrifices, feast days and vows, they are scattered throughout the story of Israel's move from Mount Sinai to the promised land. A brief outline puts the laws in boxes within the narrative:

Num 1:1–10:10	A series of laws on the order of the camp, the duties of levites, vows, feast day ceremonies and offerings.

Num 10:10–14:45	The journey from Sinai to Paran. An attempt to capture Canaan from the south fails.

Num 15	Laws on sacrifice and ritual actions.
Num 16–19	Challenge to Aaron's authority and laws for high priest and levites.

Num 20–21	Journey continues to the plains of Moab. The conquest of the kings Sihon and Og.

Num 22–24	The opposition of the Moabites and the proph-et Balaam.
Num 25	The rebellion and punishment at Baal Peor in Moab.
Num 26–30	More laws on census, inheritance, vows, sacrifices.
Num 31–34	Final conquest of the area east of the Jordan River and settling of some of the tribes there.
Num 35–36	An appendix with laws on levitical cities of refuge for accused and inheritance laws.

The outline reveals that the book keeps the shape of a journey, but that laws are mixed up throughout. The reason why the laws are in the narrative cannot be exactly known, but it surely seemed more proper to them than it does to us who are used to a clear distinction between laws and stories.

Like the laws of Leviticus, the materials gathered in Numbers come from many different ages. The oracles of Balaam with their archaic poetic lines and frozen expressions originated in the time of the judges, and the poems in Numbers 21:17–18, the "Song of the Well," and in Numbers 21:27–30, the "Lament over Heshbon," may also be quite ancient fragments. These, together with the story narrative, are from the J and E sources, while most of the laws are later and belong to the P source. P also tied the events in Numbers to the Book of Exodus by listing all of the desert stopping places of Israel in chapter 33. Altogether, there are twelve major stages in their journey up to the arrival at the promised land. Six of these lead up to Mount Sinai, and six lead away from it. P took the first six from Exodus 12–19, and the last six from Numbers 20–22, creating a single narrative out of everything in Exodus, Leviticus and Numbers.

The Murmuring in the Desert

A second indication of how closely Numbers is joined to the story of the Book of Exodus lies in the great stress that both books place on how Israel grumbled and rebelled against God during the years in the desert. In fact, the two books often parallel each other in incidents:

Exodus 14–17	Numbers 11–21
Ex 14:10 Complaint that Egyptians were about to slay them: God opens the Reed Sea.	*Num 11:1* People grumble against Yahweh at Taberah: fire punishes them.
Ex 15:23 People grumble at Elim about bitter water: Moses cures the water.	*Num 11:4* People grumble about no meat at Kibrothhattaavah: God sends quail, but also a plague.
Ex 16:3 People grumble at no food in the desert of Sin.	*Num 12* Miriam and Aaron rebel against Moses: God gives Miriam leprosy.
Ex 17:2 No water at Rephidim: God gives water from rock.	*Num 14* People rebel at desert stay: God extends the time to forty years.
	Num 16 Korah, Dathan and Abiram rebel against Moses: God consumes them in fire.
	Num 20 People grumble about lack of water: Moses strikes water from the rock.
	Num 21 People grumble about food: God sends fiery serpents.

The incidents in Exodus stress the *patience of* Yahweh, who always listens to Israel's needs and intervenes to help. Numbers 11–21, on the other hand, stresses that the people's constant rebellion led Yahweh to *punish* them time and again. But each time Moses intervenes and begs for the sake of the people, and God softens his anger and turns back his punishments or heals the victims.

Numbers 11–20 is one series of murmurings after another. Many are directed against the hard conditions of the wilderness, but some are directed against the authority and leadership of Moses himself. Some scholars believe that the traditions found in Exodus and Numbers reflect only a few of the many conflicts and struggles among the tribes during these formative years as different ones fought for leadership and superiority. Perhaps not all of the twelve tribes were slaves in Egypt and escaped with Moses. Those that had escaped sought their own kind in Sinai and across the Jordan, and so other tribes and clans joined with Moses' group and accepted for themselves the God Yahweh who had made himself known at Sinai. The leadership of Moses prevailed, but Numbers shows us that the struggle to make one nation under Yahweh was not as simple as we sometimes think.

The constant *repetition of the rebellion theme* would not have been missed by the Israelite of the sixth century for whom P wrote. They could look back on the centuries of injustice, disobedience and false worship, the condemnations of the prophets, the failures of the kings, and know that the loss of their freedom and land in exile had been richly deserved. God cannot be pushed too far without asserting his own justice and honor. Yet even at a late hour, he could turn from his anger and spare them, if they would only turn to him. More than most books of the Old Testament, Numbers lets us see why the Pentateuch came to be the way it is—a gathering of very old traditions and much later added developments. For Israel, each part of the ancient faith tradition had a message for later generations.

At the end of Numbers, Moses dies, the leadership passes to a new war captain and trusted follower, Joshua, and a new chapter is about to begin for Israel: the conquest of the land.

The Book of Deuteronomy

The final book of the Pentateuch is Deuteronomy, which is written as the last speech and warning by Moses to the people on how to live in the land they are about to conquer. Since it was composed in the seventh century as a kind of commentary on the meaning of the Pentateuch and as a summary of its message, we shall treat it below in Chapter 17. Looking back from the troubled times of the last kings of Judah, it offered hope to a discouraged seventh century Israel, a new chance to obey the covenant and a lesson that God's punishment was not final. For these reasons, it stresses the divine word that never fails. It stands apart from the story structure of Genesis through Numbers in the form of a warning speech. It emphasizes how God tested Israel in the early days of its existence, yet did not destroy the people no matter how often they failed. The real meaning of the years in the desert can be found in the lesson God himself had taught there: "A person does not live by bread alone, but by every word that proceeds from the mouth of Yahweh" (Dt 8:2–3).

STUDY QUESTIONS

1. What is the significance of the Sinai Covenant? How do the different sources (J, E, P) treat this event?
2. Describe what is meant by the term "covenant". What are its essential, constitutive elements?
3. What are the two major types of ancient treaties? How do they differ? Give examples to illustrate this difference.
4. How does Israel's covenant with Yahweh compare with Hittite and Assyrian treaties?
5. Compare and contrast the J and E accounts of the presentation of the covenant.
6. Describe the Ark of the Covenant and Tent of Meeting.
7. Briefly describe the different types of law found in the Pentateuch.
8. What are case law and apodictic law? How do they differ?
9. Briefly describe the Book of Leviticus. What is its structure? What does it contain?
10. What is contained in the Book of Numbers? What is its purpose or goal?
11. Briefly describe the contents of the Book of Deuteronomy. When was it written? What is its aim or purpose?

Chapter 10

THE ISRAELITE POSSESSION OF CANAAN
THE BOOKS OF JOSHUA AND JUDGES

Suggested Scripture Readings:

Joshua 6–8
Joshua 22–24
Judges 1–5

The "Historical Books"

The Book of Joshua opens a new section of the Scriptures, often labeled simply the "Historical Books." They include all the books that the Jews call the Former Prophets: Joshua, Judges, 1 and 2 Samuel, 1 and 2 Kings. These belong together because they were originally edited as a single continuous history of Israel from the days of Moses down to the Babylonian exile. They are strongly influenced by the preaching of the great prophets of the eighth and seventh centuries. Modern scholars agree that they were put together by the same school of thought that edited the Book of Deuteronomy, and so they are sometimes called as well the Deuteronomic History. They will be treated briefly below and again in more detail in Chapter 18.

Following the practice of the Greek Septuagint, however, most modern English translations also include 1 and 2 Chronicles, Ezra, Nehemiah, Ruth, Esther and the four works in Greek only, Judith, Tobit and 1 and 2 Maccabees, as historical books and place them with the Former Prophets.

In studying the historical remembrances of the early period in Joshua and Judges we are faced with their claims that Israel took the land of Palestine by violent assault. Many scholars today offer other possible means by which Israel gained possession of its land. The evidence is complex and difficult to use because there is so little on which to base a conclusion. The newer theories point out the problems with a military conquest of the land, but their own counter-proposals are even less certain.

The Book of Joshua

The Book of Joshua falls naturally into two major sections. Chapters 2–12 describe the miraculous conquest of the land by the tribes under Joshua's leadership, and chapters 13–22 tell how Joshua divided the land among the tribes and settled all the boundary and territorial disputes. But the collectors of these traditions have added a preface in chapter 1 and an epilogue in chapters 23–24 which set the meaning of these events in a theological context. Both are done in the forms of speeches by Joshua himself. In chapter 1, he promises that God will make the victory possible if the people will obey the law given by Moses which they have accepted (see the details of this law in the Book of Deuteronomy). In chapters 23–24, Joshua gives his final words, his last will and testament, in which he exhorts Israel to remain faithful after his death, and makes the people solemnly renew their covenant promise to God.

From the description in Joshua 2–12, we might easily get the impression that the conquest was swift and decisive, and that Israel's armies were able to defeat every opponent. The Jordan River is crossed in a miraculous way that parallels Israel's escape from Egypt through the Red Sea; a major shrine is dedicated to Yahweh at Gilgal; Jericho falls to the power of God's ark of the covenant; Ai is defeated; and now the local peoples stand terrified at Yahweh's might. The citizens of Gideon make peace with Israel by a trick in order to save their lives, and in two lightning campaigns to the north and south, Joshua defeats the major Canaanite kings and their allies. Chapter 12 closes this section with an impressive list of the captured peoples. The stage is now set for his division of the land among the tribes which follows in chapters 13–22. Many readers regard these chapters as among the most uninteresting sections of the Bible with long lists of town and place names, but they contain invaluable help to the historian and geographer in locating many ancient cities and identifying the boundaries of the tribes who lived in Palestine.

However, we must be cautious about the Book of Joshua's account of Israel's invasion of the land. For one thing, the land area that Joshua captures is far less than the land he divides among the tribes. No mention is made in chapters 2–12 about taking Shechem or the central hill country, nor of capturing any cities on the coastal plains, nor of taking many major cities in the Jezreel Valley in the north. Despite his victories over the kings of some major strongholds such as Megiddo, Taanach and Gezer, short references in the second half of the book make it clear that Israel often failed to drive out the Canaanites because they had walled cities and chariot brigades (see 13:2–6; 15:63; 16:10; 17:11–13; 17:16–18). Many areas were only half conquered, and the biggest victories seemed to be in the mountain areas on the eastern part of the land. The Book of Joshua idealizes the early victories but the reality at first fell far short of this account.

The reason for such an exalted telling of the story lies in the religious purpose of the book. Israel was not fighting on its own; it was God who gave the help and strength for this small band of tribes to overcome much more powerful enemies. Even if the battles gave Israel control over only a quarter of the land that the book describes, the victory was unbelievable unless God had helped. The city and town lists given for each tribe come from a later time when people were well established in the land and probably describe the settled conditions of the Israelites near the time of David about 1000 B.C. They reveal an Israel that claimed title to the whole land of Palestine because they had won it with the help of God who fought on their side. Just as the exodus story speaks about God as a warrior who fights on behalf of his people (Ex 15), so the story of the conquest portrays God directing the battles needed to gain a foothold in the territory controlled by the Canaanites.

The people responsible for carrying on the ancient traditions of the conquest emphasized that the victories came from God and that Joshua and the tribes followed God's directions carefully and always dedicated their military victories as a sacrifice to God in thanksgiving for his aid. This is the terrible custom of the "ban," called in Hebrew a *herem,* in which the Israelites were to slay everyone in the defeated towns. It was practiced to show that Israel put all its trust in God alone during the war and sought nothing for itself.

Modern people are shocked by such brutality, but it is necessary to remember that the ancient world did not share our outlook. Their ethical principles often placed national survival above any personal goods, and identified success in war or politics with the will

OUTLINE OF THE BOOK OF JOSHUA

I.   1:1–18   Introduction: the authority of Joshua

II. 2:1–12:24   The Conquest of the Promised Land

III. 13:1–21:45   The Division of the conquered lands to the tribes

IV. 22:1–24:33   Joshua's Farewell and renewal of the Covenant

of their god or gods. The Book of Joshua is not the only ancient example in which the victors dedicated a defeated enemy as a total sacrifice to the god in payment for victory. A black stone that can be dated to the middle of the ninth century B.C., found in 1888, carried an inscription of King Mesha of Moab that told how Mesha had fought against certain towns of Israel and defeated them and made them all a *herem* in honor of the Moabite god Chemosh (see below, Chapter 15). Naturally, if such policies were followed too often, very few people would survive the many wars between small nations in the ancient Near East, so we can be sure that the ban was rarely carried out in practice, and only in moments of great peril. Indeed, since the purpose of the Joshua narrative is to glorify Yahweh who gives Israel its victories and its lands, we can be absolutely sure that the editors and authors have magnified the victories and downplayed the defeats a great deal.

The Book of Judges

The Book of Judges continues the story of Israel's conquest and gradual occupation of the whole land. It tells the stories and legends of Israel's time of tribal life in Palestine which lasted about two hundred years, from 1250 down to a little after 1050 B.C.

Altogether, the book follows the exploits of twelve judges during this period. Six are hardly more than names attached to a single incident only barely remembered: Shamgar, Tola, Jair, Ibzan, Elon and Abdon. As a result these are usually called the "Minor Judges." The other six are the "Major Judges": Othniel, Ehud, Barak (with Deborah), Gideon, Jephthah and Samson. They were renowned for their brave exploits in battle and were really not legal judges primarily but warlords. They were leaders who arose in times of great need and led the tribes to victory in one or more battles. Because God had marked them out charismatically, they stayed on to guide the tribes during the rest of their lifetimes. Because of their recognized authority as war leaders, they also exercised power in legal disputes between tribes and in political squabbles.

The Book of Judges can be divided into three major parts. Chapters 1–2 set the stage by describing the situation of Israel after Joshua dies. Chapters 3–16 tell the stories of the twelve judges. Chapters 17–21 give some extra legends about the two tribes of Dan and Benjamin. All three sections illustrate the same lesson for Israel, namely that God stood by them when they were faithful and obedient to him, but allowed them to fall into disaster and the results of their own sins when they turned from his covenant and disobeyed.

The opening two chapters make clear what we have already suspected from the Book of Joshua—that the tribes did indeed fail to conquer many of the cities and people who dwelt in Palestine. They settled down instead to a long period of co-existence and only very gradually gained control over the Canaanites. In fact, it was not until the days of Saul and David, after the Book of Judges ends, that Israel began making really significant gains again as they had under Joshua.

The editors who recorded these traditions saw that the period of the judges represented a spirit of compromise with the pagan culture of the land. It was the greatest sin of the tribes and one which would be repeated again and again in Israel's later history. For this reason, the editors repeatedly used a pattern to describe the period: *the people sin, bring down Yahweh's wrath upon themselves, later repent, are delivered by a judge sent by God, and finally gain peace while the judge lives.* Naturally the real history of the times was much more complex, with many ups and downs that are not recorded in this book. It seems that most of the stories we do have involved only a few tribes and came from local memories rather than from wars waged by Israel as a whole. These were passed on orally at first among the tribes, and some have developed into full-blown hero legends in which the judge is bigger and more glorious than any normal person. Such is the case with the story of Gideon in Judges 6–8 and of Samson in Judges 13–16.

The picture that emerges shows an Israelite confederation of twelve tribes still struggling to find unity among themselves at the same time they fought for footholds in different parts of the Canaanite territory. It was a time of small local wars and defensive fighting against desert nomads. The Song of Deborah in Judges 5 reveals

OUTLINE OF THE BOOK OF JUDGES

I. **General Introduction**   1:1–2–5
   Summary of conquest and explanation of its failures

II. **Prologue of the Deuteronomist to Tales of Judges:**   2:6–3:6
    sin-punishment-repentance-deliverance;
        why some nations not conquered

III. **The stories of the Judges:**   3:7–16:31
Othniel	major judge	3:7–11
Ehud	major judge	3:12–30
Shamgar	minor judge	3:31
Barak (Deborah)	major judge	4:1–5:31
Gideon	major judge	6:1–8:35
Abimelech	usurper and tyrant	9:1–57
Tola and Jair	minor judges	10:1–16
Jephthah	major judge	11:1–12:7
Ibzan, Elon, Abdon	minor judges	12:8–15
Samson	major judge	13:1–16:31

IV. **The Tribal History of Dan and its Idolatry**   17:1–18:31
    The levite, his idol, the migration of Dan

V. **The Tribe of Benjamin and its Atrocity**   19:1–21:25
   The levite and his concubine outraged;
   War of all Israel with Benjamin

that often one or more of the tribes would not come to the aid of others. The violent story of Abimelech in Judges 9 and the terrible incident of the Benjaminites in chapters 19–21 both picture tribes in open conflict with one another. Strife was the name of the game throughout the age of the judges. As one writer has remarked, it was like the wild west of American folklore.

Evaluating the Difference Between Joshua and Judges

The archaeological evidence for the Early Iron Age (the period from 1250 down to 1000) is quite mixed. During the Late Bronze Age (1450–1250) which preceded it, many large Canaanite cities flourished. But at the beginning of the Iron Age, the towns of Bethel, Tell Beit Mirsim, Lachish, Hazor, Debir, and what is probably Eglon all fell violently. At the same time, other major centers such as Shechem or Gideon showed no destruction. Ai, which figures prominently in Joshua 7–8, did not even seem to be settled in the thirteenth century, while Jericho, the first major city reportedly sacked by Israel, has left no surviving walls from that century, although it may well have simply reused the massive walls of the fifteenth and fourteenth century city that had been on the same site.

In the far south of the country, in the Negev desert region, excavations have disclosed little or no evidence of fortified cities during this whole time period. The account of major forts and strong cities in the Negev reported in Numbers 13:28, including some which had repelled the attack of the Israelites from the south, seem to be a memory from an earlier period about the sixteenth century, the only early period when such conditions existed. At the same time, a new style of house with three or four rooms appeared in the Negev in the thirteenth to eleventh centuries, a style associated with the Israelite settlement.

In the far northern area of Galilee, archaeological surveys show that many new villages sprang up in the hills and wooded areas, but that the major cities were not generally changed to any degree.

All of this confirms the questions about the swift and sure invasion story in Joshua and fits better the type of uncertain struggle and slow conquest pictured by the Book of Judges. Yet, the evidence from archaeology is still too little and too hard to interpret for much to be claimed one way or the other. Many archaeologists, such as Yigael Yadin and William Foxwell Albright, believe that the evidence of destruction for such great cities as Hazor supports the biblical tradition of a major invasion by Joshua and his tribes. This does not mean, however, that the whole land was conquered at once and held onto. The initial successes, including a few major battles, may have allowed some tribes to gain a foothold in the mountainous areas which were sparsely settled and weakly defended. It took two centuries for Israel to become strong enough to actually control the major part of Palestine. This did not occur under the judges but had to wait until the military successes of Saul, the first king, against the Philistines which are narrated in 1 Samuel. This took place as late as 1020 B.C.

Joshua and the Conquest of Palestine

Generally, if we look at the picture of the big powers, Egypt and Mesopotamia, in the thirteenth and twelfth centuries, the conditions were good for a small people such as Israel to attempt an invasion of Palestine. The Assyrians were very weak, the Egyptians had blocked a Hittite threat from the north in the Battle of Qadesh about 1295, and Egypt herself was now under attack from a wave of invaders called the "Sea Peoples" who came by ship from Crete and Greece and western Turkey. In Palestine itself, there was little order among the city-states. The Amarna letters have already shown us the constant bickering among the small kings and the threat from groups of lawless Apiru outside the cities. The Sea Peoples who were thrown back from the Egyptian shores were landing along the coast of Palestine, setting up a series of small, but closely united, city-states at the expense of the older Canaanites.

These new invaders are known to us as the Philistines. From them the land gets its name Palestine during the Greek period. They formed a league of five cities near the coast in the south: Ekron, Ashdod, Ashkelon, Gath and Gaza. Although at first they did not rule much territory, they possessed a great power over the other inhabitants of the land. They brought with them the secret of making *iron* tools, and thus their weapons were far superior to the soft bronze weapons of the local Canaanites, and, for that matter, of

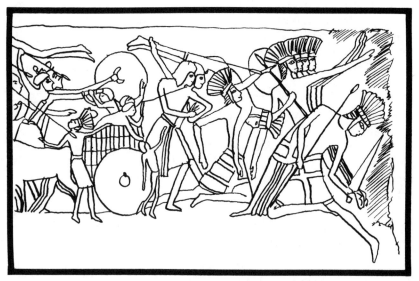

Battle of the "Sea People" against Egypt about 1150 B.C. Defeated by the Egyptians, many settled in southern Palestine and became known as *Philistines.*

the Israelites (cf. 1 Sam 13:19–22). Eventually the Philistines would become the arch-enemies of Israel, but at first they proved a help by weakening the larger Canaanite city-states in the coastal plains and valleys.

Israel was also helped by the fact that most of the cities were away from the mountainous areas near the Jordan. City-states had grown up in the western part of the country where the soil was able to be farmed profitably, but they were rare in the stony and poorly watered mountain country. All that stood between an Israelite invasion force from the east and a space to live in the mountains were a series of cities near the Jordan Valley: Jericho, Bethel, Ai.

Theories of a Peaceful Settlement or Internal Revolt

In recent years, other suggestions have been proposed to account for the complex traditions about the conquest and settlement. A popular proposal of Albrecht Alt, Martin Noth and Yohanon Aharoni, among others, sees Israel's invasion of Palestine as peaceful. The separate groups of tribes did not all enter at once. Some had come out of Egypt with Joshua and Moses and attacked across the Jordan, others infiltrated from the south into the areas of Beer-sheba and Hebron, still others moved into the northern areas of Galilee. A few had never left the land nor been among those in Egyptian slavery, but joined the invading tribes upon their arrival. These were moved by many motives, including religious conversion to Yahweh, forced union by the power of the invaders (cf. Jos 9), and dissatisfaction with the Canaanite oppression of peasants and small villages.

Another possibility has been raised in view of many clues in the Amarna letters that there were disaffected groups in Palestine, landless bands of mercenary troops, and much unrest and strife between the major Canaanite city-states. Using modern sociological models, scholars such as George Mendenhall and Norman Gottwald propose that these stem from a growing conflict between a minority who controlled urban power and the economically deprived, or even oppressed, peasants who worked the land and populated the outlying villages. This led to widespread peasant revolts. These scholars place Israel's conquest tradition in this setting, pointing out how Yahweh, the God of Israel, became a perfect focus for the hopes of a powerless population because he was a God who liberated his followers from slavery. What he had done in Egypt for some

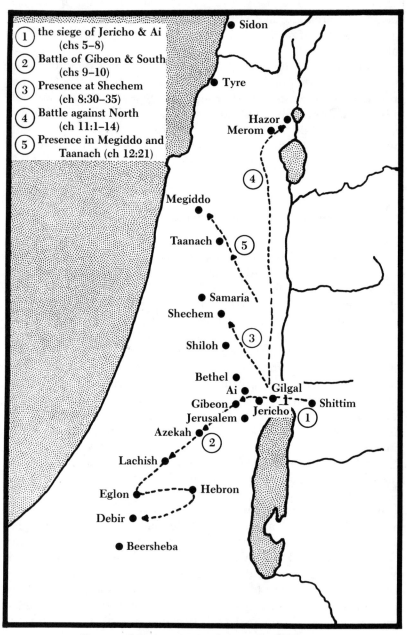

Route of Conquest in the Book of Joshua

tribes, he could do for all peoples who would join in faith to him. Israel was born out of this mix of a small number of invading or migrating tribes coming with Joshua, many local villages and rural political groups, as well as some urban poor, who accepted the Yahwist faith and established new political orders and settlements in the land.

The actual situation perhaps involves elements of all these theories: invasion, gradual infiltration of outside tribes, uprising and confederation of peasants breaking free from the urban powers. Certainly the evidence of Judges 1 that Israel could not take Megiddo, Beth Shan, Taanach, Gezer and Dor forces us to modify any simple idea of the conquest. Also the failure of the Book of Judges to mention Shechem could mean that the Israelites did not need to conquer that area because they or related groups were already present in the area before this time. Other inconsistencies also abound. Joshua 10:36f claims that Joshua took Hebron, while Judges 1:10 has the tribe of Judah capture it much later. Joshua 10:38f has Joshua take Debir, while Joshua 15:13–19 awards the victory to Othniel still later. Judges 4 and Joshua 11 report the same conquest of the north but hardly agree at all in their stories.

We can conclude that Israel preserved two related but separate traditions that have been gathered and harmonized to some extent but which still show their original differences when examined closely. One stressed how God was with them from the exodus through the taking of the land, and how they gained possession of their new homeland entirely by divine aid and according to a divine plan that could not be thwarted and through leaders especially blessed and anointed. The other tradition stressed the smallness and weakness of Israel and its constant problems with the Canaanites over many years. But here, too, the glory of survival and gradual rise to power belonged to Yahweh and his aid in times of need.

"The Deuteronomic History" in Joshua and Judges

Characteristic of both Deuteronomy and the Books of Joshua and Judges are the strong moral notes, the sermonic style and the emphasis on the word of God spoken through the *leader*, whether Moses or Joshua or one of the judges. These give a theological emphasis to the ancient stories so that the reader will not miss the action of God in a given situation. The authors have used very old and authentic traditions, but at crucial points have added comments and judgments according to the thought of Deuteronomy. One of their favorite means of adding their comment to the original story was to place a *speech in the mouth of one of the heroes* that gives warning to the people.

Some examples of the Deuteronomic editors' work can be seen in important moments in the story. For example, in Joshua 1, the narrative begins with a word from Yahweh promising to be with the people in the wars ahead, but warning them to observe all the laws which Moses had given them. There then follow several chapters of older conquest traditions. Again, in the middle of the book (Jos 12), after all the land is conquered, God again speaks to Joshua a word about dividing the land among all the tribes. Finally at the end of the book, the editors place a final speech in the mouth of Joshua (Jos 23) in which he exhorts the people to obey the law, to be faithful to Yahweh, and to renew the covenant. He warns that God will punish them if they turn away from the covenant. Thus, by means of speeches in the mouths of either the Lord or of Joshua, the editors gave a meaning and a purpose to the collection of traditional stories they had joined together.

The hand of the editors is even more apparent in the Book of Judges, where the message that God will be with Israel if they are faithful, but will abandon them to their enemies if they are not, is carefully noted by placing each separate story into an identical pattern whose basic outline has five parts:

1. The people did evil in the sight of Yahweh.
2. God in his anger delivered them to an oppressor.
3. The people cried out to Yahweh.
4. Yahweh sent a hero to deliver them.
5. The land had peace all the days of the judge's life.

But soon the pattern would start all over again. A sample of the full formula can be found in the story of the judge Othniel in Judges 3:7–11:

> And the people of Israel did what was evil in the sight of Yahweh, forgetting Yahweh their God, and worshiping the baals and the asherahs. And Yahweh was angry with Israel and delivered them into the hands of Cushan Rishtayim, king of Aram Naharayim. And the people of Israel served Cushan Rishtayim for eight years. But the people of Israel cried out to Yahweh and he raised a deliverer for Israel,

Othniel, son of Kenaz, the younger brother of Caleb, and he rescued them. The spirit of Yahweh came on him, he judged Israel, he went to war, and Yahweh gave Cushan Rishtayim, king of Aram, into his hand. His hand prevailed over Cushan Rishtayim so that the land had rest for forty years until Othniel, the son of Kenaz, died.

The editors of Judges have placed a long explanation of this pattern in Judges 2:10–23 to serve as a general introduction to the individual judges. It stresses the faithfulness and mercy of God to the people and to the judge, but points out that the people forgot quickly the lesson and turned back to their evil ways, following after other gods and sinning worse than earlier generations had done.

The Twelve Tribes

The problem of the conquest's actual course of events also raises questions about the different tribes involved. Biblical tradition consistently affirms that Israel was made up of twelve tribes. In Genesis these are named after the twelve sons of Jacob. However, the actual listings often show variations, of which the most important are the omission of Joseph in most lists after the Book of Exodus, replaced by his sons Manasseh and Ephraim, and the omission of either Levi or Simeon to make room for the extra son. Thus:

Gen 49:1–27	Num 1:5–15	Dt 33:1–29
Reuben	Reuben	Reuben
Simeon	Simeon	Judah
Levi	Judah	Levi
Judah	Issachar	Benjamin
Zebulon	Zebulon	*Ephraim*
Issachar	*Ephraim*	*Manasseh*
Dan	*Manasseh*	Zebulon
Gad	Benjamin	Issachar
Asher	Dan	Gad
Naphtali	Asher	Dan
Joseph	Gad	Naphtali
Benjamin	Naphtali	Asher

According to the story of Genesis 29–30, the twelve sons of Jacob came from four different mothers. Thus Jacob's older wife

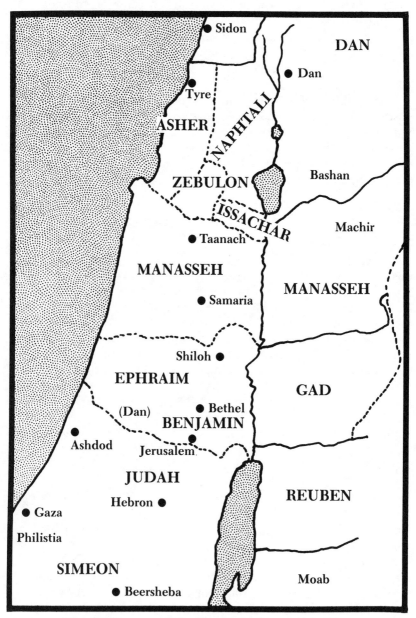

The Settlement of the Twelve Tribes in Palestine

Leah gave birth to Reuben, Simeon, Levi, Judah, Issachar and Zebulon, while her servant girl Zilpah bore Gad and Asher. The younger wife Rachel was the mother of Joseph and Benjamin, while her maid Bilhah bore Dan and Naphtali. The names were all relatively common in the patriarchal period. They are Semitic and properly belong in the Palestine area for their origin. As with so many biblical genealogies in the Book of Genesis, we must reckon that each "son" really represents a whole tribe or clan, and that the twelve-tribe family understood themselves as equals ("brother") in some form of federation. In a similar manner, Jacob and Esau as brothers also stood for how Israel and Edom were related and Isaac and Ishmael as half-brothers expressed the same relationship that Israel understood that it had with the Arab tribes to the east. The story of Jacob and Laban in Genesis 30–31 recognized that the Israelites were "cousins" to the people of Aram in Mesopotamia. The traditional story of the two wives and two maids may reflect some more primitive groupings of tribes before the final twelve.

On the question of differences in the lists of tribes, we need to note that it may have taken many decades for all twelve tribes to be united. The replacement of Joseph by Ephraim and Manasseh, named as his two sons in Genesis 47, may mean that these two powerful tribes were late additions to the "league." Simeon disappears in lists such as Deuteronomy 33 altogether, perhaps a sign that the tribe itself was wiped out or died out. Levi loses its status as one of the twelve but continues on in later Israelite life as a *class* of priests. These differences and what led to them cannot all be explained at this time, but they do let us know that the simple stories of Jacob and his sons mask a long history of groups and individuals coming together to form what emerges at the end of the period of the judges as the nation of Israel.

The Tribal League

Many scholars have proposed that Israel's twelve tribes were part of a league similar to several that we know of from the Greek city-states many centuries later. The tribes would have formed a loose federation centered around the worship of Yahweh. Each year delegates would meet at a central sanctuary and offer renewed devotion and sacrifice to God, pledge themselves to one another and to God anew, and submit all disputes and problems of common concern to a decision there before God. The evidence for such a league, usually called an amphictyony, after the Greek models, is quite slim, especially since the Book of Judges makes it obvious that most of the tribes did not cooperate with one another. However, the worship of Yahweh set these twelve tribes off from the rest of the Canaanite population, and even if there was no formal league, they did recognize some central place where the ark of the covenant was kept (first at Shechem in Joshua 23–24, later at Shiloh in 1 Samuel 1–4).

The Significance of the Land for Israel

Before moving on to the story of Samuel and the beginnings of kingship in Israel, we must pause and consider how important the taking of the land is to biblical theology.

We can gain important insights into the central role that owning land has for ancient society in order to properly worship its gods by looking at some instances involving the place of Yahweh in the land. The story of the prophet Elisha and Naaman the Syrian general in 2 Kings 5 recounts how the Syrian did not believe he could worship Yahweh unless he took some of the soil of Israel home with him to Damascus. In 2 Kings 18:25, the Assyrian general tries to win over the citizens of Jerusalem to the idea of surrender by claiming that Yahweh was so angry with their stewardship of the land that he had handed it over to Assyria as spoil. Still another aspect of this connection between Israel, its God, and the land is revealed in the terrible sense of loss and helplessness that exile from the land brings. Psalm 137 and the Book of Lamentations express this feeling in deeply moving poetry.

Israel always understood the land to be a gift from Yahweh. Before the conquest, the patriarchs in Genesis are regularly portrayed as *landless:* Abraham the sojourner from a distant country, Jacob and his family settling in Egypt by special grant of the pharaoh. The patriarchal narratives stress the *hope* of land as a promise given by Yahweh (cf. Gen 15). Yet, as God guides them toward the promised land after the exodus, the *conditional* nature of this gift is brought out. People must choose between slavery in Egypt or wandering in the wilderness (see Ex 16–18 and Num 11–20).

Again when they are poised at the edge of the new land, the Book of Deuteronomy insists that they must choose their course carefully. The land will be a gift of Yahweh, sacred, blessed and made fruitful, but it will also be a source of temptation to forget

Yahweh and follow Baal and other pagan deities when the people prosper there. The land will also be a sacred responsibility of *stewardship* under Yahweh. It is the land of the covenant, so that possession of the land and obedience to Yahweh's covenant law go hand in hand. Sabbath rest, care for the poor, protection of the widow and the stranger, and keeping the whole body of law found in Deuteronomy 12–25 come with the right to the land.

But from the moment that Israel entered the land, the actual history was seen as a story of greed and progressive betrayal of Yahweh who was the owner of the earth and the gift giver. The Deuteronomic editors remember the time of the judges, for example, as a period of petty strife when tribes refused to bear the burdens of the covenant. The dismal picture of the other tribes warring against Benjamin closes the Book of Judges, and the author adds as a final, very negative summary: "In those days there was no king in Israel; everyone did what was best in his own eyes" (Jgs 21:25).

But the same judgment would be leveled against the rule of the kings in the Books of Kings, and against the landowners, prophets and priests in the Prophetic Books. The prophets even began to announce that Israel must lose the land and suffer severe punishment and exile before there could be any hope that God would restore it. Indeed, the prophets Jeremiah and Ezekiel, writing near the final end of Judah in 586 B.C., already place more emphasis on the holiness and justice of the people as a community than on their possession of the promised land. Books written after the exile to Babylon from 586 to 539 stress the law and the purity of the people, and often speak of the restoration of the land only in the far-distant future.

The experience of the people's failure in the land because of sin led the religious leaders in the time of exile and after to steer a new direction. They emphasized the need for faith based on interior devotion to Yahweh and personal responsibility for keeping the law. Indeed it led to the development and establishment of a *written book* of revelation that would be a permanent guide for Israel, the Pentateuch (*Torah*). This took place by the time of Ezra (450–400 B.C.), and was followed shortly by the addition of the Prophetic Books, and after several centuries by the rest of the Old Testament books. This was to be the primary heritage of Israel, "The People of the Book," rather than the uncertainties of the land. Nevertheless, the tie between the law and the land was and is intimate. Even in post-exilic authors, the hope of a restoration of the land to its former glory was strong. The dream of an independent Israel led to strong currents of messianism which took one of two forms: either *political* overthrow of the pagan nations and a new era of empire such as David had ruled, or the *apocalyptic* hope of an end to the present world and the re-creation of a new world by God in which Israel would dominate.

The Pentateuch narrative leaves Israel not yet in possession of the promised land. One reason why the Old Testament divides these five books from the following history in the land found in Joshua, Judges, 1 and 2 Samuel and 1 and 2 Kings is to show that Yahweh's saving grace and covenant law did not need Israel to be in possession of land in order to be binding and valid.

STUDY QUESTIONS?

1. What is meant by the term "Historical Books"? What books fall under this classification? Why?
2. Describe the contents and purpose of the Book of Joshua.
3. What is contained in the Book of Judges? What are its major divisions?
4. Evaluate the archaeological evidence regarding the events narrated in the Books of Joshua and Judges.
5. Briefly describe why the conditions were conducive for Palestine to be conquered.
6. What are the different theories proposed for the Israelite conquest and settlement of Canaan?
7. What are some important characteristics of the "Deuteronomic History"?
8. Explain why the listings of the Twelve Tribes differ.
9. What is the importance of the land for Israel?

Chapter 11

CANAANITE RELIGION AND CULTURE

Suggested Scripture Readings:

Jeremiah 10:1–17
Isaiah 44:9–20
Ezekiel 8
Wisdom of Solomon 13–15

"A Land Flowing with Milk and Honey"

Canaan was an attractive land. The Book of Exodus calls it "a good and spacious land, a land flowing with milk and honey" (Ex 3:8), and a little later says, "I have decided to lead you up out of the misery of Egypt into the land of the Canaanites . . . a land flowing with milk and honey" (Ex 3:17). It appeared to the spies sent to scout the southern borders in Numbers 13–14 as a "fine, rich land" (Num 14:7) and one with grapes so large that two men had to carry each bunch (Num 13:23). Even if this last point is slightly exaggerated, it backs up what we know from other sources. Many large towns with flourishing cultures stood in the major valleys and along the seacoast. These cities carried on extensive trade with Egypt to the south and the cities of Lebanon and Syria to the north. In fact, the word "Canaan" should not be identified with just modern Israel. It really refers to the whole Mediterranean coast from Turkey down to the border of Egypt. The language and cultures were all related, from Ugarit in the northern edge down through the Phoenician cities of Byblos, Tyre and Sidon to the important centers of Megiddo, Hazor, Lachish and Gezer in the southern area we call Palestine today. The word "Canaanite" means a "trader" in the Semitic language, and captures in a name how other ancient peoples saw them. It was only in later times that the single coastal culture was divided in people's thinking so that the southern part was named Palestine after the Philistine cities there, and the north became Phoenicia, from the Greek name of the murex snail used to make purple dye, which was a major export of the area around Tyre and Sidon.

The material culture of the Canaanites was evident to the Israelites as well. The strong walled cities and impressive buildings made them fearful (Num 13:28). Fine, many-roomed mansions stood side by side with crowded tenement districts. In the ruins, archaeologists have found the remains of vases and bowls of excellent workmanship from Crete, statues and amulets from Egypt, tablets of treasured literature from Babylon, and fine ivory work done by local artists. It is no wonder then that the Bible recalls how forcefully the simple, relatively poor tribes of Israel were struck by the wealth they saw among the Canaanites. But along with the glittering and prosperous material achievements came religious beliefs— beliefs that clashed almost entirely with Israel's stark faith in one God, who was ruler, patriarch, warrior, and protective mother all in one and who had declared that no other gods nor their images were to be before him (Ex 20:2–3).

The Lure of Canaanite Religion

The prophet Hosea in the eighth century B.C. protested violently against Israelite religious practices:

> My people consult a piece of wood, and their staff gives them oracles, for the spirit of harlotry has led them astray, and by playing the prostitute they forsake their God. They offer sacrifice on the mountaintops and burn incense on the hills beneath the oaks, poplars and terebinth trees because of their refreshing shade. Thus it is that your daughters are harlots, and your brides are prostitutes (Hos 4:12–13).

And the Book of Deuteronomy, a century later, included a law that demanded:

> There are to be no cult prostitutes among the daughters of Israel, nor a cult prostitute among the sons of Israel. You

may not offer the fee of a cult prostitute (a woman) nor that of a dog (the male prostitute) in the house of the Lord your God as payment for a vow. Both of these are an abomination to the Lord your God (Dt 23:17–18).

Similar charges can be found in other prophets—see Micah 1:7; Jeremiah 2:7–8; 2:23–24; 11:13; etc. All of these condemnations stem from prophetic disgust with those people who had turned away from devotion to Yahweh to go after the delights and attractions of the cults of Baal, Asherah and other gods of the Canaanites.

It may seem surprising that the pagan gods could still have such power some five or six hundred years after Joshua and the tribes had established themselves in Palestine and brought the Canaanite peoples slowly but surely under their control. But the evidence from the Bible is overwhelming that Israel struggled against the religious practices of the pagans almost continuously down to the end of its own independence in 586 B.C. The Books of Deuteronomy and Kings and the prophets Hosea, Amos, Micah, Ezekiel and Jeremiah all testify to widespread idolatry on the part of Israel. Moreover, archaeological digs regularly turn up large numbers of small amulets and idols of pagan gods and goddesses in almost every Israelite city that has been discovered.

How are we to explain this when the Old Testament makes such a point that worship of Yahweh demanded the exclusion of all other gods? Probably several factors were at work. On one hand, we must remember that the Bible emphasizes the *ideal* worship, but Israel often fell far short of this complete devotion. On the other, many different groups and towns were added to Israel's faith from early times, and these brought their pagan customs and beliefs along with them without really changing inside. It was very common in the ancient world to identify the local gods and goddesses of a people with the new gods of a conqueror or victor in war. People simply transferred their loyalty and public allegiance to a new god but understood that really no change had taken place. The Canaanite god Baal could be identified with the Babylonian Marduk or the Assyrian Ashur as storm gods or sky gods without any major difficulty. So, undoubtedly, many former pagans found little difficulty claiming loyalty to Yahweh with no real intention of abandoning all of their old beliefs in the bargain. Similarly, many Israelites would have found it easy to add a pagan practice or two as part of their devotion to Yahweh.

Canaanite Nature Religion

Canaan had as rich a set of religious beliefs as it had material success. The basic principle which gave shape to their religious system was the worship of gods who controlled the forces of nature, especially those that affected the climate and annual cycle of rain and drought in the coastal areas. There is almost no rain from April until October and so the year falls naturally into two real seasons, the dry season and the wet season, during which the storms bring rain from the west across the Mediterranean. Almost all of the gods who were important to the Canaanites were gods involved in this rhythm of nature. Typically their religion pictured the gods as little more than the *personified power* of the storm, the drought, the growing crops, sexual fertility and the like. Around these gods and goddesses myths and rituals were developed which tried to reflect an orderly and proper way to bring such natural forces into proper balance during the year, so that rain and dryness alternated without an excess of one or the other.

This can be loosely termed a "nature religion" but might be better described as "cosmological," meaning that it focuses on the proper relation between the divine ordering of the universe and human response. The gods act on a cosmic scale, directing the fates of the entire created world; it is the task of human religion to win their favor and bring a favorable blessing and order on our small creaturely presence. The result was that Canaanite religion, much like Babylonian, involved very elaborate stories and cultic practices designed to insure that the gods acted favorably toward the people and land of Canaan. Many rituals dealt with sacrifices or duties toward dead parents and ancestors, but among the chief concerns was fertility, both of the soil and of the animal and human populations. Failure in crops or flocks could mean starvation, while human birth rates had to remain high to offset the terrible infancy and childhood mortality rate. Naturally then emphasis was centered on performing sexual actions that would bring about *fertility* by human *imitation* of the divine powers that bestowed fertilizing seed and life on the land.

The discovery of the Ugaritic tablets in 1929 has given us a good idea of the myths and the rites used by the Canaanites. Both involve generous amounts of magical imitation in which priests and worshipers represent sexual matings of the gods. One example would be the annual New Year's festival in which the king, as Baal's representative, would unite himself with a high priestess in a "sacred marriage" to guarantee the land's prosperity and fertility for the coming year. At the same time, other worshipers would abandon themselves to sexual license with official cult prostitutes, both men and women, in order to fulfill prayers or vows asking for children, or better crops, or an end to drought. Similar festivals would be held at various times throughout the year, often at important times of the agricultural seasons: harvest, planting, change from wet to rainy season, etc.

The Canaanite Gods

Because of the fortunate find of religious myths at Ugarit, we no longer have to rely only upon the negative descriptions by Israel's prophets to understand Canaanite beliefs. We have Canaan's own positive version, so to speak, and it makes the picture much clearer. The tablets reveal literally hundreds of gods, some native and some borrowed from Babylon and other powerful neighbors. A few of these gods are truly cosmic deities, having responsibility for major forces of nature all over the world, but most are local gods of a single place, some of them not much more than demons or river spirits. There is a remarkable fluidity in the descriptions of the different gods and goddesses, with the characteristics of one often

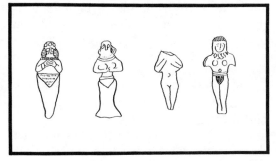

Astarte or Mother Goddess figurines from the Ancient Near East.

A small amulet from Babylon showing the demon Pazazu, a dangerous bringer of disease.

reappearing in descriptions of others, and many times it is not even easy to separate their roles apart. A few of the more important ones at Ugarit were:

(1) *El,* the father of the gods and creator of all creatures. He appears as the highest god and final judge in all disputes among the divine beings. But he also seems to be remote and not directly involved in human affairs. He dwells at the source of the two cosmic rivers that make up the ocean on a sacred mountain far away. Generally, he is kindly and merciful in his rule over the assembly of the gods.

(2) *Baal,* the god of the storm, who is the day-to-day king of the gods. It is he that controls the annual rainstorm and fertility cycle of the earth, and on him depends the yearly agricultural success. Like El, he receives the titles "king," "eternal one," and "lord of heaven and earth." Above all he is *Aliyan Baal,* "Baal the prevailer," and he is often portrayed with an arm upraised holding a war club, the symbol of thunder, and with a twisted staff in his other hand, symbolizing the forked lightning.

(3) *Asherah,* the goddess over the sea, and wife of El. This goddess does not appear to play a large role in the fertility rites at Ugarit, but has an important voice in influencing El's decisions, and needs to be won over to Baal's side. Later, however, the Hebrew prophets frequently identify the fertility cults of the pagans simply as the "worship of the Asherahs."

(4) *Anat,* the sister or wife of Baal. She seems to be both sister and wife of the god. She certainly acts as a warrior in her blood-thirsty battles on behalf of Baal, but can also be identified with sexual charms. Much like the Babylonian goddess Ishtar, she combines the dual role of a goddess of love and war at the same time.

(5) *Astarte,* a third goddess, is also identified strongly with the fertility rites. Her cult was widespread in Canaanite areas, often identified by the discovery of many small hand-sized statuettes of a naked goddess holding her breasts out to the worshiper. But these idols are just as common in the ruins of Israelite settlements! She shares many aspects in common with Anat.

The three goddesses manifest the feminine side of Canaanite religion, combining the roles of mother goddess, protectors of childbirth, givers of fertility to women, and helpers with sexual charm. Though each has some warrior traits, more often they are shown as sacred prostitutes looking out of their windows to entice passers-by in.

The Religious Myth of Baal

The most important Ugaritic religious text for understanding Canaanite beliefs is *The Epic of Baal,* a series of texts about the role of Baal, the storm god. They are on tablets of clay, which have many broken pieces, and so the exact order of events cannot be arranged with absolute certainty, but the following is a short summary of how the story probably went.

It opens with some kind of conflict between Yamm, the god of the sea, and Baal, god of storm and vegetation, over which one should be the king of the earth. Yamm seems to gain the upper hand at first but is challenged by Baal to battle. Baal wins with the help of magical weapons made by the divine blacksmith and puts Yamm under permanent restraint. This phase of the myth symbolizes the victory of divine order over the chaotic rampages of the untamable ocean.

Now that Baal has won the kingship, he needs a palace to dwell in. He gets his sisters (or wives), Anat and Astarte, to win over Asherah, the wife of El, to his cause. She persuades El, the father of gods and men, to grant Baal's request. El concedes, and the blacksmith god builds a fine palace of gold and silver. To celebrate, Baal holds a great feast for the gods in which his kingship is acknowledged. Now order and peace prevail.

But this is short-lived, for soon a new threat looms in the person of the god Mot, the personification of death. He is unhappy that Baal got the kingship and believes he has better right to it because he is more powerful. He demands that El and the assembly of the gods hand Baal over to his power. Baal accepts the challenge and descends to the netherworld to battle Mot, but eats the bread of death and is overcome. The earth wilts and fades for lack of rain, and the gods go into mourning over his death.

At this point, his sister Anat goes in search of her missing brother, and with the help of the sun goddess Shapash, who is able to travel each night through the underworld from west to east, she locates him and somehow frees him from Mot's kingdom of the dead. Meanwhile, back on the sacred mountain, the god of artificial irrigation, Ashtar, tries to take Baal's place as king. But his feet cannot even reach down to Baal's footstool and so he is found inadequate. The canals will never replace the natural rains!

Anat now does battle with Mot and slays him, winnows him like wheat and sprinkles his remains like seed across the fields:

Like the heart of a cow for her calf,
   Like the heart of a ewe for her lamb,
   So's the heart of Anat for Baal.
She seizes the Godly Mot—
   With sword she doth cleave him.
With fan she doth winnow him—
   With fire she doth burn him.
With hand-mill she grinds him—
   In the field she doth sow him (ANET 140).

As Baal revives and returns to his kingship, the earth once again
flourishes and lives:

The heavens fat did rain,
   The wadies flow with honey!
The Kindly One El Benign's glad.
   His feet on the footstool he sets,
   And parts his jaws and laughs.
He lifts up his voice and cries:
"Now will I sit and rest
   And my soul be at ease in my breast.
For alive is Puissant Baal,
   Existent the Prince, Lord of Earth!" (ANET 140).

A separate incident, in which Baal himself fights against Mot,
ends with both still battling fiercely when night falls. Shapash, the
sun goddess, begs El not to let death rule the earth, and so El forces
Mot to go back to ruling the realm of the dead. This symbolizes the
triumph of the rains and life-giving forces over the killing heat and
dryness of summer and early fall. Baal may disappear each year
from April to October, but he always returns.

Whether it is Anat or Baal who actually defeats Mot in the
"official" version of the myth is less important than the significance
of the story as a whole. It dramatizes the conflict between the "wet"
and the "dry" seasons. For civilization to survive, it is absolutely
essential that Baal triumph at the end. Perhaps the entire myth was
recited at some festival, or else parts of it may have been used at
several feasts over the course of a year. Parts may even have been
acted out.

A stele from Ugarit showing the god Baal holding the club of thunder and the staff of lightning, symbol of the god of the storm.

The storm-god Hadad, or Adad, on the back of a bull with forked-lightning in his hands. From Arslan Tash, Syria, 8th century B.C.

Israelite Echoes of the Myth

Graphic imagery in the Bible often describes God as a warrior who triumphs over the enemies of Israel and over the forces of nature. The Hebrew writers owe much in these passages to the Canaanite myth whose language they undoubtedly borrow. The closest and most dramatic example is found in Isaiah 27:1, which describes the sea-monster of chaos, Leviathan, well known in Ugaritic myths under the spelling Lotan:

In that day, the Lord
with his sharp, great and strong sword
will punish Leviathan, the fleeing serpent,
Leviathan, the twisting serpent,
and he will slay the dragon of the sea.

With this compare a text from the Baal epic:

> If you smote Lotan, the twisting serpent,
> destroy the writhing serpent,
> Shalyat of the seven heads . . .

Psalm 74:13–14 expresses a like idea: "You divided the sea with your might, you broke the heads of the dragons in the waters; you crushed the heads of Leviathan, you gave him as food to the beasts of the wilderness." Isaiah 51:9–10 borrows the same image to describe God's victory over the Egyptians in the exodus: "Awake, awake, put on strength, O arm of the Lord; awake as in days of old, the generations of long ago. Was it not you who cut Rahab in pieces, and pierced the dragon? Was it not you who dried up the sea, the waters of the great deep? You made the depths of the sea a path for the redeemed to pass over."

The same metaphor of divine victory over the forces of evil, personified as the gods Sea or Death, lies behind other passages such as Job 41 and its description of Leviathan, Psalm 89:9–10 and its praise of God's might, and Isaiah 38:9–19 with its victory hymn over the power of death. While rejecting the multiple gods and the nature myths of Canaan, Israel felt itself free to use many of the themes to enhance the power of Yahweh. Thus Yahweh is sometimes called Baal ("Lord") over the earth (Hos 2:16), or even El (Is 14:13). He can use thunder and lightning for weapons (Ps 18:13–14), he brings the rain (Ps 68:9–10), and he rules over the sea (Pss 93:3–4; 98:7–8; 74:13–14). Psalm 29 was probably a poem to the storm god Baal taken over by Israel and applied to Yahweh in order to emphasize that Yahweh and not Baal rules creation.

None of this wholesale borrowing should cause us much difficulty. After all, the Christians chose the feast of the newly reborn sun god in the Roman calendar to be the feast day of Christmas, since Christ is the true sun that dawns on the world. Such theft of pagan feasts not only helps to transfer people's loyalty away from their old practices, but keeps a continuity in their lives, especially by preserving the favorite holidays. One does not have to give up all celebration in order to follow Christ.

Other Religious Practices

The *fertility rites* in honor of Baal and his wives were the elements of Canaanite religion that most horrified the Israelites, who had a very strict idea of the sacredness of sex and its connection to marriage. Yet many other practices were shared by both peoples. *Sacrifice* played a large role in both religions: Leviticus 1–8 details the rules of sacrifice for Israel, while Ugarit has yielded quite a few sacrifice lists giving the proper offering for each god. *Altars* were often similar in shape: the altars found in Canaanite cities had four sharp projections at the corners called "horns," and the Bible describes Israelite altars in the same way (Ex 27:2; Lev 9:9; Ps 118:27; 1 Kgs 8:31). Both religions had altars for incense. Both had *temples* made up of three parts: a porch, a regular sanctuary, and a special inner sanctuary which in Israel was called the "holy of holies."

But Israel condemned other practices that they found disgusting. One was child sacrifice, widespread in Canaanite areas. Apparently parents offered up a small child to be burned before a cult statue of the god in payment for the deity's aid in a moment of crisis, often as a result of a vow they had made. This seems to have been especially common in Carthage, a Phoenician (Canaanite) colony in North Africa, but undoubtedly took place back in the mother country as well, although archaeological exploration of Phoenicia has been very limited because many modern Lebanese cities are built on the same sites as the ancient cities were, and so digging has been impossible there. The Bible records one incident in which a Moabite king offered up his son to ask divine protection against an Israelite attack (2 Kgs 3:27). Several times the Israelites themselves descended to the same practice (Jgs 11:30–39; 1 Kgs 16:34; 2 Sam 21:1–9). But both the prophets and the law condemned the practice totally (Lev 18:21; 20:2–5; Dt 12:31; Ez 16:20; Ps 106:37–38).

The prophets often mention the massebah, a Canaanite pillar symbol, among the objects they condemn. Examples of these stones, looking much like grave markers, occur at many Canaanite ruins, e.g., Megiddo, Hazor, Gezer and Shechem. Early traditions record that Israel too used such markers as memorials of important places where God had appeared (Gen 28:18, 22; 35:14; Ex 24:4), but when Israel settled in Palestine, the prophets condemned the use of massebah stones because they were symbols of the male fertility gods (Hos 3:4; 10:1–2; Ex 23:24; 34:13; Lev 26:1; Dt 7:5; 12:3; 16:22; 1 Kgs 14:23). Besides the fertility cult use, massebah pillars may have been used as memorial stones in a cult of dead ancestors. Along with these pillars, the prophets often condemn Israel's use of "high places," which were raised outdoor altars (Is 1:29–30; Jer 2:20; Ez 6:13; 16:16; Hos 4:13). The Canaanites had worshiped on these

Statue and standing stones in Canaanite temple at Hazor (13th century B.C.)

Altar with horns from Megiddo (10th–9th centuries B.C.)

altars, and at first Israel accepted them easily (1 Sam 9:12; 1 Kgs 3:4–5; 18:30). Only when the people began to combine the worship of Yahweh with that of Baal did the prophets take entirely negative stands (Jgs 6:25; 2 Kgs 23:8; Am 7:9).

Other common practices taken over by the Israelites from their pagan neighbors include the burning of incense before a female goddess and offering baked cakes (Is 17:8; Ez 6:4; Jer 44:15), burning incense to the storm god Baal (Jer 44:3, 8), or worshiping the sun, moon and stars as gods (Dt 4:19; 17:3; Zeph 1:5; Jer 8:2; 2 Kgs 23:5).

Exodus 20:4 condemns the making of any image or idol of Yahweh, but often the prophets and psalmists had to warn against attempts either to put some image of Yahweh in the temple or to replace his worship with devotion to a statue of a foreign god who could be seen and carried about (see Jer 2:5, 11; Dt 32:17; Is 44:9–20; 40:18–20). Exodus 20:26 forbids Israelite priests to go before the altar naked as did many pagan priests.

On the other hand, Canaanite religious practice also had a high regard for the duty of children to care for their parents in old age and after death. The particular duty of seeing to the burial of the parents and maintenance of the tombs fell on the sons. This filial piety is well demonstrated in a text from the Ugaritic epic of Aqhat which lists a son's duties to his father:

> So shall there be a son in his house,
>   A scion in the midst of his palace:
> Who sets up the stelae of his ancestral spirits,
>   In the holy place the protectors of his clan;
> Who frees his spirit from the earth,
>   From the dust guards his footsteps;
> Who smothers the life-force of his detractor,
>   Drives off who attacks his abode;
> Who takes him by the hand when he's drunk,
>   Carries him when he's sated with wine;
> Consumes his funerary offering in Baal's house,
>   (Even) his portion in El's house;
> Who plasters his roof when it leaks,
>   Washes his clothes when they're soiled (ANET 150).

In the same way the Old Testament makes a special point of warning children to respect and care for their parents (Ex 20:12; Lev 19:3; Dt 5:16; Prv 1:8; 6:20; Sir 3:1–16).

Summary

The innumerable examples of amulets, statues, and other small offerings left in Canaanite temples as thanksgiving tokens from devoted worshipers reveal to us a side of pagan worship which was not primarily sexual orgy but a real devotional life offering trust in divine help. Archaeologists have brought to light much about Canaanite faith that we simply did not know sixty years ago. The tablets from Ugarit, the objects and altars, all reveal a people filled with the same worries and hopes that we all have.

But their religion also reveals itself strongly dependent on the forces of nature. It sought to control those forces by turning the hearts and wills of the divine beings to look favorably on the worshipers. Ancient peoples lived with a great deal of uncertainty about the power of the gods, always celebrating their return from powerlessness, as when Baal escaped from the hands of death. They relied on magical recitation of prayers and rituals, and indulged in degrading sexual practices, hoping to achieve union with the gods. Israel, with its strong Mosaic faith in the complete power and compassion of the one God Yahweh who stood above all natural forces, saw through the weaknesses of Canaan's desperate search for security in life and rejected any worship of nature.

Israel instead insisted upon a God who stood above the frailties and temptations of human beings, who was not chained to the patterns of the seasons, who ruled over all of creation, and who controlled the histories of each nation. He was unfailingly merciful and faithful, never capricious or uncertain, and he demanded strict moral standards of conduct from his people. Sex was subordinated to marriage and the social good of the families, and drunkenness and other revelry was ruled out as part of worship.

It is easy enough for us to see now that Israel's idea of God was superior to that of the people of Canaan, but we must remember that it was not so easy then for Israel always to keep this clear. The prosperity of the land of Canaan could be interpreted as a blessing from Baal, while the intimate relationship between a farming economy and the annual religious rites of fertility and sacrifice made a very satisfying set of beliefs. Also, the loosening of ethical demands from religious celebrations made it much easier to practice—and enjoy. If Israel managed to save its faith against such odds, the biblical testimony is that only God's gracious fidelity brought it about.

STUDY QUESTIONS

1. Identify the following: Canaan, Canaanite, Palestine, Phoenicia, Ugaritic tablets, *Epic of Baal.*
2. Briefly describe some key characteristics and elements of the Canaanite religion. Why did it seem appealing to the people of Israel?
3. Who were some of the major gods and goddesses in the Canaanite religion? What were their roles?
4. Briefly describe how Canaanite myth influenced the Hebrew writers.
5. What religious practices did the Canaanite religion and Israelites have in common? Which Canaanite practices did Israelites condemn? Why?
6. "Canaanite religion and culture was totally inconsistent and abhorrent to the way of life of Israel." Assess the validity of this statement. Do you agree or disagree? Why? Give reasons for your position.

Chapter 12

"A KING LIKE THOSE
OF OTHER NATIONS":
THE BOOKS OF SAMUEL AND KINGS

Suggested Scripture Readings:

1 Samuel 7–12
2 Samuel 7–12
1 Kings 3–9

A. THE BOOKS OF SAMUEL AND KINGS

A Changing World

The two Books of Samuel and the two Books of Kings trace the last days of the period of the judges and the first days of Israel as a monarchy. It is a fateful moment of change, and the high drama is helped by the stunning reversal in fortune that the change made. The period of Samuel, the last judge, and of Saul, the first king, marked the most desperate moments of danger Israel had ever faced; the following reign of David and his son Solomon marked the highest success the nation would ever achieve in its long history. But kings would prove to be a mixed blessing for an Israel that prided itself on being a league of tribes with a great deal of local freedom and equality. While kings provided strong government, they did it at the expense of every Israelite's jealously guarded rights. Since many of these rights were rooted in the covenant with Yahweh in which all the people shared, the religious meaning of kingship had to be worked out so as to preserve the more basic belief that Israel was a people subject to one king only, Yahweh himself.

The Life of Samuel

The First and Second Books of Samuel form a transition from the loose tribal league in force since the time of Joshua to the strong, centralized state forged by David and Solomon. The major figure in this period of change was Samuel, a prophetic and religious leader as well as the most important political voice of the late eleventh century B.C.

1 Samuel opens at the shrine of Shiloh, where Eli the priest guards the ark of the covenant so that members of the twelve tribes can come to worship on the great feast days of the year. One mother, Hannah, whom God has blessed with a child after many years of barrenness, dedicates her child to serve at the shrine under Eli. There the boy Samuel receives a special call from God and develops into both a priest and a seer. In a desperate moment, Eli allows the tribes to take the ark into battle against overwhelming Philistine forces, and the Philistines destroy Israel's forces, capture the ark and kill Eli's sons. This terrible defeat leads to Eli's own sudden death on hearing the news, and Samuel emerges as the one religious force in the country. He not only presides at sacrifices, uses his powers of "seeing" to find lost objects, and "judges" disputes, but effectively controls political decisions for the stunned and desperate tribes as well.

Chapters 8 through 15 then move on to describe how Israel got a king. The danger from the Philistines was so great that the tribes themselves realized they would not have a chance unless their forces were united more effectively under a single military leader. They even lacked iron weapons such as the Philistines had, having to fight with less effective bronze (1 Sam 13:19–22). The people begged Samuel to give them a king "as other nations have" (1 Sam 8:5). Samuel warns them of the dangers of giving so much power to one person, but they insist, and God gives in, telling Samuel: "At this time tomorrow I will send you a man from the land of Benjamin whom you are to anoint as commander of my people Israel. He will save my people from the hands of the Philistines for I have witnessed their misery and heard their cry for help" (2 Sam 9:16). Yet only a chapter later, Samuel says, "Today you have rejected the Lord your God who delivers you from all your evil and disasters, by telling him, 'No! Set a king over us' " (1 Sam 10:19). Thus even the early traditions show a mixed reaction to the decision to have a king.

Most scholars see at least two separate strands of tradition. One can be called the *pro-Saul* version. It is found in 1 Samuel 9:1–10:16

and 11:1–15. The other version is an *anti-Saul* source found in 1
Samuel 8:1–22, 10:17–26, and 12:1–25. The book's editors have
joined these two accounts and made them into a statement which
gives both sides of the issue. It reveals that Samuel was reluctant to
have a king, but accepted the people's demands when God made
the choice evident in Saul, who stood "head and shoulders above
the rest of Israel" (1 Sam 9:2).

THE PRO-KINGSHIP SOURCE AND THE ANTI-KINGSHIP

Pro-kingship Source	**Anti-kingship Source**
1 Sam 9:1–10:6 Saul becomes king with the blessing and secret anointing by Samuel	*1 Sam 8:1–8:22* Philistines grow stronger under Samuel and people want a king against Samuel's wish.
1 Sam 11:1–15 Saul proves himself a great military leader and is made king at Gilgal.	*1 Sam 10:17–27* Lots cast for the choice of a king after Samuel tells people that they have rejected God.
	1 Sam 12:1–25 Samuel's farewell speech warning of the dangers of having a king like other nations.

The Story of Saul

Saul proves himself a valiant warrior and manages to rescue the
Israelites of Jabesh-gilead from the Ammonite army, and to win a
number of battles against the Philistines, but he never manages to
gain that final victory he needs to unite Israel. Meanwhile his own
moody, rash temperament and lack of organizational ability become
his undoing. He turns Samuel against him by his arrogance, he
almost executes his own son Jonathan because of a rash oath he took,
and he persecutes his own most promising young follower, David.
This proves to be a fatal mistake. David first appears as a young aide
of Saul's, his armor bearer and musician. David quickly reveals that

he has both a winning personality and great skill as a warrior. He kills the Philistine hero Goliath with a slingshot in a single combat. This makes David very popular with the people, and provokes Saul to rages of envy. As 1 Samuel 18:7 puts it: "Saul has slain his thousands, but David his tens of thousands!" Saul becomes the victim of black moods and violent rages, mostly directed against David.

The second half of the book, 1 Samuel 16–31, traces David's rise to power as Saul's fortunes decline. Samuel transfers his blessing and anointing from Saul to David; as a result, David is forced to flee. At the same time he begins to build his own power base in the desert areas of Judah, even serving as a mercenary army leader for the Philistine king of Gath. But he does protect the southern tribes from desert raids and from Philistine attacks while making his Philistine overlord think that he is completely loyal to him. Meanwhile Saul wastes his resources and energy searching for David while the Philistines regroup their forces. The end for Saul finally comes in a great battle on Mount Gilboa in the center of the country. Saul and Jonathan are both killed and the army routed. The era of Saul has ended and that of David has begun.

David's Rise to Power

The Book of 2 Samuel centers on the reign of David. It can be divided into two parts. Chapters 1–8 show how he managed to

OUTLINE OF THE BOOKS OF SAMUEL	
1 Sam 1–3	The childhood and prophetic call of Samuel
1 Sam 4–6	The story of the Ark of the Covenant in battle
1 Sam 7–12	Samuel and Israel's decision to have a king
1 Sam 13–31	The story of Saul's failure and David's rise to power
2 Sam 1–8	David's period of kingship over all Israel
2 Sam 9–20	The "Succession Narrative" of David's sons
2 Sam 21–24	Appendix of other David traditions

consolidate power in his own hands and to win a large empire for the newly united Israel. Chapters 9–20 record the downfall of many of his hopes as struggles in his own family weaken his reign. It is the story of how his sons fight to become his successor on the throne. Much of the tragic outcome develops from David's own sin.

The rise of David to power showed that he was both a military and a political genius. He defeated his Philistine masters and extended the borders of Israel across all the small states of Syria and Transjordan. He could really be said to rule from the "river of Egypt to the Euphrates" (Gen 15:18; Jos 1:4). Thus the dreams of Israel were fulfilled in David. But even greater than his military conquests was his gift of winning over others to his cause. He had won the loyalty of the south by showering them with benefits while nominally a servant of the Philistines, and was crowned king of Judah at Hebron shortly after Saul's death. He then patiently maneuvered and waited for the collapse of the badly run remnant of a state set up by Saul's surviving son, Ishbaal. 2 Samuel 3:1 expresses this period succinctly, "There followed a long war between the house of Saul and the house of David, in which David grew stronger and the house of Saul weaker." Finally, Ishbaal's general, Abner, turned traitor and joined David, Ishbaal was killed, and the northern tribes came to Hebron and offered to make David their king also. The fact that he became king by *mutual* agreement was very important in the centuries ahead since he took the throne not by right nor by conquest, but by the free consent of these tribes. Later they would withdraw from his kingdom and form an independent state.

David then accomplished a second brilliant move. He captured the Canaanite city of Jerusalem from a group called the Jebusites. It stood on the border between Judah and the northern tribes and yet was not part of either. David made it his capital, and from then on it was popularly called the city of David. He brought the ark of the covenant into the city to his palace grounds and placed it in a tent, perhaps the very tent that had been known during the desert wanderings in the time of Moses. An oracle by his prophet Nathan prevented him from constructing the magnificent temple he wished, but God did promise him an even greater blessing in 2 Samuel 7, a dynasty that would not end.

> I will give you offspring after you, and he shall come forth from your body and I will establish his kingdom. . . . I will not take my steadfast love from him as I took it from Saul

whom I defeated for you. Your house and your kingdom will stand before me always and your throne will be established forever (2 Sam 7:12, 15–16).

This special promise to David forms the high point of the Books of Samuel and was celebrated and remembered in the psalms and worship of Judah as the basis of God's special relationship with them. It was looked to as a sign of divine protection in many difficult periods during later centuries (see Is 37:33–35). As a further effort at reconciliation and healing for all segments, David took under his care the last son of Saul, Meribbaal, and the remaining sons of Eli, the priest of Shiloh who had cared for the ark.

The Dark Side of David

The picture of David, however, is not all rosy. Because of his successes, legends of greatness grew up around him, just as the *Iliad* and *Odyssey* report the great legends about Achilles and Odysseus in ancient Greece, and the French national epic of Roland and the Spanish national epic of the Cid tell of Charlemagne's leadership in the Dark Ages. Despite the high praises of the Bible, David may well have been a very scheming and calculating war lord who rose to power by less than fully honest means. Many scholars believe that he played off Saul against the Philistines, bought his loyalties in the south, created a personal army loyal to no cause but his own person, exploited the deaths of Saul and Jonathan to become king in place of the rightful heir, and perhaps could have arranged the death of Ishbaal with Abner. While most of this is only hinted at behind the current story, the text does show his bloodthirsty ambition at work when he murders Uriah to get his beautiful wife Bathsheba (2 Sam 11). The revolts by his own sons and the widespread support they received also suggests that many were unhappy with his despotic rule, especially among the northern tribes (2 Sam 15–18). His forced labor gangs (2 Sam 20) and establishment of a military draft after taking a census (2 Sam 24) became hated elements of the monarchy.

Much of this material is gathered in the second part of 2 Samuel in a single narrative story which many authors today call "The Court History of David" or "The Succession Narrative." It extends from 2 Samuel 9 through 1 Kings 2, with several appendices inserted at 2 Samuel 21–24. The anonymous author dramatically shows how David was able to conquer all external foes and heal the

PASSAGES IN THE BOOKS OF KINGS THAT PRAISE DAVID AS THE IDEAL OF FIDELITY TO YAHWEH

I Kings 3:3	We read that Solomon walked in the statutes of David his father.
I Kings 3:14	Tells us that David walked in the statutes and ordinances of Yahweh.
I Kings 5:3	(Hebr. 5:17) David was prevented by his wars from building the temple, but is its real spiritual founder.
I Kings 8:17ff	David intended to build the temple, and did well in so doing.
I Kings 9:4	David walked before Yahweh "with integrity of heart and uprightness."
I Kings 11:4	David's heart was wholly true to Yahweh.
I Kings 11:6	David followed Yahweh wholly.
I Kings 11:33	David walked in the ways of Yahweh, and did what was right in his sight.
I Kings 11:38	David walked in the ways of Yahweh, did what was right in his eyes and kept his statutes and commandments.
I Kings 14:8	David kept Yahweh's commandments and followed him with all his heart, doing only that which was right in his eyes.
I Kings 15:3	David's heart was wholly true to Yahweh.
I Kings 15:5	David did what was right in the eyes of Yahweh, and did not turn aside from anything that he commanded him all the days of his life, except in the matter of Uriah the Hittite.
I Kings 15:11	Asa did what was right in the eyes of Yahweh, as David his father had done.
II Kings 14:3	Amaziah did what was right in the eyes of Yahweh, yet not like David his father.
II Kings 16:2	Ahaz did not do what was right in the eyes of Yahweh, as his father David had done.
II Kings 18:3	Hezekiah did what was right in the eyes of Yahweh, just as David had done.
II Kings 21:7	Yahweh said to David (!) and to Solomon his son: "In this house and in Jerusalem, which I have chosen out of all the tribes of Israel, I will put my name for ever."
II Kings 22:2	Josiah walked in all the ways of David his father.

national wounds with the family of Saul, but could not keep peace in his own family. The story begins with a terrible sin by David, the murder of Uriah. When confronted by the prophet Nathan, David repents and does penance (2 Sam 12). God's judgment through the word of the prophet will not disappear, however: "Now the sword shall never depart from your house, because you have despised me in taking the wife of Uriah to be your wife. I will bring evil upon you *out of your own house"* (2 Sam 12:10–11). God will stand by David, but the seeds of his own evil cannot be so easily wiped out. His son Amnon rapes a half-sister Tamar, and in turn Tamar's brother Absalom slays Amnon. One son has killed another. Absalom is spared by David but lives to plot against his father later. When he too is slain, this time by David's loyal general Joab, David blames Joab who saved his life. He utters one of the most moving lines of the Old Testament: "Absalom my son! My son, my son Absalom. If only I had died instead of you, Absalom, my son, my son" (2 Sam 19:1). In his old age still another son, Adonijah, tries to take over David's throne. This time David is saved by the help of Nathan and Zadok the priest who rush Solomon to be crowned before Adonijah can seize power.

The Court History is a skillful piece of narrative, filled with dramatic tension as it unfolds the flaws and weaknesses in David while still showing God's constant protection for him and the dynasty which he had founded. David was not perfect, but God's fidelity and promise never wavered. It is one of the best pieces of ancient literature, probably being composed during the reign of Solomon between 960–930 B.C. It is the fruit of the new culture that David brought to Israel as he established schools in the prosperity of empire.

King David's Glory

David appears often in the psalms as a symbol of God's love for Israel. Psalm 89 is a song in praise of God's promise to David and his family. It goes so far as to claim:

> I will make him my first-born son,
>   the greatest king in the entire world.
> My steadfast love I will show him forever,
>   and my covenant will stand firm for him.
> I will establish his descendants forever (Ps 89:28–30).

Similar thoughts are expressed in Psalms 20, 21, 78, and 132. The special promise of a dynasty that would endure forever is also found in the so-called "messianic" Psalms 2 and 110:

> I will tell of the Lord's decree;
>   he said to me, "You are my son;
>   today I have begotten you" (Ps 2:7).

> The Lord said to my lord: "Sit at my right hand
>   while I make your enemies your footstool."
> The Lord sends from Zion your royal sceptre:
>   "Rule over the gathering of your enemies" (Ps 110:1–2).

How did David receive such high praise in the Old Testament tradition when he had so many dubious qualities about him? Key to the biblical portrait is David's blessing from Yahweh and his complete loyalty to Yahweh in return. He sinned, often seriously, but he never forsook this primary loyalty. As a great warrior, he brought

---

**PARALLELS BETWEEN DAVID AND JESUS
IN THE NEW TESTAMENT**

The story of Absalom's rebellion against his own father David is told in 2 Samuel 15–19. It is a touching story of David's suffering and his forgiveness of his son's actions. The New Testament tradition uses the elements of this story to describe the mission and suffering of Jesus:

John 18:1	Jesus passes over the Kidron Valley during his passion.	2 Sam 15:23
Luke 22:39	Jesus goes up the Mount of Olives weeping and praying.	2 Sam 15:30
Luke 23:35	Jesus bears curses from the people.	2 Sam 16:5–13
Matt 27:5	Jesus' betrayer hangs himself as does Ahitophel.	2 Sam 17:23
Rev 21	The Lord returns in glory to Jerusalem.	2 Sam 19:2–44

the rule of Yahweh to many surrounding nations. As a king he received a promise of divine protection that actually lasted four hundred years down to the final end of Judah and Jerusalem at the hands of the Babylonians in 586 B.C. He established Jerusalem and the central sanctuary of worship for Yahweh and became famous as a composer of psalms and prayers. Israel's memory of David is most influenced by these elements of divine help through which the nation was established soundly. The memory tends to forget or to downplay his weaknesses in the "The Succession Narrative," but it does remember that the primary meaning of both his successes and failures was not that David deserved the praise but God who used the weak king to accomplish his divine purpose. There are signs of this even in the way the Yahwist author tells the patriarchal stories in Genesis. The emphasis always falls on how Isaac was chosen over an older brother Ishmael, and Jacob over Esau, and Joseph over ten older brothers. It also stresses that the promises made to Noah and Abraham and Jacob will never be fulfilled until the land is an empire and its people as numerous as the stars—a reality that only fits the descriptions of the empire of David and his son Solomon.

Solomon and Israel's Age of Glory

The story of Solomon opens in 1 Kings 2:12, with clear hints of what is to come: "When Solomon was seated upon the throne of his father David, with his rule firmly established . . . " Above all, he was *decisive.* He put to death through one excuse or another almost all of the powerful or dangerous rivals from his father's time: Adonijah, his scheming brother; Joab the general who had made most of David's victories possible; the former rebel Shimei. He also exiled the Shiloh priest Abiathar back to his home. Next he cemented his relations with neighboring kings, entering into a treaty with Hiram of Tyre to the north, and taking a daughter of the pharaoh of Egypt to be his wife. He did more than make peace with Egypt, however. 1 Kings 4 tells how Solomon organized the new empire of Israel along the lines of administration used in Egypt. David had already set up several officials modeled on Egyptian offices (see 2 Sam 8:16–20; 20:23–26); Solomon added a prime minister, called, as in Egypt itself, the "one over the house."

This move was the beginning in a whole series of decisions to borrow practices and imitate the ways of foreign powers. Ultimately it led to a revolt within Israel against the introduction of pagan ways. Even the final judgment of the First Book of Kings was that Solomon had been the reason why Israel turned away from the faithful obedience to Yahweh that David his father had observed (1 Kgs 11).

Solomon however was remembered for two outstanding achievements: his *wisdom was legendary;* and he *built the temple* that became the focal point of Israel's religious life. Wisdom was the quality of kingship par excellence. From his first days as king, Solomon was accredited with special wisdom. God bestowed it on him as a gift after a dream in Gibeon (1 Kgs 3). He soon showed his ability to make wise decisions in the famous story of how he discovered the true mother of a baby by threatening to split it into two and give part to each claimant (1 Kgs 3). It is affirmed again when he is said to be the author of thousands of proverbs and songs, and to have knowledge of all plants and animals (1 Kgs 4).

Solomon was also a major builder. He constructed the wall around the city of Jerusalem, fortified the major centers of Megiddo, Gezer and Hazor as military bases for his chariot divisions, and created an enormous palace and temple complex north of the city of David on a hill called Zion. Here artisans and craftsmen from Tyre and Sidon worked for twenty years with forced labor gangs from throughout the kingdom. The stories of Solomon center on this impressive building project. 1 Kings 6 and 7 give detailed descriptions of the buildings and their furnishings, and the editors have included an elaborate and lengthy speech in chapter 8 at the dedication of the temple itself. In this speech, Solomon asks God to hear the prayers and accept the sacrifices offered in the temple, and echoes the warning message of Deuteronomy that God has fulfilled all his promises and now demands obedience to his law if prosperity is to continue (1 Kgs 8:56–61).

Solomon also developed extensive trade with foreign countries. He commissioned a fleet on the Red Sea to bring back the wealth of Arabia and East Africa. He also taxed and regulated the caravans going from Arabia northward, made commercial treaties with Hiram of Tyre to share in the sea trade of the Mediterranean, and, according to 1 Kings 10, traded in horses and chariots between Cilicia in Turkey and Egypt. Part of the splendor of Solomon's reign can be seen in 1 Kings 10, the story of the queen of Sheba who came all the way from Arabia to see the magnificence of his court and perhaps even to work out some favorable trade arrangements.

Above all, Solomon seemed to have escaped any major wars, enjoying a long period of peace throughout his reign.

Evaluating Solomon's Reign

If we had only chapters 3 to 10 of 1 Kings, Solomon would appear to be an ideal ruler, wise in every respect, lordly in style, pious in his devotion to Yahweh, a king who thought only of the protection of his kingdom, the honor of his God, and the welfare of his people. Even with several passages added in by the Deuteronomic editors that warn the king that prosperity would depend on obedience to God's laws and commands (1 Kings 3:14; 9:4–9), the overall picture is one of complete admiration for Solomon's kingship. This praise stems from the central place given to the building of the temple in the history of the Old Testament. Solomon was great because he established Yahweh's house, which was the center of the nation's worship, faith and hope in their God. Solomon's blessing was understood in the light of God's giving of the temple.

But in chapter 11 a different mood prevails. This chapter shows us another side of Solomon which the tradition condemned. It is also likely to be closer to the real truth about him than the ideal picture drawn in earlier chapters. He becomes a tyrant who outdoes even pagan kings in the luxury of his lifestyle with a thousand wives and concubines. In this, he violated the law of Moses about intermarrying with foreign peoples. But even worse, he built temples for all of their gods as they wished: to Chemosh, god of Moab, and to Moloch, god of Ammon, and to others. 1 Kings 11:5 even records that he performed rites for Astarte and Milcom. At the same time, he required vast amounts of supplies to feed and support the large bureaucracy he created, and these had to be obtained by taxing the citizens. Even worse in the eyes of most Israelites were the forced labor gangs he used to build his great projects. But the major friction created by Solomon's policies came when he transferred rights and privileges from the tribes to the person of the king. Where David had been careful to respect the tribes and their ideals, to win their agreement to him as king, and to avoid favoring one section against another, Solomon aggressively did the opposite. He laid down new boundaries for provinces which split tribes apart, and he seemed to favor the ways of Canaanites and other foreigners over Israel's traditions. He even encouraged religious practices that opposed the worship of Yahweh as the sole God in Israel. He probably was a sincere believer in Yahweh, but he adopted so many pagan practices of ritual and decoration for the temple that he neglected the simple and severe demands of Yahweh's faith that centered on the covenant and the people as a community.

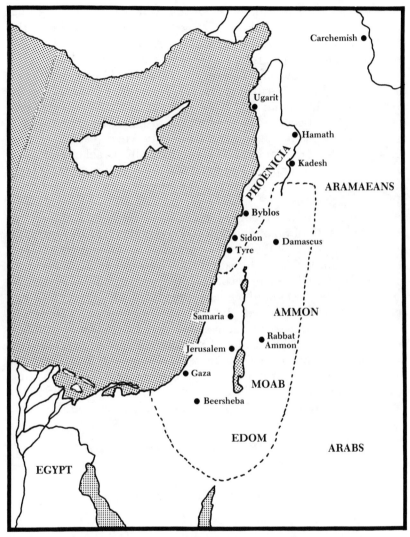

**The Empire of Israel under David and Solomon
(1000–930 B.C.)**

Near the end of his reign, troubles broke out everywhere. The Edomites rebelled and broke free, and the Syrians under a new king of Damascus also won their freedom. The Israelites themselves were fed up with the forced labor and a major revolt broke out under the former head of labor gangs, Jeroboam. What made this serious for Solomon was that it was incited by a prophet of the old tribal traditions, Ahijah, from the ancient cult center of Shiloh.

Solomon died at this moment, a king who had begun with great promise and brought Israel glory to an extent it had never seen before nor would again, but who died out of touch with his own people. He had become like the kings of other nations in every bad sense, just as Samuel had warned eighty years earlier (1 Sam 8:10–18)—a total master of their lives. Ironically, Israel had received what it asked for when it asked to be like other nations. But its faith, despite apparent triumph over other peoples and their gods, was now in real danger.

Solomon's life was recorded in a book of official acts of the king, called The Acts of Solomon (1 Kgs 11:43). Many of the incidents used by the authors of the Books of Kings were probably taken from this collection. It was customary all through the ancient world for kings to keep such yearly records so that events could be remembered and dates be figured out according to which year of the king's reign something happened. But the editors interpreted these raw events for us, emphasizing the blessing God gave Solomon and how success had turned his head and the allure of other gods and how other kings led him away from Yahweh's commands into a practical idolatry which was his downfall. By all human measures, Solomon was the most successful king Israel ever had, but by the Old Testament's judgment he was, if not the worst, at least among the worst.

B.   KINGSHIP IN THE ANCIENT WORLD

Kingship among Israel's Neighbors

Kingship in the Ancient Near East came in many different forms. Kings of the great nations, such as Assyria, Babylon, Egypt and the Hittite empire, often identified themselves with the great forces of nature, such as the storm god or the sun god. Kings of small nations who were subject to these great empires saw themselves as servants of a local god who specially cared for their little area. Also, many of these local kings came from a military elite who had taken control of the native population by force. Many Canaanite city kings were of this type. The gods they honored were not the same gods that the people worshiped, but were the personal gods of the king's family or original homeland. A third type of king arose from tribal or clan-oriented peoples. These could be elected or could inherit their throne, but they understood that the people's will had some part in the continuation of their kingship. Israel and a few of its bordering states, such as Moab, Edom and the Ammonites, were of this type.

Kings generally had full control over military defense, settled judicial appeals, and functioned as the chief priest in important festivals. They controlled the major economic decisions such as taxation and civic building projects. But nowhere was kingship a purely secular office. All carried out important religious duties as well. The king symbolized the presence of the god in the land and played out certain roles of the divinity for the people. In Egypt, the pharaoh was considered a divinity himself and acted as the absolute dispenser of life and law for all in the land, while in Mesopotamia and Canaan the king was understood to be only the deputy of the gods. And although Mesopotamian kings sometimes referred to themselves as a "god" in their inscriptions, they actually described the king as a servant of the god, maintainer of the divine order on behalf of the god, and the adopted son of the god. Many times kings used phrases of themselves such as "being held by the hand," or "chosen," or "suckled by the goddess," or being "born of the god." While they took on divine qualities, they remained human nevertheless.

The central role for kings in all nations was to preserve the divine order. Royal participation in the religious rites that determined divine blessings for the year was considered essential. The first in importance was the New Year's festival, when purification for all the wrongs of the past year, the suspension of the order of nature for a week as the old year changed to the new, and the re-enactment of the gods' battle for control of the universe would all take place. The reading of the creation myth formed the centerpiece of the feast. It included the battle of the chief warrior god against the sea monster of chaos, the creation of the earth and its seasons, the appointment of duties to each god, and the limiting of humans to the role of servants for the gods. This and other prayers were recited in dramatic form with many processions and rites involving the statues of the gods in order to ensure that the divine world was pleased and would bless the year ahead. In one crucial ceremony, the king was dethroned, humiliated and re-established on his throne in the god's favor for another year. In another, the king mated with a high priestess in order to imitate the divine fertilization of the crops, flocks and people. Thus by a kind of sympathetic magic, the fruitfulness and blessing of the land on all levels would be ensured for the coming year.

Kingship in Israel

Many of the testimonies of early Israel proclaim that Yahweh was king over Israel. It is clear in the poem of Exodus 15 (see esp. Ex 15:8) and in many psalms (such as Ps 18). This was already present in the first covenant which Israel understood as an agreement between God as the great king and Israel as a vassal people. Later psalms, such as Psalms 93, 95, 96, 97 and 98, make special mention of God as King. Possibly Israel itself celebrated a New Year's feast with a proclamation of Yahweh's kingship and an annual renewal of the covenant. It is also possible that New Year's day served as the coronation time of the human king. But there is no direct evidence for these possibilities in the Old Testament except from the parallels in other nations. The Feast of Booths or Tabernacles in the fall was a harvest festival that was interpreted as a memorial of the period Israel spent wandering in the desert. Near it in time was Rosh-Hashana, the actual New Year's day, but nowhere does the Bible say outright that it had any special ceremonies connected with it (see Lev 23:33–36; Num 29:12–38).

On the other hand, the psalms often mention details which might be part of such a celebration. For example, there are special hymns that praise Yahweh's kingship (Pss 47, 93, 95, 98, 99), mention the battle between Yahweh and chaos (Ps 74:13–14), make reference to the suffering and humiliation of the king before he resumes his throne (Pss 30:6–12; 89:38–45), and offer a description of a procession of the ark of God in victory to the temple (Pss 68, 15, 24, 132). Several psalms speak of the human king as God's son or as specially favored by Yahweh (Pss 2, 18, 20, 21, 89, 110, etc.). Because the king is God's elect, the psalmist prays that God will come to his aid.

Many of these attributes found in pagan literature about monarchs were used of Israel's kings in the heyday of national independence from 1000 to 586 B.C. These titles were taken directly from characteristics usually associated with the gods. Thus the person of the king was sacred and above violation; he embodied blessing for his land (see Pss 2, 110). He brought harmony to the state and so all must pray for his well-being (Pss 20:1–5; 72:15). He was an adopted son of God (Ps 2:7), protector of his people (Ps 89:18), gave fertility to the land (Ps 72:3, 16) and established justice for all (Ps 72:1–4).

The king also played a role in the cult. He offers sacrifice (1 Sam 13:10; 14:35; 2 Sam 6:13; 24:25; 1 Kgs 3:4; 8:62; 9:25; 12:32; 13:1; 2 Kgs 16:10–18). In some cases, his sons were made priests (2 Sam 8:18). The king also prayed for the nation at important moments: Solomon dedicated the temple with prayers (1 Kgs 8), and David prayed (2 Sam 6:18). Prophets and priests were considered royal officials subject to the king, as Nathan, Zadok, Gad and Abiathar had been under David. Kings also took the responsibility for reforms of the cult: Asa in 1 Kings 15:12–15, Hezekiah in 2 Kings 18:1–7, Josiah in 2 Kings 22:23.

2 Samuel 7 is the basis of all these promises of kingship to the house of David, but they are probably based on earlier ideas. The combination of a god giving an oracle of promise to a king's dynasty and the king's desire to build a temple is already found in the fifteenth century B.C. inscriptions of pharaohs Thutmose III and Amenhotep III, in which the king's conquest of his enemies is completed by building a victory temple. Similar union of victory and a house for the warrior god can be seen in the basic Canaanite Myth of Baal in the Ugaritic texts. This same pattern is echoed in Exodus 15 and Psalm 74. Even the very old creation epic pattern in Mesopotamia, represented by the *Enuma Elish,* concludes with the building of a temple for Marduk.

However, the royal ideology carefully subjected the king to Yahweh, and the kings never claimed divinity but rather saw themselves as special *deputies* of Yahweh who have his blessing (see esp. Pss 89 and 132).

None of this proves that Israel observed a New Year feast of kingship or considered the king to be sacred. The references found in the psalms may well have been said on any number of occasions of praise to God or of petition on behalf of the king. Especially the celebration of Yahweh as king over Israel is found in other biblical books. Isaiah 2, Micah 4 and Zephaniah 3:15–17 praise Yahweh's kingship; even late texts such as 1 Chronicles 17:14, 27:5, and 29:23, and 2 Chronicles 9:8 and 13:8 celebrate the kingship of Yahweh after the fall of the old state and death of the last human king.

STUDY QUESTIONS

1. Describe how Samuel represents a transition from a loose tribal league to a strong centralized state.
2. What is the significance of Saul?
3. Briefly describe David's rise to power. What were his major contributions? What were his shortcomings?
4. Describe the role of Solomon in the history of Israel. What were his significant and major achievements? What were his weaknesses?
5. "The flaws and character deficiencies of a patriarch or individual leader significantly affect Yahweh's relationship and fidelity to his people." Assess the validity of this statement.
6. What were the different forms of kingship in the ancient Near East? What characteristics are usually associated with kingship?
7. Describe how Israel understood kingship.

Chapter 13

DAILY LIFE
IN ANCIENT ISRAEL

Suggested Scripture Readings:

Genesis 24 (married love)
Proverbs 31 (wives)
Isaiah 38 (sickness)
Sirach 38 (sickness)
Qoheleth 12 (old age)

Changing Patterns of Life

The Israel that emerged from the period of the judges was a people settled mainly in small villages and dependent on farming or shepherding for a living. But the new kingdom established by David and Solomon added many large cities taken over from Canaanite control, and the great economic and political weight that they carried shifted the power balance toward urban centers and their interests. No doubt many pagans in the cities were converted to faith in Yahweh during David's reign, and these did not share the older tribal loyalties that had been at the center of Israel's national identity and her religious traditions. This difference between tribe and city led naturally to many tensions that caused trouble for centuries to come. The Israelites from the villages and rural lands maintained much of their older tribal loyalty to Yahweh as king above any earthly rulers, and resisted any moves by human kings to adopt pagan practices into their courts and into Israel's government structures. In the last years of the kingdom (about 600 B.C.), we can see an example of this tension at work in the role of the "people of the land." They were the major rural landholders or chief citizens of towns and villages. They opposed many policies of the Jerusalem kings, but were fiercely loyal to the house of David itself, rebelling against any attempted usurpers (2 Kgs 11). Even more traditional and extreme were the Rechabites, a group who opposed all city customs and tried to live as in the days of the desert wanderings, drinking no wine, refusing to cut their hair, and rejecting any permanent houses (Jer 35).

City Life

The ancient town was most often a community of one to three thousand people crowded inside walls on the top of a small hill near a stream or permanent spring. Some of these "hills" were really tells, the layered mounds built up by many generations of life on the same spot, created as each town was torn down and rebuilt several times over the centuries. As the mounds grew higher they also grew narrower at the top so that more and more houses were crammed side by side with little more than alleys twisting between them. There were few open spaces inside the walls since that would have been wasted area. Sometimes houses were even built directly into the walls to fit more people in. Such a house is described in the story of Rahab and the two spies (Jos 2). A typical house in the town had a stone base on which were built mudbrick walls and a flat roof, made of either mud or sticks and thatch. In hot weather it provided a cool place to sleep.

After the conquest of the land, a typical Israelite-style house began to appear in areas where they had settled. It had three or four rooms around a small courtyard, and may have stood two stories high. Probably only the wealthy could afford such luxury as a house with a courtyard, and everyone else lived crowded in smaller blocks.

The major public square was often located in a space just outside the main gate of the town in an area protected by an outer set of gates raised for defense. In this small plaza, the elders had seats to hear cases and make judgments (see Ru 4), and even marketing was done there, just as it frequently is today in Arab towns of the Near East. A few of the major cities, such as Megiddo, have revealed several other wide plazas, often in the courtyards of important buildings. Some evidence of drains to take sewage and street water away have also been found in larger towns, but generally towns were crowded, probably garbage-infested, and with few comforts by modern standards.

The Human Person in Israelite Thinking

Hebrew descriptions of the human person were very concrete. Most often, words such as "heart," "throat," "neck," "kidneys," "flesh," and "breath"were used for the psychological and spiritual aspects of the individual. Choosing parts of the body to describe our inner thoughts and feelings may sometimes seem strange to modern readers. For example, the Song of Songs describes the bride in vivid images:

> Your neck is like an ivory tower . . .
> Your nose is like the tower of Lebanon . . .
> The hair of your head is like royal purple . . . (Song 7:5–6).

But we must remember that the author is not thinking of the *shape* or *color* of the woman. A nose like a tower does *not* mean her nose is too long! The image involves the *function* or inner quality of the object, so that her nose has a tower's nobility and dignity, while her hair has the same beauty and importance as the rare and expensive purple dye used only for kings and nobles.

The same use of bodily parts for inner qualities is found in biblical passages that describe the person as living "flesh" or "spirit," or declare that someone's "heart" planned evil or "kidneys" rejoiced. Humans are made up of flesh (*basar*), spirit (*ruah*), heart (*leb*) and soul (*nepesh*). All of these words have many different meanings, and each passage must be treated separately to understand what the authors mean to say about a person. Psalm 56:4, for example, says "I hope in God without fear, for what can *flesh* do to me?" Here, clearly, the author means that no *mere mortal* person can harm him or her. When Jeremiah cries out in anguish, "My heart is beating wildly, I cannot keep quiet," he expresses his fear and sorrow over the people's sins by the literal action of his heart. But Proverbs 16:9 chooses a different sense of "heart": "A person's heart plans his way, but Yahweh guides his steps." Here the biblical sense of "heart" is the power to think and reason. To an ancient, the brain had no thinking role; it ran the senses of hearing and seeing and smelling. The heart did the thinking, and the kidneys gave the emotional feelings of joy, fear and sorrow. Some trace of this remains in the modern expression to "feel fear in the pit of our stomach."

The basic quality of human life is described by the word *nephesh*, usually translated as "soul." The word originally meant the "throat," and signified hunger or thirst, and then naturally was used for any desire or lust, and then for feelings and breathing (panting), then for life itself which depends on breath, and finally for the very idea of the person and one's inner spirit, the soul. Genesis 2:6 says:

> The Lord God formed the man from the dust of the earth and breathed into his nostrils the breath of life, and the man became a living soul (*nephesh*).

Here, the final word "soul" expressed all the qualities of life, desire, feeling, weakness and need for nourishment and help that the Hebrew knew was part of being a *nephesh*.

In the same way, a person can be described as a "spirit" (*ruah*), a word which sometimes means the wind, at other times, breath, or vitality and life-giving power, and, at still others, human will and determination, or its opposite, dejection and despair. It is the sum of all the inner power of the human spirit to act and carry through with its decisions. The psalmist can pray:

> Create a pure heart in me, O God,
>   and put a new and steadfast *spirit* within me.
> Cast me not out from before you,
>   and do not take from me your holy *spirit* (Ps 51:10–11).

Humans are weak flesh in need of God, but the spirit is God's own power to live the divine life God has given. Out of the experience of coping with the limits of our bodies and the powers of our inner desires and hopes came the Israelite view of a person as unified in flesh and spirit.

Sickness and Old Age

Since the ancient peoples knew so little about the causes of disease and death, their medicine and healing depended largely on the use of natural roots and plants that had proven useful in the past for certain symptoms. For wounds and external sores, they had many useful remedies, including the famed balm of Gilead that

Jeremiah mentions in his oracles (Jer 8:22). But for fevers and viral diseases, there was little that they could do since they did not even guess the causes. For these dangerous and often fatal illnesses, the ancient world either tried fantastic cures, using strange and exotic animal parts almost as though one could stop the strange disease by an even stranger medicine, or else they resorted to prayer, begging the gods for mercy and healing.

To the ancient mind such sicknesses as the plague or pneumonia or liver ailments came on without any external physical cause such as an animal bite or a wound. They were explained by accusing evil spirits of creating the illness, or even by suggesting that God himself sent it as a punishment (Ps 39:10–11). For most of these illnesses, one might get some help from a doctor, but the primary source of healing would be God. The psalms are filled with reference to the suffering of the individual who seeks God's healing (see Pss 32, 38, 88, 91 and the prayer of Hezekiah in Isaiah 38). Israel generally condemned any recourse to demons, but at times the Old Testament certainly suggests that people believed that evil spirits associated with human suffering did exist. Psalm 91 mentions "plague" and "pestilence" stalking victims, and Leviticus 16 describes Azalel as a desert demon to whom the high priest annually sends the sins of Israel on the feast of Yom Kippur. These, however, are rare mentions, and are always connected with a reference to the power of Yahweh to heal. Doctors are fine, but the ultimate power over life, sickness, and death lies in the hands of Yahweh.

The same is true of old age. Because of the hardships of life and the dangers of disease, life was short in the ancient world. The average lifespan of people during the time of Israel's kings was certainly not over forty-five years if we can judge from the ages of the kings listed in the Books of Kings. Although ages of seventy or eighty were not uncommon, they were certainly the exception. When Psalm 90:10 declares that the years of a lifetime are seventy or eighty years, it is speaking of the ideal blessing, for the rest of the psalm makes it evident that life is short and uncertain and in desperate need of God's mercy. When David fled from his son Absalom, the eighty year old Barzillai helped him with food, and David wanted to honor him back in Jerusalem, but the old man refused the honor, wishing only to die near his home (2 Sam 19:31–37). Famous men such as Abraham or Moses are said to have died at a great age—one hundred and seventy-five years old for Abraham and one hundred and twenty years old for Moses. These ages were not so much intended to be the actual age at death but a symbolic way of showing how God's blessing gave such faithful servants a long life. Abraham died "in a good old age, elderly and full of years" (Gen 25:8), while Moses died with his eye undimmed and his sexual vigor still strong (Dt 34:7).

Yet more often than not, old age was seen as a time of failing strength with loss of eyesight, inability to eat, and growing weakness. The Bible has several great poems and essays on the trials of old age: Psalm 71, Ecclesiastes 12 and Sirach 41. But despite their failing health, the elderly were respected for their wisdom. Proverbs 16:31 praises the gray hair of a man as "a crown of glory gained in an upright life," and Job 12:12 declares that "wisdom is with the elderly, and understanding comes with length of days."

Death and Afterlife

The most striking feature in Israel's thinking about the question of death was how *final* death was thought to be throughout most of the Old Testament period. There is very little evidence that Israel held out hope for an afterlife before a quite late time in the post-exilic age. This is all the more amazing when it is compared with the thinking of the pagan peoples around them. Almost all ancient nations had elaborate burial customs and rules for honoring relatives who had died, which included sacrifices and feasts in their honor. Egypt had a very developed belief in a blessed afterlife where the dead person would live on much as he or she had in life. The peoples of Mesopotamia and Syria had *at least some hope* of happiness for the great and the heroic in the next life, but mostly thought of death for the ordinary person as a rest for the spirit. The Sumerian and Babylonian myth of Gilgamesh records one incident in which the hero hears about the underworld from his dead friend Enkidu. The conditions for those who have died range from lying on mud and broken brick beds up to enjoying comfort and finally to feasting, depending on the state of the person at death.

Israel in contrast avoids all mention of a place of joy after death. The grave is a pit or swamp (Ps 40:3; Lam 3:43), and a person returns to the dust of the earth (Jb 10:9; 34:14; Sir 12:17). Death is destruction (Pss 16:10; 55:24; Jb 9:31) and has jaws wide open to swallow up a person (Ps 41:3; Hb 2:5; Is 5:14). Death is a place of emptiness where no memory of God exists and no praise is sung (Ps 6:6; Is 38:18). The place of the dead is usually named Sheol, which probably meant the place of ordeal. In general, it appears to be a place of stillness, darkness and total helplessness where the spirit of a person lies after the grave has taken the body. Both Isaiah 14 and Ezekiel 32 give elaborate descriptions of Sheol as a place where bodies lie row on row, with no power and no hope. Even the possibility of hope in God's power is denied them:

> ... like one forgotten among the dead,
> like the slain that lie in the grave,
> like those whom you remember no more (Ps 88:5).

In this idea of death, Israel was close to the descriptions found in the *Epic of Gilgamesh* and in the Greek idea of Hades as pictured in the *Odyssey* of Homer.

But behind the power of the grave and Sheol stands the even more powerful image of death itself. In the Canaanite thought of Ugarit, death was personified as a god that opposes the great Baal and even overcomes him for a while in the annual struggle between rain and drought (i.e., Baal versus death). In the same way, death was personified in Hebrew thought. Isaiah 28:15 says:

> We have made a covenant with death,
> and an agreement with Sheol.

Jeremiah 9:20–21 quotes the wailing of the people:

> Death has climbed up through our windows
> and entered into our palaces.
> He has cut off the children from the street,
> and the young men from the city squares.

Death grabs hold of a people and swallows them or imprisons them forever (see Hos 13:14; Is 5:14; Ps 89:49). But death is powerless before Yahweh. The psalms in particular praise God for rescuing the faithful from the grasp of death (Pss 88:10–12; 73:24–25; 49:15; Is 25:8). For this reason it is forbidden to offer any sacrifices to the dead or to consult the spirits of the dead as did the pagan peoples (Is 8:19–20; Dt 14:1–2; Lev 19:27–28; 1 Sam 28:4–6).

Death comes fully when the spirit of a person leaves the body, but in the ancient way of thinking the power of death has already grabbed hold of someone who suffers sickness or faces grave danger to life. Death has gained power over the individual and it is just a matter of time before the end will come. Many psalms talk about

the terrors of death when describing illness. Psalm 18:4 says that the
"cords of death encircled me." Psalm 116:3 not only repeats this
statement, but goes on to say: "But you have delivered my soul from
death, my eyes from tears and my feet from tripping" (Ps 116:8).
God the healer is praised again and again for delivering the life of
the psalmist from death.

But for whatever reason Israel had earlier resisted any hope of a
life of happiness after death—perhaps in reaction against the Egyptian overemphasis on the afterlife—its views began to change after
the exile. The prophets of the time, Jeremiah and Ezekiel, had
placed strong emphasis on the fate of the individual rather than of
the whole people. From the exile on, the good or evil life of each
person mattered before God and led naturally enough to the question of what happened to the good person who died without any
recognition or blessing in this life. From this came a renewed
interest in God's justice that would not forget the faithful in the next
life. This new understanding took shape in the Book of Daniel,
helped by the questions of persecution and martyrdom, and with
some outside influence from Persian and Greek ideas on the afterlife and immortality of the human spirit. In passages such as Psalms
16:10, 49:9, 73:26, Isaiah 26:19 and Daniel 12, a new hope for the
resurrection of all the dead to a new life of blessedness with God on
earth took shape. In the Old Testament it was a small beginning, but
it became much more central and important in later Judaism and in
Christianity.

Daily Work

The primary area in which a person expressed himself or herself was daily work. In the creation stories of Genesis 1 and 2, the
purpose of men and women is clearly said to be the domination of
the earth and its cultivation:

> God blessed them and said to them, "Be fruitful and multi-
> ply, fill the earth and control it, and rule over the fish of the
> sea, birds of the air and over every living thing that moves
> on the earth" (Gen 1:28).

More explicitly in Genesis 2 it states:

> And the Lord God took the man and put him in the garden
> of Eden to till the land and protect it (Gen 2:15).

But after the sin of Adam and Eve, the authors of Genesis express the *burden* of work for both men and women:

> To the woman he said, "I will magnify greatly your anguish in bearing children, and you will give birth to them in pain." ... And to the man he said, "Cursed is the ground because of you; in toil you shall eat of it all the days of your life" (Gen 3:16–17).

In this way, the Old Testament views human labor as both a source of *blessing* (the gift of dominating and caring for the earth) and of *curse* (the penalty of sin and disobedience renders the task difficult and painful).

From the viewpoint of Genesis 1 and 2, the major field of labor was raising food through farming or tending flocks (the models of this are Cain and Abel in Genesis 4). Such images of the agricultural world were often used to describe both God and Israel. God is the true shepherd who guards and guides his flocks:

> (Yahweh) will feed his flock like a shepherd,
>   he will gather the lambs in his arms.
> He will carry them in his bosom,
>   and gently guide those that are with young (Is 40:11).

The prophets Jeremiah and Ezekiel foresee a day when God will become a shepherd to restore Israel back to its proper land (Jer 23:3; Ez 34:11–22). But the kings are also to be good shepherds. Ezekiel says of a new king,

> My servant David shall be king over them, and they shall all have but one shepherd" (Ez 37:24).

To express the joy of faith in Yahweh, Psalm 126 borrows the images of the farm:

> May those who sow seed in tears
>   reap with shouts of joy (Ps 126:5).

One of the earliest inscriptions ever found in Palestine was a small calendar carved on a limestone tablet and which can be dated to the time of David. It lists the twelve months of the farming year, beginning in October:

Two months of harvesting
Two months of sowing
Two months for later planting
A month for gathering flax
A month for reaping barley
A month for harvesting and gathering
Two months for pruning the vines
A month for gathering summer fruit

Indeed, for those who are faithful and obedient to God, labor becomes a source of deep blessing and happiness:

You shall eat the fruit of your labor by hand,
    you shall be happy and all will go well for you.
Your wife will be like a fruitful vine in your house,
    your children like olive branches around your table (Ps 128:2–3).

This last psalm expresses the most common view of woman's work in Israel: caring for the home and raising (and educating)

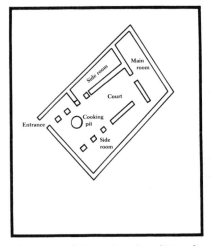

Floor plan of the unique Israelite style house of four rooms. It appears suddenly in Canaan after the time of the Conquest. It is approximately 30 × 50 feet.

The Gezer Calendar, giving the agricultural chores of each season (10th century).

children. Perhaps the most complete description of the honor a woman's work for the family gained is found in the long poem in praise of a wife in Proverbs 31.

Other occupations are mentioned in the Bible. The skilled labor of metalworkers and artisans is praised in the Book of Exodus in its description of the building of the tent of meeting and the ark of the covenant (Ex 25–31, 35–40). Scribes are praised highly by the Book of Sirach (Sir 38:24–39:11). The Book of Proverbs extols good workers and condemns the lazy or greedy (Prv 10:4; 13:4; 24:30–34). All human labor is a call from God to share in the responsibility of caring for the world. By itself work leads only to frustration, but under God it is a sharing in the blessing of creation.

The Family in Israel

Family life was patriarchal in structure. The father had a final power of decision under Mosaic law that was denied to a woman. Only men, for example, could divorce their wives, never a wife her husband. Yet the family maintained a strong clan loyalty for protection of all its members. Genesis 35 tells how Jacob's twelve sons came to the rescue of their sister Dinah when she was forcibly taken by the prince of Shechem. But such clan identity can also lead to woe, as when Achan's whole family, including children and grandchildren, were executed with him as punishment for his theft (Jos 6–7).

The Old Testament, however, also shows numerous instances of deep love between a husband and wife. Rebecca and Isaac are portrayed tenderly in Genesis 24, while Proverbs 31 preserves a beautiful hymn in honor of the ideal wife. The Song of Songs contains a series of love songs between a young man and woman which express deep emotion and care for one another. Chapter 8 of the Book of Tobit describes a loving marriage between two young Israelites. And the Book of Ruth relates a story of deep loyalty, love and sense of respect among in-laws. There was also a strong sense of duty to protect and care for widows, and custom demanded that the nearest male relative had to take the widow of a childless brother into his home and treat her as his own wife and raise children through her in the name of his brother. This custom was called a levirate marriage, and in the Book of Ruth, Boaz accepts Ruth as his own wife and takes her in to fulfill this obligation.

Children also had a place in the family, but the biblical emphasis falls on educating them to be responsible adults. The Book of Proverbs is filled with advice on the proper behavior expected from children and the importance of discipline in their upbringing:

> He who spares the rod hates his child,
>> but he who loves is diligent to discipline the child (Prv 13:24).

The Hebrew view did not see children as innocent and cute, but as headstrong and full of self-will. Parental training would root out foolishness and teach the right way of life and punish stubborn wills (Prv 22:6, 15; Sir 30:1–13). Listening and obedience headed the list of desirable qualities in a child.

Education for children took place in a number of different ways. For both boys and girls, the parents passed on the traditions of the nation and of covenant faith, and constantly explained the meaning of what God had done (Ex 12:14; Dt 6:4–7). Education also involved sharing in the religious celebrations and learning from them. This was very important in the feast of Passover where children played a major role, and also in pilgrimages and processions (see 1 Sam 2). Finally, for a lucky few boys, formal education was a possibility. At schools they would be taught how to read and write and learn to master the wisdom of the people.

But children did not just receive training and care; they were expected to do their share. Exodus 21:15 specifies the death penalty for children who do not reverence and obey their parents. To "honor" meant above all to care for their needs, especially in old age. So seriously did Israel take these duties that the law made a special exception for priests to touch the body of a dead relative even though it would defile him in doing so (Lev 21:2–3). These obligations extended to all members of the family. The basic unit of Israelite society was the extended family, so that "brothers and sisters" included cousins, uncles, aunts and other relatives.

The ideal family was a large family, which fulfilled the command of Genesis 1:28 to "be fertile and multiply and fill the earth."

> Your wife will be a fruitful vine in your home,
>> your children like olive branches around your table (Ps 128:3).

And although there are cases of a tender love for a daughter in the Bible (such as Jacob's love for Dinah in Genesis 35), sons were far more desired because they would add to the strength of the clan. A daughter, on the other hand, had to be given in marriage to a man from another clan and was thus lost to her parents' family.

Nevertheless, despite the legal limitations imposed on women in ancient society, there are few examples in the Bible where any woman is treated with disrespect or contempt. In many cases women rose to perform important social functions. The role of queen mother in the southern kingdom of Judah was a high office of the realm. Judith and Esther are whole books built around women who led Israel in moments of great danger. One of the oldest poems in the Bible tells the war exploits of the judge Deborah (Jgs 5). Many times, too, women acted as prophets giving advice to the state. This is told of Deborah in Judges 4 and of Miriam in Exodus 15, and of Huldah much later in the time of King Josiah of Judah (2 Kgs 22), as well as the wise woman from Tekoa who approached King David (2 Sam 14).

Sexual Attitudes

Sexual behavior was carefully regulated. The law codes take an especially strict line on any violation of the marriage vows by either husband or wife. Although prostitution was not condemned for the most part (indicating a double standard that was easier on men), any sexual relations of a couple before marriage carried with it the obligation to marry that person. See the laws on marriage and sexual practices in Leviticus 20:10–14 and Deuteronomy 22:13–30.

Other sexually-oriented acts were usually condemned very strongly. Homosexuality is outlawed by Leviticus 18:22, and two examples of it are part of the stories in Judges 19:22 and Genesis 19:4–5. In both of these cases, the people of a town make homosexual demands on a visiting stranger. Despite the attempts of some authors in recent years to put the Bible's condemnation solely against the abuse of hospitality to a guest, it seems clear that the passages also denounce the homosexual behavior as wrong. It is even more reprehensible when it involves abusing a guest under the protection of one's house. Indeed, both texts suggest that it is better to hand over your daughter to be raped than to allow a crime of such proportion to be done at all.

The Mosaic law also condemned many other sexual practices that were considered unnatural, such as bestiality (Lev 18:23), or males wearing the clothes of women (Dt 22:5). It also condemned acts considered shameful, such as nakedness and exposure of the sexual organs (Gen 9:21-23; 2 Sam 6:20). Health considerations made taboo any sexual relations with a woman in menstruation (Lev 18:19), and an ideal of single-minded dedication to God made sexual activity out of the question for a warrior engaged in a "holy war" (1 Sam 21:6; 2 Sam 11:11). Israel itself understood the sexual drive to be unruly as a result of the sin of Adam and Eve, and in need of the regulation of marriage. This becomes clear through the story of the Garden of Eden in Genesis 3, in which the pair immediately were ashamed of their nakedness as a result of disobeying God (Gen 3:10). In turn, God's punishment in throwing them out of the garden was tempered by his mercy when he helped them to begin a family as a couple shortly after (Gen 3:21; 4:1).

In marriage, however, love, if not already present between the couple because the match was arranged by the parents, was expected to grow and bring the two closer together. The prophets Hosea and Jeremiah especially show us the ideal of a loving marriage by comparing it to the love that God has for Israel.

Marriage Customs

Marriage, as pictured in Genesis 1 and 2, was ideally between a man and one wife. Since these passages were written about the time of King David in the year 1000 B.C. or so, it seems that this became standard practice at least from that time on. Certainly there are no cases of a man marrying more than one wife after that time except among kings. David himself took many wives, as did his son Solomon, and perhaps some others (2 Sam 11:27; 1 Kgs 11:3; 2 Chr 24:3). And Israel certainly remembered an earlier time when polygamy was common. The patriarchs Abraham and Jacob had more than one wife, and this was common throughout the Ancient Near East of the second millennium before Christ. However, even the ancient law codes preserved from the time of Hammurabi of Babylon (about 1700 B.C.) or the Assyrian laws (about 1100 B.C.) involve many restrictions on the treatment of multiple wives. The first wife was protected and had special rights, and second wives were generally taken *in order to bear children* if the first wife was unable to. The story of Abraham in Genesis 16 shows this side of ancient custom in practice. Only because Sarah is barren does she (not Abraham himself) arrange for a second and clearly subordinate servant girl to be given to Abraham for a wife.

The ideal was monogamy because of the covenant bonds, and if royalty did not always pay attention to this rule, it was because kings are kings, and often claim special privilege for reasons of political alliances. But the Book of Proverbs and other Wisdom books reflecting on the life of the family always envision a father, one mother and their children (Prv 5:15–19; Sir 26:1–4).

The marriage ceremonies themselves were a time of rejoicing. The parents had often arranged the marriage since children married young, perhaps at thirteen or fourteen, although the love and attraction of the couple can also be a reason for marriage (Gen 34:4; 1 Sam 18:26). A contract was drawn up and the husband was made to publicly declare his obligation to take this wife and care for her. He paid a sum of money to the parents of the bride as a token of his seriousness, and the bride brought a dowry to give to the husband to manage. But the dowry money remained hers in title as support in case her husband divorced her or died. The marriage day itself involved processions of the groom and his friends and the bringing of the bride to the groom's home—often accompanied by singing of love songs and playing of musical instruments. The poetry of the Song of Songs may be taken from these marriage songs, and Psalm 45 may actually give us a glimpse into a king's wedding party:

> The king's daughter in her chamber
>   is dressed with golden robes.
> In rich garments she is led to the king,
>   her bridesmaids are her escort.
> They bring her forward in joy
>   as they enter the palace of the king (Ps 45:13–15).

Friends and Enemies

Israel's basic bonds of loyalty are found in the family, so that the relations of brothers to one another gets much attention in the Bible. Deuteronomy 21 lays down several laws on the rights of brothers, but the basic rule is that all brothers must be treated equally by their father even if they have different mothers from among the father's wives. The responsibility of a person to his brother (and less so to a sister) is seen in the special obligation of a man to marry the wife of his brother who has died so that she can bear a child that will have the dead brother's name (Dt 25:5–10; Gen 38). The ideal of primary loyalty and love between brothers gave added meaning to the story of Cain and Abel where brotherly hatred leads to the first crime upon the earth (Gen 4) and to the dramatic story of Joseph and his brothers in Genesis 37–50, where God shows his power to turn even brotherly hate to forgiveness and good.

This aspect naturally led to the use of "brother" to describe a fellow Israelite, especially as a fellow member of Yahweh's covenant (Ex 2:11; 2 Sam 19:42). Deuteronomy constantly describes the covenant duties of one person to another in terms of concern for brothers (Dt 22:1–4; 24:7). The high point of such a beautiful insight is found in the command of Leviticus 19:17–18:

> Do not hate your brother in your heart. You shall try to reason with your neighbor lest you sin on his account. Do not take vengeance or hold to anger against your own people, but you are to love your neighbor as yourself. I am Yahweh.

If such a command must be obeyed toward all Israelites, how much greater will be the loyalty and love for one's own special friends! The Book of Proverbs is filled with advice on friendship, most of it warning not to abuse and destroy the good friendship of others. Proverbs 17:17 even goes so far as to suggest that "a friend loves all the time, but a brother is born for the time of hardship." There are many fine examples of friendship in the Old Testament, including the bonds between David and Jonathan, the son of Saul, who was as dear to David as "his own self" (1 Sam 18:1). Shaphan, a high official of King Josiah, and his sons were good friends to Jeremiah, and Joshua is regularly portrayed as the close friend of Moses as well as his disciple.

But a person can have enemies as well. Saul became a bitter foe of David and went so far as to try to kill him. In fact, his fear and hatred of David became so deep that Saul allowed the kingdom to fall apart while he pursued his mad chase after the young warrior. The entire sad story of how that hatred turned a life to disaster is told in 1 Samuel 13–31. The psalms, too, are rich with language of hatred against enemies, whether they be sickness and disease or real people. Psalm 109 is particularly strong:

> Wicked and lying mouths are open against me,
>   they attack me with words of hate . . .

May his days be few and another seize his goods,
   may his children wander homeless and have to beg,
   may they be driven out of the ruins they live in . . .
He loved to curse, let curses come upon him (Ps 109:2–3,
   8–10, 17).

But at times, too, the Old Testament rises to a very high level of concern for one's enemy. Proverbs 25:21–22 asks all Israelites to overcome their hatred and offer help to a hated foe:

If your enemy is hungry, give him food to eat,
   and if he is thirsty, give him water to drink.
For you will heap hot coals on his head
   and Yahweh will bless you.

The coals were used in ancient rites as a sign of repentance. Here the good deed of a person will lead his or her enemy to repentance and reconciliation.

Legal Justice in Early Israel

Despite the great interest in torah, or legal teaching, in the Old Testament, there is much less on how actual cases of law were handled. Most of the information comes from a number of individual cases here and there. The easiest way to organize what information we do have is to distinguish the legal practice in the time before King David from the practices during the period of the monarchy.

Before Israel had a central royal authority with all the organs of government to administer justice, crime and legal disputes were handled on either the family or the clan level. In the story of Abraham, Sarah brings an accusation against her maid and substitute-wife Hagar directly to the patriarch. Abraham decides the case on his own authority as head of the local family group by giving Sarah power to get rid of Hagar (Gen 16:5–6). The same kind of total power of judgment can be seen in the case of Judah and his daughter-in-law Tamar in Genesis 38. Perhaps, too, the custom of the blood-revenge in which a family avenged the murder of one of its members by killing someone from the family of the murderer developed out of the need for families to defend their own rights.

The right of blood-revenge was very old, and some biblical passages make a point that its use was still reserved to the family even after law courts were established (Num 35:19; Dt 19:12).

But in general the older family law gave way to a larger clan or tribal system from the time of the judges on. Just before the exile, the Book of Deuteronomy has several passages in which rights that a parent used to exercise are now decided by elders of the town (Dt 21:18–21; 24:16). The larger clan level usually exercised the power of judgment through such elders. The Book of Ruth describes the role of Boaz, her husband-to-be, as an elder of his town. In Ruth 4, he calls a legal assembly together in the gates of the city by stopping ten elders like himself and asking them to come and sit in judgment on the claims of Ruth. The chief means of reaching a decision was the testimony of the parties and their witnesses, as well as the presentation of any written contracts or deeds if such existed. Generally, the process relied more on the oral arguments, and written records were secondary. This may explain why the law codes that survive from the ancient world are not complete written collections but more like selections. Because legal judgments were based on custom and tradition, the written laws served only as models on which the elders would base new decisions.

Since the city gate was the only large space in town and was also used as the marketplace and public assembly, it was natural for a court to be convened on the spot from among the town's elders who were present (see Am 5:10; Dt 21:19). The elders were the male heads of family groups and they alone could serve. Women, children, and foreigners did not take part as judges, nor presumably as witnesses. Strangely enough, the elders who sat as judges might also play the role of defendant, accuser or even witness at the same time. Nobody took an oath that what he said was the truth, but occasionally the trial was settled when the accused person took an oath declaring his or her innocence.

Penalties in biblical law were generally less severe than in many of the neighboring countries. The death penalty was demanded for only a few cases (murder, blasphemy against God, adultery of a woman or man, dishonor of parents). Many times the penalty would be payment of money to the offended party or perhaps some flogging of the guilty person. If the death penalty was demanded, it usually was carried out by stoning, although burning to death is required for the particular crimes of incest and cultic prostitution in Leviticus 20:14 and 21:9.

Royal Justice

Even during the time of the judges, it seems that clan leaders or war commanders such as Gideon exercised the power of making legal judgments in disputes that could not be handled at lower levels. So, too, Samuel made his rounds from town to town conducting sacrifices and settling judgments (1 Sam 7:15–17). Possibly there were even formal men who served as official judges in some places. Exodus 18:13–26 holds that Moses set up such officials at the urging of his father-in-law Jethro. It is not surprising, then, that when kings began to rule, the ultimate power of judgment passed to them. Solomon sat in judgment on cases (1 Kgs 3:16–28), and young Absalom tried to take his father's throne from him by getting the people to come to him for justice rather than to David (2 Sam 15:1–6). In 2 Kings 6:26–30, King Jehoshaphat of Judah acts as the judge in the case of a woman who ate her own child. Finally, a late source, the Second Book of Chronicles, claimed that Jehoshaphat appointed judges in all the major towns of the country (2 Chr 19:5). All of this indicates that the kings took an active interest in the administration of justice in their lands, and that they themselves were often called on to make judgments in particular cases.

But this by no means suggests that the kings took over the local justice that had become established in the towns and villages through the elders from the earlier days. The kings are never said to have made laws for the nation, so it seems proper to conclude that the law was built on the age-old customs and judgments and that royal additions came only in cases that needed new solutions or had never occurred before. Once again, the Book of Deuteronomy gives evidence that Israel's religious leaders understood that the law came from God and was to be decided by judges on a local level where possible (Dt 16:18–20), and that difficult cases should not be taken to the king but to the priests who would pass judgment for God (Dt 17:8–12). Thus the power of the king was considered limited.

This ultimate authority of the law and justice was religious and based on the covenant rights of each individual in Israel. This explains why so often the laws are devoted to concern about injustice to widows, orphans and strangers—people with little protection from any clan or tribe, and who therefore must trust in God as their protector through the laws he has given.

Slavery

Unfortunately, Israel did not free itself from one very bad feature of ancient life: slavery. Nearly every nation in the Near East permitted slavery, and the best we can say about biblical teaching on the subject is that Israel limited its use and tried to keep slavery at a minimum. Leviticus 25:39–40 forbids Israelites to make any of their own people slaves, but goes on to permit owning foreigners as slaves. Other passages, however, such as Exodus 21:1–6 and Deuteronomy 15:2–5 clearly allow for an Israelite to sell himself into slavery to pay debts. These texts limit the period of slavery to seven years, but after that time a slave may choose to stay a slave for life (Dt 15:16–17).

Conditions of the slave in Israel are unknown. Perhaps it was not much more difficult a life than other people lived, especially the poor. But it was opposed to the very basis of the covenant—that God had given his blessing to all in Israel *equally* and that *all* must share in that blessing. The slave was property with no legal rights over his or her own person. If someone married while a slave, the children belonged to the owner of the slave and could not go free when the seven years were over. This in turn probably forced many families to remain slaves for life in order to keep their children. Even if the master killed a slave, the punishment for this murder was less that if the victim had been a free person (Ex 21:20–21). Female slaves taken in as second wives had no right to go free, but they were generally protected better than men by endless laws designed to guard the rights of their children (Ex 21:7–11; Dt 21:10–14).

The biblical narratives outside of the law codes almost never mention slaves, however, and so it is a reasonable guess that slavery was rare in Israel and usually found under only one of two conditions: (1) poverty that forced a person into slavery just to live, and (2) prisoners of war, made to work for the state. In the first case, the slave was an Israelite and usually treated with a certain amount of dignity (see Lev 25:39–43) during the temporary time that the slavery lasted. In the second case, Israel did not differ much from its neighboring countries and often forced these foreign slaves to do the hard work of the state, such as mining and rowing ships, for the rest of their lives. Both types of slavery gradually disappeared after the exile when Israel no longer had political independence and social conditions changed. However, some cases must still have occurred during Roman times since the Talmud sets further limits to how a slave must be treated.

STUDY QUESTIONS

1. How did changes in society, such as the emergence of cities, affect the life of Israel?
2. Describe the Hebrew understanding of the human person.
3. Briefly describe how a typical ancient Israelite would understand sickness, old age, death, afterlife, daily work, slavery.
4. What role did the family play in the life of Israel? What were the structure and relationships in family life? What were the obligations for different family members?
5. What were the Israelite's attitudes and understanding of sexuality and marriage?
6. Identify the following: Sheol, dowry, monogamy, Israelite understanding of friends and enemies, elders.
7. Describe legal and royal justice in Israel.

Chapter 14

ISRAELITE WORSHIP AND PRAYER

Suggested Scripture Readings:
1 Kings 5–8 (The Temple)
Psalms 1, 8, 18, 22, 23,
51, 91, 95, 104, 137, 145

A. THE DEVELOPMENT OF ISRAELITE WORSHIP

The cultic aspects of Israel's worship can be divided into four periods or stages. The first covers the early period associated with the patriarchs. A second describes the Yahweh faith established under Moses and carried down through the tribal period until the time of David. The third stage runs from the building of the temple under Solomon until its destruction and the people's exile in 586 B.C. Finally, a fourth covers the new forms and renewed cult and worship in the period after the exile.

From the Beginnings to David

The Book of Genesis describes Abraham stopping at the "oak of vision" in Shechem where God appeared to him (Gen 12:6). He later builds another shrine at the "oak of Mamre" near Hebron (Gen 13:18) and at Ai (Gen 12:8). Still later he plants a tamarisk tree near an altar in Beer-sheba (Gen 21:33). His son Isaac worships in the same place, and Jacob dedicates another memorial to Yahweh with a stone at Bethel to commemorate his vision of the ladder there (Gen 28:12–13). Joshua much later sets up memorial stones to Yahweh at Gilgal to commemorate the victory crossing of the Jordan River to conquer the promised land.

These shrines at sacred places where an ancestor had worshiped God or experienced special vision were often associated with trees or groves of trees. Special mountains also play an important role. Genesis 22 relates the story of Abraham's readiness to sacrifice Isaac on Mount Moriah, and of course the most important revelation of all, the covenant to Moses, comes on Mount Sinai. In general, the Canaanite world and the patriarchal stories share a common respect for sacred trees, springs or mountains as places in which the gods could be encountered. The settled peoples of Canaan mostly identified their gods with particular shrines—e.g., Baal had a home on Mount Saphon on the northern coast of Syria. Nomadic tribes, on the other hand, regularly worshiped their tribal gods at any place that was so imposing or strange that it seemed to be filled with a mysterious presence of the god. Israelite tradition remembers the patriarchs as referring to their God as the God "of the fathers," a name which suggests that their God Yahweh was more associated with the people of the clan than with any one place. They did not localize Yahweh at one shrine, but could honor any place that he chose to meet them.

The patriarchal stories also reveal many different names for God. The name Yahweh was revealed to Moses by God at the burning bush in Exodus 3 according to reliable tradition, and so the frequent use of the divine name earlier in Genesis is really out of place and reflects the thinking of people much later in time. Names such as El Shaddai (Gen 17), the Fear of Isaac (Gen 31:42), and the Bull of Jacob (Gen 49:24) were all associated with certain areas of the country and may originate in different tribal names for their individual gods. From time immemorial, people had worshiped the god of their clan under a certain name, often at a certain place. Interesting in this regard is the story in Genesis 14 in which Melchisedek, the king of "Salem" (Jerusalem?), invites Abraham to share in the offering of bread and wine to El Elyon, i.e., "God Most High," probably the local god of Jerusalem.

With the understanding brought by Moses and the covenant experience at Mount Sinai, worship took on a unified aspect in Israel. God was now called by a proper name, "Yahweh," which means "He who causes to be," or "He who is present to you," or the like (see Ex 3:13–15). There were ceremonies associated with the covenant that could be renewed, including the sprinkling with blood and renewal of pledges to Yahweh (see Ex 24 and Jos 24). The

Book of Exodus devotes considerable space to the construction of two important early shrines of worship: the tent shrine and the ark of the covenant.

The tent or desert sanctuary is described in detail in Exodus 25–28. The current picture, written by later hands, makes it sound like a small version of the temple of Solomon. It must have been a much simpler building that was portable enough to be moved. According to Numbers 11:24–30, this tent was a place of meeting where God spoke to the elders or to Moses and his spirit came down on them there. It was not a town meeting hall! But mention of this sanctuary disappears after the Pentateuch, and we can only guess that its role was gradually taken over in the time of the judges by a more solid structure. This stood perhaps first at Shechem and later at Shiloh, at least until the time of Samuel.

The ark of the covenant was a chest or box on poles that was carried in solemn moments of war in front of the marching Israelites, and, when at rest, was a place for the people to go to seek Yahweh's will. In the period before Mohammed, Arabian pagans would carry a shrine box of their tribal god on the back of a camel wherever they went. In wartime the box would accompany the soldiers to battle. The same functions seem to have been true for Israel's ark. Joshua has the ark carried to the battle of Jericho (Jos 4), and Eli lets the ark go to the battle of Ebenezer (1 Sam 4), only to be lost to the Philistines. According to later theology, it was a place for the ten commandments of the law, written on the two stone tablets, to be stored (Dt 10:1–5), but more often and more originally, the ark seems to have been understood as a throne on which Yahweh placed his glory. Though invisible himself, God would manifest his presence to the people by the power associated with the ark. Throughout the Ancient Near East, gods were often shown seated or standing on sacred animals such as a lion or a bull, or on a high mountain. These became the platform or special throne for the god. Many times, too, kings pictured themselves seated on special thrones built on cherubim, the winged bull-lion-man-eagle. Archaeologists found a very fine example belonging to King Ahiram of Phoenicia who lived about the time of Solomon. A cherubim throne was a sign of royal glory as the representative of the gods, and marked the king's share in their divine power. Israel shared in these ancient ideas, and it wasn't until the seventh century B.C. that Israelite theology had advanced far enough to carefully set aside the older explanation of how God was present in person over the animals. By then, Deuteronomy held rather that God dwelled in

Ahiram, king of Tyre, seated on his throne (c. 1000 B.C.)

Assyrian Cherubim: human-headed lion with wings (882–858 B.C.)

heaven above all the peoples of the earth and only his *name* was enthroned in the temple upon the ark. The ark was merely a box for the two tables of stone.

Some authors think that the tent and the ark were really descriptions of the same shrine. Thus the two major sources of the Pentateuch each remembered a different version. The Elohist from the north stressed the ark as a shrine, while the Yahwist in the south saved a tradition that Moses set up a tent especially for receiving oracles from God. Both would fulfill the same function. At some point, editors combined the two accounts together into our present text. However, it is just as possible that they really did exist at the same time but among different groups of tribes. David, as part of his genius, managed to combine the two into one—bringing the ark (northern tribes) from its resting place up to Jerusalem, and placing it in the remnants of the tent shrine (southern tribe of Judah).

The Temple of Solomon

Worship during the time of Israel's kings continued many earlier practices that had become popular with the people. The major shrines at Shechem, Bethel, Beer-sheba, and Gilgal continued to enjoy popularity among the people as places of pilgrimage. New ones gained prestige at Gibeon, favored by Solomon, and at Dan, where Jeroboam I, king of northern Israel, had set up a golden calf after Solomon's death to prevent the people from going to Jerusalem. The prophet Samuel at the dawn of this period is shown in 1

Samuel 7:15–17 traveling each year on regular rounds from Ramah to Bethel, Gilgal, and Mizpah and back to Ramah. At each place he presumably offered sacrifices and decided religious cases. At the same time, by far the most significant center of worship developed in Jerusalem itself under the influence of David and Solomon. David dreamed of, and Solomon built, a huge temple, the ark was given a place of honor at its center and the liturgy proclaimed the eternal promise of protection to the house of David prophesied by Nathan in 2 Samuel 7 as the cornerstone of God's covenant with Israel.

Solomon's arrangements for the construction of the temple are narrated in 1 Kings 5–8 and give a good idea of the cost and magnificence of the building. Solomon employed Phoenicians from Tyre and Sidon, the most famous architects and builders of the time, who constructed a typical Syrian style of temple with three parts: a porch, a holy place, and a holy of holies where the most sacred statue of the god would be kept. Pagan examples are known in the Near East in honor of other gods, so it was not the shape of Solomon's temple that was unique. The outer *porch* was rather narrow, not much more than a solemn entranceway. The *holy place* that followed was raised several steps, and served as the main chamber. It was forty-five feet long and contained constantly burning lampstands, a small altar of incense and a table for the showbreads, which were blessed, placed before the Lord, and changed each week. From the holy place, another set of steps led to a curtained and dark chamber without windows in which the ark of the covenant stood under two enormous statues of cherubim with their wings outspread. Since the first commandment forbade any statues of Yahweh, Israel believed that his "glory," the visible aura and numinous power of God, was present above the top of the ark and under the wingspread of the cherubim. No one went into the *holy of holies* except the high priest once a year on the feast of Yom Kippur (the day of atonement).

Outside the building proper, in the front courtyard, was a large bronze tub of water called "the sea" sitting on twelve large bronze oxen. It represented the powers of watery chaos ruled by Yahweh (Gen 1:2–3), and at the same time provided water for the services and ritual washings. Across from it stood a large altar of holocausts, reached by a series of steps, on which the animals of sacrifice were slaughtered. Directly in front of the temple porch, on each side of the door, were two tall pillars of bronze, each with a bowl at the top to hold fire or to burn incense. They were called Boaz and Jachin, names in Hebrew signifying the supports that upheld the whole

The Stevens reconstruction of the Solomonic Temple.

earth. For more details on the temple see the brief description in Exodus 40 and in Ezekiel 40–42. As buildings go today it would have seemed very modest in size, but by ancient standards it was a splendid building, richly paneled in costly wood and tapestries. Gold leaf was used freely around the walls and on the bronze objects.

While Solomon lived, his temple was the true center of worship for the whole country, but after his death, when north and south split into two, Jeroboam, the rebel king in the north, set up Bethel and Dan as countershrines to prevent his subjects from looking south to Judah for religious or political leadership.

Jeroboam's chief center was the ancient shrine city of Bethel not far from the northern capital of Samaria. It had an ancient tradition of special connection to Jacob, and even the stories of Abraham mention that he had worshiped there. During the period of the judges, the tribes kept the ark there, at least for a while (Jgs 20), and sought Yahweh's will at that shrine. Jeroboam named it a royal sanctuary, and the prophet Amos seems to have done his major prophesying at the shrine (Am 7:10–17). At the time of Elijah, in the ninth century B.C., Jezebel, the queen of Ahab and a Phoenician (Canaanite), erected a temple to her god Baal there to offset the worship of Yahweh. Thus through all this period, Bethel was a most important place of Yahweh's cult.

Interestingly enough, in light of the later condemnation of all such cult places outside of Jerusalem by Deuteronomy, the prophets who actually lived through the period such as Elijah, Amos, Hosea and Isaiah never condemn these shrines as false places of worship. The emphasis on true worship in Jerusalem comes only after the fall of the northern kingdom in 722 and the religious reforms of Hezekiah (and Josiah) in the period from 705 to 609. Instead the prophets condemn the people who turn from honoring Yahweh to worshiping Baal at the same shrine with pagan rites. The severe judgment made against the high places, groves of Asherah and the cult of the pillars comes from their association with pagan rites—not from the locations themselves.

Temple Worship

What form did worship take in Jerusalem's temple? Since Yahweh was invisible and permitted no images, there could be no question of imitating the pagan practices of offering food to the gods each day, changing their clothes, washing them, gathering the different divine images together in meetings, and forming long processions with the statues carried in an order of importance. In Israel, there is some evidence that the ark itself may have been carried in processions on solemn occasions (see Pss 89 and 132), but that cannot be absolutely proved. Music was certainly important, as well as various types of prayer services and blessings (see the lists of temple musicians in 1 Chronicles 25 and the discussion of the psalms below). But what stands out most are the regulations for the offering of sacrifice and the keeping of feast days in which the people participated in pilgrimages and processions.

Sacrifices were central. A sacrifice in Israel's thinking primarily rendered our service back to God. In the case of animal sacrifice, humans returned as a gift the life that God gave as a gift. Thus the death of the animal itself was not as important as the sprinkling of its life-carrying blood on the altar and the taking of the animal out of everyday service to give it back to God alone. The occasion was normally a time of joy signaling praise, reverence and thanksgiving to God. But sacrifices could also be offered as petitions or as sin offerings for guilt. Even if the occasion was the hope of forgiveness or relief from disease or other calamity, the note of trust and hope always played a major role in the spirit of the offering.

Sacrifices were well known throughout the ancient world, but

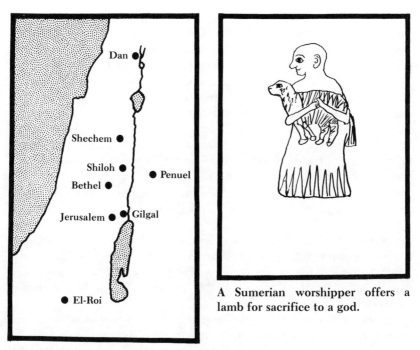

A Sumerian worshipper offers a lamb for sacrifice to a god.

Cult Places

in Israel, unlike in some Canaanite cults, the sacrifice was never considered a magical ritual that brought God to act in a certain way. The spirit of adoration and silence and the obedience of the people before Yahweh always stand out. And when the prophets do condemn abuses of sacrifice, they almost always attack that slipping over into a conviction that God must accept this gift and then do what is requested. Israel had several types of sacrifice, listed very carefully in Leviticus 1–7. This may be a list reflecting the fully developed temple rites despite its inclusion in the Pentateuch. The major types of sacrifice in Leviticus are:

Holocausts (Lev 1). An offering of an animal which is totally burned up on the altar after the priest has laid his hands on its head and its blood has been sprinkled on the altar. It serves both for the daily sacrifice of praise to the Lord on behalf of the community, and also for atonement if offered by an individual.

Grain Offerings (Lev 2). The offerer may also present cakes baked with unleavened flour together with a small portion of oil and incense. The priests present the entire offering on the altar, but

only burn a small portion of it together with the oil and incense. The
rest goes to feed the priest and his family.

Peace Offerings (Lev 3). This is an animal offered up by individuals for thanksgiving to God or to fulfill a vow that they made.
However, it is not totally consumed in fire. It is offered up and its
blood put on the altar, but only a few inner organs and the best fatty
parts are actually burned completely. The rest is shared as a meal
among the offerer and his family or guests.

Sin Offerings (Lev 4). For anyone who has become unclean by
touching a dead body or through disease or other causes listed in the
law, or who has done something forbidden by the law, or who has
rashly sworn an oath before realizing it, atonement can be made by
means of an animal offered to God. In this case, only the fat is
burned and the blood sprinkled on the altar. The rest is burned up
outside the temple area. If the offender is the whole community or
a priest, a bull is required; if an individual, it can be a female sheep
or goat. If someone is too poor to afford these animals, two doves
can be substituted or even a small amount of flour baked into a
cake.

Guilt Offerings (Lev 5). For more serious offenses, or if the
wrong actions have led to injustice or cheating someone out of
money, a further sacrifice was demanded to do penance for the
guilt of the offender. This sacrifice was to be a male ram brought to
the priest and was probably treated exactly like the sin offering.
Naturally, the sinner also had to restore whatever he stole or cheat-
ed another out of.

Sacrifices were an important part of the rites used to express
Israel's dependence on Yahweh. Every day there was a special
morning and evening sacrifice offered to the praise of God, and on
big feast days the number of animals sacrificed was increased significantly. The idea of offering animals as sacrifice is a custom much
older than the biblical period, and was well known among Israel's
Semitic neighbors in Babylon and Ugarit. The Bible itself remembers early sacrifices among the patriarchs (see Gen 4:1–6; 8:20–22;
15:9–12; 22:2–3; Ex 24:4–8; Num 23:1–6), and knew of the practice
in the period of the judges (Jgs 6:18–21; 1 Sam 13:2–14). Israel
maintained it faithfully while the temple stood, both before the
exile and then again after it was rebuilt in 516 B.C. The practice did
not stop until the Romans destroyed Jerusalem and the temple in 70
A.D. and forbade Jewish worship at the site. Today, Jews as well as
Christians worship without animal sacrifice, but with a strong belief
in the need for daily sacrifice of praise to God.

Feast Days

Feast days and special festivals were also an important part of Israel's religious life. Over the centuries there were probably quite a few of them that were celebrated for a time and have now long since been lost or forgotten. In many cases, too, private individuals may have made special trips to the temple in Jerusalem or to other shrines to celebrate anniversaries, births and other occasions of thanksgiving, as well as to plead for divine help in times of personal sickness or tragedy. An example of this kind of prayer is seen in the story of the prophet Samuel's parents, Hannah and Elkanah, who made an annual pilgrimage to the shrine of Shiloh to pray (1 Samuel 1–2).

The Bible regulates a certain number of feasts that must be observed each year. They were instituted at various times, and some have very ancient roots in pagan festivals that already existed before the Israelites came into the land. Israel turned them into days in honor of Yahweh rather than of the pagan gods. The most important of these ancient feasts, all of them originally celebrations of the harvest seasons of the year, are the feasts of Passover in the spring, Pentecost in the summer, and Booths in the fall. These are called "pilgrimage feasts," because the law (Ex 34:23; Dt 16:17) demanded that every Israelite male go to Jerusalem for their observance. This regulation is quite late and certainly did not apply completely in the period when there were two kingdoms each with its own shrines; nor did it seem to be in practice before the temple of Jerusalem was built, for Samuel goes to many shrines each year (1 Sam 7:15–17). But it became a very deep-rooted part of Israelite piety to want to go to the major shrines of Yahweh, especially Jerusalem (see the touching tragedy of a pilgrimage in Jer 41:5–8). For the time of Jesus, the New Testament records the cities filled for the festivals (Jn 11:55; Acts 2:5–11). Eventually, the later Old Testament period saw the rise of the sabbath observance as central to Israel's worship, and to this day it has remained the key factor in both Judaism's practice (sabbath = Saturday), and in Christianity's (Sunday = Christian sabbath = The Lord's Day of Resurrection).

The major feasts were:

Passover. This fell in the spring and is closely connected with an older feast of unleavened bread which was an agricultural feast celebrating the harvest of the spring barley and the making of new flour. Any of the yeast used for last year's bread had to be thrown out and new yeast developed. Israel used this occasion to celebrate the deliverance from Egypt. Details of the passover supper liturgy are included in the story of the exodus (Ex 12). The festival period lasted eight days.

Pentecost or *Weeks*. This fell fifty days after the Passover celebration and marked the early wheat harvest with a one-day feast that honored the covenant-giving at Mount Sinai. Numbers 28:26 calls it the feast of first fruits from the command to bring the best of the first harvest to God as an offering (see Dt 16:9–12; 26:1–19).

Booths or *Tabernacles*. The fall feast cycle of eight days marked the fruit, olive, wine and late grain harvest. It fell in late September or early October just before the autumn rains began to fall which would make possible the planting of seed for another year. The "booths" or "tabernacles" recalled the period of wandering in the wilderness, and it was a time of rejoicing and thanksgiving for Israel's blessing of the land. This feast was closely associated with two other feasts in the same month:

Rosh Hashana (New Year's). This marked the beginning of the year, and stressed the need for God to forgive and restore Israel from any sins or faults for the year ahead. This was followed ten days later by the solemn *day of atonement,* or

Yom Kippur. The high priest did formal penance for the people's sins and then laid them on a scapegoat which was driven out into the desert to die. Probably the Israelites believed that evil spirits lived in that wilderness and that the goat brought the evil and sin they had caused back upon them.

New Moon. A special commemoration was to be made on the first day of each month in honor of Yahweh. This is mentioned often in the Old Testament but we know little about it (see Num 28:11–15; Sir 43:6–8).

Sabbath. The custom of celebrating the seventh day of the week as special may go back long before Israel. But only in Israel do we find such stress on the sacred rest that must mark the sabbath. It is mentioned in the story of creation (Gen 1), in the giving of the manna in the desert (Ex 16) and in all the law codes (Ex 23 and 34; Lev 23; Num 28; Dt 5). In later Israel it was the sign of Jewish observance par excellence.

Purim. This is a feast established after the exile. It commemorates the day of deliverance that God gave to the Jews in Persia under Queen Esther. It takes place on the fourteenth day of the last month of the year. The only biblical mention of this popular feast is in Esther 9.

Hanukkah. In 165 B.C. Judas Maccabeus rededicated the temple in Jerusalem that had been desecrated with pagan idols by the Greek kings of Syria (1 Mc 4:52–59). This "dedication" (Hanukkah) was celebrated by lighting the lampstands in the temple, and to this day is a "Feast of Lights" in the same month as the Christian celebration of Christmas—a time of Jewish rejoicing.

The Priests and Levites

From earliest times there is evidence of a special class of priests who performed sacrifices, sought the will of God and guarded shrines, even though often enough the father of a clan or family often offered some sacrifices for his own group. The story of a levite who was hired by a certain Micah to be his private priest is told in Judges 17. Later the whole tribe of Dan takes on this same levite's services for their benefit. Samuel the prophet also offers sacrifices regularly, as did many of the kings of Israel, from Saul in 1 Samuel 13 to David in 2 Samuel 6:13, Solomon in 1 Kings 8:62–64, Jeroboam I in 1 Kings 12 and Ahaz in 2 Kings 16. When Samuel condemned Saul for offering the sacrifice, we cannot assume the reason was because Saul was not a priest; rather it was because he disobeyed the prophetic word of God through Samuel.

According to the standard biblical view presented in Exodus 28–29 and Leviticus 8–10, the high priest was to be a descendant of Aaron, as were all the priests, and they must be specially consecrated. Others from the tribe of Levi may assist in the care of the temple and its worship, but may not be priests (see also Num 18). The little story of how Korah rebelled against Aaron's role in Numbers 16 and was killed by divine anger was intended as a lesson to warn levites and others from trying to usurp priestly roles. This clear distinction certainly was the situation that prevailed after the exile of 586 to 539 B.C., but does not seem to have been so widely practiced in earlier times.

The Book of Deuteronomy, written in the seventh century B.C., does not distinguish between priests and levites, and calls them all levitical priests. Samuel was not himself a levite nor a descendant of Aaron, and Jeroboam, the first king in the north after Solomon's death, plainly set up non-levitical priests to serve his sanctuaries at Bethel and Dan. Under David, Zadok served as high priest, and it is not at all clear that he was of Aaron's family. This lets us know that the actual history of the priesthood is murky and leaves many problems yet to be solved. But from the time of the exile on, the structures become much more formal. Ezekiel, writing in exile, distinguishes between *priests* from the family of Aaron and the *levites,* who may assist but not do priestly tasks. He goes further and insists that the high priest must be of the family of Zadok himself. This same position is taken by the post-exilic writings of Ezra, Nehemiah and the Books of Chronicles.

Kings had certainly offered sacrifice while they held power. But in the same post-exilic view, this had been wrong, and the priestly office had been violated by the practice. Several stories imply this, and one passage in 2 Chronicles 26:16–20 claims that King Uzziah (about 760 B.C.) was struck with leprosy for offering an incense sacrifice in the temple. However, kings were considered sacred figures everywhere in the Ancient Near East, and regularly represented their people before God. Psalm 110 and Genesis 14 make a special mention of the ancient priest-king of Jerusalem, Melchisedek, and his sacrifice—suggesting that he was a model for the practice of the later kings of Jerusalem.

A major question today is whether the prophets were really part of the cultic staffs at shrines and even at the Jerusalem temple. In many other ancient nations we know that some of the temple priests were in charge of seeking the divine will by omens or divination or oracles in dreams and trances. Possibly the same is true in Israel. As we shall see in the chapter on prophecy below, there is some reason to believe it indeed was so.

In the period after the exile, many changes took place. Because the Babylonians had destroyed the temple and removed Israel's kingship for good, the exiles had to develop new ways of practicing their faith. They rebuilt the temple after their return and worshiped in it, but also laid greater stress on the study of their tradition particularly as it was written down officially. The fixing of the Pentateuch and its being made the "Book of the Law" of the Lord must have taken place under Ezra the scribe about 450 B.C. From then on the sacrifices took second place to the study of the law. This in turn gave rise to *synagogues* for local study and prayer, and the rise of special students and teachers of the law, who were not priests, but preferred to be called "rabbi," *master.* The priests who were members in these local synagogues could ask the blessing on the congregation but did not necessarily have the authority to teach. Among the people outside of Jerusalem, especially, the rabbis became far more important than the priests. At the same time, observance of the sabbath became the major practice, for it was a feast that could be observed at home by all, and it also allowed time for going to the synagogue to pray and study.

B. THE PSALMS AND ISRAEL'S PRAYER

The Piety of Israel

Stories in the Old Testament gave several examples of pious Israelites. Hannah, the mother of Samuel (1 Samuel 1), the widow of Sarepta in the days of Elijah (1 Kings 17), King David (2 Samuel 7–12), King Hezekiah (2 Kings 18–20; 2 Chronicles 30–31), and King Josiah (2 Kings 22–23) all reveal a religion of trust and confidence in God's care for the individual in need. This piety is seen also in the famous passages of the prophet Jeremiah which are called his "confessions" (Jeremiah 11:18–12:6; 15:10–21; 20:7–18). After the exile, several books were written to show the perfectly pious Israelite at work: Tobit, Esther, and Judith. They combine pain, trust, action and generosity at one time. But above all, the ideal of an Israelite can be seen in the beautiful prayers of the Book of Psalms which offer numerous descriptions of the just person at prayer.

The Nature of the Book of Psalms

The psalms are one hundred and fifty prayer-poems collected in a single book called the Psalter. All were probably intended to be sung or accompanied by music. But not all are alike. Many are brimming with joy and praise of God's goodness; others are filled with sorrow and lament and a spirit of contrition. Some are aimed at sickness or bad fortune in life; some were used on weddings or other special occasions. But by having them all, we are able to see a depth and width of Israel's attitude toward Yahweh not present in any other book of the Bible. In Hebrew, the Book of Psalms is called *tehillim*, that is, "Praises." The name captures the meaning of these songs better than any other word. Even in psalms of deep sorrow and distress, the note of confidence and trust in God's goodness always comes through.

As they stand today, the one hundred and fifty psalms do not seem to have any special subject order or theme development from one end to the other. It seems rather that the present book is made up from many smaller collections. For one thing, most psalms have a label at the beginning, which says "of David," "of Asaph," "of Korah," or of others. These labels do not necessarily mean that the psalm was written *by* the man, but that it came from the collection under his name—in some cases, collected by him, or written by him, or just related to the office he held. Thus many David psalms probably mean "from the royal collection," while Asaph psalms mean "of the temple collection."

For another thing, the psalms seemed to be grouped in small collections. We have eight psalms of Korah together in Psalms 42–49, and eleven by Asaph in Psalms 73–83. Psalms 120–135 make up a group called the "songs of ascent," perhaps used in processions or pilgrimages. Psalms 113–118 and 146–150 make up two "Alleluia" collections. These collections in turn have been organized at some point into five "books" of psalms so that the Psalter will match the Pentateuch in shape. Thus we have the following five-part order in the present book:

Book 1,   Psalms 1–41, an early collection of Davidic hymns.
Book 2,   Psalms 42–72, a northern collection of hymns.
Book 3,   Psalms 73–89, a collection from the temple singers.
Book 4,   Psalms 90–106, psalms from a royal collection, perhaps for New Year's.
Book 5,   Psalms 107–150, a second and expanded Davidic royal collection.

Each of these divisions is marked by a special prayer and blessing of praise that serves as the last verse. All are similar to the one in Psalm 41:14: "Blessed be the Lord the God of Israel for all eternity and forever. Amen, amen."

Another piece of evidence for originally smaller collections is seen in how some of the psalms from one "book" repeat psalms from another book. Thus Psalm 14 matches Psalm 53, and Psalm 40:12–18 matches Psalm 70. The difference between the earlier and the later versions of each is the use of the name of God. Those in book 1 (Pss 1–41) all use Yahweh, while those in book 2 (42–72) use Elohim, the word for God. This is exactly the difference between the Yahwist and Elohist authors of the Pentateuch, and reflects a southern versus a northern kingdom outlook. The same psalms appeared in both kingdoms' collections when the two were combined into the present book, so that both examples were kept.

The Variety and Richness of the Psalms

To appreciate the beauty of the psalms, we must begin to read them for two things: the beauty of their language and images, and the unique thought and individuality of each. Since to read them all the way through at one sitting would be to get a bad case of mushy message, it is important to examine each psalm on its own merits. For this reason, scholars place a great deal of emphasis on the work of form criticism so that we can identify each psalm according to its special type. There are six major types recognized by most experts: (1) hymns of praise, (2) thanksgiving hymns, (3) individual laments, (4) community laments, (5) royal psalms honoring either Yahweh as king or the earthly king as his deputy, and (6) wisdom psalms.

Other smaller types can be seen and identified also. Psalm 45 is a wedding song; Psalms 15 and 24 are processional psalms for entering the temple; Psalms 93 and 95–99 are for a festival of Yahweh's kingship; Psalms 78, 105 and 106 recite the great historical deeds of salvation. By knowing the proper type of psalm, the reader gains a better focus for what the psalmist was trying to say and how the complete poem expresses that message.

Besides identifying a general category of psalm type for each psalm, it is important to understand its internal structure. Consider the example of a psalm of individual lament. Most of these psalms have a similar structure made up of the following elements:

(a) *an address to God:* "Hear me, O God," often followed by praises.
(b) *the lament itself:* the psalmist brings his complaint to God.
(c) *confession of trust* in God and petition for relief.
(d) *exclamation of certainty* that the psalmist's prayer has been or will be heard by God.
(e) *the vow of praise:* the psalmist promises to declare God's praises to the community or to continue to praise him forever.

Other types of psalms have slightly different structures, but each different type follows its own special structure fairly closely. By paying attention to the differences as well as the common points, we learn a great deal about a psalm. For example, many people have wondered at the great emotional range in Psalm 22, in which

---

SOME PSALM CATEGORIES
ACCORDING TO LITERARY GENRE

Hymns of Praise:	Pss 8, 19, 33, 66, 100, 103, 104, 111, 113, 114, 117, 145–150.
Thanksgiving Hymns:	Pss 18, 30, 32, 34, 40, 65, 66, 67, 75, 92, 107, 116, 118, 124, 136, 138.
Individual Laments:	Pss 3, 4, 5, 6, 7, 9–10, 13, 14, 17, 22, 25, 26, 27, 28, 31, 35, 38, 39, 40, 41, 42–43, 51, 52, 53, 54, 55, 56, 57, 59, 61, 64, 69, 70, 71, 77, 86, 88, 89, 102, 109, 120, 130, 139, 141, 142, 143.
Community Laments:	Pss 12, 44, 58, 60, 74, 79, 80, 83, 85, 90, 94, 123, 126, 129, 137.
Liturgical Psalms:	Pss 15, 24, 50, 68, 81, 82, 115, 134.
Wisdom Psalms:	Pss 1, 19, 36, 37, 49, 73, 78, 112, 119, 127, 128.
Trust Songs:	Pss 11, 16, 23, 27, 62, 63, 91, 121, 125, 131.
Royal Psalms of the King:	Pss 2, 18, 20, 21, 45, 72, 78, 89, 101, 110, 132, 144.
Zion Hymns:	Pss 46, 48, 76, 84, 87, 122.
Royal Psalms of Yahweh as King:	Pss 29, 47, 93, 95–99.

---

the psalmist goes from the depth of despair to passages of absolute praise that God actually saved his life. If we recognize the lament structure in this psalm, we can see that the first twenty-two verses mix the psalmist's complaint with words of trust, while the last ten verses declare his absolute certainty that God has heard his prayer. The break between verses 22 and 23 is very sharp as a result, and many scholars have suggested that we should suppose that a priestly blessing was given over the worshiper at this moment in some temple service of healing. The praying psalmist receives the blessing and is moved to declare his confidence in God's healing, saving power.

The Liturgical Origins of the Psalms

This brings us to the burning issue in the modern study of the psalms as to whether they were primarily private prayer or instead public prayers of the temple. Of course, the temple had something to do with saving them, otherwise many would have been lost over the years as people came and went. But beyond this service as a library, there is good reason to believe that many, if not most, of the psalms originated in actual liturgical services. We know from later Jewish traditions, for example, that the levites recited the "Hallel psalms" (Pss 113–118) as the lambs were slaughtered on the feast of Passover. Indeed, themes of the exodus dominate many of these particular psalms (see Pss 115 and 116). Were they composed originally for use in such a festival? Or did they only later get adopted? A similar use at Passover could account for Psalm 136 with its narration of the great saving deeds of Yahweh. At the same time, the fall feasts of Rosh Hashana (New Year's) and of Booths may well have been specially dedicated to celebrating the kingship of Yahweh and his creation of the world, as well as the coronation and power of his delegates, the earthly king. Many psalms would ideally suit such a feast: Pss 95–99 on Yahweh's kingship, or Pss 47 and 29 on God's rule over creation, or Pss 2 and 110 on the king's royal powers. This fall feast or one like it may also have been a celebration of renewing the covenant God made with King David (2 Sam 7). Psalms 89 and 132 would fit perfectly that idea.

Other possible festival or liturgical ceremonies include:

(1) *Purification and Sin Healing.* The themes in Psalms 81 and 106 stress the people's repentance for their long history of infidelity, while psalms such as 76 or 82 celebrate God as judge of the universe who will punish wicked nations for their evil. Psalm 50 may even be part of a day of atonement.

(2) *Pilgrimages.* Exodus 23:17 requires every male to go up for the three major feasts each year. The title "song of ascents" in Psalms 120–134 has often been associated with the coming of groups to the temple for the big feasts. These psalms contain themes of looking forward to the city or to what Yahweh has done, or remember the processions of the ark.

(3) *Entrance Liturgies.* Psalms 15 and 24, in particular, seem to be sung at the gate of the temple by alternate choirs. One group on the outside asks permission to enter by singing God's praise; the second choir inside the gates demands that they be purified and worthy to enter. Then the gates open.

(4) *Zion Celebration Hymns.* Psalms 46, 48, 76, 87, 125 and others extol the temple and its special place in Jerusalem on the Mount of Zion. These praise the lasting promise of God to be with Israel and to make his home on Zion. It is hard to imagine that these could have been celebrated anywhere but on the temple grounds. A late psalm written in exile conveys some of the deep sense of security that Zion had meant to Israel before the Babylonians destroyed it:

> By the streams of Babylon
> > we sat and wept
> > as we remembered Zion.
> On the aspens of that land
> > we hung up our harps,
> Though our captors there asked us
> > the lyrics to our songs,
> And our despoilers urged us to rejoice,
> > "Sing for us the songs of Zion."
> How could we sing a song of the Lord
> > in a foreign land? (Ps 137:1–4).

(5) *Wedding Songs.* Psalm 45 was probably sung on the king's wedding day.

(6) *Victory Songs.* Many songs are found in the Bible, although not always in the Psalter, that are clearly hymns of victory sung to Yahweh. Exodus 15 (the Song of Miriam) and Judges 5 (the Song of Deborah) are certainly such. Psalms 66 and 68 may also be of this type. This is not surprising. 1 Maccabees 4:24 and 13:51 tell how the armies of Judas Maccabeus sang victory hymns as they won a battle. And anyone who has ever seen the movie *The Secret of Santa Vittoria* will long remember the final scene in which the German commander in World War II is forced to leave the Italian town before he can locate their one resource, their famous wine which they have hidden. As the Germans march out, the people break into spontaneous songs and dances of rejoicing.

(7) *Hymns for the King.* Special royal songs may well have

played a major part in ceremonies at times of battles or on the king's birthday when the people prayed for his health and well-being. Psalms 20, 21, 60, 61 and 72 may belong to such a category.

Other signs that the psalms were used primarily in the temple for public worship can be found in the directions for musical accompaniment that head many psalms. Psalm 4, as an example, begins with the note, "With stringed instruments." Psalm 8 is to be played upon "the gittith." Psalm 45 is to be sung "according to the tune of 'The Lilies,' a love song." Musical accompaniment was very important to temple services, as the biblical descriptions make clear. 1 Chronicles 16 lists the temple singers who joined Asaph in singing while the ark was carried to Jerusalem. 1 Chronicles 25 gives a detailed list of temple musical personnel. Concretely, in 2 Chronicles 5:13, the temple singers sing a verse that looks as though it is part of Psalm 136: "Give thanks to the Lord for he is good, his mercy endures forever." Then, too, many of the psalms mention aspects of worship that are to be performed while the words are being sung. Processions are mentioned in Psalms 42, 68 and 132, and praying in the temple itself in Psalms 5:7 and 26:6–7. All of this makes a strong case that the primary origin of the psalms was in public worship.

Personal Piety and the Psalms

Despite their public use, most of the psalms also contain a very personal note, including strong emotions and personal concerns that express the psalmist's anguish or great joy. Quite possibly any single psalm began in the personal prayer of someone either in distress or feeling thankful, and was so appreciated and liked that it was treasured and used by all, much as modern Christians love the prayer of St. Francis of Assisi for peace, or have recited the famous "Breastplate Prayer of St. Patrick" down through the ages. The personal songs were taken up and modified for congregational use. This would be particularly true of the individual laments.

The deepest insight into the religious prayer of an ancient Israelite comes from the ways the psalmists address God. In the psalms, certain qualities of Yahweh are mentioned over and over again. Among the most important of these are:

(1) *God is holy.* He is addressed as the "Holy One of Israel" in Psalms 71:22, 78:41 and 89:19. This signifies Israel's belief that God

was not one of us, but apart from and above human life, and in him alone was the fullness of life and power. Other examples include:

Holiness befits your house, O Lord, for all ages (Ps 93:5).

Extol the Lord our God
  and bow in worship before his holy mountain,
  for the Lord our God is holy (Ps 99:9).

(2) *God is greater than all gods.*

Who is like the Lord our God enthroned on high
  who looks down upon the heavens and the earth? (Ps
    113:5–6).

There is no god like you among all the gods, O Lord,
  nor are any deeds like yours (Ps 86:8).

The mention of other gods does not mean that Israel was not truly monotheist in its faith. Psalms that affirm the greatness of God are engaged in a debate with the pagans who believe in many gods, and so they use the language of contrast. Psalm 89 certainly doesn't consider Yahweh to be only one god among many when it says:

Who in the heavens can be compared to Yahweh?
Who among the sons of God is like Yahweh—
  a God feared in the council of the holy ones?

The answer is obvious: there is no being at all like Yahweh!

(3) *God is eternal.* Yahweh is not like us humans. He has been and will be the enduring source of life and hope always:

Before the mountains were created
  or you had formed the earth and its surface,
  from eternity to eternity you are God (Ps 90:2).

God's *name* also endures forever as the power that the psalmist calls upon in times of trouble,

Save me, O God, through your name
  and deliver me by your might (Ps 54:1).

Your name, O Lord, endures forever,
and your fame, O Lord, for all ages (Ps 135:13).

(4) *God is a rock and fortress to defend us.* The psalms refer to God as a rock or a fortress or a refuge to signify his unchanging fidelity and loving protection. One of the most moving passages in the Book of Psalms is the opening of Psalm 18:

O Lord, my rock, my fortress, my savior,
my God, my rock of refuge,
my shield, my horn of salvation, my stronghold (Ps 18:2).

Protection and refuge can also be tender and gentle in the theology of the psalmists:

You who live in the shelter of God most High,
in the shadow of the Almighty,
Say to the Lord, "My refuge, my fortress,
my God in whom I trust" (Ps 91:1–2).

(5) *God is a redeemer.* Israel calls upon Yahweh to deliver them as he once delivered their ancestors at the Red Sea. But this time it could be from sickness, the snares of enemies, or death:

Incline your ear to me
and rescue me quickly.
Be a rock of refuge for me,
a strong fortress to save me. . . .
Into your hands I commit my life spirit;
you have redeemed me, Lord, faithful God (Ps 31:2–5).

(6) *God is compassionate and merciful.* The Hebrew concept of *hesed* is more than just mercy; it contains the idea of steadfast love, loyalty and kindness as well. All things reveal this kindly face of God: The earth is "full of your *hesed*, O Lord" (Ps 119:64). Psalm 136 adds after each verse the refrain, "for his *hesed* endures forever." It is the heart of the covenant relationship between Israel and Yahweh:

Satisfy us, O Lord, in the morning with your *hesed*,
that we may rejoice and be glad all our days (Ps 90:14).

(7) *God is just, and upright.* Above all else God is not wicked and deceitful as humans are. He can be trusted because he upholds what is right:

> Enter not into judgment with your servant,
>> for no living person is just before you (Ps 143:2).

> With the loyal you prove yourself loyal,
>> with the blameless you show yourself blameless,
> With the innocent, you show yourself innocent,
>> but with the wicked, you show yourself crooked (Ps 18:25–26).

Above all, God is concerned with justice for the poor and oppressed:

> He raises up the poor out of their affliction
>> and makes their families like flocks;
> The upright behold it and rejoice,
>> but the wicked stop up their mouths (Ps 108:41–42).

Many times the psalmists combine God's faithfulness, justice, mercy, love and uprightness together:

> The word of the Lord is upright,
>> all his work shows his faithfulness;
> He loves righteousness and justice;
>> the earth is full of his enduring love *(hesed)* (Ps 33:4–5).

There are many other ways to discover the religious feelings of the Israelites through the psalms. For example, the important problem questions of future hope, faith, sin and forgiveness, and divine providence could be examined. The importance of certain themes known from the prophets and the Pentateuch might be studied as they appear in the prayers of the psalms: the exodus, the "glory" *(kabod)* of God, the divine "name," or the concern with the poor and powerless *(anawim)*. A whole book in its own right would need to be devoted to these ideas in order to do them justice. But in the end, the understanding of these sides of the biblical faith would lead us straight back to the titles of Yahweh above.

The psalmists loved to speak of God under endless descriptive names: not just "rock," "fortress," "stronghold," "savior," and "redeemer," but also in dozens of others, including, "The Mighty

One," the "Most High," "my inheritance," "my portion," "my cup," "king," and "judge of the earth." In reading the psalms, it is important to be aware of the divine titles and the rich language that Israel developed to express the wonderful sense of God's mysterious goodness that they had experienced in so many ways in all aspects of their lives.

Sickness and Tragedy in the Psalms

Psalms 6, 30, 32, 38, 39, 41 and 88 are all good examples of psalms directed to a time of personal sickness. God seemed to allow sickness by turning away his face (Ps 30:8), or even by actually willing it—see also 2 Samuel 12:15 (the case of David's child by Bathsheba), or 1 Samuel 16:14 (the case of Saul). An Israelite had several places to turn in sickness. Sirach 38:1 shows that natural healing by poultices and medicines was often expected. But where no remedy can be found, the sick person can turn to God in prayer. Isaiah 38 gives us a very clear picture of King Hezekiah praying to God for healing:

O Lord, restore me to health and make me live,
    for indeed it was over my health that I was so bitter,
But you guarded my life
    from the pit of destruction (Is 38:16–17).

The Book of Sirach also gives instructions to pray for healing:

My son, when you are sick, do not be negligent,
    but pray to the Lord and he will heal you (Sir 38:9).

Prayer and medical knowledge worked hand in hand and priests often doubled as medical functionaries. Leviticus 14 and 15 gives various directions for the priestly treatment of leprosy, open sores and skin eruptions. There may even be reflections of special healing services performed at the temple present in the psalms; see Psalms 26:6 and 73:13 as samples.

Another concern that faced the psalmists was the ever-present danger from evil spirits or demons that caused sickness and death. The people of other ancient nations had elaborate rituals for driving off demons and evil spirits, and saying the proper incantations and prayers to prevent these beings from having powers over a person.

But in biblical thought, no demons can have power unless Yahweh lets them, so that psalms of persons in distress often combine a prayer of piety toward Yahweh with pleas against evil demons or forces outside the person. The faithful confess their own sins and claim their faithfulness in important matters so that God will have mercy on them and turn the evil back on the spirits or on an enemy. See examples such as Psalms 5:8–11, 6:1–11, 10:1–15, 17:10–15 and many others.

In Christian tradition, special place has been given to the so-called "Penitential Psalms" (Pss 6, 32, 38, 51, 102, 130 and 143), which express a strong personal note of penitence for sins and a heartfelt plea for mercy. Psalm 51 is the greatest of these, and reaches a particularly high note of humility in which God's mercy is readily praised as totally and freely given:

> Have mercy on me, O God, in your merciful love *(hesed)*,
>   in your abundant compassion, wipe out my sins (Ps 51:1).

No matter how low a person gets, God's faithful and compassionate love is always ready to restore and bring joy to his or her life:

> Restore to me the joy of your salvation
>   and hold me up with a willing spirit (Ps 51:12).

STUDY QUESTIONS

1. What are the four periods or stages in the cultic aspects of Israel's worship? Briefly describe the characteristics and qualities of worship in each period.
2. What is the significance of the Temple? Describe the importance of Temple worship and sacrifice.
3. What are the major types of sacrifice described in Leviticus 1–7?
4. What are some of the major feasts in Israel's religious life?
5. Describe the role and function of the priests and levites.
6. How did the Babylonian exile affect cultic worship?
7. What are the Psalms? How many are contained in the Book of Psalms? Briefly describe some characteristics and major themes of the Psalms.

8. What is the five-part order in the present Book of Psalms?
9. What are the six major types of Psalms?
10. Describe the best approach in reading the Psalms to appreciate their beauty and richness.
11. Describe the liturgical origins of the Psalms.
12. What are some qualities of Yahweh that are continually repeated in the Psalms?

Chapter 15

THE KINGDOM SPLIT
INTO TWO

Suggested Scripture Readings:

1 Kings 17–21
2 Kings 9–11
2 Kings 17–20

Collapse at the Death of Solomon

Trouble was already brewing when Solomon died after a forty year reign. His great building projects had required heavy taxes and a forced draft of skilled laborers and engineers to build them. Moreover, he needed to maintain a very large and costly army to keep the small neighboring countries which David had conquered under Israel's control. Even worse from many people's standpoint, he disregarded the religious faith and tribal roots that had made Israel what it was. His foreign wives and their pagan gods angered faithful believers, and his redivision of the country to break up the tribes and put all the governors directly under royal control offended the local identity and loyalty of the tribes.

Solomon's son Rehoboam was forced to go to Shechem and discuss the situation with the tribal leaders. When he refused to make any changes in his father's policies, the ten northern tribes broke away from the king and his tribe of Judah, declaring, "What share have we in David? ... To your tents, O Israel! Now look to your own house, O David" (1 Kgs 12:16). Rehoboam was forced to flee south to Jerusalem to save his life, while the northern leaders called on Jeroboam, a former chief of Solomon's forced labor gangs

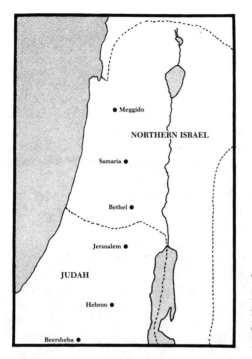

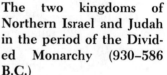

The two kingdoms of Northern Israel and Judah in the period of the Divided Monarchy (930–586 B.C.)

who had revolted and fled, to be their king. Now there were two kingdoms: a northern one which called itself Israel, after the old tribal customs, and a southern one, still loyal to the house of David and Solomon, and made up of only the tribe of Judah (and the remnants of Simeon).

Thus began a period of rivalry between the two parts of the Israelite people. The border between the two kingdoms ran only ten miles north of Jerusalem, the southern capital, and the tribal area of Benjamin which lay on the border was constantly being fought over by both nations. Judah had a far smaller population and a more rugged, desert land, but had the advantage of a closer unity among its people, a fierce loyalty to the ruling house of David, and a more isolated and protected geographical location from strong powers to the east. It also possessed the temple in Jerusalem with its ark of the covenant—the two major objects in the worship of Yahweh.

The northern kingdom contained the richer and more fertile part of Palestine, including the lush valley of Esdraelon and the green hills of Galilee. It also had a far greater population. Jeroboam, its first king, set about quickly to create a state with an identity of its own. He named two old and venerated shrine cities as the centers of worship to replace the attraction of Jerusalem: Dan and Bethel. He built two golden calves so that each shrine would have a symbol to counteract the ark of the covenant as Yahweh's seat. The bull-calf was not a pagan god in itself, but rather intended as a throne on which God's invisible presence would reside. He also set about fortifying and repairing Shechem, Bethel and Penuel, the northern cities in which Jacob had lived, so that the people would look back to their older roots in the tribes and forget the more recent Davidic covenant and claims. All in all, Jeroboam was quite successful in this task. Despite the condemnations of much later prophets from Judah, such as Jeremiah and Ezekiel, who lived long after the northern kingdom had been destroyed, no prophet who actually lived or worked in the northern kingdom, such as Elijah, Elisha, Hosea or Amos, ever condemned the shrines as false worship. Only later did Israel look back and see that this was part of the reason for God's punishment and anger against the nation.

The two hundred years from 922, when Jeroboam began to rule, down to 722, when the northern kingdom fell to the Assyrians, were mostly taken up by war: either battles against Assyria, border disputes with Judah, revolt by subject peoples such as Moab, or the struggle against the growing power of the new Aramean state of Damascus in Syria. The Arameans wanted all the border areas of Israel across the Jordan to the east. Damascus had a number of energetic kings named either Ben-hadad or Hazael whose military attacks often posed a grave threat to the very existence of the northern kingdom. But it was above all the age of the rise of Assyria, the great Mesopotamian power. Assyrian ambition was to conquer all the western lands, and it slowly but surely moved against its neighbors in the two centuries after Solomon's death.

The Books of Kings

The two Books of Kings tell the story of the period from David's death to the fall of the southern kingdom of Judah in 586 B.C. before the Babylonians. Thus, in one sense, they can be called the history of David's dynasty, although the picture they present is much larger. It includes the struggles between the northern kingdom and Judah, the rise and flourishing of prophecy, and a religious judgment on everything that happened during these four centuries.

After devoting the first eleven chapters of 1 Kings to the death

OUTLINE OF THE BOOKS OF KINGS

1 Kings 1–2	The end of the "Succession Narrative" with Solomon winning the kingship.
1 Kings 3–11	The reign of Solomon.
1 Kings 12–16	The early days of the Divided Monarchy.
1 Kings 17– 2 Kings 8	The prophetic stories of Elijah and Elisha during the days of the Aramean Wars.
2 Kings 9–17	The history of the Divided Monarchy up to the fall of Samaria in 722–721.
2 Kings 18–25	The history of Judah from the end of the Northern Kingdom to the Exile in Babylon and the Fall of Jerusalem in 586. The last incident occurs in 562.

of David and the reign of Solomon, the rest of the chapters relate the individual reigns of each king in the north and in the south by means of special formulas which begin and end the account of the king. The dates are carefully recorded and compared to the dates of the king in the other kingdom, so that we can gain a good idea of the actual history of the period from these accounts. Thus the opening formula for the kings of Israel would read:

> In the third year of Asa, king of Judah, Baasha, the son of Ahijah, began to reign over Israel in Tirzah, and he reigned twenty-four years. He did what was evil in the sight of the Lord, and walked in the way of Jeroboam (1 Kgs 15:33–34).

The closing formula would sum up:

> And Baasha slept with his fathers, and they buried him at Tirzah, and Elah his son reigned in his place (1 Kgs 16:6).

And sometimes the editor would add in the middle a third formula:

> Now the rest of the acts of Omri, which he performed, and the might he showed, are they not written in the book of the chronicles of the kings of Israel? (1 Kgs 16:27).

In between the opening and closing formulas, the editors of the Books of Kings would include one or more significant events the king had done. Besides the date of his becoming king, the year of the current king of Judah, and the length of his reign, all the kings are judged on whether they were faithful to Yahweh or not. None of the kings in the north are found pleasing to the Lord. This reflects the judgment of the authors of 1 and 2 Kings, who wrote much later from the perspective of Judah, and interpreted the separation of the northern tribes after Solomon's death as the beginning of idolatry and rejection of Yahweh and his temple, and the cause of their eventual fall to Assyria. The summary statement of this viewpoint can be found in full detail in 2 Kings 17.

The southern kings are listed with a very similar formula, but which includes also a note about who each king's mother was. So, for example, we read in the story of Abijam:

> Now in the eighteenth year of Jeroboam, son of Nebat, Abijam began his reign over Judah. He reigned three years in Jerusalem and his mother's name was Maacah, daughter of Abishalom. And he walked in all the sins which his father had done before him, and his heart was not wholly true to the Lord his God as was the heart of his father David (1 Kgs 15:1–3).

> The rest of the acts of Abijam and all that he performed, are they not written in the book of the chronicles of Judah? ... And Abijam slept with his fathers, and they buried him in the City of David, and Asa his son reigned in his place (1 Kgs 15:7–8).

In all there were twenty southern kings, including one queen-mother, Athaliah, who seized the throne illegally. All are judged by their conduct in light of David's faithfulness. Most are found wanting, except for three: Asa, Hezekiah and Josiah.

The history in the Books of Kings reveals that Judah had a much more stable sense of nationhood. The listing of the queen-mother in each king's dates shows the importance of naming the important families which intermarried with the royal house, and the place of honor and authority given to women at the government's highest level. On the other hand, northern Israel had nineteen kings in just about half the amount of time. Northern prophets and tribal leaders

THE KINGS OF NORTHERN ISRAEL
AND OF JUDAH (922–586 B.C.)

Northern Israel		Judah	
Jeroboam I	922–901	Roboam	922–915
Nadab	901–900	Abijah	915–913
Baasha	900–877	Asa	913–873
Elah	877–876	Jehoshaphat	873–849
Zimri	876	Jehoram	849–842
Omri	876–869	Ahaziah	842
Ahab	869–850	(Athaliah)	842–837
Ahaziah	850–849	Joash	837–800
Jehoram	849–842	Amaziah	800–783
Jehu	842–815	Uzziah (Azariah)	783–742
Jehoahaz	815–801	Jotham	742–732
Jehoash	801–786	Ahaz	732–715
Jeroboam II	786–746	Hezekiah	715–686
Zechariah	746–745	Manasseh	686–642
Shallum	745	Amon	642–640
Menahem	745–738	Josiah	640–609
Pekah	744–732	Jehoahaz	609
Pekahiah	738–732	Jehoiakim	609–598
Hoshea	732–722	Jehoiachin	598–562(?)
		Zedekiah	597–586

were also much harder on the kings. A large number were assassinated, and often the prophets themselves incited war leaders to kill the king and take over. Such was the case with Jehu in the time of Elisha the prophet, and it even accounts for the original choice of Jeroboam himself, who was picked out by a prophet, Ahijah, in 1 Kings 11. Northern Israel rose and fell in just about two hundred years, and most of its life was spent fighting one enemy or another. Judah survived as a kingdom under one dynasty for over four hundred years. (See the accompanying chart of the kings.)

The Prophets Elijah and Elisha

About fifty years after Solomon's death, Omri came to the throne of northern Israel, founded a new capital of Samaria and re-established a slipping Israel to power. He cemented relations with the Phoenician kingdom to the north in Lebanon by marrying his son Ahab to a daughter of the king of Tyre, Jezebel. His political sense worked well—even many years later, the Assyrians were still calling the land of Israel by the name "house of Omri." But by bringing in a queen who worshiped the pagan god Baal and permitting her to set up a temple to his cult, Omri stirred up the prophets against his house and began a contest for religious domination that finally brought down his own dynasty in a bloodbath under Jehu some thirty years later.

The central figures in this drama were the prophets Elijah and Elisha. They left no written words like many later prophets, and are found only in the great stories told *about* them in 1 Kings 17–21 and 2 Kings 1–9. Many of these stories are hero-legends, with lots of color and bravado and great deeds beyond anything performed by ordinary people. For this reason, historians are careful to sort out what probably really happened from the great mass of enthusiastic praise and often exaggerated claims in these stories. Miracles make up a large part of their way of acting, and most biblical scholars understand these to be more a means of showing how extraordinary these prophets were than to be actual events just as they are described. It should be noted that we have the words and deeds of many prophets in the years after, and none ever mention such miracles as part of their prophetic mission. No doubt Elijah and Elisha had great psychic and healing powers and did some remarkable things that made a lasting impression on their age, but the present stories have a distinct flavor of the legendary about them.

The Elijah cycle of stories has five major scenes, one each in 1 Kings 17, 18, 19, and 21, and in 2 Kings 1. The first scene in 1 Kings 17 portrays Elijah as powerfully blessed with the spirit of Yahweh. He commands a drought for three years as God's punishment on northern Israel. Yet he performs miracles of healing and multiplying food for the widow in Sidon who is faithful and humble through it all.

The second scene is the greatest. Elijah confronts the prophets of the god Baal on Mount Carmel in a contest to the death in 1 Kings 18. It is a crisis moment for followers of Yahweh. Although King Ahab was probably still a worshiper of Yahweh, he had permitted his pagan wife Jezebel to persecute and kill many of the prophets of Yahweh. Few had escaped. Elijah alone stands forth to challenge them to match their god against Yahweh. In a dramatic moment, we watch the prophets of Baal dance and shout the name of their god, slash themselves to draw blood, and beg Baal to send fire down on their altar to consume the bull that is sacrificed. Nothing happens, and Elijah calls out to them to shout louder because Baal may have fallen asleep or gone to use the bathroom. Then it is Elijah's turn, and Yahweh responds immediately, sending the slain bull up in flames. The people repent and proclaim that Yahweh alone is their God, and Elijah in the fierce zeal of his faith orders all the false prophets slain on the spot. The story concludes with Elijah praying for the end of the drought, and God answering his prayer.

The third scene, in 1 Kings 19, pictures Elijah in despair, saddened because the people have not reformed their ways nor thrown out the pagan cults of Jezebel. God calls him to return to Horeb, the northern Israelite name for the mount of Sinai where Moses had received the covenant. There he is granted a vision of God himself just as Moses had received centuries earlier. Hidden in a crack in the rocks, he experiences a great wind and earthquake and fire, but God is not in those. Finally a small voice, almost silent, reveals to him that God comes not in the powers of nature but in the voice of the spirit given to prophets. Elijah returns to the land of Israel and appoints Jehu to overthrow Ahab's rule, Hazael of Damascus to overthrow his king Ben-hadad, and Elisha to be his own successor. The stage is set for God's commands to be carried out.

The fourth scene in 1 Kings 21 reveals Elijah's prophetic concern with justice. King Ahab wants the field of a poor farmer nearby, and when the farmer, Naboth, won't sell, Ahab allows Jezebel to plot his death and so get the field for the king. Suddenly Elijah appears before him, much in the way that the prophet Nathan had confronted David over killing Uriah in 2 Samuel 11–12. He hands out a divine sentence of death on Ahab and his wife. And although Ahab temporarily repents, the editors of Kings note about him harshly: "No one gave himself up to doing evil in the eyes of the Lord as did Ahab, urged on by Jezebel his wife" (1 Kgs 21:25).

The fifth scene in 2 Kings 1 tells of an incident in which Elijah delivered an oracle of judgment against the son of Ahab, Ahaziah, who had succeeded his father. The new king had been badly injured and went to ask for healing from Baalzebub, the god of the Philistines in Ekron. When Elijah condemned this idolatry and announced that the king would surely die, the king sent soldiers to seize the prophet. Twice fire came down and killed companies of fifty, but the third time Elijah spared the soldiers and went with them to give the death-sentence oracle in person. Many readers of the Scriptures are shocked at this apparent cruelty on the part of a man of God, because they forget that these are legends which emphasize the power of God and his prophet against all the human authority and military might of kings who reject God. The stories use fighting words, so to speak, to make their point. We should not conclude that the events actually ended this way for the poor battalions that had to deal with Elijah.

When we turn to the stories about Elisha, the disciple who succeeded Elijah as leading speaker for Yahwistic faith in the northern kingdom, we find a different type of person. Most are familiar with the story of how Elijah was taken to heaven in a fiery chariot and his cloak fell down upon Elisha, who then received the power of Elijah as a prophet (2 Kgs 2). But Elisha does *not* work in the style of Elijah—a wild man, wearing a hairy garment and appearing and disappearing suddenly and where least expected. Rather, Elisha seems to be settled down, often associated with a large band of followers, who work themselves into ecstasy with the help of music and dance. Elisha himself is described as a man of miraculous powers, sometimes for the good of those who seek him out and sometimes for harm. He can do all the miracles that Elijah did, raising the dead to life and multiplying food, and much more besides. He brings up heavy metal axes from the bottom of a lake, cleanses the poisoned water of a spring, and calls down bears to maul boys who laugh at him.

But Elisha was more than a wonder-worker. He was a guardian of the true faith in Yahweh. Much more so than Elijah, Elisha directly entered the political world, dealing with officials of the enemy kingdom of Damascus who came to him. These included the traitor Hazael who planned to kill his king, Ben-hadad (2 Kgs 8:7–15), and the general Naaman who needed to be cured of leprosy (2 Kgs 5:1–27). He anointed Jehu, the Israelite general, to overthrow the dynasty of Ahab and his sons (2 Kgs 9:1–37). Elisha was a prophet consulted by the elders, respected for his spirit power and famed for his prophetic word, but he always stood outside the mainstream of Israel's government. Like Elijah he was zealous for fidelity to Yahweh, but unlike Elijah he showed no special moral leadership on behalf of the poor or oppressed. The picture that emerges from the Elisha stories in the Second Book of Kings is a combination of wonder tales about a holy man and reports of momentous political changes brought about by prophetic opposition to royal policies unfaithful to the traditional faith in Yahweh.

The Theology of the Books of Kings

Amazingly, the large grouping of stories about the prophets Elijah and Elisha stand as a separate bloc (1 Kgs 17–2 Kgs 9) within the present Books of Kings and have little or none of the moral evaluation found in the formulas that surround the long line of kings, both north and south, everywhere else in the Books of Kings. However, stories about the two prophets are mixed together with narratives about the wars between Israel and Damascus in 1 Kings 20 and 22, as well as 2 Kings 3. Apparently, early editors combined the war stories with the lives of the prophets in order to emphasize the control of Yahweh during these desperate times, especially when he spoke through the words of his prophets. They were already written and well known before the author of the Books of Kings sat down to compose his history. He simply included them whole in his work.

The one thing that the author of Kings did add was the emphasis on how Elijah and Elisha carried on the role of Moses, the founder of the faith. Just as Moses was a great mediator between Yahweh and Israel, so were these heroes of faith. Elijah goes up to Mount Sinai and experiences God in the rocks as Moses did in Exodus 34; he parts the Jordan as Moses did the Red Sea in Exodus 14; he goes up to heaven in a way seen by no one, as did Moses in Deuteronomy 34; he calls down fire on those who oppose Yahweh as Moses did in Numbers 11. In similar ways, Elisha imitates Moses—he too parts the Jordan, provides water in the desert and bread for the starving, and turns water to blood. For the author or authors of Kings, these two prophets carried on the mission of Moses to defend the covenant and maintain the commandments of Yahweh among a people who constantly murmured against the Lord.

This understanding of Elijah's and Elisha's role fits well into the theology of the larger history of the kings. The Books of Kings use old records taken from a number of sources, such as the chronicles of the kings in both Judah and Israel and the legends of the prophets, but fit them into a framework which cares much more about *how faithful* these kings were than how much they *did*. Omri was undoubtedly a great power in his day, but gets barely any mention at all in 1 Kings 16:21–28, while many lesser rulers are treated at length. The only criterion seems to be whether the information will help the reader learn the lessons of history. And for the Books of Kings, the lesson above all is that *infidelity to God's covenant given through Moses will lead to disaster and destruction.* Since the last king named is Zedekiah of Judah, who lived at the time of the final fall of the kingdom and the people's exile to Babylon in 586 B.C., the book's viewpoint looks back from that moment of total defeat and loss to find out why God has allowed it to happen. The answer is given that from the first kings down to the very last, both kingdoms failed to uphold the covenant and its commandments. This answer is expressed by the judgment made on each king (except Asa, Hezekiah and Josiah, and of course, David) that he sinned by walking in the footsteps of Jeroboam or Solomon, both fallen into idolatry. The same judgment is also expressed in a few key passages which the authors have added as speeches. One such passage is 1 Kings 8, when Solomon is made to say a long prayer of explanation of the covenant; another is 2 Kings 17, when the fall of the northern kingdom is attributed to the disobedience of the people.

Above all, the authors understood that God had spoken words of both blessing and threat through the mouths of prophets, but that

THE DEUTERONOMIC THEOLOGY OF PROPHECY AND FULFILLMENT IN THE BOOKS OF KINGS

Prophecy	Fulfillment
1 Kings 11:29–31 **Ahijah:** Ten tribes to be taken from Roboam and given to Jeroboam.	1 Kings 12:15 The Lord makes "good his word" spoken to Ahijah.
1 Kings 14:6–8 **Ahijah:** Jeroboam will lose his kingdom.	1 Kings 15:29 Baasha exterminates the house of Jeroboam as Ahijah said.
1 Kings 16:1–3 **Jehu:** Predicts the fall of the dynasty of Baasha.	1 Kings 16:12 Zimri destroys the house of Baasha as Jehu predicted.
2 Kings 1:6 **Elijah:** Ahaziah, king of Judah will not recover.	2 Kings 1:17 Ahaziah dies according to the word of Elijah.
2 Kings 7:1–3 **Elisha:** Predicts that tomorrow all prices will go up greatly.	2 Kings 7:16–18 Prices went up just as Elisha had predicted.
2 Kings 11:15–18 **Hulda:** Forecasts the death of king Josiah.	2 Kings 23:30 Josiah dies at Megiddo and is buried in Jerusalem.

the people had not paid any attention to the warnings. The Books of Kings are filled with prophets, from Ahijah in the days of Solomon (1 Kgs 13), through Micaiah ben Imlah who lived at the time of Elijah (1 Kgs 22) to Hulda, a prophetess under King Josiah in the late seventh century (2 Kgs 22). As we shall see in more detail in Chapter 18 below, this stress on the *word of God* in the Books of Kings reflects the particular outlook of its authors, who also composed the other historical works of Joshua, Judges, and Samuel. These writers of the time of Josiah, who were then in exile some years later, followed the teaching of the Book of Deuteronomy that Israel would only be given the promised land to possess if it remained faithful to the covenant with Yahweh. In Deuteronomy 18 God told Moses that he would raise up another prophet like Moses who would speak to the people all the words that God commanded, just as Moses had done. It is this model that the author of Kings followed. He points out that God had indeed raised up prophets to challenge the people, the most important of whom had been Elijah, but when the people refused to listen to them, God took away their land as he had promised, first from the northern kingdom and later from the people of Judah and Jerusalem itself.

The Rise of Prophecy

Although the Books of Kings are the first major source in the Bible to mention large numbers of prophets active throughout the two kingdoms of Judah and Israel, it is not the first notice of prophetic activity among the chosen people. Already in Numbers 23–24, a pagan prophet Balaam is hired to curse Israel, and instead offers oracles of blessing. Samuel, the great leader of the last days of the judges, is interpreted as a prophet in what he does. Prophecy also played a role in the life of King David. He had two court prophets, Nathan and Gad, who offered divine guidance and sometimes condemnation in matters of royal policy. Even the events from the time of the conquest in the Books of Joshua and Judges are presented by the authors as responses to divine words. In fact, the prophetic word is made to play such an important role in all these books that Jewish tradition refers to them simply as the "Former Prophets" (Joshua, Judges, 1 and 2 Samuel and 1 and 2 Kings), as distinguished from the "Latter Prophets," whose collected oracles have come down to us in books under their individual names (Isaiah, Hosea, Jeremiah, etc.).

The first of these "Latter Prophets," Amos, marks a turning point in our knowledge of prophecy. Up to his time, the middle of the eighth century B.C., all our knowledge of prophecy depends on stories *about* the prophets. From Amos on, we can examine and study their actual words. In the following chapters we will look at the contributions of these great classical writing prophets to Israel's faith. In comparison to the rich words that they have left us, the information on earlier prophets, even an Elijah or Elisha, seems very scanty and often colored by imaginative details and folk-tale heroism.

Prophecy itself used to be considered a unique characteristic of Israel not found elsewhere in the ancient world. But that view prevailed when the Bible was our only source of knowledge of the ancient world. Since the last century, new information about prophecy in other nations has come to light as a result of archaeological digging. Babylonian and Assyrian records speak of a large class of vaguely "prophetic" persons associated with temples. Most of these sought the will of the gods through divination, that is, reading unusual signs in natural objects. Since it was difficult to know what the gods wanted human leaders to do, experts would interpret extraordinary "divine" signs such as the movement of the stars, or deformities in the livers of sheep, or the flight of a flock of birds, or the meaning of dreams. It was through these unusual signals, all free from human tampering or "fixing," that the gods could indicate what decisions should be taken. Divination was a highly technical job and the Babylonian priests have left many clay tablets of instructions on how to interpret such things as sheep livers. But beyond this type of seeking God's word, it was also recognized that God might speak directly to individuals in dreams or trances. In the Atrahasis epic, a version of the Babylonian flood story, the god Enki speaks to the hero in sleep. In eighteenth century B.C. letters from the great Babylonian city of Mari, located on the Euphrates River, numerous prophets and prophetesses send oracles to their king, Zimri-Lim, to communicate special commands from the gods. Usually these were given in a trance in a temple setting, and copied down by the priest and sent on to the king along with a piece of the speaker's hair and clothes, to make sure that the person was not lying. One such oracle reads:

> Speak to my lord: Thus Mukannishum your servant. I of-
> fered a sacrifice to Dagan for the life of my lord, and then
> the *aplum* (prophet) of Dagan of Tuttul arose and spoke as

follows: "O Babylon! How must you be constantly treated?
I am going to gather you into a net. . . . I will deliver into
the power of Zimri-Lim the houses of the seven confeder-
ates and all their possessions" (ANET 625).

Here the local priest is performing the daily sacrifice on behalf of
the king's welfare, when a prophetic person is inspired to deliver an
oracle against the enemy state of Babylon which predicts a victory
for Mari's ruler over the Babylonian confederation. Many of these
pagan prophets seem to be part of the official priesthood of temples,
but others, especially the ecstatics, were ordinary people with special gifts of clairvoyance or other psychic powers.

In the Bible itself, the earliest mention of prophetic roles comes
in the form of divinations to discover the divine will. The story of
Gideon in Judges 6 tells how Gideon requested a sign from God by
letting his fleece remain dry overnight while the ground nearby was
covered with dew. The Books of Samuel mention the *urim* and
thummim as a means of asking God for a yes or no answer on
several occasions (1 Sam 14:18, 36–37, 41; 23:10–13). Apparently
they were a white and black ball, and drawing a white ball meant
"yes." This was a formal way to "seek Yahweh's will" (Jgs 1:1–2; 1
Sam 10:22–23), and, according to directions in Exodus 28, was
reserved to the high priest.

More strictly prophetic is the story of Balaam in Numbers
22–24. The king of Moab hires a famous "seer" to curse Israel.
Balaam offers sacrifices, has a vision and speaks words that come
from outside himself. Unfortunately for the king of Moab, the
prophet utters blessings instead of curses on Israel. The text explicitly says in Numbers 23:5 that "God put a word in Balaam's mouth."
He does not speak his own thoughts but becomes a mouthpiece for
God. In Numbers 24 the text of the oldest oracles goes on to suggest
that this word came in the form of a visionary trance:

The oracle of Balaam, son of Beor,
    the oracle of the one whose eye is opened,
The oracle of one who hears God's words
    and sees a vision of the almighty,
    swooning but with his eye uncovered (Num 24:15–16).

This is the classic definition of a "seer" whose prophetic insight
comes through some sort of "third eye" vision accompanied by
words. It perfectly describes the talents of Samuel to find lost

objects and see distant events in 1 Samuel 9:5–20, and of Elisha, with his "vision" of men coming to visit him in 2 Kings 6:32, his prediction that the king will die in 2 Kings 8:10, and his vision of his servant Gehazi afar off in 2 Kings 5:26.

Closely related to this older form of prophecy are the so-called "sons of the prophets" that occur in the period from Samuel down to Elisha, about two hundred years in all. These are bands of prophets who follow a leader such as Elisha, who is called the "father" of the group. They travel about and often use musical instruments to initiate a trance-like state. This is said to be the "spirit of God" rushing upon them, and is wonderfully described in two events from Saul's life in which he meets a band of such "sons of the prophets" and goes into a trance, rolling on the ground, stripping off his clothes, and becoming "another man" (1 Sam 10:5–12; 19:23–24).

The Writing Prophets

The classical prophets after the time of Amos still use the term "spirit of God" to describe their source of prophetic messages. See, for example, Ezekiel's vision of the dry bones in Ezekiel 37. The call of Isaiah to be a prophet in Isaiah 6 clearly resembles a trance-like state. But what is surprising is how rarely such language occurs among the great writing prophets. Most of their oracles are introduced by the very simple statement: "The word of the Lord came to me," or just "Thus says the Lord." We cannot be sure how this word came, whether in a trance or a dream (as it did to the earlier Nathan in 2 Samuel 7), or whether in some sudden insight or overwhelming inspiration under more normal circumstances.

The word that they use of themselves, *nabi* (in Hebrew), means "one called" or "one who is called." The title indicates that the person does not speak his or her own words, but the words of God. Our English word for the *nabi*, "prophet," is derived from the Greek term *pro-phates*, "one who speaks on behalf of another," that is, a herald or announcer. It thus means the same. There are a number of indications within the Old Testament that this conviction that the words they spoke came directly from God was based on the prophetic experience of being summoned in some kind of a vision to hear God speak in the *heavenly throne room*. The charming story of the prophet Micaiah ben Imlah in 1 Kings 22 pits this single Yahweh prophet against hundreds of false prophets who only tell the king what he wants to hear. Micaiah claims that he is better than they because he has actually stood in heaven and heard what God was going to do. Jeremiah says the same in Jeremiah 23, and Isaiah's vision in Isaiah 6 presupposes that the prophet is looking into the heavenly throne room. The prophet participates in the decisions made by God and his angelic advisors. The best description of this whole heavenly courtroom can be found in the opening chapters of the Book of Job where Satan and God carry on their dialogue over the fate of the hero.

We must be careful when comparing early and late prophecy because it is always possible that the editors and writers of the Old Testament described early prophecy in terms of how Israel experienced the later prophecy of their own times when men like Isaiah and Jeremiah were preaching their messages. But it certainly seems safe to conclude that early forms of prophecy in Israel leaned more to the discovery of the divine will for specific occasions and for specific individuals. The prophetic personnel were marked by great psychic gifts of seeing the future and by powers of divination. Some of these prophets were members of organized groups that favored ecstatic behavior rather than "messages" to be delivered, and many were part of the payroll of kings or temples and could be called on for a vision or prediction in moments of need. This role contrasts sharply with the concerns of the writing prophets who speak to the whole nation and who see their primary task as challenging popular but false values while exhorting the people to rediscover the covenant and to reverse their evil ways. But both types have in common the concern to speak for those without a voice, i.e., the underprivileged and forgotten, the poor and the victims of injustice. They also share a strong sense of the tradition of the covenant which looks upon all Israelites as sharers in the blessings of the Lord and thus entitled to be treated with justice. Because of this standpoint which puts them outside the power centers and allows them to criticize Israel's kings and leaders as well as the common people, the prophets contributed a powerful new factor to Israel's idea of itself, namely the conviction that they are not God's people unless they are *morally* upright. From the prophets on, Israel considers the *ethical* dimension to be as important as the *worship* of Yahweh's name in cult.

STUDY QUESTIONS

1. Explain why two kingdoms developed. What were they? Briefly describe some characteristics of each kingdom.
2. Briefly describe the Book of Kings. What are its contents? What are some major characteristics?
3. Identify the following: Omri, Samaria, Ahab, Jezebel, Elijah, Elisha.
4. How are Elijah and Elisha similar to Moses?
5. What is prophecy? Is it unique to Israel?
6. How does one distinguish the "Former Prophets" from the "Latter Prophets"?
7. Explain the English derivation and meaning of the term "prophet." What are the Hebrew and Greek derivations?

Chapter 16

THE GREAT PROPHETS
OF THE EIGHTH CENTURY

Suggested Scripture Readings:

Amos 3–7
Hosea 1–4
Isaiah 1–12

The Assyrian Rise to Power

The petty border wars between Israel and Judah, and between both of them and their neighbors Damascus, Edom, Moab and the Philistine cities, all pale before the threat posed by the one great superpower in the world between 900 and 600 B.C.—Assyria. Located in northern Mesopotamia with its major cities on the Tigris River, Assyria shared the general Babylonian culture but had a fierce tradition of independence from its more cultured and dominant neighbor to the south.

Under a series of strong kings in the ninth century B.C., Assyria began a program of systematic conquest and empire-buildng that spread in all four directions, but especially toward the south to control Babylon, and toward the west to gain access to the forests of Syria and Lebanon which would insure a steady supply of wood for the largely treeless homeland. By the end of the ninth century, Assyrian armies had taken over several small states in Syria and southern Turkey, and placed enough pressure on all the others to force an end to the fighting between northern Israel and Damascus. Those Syrian states that had escaped being totally absorbed as provinces of the Assyrian empire were made vassals who had to

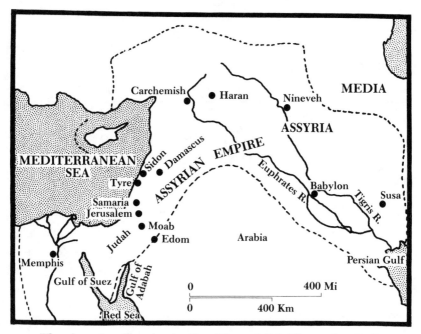

The Assyrian Empire in the 8th and 7th Centuries B.C.

pledge loyalty to the Assyrian king as their overlord and pay heavy tribute in money and goods each year. Naturally, subject nations took every opportunity they could to break free, and the strength of the Assyrian empire went up and down with the quality of the king on the throne. Every time an Assyrian king died, nations rebelled; every time a weak king ruled, the small states managed to win back most of their freedom.

But the threat of further Assyrian attacks always remained the major worry in the west. Already in the reigns of Assurnasirpal II (883–859) and Shalmaneser III (859–824), two of the strongest Assyrian monarchs, the small western nations formed defenses together against the dreaded Assyrian armies. The artwork on the palace walls of Nimrud, the Assyrian capital, shows a bloody enthusiasm for conquest and the humiliation of enemies which made Assyria infamous in the ancient world. Their reputation for barbaric cruelty was well deserved if the excellent wall-carvings of beheaded victims, impaled enemies and trampled corpses can be believed. In a less sickening way, there exists a famous carved pillar from the palace of Shalmaneser, popularly named the "Black Obelisk," which portrays King Jehu of Israel kneeling in humble pleading before the king while offering his annual tribute. This stele can be dated to 841 B.C. and indicates that by that time the northern kingdom was already a vassal of Assyria.

Israel's Age of Prosperity

By the year 800 B.C., Assyrian power weakened and the western states of the Near East enjoyed about fifty years of relief. During this time, both Israel and Judah reached their greatest prosperity since the time of Solomon under two remarkable kings, Jeroboam II of Israel and Uzziah of Judah. There was a revival of trade and commerce, towns were rebuilt, Jeroboam was able to extend his control over parts of the kingdom of Damascus, and the number of wealthy citizens increased dramatically, at least if we can believe the archaeological evidence showing that much larger private houses began to appear at this time. A tiny glimpse into the busy and prosperous economic life of Samaria, the capital of Israel, has been provided by the discovery of a number of potsherds in its ruins which list the dates and amounts of shipments containing oil and wine. These "Samaria ostraca" are among the few records of Israel that we have apart from the Bible.

Jeroboam II reigned from 786 to sometime about 750 (experts differ anywhere from 753 down to 746 B.C.). Although he brought economic success to the north, a large number of people had names with Baal as part of them. This reveals that the revolt of his great-grandfather Jehu had not wiped out the Canaanite cults among the people. It is significant that no names with Baal can be found in Judah at this time, where Uzziah (also known as Azariah) came to the throne about the same time (783–742) and also brought about a renewed vigor to the southern kingdom. He rebuilt Solomon's port city on the Red Sea at Eilat and regained control over the Edomites to his East. Near the end of his long reign, he even headed a short-lived coalition of western states who opposed Assyrian armies, but failed to stop their advance into Syria.

It was into this world that our first writing prophets enter, Amos and Hosea in the northern kingdom, Isaiah and Micah in Judah. Of all these, only Amos seems to have begun his prophetic mission before the deaths of the great kings Jeroboam and Uzziah, although it is possible that Hosea began prophesying about 750 also. Each of these four had his own specific message to bring, but each also faced the difficult problems of an age that had known great prosperity, but was now under a renewed pressure from Assyrian power which robbed Israel of independent movement. Beyond this, the prophets to the north also faced a chaotic failure of government in the wake of Jeroboam II's death. Civil war, assassinations and internal fighting between groups which supported Assyrian policies or opposed any capitulation to them racked the northern state. Both Amos and Hosea could see that the end was not far ahead for a people bent on their own ruin.

The deaths of Jeroboam and Uzziah in the 740's came at the very moment when Assyria regained her power and renewed her push to the west. Angered by the weakness of his country, an Assyrian general revolted and overthrew the current king in 745, and took the throne himself under the name Tiglath-pileser III. It was a name to be remembered. In yearly military campaigns conducted until he was killed in battle against Urartu in 728, Tiglath-

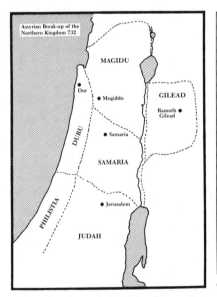

After the attack by Northern Israel on Judah in 734–732, Assyria invaded and broke up the Northern kingdom into 4 provinces: Magidu, Duru, Gilead and Samaria. Israel ruled only the latter.

The Black Obelisk of King Shalmaneser III (858–824 B.C.), showing King Jehu of Israel bowing down in homage and paying tribute to the Assyrians.

pileser conquered one nation after another. He introduced a new terror tactic into Assyrian policy. Instead of attacking a vassal kingdom that rebelled against him and executing only the unfaithful king and replacing him with a new and more friendly king, Tiglathpileser began holding entire cities responsible if they did not surrender the rebelling king to him. He would often wipe out a whole population or deport them to far-off lands and replace them with peoples conquered in still other parts of his empire.

Under this pressure, Israel experienced six kings in only twenty years after the death of Jeroboam. Four of these were assassinated by opponents, depending on whether those who favored rebellion against Assyria gained or lost the upper hand to those who wanted peaceful submission. At one point, King Menahem rebelled against Assyria in 738, but surrendered and paid a huge ransom to be allowed to retain his throne. In a second revolt in 734, Pekah the new king joined with Damascus to try to stop Assyrian armies in the west but lost badly. As a result, the Assyrians took away three-quarters of Israel's lands and made them into Assyrian provinces directly governed by the king's aides.

Collecting and Editing the Prophet's Words

With the appearance of Amos, we enter the period of Israel's history that is usually called "Classical Prophecy." It gets this name because the writings left by individual prophets became the standard for interpreting Israel's faith by both later Jews and Christians. When trying to capture the spirit of the prophet's thought, readers often assume that every word comes from the prophet himself. Yet the titles of books under individual names such as Amos or Hosea do not imply that they contain just the words *of* Amos and Hosea, but also words *about,* and in the *tradition of,* the prophet. Nor are the oracles and sayings necessarily in the logical or chronological order that we would like. Ancient editors have collected and arranged words spoken by these prophets in an order that seemed important to them but often escapes us. Editors frequently added words taken from disciples of the prophet, or even unknown prophetic words that are similar in theme and which add to the thought of the prophet in whose book they are included. Even more dramatically, later generations who cherished the words of an Amos or Micah occasionally added new applications and comments from their own centuries to the collected words of the long-dead prophet. This was a natural development. Each prophet had faced a specific need in his day, whether it was a certain king's greed or the attack of an Assyrian army or whatever. When kings were no more and Assyrians had long ago become notes in history books, Israel still read the words of the prophets as inspired guides for a new age, but they needed to show that those words now applied to life in exile or without a temple and royal family. It is much the same as when Christians apply the meaning of Jesus' Gospel to problems that never existed in his own time: nuclear war, abortion, test tube babies and others.

The most notable example of this process of editing and expanding the thought of a prophet can be seen in the Book of Isaiah. Careful scholarship has identified three separate collections of oracles, and perhaps more, joined together as one book. Each collection has its own special style and references to dates and events that makes its historical setting in life different from the other two parts. The first and most important grouping is from the great prophet Isaiah himself, found in chapters 1 through 39, and includes oracles and words that he spoke plus several later oracles, such as chapters 24 through 27.

A second major section is found in chapters 40–55. These chapters speak of Babylon rather than Assyria, and hope for a Persian liberator, Cyrus, to come and free Israel from exile. The author uses a distinctive style which mixes hymns of praise with courtroom lawsuits. Whoever this great genius was, he lived some two hundred years after the original Isaiah, and carried the earlier message of trust in a holy God who loved Zion to a terrible new age of exile and total loss of Zion which Israel suffered under the Babylonians in 586 B.C.

The last major division, Isaiah 56–66, makes still a third collection, spoken and kept in the years after Israel was freed from exile by the Persian king, Cyrus the Great, in 539 and had returned to the ruined and desperately poor homeland of Judah. It has a much more somber and penitential mood than Second Isaiah had in chapters 40–55, but at times it also moves to moments of great hope and a vision of the restored glory at Zion that will someday come about, more typical of First Isaiah's message.

We can learn much by paying attention to the different levels in a prophetic book. It helps us understand how God's people heard the oracles of a prophet, kept them, saw new meanings in them as the years went by, and constantly reminded themselves that God's word did not die but lived anew for each generation just as powerfully as when the prophet had first spoken it. Because of this living force of the divine speech, different levels are never seen as different and separated messages, but form a single book where each part helps the reader understand the other parts in a larger vision of history. It creates a dynamic forward motion of the word through time. Proof of the importance of this union of different parts into one whole can easily be seen in the fact that both Jews and Christians have traditionally understood the prophets as messengers of God's promise and hope, predicters of future restoration, even though most of the words are judgment and damnation and warnings of destruction. Why is this? Because a combination of words from several periods of time reveals not a single final judgment, but a record of God's mercy which returns again and again to speak to Israel in new ways.

Amos: Prophet of God's Justice

The first thing we discover about prophets is that they tell us almost nothing about themselves. Generally the books reveal little beyond when a prophet spoke and to whom. The message was everything, the messenger very little. Amos was no exception. The book notes that he came from a small village named Tekoa in Judah to preach in the northern kingdom at the shrine of Bethel, and that he was *not* a professional prophet attached to some temple but a farmer and herdsman by trade. Chapter 7 gives a single biographical incident from his life when he is challenged by the royal priest of Bethel about his right to prophesy. Amos protests that he had not chosen to come so far from home to preach; on the contrary, God had forced this mission upon him: "I am no prophet, nor the son of a prophet! I am a herdsman and a tender of sycamore figs, and the Lord brought me from behind the flock and said to me: Go! Prophesy to my people in Israel" (Am 7:14–15). Amos then delivers strong words of judgment against both the king and the people of northern Israel: you shall lose your land and be sent into exile and your leaders shall be killed. Amaziah the priest is naturally unhappy with these words and warns Amos to leave and make his living prophesying in his own country, but he never challenges Amos' claim that God was speaking through him. Clearly the political division between north and south did not mean that the two kingdoms rejected the idea that they were still one people of Yahweh.

Since Amos makes little reference to the terror of Assyrian

attack, he probably lived just before the rise of Tiglath-pileser III, perhaps in the period from 760 to 745. If we can learn little about the personality of the prophet himself, we can at least find out what he thought by the examination of his oracles. The book contains numerous individual messages delivered on different occasions. It has an order, but it is not one that attracts modern readers. It does not follow the oracles in order of time from earliest to latest, nor does it collect all the words on one subject or theme together in one chapter and then move on to new topics. It rather moves in dramatic fashion from a large scale condemnation of the evil in other nations (chapter 1), to the terrible injustice and evil found in Israel (chapters 2–6), to visions of the divine punishment coming upon the people (chapters 7–9).

The basic message of Amos stresses God's moral rule over the entire world and the divine demands for justice and concern for the outcast or oppressed. Amos has a surprising universalism in his outlook. God cares for every nation: "Are you not like the people of Ethiopia to me, O Israel, says the Lord. Did I not lead Israel out from the land of Egypt, the Philistines from Caphtor, and the Syrians from Kir?" (Am 9:7).

And yet, since God has specially chosen Israel and entered into a relationship of knowing and loving them, he holds the nation particularly responsible for a just and upright way of life. "You only have I known among all the families of the earth; therefore I am going to punish you for all your wickedness" (3:2). Amos connects

---

OUTLINE OF THE BOOK OF AMOS

Amos 1:1–2   Title and label.

Amos 1:3–2:3   Oracles against foreign nations surrounding Israel.

Amos 2:6–4:13   Judgment oracles against idolatry and injustice in Israel.

Amos 5:1–9   A call to return to God.

Amos 5:10–6:14 Further judgment oracles against injustice and idolatry.

Amos 7:1–9:6   Series of visions of judgment
                (7:1–10) a short biographical story of Amos at Bethel.

Amos 9:7–15   An oracle of hope, perhaps added later.

the injustice he sees around him to a society bent on wealth and prosperity and forgetful of the true worship of God. No more powerful condemnation has been spoken than Amos' first words against Israel: " . . . they sell the just person for money and the poor for a pair of shoes, and trample the heads of the impoverished into the dust of the ground and shove the afflicted aside on the road; a man and his father sleep with the same slave girl so that my holy name is profaned . . . and drink wine in God's house taken from those who are in their debt" (2:6–8). He condemns the selfish luxury of the women of the nobility: "You cows of Bashan, who live on the mount of Samaria, who oppress the poor, crush the needy, and demand of their husbands, 'Bring more drink!' " (Amos 4:1). He lashes out at the merchants who can hardly wait until the sabbath ends so that they can make "the ephah small and the shekel great and use false weights to cheat people; that we may buy the poor for money and the impoverished for a pair of sandals and sell worthless wheat" (Am 8:5–6).

Amos and the Tradition of Prophetic Language

Although Amos never mentions the ten commandments by name, his charges reflect them in every chapter. The people violate all the demands that God has made upon them in the great covenant on Mount Sinai. His words touch moral failure in every level of society: the law, the leadership, the economic life, and even worship. Northern Israel is a people confident that God will protect them no matter what they do because of the covenant bonds between them and God. But Amos understands it differently. He speaks again and again of the times that they have suffered attacks from their enemies and natural disasters in punishment for their evil ways and yet remain unmoved (Am 3:3–8; 4:6–13), he sings a mock funeral song over the people to warn them of their coming death (Am 5:1–5), and he attacks their most cherished liturgical celebrations. In a moving passage (Am 5:18–20), he flatly contradicts the hope proclaimed on their feast days that Yahweh will be a warrior God who will fight for Israel against all of its enemies on a great day of victory and light. Instead, the "Day of the Lord" they celebrate and hope for will be a day when God *will turn on them* and destroy them for their sins. And he has no use for worship and sacrifices that are empty and meaningless: "Take away from me the noise of your festal songs, I will not listen to the melody of your harps; rather let justice flow down like a stream of water, and uprightness like an ever-flowing river" (Am 5:23–24).

Because the picture of faithlessness to the covenant seemed so bleak to him, Amos was forced to use strong language to shock people out of their pride and complacent attitudes. He borrows the language of battle and cursing from ancient traditions, and warns of cities engulfed in flames, houses smashed, women and children led away with hooks in their noses, corpses left unburied and rotting, the land devastated and abandoned. Amos realizes that God does not stand idly by and watch evil go on. The political moves of Assyria and its fearful military victories are not accidents of history but permitted and directed by God to punish Israel. His is not a message full of hope. Amos once or twice raises the possibility that Israel could turn back to God and find forgiveness (see Am 3:9–11, 5:4–5, and especially 7:2–6). But mostly he holds out little hope, and sees a time when God will save only a tiny remnant without much promise as the sign of his loyalty to this people, "as the shepherd rescues two legs or a piece of an ear from the mouth of the lion" (Am 3:12).

There is a tremendous amount of drama and imagery in Amos' use of prophetic language. Chapter 1 is an excellent example. One can almost feel the people of Bethel swelling with pride as the prophet denounces one foreign power after another. Six times Amos thunders out Yahweh's judgment against an *enemy* people—Damascus, Gaza, Tyre, etc.; then he turns on a seventh—Judah. That seemed close to home, but, after all, the southerners deserved punishment since they did oppose most of what the north did. Suddenly, the prophet continues: "For three sins of Israel and for four, I will not revoke punishment against them" (Am 2:6). Such was not supposed to be. Prophets were to condemn and give judgment against others, but not to turn on one's own. Amos knows how to make his point vividly.

Amos and the Radical New Direction of Prophecy

Since the Book of Amos breaks new ground in Israelite history, scholars have long puzzled over what led him to preach in this new way. One important reason for Amos' new directions came from his background in the rural lands of Judah. He may have learned his faith from the teaching of the elders and heads of the villages in his native area around Tekoa. It was "clan wisdom," passed on by the father or village elder according to traditional ways and using ancient proverbs and sayings. The Book of Amos shares with the wisdom writings of the Old Testament a love for rhetorical questions, illustrations from nature, and the conviction that God deals with other nations in the same way as he does with Israel. It is a broader perspective than local loyalty alone; it draws on older reflections that have been passed down for centuries. By looking through the Book of Proverbs, a person can easily detect the similarity of themes and outlook found there to the words of Amos. Proverbs 16:11 and 20:23 condemn injustice; Proverbs 14:31, 22:22 and 30:14 condemn oppression of the poor and needy; Proverbs 15:8 opposes empty cultic worship; Proverbs 21:17 and 31:4–5 warn against luxury. Amos addresses the people of the north with a wisdom that they have forgotten, namely that the covenant with Yahweh was a way of life that involved the ethical behavior of individual to individual, and that it was based on a covenant law that had to be learned at home if it was to have effect in the market or palace or temple.

Scholars have also wondered what caused people to begin to preserve the actual words of the prophet for future generations just at this time when they had never bothered to do so for earlier men such as Elijah. Apparently, the major reason for keeping his words lies in the fact that they were addressed not to the king or to an individual priest but to the whole people. Amos strikes out in a new direction. No longer will God punish only the king or leader for a nation's evil, but he will hold the people as a whole responsible. Perhaps Amos imitated the new policies set up by Tiglath-pileser III when he held entire cities guilty of rebellion if their king rebelled. God's covenant wasn't just with the leaders representing the people, but was with all the people of Israel equally, and all must bear the task of keeping that covenant alive.

Those who collected the words of Amos and their harsh warnings of divine judgment added on a small oracle in Amos 9:11–15 which ends the book on a note of hope and promise. This short message picks up many of the themes found earlier about the depopulated and devastated land of Israel and looks ahead to a day when they shall be restored. It may not be from Amos himself, but it reflects later belief that Amos' message held out the hope that after punishment God's mercy and forgiveness will again bring blessing to Israel.

Hosea and the Knowledge of God

We know as little about Hosea as we do about Amos. He was born and raised and preached in the northern kingdom all his life, unlike Amos, and so he is unique among the prophets whose words have come down to us since he alone represents the thinking of a *purely northern prophet*. The opening label in Hosea 1:1 tells us that he worked from about 745 down to at least the fall of the north in 722 B.C. and perhaps longer. This makes him a younger contemporary of Amos, and they do share a common passion for the commandments of the covenant. From the personal details in chapters 1–3, it seems that he experienced a very painful marriage in which his wife proved unfaithful on more than one occasion. If the story reflects his real-life situation, then it may help us to understand the special emphasis that this prophet gives to the tender bond of love between God and Israel and how seriously sin affects the covenant relationship. But Hosea, like all the prophets, uses a colorful language that shares images and words with the psalms and treaty curses and the law courts, and it is just possible, though unlikely, that he used a parable of married love to get across the revelation he had received from Yahweh without ever having been through the great trial himself.

The book is divided into three sections:

(A) Chapters 1–3 describe in different ways the broken marriage between God and his people and serve as a kind of preface to the rest of the book.

(B) Chapters 4–13 gather the actual oracles delivered by Hosea throughout his ministry.

(C) Chapter 14 stands as a closing vision of hope after judgment.

When considered as a whole, Hosea preaches the same message of judgment that Amos uttered, listing the violations of justice and the oppression of the poor, pointing to the broken commandments and calling for a return to covenant fidelity and obedience to God. But there are many differences as well. Hosea brings out the compassion of Yahweh and his sorrow at having to punish Israel for its sins much more than does Amos. He really hopes that Israel will return to the Sinai covenant, and he uses many images taken from the desert wanderings to recall people's memory to Yahweh. He also borrows freely from the language of the law case and the

---

THE KINGS OF ASSYRIA 883 to 628 B.C.

Assurnasirpal II	883–859	Period of Assyrian expansion
Shalmaneser III	858–824	to the West
Shamsi-Adad V	823–811	
Adad-Nirari III	810–783	
Shalmaneser IV	782–773	Period of internal Assyrian
Assur-Dan III	772–755	weakness and withdrawal
Assur-Nirari V	754–745	
Tiglath-Pileser III	744–727	Usurper restores power
Shalmaneser V	726–722	
Sargon II	721–705	Fall of Samaria 722–721
Sennacherib	704–681	Attack on Jerusalem in 701
Esarhaddon	680–669	
Assurbanipal	668–628	Last great king of Assyria

Babylonians and Medes take Nineveh
in 612 B.C.

---

courtroom to demand that Israel live up to its legal duty in the covenant.

All of this is summarized beautifully in the opening oracle of the collection that comprises chapters 4–13:

> Hear the word of the Lord, people of Israel.
> The Lord has a *lawsuit* against the inhabitants of this land.
> There is neither fidelity nor loving compassion,
>   and no knowledge of God in the land.
> There is instead swearing oaths, lying, killing, stealing and
>   adultery;
>   there is violence and murder upon murder.
> Therefore the land fails and all its inhabitants perish;
>   even wild beasts, birds of the air, and the fish in the sea die
>   (Hos 4:1–3).

Not only does the prophet recite most of the ten commandments here, but he also singles out three special covenant qualities that cannot be found anywhere: *fidelity, loving compassion* and the *knowledge of God*. Of these, the most important for Hosea is knowing God. This does not refer to book learning or memorizing the laws and the history of the exodus, but to personal relationship. We really understand those who are close to us—I know my friend well, or my wife, my husband, my child, my parent. This realization leads Hosea to utter very strong words against the kings, nobles, priests and other prophets who are in special positions and should know God and God's will more deeply than most. It also leads him to some of the strongest oracles in the Bible against an empty and vain church-going in which a person continues to sin and do evil while never missing a sabbath or a feast day. He pleads in Yahweh's name: "I desire loving compassion and not sacrifice, the knowledge of God and not burnt offerings" (Hos 6:6).

Such infidelity to the real meaning of the covenant is like sexual perversion or the breaking of marriage vows: "I will not punish your daughters when they play the prostitute, nor your brides when they commit adultery; for the men themselves go in to prostitutes and make sacrifices with cult harlots; and a people who lack understanding shall come to ruin" (Hos 4:14). "The spirit of a harlot is in them and they do not know the Lord" (Hos 5:4). "In the house of Israel I have seen a terrible thing: Ephraim the harlot, Israel defiling herself" (Hos 6:10).

Hosea blames this rebellion against the very heart of God's covenant on Israel's selfishness and its forgetting. The nation is so tied up in what it can get for itself right now that it throws aside all that God has done and abandons him for the pleasures and profits offered by pagan gods and peoples. Their behavior is stupid and senseless and will only bring them to ruin. "Ephraim is like a dove, silly and senseless" (Hos 7:11), says the prophet as he calls tenderly to the people of Israel by their old tribal name of Ephraim (the place where the capital city of Samaria was located). He laments: "They sow the wind and shall reap the whirlwind" (Hos 8:7). "Ephraim herds the wind and pursues the east wind all day long" (Hos 12:1). "Your love is like the cloud at dawn, like the dew that disappears early in the day" (Hos 6:4). The emptiness in what they do seems so clear to Hosea.

The Prophet of Divine Compassion

Yet God does not forget Israel nor lose the hope of recovering its love again! "What shall I do with you, Ephraim? What shall I do with you, Judah? I would restore the fortunes of my people" (Hos 6:4, 11).

> How can I give you up, Ephraim,
>   or hand you over, Israel?
> How can I make you like Admah
>   or treat you like Zeboiim?
> My heart retreats within me,
>   my compassion burns with tenderness.
> I will not punish you in anger
>   or destroy Ephraim again.
> For I am God and not a human person,
>   the Holy One among you;
> I will not come to destroy (Hos 11:8–9).

Such deep feeling for God's love of Israel leads the prophet to picture Yahweh watching over his people like a father over his young son in chapter 11, and like a husband in love with a flighty and unfaithful wife in chapters 1–3. This latter image becomes the key to Hosea's message and has been placed at the beginning of the book to emphasize how important an idea it is. It is presented in three different ways in each of the three chapters. Chapter 1 tells a story of Hosea taking a prostitute for a wife and raising three children by her whose symbolic names tell the parallel story of Israel's infidelity: "Jezreel," to recall King Jehu's battle in the Jezreel Valley against the cult of the god Baal; "Not-pitied," to show that God has withdrawn his forgiveness; and "Not my people," to reveal the final breakdown of the covenant itself. Chapter 2 contains an oracle which describes Israel as a prostitute in vivid words of judgment, and chapter 3 gives a first-person account of Hosea's return to his wife as a promise that God will once more return and forgive Israel.

Hosea's theology grew out of a firm belief that God had *chosen* Israel and blessed her with his love and saving acts of kindness at the exodus and that this love had continued unbroken right up to the prophet's own time. But this covenant in love was not merely a legal arrangement with duties on both sides; it was a truly personal relationship that carried far deeper obligations of love and concern for one another. It endures freely and despite setbacks. It requires trust and "knowing" on the part of Israel. Yet Hosea paints a bleak picture of the distrust, instability, idolatry and evil practices seen everywhere in the last days of the northern kingdom. To try to reverse this direction in Israel's life, Hosea pointed out the many acts of love done by God in the past, and the equally large number of rebellions on the part of Israel over the years. He points out that even a God who is a loving husband or father can also discipline a child to bring it back to its senses. At the same time, the punishment that surely lay ahead for this stubborn people was always balanced by God's willingness to turn around and forgive them. Where Amos had seen little chance for Israel, Hosea almost begged the people to give God a try.

Hosea boldly proposed his marriage imagery. Probably he was fighting directly against the religious practices of the followers of the Canaanite god Baal who regularly slept with temple priestesses hoping to win over the god's favor and gain fertile or healthy new children for the year ahead by means of the sexual rites. He could see the effects of this apostasy on the morals of society as injustice and dishonesty increased. On top of this, his own personal pain and anguish made the rejection of God seem all the more searing to him. Hosea lived in a time of crisis and no doubt saw one king after another change loyalties for and against Assyria, saw the violence of assassination destroy the inner spirit of the country, and watched as little by little the Assyrians conquered and deported parts of the kingdom until the capital itself went down in flames in 722. To his eye, trained to see the hand of God at work, all this disaster stemmed from the loss of their religious loyalty and faith. A healthy covenant people, living up to the commandments of the Lord, would never have fallen into such heedless and self-destructive ways.

Hosea failed to change the fate of Israel, but his words captured so powerfully the enduring meaning of the covenant and the tension between human sin and the search for God's love that they have become a treasured source of reflection for both the Jewish and Christian communities ever since.

Isaiah of Jerusalem

While Amos and Hosea prophesied in the north, Isaiah, son of Amoz, was active in the kingdom of Judah. Isaiah began his ministry sometime after 740 and continued down to at least the year 700. The book under his name is the largest work of prophecy in the Bible, and naturally also the richest in prophetic thought. As noted earlier, its sixty-six chapters grew over several centuries, and we must search for the life and work of the original Isaiah of Jerusalem only in the first thirty-nine chapters of the present book. Even in these chapters, scholars believe that many passages come from much later times.

The material in First Isaiah, as chapters 1–39 are called, can be divided into the following sections:

Chapters

1–12 Oracles against Judah mostly from Isaiah's early years (740–732)

13–23 Oracles against foreign nations, many from his middle years (724–705)

24–27 A "Little Apocalypse" added at a much later date, perhaps in the sixth century

28–33 Oracles from Isaiah's later ministry (705–700)

34–35 A vision of Zion, perhaps a later addition

36–39 Stories of Isaiah's life, some from the Book of Kings (see 2 Kgs 18–19)

Like his colleagues in the north, Isaiah was passionately involved in the political life of his day. In many cases he seemed to have direct access to the king and so may well have been from a noble family himself. He lived through several major crises including the fall of Samaria in 722. But the oracles that have been preserved for us stress just *two* of these events. One was the war declared jointly by King Hoshea of northern Israel and the king of Damascus against Judah in 734. They wished to rebel against Assyrian rule but were afraid of a hostile Judah at their back if it would not become their ally. When King Ahaz of Judah refused to join the rebellion, they decided to attack Judah first. The evil outcome of this event in the eyes of Isaiah was the tragic, desperate decision of Ahaz to call on Assyria to come to his aid, and thus to ally himself with the pagan faith of that country.

Assyria did defeat the two kingdoms of Israel and Damascus and saved Ahaz from defeat, but at a terrible cost. Tiglath-pileser III destroyed the kingdom of Damascus altogether and divided northern Israel into three Assyrian provinces ruled directly by a governor from Nineveh, with only a small territory around the capital city of Samaria left as a kingdom to King Hoshea. At the same time, Ahaz became a vassal of Assyria and had to pay a large sum of tribute money each year and pledge loyalty to the Assyrian monarch. The pleas of Isaiah to avoid any involvement with Assyria had fallen on deaf ears, and the result was a worse situation than before. Chapters 6–11 of Isaiah capture this period of the prophet's life most fully.

The second great event was a later attempt by King Hezekiah of Judah, the son of Ahaz, to free himself from the subjection to Assyria that his father's actions had inflicted upon the country. Hezekiah revolted and declared freedom in 705 B.C., the year that the Assyrian king died and his son Sennacherib took the throne. Judah was not the only nation to try for independence at the time, and it took Sennacherib four years to get control of his homeland and the eastern parts of the Assyrian empire. But then in 701 he appeared in Palestine with his army and began the siege of Judah. He took all the major cities and surrounded Jerusalem for a final assault, intending to wipe out Judah forever. Lord Byron captured the scene forever in his great poem, *Sennacherib:*

> The Assyrian came down like the wolf on the fold,
> And his cohorts were gleaming in purple and gold;
> And the sheen of their spears was like the stars on the sea,
> When the blue wave rolls nightly on deep Galilee.

The story of this attack, found in Isaiah 36–37, ends with a miraculous plague that wiped out much of the Assyrian army and forced them to return home without taking Jerusalem. Such a result, in answer to both the prayers of the king and the prophecy of Isaiah, strengthened the conviction of the people of Judah that Yahweh indeed loved the city of Jerusalem because of his temple and would protect it at all costs.

But Judah did not escape from Sennacherib without great cost. First of all, every city except Jerusalem was attacked and destroyed; secondly, Hezekiah had to pay a huge sum of money to the Assyrians to maintain his throne and keep them from attacking again; finally, the people's joy made them forget the warnings of the prophets about injustice and evil. They began to trust too much that God would put up with anything. This attitude grew worse in the following decades and led to even more dire prophetic words of judgment in the days of Jeremiah and Ezekiel a hundred years later.

Isaiah and the Historian

This time in the history of the Old Testament stands out vividly for the historian. There are a number of important monuments and inscriptions that throw light on events mentioned in the Book of Isaiah. Sennacherib, the Assyrian king, left a whole throne room in his palace covered with detailed scenes of his assault on the second largest city in Judah, Lachish. These can now be seen in the British Museum where the remains of the palace from Nineveh are on display. He also left a pillar covered on six sides with an account of his battle against Hezekiah. In an indirect reference to the disaster that ended his attack, he never claims to have actually captured Jerusalem but only to have trapped Hezekiah inside "like a bird in a cage" (see accompanying chart).

The longest known Hebrew inscription from the time of the Israelite kings comes from this battle also. Hezekiah is reported to have covered over the water supply of the city which lay outside the walls in order to protect it against the possibility that the Assyrians would cut if off and so force the city into surrender through thirst (2 Kgs 20:22; 2 Chr 33:30). Hezekiah then dug a tunnel underground leading the water within the walls of Jerusalem to a pool at Siloam. In 1880 some boys discovered a description carved into the wall of the Siloam tunnel. It explains in lively terms the problems the diggers ran into:

> ... while there were still three cubits to be cut through, (there was heard) the voice of a man calling to his fellow, for there was an overlap in the rock to the right. And when the tunnel was driven through, the quarrymen hewed, each man toward his fellow, axe against axe; and the water flowed from the spring toward the reservoir for twelve hundred cubits ... (ANET 321).

Visitors can still go through the tunnel into the pool of Siloam today.

Finally, close by on a hill facing the walls of Jerusalem stands a tomb from Hezekiah's time. A broken inscription notes that it is the tomb of "(?)-yah, who is over the house." Though the name cannot be completely made out, it may well be the tomb of Shebnah, the steward over the royal palace, whom the prophet denounces (Is 22:15–16) for building his tomb facing the city.

The Message of Isaiah

Isaiah is often considered the greatest of the Old Testament prophets because of the sheer range and vision of his prophecy. He

SENNACHERIB'S ATTACK ON JERUSALEM IN 701

The Assyrians left a record of their attack on Jerusalem in 701 that agrees almost completely with the account in 2 Kings 18:13–16. The only difference is in the amount of tribute, and that may be due to either Assyrian exaggeration or a difference in weighing the talent.

Taylor Prism

Since Ha-za-qi-ia-u (Hezekiah) did not submit to my yoke, I besieged forty-six of his strongholds, fortified places, and innumerable small villages at their gates. I took them by means of ramps, battering rams, together with assaults by foot-soldiers using mines and saps. I captured and removed 200,150 persons, young and old, men and women, horses, mules, asses, camels large and small stock without number and I took them as plunder. The king himself (Hezekiah) I shut up in Jerusalem, his royal city, like a bird in a cage. I built towers against him, and anyone who came out of the main gate of the town, I chastised. The towns which I raided I cut off from his country and gave them to Mi-ti-in-ti, king of Ashdod and Padi-i, king of Acheron and Is-mi-en, king of Gaza. I diminished his country but I increased the tribute and the gifts due to me as his overlord. These I required of him over and above the tribute paid every year. Hezekiah, overcome by the glory and the terror of my sovereignty, and because his picked troops and the irregular forces which he had concentrated at Jerusalem to defend it, had deserted, sent to me, afterwards, at Ninevah my imperial city: 30 talents of gold, 800 talents of silver, precious stones, antimony, daqgas-si stone, large slabs of porphyry, beds inlaid with ivory, ceremonial thrones of ivory, elephant hides, ebony-wood and boxwood, coloured garments, dyed tunics—violet and crimson—objects of copper, iron, bronze, and lead, chariots, bucklers, lances, body armour, daggers, belts, bows and arrows, innumerable weapons of war, as well as his daughters, concubines, musicians both male and female. He sent his envoys to bear the tribute and do obeisance.

13. Now in the fourteenth year of Hezekiah, Sennacherib, king of Assyria, attacked all the strongholds of Judah and took them.

14. Then Hezekiah, king of Judah, sent messengers to the king of Assyria at Lachish, bidding them say to him: 'I have sinned; cease from attacking me. Everything you put on me I will submit to it.' The king of Assyria caused Hezekiah king of Judah, to pay 300 talents of silver and 30 talents of gold.

15. Hezekiah gave him all the silver that was found in the house of Yahweh and in the store-house of the king's palace.

16. At that time Hezekiah stripped (of their plating) the doors of the sanctuary of Yahweh, as well as the pillars which ... the king of Judah had covered (with metal) and he sent it all to the king of Assyria.

matches Amos and Hosea for intense anger against oppression and injustice. In Isaiah 3:15, for example, he asks: "What do you mean by crushing my people, by grinding down the faces of the poor? says the Lord God of Hosts." He can match their denunciations of idolatry and abandonment of Yahweh: "They have forsaken the Lord, they have despised the Holy One of Israel, they are utterly estranged" (Is 1:4). He, too, hates vain worship: "Bring no more empty offerings. Your incense is an abomination before me. New moon and sabbath and the calling of assemblies—I cannot endure evil at the same time as a solemn assembly" (Is 1:13). And he shares the anguish of Hosea in trying to express how much God wants Israel to turn back. Isaiah's famous story of the vineyard in chapter 5 captures God's sorrow dramatically but also reveals his unbending demand that justice be done: "He looked for justice, and behold there was bloodshed; for righteousness, but behold, an outcry" (Is 5:7).

Beyond these traditional concerns, Isaiah concentrated on God's *plan* for the whole world. He could speak freely of Assyria as God's instrument sent to punish the chosen people (see Is 10:5–15), and of God's control over all nations great and small, and of how just as he blessed nations and gave them good things, he could also punish them for their evils and abuses (Isaiah 14:24–27 and 28:14–21 are good examples of this). Isaiah's theology demanded that Israel and Judah place their trust only in God and not in foreign powers. In the great crises of 734 and 701, Isaiah warned against playing power politics. He told Ahaz not to get help from Assyria in 734, and again in 701 he warned Hezekiah not to seek aid from Egypt against Assyria. The beautiful visions of Immanuel that fill chapters 7, 9 and 11 came about because Isaiah tried to show Judah's kings that God would stand by them if they remained faithful and would bring about a better day. Ahaz angrily rejected Isaiah's words; Hezekiah couldn't find the courage to believe them. As a result, Isaiah turned his hopes to a future king who *would obey* Yahweh. From this moment, the words of Isaiah inspired hopes of a messiah, a new king in Israel's future who would better serve God and bring about a full measure of the divine blessing on the land (see Is 9:1–6 and 11:1–9).

Together with the vision of hope in Isaiah, the theme of God's holiness stands out. Again and again, Isaiah calls God the "Holy One of Israel" (Is 5:16, 19, 24; 6:3; 10:20, etc.). This phrase sums up the majesty of God as king of the universe and as the one who resides in the midst of his people in glory. For Isaiah, Yahweh is both the all-powerful Creator whom we worship and the intimate Savior whom we can approach in the temple and in prayer. Moreover, because God is holy and has made his home in the midst of Israel, he demands of all the chosen people a holiness and right living that imitates his own. This insight leads Isaiah to blast the human pride that puts itself against God's ways and exalts itself:

> The haughty stares of a man shall fall,
>   and people's pride will be humbled,
>   and the Lord alone will be exalted on that day.
> For the Lord of hosts sets a day
>   against all that is proud and raised up (Is 2:11–12).

It also makes Isaiah keenly aware of the oppression and injustice committed by wealthy classes against the poor in the name of good business and profit:

> Woe to those who call evil good and good evil,
>   claim darkness as light and light as darkness,
>   put bitter for sweet and sweet for bitter. . . .
> Therefore the anger of the Lord is aroused against his own
>   people,
>   and he has stretched out his hand against them and struck
>   them down (Is 5:20, 25).

God's punishment can be expected, not because God hates this people or rejects his covenant with them, but because "the Lord of hosts is exalted in justice and the Holy God reveals his holiness in righteousness" (Is 5:16).

As a result of this understanding, Isaiah predicted the downfall of both kingdoms, but also foresaw a day when God would rebuild a *remnant* that would be holy and righteous before God:

> And he who is left in Zion
>   and remains in Jerusalem shall be called holy,
>   anyone who is marked off for life in Jerusalem,
> When the Lord washes away
>   the dirt from the daughters of Zion
> And cleanses the blood from the midst of Jerusalem
>   with a spirit of judgment and a spirit of scorching (Is 4:3–4).

This remnant can be very small indeed, only a stump from the original tree of Judah: "And though a tenth of it remain, it will be burned again" (Is 6:13).

Yet this remnant would also be the source of hope for Israel because it represents God's promise that he will not destroy Jerusalem or the temple on Mount Zion completely. Isaiah ends the first collection of his oracles of judgment against Judah with a great vision of the people restored in glory on Mount Zion, shouting out their praise: "Cry out and sing for joy, O dweller of Zion, for great in your midst is the Holy One of Israel" (Is 12:6).

Isaiah and the Royal Traditions of Jerusalem

The combination of the Holy One of Israel, the greatness of Mount Zion, and the dream of Immanuel, the faithful king, sets Isaiah off from the thought patterns of an Amos or Hosea. Because he was a citizen of Jerusalem, he made use of the special royal traditions associated with the capital city and with the royal house of David much more than did prophets working in the north. Since we know that the temple stood next to the royal palace (1 Kgs 6–7), and has even been referred to as a "royal chapel" (to express the close connection between the political and religious areas of Judah's life), it should not be surprising to discover that the prayers and worship used in the temple often centered on the promises of Yahweh to the house of David. Jerusalem liturgy especially celebrated the oracle of the prophet Nathan promising a lasting throne to the kings who came from the family of David (2 Sam 7). We gain a small glimpse of this royal theology in Psalms 89 and 132, which praise the covenant of David, but also in many psalms that pray for the welfare of the king, such as Psalms 20, 21, and 45. Closely tied to this concern for the king are the psalms that extol Zion as the dwelling place of Yahweh and the source of protection for Israel: Psalms 46, 47, and 48, for example.

Isaiah makes use of these traditions throughout his prophetic oracles. He almost never mentions ideas directly tied to the covenant with Moses at Mount Sinai, but rather draws a picture of Yahweh passionately concerned with the failures of the king and angered because the people turn from his presence as their God on Mount Zion to other nations and their kings. Isaiah proclaims the need for trust in the God of Zion:

For thus says the Lord God,
  the Holy One of Israel:
In turning back to me and in quiet you shall be saved;
  in silence and trust shall be your strength (Is 30:15).

Yes, people of Zion who dwell in Jerusalem:
  you will no longer weep,
For he will give you favor when you cry out
  and answer you when he hears you (Is 30:19).

At the same time, he emphasizes that God will not abandon the house of David but will raise up a king who will obey Yahweh and give glory to his name:

There shall come forth a shoot from the stump of Jesse
  and a blossom shall spring from his roots.
And the spirit of the Lord shall come upon him:
  the spirit of wisdom and understanding,
The spirit of counsel and power,
  the spirit of knowledge and fear of the Lord,
  and the fear of the Lord shall be his delight (Is 11:1–2).

While Isaiah seems to have been totally disappointed in Ahaz and his response to the prophet's words in 734, Isaiah's later oracles directed to his son Hezekiah seem more hopeful despite the greater time of danger that Sennacherib's attack of 701 posed to both king and state. The oracles in chapters 28–32 still contain warnings of judgment and disaster, but the following chapters go out of their way to reassure Israel and Judah that God will not abandon his promises to Zion and to the king. Chapters 33–35 are songs of praise of Zion, and chapters 36–39 tell the story of how God delivered Hezekiah from the Assyrians. These were perhaps added later than the oracles of judgment in order to emphasize the grounds for continued trust in Yahweh. They may even be expanded beyond Isaiah's original words but are solidly based on his preaching and echo the themes found in the Immanuel prophecies of chapters 7–11.

The Second Book of Kings notes that Hezekiah began a major reform of religious abuses in Judah, but that these did not take hold

The *Siloam Inscription* from the days of King Hezekiah of Judah describing the digging of a secure water tunnel from the springs outside the city walls to a pool inside the city. This was essential if Jerusalem was to withstand the attack of the Assyrian king Sennacherib. It was found just inside the tunnel carved into the wall.

for long. Part of the reason no doubt was the devastation caused by the Assyrian attack in 701; another was the quick rejection of these reforms by Hezekiah's son and successor, Manasseh, who ruled from 687 to 642. There is even a legend that Manasseh martyred the prophet Isaiah shortly after taking the throne.

The true importance of Isaiah, however, does not depend on whether or not he was able to reform the thinking of the king and people of Judah during his own lifetime. His words contained that rare mix of ethical insight, realistic warning of disaster, and long-range hopefulness that mark his as the most profound vision of the Old Testament. The words of Isaiah did not fall forgotten by the wayside, but became the basis for Israel's later reflection and speculation. His oracles provided the foundations for hope in the time of exile to later prophets such as the authors of the last half of the Book of Isaiah in chapters 40–55 and 56–66. They also stirred the messianic hopes of post-exilic prophets such as Haggai and Zechariah, and of the early Christians who quoted Isaiah more than any other book of the Old Testament to explain the meaning of Jesus.

Micah of Moresheth

If Isaiah seemed to be totally concerned with the behavior and life of Jerusalem the capital city, and with the presence of the holy God that dwelled in its midst, Micah seems nearly the opposite. Except for the long poem on Zion that fills chapter 4 of his book and which many scholars doubt is original to Micah, hardly a mention of Jerusalem or the temple occurs anywhere. Instead, he talks of the villages and small towns, the tribal territories and the border cities of the Philistines to the west. The label that heads the book in Micah 1:1 tells us that he preached his message at the same time as did Isaiah, but the two prophets must have been very different types of people. Micah's town of Moresheth-gath was probably quite small and more concerned with the agricultural year and the weather than with the affairs of state. Where Isaiah might cry out against injustice in urban vocabulary, "How the faithful *city* has become a prostitute, who used to be full of justice; righteousness lived in her, but now murderers!" (Is 1:21), Micah would rather choose to say, "We are utterly ruined; he takes away the inheritance of my people and removes it from me; among our captors he divides our *fields*" (Mi 2:4).

But Micah looked out at the same nation as Isaiah and saw the same injustices and evil everywhere. His charges are leveled above all against the landlords who take advantage of the poor, and he foresees the same divine judgment coming against the people and their leaders as Isaiah did. Indeed, the two prophets stand so close in their understanding of what was happening in Judah that we can hardly doubt that each one was reporting very accurately what was going on. Micah's message was powerful and uncompromising. He declares that even if the whole nation should become corrupt and turn from Yahweh, he will wait and trust only in the Lord (Mi 7:7). Even a hundred years later, the Book of Jeremiah remembers the power of Micah's message that encouraged King Hezekiah to begin his reform movement (Jer 26:18–19).

The Book of Micah can be divided conveniently into four parts which alternate between judgment and hope:

1:1–3:12   Oracles of judgment against both Samaria and Judah
4:1–5:15   Oracles of hope and restoration
6:1–7:7   A legal trial against Israel for its sins
7:8–20   A vision of God's victory over Israel's enemies

Chapters 1–3 open with a condemnation of the leaders of Judah for their sins. Micah lists a whole series of cities and towns and announces their day of judgment. In many ways he sounds much like an angry resident of a small town expressing his grievances against large cities when he asserts that the two chief sins of both the northern kingdom and of Judah are their two capital *cities,* Samaria and Jerusalem (Mi 1:5). People in power use their position to take the inheritances belonging to the weak and powerless. People are forced from their homes and family farms because of the greed of civic officials, priests, diviners and even other prophets! This shocking series of oracles ends in a final climactic vision in 3:12 that sees the total destruction of Jerusalem and the end of the temple. In this he goes further than Isaiah usually did, although Isaiah himself often hinted that God's punishment might affect the whole land.

Following immediately after this horrible prediction, chapters 4–5 reverse the picture and describe a time of rebuilding Zion and Judah more gloriously than ever before. Not only shall the great capital of Jerusalem shine, but even the small towns and villages will live in peace and prosperity undreamed of in the past. The only condition that Micah lays down is that all false worship and idols be banished from the land. Many scholars are convinced that such a hopeful series of oracles can only come from a later date after Israel won back its freedom from exile under King Cyrus the Great of Persia in 539. But the heart of the vision in Micah 4:1–4 can also be found in the exact same words in Isaiah 2:2–4 and probably belongs originally to the eighth century conditions in Judah. A situation of widespread worship of the pillars and statues of the Canaanites fits much better the age of Micah than the time of exile or after when such practices found very few followers. So although it is very possible that these oracles were edited and put into their final written form sometime later than the prophet himself, their basic message still reflects the original preaching of Micah.

Chapters 6 and 7:1–7 begin with the language of the lawcourt in which God speaks as though he were both prosecutor and presiding judge. Words such as "case," "controversy," "contend" and "plea" which fill verses 1–2 of chapter 6 (depending on which translation is used) are all legal terms. The "trial" then takes place in three stages in the rest of the chapter. Verses 3–5 portray God defending his own side of the issue; verses 6–8 shift to the defendant's own admission of what human conduct should be; verses 9–16 deliver God's verdict and punishment on Israel. Many times God has shown himself a faithful and caring God from the days of the exodus on, but what has Israel done in return? The people have come with hands full of sacrifices but hearts empty of goodness and justice, and they expect God to forgive them and forget the pleas of the victims of their injustice. Micah 6:8 has long been recognized as an important statement of what the covenant should be: *to do right, love goodness,* and *walk humbly before God.* The rabbis who commented on this verse in the early centuries of the Christian era called it a one-line summary of the whole Law.

Chapter 7:1–7 concludes this judgment trial with a catalogue of all the different groups in Israelite society who have corrupted their ways. As with the prophets before him, it leaves very few untouched. It ends with a strong resolution by the prophet to stand against the popular practices and common belief that "since everyone does it, it's okay." He will look only to the Lord and trust in the God who alone can save, and he is sure that God will listen to him.

This act of faith serves both to conclude Micah's words against his own people and to introduce the final section, a promise of God to return and restore Israel after he has punished its evil by means of an enemy attack. The vision contained in Micah 7:8–20 sees a new day of the Lord, when God will rebuild the walls of a fallen city and repopulate the empty ruins of the land. Because this vision seems to reflect a period when much of the population has been thrown off the land or killed, it could be a later comment from the time of the Babylonian exile that has been added to recall Micah's words of judgment and promise in order to give hope to a people who are despairing that God will ever act again on their behalf. Nevertheless, it might just as well reflect the desperate times under Hezekiah when the northern kingdom has been destroyed and its people exiled, and Judah has been almost totally wiped out by the Assyrian attack of Sennacherib. As in chapters 5 and 6, there are many similarities in this passage to Isaiah's vision of Immanuel and the coming days of rejoicing (see the hymns in Isaiah 4, 12, and 35). Out of the tragedy of the late eighth century, Isaiah and Micah fashioned a new message based on a combination of severe punishment for evil and confidence in the future based on the promises to David that God would not permanently abandon his people and his special city of Zion. Perhaps in this, they built upon two foundations; one was the prayers and songs used in the Jerusalem temple with their words of joyful confidence in the kingship of God; the other was the prophetic call to ethical uprightness derived from the heart of the covenant of Mount Sinai.

STUDY QUESTIONS

1. Briefly describe Assyria's rise to power.
2. What is "Classical Prophecy"? Describe its major characteristics.
3. Explain the importance of distinguishing the different levels in a prophetic book.
4. Who was Amos? What role does he play in Israel's history? What is his central message?
5. How did Amos revolutionize or change prophecy? Briefly describe his style of prophecy.
6. Who was Hosea? Briefly describe his role and contributions in the history of Israel.
7. Who was Isaiah? What is his central message? What role does he play in Israel's history? Briefly describe the characteristics of his prophecy.
8. Who was Micah? Briefly describe the major characteristics and elements in his prophecy. What is his central message?
9. Compare Amos, Hosea, Isaiah, and Micah. What were their messages? How are they similar? How do they differ?

Chapter 17

THE LAST DAYS
OF THE KINGDOM OF JUDAH

Suggested Scripture Readings:

Deuteronomy 4–11
Deuteronomy 29–31
2 Kings 22–23
Habakkuk 1–3

The First Half of the Seventh Century

After all the attention that biblical tradition gave to events in the last part of the eighth century, including at least three major wars (the attack by Israel and Damascus against Judah in 734, the Assyrian destruction of Samaria in 722, and the invasion of Judah by Sennacherib in 701) and four significant prophets (Amos, Hosea, Isaiah and Micah), it is surprising that there is so little information about the next seventy years. King Hezekiah and Isaiah disappear without any mention of their final years. Scholars have sometimes found clues of a second Assyrian attack on Judah in the 680's, but these suggestions have not convinced most historians. Jewish legends grew up about the martyrdom of Isaiah by the wicked son of Hezekiah, Manasseh, but again no proof has ever been found that would back up such stories.

The seventh century was dominated by the reign of King Manasseh. He sat on the throne for fifty-five years according to the Second Book of Kings (2 Kgs 21:1), the longest rule of any king in Israel's or Judah's history. Probably part of this time he served as the

338

acting king (co-regent) during Hezekiah's last years (from 697 to
686) while he was still the crown prince. At his father's death in 686,
he became king in his own right and lived until 642, a total of forty-
four years. His reign was judged by the deeply religious editors of
the Second Book of Kings to be the worst in the nation's history, and
Manasseh himself to be the chief supporter of false gods and most
ardent enemy of the demands of the covenant. 2 Kings 21 describes
how he rebuilt all of the altars and shrines to the pagan gods which
Hezekiah had torn down, even putting them in the temple in
Jerusalem. He consulted magicians and astrologers, murdered many
innocent people and sacrificed his own son to some pagan deity.
The authors conclude that he did more evil than all the Canaanites
before him, made Judah fall into the same sins, and therefore
became the major cause of the destruction and exile that later befell
the nation in 586 B.C. (2 Kgs 21:10–15).

This is a very harsh judgment on the king, and there is not
much information about this period that can clear up the reasons
why the Bible passes over its longest-ruling king so quickly and so
negatively. 2 Chronicles 33 may help a bit when it tells how the
Assyrians came and took Manasseh in chains to Assyria until he
pledged full loyalty to them. He then was allowed to keep his
throne. Some scholars have thought that as a result of such an abject
humbling, Manasseh was forced to build shrines to various Assyrian
gods as proof of his loyalty. This is doubtful, however, since Assyrian
documents show that they never forced vassal states to worship
their gods instead of the local god. On the other hand, two major
inscriptions of the Assyrian kings Esarhaddon and Ashurbanipal list
Manasseh among their subject kings forced to give tribute money
and soldiers to Assyria. Perhaps in a way that we still do not
completely understand, Manasseh did feel forced to introduce the
worship of Assyrian and Canaanite gods alongside that of Yahweh in
order to make his little kingdom more like that of other Near
Eastern states and so secure more favor from the Assyrian governors
and overlords who watched him carefully.

Manasseh may have kept the nation at peace by being so docile
toward Assyria, but it led to the suppression of many rights and the
loss of religious devotion to Yahweh. It certainly seems to have been
a silent time in the history of prophecy. No prophetic voice was
recorded between 700 and 650, although it is highly unlikely that
none were present in the land. The king may have persecuted
them, or else accounts of their words just did not survive for the

authors of the Second Book of Kings to use. When prophecy reappears with Zephaniah and Nahum between 650 and 625, Manasseh had either died or was near the end of his life. It had been a dark age for loyal believers in Yahweh.

Manasseh was succeeded in 642 by his son Amon who continued his father's policies. Amon had waited a long time to become king and may well have co-ruled with his aging father for a number of years. He had no intention of making major changes. But the people had had enough of Assyrian pressure, and Amon was assassinated only two years later by members of his own royal court. They then placed his eight year old son, Josiah, on the throne. The officials no doubt considered that they could both keep the continuity of the royal line of David and also direct such a young boy's policies along more patriotic and nationalistic lines. Josiah eventually did set up a very independent and anti-Assyrian policy, but only many years later when Assyria was dramatically and quickly falling apart in front of the whole world. From 640, when he became king, until 628, when he became old enough to act on his own at the age of 20, Josiah and the regents who ruled in his name followed a very quiet and apparently loyal policy toward Assyria.

The Book of Zephaniah

About the time of Josiah's crowning, the Book of Zephaniah records for us the voice of reaction against the idolatry practiced in Manasseh's years. Zephaniah was a fiery preacher whose wrath against pagan practices and hatred of Assyria were matched only by his devotion to Yahweh. The book under his name contains a number of oracles delivered at unknown times and places but which fit best the period of Josiah's early years from 640 to 625. Quite possibly, Zephaniah thundered his words all in a short period of a few weeks or months. In any case, the complete collection is only three chapters long and may not represent everything that he had to say. Many experts think that Zephaniah was a prophet who spoke during the temple liturgy on some special occasion. Unlike Amos or Hosea or Isaiah in the earlier times, who were remarkably free from the interests of temple or priesthood, Zephaniah, together with the slightly later Nahum and Habakkuk, may well represent cultic prophets who were in some way attached to the temple and its liturgical rites, especially on feast days.

The Book of Zephaniah can be divided into three sections:

(1) Oracles against the sins of Judah   (1:2–2:3 + 3:1–8)
(2) Oracles against enemy nations   (2:4–15)
(3) Promises of deliverance   (3:9–20)

All of these sections revolve around a single major theme: the coming day of the Lord. As Amos had first proclaimed (Am 5:18–20) and Isaiah had repeated (Is 2:6–22), the day of divine judgment against sinners would come in destruction if the people did not repent. Zephaniah has a worldwide vision. He opens chapter 1 by stressing that the good order of God's creation recounted in Genesis has been reversed and that instead chaos rules. But Yahweh will sweep away all who have perverted his goodness, especially the worshipers of false gods wherever they live. So Zephaniah warns the people of Judah first:

> I will extend my hand against Judah
>   and against all who dwell in Jerusalem;
> I will cut off from this place the remnant of Baal,
>   and the names of all idolatrous priests (Zep 1:4).

God will "search Jerusalem with lamps" (Zep 1:12) to find the guilty and punish them drastically, "their blood poured out like dust, and their flesh like dung" (Zep 1:17).

But the prophet preaches just as boldly against foreign nations, predicting that the same terror and destruction shall fall upon them. Zephaniah names the traditional enemies of Judah—Philistines, Moabites, Ammonites and Egyptians—and ends with a dramatic announcement of the destruction of the superpower itself, Assyria:

> And he will extend his arm to the north
>   and destroy Assyria,
> And make Nineveh a deserted and arid waste
>   like the desert (Zep 2:13).

Assyria takes the place of honor—or, better, infamy— at the end of the list because its pride and arrogance against Yahweh far exceeds any other nation's. With great irony, Zephaniah quotes Nineveh's claim: "This is the exultant city that sits in safety and says to herself, 'I am and there is no other!' " (Zep 2:15).

He returns in chapter 3 to list all the corruption at every level of society, and declares that the whole earth shall be consumed by fire for its evil (Zep 3:8). But immediately, he includes a promise of hope that God will purify Israel, restore all who have been sent into exile, and give peace to the land. It will be a time of rejoicing and not fear:

> The Lord your God is in your midst,
> > a warrior who brings victory,
> Who will rejoice and be glad with you,
> > and once again show you his love;
> He will shout with joyful song over you,
> > as on the great feast days (Zep 3:17).

The entire message of the prophet ends as it had begun, with praise for God who rules the entire universe. Perhaps the whole series of oracles were delivered during a week of celebration of the kingship of Yahweh, a feast for which we have no exact information but many hints in the Old Testament. It would have taken place in the fall, connected to the New Year's festival, and would be a fitting occasion for proclaiming both God's punishment of all sin everywhere in the world and his victory over Assyria sometime ahead.

Zephaniah's message has the power of a great orator speaking with passion. Most of his themes are very traditional, and the crowds of Israelites who heard him would have applauded his thought as one with their own. His central concern with the day of the Lord borrows heavily from Isaiah, some eighty years earlier. Listen to Zephaniah's words, and then compare them to Amos and Isaiah:

> The great day of the Lord draws near,
> > it is near and coming fast;
> The sound on the day of the Lord is bitter,
> > the warrior shouts aloud;
> A day of wrath, a day of distress and anguish,
> > a day of ruin, devastation, darkness and gloom;
> A day of clouds and dense fog,
> > of trumpet blast and battle cry,
> Against the fortified cities
> > and against their high towers (Zep 1:14–15).

> Is not the day of the Lord darkness and not light,
> > a day of gloom without any brightness? (Am 5:20).

> For the Lord of Hosts has a day against all the proud,
>   against all the proud and lofty,
>   against all that is high and lifted up (Is 2:12).

Zephaniah represents the best of Israel's values brought together in a time of great difficulty. He has sensitivity to evil among his own people, trust in Yahweh to protect the nation, and a conviction that necessary as punishment may be, there will always be a new time of God's favor for the people of the covenant.

King Josiah's Reform

While Zephaniah probably lived before Josiah had asserted his independence and made any major religious reforms, his words certainly reflected the terrible state of religion in the king's early years when the pagan cults set up by Manasseh flourished. 2 Kings 22 tells the story of how Josiah began his reforming efforts. In his eighteenth year, which would be 622, he decided to repair the temple which was in poor shape. He spared no expense in the effort, and shortly after he had begun the task, the high priest Hilkiah brought out a book which had been found hidden somewhere in the temple. The Second Book of Kings is not clear whether it had lain there lost in a corner for a long time or whether the high priest had known about it all along and only risked showing it to the king when he was certain that Josiah was serious about religious reform.

After Josiah had read the book, he tore his clothes in distress because it threatened God's wrath on any who did not obey its words (2 Kgs 22:13). When he asked the prophetess Huldah to seek a word from God about the book, she answered that God would destroy Jerusalem for its idolatry but that the king would be spared because he had repented. Then the king gathered all the people and made them renew the covenant and promise to obey all its divine laws and statutes (2 Kgs 23:2–3). Finally he began a bold effort to remove all pagan shrines and cult objects from the land and to restore the worship of Yahweh alone (2 Kgs 23:4–20).

What exactly was this book that had such a shattering effect on the king? At different places in the text, the Second Book of Kings calls it the "book of the law," "this book," and "the book of the covenant,"and once it says that Josiah did all according to "the law of Moses" (2 Kgs 23:25). Thus it certainly reflects the traditions of the covenant given at Mount Sinai. A close comparison of the language used about the book in 2 Kings 22–23 with the contents of the Pentateuch shows the most similarities to the words of Deuteronomy. This is particularly true in terms of the various actions that Josiah undertakes to rid the land of pagan objects. Note the demands listed in Deuteronomy side by side with 2 Kings 23:

The king abolishes the asherim idols	Dt 7:15	2 Kgs 23:4,6–7
He ends the cult of the stars	Dt 17:3	2 Kgs 23:4–5
He ends worship of sun and moon	Dt 17:3	2 Kgs 23:5,11
He destroys cult prostitution	Dt 23:18	2 Kgs 23:7
He defiles the Moloch cult place	Dt 12:31	2 Kgs 23:10
He tears down the high places	Dt 7:15	2 Kgs 23:13
He removes all foreign idols	Dt 12:1–32	2 Kgs 23:13
He breaks the pillar idols	Dt 12:3	2 Kgs 23:14
He renews the feast of Passover	Dt 16:1–8	2 Kgs 23:21–22
He forbids the cult of the dead	Dt 18:11	2 Kgs 23:24

It seems that Josiah's "lawbook" was some form of the Book of Deuteronomy, probably the middle sections that run from chapter 4 through 28, and that the king's reforms were a serious attempt to return to a faithful understanding of the covenant of Moses as it was described by the authors of Deuteronomy. The energy which Josiah gave to his movement shows that he did indeed undergo a sincere conversion from the ways of his fathers, and the later authors of the Second Book of Kings remember Josiah as the greatest king in the history of the people after David himself. Thus 2 Kings 23:25 says:

> Before him there was no king like him who turned to the Lord with all his heart and all his soul and all his might, according to the law of Moses; nor did any like him arise after him (RSV translation; compare the language of Deuteronomy 6:5–6).

Josiah's Political Gains

But the time was also ripe for major change from a political standpoint. Sometime between 632 and 628, the last great king of Assyria, Ashurbanipal, died. His sons and successors were weak leaders, and by 625 it had become clear that two new powers were rising to challenge the control of Assyria over the Near East. One

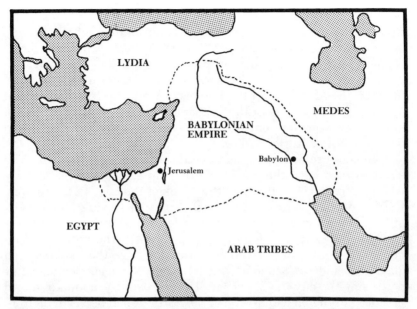

The extent of the Babylonian Empire under Nebuchadnezzar II (605–562 B.C.)

was the kingdom of the Medes in northern Iran. In the middle of the seventh century they had moved quickly to build a large empire in Iran and eastern Turkey, and they now cast greedy eyes toward the rich lands of Assyria and Babylon. The second power was Babylon itself. Under a new local ruler, Nabopolassar, it drove out the Assyrian army and dreamed of recreating the mighty Babylon of Hammurapi's day some thousand years earlier. Each year from 625 on, Nabopolassar sent his forces out to attack another part of Assyria's crumbling empire. All the nations to the West who had been forced to submit to the tyranny of the Assyrians took heart and began to dream of a chance for independence. Little Judah was among these nations. 2 Kings 21:23–24 describes how the "people of the land" punished those who had assassinated King Amon in 640 and made sure that the Davidic dynasty continued in his son Josiah. It is these landowners and farmers who preserved the traditions and hopes for independence through all the long years of Manasseh's kingship, and who were probably the strongest supporters of a new move to regain some freedom as the Assyrians grew weaker.

Josiah is said to have forced his reforms on both Judah and the territory of the former kingdom of Israel in the North which had been an Assyrian province since the fall of Samaria in 722–721. This suggests that he extended his rule and control over all of Palestine as soon as he could. Since at no time does Josiah come into direct conflict with the Assyrians, he must have retaken the land as a "caretaker" in the name of Assyria as the conquerors had to withdraw bit by bit to defend the homeland from the Babylonians and Medes. That way he kept the appearance of true loyalty to Assyria but in fact won full control of the territory ruled by David and Solomon four centuries earlier.

Religious reform went side by side with political freedom. The effort to take back the northern area was surely well under way when the priest Hilkiah found the "book of the law" in the temple. Josiah took the chance to restore the unity of David's kingdom by insisting on a return to the full obedience to the covenant among both the people of Judah and the population of the northern kingdom. This would not have been an easy job since the Assyrians had filled the lands of Samaria with all kinds of pagan peoples after destroying the city in 722. For well over a century, a kind of mixed practice of religion had existed in the north. It had been cut off from any contact with the temple and priests in Jerusalem, and was served by a variety of levites and priests who kept some of the religious heritage alive at the old shrines such as Bethel and Dan. To insure that all worship was properly orthodox and right, Josiah removed these temple professionals from their shrines and local towns and forced all major religious celebrations to be held in Jerusalem at the temple. Many of the levites, who represented temple singers, caretakers and sometimes even priestly officials, were simply deposed; others were allowed to come to Jerusalem and serve in the temple. By this move, Josiah was able to remove the chief centers of pagan worship and at the same time focus the whole nation's loyalty on Jerusalem and its combination of royal rule and true worship. He fulfilled completely the central demand of the Book of Deuteronomy's law code:

> You shall search out the place which the Lord your God chooses out of all your tribes to place his name and his dwelling there. There you will go up and bring your holocausts and sacrifices, your taxes and the offerings you give, your gifts and first-born of your herds and flocks; and there you will eat before the Lord your God and rejoice, you and all your households (Dt 12:5–7).

The Book of Deuteronomy

It is necessary to look more closely at Deuteronomy since it seems to have played such an important part in the time of Josiah. As it stands, it is written as a single speech of Moses on the banks of the Jordan just before the people are to cross over to begin the great conquest of the promised land. In form, it is Moses' farewell speech, his last will and testament to the Israel that he has led out of Egyptian slavery and through the harsh desert of Sinai. He has brought Yahweh's special covenant to them and more than once intervened to save them from God's anger when they had been unfaithful. However, anyone who has looked closely at the Pentateuch can see that there is an immense difference in style and vocabulary between Deuteronomy and the other four books. Only in Deuteronomy do we find expressions such as "the testimonies, the statutes and the ordinances which the Lord your God commands you," "you shall keep the commandment which I command you this day," "to love the Lord your God with all your heart and soul," "lest you perish off the good land," "if you turn aside to walk after other gods and worship them," and "for your eyes have seen the great work which the Lord worked."

Deuteronomy favors long speeches with much urging to obedience typical of a preacher delivering a sermon. This stands apart from the often short stories and incidents found in the Books of Genesis and Exodus. For at least two centuries now, scholars have known that Deuteronomy did not come from the same time as the rest of the Pentateuch, and that it actually reflects a writer or writers who look back from a much later time to the days of Moses and the conquest. In the name of the true tradition of Moses, the Book of Deuteronomy makes a call for return to the proper obedience to the covenant. The authors manage to get their message across by the very effective means of putting the warnings in the mouth of the great founder himself. This was a very common method of writing in the ancient world. It was not an attempt to deceive, but to link a writer's religious teaching to its real, and much more ancient, source and authority. The people who composed Deuteronomy did so with the full intention of presenting a program of religious reform that would restore the observance of the covenant back to the way it was given under Moses.

The Book of Deuteronomy can be divided into a number of speeches and sections. The major part runs from chapter 5 through chapter 28, and includes a long preface (4:44–11:32) and a reworking of the old covenant laws found in Exodus 20–23 (chapters 12–26). A second speech of Moses was added at the beginning to form a prologue which explained how these demands were based on the people's actions and God's promises during the forty years in the desert; it covers chapters 1 through 4. The last section of the book contains six chapters with a number of important supplements about Moses' teaching (chapters 29–34). They record a final speech, an ancient song ascribed to Moses, his final blessing and his death scene.

The core of the Book of Deuteronomy is the law code found in chapters 12–26. Because it is similar to the covenant law code in Exodus 20–23, it is called the "second law" (= deutero + nomos in Greek). A comparison of the two law collections, however, reveals that in every case the wording of the law in Deuteronomy reflects a later time than does the Exodus code. Where, for instance, the law of Exodus 23:10–11 demands that farmers leave the land unplanted every seventh year so that the poor can survive by finding some grain and wild regrowth to eat, the parallel law in Deuteronomy 15:1–11 adds elaborate regulations for forgiving debts owed by the poor every seven years, and it expands the meaning to cover foreign borrowing and lending. Clearly Deuteronomy 15 no longer has in mind a nation of small farmers, but a city population which depends on a money economy, a situation found not in the time of Moses but in the later period of the kings. The law that follows in Deuteronomy 15:12–18 deals with slaves. Where Exodus 21:1–11 gives a set of basic directions on how to free Hebrew slaves after six years of service, Deuteronomy adds a moral note that the slave-masters are to remember back to the days in Egypt when they were slaves, and so be compassionate. Obviously, Deuteronomy presupposes that a long time has passed since the people were living in the desert. The same comparisons can be made with many other laws that the two codes share in common.

Indeed the most striking aspect of Deuteronomy's style is that, although put in the mouth of Moses, the homilies are directed at a people living long after the events of the exodus, people who are urged to recall and keep the teaching of Moses. The book looks back on the conquest of the holy land as a completed event, and its legal ideas presuppose the highly developed government set up by David and Solomon. Examples of this are the rules directed at kings in chapter 17 and at a central sanctuary in Jerusalem in chapter 12, neither of which came into being until many centuries after Moses'

OUTLINE OF THE BOOK OF DEUTERONOMY

1. *General Introduction*   1:1–4:43
   - 1:1–3:29   Historical survey
   - 4:1–43   Introduction to law

2. *Particular Introduction to Deuteronomic Code* 4:44–11:32
   - 4:44–49   Introductory words
   - 5:1–33   Moses and ten commandments
   - 6:1–25   Instruction on obedience to law
   - 7:1–26   Attitude to pagans and conquest of land
   - 8:1–20   Lessons from desert wanderings—dependence on Yahweh
   - 9:1–10:22 Lesson from golden calf and idolatry-covenant
   - 11:1–32   General command to love covenant for blessing

3. *The Law Code (12–26)*
   - a. Introduction: Laws on one sanctuary   12:1–31
   - b. Laws   Idolatry laws   13:1–19
     - Ritual food taboos and tithes   14:1–29
     - Sabbatical release for poor   15:1–18
     - First-born sacrifice   15:19–23
     - Pilgrim feasts   16:1–17
     - Officials: judges, king, priest, prophet   16:18–18:22
     - Sanctuary cities   19:1–21
     - Holy war   20:1–20; 21:10–14; 23:9–14
     - Murder unknown   21:1–9
     - Special problems   21:15–22:12
     - Sexual laws   22:13–23:1
     - Community laws: poor, marriage, etc.   23:1–25:19
     - Tithes on first-fruits and tithing   26:1–15
   - c. Conclusion of the covenant summary   26:16–19
   - d. Covenant ceremony and curses   27:1–26
     - More curses and blessings   28:1–46
     - Exilic expansion   28:47–68

4. *Final Speeches*
   - a. Moses' final homily on the covenant   29–30
     - Covenant warnings for exile   29:1–27
     - Promise of mercy in exile   30:1–20
   - b. Preparation for Moses' end; Joshua picked   31:1–13, 23ff
   - c. Command to Moses for a song   31:14–22
   - d. The song of Moses   32:1–44
   - e. Moses' last view of land and blessing   32:45–33:29
   - f. Moses' death   34:1–12

Comparison of Deuteronomy with the Covenant Code of Exodus 20–23		
Ex 21:1–11	=	Dt 15:12–18
Ex 21:12–14	=	Dt 19:1–13
Ex 21:16	=	Dt 24:7
Ex 22:16f	=	Dt 22:28–29
Ex 22:21–24	=	Dt 24:17–22
Ex 22:25	=	Dt 23:19–20
Ex 22:26f	=	Dt 24:10–13
Ex 22:29f	=	Dt 15:19–23
Ex 22:31	=	Dt 14:3–21
Ex 23:1	=	Dt 19:16–21
Ex 23:2f, 6–8	=	Dt 16:18–20
Ex 23:4f	=	Dt 22:1–4
Ex 23:9	=	Dt 24:17f
Ex 23:10f	=	Dt 15:1–11
Ex 23:12	=	Dt 5:13–15
Ex 23:13	=	Dt 6:13
Ex 23:14–17	=	Dt 16:1–17
Ex 23:19a	=	Dt 26:2–10
Ex 23:19b	=	Dt 14:21b

death. In general, almost every chapter gives away the secret that the authors are really not looking ahead to a new time but are rather looking backward from deep in the time of the monarchy.

Deuteronomy and the Covenant

Because the outlook of the book comes from the seventh century B.C. and not the thirteenth, the Book of Deuteronomy's teaching does not center so much on warning against dangers *ahead* as it does on *returning* to the covenant and learning to be more faithful than their parents and grandparents had been through the years. The preface to the law code in chapters 12–26 fills all of chapters 5–11. Again and again, the author summons the people to be obedient to the "commandments, the statutes and the laws" which the Lord their God commanded Moses to teach them. Each time, he places this obedience in terms of the covenant love between Yahweh and the people. As Deuteronomy 7:12 puts it: "If you will listen to these commandments and obey them faithfully, then the Lord your God will keep with you his covenant and his constant love just as he promised to your ancestors." The relationship is very special, for God "has chosen you from all the nations on the face of the earth to be a people specially his own" (Dt 7:6). This election by God carried with it an obligation to be grateful to God and to live lives worthy of such divine favor. Deuteronomy stresses the duty of service and obedience by using words and language from the treaties made between kings in the Ancient Near East. We have already seen how the covenant on Mount Sinai shares in the idea of a treaty between a ruler and a smaller subject state. But only Deuteronomy follows the actual format of a treaty as they were commonly drawn up by the Assyrians and Hittites. The six stages of the treaty form can be found in the Book of Deuteronomy, creating a framework for the authors' message:

The preamble in which the king is named	Dt 1:1
The historical list of the king's kindnesses to the small state	Dt 1:2–4:40
The list of demands to be obeyed	Dt 4:44–26:19
Provisions to have the treaty read each year	Dt 27:8
The witness of the gods	(none)
Curses on those who break the demands and blessings on those who keep them	Dt 27–28

The great king who has agreed to enter into this covenant with Israel is Yahweh, the only God of heaven and earth, and so the central theme of Deuteronomy's law is true worship of him and rejection of any pagan idols. The heart of Israelite faith is summed up by Deuteronomy in the famous creed of Judaism, which also serves as its most treasured prayer:

Hear, O Israel, the Lord our God is one Lord, and you shall love the Lord your God with all your heart and with all your soul and with all your strength (Dt 6:4–5).

And to make sure that Israel will never forget this commandment, Deuteronomy goes on to add:

And these words which I command you today shall be put on your heart, and you shall teach them carefully to your

children, and you shall talk of them when you sit in the
house, and when you are out walking, when you lie down
at night and when you arise in the morning. And you shall
bind them on your hands, and tie them on your forehead,
and you shall write them on the doorposts of your houses
and gates (Dt 6:6–9).

Deuteronomy quotes the entire ten commandments (first
found in Exodus 20) as a heading to its message (chapter 5), but the
first commandment really forms the foundation for everything else.
Its importance can be seen in the repeated commands not to walk
after other gods, to tear down all the pagan shrines in the land, and
to remember that it was Yahweh alone who brought them out of
their slavery with a strong arm and upraised hand. Israel must not
just be loyal to Yahweh; it must also be holy as God is holy. Chapter
9 gives a long list of times that Israel had rebelled against Yahweh in
the desert period of forty years. "Ever since I have known you,"
Moses is made to say, "you have been rebels against the Lord" (Dt
9:24). He concludes with a question to all the people:

And now, Israel, what does the Lord your God ask of you,
but to fear the Lord your God, and walk in all his ways, to
love him and serve the Lord your God with all your heart
and with all your soul, and to keep the commandments and
statutes of the Lord which I have commanded you today
for your own good? (Dt 10:12–13).

And why should they love these commandments so much?

The Lord your God is God of gods and Lord of lords, the
great, the mighty and the awesome God, who shows no
favoritism and takes no bribes. He does justice for the
orphan and the widow, he loves the foreigners in your
midst and gives them food and clothing. Love the foreigner
therefore because you too were foreigners living in the
land of Egypt (Dt 10:17–19).

The Place of Worship in the Land

Another major aspect of the theology of Deuteronomy centers
on the single sanctuary. The Book of Deuteronomy never names

Jerusalem outright (since it was not a city belonging to Israel at the time of Moses), but there is no doubt that Jerusalem is meant when the authors insist on "the place that the Lord your God chooses out of all the tribes and designates as his dwelling place" (Dt 12:5). The building of the temple by Solomon and the placing of the ark of the covenant in its holy of holies does not really permit any other shrine to be "designated" by Yahweh himself. This particular law is very closely related to the reform movement of Josiah to win back the loyalty of the northern tribes who had been separated from Judah for so long, and cannot have been a very old law that dated back beyond the fall of Samaria in 722. In fact, the older law of Moses in Exodus 20:24 permitted altars to be built in many places.

A final note about Deuteronomy should mention the importance placed on the right use of the land. Obedience and right living will lead to a prosperous land, but idolatry and disobedience will lead to the loss of the land, destruction of the people, exile, and the return of the pagan peoples to power. The choices are made very plain. Obedience will lead to blessing, and blessing equals prosperity. Sin and rebellion will lead to the curse, and the curse means failure in war, in raising crops, in preserving an independent state. Yahweh may be the God of all the earth, but he has made Israel's possession of the land of Palestine conditional on their right use of nationhood. If they abuse justice, then their society will fail. It is put most forcefully in terms of life and death in chapter 30:

> See, I place before you today life and good, death and evil. If you obey the commandments of the Lord your God which I command this day by loving the Lord your God, and by walking in his ways and keeping his commandments and his decrees and his laws, then you shall live and increase and the Lord will bless you in the land which you are about to occupy. But if your heart turns away and you do not listen, but follow after other gods and serve them, then I declare to you this day that you shall perish; you will not live in the land which you are crossing the Jordan to possess (Dt 30:15–18).

This is a very harsh warning, and almost too simple to be real. Everyone knows that good people do not always receive blessing and that the wicked do not always end up punished. But Deuteronomy is not really saying that God will always act in one way or another in every situation in life. No, Deuteronomy is looking back at a very special situation that has *already happened* and he knows that God asked for obedience and Israel has many times disobeyed and turned away. So the argument is more of an explanation for Israel's problems—its state of subjection to foreign powers, its many corrupt kings over the years, its injustices and its failures. Deuteronomy points out that things could have been different if the people had taken their religious covenant more seriously and lived according to the law of the covenant over the centuries past. Not just in chapter 30, but in many of the passages in chapters 28 and 29 as well, it is very difficult not to get the impression that the warnings of exile and affliction come from the actual experience of the writers who have seen it and know the devastation personally. At the same time, they hold out hope that Israel can change and return and God may relent and gather the exiles back to the land.

Who Wrote Deuteronomy?

Deuteronomy is a rich mixture of references to the old covenant laws of the Book of Exodus and the evils of much later idolatry and unfaithfulness in the promised land. It claims to be a speech from the lips of Moses, but has none of the early style or flavor of the old Yahwist or Elohist traditions that tell the story of Moses. It is full of warlike images, calling the people to do battle and conquer in a "holy war" (see Dt 20:1–20, 21:10–14, 23:10–15, and most of chapter 7), yet it speaks often of coming exile and disaster (see 4:26–31, 28:47–53 and 30:1–10). Do we have any hope of finding the real Deuteronomy in all of this? At least one important help comes from simply sorting out the different concerns of the book into groups according to which traditions of the Pentateuch they are most like, the Yahwist or the Elohist. These two sources represent, on one hand, the outlook of the southern tribe of Judah with its house of David and the temple, versus, on the other, the outlook of the northern tribes who had broken away from Solomon in the 900's. It leads to the conclusion that *both* traditions are strong in Deuteronomy:

Northern Connections:

(a) similarity to the language of Hosea on the love of God and the covenant

(b) use of "Horeb" for Mount Sinai, typical of the Elohist source

THE LAST DAYS OF JUDAH

   (c)   strong polemic against worship of the baals as in the story of Elijah

   (d)   the war-language, found most strongly in the Elijah/Elisha cycle

   (e)   a very favorable view toward the role of prophets

   (f)   a negative view of the moral goodness of kings (chapter 17)

   (g)   high regard for Moses as the charismatic leader of all Israel

   (h)   use of the northern mountains of Gerizim and Ebal for the covenant renewal ceremony (chapter 27)

   (i)   similarity to the covenant renewal ideas of Shechem, a northern city, in Joshua 23–24

   (j)   no mention of the Davidic house as a special covenant

   (k)   the summons to "all Israel" in a typical northern style

Southern (Judah) Connections:

   (a)   Jerusalem as the place where God placed his name

   (b)   use of the ark of the covenant which was in the temple

   (c)   a teaching style that many think was typical of the rural areas of Judah, nationalistic but not legalistic, and very moralistic, perhaps done by levites

   (d)   use of the word "elect" or "chosen" for Israel, a word used only of David's election as king before this (2 Sam 7)

   (e)   the very precise link between Deuteronomy and the law book found in the temple

Since the book has ties to both the northern traditions before the fall of that kingdom in 722 and to the problems of Judah in the time of Josiah a hundred years later, scholars generally agree that the roots of Deuteronomy's thought lie first in the north, coming from the same background that produced the Elohist ideas in the Pentateuch, the prophet Hosea with his deep sense of the covenant love of God, and the fiery traditions of zeal for Yahweh seen in the Elijah and Elisha stories of 1 Kings 17 through 2 Kings 10. At some point these ideas were brought into Judah and put together as the basis for a reform of the southern kingdom. The most likely course of events is as follows.

Northern prophets and their followers, together with the religious leaders (priests and levites), developed the set of laws that make up Deuteronomy 12–26 together with the basic call to reform that is found in its preface in Deuteronomy 5–11. When Samaria fell to the Assyrians, many of these prophets, levites and others fled south to Judah for safety, bringing their program and their ideas with them. At this point, King Hezekiah of Judah took over the basic ideas and began his own reform sometime between 720 and 700 B.C. Both 2 Kings 18–20 and 2 Chronicles 29–32 stress that he undertook a serious religious renewal against pagan cults very much like that later credited to Josiah. Hezekiah no doubt wanted to bring together the best of the northern tradition and the best of the southern vision of temple and monarchy now that the kingdom of Samaria had been destroyed for good. Most experts believe that it was under Hezekiah that the "J" and the "E" sources were combined to form the Books of Genesis, Exodus, Leviticus and Numbers. There is also some evidence that Hezekiah desired to save older traditions in the label found in the Book of Proverbs (25:1) that "the men of Hezekiah transmitted these proverbs of Solomon." Possibly then it was under Hezekiah that chapters 5 through 26 (with chapter 28) were written down as the basis of the reform. When Hezekiah died and his son Manasseh began an age of persecution of true Yahwism and violent rejection of the Deuteronomic program, the book was hidden away in the temple, or simply lost and forgotten in a corner, or still more probably was guarded by the priests and levites until a better moment came. That moment happened under Josiah. The book's reappearance had a moving effect on the young king, and he followed its program fully.

The Results of Josiah's Reform

While Josiah lived, he fought hard to make his reform work. The Second Book of Kings remembered him as the greatest king that Judah and Israel ever had after David himself (2 Kgs 23:25). But unfortunately his political decisions were not as good as his religious ideas, and he died in a hopeless battle to stop the Egyptian army from going to help the now-desperate Assyrian empire in 609. His reform had lasted only thirteen years, and if we can believe prophets such as Nahum, Habakkuk and Jeremiah, it seemed to have died with its founder.

On the international scene, these were difficult times. The Babylonians had won victory after victory under Nabopolassar, and in 612 B.C. the combined armies of Babylon and the Medes captured and burned to the ground the great city of Nineveh itself. The remnant of the Assyrian forces gathered in Haran, the city of Abraham, for a last stand. The Egyptian pharaoh, Necho, who had the great dreams of an Egypt free from all foreign powers, did not want to see Babylon become too strong and replace Assyria as the terrible world power that would then try to take Egypt as well. He preferred a weak Assyria that survived to no Assyria at all, and sent his forces north to help save the day. They failed and the Babylonians smashed Assyria forever in 609. But Egypt did not leave Palestine. It decided to control the kingdom of Judah as a buffer against the Babylonians now that its king had died. Thus began the last years of Judah, caught in a conflict between Egypt and Babylon, trying to play off both sides to win back its freedom, and getting more and more dangerously close to disaster. We will follow the sad train of events in those final days in the next chapter on Jeremiah, but first there are two more voices raised in Judah on behalf of Yahweh during Josiah's reform that have been preserved in the Bible: Nahum of Elkosh and Habakkuk.

The Prophet Nahum

Zephaniah had lived before Josiah's reform and focused his zeal mostly against the evils of idolatry and faithlessness in Judah itself. Nahum provides a different view taken from within the time of reform and directed mostly against the evil of Assyria. This is one of the most colorful and dramatic books in the Old Testament with its ferocious description of the Babylonian siege of Nineveh. A short book of three chapters, it contains mostly angry and impassioned hatred against Assyria. The first chapter pictures Yahweh coming as a divine warrior to punish idolators and deliver Judah from its enemies. The second chapter describes the battle for Nineveh, and the third mixes battle scenes with reasons for God's wrath.

While it can be counted among the most stirring sections of the Bible, Nahum remains somewhat of a mystery book. We know nothing about the author except his name; he gives us no personal details, and no message of comfort about the God of the covenant and his mercy. Because it is so unified, it probably was written or spoken all on one occasion, perhaps as a long poem, at some festival in the temple. It takes the form of a battle curse, known to be part of the message of prophets in many ancient nations. Before battle or in time of great danger, the prophet delivers an oracle of doom against the enemy and makes it into a word of comfort and hope for his own people. It often serves to lift the morale of an army before battle. In this case, the description of Nineveh and its fall is so clear that Nahum possibly spoke it very near the date of the event. Since Nineveh fell in 612, we can guess that Nahum delivered these words sometime between 615 and 610. Because of their power and their deep trust in the protection of God, they were saved and made part of the collection of prophets so that future generations could know what God had done, and learn to trust as Nahum had.

The Prophet Habakkuk

Habakkuk lived shortly after Nahum and describes a time when Babylon was taking over the Near East from the fallen Assyrians. Habakkuk 1:6–11 describes Babylon as the scourge of God causing terror everywhere. God declares that the Babylonians will be his instruments of punishment: "For I am doing a work in your days that you would not believe if I told it" (Hb 1:5). But Habakkuk also complains how the wicked continue to persecute those who seek justice and how idolatry abounds (Hb 2:6–11). Who are these wicked? Perhaps the people of Judah themselves, fallen back into evil after the death of Josiah. But also they are the Babylonians. God may use them, but that doesn't mean Habakkuk thought of them as saints. God's plan must be carried out, but he will punish the evil and the idolatry of the Babylonians just as much as that of his own people (see Hb 1:11; 2:5).

Chapter 3 is a hymn in honor of Yahweh as the divine warrior. It describes the Lord's march across the earth to do battle against his enemies, assisted by his allies of storm, pestilence and plague (Hb 3:4–5). The poet is terrified at the vision and yet ends with a deep trust that the coming of the Lord will bring salvation and rejoicing (Hb 3:16–18). Habakkuk thus shares many elements with Nahum. His oracles are very close to the style of psalms of trust and lament, and may also reflect the role of the prophet in liturgy. In a ceremony of prayer or sacrifice to God in a time of some great danger, the prophet was inspired by God to deliver an oracle that both condemned evil and asked for trust in Yahweh's saving power. But the heart of his message, found in Habakkuk 2:1–5, is purely prophetic. Habakkuk climbs his watchtower to wait for a word from the Lord. God sends the word that is to be declared clearly and plainly to all even if it is very slow in coming about: *the righteous who believe will live, the wicked will not succeed.*

Zephaniah, Nahum and Habakkuk represent a resurgence of trust in the mighty power of Yahweh to turn the tide of world tyrants. To make their point, they have returned to the ancient language of God as a divine warrior. Filled with the reforming zeal of Josiah and Deuteronomy, they declare that fidelity to Yahweh will be more lasting than any empire. There is not much evidence that many listened to their words, especially those in the high offices of the royal palace. Judah continued to trust more in powerful nations than in a quiet attempt to build a just society. We turn now to the most tragic, but perhaps also the greatest, of the prophets, Jeremiah. He lived through Josiah's reform, through the period of failure, and through the collapse of the whole nation—all in one lifetime! He left us a record unequaled for both prophetic and personal pain.

STUDY QUESTIONS

1. Identify the following: Manasseh, Amon, Josiah, Zephaniah, Nahum, Habakkuk.
2. Briefly describe the Book of Zephaniah. What are its contents?
3. How does Zephaniah compare with Amos and Isaiah?
4. How is Josiah's reform similar to the law of Moses?
5. Briefly describe the significance and characteristics of the Book of Deuteronomy. What are its contents? When was it written? What is its relationship to the other four books of the Pentateuch?
6. How does the Book of Deuteronomy view the covenant?
7. Who wrote the Book of Deuteronomy?

Chapter 18

JEREMIAH AND THE
DEUTERONOMIC HISTORY

Suggested Scripture Readings:

Jeremiah 1–3, 7–8
Jeremiah 18–20, 26–29
Jeremiah 30–31

A. JEREMIAH THE PROPHET

The Background of the Book of Jeremiah

Jeremiah's book opens with his call as a prophet in the thirteenth year of King Josiah about 627 B.C. He claims to be young, too young (Jer 1:6), and some scholars believe this date actually refers to his birth (he is "called from the womb" in Jeremiah 1:5), but the majority opinion still sees 627 as the beginning of his actual ministry. Since he continues to preach down past the final exile in 586 and doesn't disappear from sight until about 582 B.C., he holds the biblical record for prophetic activity, some forty-five years in all. His book is remarkable not only because it covers the drama of Josiah's reform, the failures of the kings that followed him and the final collapse of the whole nation, but because it reveals a side to prophets that is rarely seen: the emotionally powerful feelings that went with their zeal for Yahweh's word. This reveals more of the individual than any other Old Testament book. It shows Jeremiah to be "a man born out of his due time," a person in ancient dress with whom modern readers can readily identify.

360

But while we gain a sympathy and understanding of the man Jeremiah, we must still wrestle with the difficult way the book is put together. Ancients did not have the same sense of order as modern people do, and they often seem to simply gather words in any old way. Indeed, the present material, like most prophetic books, really had first appeared in smaller collections taken from various sources, and the editors had to organize it as best they could without destroying the earlier parts altogether. They worked according to their ideas of how to best present the prophet's message for their own time, and the reasoning they used is not always clear to modern readers or scholars today. Several different types of divisions can be discovered in the text.

First of all, there are three major time periods in which Jeremiah worked. The first takes place during the reign of Josiah, from the time of his call in 627 down to at least 622 and the beginning of the reform, and perhaps down even to the death of Josiah in 609. We do not know much about this period except that many of the early oracles in chapters 1–6 probably reflect Jeremiah's demands for conversion and reform. The second period is during the reign of Josiah's son, King Jehoiakim, from 609 down to 598. During this period, Josiah's reform collapsed and Jehoiakim seems to have purposely moved in the opposite direction and re-established many pagan practices. The third and final period of Jeremiah's ministry took place in the twelve years between the first destruction of Jerusalem by the Babylonians in 598 and its second and final ruin in 586, with a short period of activity in the following years of 586 to 582.

These three periods form a bare skeleton for Jeremiah's life. The oracles and stories about the prophets, however, do not actually appear in their proper order as he delivered them. They have been collected and arranged by other principles than a time-line—although some effort was made to keep as many events in order as possible. Thus we have much from the last two periods of Jeremiah's life but not much from the first. A brief outline of the whole book of fifty-two chapters gives five divisions, each with its own type of materials:

1. Chapters 1–25   Oracles and accounts involving the evil of Judah under three kings: Josiah (1–6), Jehoiakim (7–20), and Zedekiah (21–24).

2. Chapters 26–36   Stories about the prophet and oracles from the times of Jehoiakim and Zedekiah.

3. Chapters 37–45   The story of Jeremiah's last days (told by Baruch?).

4. Chapters 46–51   Oracles against foreign nations.

5. Chapter 52   An appendix describing the fall of Jerusalem in 586 (taken from 2 Kings 25 to complete the story of Jeremiah's words).

But even within these five sections, the materials are not always the same kind. Oracles delivered in poetry stand side by side with stories about the prophet's life in prose, and oracles in prose are mixed with homily material very similar to the Book of Deuteronomy. It has become common for scholars to discuss three special types of material that can be found scattered through the book:

Type A material   *Original oracles* of Jeremiah, preserved as he gave them, almost always in poetry. These are most common in chapters 1–25 and 46–51.

Type B material   *Memoirs or biographical accounts* about the prophet's work or personal suffering. These fall mostly in chapters 26–45. They are from someone else than Jeremiah, usually thought to be his scribe Baruch (named in Jer 36:4), but they are not completely orderly, so may well come from several different sources.

Type C material   *Prose oracles* that have been handed down and edited, often extensively, by members of the school of Deuteronomy. They usually appear in prose and contain many typical Deuteronomic words. They can be found in chapters 1–25 at places such as chapters 7, 16 and 21, but also later, as in chapter 32.

All of this must make us realize that this is a collection *about* Jeremiah as much as it is an anthology *of* his own sayings and writings. Some of the oracles in prose form will be more in the way of a third-person report about what Jeremiah said on a certain day, or even what he *would have said* about some evil situation—but the editors no longer had his words, so they composed it in his style. This is close to the method used by Deuteronomy and seems to have been very popular in the late monarchy period. The fact that some oracles were not actually said just the way they were written down does not mean that we cannot know Jeremiah; they rather add to his own words a number of important insights into his message made by his followers at the time. Their value is great, for without them his oracles may never have been saved for future generations.

The Political Situation of Jeremiah's Day

During Jeremiah's ministry of forty-five years, the world changed dramatically. When he began, Assyria was still the world's greatest power, but by the time he died in exile in Egypt, Babylon stood supreme. Facing Babylon, however, in the moment of victory was the Egyptian army of Pharaoh Necho who had rushed to help the weakened Assyrian army stop the Babylonians from winning a total victory. Egypt failed in that but did hold onto most of Syria and Palestine. The small countries, who had hoped so much for their freedom as Assyria fell, learned the hard lesson that they were going to simply change masters. But there was no room for two great powers in the Near East, and after four years (609–605), Nabopolassar's son and crown prince, Nebuchadnezzar, defeated the Egyptian armies near the Syrian city of Carchemesh.

The old King Nabopolassar died shortly after, and Nebuchadnezzar took the throne of Babylon in 605 to begin a forty-three year reign. He restored the ancient splendor of Babylon and built his famous "hanging gardens," one of the seven wonders of the ancient world. But it was not a time of hope or joy in Judah, which had barely freed itself from Assyrian control when it was forced to submit first to Egypt, then to Babylon.

While Josiah lived, the political situation in Judah remained calm. But the king died young trying to play a role in the battle for control of the falling Assyrian empire. His sons inherited a much changed situation, and were much less stable: three of them plus a grandson sat on the throne of David in the next twenty years. The dates they ruled can be diagrammed as follows:

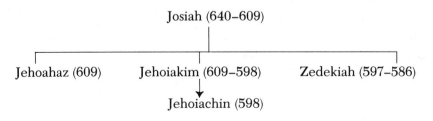

Josiah (640–609)

Jehoahaz (609)   Jehoiakim (609–598)   Zedekiah (597–586)

Jehoiachin (598)

At Josiah's death fighting the Egyptians, his son Jehoahaz was named to succeed him even though he was not the oldest son. This was probably because he promised to continue his father's policies. But the Egyptians who now controlled Palestine would not permit a leader who favored Babylon, so they removed Jehoahaz from the throne almost immediately (after a three month rule) and named his older brother Jehoiakim to be king. Jehoiakim readily reversed his father Josiah's policies and became an obedient subject of Egypt. But when the Babylonians drove Egypt out of Asia at the battle of Carchemesh in 605, Jehoiakim immediately reversed himself again and pledged loyalty to Babylon. It must have been done unwillingly, however, for not long after this he began to plot toward breaking free of foreign control. When he finally refused to pay the annual tribute money to Babylon in 599, it was open revolt. The Babylonian army appeared the next spring, in 598, and, after a short siege, forced the city of Jerusalem to surrender, took many of the leading citizens away as exiles to Babylon (2 Kings 24:10–16), and stripped the temple of all its treasures. In the middle of this rebellion, Jehoiakim died and left his young son Jehoiachin to become king just in time to surrender. Nebuchadnezzar took the boy-king into exile and placed his uncle, Jehoiakim's brother Zedekiah, on the throne in his place.

Archaeology has provided us with a first-hand account of this battle for Jerusalem in 598 from the records of King Nebuchadnezzar himself. It is part of the Babylonian Chronicle, the yearly list of the king's activities, and the part that relates to Jerusalem comes in the seventh year of the king's reign:

> In the seventh year, in the month Kislev, the king of Akkad mustered his troops, marched to Hatti-land, and besieged the city of Judah and on the second day of the month Adar he captured the city and seized its king. He appointed there a king after his own heart, received its heavy tribute and sent it to Babylon.

The twelve years between the first fall of the city of Jerusalem in 598 and its final destruction in 586 was a troubled time with many people still hoping for victory over Babylon and complete independence. Zedekiah, as he is seen in the Book of Jeremiah, proved to be a weak and uncertain man who first leaned one way and then another. But finally he too broke with Babylon about 589 B.C. under the prodding of the new Egyptian pharaoh, Hophra.

Nebuchadnezzar moved quickly to deal with this rebellion because he feared Egyptian designs on Palestine. He captured all the cities of Judah, surrounded Jerusalem and for two years starved the people into defeat. When all was lost, Zedekiah tried to flee at night to safety but the Babylonian army caught him near Jericho and he had to watch while his sons were executed before his eyes, then have his own eyes put out and finally be led away to die a captive in a Babylonian prison. Nebuchadnezzar took more people into exile, this time leaving only a remnant, including Jeremiah, to make some kind of a living in the land. He tore down the city walls and leveled the temple to the ground so that Jerusalem would no longer serve as a center for Jewish hopes. But despite his efforts, many still waited for the day when God would restore the city (cf. Jer 41:4–8).

Jeremiah's Message

Jeremiah came from Anathoth, a small town north of Jerusalem that actually lay in the old northern tribe of Benjamin. Perhaps his father, who was a priest, had learned much the same traditions as are now found in Deuteronomy. In any case, Jeremiah proved to be both a great defender of the best of the northern tradition of Hosea and Deuteronomy and a true southerner in love with Zion and Jerusalem. In style he favors longer oracles than did the earlier prophets, with a great deal of emotional drama in them. He prepares the way for his younger contemporary, Ezekiel, who brings the art of the elevated and literary oracle to perfection. But Jeremiah was not so much a writer as a speaker. He used colorful imagery of battle, plague, and the terrors of war, as well as the everyday pictures drawn from potmaking, cooking, metalwork and sexuality. We gain a good picture of the man Jeremiah in his book because we

JEREMIAH'S USE OF VISIONS AND PARABLES FOR HIS MESSAGE			
Visions		*Parables*	
The almond tree	1:11–12	Jeremiah's bachelorhood	16:1–4
The boiling pot	1:13–19	The potter at work	18:1–12
The loin cloth	13:1–7	The broken pot	19:1–20:6
The basket of figs	24:1–10	The yoke of iron	27:1–28:17
The wine-drinkers	25:15–38	The field purchase	32:6–44
		The pile of stones	43:8–13
		The book in the river	51:59–64

see him through many eyes at slightly different angles: we have his own oracles, the stories about him by Baruch, and the theological reflections on him by the Deuteronomic writers.

But all three agree on his singleminded sense of mission. He never stopped preaching against the two major evils of his day: *idolatry* and *injustice*. He was relentless even when it led to great personal suffering and persecution. But he was also tender and filled with compassion for the people, and he often pleaded for people to be converted and come back to the covenant, so that Yahweh would have mercy. He had great sensitivity both to what God asks and to what humans need to find. Abraham Heschel, the great Jewish Old Testament scholar, describes Jeremiah as the prophet of God's *pathos*—the divine sympathy. When the people refused to hear his words, Jeremiah felt the anguish personally. But he felt the pain borne by the God they had rejected even more. In one moving event of his life, God demands of Jeremiah that he remain unmarried as a witness to terrible conditions that are coming on the land to make the raising of children a horror instead of a joy (Jer 16:1–4).

Above all, Jeremiah's message was one of obedience to the divine will expressed in the covenant God had made with Israel. In this he stood in the shoes of all the prophets before him. But in a special way he continued the approach of Hosea, stressing the tender love of God and the divine willingness to receive the people back. Yahweh desires to forgive and treat Israel as a beloved wife:

> Thus says the Lord,
> I remember the faithfulness of your youth,
>   your love as a bride,
> How you followed me in the desert,
>   in the wilderness.
> Israel was holy to the Lord (Jer 2:2–3).

> Return, faithless Israel, says the Lord.
>   I will not look upon you with anger,
> For I am compassionate.
>   I will not be angry forever (Jer 3:12).

> And I thought you would call me, "my father,"
>   and would not turn away from following me.
> Indeed as a faithless wife deserts her husband,
>   so you have been unfaithful
>   to me, O house of Israel (Jer 3:19–20).

Because the people did not respond to the call of Yahweh, Jeremiah's words of hope for repentance became fewer and fewer. By the time of Jehoiakim and Zedekiah, he had despaired that anything could turn back the punishment that the people deserved for their sins. In several passages, Jeremiah even declares that God ordered him not to intercede on behalf of the people any longer (Jer 7:6; 11:14).

Jeremiah's condemnations were just as strong as those of Amos, Hosea or Isaiah before him. He warns against the policies of going first to Assyria and then to Egypt for political gain (Jer 2:17–18), he compares the people to a camel in heat for their lust after pagan idols (Jer 2:23–24), and he condemns the oppression of the poor and powerless (Jer 2:33–34), widespread adultery and fornication (Jer 5:7–8) and the stubborn rebellion against the covenant (Jer 5:23). In between each condemnation, he calls on the people to turn back to Yahweh (Jer 3:22; 4:1; 7:3; 8:5; 18:8). But his greatest scorn is kept for those who turn to pagan statues and idols for strength. He describes the piety of people who call a piece of wood "father" (Jer 2:27–28) and bow down before a gilded and richly clothed idol which is as dead and unmoving as a scarecrow in a cornfield (Jer 10:3–5). To regain their loyalty to Yahweh he calls up the memory of the exodus and the tender care of God in the desert years, hoping to move them (see Jer 2:27–28; 7:16–19; 10:1–5; 11:1–5; 19:4–5).

If Judah will not hear and listen to the word that Jeremiah brings, then God will surely permit an enemy to destroy them. The prophet sees a vision of a foe from the north pouring destruction over the land like a pot of boiling water being tipped on its side (Jer 1:13–15). This "foe from the north" is never named but could be none other than the Babylonian army on the march. Jeremiah returns to the theme often (Jer 4:5–8; 4:13; 5:15; 6:22; 10:22), and often resembles fiery Nahum with his battle scenes against Judah (Jer 4:5–29; 6:1–5). Like a schoolteacher repeating the lessons again and again, Jeremiah drums the warning into the ears of his people. Another favorite image is borrowed from the work of forging metal objects. Just as ores have to be burned so that the metal in them will melt and separate and be able to be shaped into tools and weapons, so God will burn away the bad ore of Israel and Judah to get good metal (Jer 6:27–30). He warns repeatedly that the punishment God sends will be so severe that it can be named "Terror on every side" (Jer 6:25; 20:3, 10; 46:5; 49:29).

Sometimes the prophet seems near despair over the evil that he sees around him. He cries out that "death" has climbed up into the windows, has walked into our palaces (Jer 9:20); he laments the incurable wound that only gets worse until the patient dies, and no healing oils can be found anywhere (Jer 8:22; 30:12–13). He imitates the funeral laments for the dead: "Take up lamenting and weeping for the mountains, and wailing for the desert pastures, because they have been laid waste so no one can pass by" (Jer 9:10).

The Temple Sermon

Soon after Jehoiakim became king and began to turn back from Josiah's reform, Jeremiah went to the temple to proclaim a word of warning. This "temple sermon" was so powerful and shocking that the editors included two different accounts of it, once in chapter 7, and again in chapter 26. He shocked his audience of religious people who had come to the temple to pray by declaring that their trust in God's protection was in vain. Instead, Jeremiah declares, God will wipe out the Jerusalem temple just as he had earlier destroyed the sanctuary of Shiloh where the ark of the covenant had been kept in the time of Samuel. Chapter 7 develops Jeremiah's arguments at great length, pointing out the constant idolatry and hypocrisy of the people, and promising that the wrath of God's justice cannot be stopped. Chapter 26 is shorter and probably closer to the actual original words of Jeremiah. It also includes the reactions of both those who heard the oracle and the authorities who had to deal with it. Jeremiah's words angered the people, the priests, and the prophets who were attached to the temple and they seized him and threatened his life (Jer 26:8). The princes, who were the civil authorities, rushed up to the gate of the temple where law cases were heard, and held a trial right on the spot. The priests and prophets pushed for his death. But when Jeremiah said in his own defense that he had acted on God's command when he called them to return to the ways of the Lord, he convinced both the princes and the crowds that he was a prophet and should be spared. They argued that Micah the prophet had spoken the same way a hundred years earlier and King Hezekiah had feared to put him to death. But although on this occasion the princes decided to let Jeremiah go, they failed to convince the priests and prophets, who continued to be major opponents of Jeremiah's mission.

This incident added to Jeremiah's anguish but did not stop him from speaking again. The oracles gathered together in chapters 20–23 show that he often singled out the leaders, priests and prophets for particular warning. It makes it easy to understand why he constantly faced strong opposition. He was persistent and fearless in his duty to announce all violations of the covenant and the coming fall of Judah and its capital city of Jerusalem. This made him unpopular and even considered a traitor by many royal officials. They wanted to convict him of high treason for undermining government policy and the will of the people to fight for the city. At times he had even predicted that the Davidic dynasty was to end forever:

> Thus says the Lord:
> Write this man (King Jehoiachin) down as childless,
>   whose life will never prosper;
> He will leave no descendants to sit
>   on the throne of David to rule Judah (Jer 22:30).

At other times he had advised surrender:

> To Zedekiah, king of Judah, I spoke similarly: "Bring your neck under the yoke of the king of Babylon and serve him and his nation and live" (Jer 27:12).

> Then Jeremiah said to Zedekiah, "Thus says the Lord, the God of hosts, the God of Israel: If you surrender to the generals of the king of Babylon, your life will be spared and this city will not be burned to the ground, and you and your house shall survive" (Jer 38:17).

King Jehoiakim earlier had sought to arrest him, probably to execute him, but friends in high places had warned Jeremiah and hidden him away (Jer 36). Later, Jeremiah was arrested several times, thrown into a prison or even into an open water cistern (Jer 37–39), and saved only because King Zedekiah considered him a prophet and was afraid to have him killed. The kings and their officials were most disturbed because other prophets spoke words of encouragement and support for the national war for independence. Jeremiah not only stood aside from these but denounced them as false prophets. Perhaps his strongest words against any group were directed at prophets who claimed to speak God's word but came out with only comfort and pats on the back for the people they served. In chapter 23 he levels his most serious attacks on the integrity of prophets who claim to have dreams or visions but in fact simply repeat old formulas and official sounding phrases (Jer 23:26, 30), while they themselves live lives of adultery, dishonesty, and even idolatry (Jer 23:14).

Chapter 28 tells how Jeremiah denounced the message of Hananiah, a prophet who was loudly proclaiming that God would soon defeat the Babylonians. Since both prophets did symbolic actions (Jeremiah wore a yoke on his neck to show the years of slavery ahead; Hananiah broke it in two to show the coming liberation), and both spoke with authority, "Thus says the Lord," it was difficult for people to know whom to believe. Jeremiah used two proofs against Hananiah: first, he predicted that God would strike him dead as a sign that his message was false (Jer 28:16); second, he challenged the right of a prophet to proclaim a word of salvation unless he can make it come to pass. He says:

> Now hear this word which I speak before you and all the people. The prophets who have gone before you and me from earliest times have prophesied war, famine and plague against many nations and mighty kingdoms. As for the prophet who prophesies peace, when that word of the prophet actually happens, then it will be known that the Lord sent him (Jer 28:7–9).

In chapter 23 Jeremiah uses one other major argument to back up his right to oppose the prophets of hope. He claims to have stood in the heavenly court when God made his decisions and to have been sent back to speak the divine word of judgment. This is very similar to the scene described in 1 Kings 22 about the prophet Micaiah ben Imlah. Micaiah had opposed four hundred prophets of the king who supported the royal plans to go to war. He argued that his word was true and theirs were false because he had known first-hand that God had decided in heaven to send a lying spirit into their mouths and give the true word to Micaiah. For both Micaiah and Jeremiah, the ultimate test of the prophetic office is to hear and understand the divine word while being in some way taken up into the actual presence of God and his angels who are deciding what to do on earth. It is the claim to be the *messenger* of the divine decisions from heaven to earth. And it goes far to explain why the prophets that have been preserved in the Bible use such formulas as "Thus says the Lord" or "This is the oracle of the Lord." These are formulas used by messengers and heralds all over the Ancient Near East. The prophetic role is primarily one of speaking what God has already spoken. It is a message addressed from the plans and appeals of a caring God to the hearts and minds of human peoples. It must be thought about and pondered, not just "enjoyed."

Jeremiah's "Confessions"

Jeremiah was persecuted by both King Jehoiakim and King Zedekiah. But Zedekiah at least respected his prophetic office as genuine even while keeping him in prison. Jehoiakim, as Jeremiah 36 makes clear, actively hated Jeremiah and sought to silence him somehow without going so far as to murder him. Jeremiah, in turn, saw Jehoiakim as the chief offender against Josiah's reforms and had few kind words for the king. So it is no wonder that this monarch's years were also the most difficult for Jeremiah. The oracles collected in chapters 11–20 catalogue moments of loneliness and feelings of despair that sometimes gripped the prophet. A few passages in particular stand out as deeply moving expressions of the prophetic trust in God mixed with a sense of total aloneness: Jeremiah 11:18–12:6; 15:10–21; 17:14–18; 18:18–23; 20:7–18. These five "confessions" borrow many expressions from the psalms of lament and trust and so we must be careful not to overstate how emotionally worked up Jeremiah seems to be. He hid behind the traditional phrases of the psalms so that the attention would focus on the point that God will surely deliver the prophet out of these terrible situations because God loves and guards Jeremiah while he proclaims the divine word.

But at the same time we can readily believe that the descriptions of how the people have tried to kill him (Jer 11:18–20; 18:18–20), how he was left in anguish while his enemies prospered (Jer 12:1–6), how he is mocked and made a fool of (Jer 20:7), how he wishes God would wipe out his foes and destroy them (Jer 17:18; 18:22–23; 20:12), and how even God seems to have betrayed him (Jer 10:7) all come straight from the heart of the man. They sound like someone on the edge of giving up altogether, of throwing away his work as a prophet and calling it quits. But through it all, Jeremiah clearly lasted and endured the awful burden God had put upon his back. The nature of these "confessions" as a personal testimony to the inner struggle of the prophet is unique among the books of the Old Testament. Even Jeremiah's great model, Hosea, never tells us so much about his own personal life.

Jeremiah's trials are told in great depth in the section called Baruch's biography (chapters 36–45), and his own words reveal much about his sense of mission. Jeremiah was no silent sufferer; he sometimes yelled loudly. He had longings to return and live on the land far from the danger and agony of the capital city (Jer 32), but it was not to be. Despite the loneliness, the sense of frustration and the very real horror of having to tell his own people that God was going to wipe out their country, Jeremiah kept his first and greatest loyalty to the word that God had given him to speak—like it or not!

The Call of the Prophet

It is time to return to the opening scene in the Book of Jeremiah to understand Jeremiah's life and preaching. The first chapter stands as a preface to his words, laying out the core of meaning that the reader is to find in the chapters which follow. It is built around the special call that Jeremiah received to the office of prophet. It has two scenes, verses 5–10 and 11–19. In the first, God speaks to Jeremiah as a young man and tells him that he has been set aside for the task of prophet from before his birth. Jeremiah objects that he is too young and that he has no training in speaking. God overrules him and promises to give the words which he will say. The prophecy will not be Jeremiah's but God's. It will be a task much greater than anything he could do on his own, for he shall speak to many nations, not just to Judah and Israel. But he will have to speak judgment as well as hope.

This first scene can be compared to the call stories of Isaiah (Is 6) and of Ezekiel (Ez 1–3). In each case, God overcomes the weakness or shortcomings of the prophet and gives him courage. Note how God says to Jeremiah in verse 8, "Fear not, I am with you!" It also points us back to the great figure of Moses, who needed God's reassurance in order to go back and proclaim God's message of freedom to his people and who declared he did not know how to speak and asked God to let his brother Aaron come with him (Ex 3–6). The prophet Jeremiah in this description will be a new Moses, both declaring God's words *and* interceding for the people when they are evil, as Moses had to do again and again in the wilderness when the Israelites rebelled out of hunger and tiredness (Num 11–14).

The second scene in verses 11–19 adds new aspects to Jeremiah's call. In a vision of the almond tree, whose blossoms come out like hundreds of eyes a month before other trees awake in the spring, he discovers he is to be a watchman for Israel, to call out warning to the city. In a second vision, he sees a boiling pot, and discovers that God will use the Babylonians as an instrument to punish Israel for its sins. Finally, God promises to make him a "fortified city, with iron pillars and a wall of bronze against the whole land of Judah" (Jer 1:18). Yahweh does not abandon his chosen ones in the hour of need, but he also did not tell Jeremiah at what price his courage would be tested.

Jeremiah's Words of Hope

Chapter 1 sums up the task of Jeremiah in the expression: "I have set you this day over nations and kingdoms, to uproot and break down, to demolish and destroy, to build and to plant" (Jer 1:10). For most of his career, at least from the days of Josiah down to the final fall of Jerusalem in 586, he was engaged in the first task of warning against the evils in Judah. His theology, firmly rooted in the mystery of the exodus as a time when God saved and yet punished rebellion, made him understand that God could indeed destroy Jerusalem. But just as the forty years in the desert were not a total end, but only the end of one generation, Jeremiah held out the longer hope that God would restore the people.

Most of these oracles of hope and comfort come from Jeremiah's last years when the doom was so certain or perhaps had even already come, that no more warning needed to be said. His message of promise takes several different forms. In the simplest example, he buys a family farm in chapter 32 despite the fact that the Babylonians had already captured it. It was Jeremiah's conviction that a day would come when he could farm it again. A second example comes from his call to surrender to Babylon because their rule will be limited. Chapter 29 contains a letter to those already in exile in Babylon after 598. In it, Jeremiah sees only seventy years before God will restore the people back to the land of their inheritance, Palestine.

Chapters 30 and 31 are often called Jeremiah's "Book of Consolation." Here are gathered many of his words of hope from a variety of different times and occasions. Some of these are addressed to "Israel" and probably were from the early days of his prophetic work under Josiah when he spoke to the remnants of the northern kingdom of Israel (Jer 30:10, 18; 31:7). Later Jeremiah reused them to comfort the exiles of Judah who would be a new Israel of the future. These oracles are filled with words of healing, visions of fruitful fields, the joy of singing, hopes for free travel to Jerusalem for feasts and a return to the great days of David and Solomon when the nation was one.

But the most vital and moving of the visions is found in Jeremiah 31:31–34, the oracle about a "new" covenant. Jeremiah sees a time when God will renew his covenant with Israel but it will be unlike the first covenant at Sinai which demanded that Israel obey the Lord with all its heart and soul and strength. Instead, it will be written in the heart and given power by God's spirit. In the past Israel had never been able to achieve full obedience by its own strength, so now God will not only give the covenant but will also give the grace to live it fully. It is a beautiful vision of the mercy of God reaching out. Such a vision has also had profound influence on later Christian interpretation of Jesus. Jesus gives a new covenant which can best be described by language borrowed from Jeremiah 31: it depends on the grace of God, it heals the heart and it gives the Spirit.

Jeremiah addresses his words to the future, but he never includes the people left at home after Babylon has sent the leading citizens into exile. Apparently after 598, and especially after 586, he became convinced that those left behind would never provide the reform and leadership needed to create the future. In chapter 24 he relates a vision of two baskets of figs, one good and one rotten. The good figs are the exiled citizens; the bad figs those still in the ruined country of Judah (see also Jer 25:1–14, 29:1–14 and 32:36–46). Nor at the final end of his life, when he was dragged to Egypt against his will (chapters 43–45), would he allow any word of encouragement to those who had sought safety there. For Jeremiah, God's plan involved a new vision that would come out of the experience of exile in Babylon, and it is to there that we must look for the continuation of biblical tradition.

B. THE DEUTERONOMIST'S HISTORY

Origins

Before looking at the great prophet of the exile, Ezekiel, it will be helpful to show the later influence of Deuteronomy and Jeremiah during that exile. Sometime near the end of the sixty years spent in Babylon, those who continued the work begun by Deuteronomy and Jeremiah put together the whole history of Israel from the time of Moses down to their own day, about 550 B.C. or even after. This work, which includes the Books of Joshua, Judges, 1 and 2 Samuel and 1 and 2 Kings, is often called the Deuteronomistic History because it gets its major inspiration from the theology of Deuteronomy and its deeply prophetic spirit from the life of Jeremiah. It was put together to show that the terrible fate of the people *can* be understood. The exile was not meaningless; it did not mean that God was powerless, nor that he simply played with Israel as his people and then cast them aside. Rather, all that had fallen on the people came as a direct result of their own sin and blindness. Naturally, this was the basic message proclaimed by both Jeremiah and Deuteronomy, but the editors and writers of the Deuteronomistic History wished to show that the same pattern could be detected throughout Israel's stay in the land of promise. In one sense, then, the whole history was organized to explain why the nation had failed and why their punishment had been deserved. But much more was intended—nothing less, in fact, than an entire explanation of how God acts in the world and how he never becomes unfaithful to his word spoken in the covenant made with Moses and carried on by the prophets whom he has sent.

The spirit of the Deuteronomistic History is profoundly prophetic. At every stage God made his promise and stood by his word; in almost every stage the people of Israel broke their word and rebelled. The lesson to be learned from the past was the teaching of Deuteronomy: "You must love the Lord your God with your whole heart and soul and strength" (Dt 6:5). Nothing less will do. There was set before Israel two choices, the way of life and prosperity, or the way of death and evil (Dt 30:15–20). They were asked to choose life, so that God could bless them in the land, but instead they chose the way of evil, and God's word must be fulfilled just as surely as his blessing would have been: "I declare to you this day that you will perish; you will not live in the land which you are crossing the Jordan to possess" (Dt 30:18). Because they interpret history as the continual fulfillment of the word of God, Jewish tradition rightly calls these books "Former Prophets" rather than today's milder and less adequate term, "Historical Books."

Sometime after the death of Josiah, the religious leaders of the reform movement inspired by Deuteronomy began to gather the old stories and archives of the past into a large collection. They had many different types of material to deal with. Some kinds, such as the chronicles of the kings of both kingdoms, were in well-preserved written forms; some, such as the stories of the judges, may have been only oral legends. In any case, these "Deuteronomists" gathered enough to form a continuous history of the people from the time of Joshua's conquest down to their own day. Where first-hand accounts were lacking or incomplete, they filled in the spaces with other stories and comments. They also needed to create a framework so that the readers would understand the religious significance of each step in the ancient history. They did this by putting long speeches into the mouths of the chief heroes of Israel at crucial moments. Thus Joshua gives a long speech in Joshua 23–24, Samuel in 1 Samuel 12, David in 2 Samuel 7, and Solomon in 1 Kings 8, and the editors themselves interpret for us in 2 Kings 17 and 25. The result is that all kinds of strange narratives stand side by side, some very reliable, others rather colorful and even exaggerated. They are in a chain, linked by a theological vision first of God's grace, followed by Israel's sin, followed by God's forgiveness and mercy, followed by more sin, etc.

The major focus of the history was created by putting the Book of Deuteronomy at the head as a prologue to the whole. By a close study of Deuteronomy anyone can have a true understanding of the two most important elements of Israel's faith: (1) the *covenant* between God and the people—and why God has punished Israel for infidelity; (2) *the promise of the land*—and why they have lost it. The Book of Deuteronomy was well suited to play the role of "interpreter" for the hundreds of years of Israelite history because it combined both the authority of the lawgiver Moses himself, a clear explanation of the covenant laws and demands tied to blessing and curse, and a spirit of prophecy that could both foresee what would happen and warn against it.

The Pattern of the Deuteronomic History

Building on the vision of Deuteronomy, the editors of the new history divided their work into five stages. First came the great conquest under Joshua related in the Book of Joshua. Second was the period of the judges, a troubled time of ups and downs when leadership was weak. This is treated in the Book of Judges and 1 Samuel. The third stage was the high point of God's blessing of the land under King David. This is mostly told in 2 Samuel. A fourth stage was the period of the kings, beginning with Solomon and continuing through the divided monarchy down to the fall of Jerusalem in 586 B.C. The fifth and last stage, barely touched but always looming over everything described in the first four periods, is the exile. These five stages represent Israel at its best and at its worst, and the Deuteronomists are eager and willing to report both.

Stage 1: Joshua. Naturally, the first scene was a time of great glory and pride for Israel. Under Joshua, Israel made its place in the land and proved its superiority to the Canaanites already living there. All of this is interpreted as a blessing from Yahweh and regularly emphasizes that Joshua and the people only achieved victory when they obeyed God and were faithful to him. This is stated clearly in Joshua 1 and again at the end in chapters 22–24, which the Deuteronomists have added. Moreover, the authors have chosen their stories carefully, including not just great battles won, but also the role of the ark of the covenant as a help from God (chapters 3 and 6), the importance of places of worship such as Gilgal (chapters 4–5), and even stories of warning, such as the punishment of Achan (chapter 7). The final speech of Joshua in chapters 22–24 underlines the message of Deuteronomy in red ink: No altars but the one which the Lord commands are to be built (Jos 22 = Dt 12), and the people are to renew the covenant with all their hearts (Jos 23–24 = Dt 4–11). This final speech of Joshua on his deathbed matches the last will and testament of Moses on his in Deuteronomy.

Stage 2: The Judges. While Joshua represents a time of blessing and obedience for the most part, Stage 2 reveals a spirit of rebellion and disobedience among the next generation of Israelites. As seen above in Chapter 10, the Book of Judges takes a different viewpoint toward the conquest. Where the Book of Joshua stressed the power of God to overcome all enemies, Judges pictures a long slow process of settlement, local uprisings, and a growing strength with many setbacks along the way. The Deuteronomists did not feel that any real contradiction existed between these two ways of looking at the time of settlement. By comparing Joshua with Judges, the reader could see the different responses to the covenant from one generation to the next. The wonderful adventures of the old heroes in the Book of Judges did not have to be thrown out but could be interpreted to show how often Israel had sinned and needed God to rescue them from their own folly. Thus the pattern of sin, punishment, call for help, raising up of the judge, victory and peace, followed again by sin and punishment, etc., illustrated perfectly the warnings that Deuteronomy had given. Samuel is the last and greatest judge in this stage of history, and he faced the difficult task of setting up a king over them. But the Deuteronomists have him issue a final warning: "If you will not pay heed to the word of the Lord, but instead rebel against his commands, he will raise his hand against you as he did against your fathers" (1 Sam 12:15).

Stage 3: King David. The time of King David was a high point of fidelity to the covenant, and a time of God's greatest blessing on the land. The authors had before them very well-written stories of the life of King David, including the story of his battle against King Saul for the throne (1 Sam 13–31) and of the fight among his own sons for the right to succeed their father (2 Sam 9–20). These older histories already told how God had stood by David and protected him through the evils plotted by Saul and by his own offspring. At the center, the Deuteronomists placed the personal covenant that Yahweh had made with David to establish his own family on the throne of Israel for all time (2 Sam 7). They carefully note that this promise to David does not replace the covenant of Moses, but becomes a sign of God's care for the people through the visible leadership of the kings. There is a very high regard for both David and for the possible good that his dynasty can do behind this view of the kingship. The Deuteronomists would agree with the view of Psalm 89:

> My faithful and enduring love will be with him,
>   and in my name his horn will be exalted.
> I will set his hand over the sea
>   and his right hand over the rivers;
> He will call to me, "You are my father,
>   my God, my rock, my salvation" (Ps 89:24–26).

But they are careful to warn that God will punish any evil that the kings do (2 Sam 7:14), and after David's death they even announce that God may withdraw his covenant altogether if they turn totally aside from him (1 Kgs 9:6–8).

Stage 4: The Kings. At this stage the Deuteronomists had available the books which listed all the major events of each king's reign, for both the time of Solomon and for the separate kingdoms that split apart at his death. The Deuteronomists often pass over important works that a king performed with barely a mention (an example is the reign of Omri, an important king in the northern kingdom—1 Kings 16 notes in one verse that he founded the great capital city of Samaria). Instead, they concentrate on how well the kings obeyed the demands of the covenant to avoid all false worship. The northern kings of Israel were all rated as evil, and of the kings of Judah really only three made a positive grade: Asa, Hezekiah and Josiah. These three all "walked in the footsteps of David their father."

However, the *real* history of the days of the kings centered on the *prophets* that God sent again and again to warn the people away from pagan cults. The great prophetic hero was, of course, Elijah who had faced the entire array of devotees of the god Baal and won. Thus this stage of the Deuteronomic History can be properly called the "victory of God's word." The prophets speak both warning and promise, but whatever they speak God really performs. His words are never uttered in vain. Some examples of this pattern can be listed here to show what the authors were doing:

PROPHECY	FULFILLMENT
1. 1 Kgs 11:29ff: Ahijah predicts ten tribes to be taken from Rehoboam.	1. 1 Kgs 12:15b: Yahweh fulfills what is spoken by Ahijah.
2. 1 Kgs 13:3: Unknown prophet says Josiah to slay false prophets.	2. 2 Kgs 23:16–18: Josiah acts according to word of prophet.
3. 1 Kgs 14:6ff: Ahijah predicts Jeroboam to lose kingdom.	3. 1 Kgs 15:29 Baasha exterminates Jeroboam's house.
4. 1 Kgs 14:12: Jeroboam's child shall die.	4. 1 Kgs 14:18: Child dies as prophet spoke.
5. 1 Kgs 16:1ff: Prophet Jehu predicts fall of Baasha's house.	5. 1 Kgs 16:12: Zimri destroys Baasha's house.
6. 1 Kgs 21:23: Elijah says dogs will eat the flesh and blood of Ahab.	6. 2 Kgs 9:36: Fulfilled according to word of Lord.
7. 2 Kgs 1:6, 16: Elijah predicts Ahaziah of Judah will die.	7. 2 Kgs 1:17: Ahaziah dies according to word of Elijah.
8. 2 Kgs 10:30: Predicts four generations for Jehu family.	8. 2 Kgs 15:12: So it came to pass as Lord said to Jehu.

PROPHECY	FULFILLMENT
9. 2 Kgs 31:10ff: Unknown prophet says Jerusalem will have great evil because of Manasseh's sin.	9. 2 Kgs 24:2: Yahweh summons Babylon according to word of his prophets (and add 2 Kgs 23:26).
10. 2 Kgs 22:15ff: Hulda predicts death of Josiah.	10. 2 Kgs 23:30: Josiah dies at Megiddo.

Stage 5: Fall and Exile. The Second Book of Kings tells it the way it is. As it draws to an end, the evil practices have not ceased, but have rather increased, and even the reforming zeal and fidelity of Josiah, the last and greatest of David's "good" descendants, cannot stop the divine punishment that the people have brought down on themselves through their kings (see 2 Kgs 23:26–27).

Conclusion

Most scholars recognize that the purpose of the Deuteronomic History is at least in part to explain *why the kingdom failed and the people were exiled despite God's covenant promises.* But they disagree on what exactly the Deuteronomists really thought God was going to do, or what the people might do, after it had happened. The ending of 2 Kings is very ambiguous. King Jehoiachin is let out of prison to spend his last days as a prisoner of Babylon in some comfort. Does this show hope that God would someday restore the royal family back to the throne? Or does it merely show that the last king had grown so old and feeble that no more hope could be placed in his return? One reason why it is hard to answer this question is that the Deuteronomic History was completed while the exile was still on and so the authors just did not know what God would do. On the pessimistic side, most of the great story from Joshua to 2 Kings is critical of kings and people alike and sees destruction as the justifiable outcome of their sins. On the other hand, the authors value the covenant highly and any hints of hope should be taken seriously. The calls to repent that fill Deuteronomy and Joshua and the Books of Kings most likely signal a real conviction that God would restore Israel to its land and bless it as a people again.

This can be confirmed by a second look at the Book of Deuteronomy itself. It already includes several hints about what God might do that have been edited into the final form of the book by the authors of the Deuteronomic History. These include chapters 1–3 which trace how God generously led the people in the wilderness after the exodus and forgave them again and again. It also includes some very concrete references to the exile in other chapters, especially Deuteronomy 4:27–30 and 30:1–10, which hold out hope for a day of return if and when the people repent. God is a compassionate God and he will renew the hearts of the people to accept again his covenant. In this view, closely linked to the thought of Jeremiah 31:31–34, the future of Israel will not depend so much on the land or the kings but on the obedience of the heart—an obedience possible because God will give the grace to make it possible.

This Deuteronomic History was a major effort of the biblical tradition to relook at its beliefs and understand the ups and downs of history in a new light. An older belief that God had fought for Israel as a warrior, defeating all enemies and promising all blessing, had given way in the sober facts of defeat to a deeper and more spiritual view of God's actions in the world. It did not develop overnight. The major stages can be easily defined:

1. An early stage of reform recorded in Deuteronomy 5–26 (700's).
2. The application of this reform in Judah by King Josiah and the beginning of the Deuteronomic History (600's).
3. A final edition of the Deuteronomic History and some additions to Deuteronomy during the exile period (500's).

This masterpiece helped Israel understand that God was not bound to a special land or a special king, but that above all he wanted the voluntary loyalty of each person in the community. Such an understanding prepared the way for the work of Ezekiel among the exiles.

STUDY QUESTIONS

1. Briefly describe the three major time periods in which Jeremiah worked. What were they?
2. What are the different types of materials found in the Book of Jeremiah?
3. What was the political situation in the time of Jeremiah?

4. Who was Jeremiah? Briefly describe the characteristics of his prophecy. What is his central message?
5. What was the "Temple sermon"?
6. Identify the following: Jehoiakim, Hananiah, Micaiah, Zedekiah.
7. "A prophet is always ready to speak and proclaim God's message." Assess the validity of this statement. Give examples and reasons to support your position.
8. Explain what is meant by Deuteronomic History. What are its five stages?
9. What is the significance of the Deuteronomic History? What is its purpose?

Chapter 19

PROPHECY DURING THE BABYLONIAN EXILE

Suggested Scripture Readings:

Ezekiel 1–5
Ezekiel 16–18
Ezekiel 36–37

A. DEALING WITH LOSS

On Living in Exile

Judah was a small country and its educated and skilled citizens could not have been many. 2 Kings 24 claims that Nebuchadnezzar took away between eight and ten thousand people in his first attack of 598, but the parallel account in Jeremiah 52 lowered the total amount to three thousand. Several thousand more would have been taken to Babylon in later deportations of 586 and 582 B.C. These would have been by far the great majority of all leading persons in the nation.

The exiles were settled in villages and rural areas near Babylon itself. By modern standards their fate would have been easy. For unlike the refugee camps where modern governments keep today's escapees and exiles imprisoned and under strict control, the Israelites were allowed to live normal lives and run their own small towns as long as they did not try to return to their homeland. Moreover, there is good evidence that conditions were not as bad under the Babylonians as under the earlier Assyrians, who had begun the practice of mass deportations of conquered people back in the eighth century. As one example, King Jehoiachin, who had been carried off to Babylon as a prisoner in 598, seemed to have been treated with dignity and allowed to live in ease. A small Babylonian clay tablet found in the 1930's listed a daily gift of food for his household from the royal palace.

The prophet Ezekiel, as we shall see, also moved and spoke with considerable freedom in his place of exile. And Jeremiah, back in Palestine, kept up contacts with the exiles in the years from 598 to 586 (Jer 29). In fact, Jeremiah counseled the exiles to "build houses and settle in them; plant gardens and eat their produce. Marry and have sons and daughters . . . and seek the peace of the city to which I have sent you in exile" (Jer 29:5–7).

Many apparently did settle down contentedly and make a home in Babylon. Certainly the length of the total stay in exile, some sixty years for the first deportees, and forty-five for those who were taken in 586, convinces us that all but a very few died in Babylon and that most of their children *never knew any other home* than that of the exile. The records of the Murashu family, a Babylonian banking firm of the fifth century B.C., were found by archaeologists in Nippur, a Babylonian town, and they list several prominent Jewish families among their clients about the years 450 to 400 B.C. We can reasonably conclude from this that the opportunities to get ahead were available to the exiles if they wished to settle down and become part of the local people.

The First Jewish "Diaspora"

Jewish settlement outside of Palestine did not begin with the Babylonian exile. Already 2 Kings 17:6 relates the earlier exile of the northern kingdom: "In the ninth year of Hoshea, the king of Assyria captured Samaria and carried the Israelites back to Assyria, and settled them in Halah, on the Habur River in Gozan and in the cities of the Medes." This was the year 721 B.C., and Sargon II, the king of Assyria, recorded that he deported a total of 27,290 inhabitants of Samaria. To later generations, these have become the "ten lost tribes of Israel" and many legends have grown up around their fate. But they are never mentioned again in the Bible.

The prophets often included the threat of exile among their warnings. No doubt it was considered one of the most terrible of fates. But we must also remember that ordinary travel itself was a

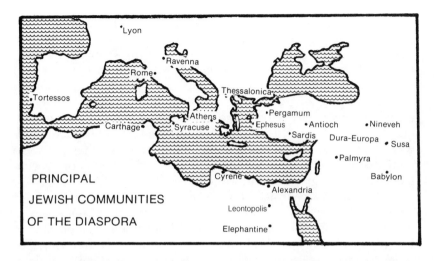

PRINCIPAL

JEWISH COMMUNITIES

OF THE DIASPORA

dangerous business in the ancient world, and even reaching one's destination did not give much security. The foreigner was often not protected fully by the local laws, and had no family to support his or her case if trouble with the local population developed. The Book of Ruth in the Bible is a very short story of four chapters which brings home all of the problems that had to be faced. Ruth is a Moabitess who had been married to an Israelite but is now left a widow. Her only hope is to throw herself on the mercy of her dead husband's relatives. It is part of the charm of the story and also its lesson that God arranges a happy ending because she kept her integrity and trusted in the rights granted by the covenant.

The Bible often mentions the extra protection needed for the foreigners living in Israel, no doubt because they had little else to fall back on. While it is true that the patriarchal stories of Genesis picture Abraham and Jacob frequently on the move, this was always in large clan groups for safety reasons. David gathered people to him in the wilderness areas of Judah, but these were mostly soldiers. Usually lone individuals would rarely leave home or family, and only under the most carefully worked out treaty conditions. The largest group of people regularly found in other countries were merchants who conducted trade by caravan or ship. Ancient treaties very explicitly mention the rights granted to these all-important professionals.

Despite the normal limits to movement, however, there was one interesting example of Jewish migration from Israel that seems to have been by choice. A number of documents have turned up in

southern Egypt at the town of Aswan which inform us about a
Jewish military colony stationed nearby on the island of Elephantine
in the fifth century B.C. One of the claims of this group is that they
had lived there since before the Persians conquered Egypt in 525
B.C. This would mean that a group had gone down sometime
during the time of exile and made their home there. They could
even have been part of the large number that fled to Egypt in 582,
taking Jeremiah against his will (Jer 41:16–44:30). This community
was well organized and many of the documents that they left were
family contracts. Long after the exile was over, they kept up contacts with the high priest in Jerusalem.

Thus, in the century after the exile, there were at least two
major centers of Jewish life outside of Palestine itself. One was in
Babylon and the other in Egypt. It would never again be possible to
identify God's covenant and promise just with the land of Israel, or
religious practice just in terms of loyalty to the temple in Jerusalem.
A newer and more personal side of faith that looked beyond temple,
kingship, and land, and that touched everyone at home or in exile,
was needed. It is Ezekiel who begins this process from among the
exiles of Babylon.

B.   EZEKIEL THE PROPHET

The Prophet Called in Exile (Ez 1–3)

The most remarkable individual during Israel's period of exile
was the prophet Ezekiel. The opening lines of his book tell us that
he was called in the fifth year of the exile, i.e., 593 B.C., at a Jewish
settlement on the Chebar (Kebar) River, one of the great canals that
brought water from the Euphrates to irrigate the lands around
Babylon. He was, like Jeremiah, both a priest and a prophet, although he shows distinct differences from Jeremiah by making
more use of his priestly training in his message. On the other hand,
many of his oracles are clearly influenced by, and drawn from the
work of, his older contemporary Jeremiah. He spoke with a great
deal of freedom and seemed to have been very well informed about
what was going on back in Jerusalem, sometimes describing scenes
in the temple and city that are just like eyewitness accounts. We
know that Jeremiah wrote letters to the exiles, and Ezekiel himself
mentions messengers who traveled back and forth (Ez 33), so it is
most likely that he received word through travelers and used this

plus a first-hand knowledge of the temple from the days before he was exiled. But some scholars are so impressed at how vivid his knowledge of Jerusalem is (in chapter 8, for example) that they doubt he could have been anywhere else than in Jerusalem during the last days of Judah.

One reason that they believe this stems from the personality of the prophet as it is described for us in his book. Ezekiel shows strong tendencies toward psychic powers and an older style of prophetic behavior which includes dreams, trances, ecstasy and fantastic visions. He speaks of the hand of the Lord lifting him up and transporting him places, or of the spirit of the Lord moving him. He does symbolic actions which seem impossible for an ordinary person, such as lying on his side for three hundred and ninety days (chapter 4) or not speaking for long periods (chapter 24). Because of these kinds of behavior, many commentators have called Ezekiel a psychotic person, or at least highly neurotic. But they miss an important factor by doing popular psychoanalysis on the prophet. All of his actions and visions draw on very old traditional language used by prophets in earlier centuries. Elijah and Elisha stories often refer to the work of the spirit of God or of the hand of the Lord. Visions and ecstasy are recorded for prophets in the days of both Samuel and Elijah. Many of his own words of warning and judgment are borrowed from the old curses attached to treaties, or from covenant ceremonies of one type or another.

In short, Ezekiel was not crazy, he was very skillfully trying to *recreate a sense of trust* that God still worked as he always had, and that he still spoke with as much authority and power as he always had. This was no easy task for Ezekiel. The people had seen—and were suffering themselves because of it—how empty and false were most of the comforting words of hope that prophets had spoken to them. It was true that Jeremiah had given warning, but what about the others? Hananiah of Jeremiah 28 and countless more spoke only of the coming victory of God—and never of defeat. Ezekiel sought to restore to prophecy some trust and some leadership for the exiles.

Ezekiel was the first prophet to preach to the people without either the temple or the promised land to show God's presence. For this reason, the story of his call to be a prophet has an even more important place to play in his book than does that of Jeremiah. In one of the greatest scenes in the Old Testament, Ezekiel describes the appearance of God in majesty upon a chariot throne. The vision of God's holiness and terrible power overwhelms the prophet, and his description is full of color and shape and motion as he tries to capture the experience. The whole vision takes three chapters to complete, and Jewish tradition has considered it so full of mystical meaning that a person was not allowed to study it until he or she is a mature thirty years old. It shares many qualities with the call of Isaiah in Isaiah 6. God is the Holy One, not like us, but Lord of the world before whom we bow down in humble acceptance of his will. As did Isaiah, Ezekiel eagerly accepts what God sends him, and like Isaiah it turns out to be a message written on a scroll that reads "Lamentation and wailing and woe" (Ez 2:10). God sends him to "a nation of rebels, who have rebelled against me to this very day" (Ez 2:3). "Hard of face and stubborn of heart are they to whom I send you" (Ez 2:4). Just as God made Jeremiah a wall of iron and brass against the whole land (Jer 1:18), so God makes Ezekiel's "face hard against their faces, and your forehead hard against their foreheads; like stone harder than flint I have made your forehead" (Ez 3:8–9).

It was not a commission designed to make Ezekiel any more popular than Jeremiah had been. As the vision ended he went away in "bitterness of spirit, for the hand of the Lord was heavy upon him" (Ez 3:14). Finally, after seven days of shocked meditation, God spoke to him a second time and told him that his role was to be the watchman over Israel. Just as Jeremiah was to have been a "watching tree" (the almond vision of Jeremiah 1:11–12), and Habakkuk had stood in his watchtower (Hb 2:1), so Ezekiel had to sound a warning when he saw what God was about to do. This concept of the prophet's task stands at the heart of Ezekiel's thought. He repeats it, not only in chapter 3 when he warns of danger and disaster ahead, but again in chapter 33 when he offers words of hope and future restoration. But he must speak whether anyone listens or not. He has his duty and the people have theirs. If the people fail to hear, that will be their problem, but if he fails to preach, the responsibility will be his.

The Nature of the Book of Ezekiel

Ezekiel is one of the most highly ordered books in the Bible. It has a basic three-part structure which follows the general course of the prophet's career:

Chapters 1–24:	Oracles against Judah and Jerusalem before 586 B.C.
Chapters 25–32:	Oracles against foreign nations
Chapters 33–48:	Oracles of hope and restoration for Judah

THE DATES OF EZEKIEL'S ORACLES

(The following dates are from the time of Jehoiachin's coronation, 598)

Ezek 1:2	5th year	July	593	Chariot vision and call
Ezek 3:16	5th year	July	593	Watchman appointed for Israel
Ezek 8:1	6th year	Sept.	592	Vision of judgment of Jerusalem
Ezek 20:1	7th year	Aug.	591	Prophecy on the new Exodus
Ezek 24:1	9th year	Jan.	588	Siege of Jerusalem begins
Ezek 26:1	11th year		587–586	Prophecy against Tyre
Ezek 29:1	10th year	Jan.	587	Prophecy against Egypt as ally
Ezek 29:17	27th year	Apr.	571	Prediction of Egypt's capture
Ezek 30:20	11th year	Apr.	587	Egypt with broken arms
Ezek 31:1	11th year	June	587	Egypt as a great tree cut down
Ezek 32:1	12th year	Mar.	585	Funeral lament over pharaoh
Ezek 32:17	12th year	Mar.	585	Pharaoh's descent into Sheol
Ezek 33:21	12th year	Jan.	585	News of Jerusalem's capture
Ezek 40:1	25th year	Oct.	573	Vision of the new Temple
Ezek 1:1	30th year		593?	This is the general heading for the whole book and may be dated as (1) 30th year from Josiah's reform in 622; (2) Ezekiel's age in 593; (3) 30th year of his call to be a prophet (563); (4) 30th year of Jehoiachin as king (568).

We cannot be sure that Ezekiel himself had a hand in arranging his oracles in this exact way, but if he did not do it personally, it must have been done very soon after his death. The plan is very carefully modeled on the Book of Joshua which tells of the holy war for possession of the promised land. So, too, Ezekiel first preaches against the people's sins in order to purify them for the battle; then he denounces the power of the foreign nations and rids the holy land of its enemies; lastly, he portions out the land to the tribes of Israel.

Beyond this basic outline, several oracles have dates connected with them so that we can follow the progress of the prophet's thought. This is especially true of the oracles in chapters 25–32, almost all of which are dated to the period of greatest crisis just before the final fall of Jerusalem in 586 and 585 B.C. They give such a clear picture of the times that there is no need to doubt that many of these oracles came directly from the prophet's own hands.

Ezekiel's style is also unique. It is elaborate and favors long oracles with many repetitions and literary allegories and images. Unlike the shorter and more direct words of an Amos or Hosea or Isaiah, Ezekiel creates very dramatic picture stories, in which he uses other people's words, or a favorite proverb, or even pagan myths about the gods, to get his point across. Examples of this are the allegory of the two eagles in chapter 17, the great mythical cedar tree in chapter 31, or his description of Egypt as the great sea monster Leviathan in chapters 29 and 32. He describes the city of Tyre as a great ship sinking with all its cargo, and compares the two kingdoms of Israel and Judah to two sisters who choose to live as prostitutes (chapters 16 and 23).

Another striking feature in Ezekiel is his use of symbolic actions and visions. He draws diagrams on a brick to show how the city will be taken (chapter 4), he cuts his beard into three parts and burns one part, chops up another, and throws the rest to the wind to show what will happen to the city (chapter 5), and he puts on a backpack and breaks through the walls of his own house to imitate the attempts people will make to escape during the coming siege by Babylon (chapter 12). He not only has the vision of Yahweh in his chariot in chapters 1–3 but another vision of the divine angels marking off the city of Jerusalem for destruction in chapter 8, a vision of the priests performing pagan worship in the temple itself in the same chapter, and a vision of God's glory leaving the city in chapter 11 and its return again in chapter 43. He sees a famous vision of dead bones that come to life in chapter 37. Through the symbolic actions and the visions the prophet conveys the seriousness of his message and also shows the continuity of God's care—he can be seen guiding and controlling both the punishment and the restoration as different stages of his plan.

When all of these aspects are considered closely, the Book of Ezekiel has a great deal more unity than most other prophetic books, even those much shorter, and confirms the earlier remark that Ezekiel himself is responsible for a good part of its order. This is just the opposite of the Book of Jeremiah, which was edited and arranged long after his death by others. It is therefore worthwhile to describe this order in some further detail:

I. *Call Narrative*

Chapter(s)

1:1–3:27   The call as a solemn preface outlining the prophet's mission as watchman.

II. *Oracles of Judgments*

4:1–5:17   Symbolic actions warning of divine punishment of Judah and Jerusalem for their sins.

6:1–7:27   Oracles of judgment that announce the day of the Lord for Israel's total destruction.

8:1–11:25   A vision of the angels investigating Jerusalem for its sins and idolatry; they find it guilty and God withdraws his presence from the temple.

12:1–14:23   A series of oracles and symbolic actions that describe the guilt and evil of King Zedekiah, the prophets, priests and people.

15:1–17:24   A series of three parables or allegories—of the wood from a vine, of the orphan daughter and bride who is unfaithful, and of the two eagles—which show the lack of faithfulness in Judah.

18:1–20:44   Three lengthy theological reflections on Israel's guilt built upon popular sayings or metaphors: chapter 18 on individual responsibility, chapter 19 as a lament for the end of the kingdom, chapter 20 on the failure of the exodus.

21:1–24:14   Oracles warning about the coming attack of Babylon and explaining why the city must fall because of its guilt.

24:15–27   The end of stage one. The prophet's wife dies and he must not mourn her or the city about to die.

III. *Oracles Against Nations*

25:1–17   Oracles against Ammon, Moab, Edom and the Philistines.

26:1–28:26   Oracles against Tyre and Sidon.

29:1–32:32   Oracles against Egypt.

IV. *Oracles of Restoration*

33:1–33	The second preface, announcing Ezekiel as a watchman for God's new acts of salvation and hope.
34:1–31	The contrast between the old shepherds and the new shepherds that God will give Israel.
35:1–36:38	The healing of the land of Israel and the new covenant in the land.
37:1–28	The vision of the restored Israel as the dead bones come to life (verses 1–14) and the union of the two kingdoms as one again (verses 15–28).
38:1–39:29	The invasion of Gog of Magog—the final battle for control of the world fought in Palestine.

V. *The New Community*

40:1–43:12	A new vision of the return of God to the temple and its restoration to perfect shape.
43:13–46:24	The establishment of the proper order of worship and sacrifice, the rules governing the priests and levites for the new temple.
47:1–12	The vision of the waters of life streaming from the temple renewing the earth.
47:13–48:35	The land is divided up among the tribes with the temple at its center and the prince over Israel at its service.

Ezekiel's Theology of Judgment

The major portion of the Book of Ezekiel is given over to oracles of judgment similar to those of Jeremiah. Since Ezekiel only preached in the last few years before the fall, from 593 to 586, he lacks the great depth of Jeremiah born from years of disappointment, but he makes up for it with the fierce power of his images and words. He also gives us a fuller picture of the conditions in Judah under King Zedekiah. Chapter 8 reveals how pagan cults had even reached the temple grounds and were being supported by the priests themselves; chapter 13 attacks the widespread use of magicians and fortune-tellers and other false voices of authority; chapter 14 shows the number of prophets who went about preaching that all would be well despite widespread evil. Again and again Ezekiel returns to the same theme that had occupied Jeremiah before him: pagan idolatry. Judah is worse than Samaria had been, and even worse than Sodom (chapters 16 and 23). He describes the weak and uncertain nature of the king trying to escape in the middle of the night while the rest of the city perishes (chapter 12). He takes up the theme of the day of the Lord, used by the prophets before him, to predict God's final and total rejection of his people (chapter 7). Nor does he neglect to condemn the sins against justice so common in other prophets. He often speaks of them in general terms—bloodshed, violence, evil conduct—but on occasion he gets very specific—bribery, usury, stealing from the poor (chapters 5, 6, 7, and 18). At times he mentions concrete violations of religious worship: failing to honor the sabbath, breaking the law, building idols, eating at high places (chapter 18).

This last group of sins calls attention to the central characteristic of Ezekiel's thought—it most closely resembles the Priestly source in the Pentateuch, especially the famous Holiness Code in Leviticus 17–26. Many of the same words and phrases found in Leviticus 26, for example, are found sprinkled throughout the Book of Ezekiel. Ezekiel often repeats certain formulas such as "I the Lord am holy," or "I am the Lord your God," both present in Leviticus. Most of all, Ezekiel uses the expression, "so that you (or they) will know that I the Lord am God." It captures the essence of the thought of Ezekiel, and he ends almost every single oracle with it. Only when the people turn back to God and recognize the divine hand behind events that are happening will they understand these events. This reflects both the Priestly tradition that Israel must always act in an obedient and holy manner because God himself gives us the lesson and model to follow by his holiness toward Israel, and also the prophetic spirit of Hosea, Isaiah and Jeremiah that Israel's sin comes from not-knowing its God. They have forgotten God, that is, given up the love relationship with him.

Another striking side of Ezekiel's message is the importance he attaches to individual responsibility. He quotes a proverb, used also by Jeremiah, "The fathers ate the sour grapes, but the children's teeth shuddered" (Ez 18:2; Jer 31:30). He then forbids anyone to speak it again. No longer will one generation have to bear the sins of another, nor the whole people suffer because of the sins of a few. It is important to recall that Israel had often demanded responsibility on the part of individuals—all the law codes show that; but it also had a general belief that God did at times hold the entire people guilty of the acts of a few. Achan had sinned against Joshua in Joshua 7, and the entire army had met defeat as a result. Amos had warned that God would leave a remnant of northern Israel when he brought punishment, but it would be no more than a piece of an ear or two tips of legs in the mouth of a lion (Am 3:12)—not very much and by no means the best part. Of course, Ezekiel does not reject the idea of Israel as a nation. He has a strong sense of Israel as a community of faith and foresees both loss for all and restoration for all. But at the same time he gives a new accent to the role of the individual person in the community. Each must decide for or against God; each must take the law into his or her heart and be able to keep it no matter what the community is doing. In chapters 14, 18 and 33 he repeats this forcefully so that when the exile came, and the community was broken up—no temple, no king, no land of their own—each would still be able to find God and his promises and law as something to live by.

This brings us to the last note of his theology of judgment. Chapter 20 retells the history of Israel from the days of the exodus. But Ezekiel does not praise a people who held close to the Lord and remained faithful during the long forty years in the desert as does Hosea 11 or Jeremiah 2. He instead asserts that Israel has always been unfaithful to the covenant, and that God had to punish Israel repeatedly in the desert years for rebellion and sin. God had acted for the sake of "his name" in saving them from Egypt and guiding them through the wilderness and giving them their land—not because they were such a worthwhile people, but to show his fidelity and his power as God. Yet they would not recognize this and obey him, but constantly turned from him. More than once his wrath could have destroyed them but each time he had compassion and forgave. Ezekiel then asks what right they have now to come near to God and seek mercy (Ez 20:31). Instead God will make a judgment in a new wilderness and purge out the rebels from the midst of the people. Before there can be restoration, the evil must be purified from Israel. It is Ezekiel's way of saying that God would not stop the Babylonian invasion, but would use them to make Israel know the Lord their God (Ez 20:44).

As was the case with Jeremiah, Ezekiel did not oppose Babylonian power. He saw it as an instrument that God used to bring about his purpose. Chapter 21 described God giving Babylon the signal to attack Jerusalem rather than the Ammonites (Ez 21:18–23); a short while earlier he utters a final prophecy condemning the king: "I will strike man and beast, the dwellers of this city; they shall die of pestilence. After that I will hand over Zedekiah and his ministers and all the people who survive the pestilence, sword and famine in this city, to Nebuchadnezzar, king of Babylon" (Ez 21:6–7). Only after *all* was destroyed would God begin his work of rebuilding.

The Plan of Restoration

The oracles against foreign nations in chapters 25–32 contain some of Ezekiel's most stunning imagery. He hurls threats against seven nations: Ammon, Moab, Edom, Philistia, Tyre, Sidon and Egypt. These represent the foreign powers that oppose Israel in the promised land. In some ways Ezekiel must have had in the back of his mind the famous command of Deuteronomy that Israel was to destroy the seven peoples in the promised land who were greater and mightier than itself, and make no covenant with them and show no mercy toward them (Dt 7:1–2). As Joshua had conquered the Canaanite peoples, so now God would defeat the foreign nations as a sign of his renewed gift to those in exile. Ezekiel uses these oracles against foreign nations as a prelude to the new covenant and the new blessing of the people when he brings them back from exile. Each oracle was given on a particular occasion. Some of them we can guess. Ezekiel 29:17–21 against Egypt was given when Nebuchadnezzar had to give up his attack on the island city of Tyre after thirteen years of siege in 572. Ezekiel 29:1–9 was uttered when the Egyptians sent a relief column to help Jerusalem escape the Babylonian attack of 588–586 and it failed.

Of all these nations, Tyre and Egypt come under the most severe judgment. Both represented the allure of pagan gods. Tyre was the home of the cult of Baal, against whom the prophets had thundered for centuries. Egypt's ruler claimed to be himself a god with unlimited power. Ezekiel says of him in mockery: "The pharaoh bragged, 'The Nile is mine; I made it,' but God will drag him out of it like a fish on a hook" (Ez 29:3–4). Over and over Ezekiel denounces the arrogant pride of Egypt and Tyre who think they are more powerful than Yahweh. He quotes their own religious myths back to them to show how shallow are their beliefs: pharaoh is the great sea monster (chapter 29), or the tree of life (chapter 31); the king of Tyre is the wisest of all men (chapter 28), perfect in all virtues (chapter 27).

Ezekiel's actual words of hope to the people are not uttered until the city has fallen. When word reached Ezekiel in Babylon that all was lost (chapter 33) he immediately turned to the future to find God's promise still alive. He foresaw a twofold plan of God. The first was to bring the exiles back from captivity and purify their sense of the covenant. For this reason, chapters 33–39 concentrate on conversion and change. There will be a new David to shepherd the people; God will abolish idols and abominations; old hearts will be removed so that new hearts and a new obedience can be given to the people, and God will drive all the arrogant pagans from the land and make his people secure in peace. Of all of these, the passage about the new heart in Ezekiel 36:22–32 is the most important. It takes up the work of Jeremiah and extends it to all areas of life. Where Jeremiah foresaw a new covenant written on the heart (Jer 31:31), Ezekiel adds that it will also result in total purity under the law, holiness, and even abundance in crops and flocks.

The second part of the plan is laid out in chapters 40–48. These are written in a prose style that may be from a disciple of Ezekiel but certainly follow the master's thought. Once the people have returned to the covenant, made possible by God's power alone and not by their own good will, then he shall give the land its order—a new temple at the center of a renewed nation in which everyone has his or her place. At the center of this vision, parallel to the new heart in the first part of the plan, are life-giving waters that flow from the temple to touch every living thing in the land (Ez 47:1–12). The source of hope and prosperity will be God alone truly worshiped.

Ezekiel's importance should not be underestimated. Many modern writers give the impression that he was more interested in legal questions than in the true spirit of the covenant. But this is not true. He shared many of the ideals of Jeremiah and was profoundly influenced by oracles and sermons that came from Jeremiah; but Ezekiel, unlike Jeremiah, was in exile and lived on to speak to a people who had no chance to escape the punishment. He had to face the task of picking up the pieces. His answer was to show that Israel's entire history had been a failure to heed the everyday living out of the covenant. Israel's political history had shown how often the chosen people had fallen into injustice and idolatry while claiming devotion to kingly rule and possession of the land. A new way had to be found now that these had been lost, a better way so that the violations and failures would not happen again.

Ezekiel found a key for understanding the new covenant to be written on the hearts of the people in its *interior*-ness. No longer was religion to be a matter of what the community did externally,

Ezekiel's Vision of the Temple (Ezek 40:1–42: 20)

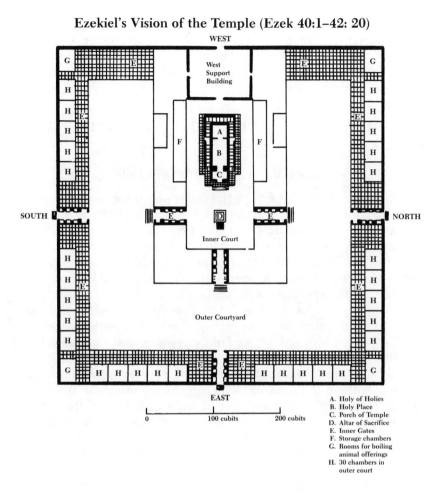

WEST

West Support Building

A
B
C

F   F

SOUTH   NORTH

E   D   E

Inner Court

Outer Courtyard

G   H H H H H   E   E   H H H H H   G

EAST

```
|_____|_____|
0            100 cubits        200 cubits
```

A. Holy of Holies
B. Holy Place
C. Porch of Temple
D. Altar of Sacrifice
E. Inner Gates
F. Storage chambers
G. Rooms for boiling animal offerings
H. 30 chambers in outer court

but was to be really from the heart. Ezekiel stressed the roles of the sabbath as a day of rest, reflective meditation on the covenant, personal uprightness, purity, and holiness. The temple and the land would have a place only when people acknowledged that "the Lord is God." They first must take on the *spirit* of the covenant, and for that prayer and study would be more important than bloodlines. God would no longer accept people because they were born Israelites; now they must decide for God in order to live (see chapter 18).

Ezekiel's new vision was priestly insofar as it stressed the union of the moral demands of the covenant with personal devotion to the daily practices of worship in the temple. His program had an important effect on the Priestly school's arrangement of the Pentateuch which placed the law on Mount Sinai at its center point. In more than one way, Ezekiel was the last of the great prophets and the first of the new priestly visionaries that would create modern Judaism as we know it today.

C. THE "PRIESTLY" EDITION OF THE PENTATEUCH

A New Interpretation of Israel's Faith

The work of Ezekiel among the exiles began the much needed task of looking beyond the dreams of the past as a basis for faith in Yahweh. No longer should Israel count on running its own nation and having its own king as signs of God's promise to be with them. A new vision was called for which would allow Israel to practice its religion no matter what happened to the land. Building on the preaching of Ezekiel, the priests and levites took the traditions that had been handed down through the Yahwist and Elohist and expanded it with much new material gathered from other areas of Israel's life: the liturgies, songs, family records, and especially the laws that had been worked out over the centuries. In the process, they created the Pentateuch much as we have it today, although probably without the Book of Deuteronomy yet attached. We have already seen how the experience of exile called forth the great Deuteronomic History as one means of explaining the disaster that had come upon Israel; it also called forth the equally great Priestly edition of the Pentateuch as a second means of explaining the exile and lasting value of the covenant idea.

This important task was taken over by the priests and levites because it was they who were most involved in the dual roles of guarding the traditions of the past and keeping them alive in present liturgy and teaching. In the period after the exile, priests and levites developed separate roles. The priests performed the religious acts in the temple, and levites did the support work of sacristans, musicians, etc. But earlier times suggest that both priests and levites also shared in teaching. Nehemiah 8 describes a day in the fifth century when the levites "instructed the people in the law" (Neh 8:7-8). And it is exactly this aim of giving a deeper meaning to the Torah, the "law," that led to the new Priestly reworking of the J and E stories of the patriarchs and the exodus.

The Shape of the Priestly Pentateuch

The "P" edition *did not rewrite* the narrative stories but generally kept them as they had come down. Instead, it mostly *added* lists of things that would fill out and develop important themes already found in the earlier works. Thus it put in census lists, old genealogy lists, inventory lists of temple items, and varied law codes, as well as a number of hymns and poems. But especially it added materials that related to liturgical practice and the cult. The Priestly writers attached the story of creation in Genesis 1 to the older version of the Garden of Eden in chapters 2–3 in order to stress both the careful divine order that God established and the sacred origins of worship with its special weekly sabbath. They added to the old flood story of Noah a new series of dates that stress an *annual* calendar so that the earth becomes dry exactly on New Year's Day (Gen 8:13). They devoted great attention in the exodus story to the proper way of celebrating this passover in the future (Ex 12). P gives nearly ten chapters, and repeats its message twice, to the building of the ark of the covenant and the tent in the desert as the climax and high point of the events at Mount Sinai (Ex 25–30, 35–40). Where it does add a narrative story, such as in Genesis 17, it supplies important ritual information. Abraham is told that circumcision must be part of the covenant.

Above all P loves order. It links the great events of the primeval history in Genesis 1–11 by five genealogy lists for the early peoples (Gen 2:4; 5:1; 6:9; 10:1; 11:10) and five lists for the patriarchs in Genesis 12–50 (Gen 11:27; 25:12; 25:19; 36:1; 37:2). In the story of the wanderings in the desert for forty years, it lists twelve major stopping places: six on the way to Mount Sinai and six from Sinai to the promised land. It loves the use of symbolic numbers: there are ten patriarchs before the flood (Gen 5) and ten after; God gives ten commands to create the world in Genesis 1; there are three sons of Noah, of Terah, and of Aaron. It emphasizes the twelve stopping places and the twelve tribes.

P is also very conscious of historical changes. It divides the world into different ages. There are several patterns that list the stages of revelation for Israel.

(1) *The first pattern involves the names by which God is known:*
   (a) people first call God *'elohim* (Gen 9), the most general name;

(b)   Abraham is later allowed to know him as *El Shaddai* (Gen 17), "the powerful one";

(c)   to Moses, God finally reveals his name as Yahweh (Ex 3).

(2)   *A second pattern lists the covenants God has made:*

(a)   to Adam in the form of blessing and promise (Gen 1:28–30);

(b)   to Noah in the repetition of Genesis 1:28 plus a promise never to desert the people again;

(c)   to Abraham with the promise of a son, land and great nationhood (Gen 17);

(d)   to Moses on Mount Sinai with the promise of land and a permanent relationship: "I will be your God and you will be my people" (Ex 6).

(3)   *A third pattern lists the obligations God sets upon the world:*

(a)   in return for the gift of creation, people are to keep the sabbath holy (Gen 1);

(b)   in return for the rainbow as a promise of no worldwide destruction again, people are to offer sacrifice to God (Gen 9);

(c)   in return for the special election as a chosen people, Abraham and his descendants are to practice circumcision (Gen 17);

(d)   in return for the gift of God's presence always with them, the people must keep the law of Mount Sinai (Ex 19—Num 10).

In between these moments of special grace from God, all the great events of the past take place: between creation and the covenant with Noah is the flood; between Noah and the covenant with Abraham is the special call to be a chosen people; between Abraham and Moses on Mount Sinai is the exodus from Egypt.

The Theology of the Priestly Writers

When we ask why the Priestly leaders took the trouble to add so much to the older traditions of Israel's beginnings, the answer must be sought in their situation as exiles. They saw that it was no longer enough to have the central core of their faith be a story of how God brought them into the land of Canaan by great power and majesty and gave them blessing there. This had been fine before the nation was destroyed but would hardly convince anyone again. The loss of the land and king showed that God was not just a God of territory. In the days of the kings, it had been good enough to hear religious leaders recite the traditional epic of God's promises to the fathers followed by the great saving deeds of the exodus and the guidance through the desert to the promised land and the special covenant relationship. The possession of the land, the family of King David, the temple, and even the moral demands of the covenant had all been blessings that could be seen or touched or given shape in the social structure built upon political control of Palestine. Once that political independence collapsed, Israel faced the choice of abandoning Yahweh because he had failed to keep his material and political blessings, or trying to understand a deeper meaning to the covenant that did not require such supports.

The prophets had already led the way with their preaching about the inner spirit of the covenant as obedience to God, moral uprightness, social concern, and trust in divine leadership. Especially in Judah, the prophets Isaiah and Ezekiel had linked such prophetic challenges to the holiness of God and to proper attitudes of worship. So had the teaching of Deuteronomy. These provided the bases on which the P writers built their new vision. Israel must be primarily a *religious* community, not a political power, and a *priestly* community whose focus on Jerusalem and the temple must be geared toward true worship and a careful observance of all the proper rites and ceremonies that give reverence and honor to the God who is *holy*. P knew that Israel in the past often proved unfaithful to even the most basic demands of the covenant of Mount Sinai. The people often fell into pagan practices that led them far from the ethical ideals of the covenant. The new Israel that will come out of exile must be a "holy" community whose life will be regulated by Torah, the "teaching" or "way of living" proposed by Moses and expressed in the laws of both ethical and ritual types (sacrifices, purification, vows, feast days, circumcision, sabbath, etc.).

In this spirit, the Priestly writers reorganized and enlarged the Pentateuch tradition. History is seen as a series of ages that have been blessed by Yahweh. They stretch from creation until the time of Israel's covenant, and despite failure in each period, God always promises to begin again. The high point of the story is the period in the wilderness when Israel was exiled from both Egypt and the promised land. It is here that God gives the laws by which one can live, including everything from proper sacrifice to moral obligations toward the poor. Special attention is given to the building of the ark of the covenant and to the tent-shrine. God's presence over the ark meant that he would be with the people wherever they wandered and the "glory" of God could be seen and felt in the tent. It is the same "glory" that P tells us again and again went with Israel on their journey to protect them (Ex 16:6–7; 24:15–18; Lev 9; Num 9 and 14; Dt 34). At the most dramatic moment of P's story, Yahweh's glory takes up residence in the newly completed tent (Ex 40:34–38). The whole story of the ark and tent can be seen as a model for the later building of the temple of Solomon and God's dwelling in Jerusalem, with one major difference—that in the desert God was free to move *anywhere* to be with his people.

A glance at the chart of P additions to the earlier traditions will also show how often directions for priests and levites (above all Aaron the high priest) are included. The priests will be the true leaders of Israel as a religious community in the future, and they must have a deep sense of God's holiness and their own obligation to careful and reverent service. Another easily observed aspect is order. Genealogy lists, census reports, stages of human history, marching order of the tribes, places to stop at in the desert, and boundary lists for the promised land all play a part in creating confidence that God has everything under control—he always *has* and he always *will.* The centerpiece of this lesson is the story of creation in Genesis 1. P places it at the head of the whole biblical tradition to stand as a preface that will state the theme for everything else. God has created the world with ease, with a perfect plan expressed by his *word,* shaped by the proper weekly worship, and full of blessing for the future. It is not just a story—it is a hymn of praise and trust that expresses all the hopes of Israel that God will re-create just as he has spoken by his word through Abraham, Isaac, Jacob, Moses, and the law.

For Israel trapped in exile, P's message was clear enough: *Don't give up on Yahweh!* His promise has always proved faithful and true in the past. The covenant endures forever, with or without the land and the king. His word speaks not only of sin and mercy (the message of J and E) but of renewed blessing as well. God gives his covenant freely, and all he asks in return is an obedient response to the way of life which he has revealed to Israel for its own blessing.

The Priestly achievement was remarkable. It brought together the best of the prophets, of Deuteronomy, of the old covenant traditions, and of the temple worship practices, and laid the foundations for a new community of Israel at the end of its exile.

THE FINAL GROWTH OF THE PENTATEUCH
UNDER "P" EDITORS

Israel's Fundamental Tradition up to the Exile		"P" Additions to the Pentateuch in the Exile	
GEN 2–3	The Garden of Eden	GEN 1:1–2:4	Creation of the World
GEN 4	Cain & The Nations	GEN 5	List of Ancestors
GEN 6–9	Flood Story—Noah	GEN 6–9	Calendar additions to the Flood Story
GEN 10	The Nations spread	GEN 11:10–27	Table of Nations
GEN 11	Tower of Babel	GEN 17:1–17	Covenant with Abraham
GEN 12–25	Abraham Stories	GEN 35:22–36:43	Lists of Jacob's and Esau's descendants
GEN 24 & 26	Isaac Stories		
GEN 25, 27–35	Jacob Stories		
GEN 37–48, 50	Joseph Stories		
GEN 49	Tribal Blessings		
EXOD 1–3	Israel's slavery & the Call of Moses	EXOD 6:2–7:13	Second call of Moses & Aaron's help
EXOD 4–5, 8–11	Moses' mission & the plagues on Egypt	EXOD 12	Passover Liturgy
EXOD 13–15	The Exodus	EXOD 16	Murmuring events (all moved from Num 10–20)
EXOD 17–18	Journey to Sinai		
EXOD 19–24	Covenant on Mt. Sinai & Laws	EXOD 25–31, 35–40	Directions & building of the Ark & Tent
EXOD 32–34	Breaking & Renewal of the Covenant		
		LEV 1–16	Sacrifice & Cult Laws
		LEV 17–26	Holiniess Code = ethical demands of Law
		LEV 27	Additional Law on vows
NUM 10–16	Wilderness & Murmuring traditions	NUM 1–10	Census, priests, Levites & tribes
NUM 20–21	Further Wilderness adventures	NUM 17–19	Directions for Aaron, priests & Levites
NUM 22–24	Balaam Oracles on the Conquest	NUM 25–31	Census & laws on vows priests & feasts
NUM 32	First conquest of Transjordan	NUM 33–36	Order of march, the stops on journey & cultic rules for the conquest
DEUT 1–33	D-Source speech of Moses and Second Law as new covenant		
DEUT 34	The Death of Moses		

STUDY QUESTIONS

1. Briefly describe life during the Babylonian exile.
2. What is the Book of Ruth?
3. Who was Ezekiel? Describe the characteristics and major features of his prophecy. What is his central message?
4. How did Ezekiel view and understand judgment? How did he see Babylon?
5. Briefly describe how Ezekiel understood the plan of restoration.
6. Explain the origins of the Priestly edition of the Pentateuch. What are its characteristics?
7. How would one describe the theology of P? What is P's understanding of history?

Chapter 20

SING US A SONG OF ZION!

Suggested Scripture Readings:

Lamentations 1–2
Isaiah 40–41
Isaiah 51–55

A. OTHER RESPONSES TO THE EXILE

The Devastation of Judah

Many archaeologists who have excavated in the holy land have pointed to the great number of towns and cities that were destroyed during the sixth century B.C. and never rebuilt again. It is a dramatic sign of the widespread loss of life and the violence that left the cities burned and lifeless. The best citizens were deported to Babylon, and those left behind were so few that they could not even rebuild. The land of Judah was reduced to an area of only about twenty-five miles long by twenty miles wide, stretching from Jerusalem down to Hebron. Where in earlier days the "people of the land" had been wealthy or at least successful farmers and landowners, now the term came to mean only the lowly survivors who scratched out a living in the countryside.

The Book of Jeremiah (chapters 40 and 41) tells us that the Babylonians set up a native prince, Gedaliah, who came from a family that had been closely tied to the reforms of King Josiah, as the governor of the newly-made Babylonian province created out of the wreckage of 586 B.C. Jeremiah was set free from prison and chose to stay in Palestine to help, but this new beginning did not last long. A zealous patriot named Ishmael, with the support of the king of Edom across the Dead Sea, led Gedeliah into a trap and assassinated him only some three years later. Ishmael escaped to Edom for protection, while the Judean leaders who were left became so frightened of the possible Babylonian response that they fled to Egypt, taking Jeremiah with them.

The province was then put under a Babylonian governor in Samaria to the north and lost its independence altogether. This eventually led to many conflicts when the Judeans returned from exile fifty years later, for the governors of Samaria did not like the idea of losing a good part of their province.

The Book of Lamentations

One of our most important sources of information about the terrible conditions in Jerusalem and Judah after the Babylonian attack comes from the Book of Lamentations. It is a short book of five chapters, each of which is a poem built upon the letters of the alphabet, and which expresses the deep pain and grief of those who survived in the land. The alphabet form, called "acrostic" in books on Hebrew poetry, starts each line or stanza with the next letter in order. This gives a very strong sense of controlled emotion in which anger, anguish and agony all struggle to burst out but cannot find a way. To intensify the grief the author or authors of these poems have chosen the forms of funeral laments as well. This adds to the power they have on the reader. It is truly grief for what is dead—Jerusalem, the temple, the king, the way of life.

But instead of picturing the city of Jerusalem as the dead body, Lamentations describes it as the widow. Personified as "daughter Zion," she weeps bitterly. Alone and afflicted by her total loss of everything and everybody, she finds no one who can comfort her:

How like a widow she is,
    once so great among the nations!
Once a queen among states,
    she has become a slave.
She weeps bitterly at night,
    tears on her cheeks;
Among all her lovers;
    she has no one to comfort her.

The Territory of Judah after the Exile

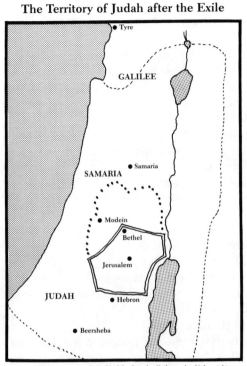

Borders of Judah after the Exile (under Nehemiah)
•••••••••••••• The area of Judah under the Greek Seleucids
----------------- The area taken by the Hasmonean kings

All her friends have betrayed her
  and become her enemies (Lam 1:1–2).

This is why I weep
  and my eyes run with tears:
Far away is anyone to comfort me
  or revive my spirit,
My children are devastated
  because the enemy has triumphed (Lam 1:16).

The poets give us a stark and terrifying picture of the conditions in the land after Jerusalem has fallen:

All her people groan
  while they search for bread,

They trade their wealth for food
   to keep themselves alive (Lam 1:11).

My heart is poured out on the ground
   because my people are destroyed,
Because children and infants faint
   in the city streets.
They call to their mothers:
   "Where is bread and wine?"
As they faint like wounded men
   in the city streets,
As their lives ebb away
   in their mothers' arms (Lam 2:11–12).

Those killed by the sword are better off
   than those who die of famine.
Starving, they waste away
   for lack of any food to harvest.
Out of compassion women have cooked their children
   with their own hands
And eaten them as food
   while my daughter, my people were destroyed (Lam
     4:9–10).

But even in the midst of disaster, Lamentations holds out hope
that God will turn from his anger and wrath and restore his people.
There is no hiding from the truth that God punished them justly.
"Jerusalem has sinned greatly and become unclean. . . . Her filthi-
ness clung to her skirts, she did not give thought to her future"
(1:8–9). "Let us lift up both our hearts and hands to God in heaven
and say, 'We have sinned and rebelled and you have not forgiven
us' " (3:41–42). Nor do they try to deny that God can be very hard:
"You have slain them in the day of your anger, and slaughtered
them without pity" (2:21). "The Lord has given full vent to his
wrath, he poured out his blazing anger, he kindled a fire in Zion
that consumed its foundations" (4:11). And yet in the same breath
they can express their trust that God will not leave them forever:

Yet this I will call to mind
   and therefore keep hope:
Because of the Lord's great love
   we have not been destroyed,

For his mercy never fails,
  they are new each morning; great is your faithfulness.
I say to myself, "The Lord is my portion,
  therefore I will hope in him" (Lam 3:21–24).

Because such expressions are so vivid and real, most scholars have believed that the authors were eyewitnesses of the fall of Jerusalem. The poems date from a time shortly after 586 and were written down in Judah itself, but we cannot be sure who exactly was the author. A very ancient tradition associates the book with Jeremiah, and so our modern Bibles, following the Greek Septuagint and other ancient authorities, usually place Lamentations right next to the Book of Jeremiah. One biblical passage actually remarks that Jeremiah had written several laments (2 Chr 35:25)—but these were over Josiah and not over Jerusalem. Still many of the phrases in Lamentations do resemble the style of Jeremiah:

To what can I compare you that I might comfort you,
  O daughter Zion?
Your wound is as deep as the ocean;
  who can heal you? (Lam 2:13; cf. Jer 8:22; 30:13).

The visions of your prophets
  were false and empty,
They did not reveal your sin
  and prevent your captivity.
The oracles they gave you
  were false and lying (Lam 2:14; cf. Jer 23:11, 14, 16).

Cry out to the Lord,
  O remorseful Zion, from your heart!
Pour out your heart with tears
  day and night before the Lord (Lam 2:18; cf. Jer 9:1).

However, it is difficult to believe that Jeremiah would have trusted in Egypt or Babylon as a hope (Lam 4:17) or had much sympathy with the fate of the king (Lam 4:20) or mourned greatly over the fates of the prophets and priests who had led the people astray (Lam 2:20). But whether Jeremiah actually had any role in writing Lamentations or not, the language and thought of both books are close together and reveal much the same picture. To understand what

Jeremiah was seeing in his visions of God's judgments, one needs to read Lamentations.

The Prophet Obadiah

The small Book of Obadiah, whose twenty-one verses make it the shortest book in the Old Testament, gives us another picture of the terrible conditions in Judah during the period of exile. The message of Obadiah is aimed totally at the Edomites whose land was on the other side of the Dead Sea and below it. Their kingdom thus lay between the Arabian tribes in the deserts to the east and the Negev area of Judah. It was a harsh land, and the very name "edom" which means "red land" describes the poor sandy soil unfit for farming. Apparently at the same time that the Babylonian armies captured Jerusalem in 586, the king of Edom took the chance to seize large parts of the southern area of Judah. He may even have sent troops to help the Babylonians. Verses 13 and 14 suggest that Edomites were part of the forces that sacked Jerusalem.

Israel's relations with the kingdom of Edom had always been difficult. The prophetic books contain many oracles directed against the Edomites in the strongest language used against any group in the Bible. Amos 1:11 accuses Edom of "pursuing his brother with the sword and casting off all pity." Ezekiel 25 charges that "Edom has acted vengefully against the house of Judah and has seriously sinned in taking vegeance." Lamentations 4 ends with the cry of the author, "But your iniquity, O daughter Edom, he will punish when he strips you bare in your sin."

But no book reaches the peak of anger found in Obadiah. Much of his oracle is found repeated in Jeremiah 46, so that the two prophets may have used an older poem that was well known as the basis of their separate judgments against Edom. But many scholars believe that Jeremiah may have borrowed from Obadiah's oracle because the latter seems so original in its power of expression. Verses 1–4 summon all the nations to fight against Edom in her mountain strongholds. Verses 5–9 go on to describe the people plundering her of all her riches. This is followed in verses 10–14 with a series of reasons why Edom has been condemned by God:

> For the violence done to your brother Jacob
>   shame will cover you
>   and you will be cut off forever (v. 10).

You should not have gloated over the day of your brother,
in the time of his misfortune (v. 12).

You should not have looted his possessions
in the day of his disaster (v. 13).

You should not have delivered up his survivors
on the day of defeat (v. 14).

Finally, the book ends with an oracle in verses 15–20 that sees a day coming when Israel shall conquer Edom and rule over her land. This final poem does not react to the present situation of exile but looks ahead to a better time when the Lord would return as a warrior on his day of battle to defeat all of Israel's enemies and make her once again powerful as in the times of David and Solomon:

In Mount Zion shall dwell all who have escaped, and it shall
be called holy,
and the house of Jacob shall possess their own possessions.
The house of Jacob shall be a fire
and the house of Joseph a flame
that shall burn and consume them.
And there shall be no survivors
of the House of Esau (vss. 17–18).

Israel's hatred of Edom no doubt had deep roots in earlier conflicts. The Book of Numbers tells at great length how the Edomites refused to let Israel pass through their territory on the journey to the promised land (Num 20:14–21). Later David defeated the Edomites and made them part of his empire (2 Sam 8:13–14; 1 Kgs 11:15–18). Two centuries later, Edom managed to revolt and free itself from Judah's control for good (2 Kgs 8:20–24). In all of these battles, an undying hatred was born between the two nations. And yet the Bible remembers that the two peoples, Israel and Edom, were once brothers. The story of Jacob (Israel) and Esau (Edom) in Genesis 25 and 27 makes them twins from the same ancestor. But, of course, since a patriotic Israelite is telling the story, Jacob proves to be the better and smarter son whom God blesses, while Esau is scorned and laughed at as a kind of rough country bumpkin.

Edom's power was short-lived after the fall of Jerusalem. Within

the next forty years or so, Arab tribes from the east attacked and
drove most of the Edomites out of their homeland and forced them
to flee across to Judah's Negev desert area. Since Judah was unable
to stop them, they settled down there. In later centuries the area
became known as Idumea—the home birthplace of Herod the
Great at the time of Jesus.

Obadiah stresses God's sense of justice against the wrongs committed by nations. The prophet prays not only for Edom's immediate punishment but also in the long run for a reversal of her state so
that she may become nothing again and Israel may be restored to
greatness. It is not a book of easy rejoicing or the praise of a God of
mercy, but it does reveal in its passion and anger a deep trust that
God cares for those who suffer and will bring justice to the world
sooner or later.

Psalm 137

A few of the psalms can be dated to the time of the exile
because they sing in anguish of being in exile and unable to go to
Jerusalem. Some of these are Psalms 42, 43, 80, 85, 126 and 137. But
of them all, only Psalm 137 clearly states that it is sung by exiles in
Babylon. Its vivid descriptions agree with those in Obadiah and
Lamentations:

> How will we sing a song of the Lord
>   in a foreign land?
> If I forget you, Jerusalem
>   may my right hand wither;
> May my tongue stick to the roof of my mouth
>   if I do not remember you,
> If I do not set Jerusalem
>   above my greatest joy.
> Remember, Lord, against Edom
>   the day of Jerusalem,
> When they said, "Destroy it, destroy it
>   down to its foundations."
> O daughter Babylon, doomed to destruction,
>   happy the one who will repay you for what you did to us,
>   happy the one who dashes your babies against the rocks (Ps
>   137:4–9).

The thoughts are not pious thoughts but they come from the heart of people who have suffered greatly.

The Exile Nears Its End

In 562 B.C., Nebuchadnezzar died after a reign of forty-three years. His sons and successors were not able to match his ability, and the empire he had created slowly but surely began to fall apart. One sign of change was the more relaxed attitude toward conquered peoples taken by the new king Amel-marduk (or Evil-merodach, as he is called in the Hebrew language). The Second Book of Kings ends its entire history of Israel from Joshua to the exile with a notice that the Babylonians began to treat the aging prisoner and one-time king of Judah, Jehoiachin, with more honor:

> In the thirty-seventh year of Jehoiachin's exile as king of Judah, in the year that Evil-merodach became king of Babylon, he released Jehoiachin from prison on the twenty-seventh day of the twelfth month. He spoke to him in kindness and seated him at a higher place than those of the other kings who were with him in Babylon. Thus Jehoiachin laid aside his prison garb and for the rest of his life ate daily at the king's table. And the king gave Jehoiachin a daily allowance as long as he lived (2 Kgs 25:27–30).

But it was not a time of peace. Three kings took the throne of Babylon in six years, until finally one of the generals, Nabonidus, seized power in 555. He held it until the end of Babylonian rule in 539.

Nabonidus was a strange man who must have been from the outer parts of the empire because he had no special love for the city of Babylon itself, and felt uncomfortable and threatened there. After some years he moved his capital to Tema, an oasis in the Arabian desert far to the south. From there he not only fought to control the Arab tribes but to control his large empire to the north. That their king was an "absentee landlord" did not sit well with the people of Mesopotamia. What was worse, his self-imposed "exile" made him miss the all-important annual New Year's feast of Marduk in Babylon for a number of years. It was at this feast that the Babylonians believed Marduk blessed the land for the year ahead. It renewed its power when the god "took the hand of" the king in the special ceremonies at the temple of Marduk. Without the presence of the king, Marduk would not give blessing and might even be angered enough to send punishment upon the land.

The Rise of Persia as a World Power

The greatest threat to Babylon, however, came from outside. A century earlier than Nabonidus, the king of the Medes, Cyaxares, created a large empire in the lands to the east of Babylon and Assyria, in the northern part of modern Iran and across much of Turkey and southern Russia. He had fought beside the Babylonians in the attacks against Assyria which led to its downfall in 612 B.C. By mutual agreement, Babylon had taken control of the west and left the Medes to rule the east and north. The capital of the Medes was in Ecbatana, now the modern city of Hamadan in Iran. In the early part of the sixth century, the Median king Astyages married his daughter to one of his vassals, Cambyses, king of Anshan, a Persian tribe in southern Iran. The child of this royal marriage was Cyrus, who became king of Anshan at his father's death in 559 B.C.

Cyrus was ambitious and Astyages was old and weak. In 550 Cyrus saw his chance and made an alliance with the Babylonian king Nabonidus to support a revolt against his father-in-law. Astyages sent two armies to attack Cyrus, but, through persuasion, Cyrus convinced them instead to join him and hand Astyages over as a prisoner. He was now king of the whole Median-Persian empire. Cyrus' talent at winning others over to his side became the hallmark of his rule and enabled him to win many battles with the promise of mercy.

Nabonidus was now frightened and joined with Egypt and the kingdom of Lydia in western Turkey in an alliance to stop Cyrus. But Cyrus acted quickly, taking northern Mesopotamia and Syria in 547. Then, in the dead of winter, when everyone thought that the snows made war impossible, Cyrus marched his army across Turkey and attacked the capital city of Lydia, Sardis. Taken completely by surprise, its king, Croesus, the man fabled for his great wealth, set fire to his palace and died in its flames rather than be captured. There is little information about what Cyrus did next, but when we next hear of his activities in the year 540, his empire included all of modern Pakistan and Afghanistan to the east of Iran. He must have spent the years from 546 to 540 fighting in those lands. Cyrus now

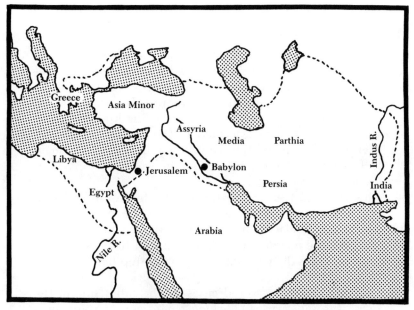

The Persian Empire

ruled the largest empire the world had ever seen, and it was obvious to all, including the unknown prophet who wrote Isaiah 40–55, that it was merely a matter of time before Babylon itself became the next victim.

By 540 he was again marching in the west. He defeated the Babylonians in Mesopotamia at Opis along the Tigris River. In this battle the Persians used a new weapon, fire, and broke the morale of the Babylonian army. Already angered and betrayed by their own king's failure to honor Marduk and his capital city, Babylon's citizens did not even put up a fight but opened the gates to Cyrus' army in October 539. Nabonidus had already fled south to escape, and Babylon was well treated. The temple services in honor of Marduk were continued, no sacrileges were committed, and two weeks later Cyrus himself arrived to "take the hand of the god" and proclaim himself king of Babylon. As a result, the people accepted him as Marduk's choice and never considered him to be a "foreign" conqueror.

Cyrus left an account of his victory over Babylon that has survived the centuries and was found amid the ruins of the city. Naturally it exalts the role of Cyrus as the beloved of Marduk and can be considered an example of early propaganda written to win support for his rule. Some excerpts will give a flavor for the whole, which is quite long:

> Marduk . . . on account of the fact that the sanctuaries of all their settlements were in ruins and the inhabitants of Sumer and Akkad had become like (living) dead, turned back, his anger (abated) and he had mercy. He scanned and looked through all the countries, searching for a righteous ruler willing to lead (Marduk) in the annual procession. Then he pronounced the name of Cyrus, king of Anshan; declared him to be the ruler of all the world . . .

> When I (Cyrus) entered Babylon as a friend and when I established the seat of government in the palace of the ruler under jubilation and rejoicing, Marduk the great lord (induced) the magnanimous inhabitants of Babylon (to love me), and I was daily endeavoring to worship him . . .

> I returned to these sacred cities on the other side of the Tigris, the sanctuaries of which have been in ruins for a long time, the images (of the gods) which live therein, and established for them permanent sanctuaries. I (also) gathered all their (former) inhabitants and returned (to them) their habitations. Furthermore, I resettled upon the command of Marduk, the great lord, all the gods of Sumer and Akkad whom Nabonidus has brought to Babylon . . . (ANET 315–316).

B. SECOND ISAIAH (ISAIAH 40–55)

Who Was Second Isaiah?

Chapters 40–55 of Isaiah are often called the "Book of Consolation" because the prophet offers no judgment and condemnation of Israel, but only a message of trust and confident hope that God is about to end the exile. These chapters have long been recognized as a single work that has its own special style, much different from the sharper words spoken by the earlier Isaiah of Jerusalem in chapters 1–39. The language soars on long strings of adjectives and titles for God. It is filled with images of rebuilding, restoring, renewing, and recreating. The poems of this author almost have the quality of hymns or psalms of praise.

When these are compared to the oracles of First Isaiah in the eighth century B.C., striking differences appear. Second Isaiah never mentions the political events of Kings Ahaz or Hezekiah, never mentions the Assyrians and their attacks, and never mentions the threats from Damascus or the northern kingdom of Israel. On the other hand, Second Isaiah clearly refers to the capture and destruction of Jerusalem as a past event (Is 40:1–2; 47:6; 48:20), and the present state of the people as exiles in Babylon (Is 43:14; 47:1–4; 48:20). It praises Cyrus the Persian as a deliverer for Israel (Is 44:28; 45:1–7), and places major emphasis on the return home to Palestine for all the exiles in Babylon (Is 41:17–20; 42:14–17).

In short, the setting is certainly that of the middle of the sixth century and not the middle of the eighth. Moreover, such clear and accurate references to specific events of the exile are unknown in other prophets such as Ezekiel or Jeremiah. It is not the prophetic method to predict small details of the future, and the belief, held by Christians of the Middle Ages, that the original Isaiah of Jerusalem predicted all that would happen one hundred and fifty years after his death has been abandoned by modern biblical scholarship. Instead, scholars understand that our present Book of Isaiah has been formed by combining the prophecies of Isaiah with those of a second prophet who lived at the time of the exile. Still a third edition was made when the exiles had returned to their homeland in Jerusalem. This makes up chapters 56–66, and we call the author of this section "Third Isaiah" (see next chapter).

This so-called Second Isaiah (or "deutero-Isaiah") was a disciple and follower of the thought of Isaiah. He stresses the same central ideas that Isaiah had earlier emphasized: (1) God is the Holy One of Israel; (2) God uses foreign rulers and nations as his instruments to punish Israel, but will in turn punish the evil that those nations do in excess; (3) he makes his home in Jerusalem on Mount Zion and from there his salvation goes forth. The times may have changed, but the message still endured: God will act for his people as he has promised, and as he has actually done so often in the past.

We do not know the name of this Second Isaiah, or how long he preached, or anything about his background except that he was among the exiles in Babylon. He has hidden his own identity behind that of the great prophet Isaiah so that those who hear or read his prophecies will see only the continuity of what God is doing from

Isaiah's age to his own. From the note of excitement and urgency in his message, we can be sure that the prophet was working just before the final end of Babylon in 539. He can see the victories of Cyrus already won, and he expects the fall of Babylon at any moment. In fact, some of the oracles may actually have been given after the Persian armies had already entered the city. The description of the Babylonian gods going into exile in chapter 46 looks like an eyewitness account!

The Outline of the Book

There are two major divisions in Second Isaiah, chapters 40–48 and chapters 49–55. In the first, emphasis falls on the whole nation Israel, in the second, on Jerusalem and Zion in particular. But the book is quite a bit more difficult than such a simple outline shows. Scholars disagree whether it is made up of fifty or more short oracles strung together like pearls on a necklace or whether it is really a small number of very long poems with many variations within each. Close examination does reveal the following patterns:

1. A matching introduction and conclusion stresses the power of God's word over everything (Is 40:1-8 and 55:6-11):

> The grass withers and the flower fades,
>> but the word of our God stands forever (Is 40:8).

> So also will be my word that I speak.
>> It will not return to me empty,
> But it will accomplish what I have intended,
>> and it will succeed in what I have sent it to do (Is 55:11).

2. A second pair of introductory and closing passages depict a herald announcing salvation to Jerusalem (Is 40:9–10 and 52:7–10):

> Go up to a high mountain,
>> Zion, herald of good news,
>> And cry out loudly,
>> Jerusalem, herald of good news.
> Cry out and do not be afraid.
>> Say to the cities of Judah:
>> "Behold your God" (Is 40:9).

How wonderful on the mountains
   are the feet of the messenger of good news,
Who proclaims peace, announces the coming good,
   proclaims salvation and says to Zion,
   "Your God is king" (Is 52:7).

3. Fragments of hymns serve to divide one section from another. Examples include Isaiah 42:10–13, 44:23, 45:8, 48:20–21, 49:13, and 51:3.

4. The center of the book stresses the role of the foreign nations, especially the collapse of Babylon and its idols, and the rise of Cyrus of Persia as God's chosen instrument (chapters 44–47).

5. A series of four "servant songs" are inserted at important places in the book to make personal the message of the prophet. These are found in Isaiah 42:1–4, 49:1–6, 50:4–9, and 52:13–53:12.

6. Several examples of the longer poems that combine shorter units within them can be identified. One is chapter 40 as a whole, which serves as a general introduction to the prophet's thought and joins together the short oracle on God's word as powerful in 40:1–9 and a longer poem on God's rule over all creation in 40:10–31. Together they make up a great hymn of praise that exalts God's power to act. Another example is the combined chapters 54 and 55, which join together a number of hymns praising God's majesty and achievements, and inviting Israel to trust completely in him.

Beyond these larger patterns, many special literary forms can be found in Second Isaiah. The prophet is fond of using trial speeches and lawsuit language. Many of these may come from actual courtroom practices of his day, but it is just as possible that they were traditional prophetic ways of expressing the guilt of Israel for violation of its greatest legal contract, the covenant with Yahweh. The prophets Hosea and Micah had used similar forms in their prophecies. But Second Isaiah does not accuse Israel as other prophets had; instead he turns the lawsuit against the pagan gods to prove that their claims to power were false.

Second Isaiah also likes special forms that declare God's intention to save Israel. One type is called a proclamation of salvation, and is arranged as a formal answer to the people's complaints that God has abandoned them or let them down. It always mentions what people are disturbed about, and then follows this with a declaration that God has heard and does intervene for them. A second type is labeled an oracle of salvation, and imitates the formal prayer for help that a prophet or priest would have said over

Trial Speeches (41:1–5, 41:21–29, 42:18–25; 43:8–13, 43:22–28, 45:18–25):

The Accusation	Hearing the Charges	Calling of Witnesses	The Decision
41:21	41:22–23	41:25–28	41:29
42:18	42:19–20	42:21–24	42:25
43:22a	43:22b–24	43:26–27	43:28

Lawsuits (40:12–31, 44:24–28, 45:9–13, 46:5–11, 48:1–11, 48:12–15, 55:8–13):

Basis for the Charges	The Outcome
44:24–26	44:26b–28
45:9–10	45:11–13
48:12–13	48:14–15

someone who was sick or in need of healing during a temple service. It always includes the healing word of Yahweh, "Do not be afraid." A good example of this kind of oracle is found in Isaiah 41:8–13:

Special Address: But you, Israel, my servant,
        Jacob, whom I have chosen,
        descendant of Abraham my friend (Is 41:8).

    You, whom I have taken from the ends of the earth
    and called from its remote corners,
    And to whom I have said, "You are my servant,
        I have chosen you and not rejected you" (Is 41:9).

Word of
Assurance: "Do not fear! For I am with you;
        do not be afraid, for I am your God."
    I strengthen you, I help you,
        I uphold you with my victorious right hand (Is 41:10).

The Salvation Event:	Behold they will be confounded and ashamed,
	all who rage against you.

The Salvation Event:

Behold they will be confounded and ashamed,
    all who rage against you.
They will be as nothing, and perish,
    all who dispute against you.
You will seek for them and not find them,
    those who contend with you.
They will be brought to nothing at all,
    those who war against you (Is 41:11–12).

Reassurance:

For I am Yahweh your God,
    who grasps you by the right hand,
Who says to you, "Do not fear!
    I am the one who helps you" (Is 41:13).

Proclamations of Salvation (41:17–20, 43:16–21, 49:7–12, 51:9–14, 51:17–23):

Introduction	The Community's Complaint	Proclamation of Salvation
43:16–17	43:18	43:19–21
49:7a	49:7	48:8–12
—	51:9–11	51:12–14

Oracles of Salvation

Address	Word of Assurance	The Promised Salvation
41:14	41:14	41:15–16
44:1–2	44:2	44:3–5
—	54:5–6	44:4b

Still another kind of literary form can be called idol parodies. In these, the prophet mocks the faith that pagans put in idols of wood and stone. Examples can be found in Isaiah 40:19–20, 41:6–7, 44:9–20, and 46:6–7. The passages are very colorful in their descriptions of how much *human* effort goes into making gods that have no power at all. This contrasts sharply with the ability of Yahweh to rule the world:

They pour out gold from their wallets,
    and weigh the silver on the scales.

They hire a goldsmith to make from it a god,
  then they bow down and worship.
They lift it on their shoulders and carry it around,
  they set it down and it stands there;
  it never moves from its place.
When someone prays to it, it does not answer
  nor save him from disaster (Is 46:6–7).

Finally, Second Isaiah often uses a first-person statement of praise placed in God's own mouth. "I the Lord was there at the beginning" (Is 41:6), "I alone am the Lord your God" (Is 42:8), "For I am the Lord your God, the Holy One of Israel" (Is 43:3). These formulas are especially dramatic and forceful and are used often (Is 41:4, 10, 13, 17; 42:6, 8, 9; 43:3, 11, 13, 15; 44:24; 45:3, 5, 6, 7, 18–19, 21, etc.). Any Israelite who heard the prophet speak this way would have been reminded how God himself on Mount Sinai said, "I am the Lord your God . . ." (Ex 20:2).

The Message of the Prophet

Chapter 40 is a prologue to the message of Second Isaiah, and the beauty of the opening scene sets the theme for the whole book. Although no person is given a name, we hear voices speaking, and can easily detect the typical questions used in a story about the call of a prophet, as in Isaiah 6, Jeremiah 1, or Ezekiel 2–3. God asks his heavenly council whom he should send as his messenger to announce the "good news": "Comfort, comfort my people, says your God. Speak tenderly to Jerusalem and announce to her that her slavery is ended and her sins have been pardoned" (Is 40:1–2). God's people have paid double the penalty and now shall receive salvation. What that salvation will be is made rapidly clear in verses 10–31: God is coming to be with his people; he will shepherd the flock; he will be the Creator who controls the nations; he alone will have power; he will give strength to the weary and the weak.

They who wait for the Lord will renew their strength,
  they will fly like eagles on their wings,
They will run and not grow tired,
  walk and not become faint (Is 40:31).

The prophet seems eager to be the messenger of this new word of salvation. In verse 6 he asks, "What shall I shout?" And the following verses stress that above all he is to proclaim the power of God to save. This is to be shown by recalling the great themes of Israel's faith: God as Creator, Redeemer from all enemies, Liberator from the slavery under Egypt at the exodus, Giver of the promise and the covenant. God will march again as the divine warrior who fights on behalf of his people as he did at the exodus and later in the conquest of the promised land (Ex 15; Jgs 5; see Is 42:13; 43:16–19). Second Isaiah never tires of mentioning the titles of God as Savior, Holy One, King, Creator, Lord, Redeemer, the First and Last, the Justifier, etc. It is as though he were constantly singing a song of praise of how wonderful Yahweh *is*. The key is this active *present*. Yahweh did not just do great things in the past—he is doing them now for Israel, if only the people would look about them and see!

Some of the major themes can be listed separately:

(1) *God's word is all-powerful.* The entire message of the prophet is framed by the two statements on God's word in Isaiah 40:1–9 and 55:6–11. Grass and earthly things may wither and die, even human beings, but God's word does not fail. It goes forth like rain to water and nourish and bring life to all creation. It never fails to do what God intends. Second Isaiah returns to this theme often. In Isaiah 43:1–7 he stresses that God has called to Israel; in Isaiah 41:17–20 he promises to answer the needy; in Isaiah 44:24–28 he confirms his prophetic word anew. Indeed, a careful reading of the book reveals a major stress on the idea of calling. God calls Israel, he calls his servant, he calls Cyrus, he calls Abraham; and in turn he asks the people to call on him and respond to him.

(2) *He will give mercy and forgiveness.* The single most striking aspect of Second Isaiah is that there is no judgment against Israel. From beginning to end, the prophet sounds the note of God's salvation. It begins dramatically in the first line, when he joins a double "Comfort, comfort my people" with the soothing promise that they have already suffered double what their sins deserved. The book may speak of God's power and majesty more often, but it is always based on his deep mercy and love for Israel. He is a God of compassion for the suffering nation and for each and every one who is weak, tired or unable to go on. It is in light of this fundamental truth about God that the servant figure makes sense.

(3) *God will do new things never done before.* In Isaiah 42:9 Yahweh declares, "Behold, the former things have happened, and new things I now declare; before they come forth, I announce them to you." Israel's faith is deeply rooted in remembering what God has

done. This is a key insight about Second Isaiah. Remember all the great acts of salvation that God has already done, remember all the prophetic words of Isaiah and other messengers that have come to pass, remember what God is as the only God in the entire universe—remember everything, but look to the future. In Isaiah 43:18, he commands Israel to stop living by the past and to notice what God is doing anew: "Remember not former things, nor consider what was done of old; behold I am doing a new thing; it is happening, do you not see it?" In Isaiah 48:6–7, the prophet insists that the new things are really different: "They are created now, and not long ago; before today you never heard of them!" Too often in the past, Israel rebelled despite what God had done for them; now they must recognize and trust the God who acts for them.

(4) *There will be a new exodus.* The "new thing" that God will do is lead the people from Babylon back to their homeland. Some major texts which compare this journey from slavery to freedom with the earlier escape from Egypt are Isaiah 42:10–11, 43:9–10, 43:16–21, 49:7–12, 51:9–10, 52:7–12, and 55:12–13. He will feed them with manna and water as Moses did long ago (Is 41:17–20; 43:18–20; 48:20–21; 49:10). He will guide them through the unknown ways of the wilderness like a shepherd (Is 40:11; 49:9–11; 43:16–21). They will pass through fire and water (Is 43:1–3), there will be a new victory at the Red Sea over the watery terror (Is 51:9–10), and there will be a new conquest of the promised land (Is 49:8–12).

(5) *Yahweh is the Redeemer of Israel.* No one uses the term "redeemer" more often than Second Isaiah. The Pentateuch directs the nearest relative to "redeem" members of his family or clan that have been forced into slavery (Lev 25:47–55), or to "redeem" their property (Lev 25:23–34), or to marry the widow of a childless brother in order to "redeem" his family name with children (Dt 25:5–10; cf. the Book of Ruth and Genesis 38), or to take vengeance on the murderer of a relative to "redeem" the nearest blood kin (Num 35:31–34). All of these imply the duty of standing by the family and protecting its rights against the attempts of others to steal them away. It is a personal obligation falling on the next of kin. The Book of Exodus talks about God's saving deeds with a verb meaning to "free" (*padah*), but Second Isaiah always uses the more personal term for "redeemer" found in Leviticus (*ga'al*). God declares that he is the personal relation of Israel, and his promise to stand by and protect them is linked to being married to Israel as a husband (Is 54:1–10), to the election of Israel as God's chosen people

(Is 43:20–21; 44:1–5), and to God as Creator of all (Is 43:1–7; 45:9–13).

This takes special shape in God's choice of Cyrus the Persian as his human redeemer. Isaiah 44:24–28 is a poem about God the Redeemer who picks Cyrus to be his shepherd to fulfill all that God has promised. Isaiah 45:1–7 goes further and names Cyrus as God's anointed one, his messiah, and announces over him the same oracle of salvation that has been given to Israel. This is clearly a radical proposal, for in effect God replaces the king and the house of David with a foreign ruler, and a pagan besides! Historically, the exiles must have rejoiced greatly at the thought of Cyrus winning the war against Babylon. He had a reputation for mercy toward the defeated rulers and their people, and he followed a regular policy of letting nations that had been exiled and resettled by the Babylonians and Assyrians return to their native lands. It is no wonder that the prophet sees the hand of the compassionate Yahweh behind everything that is coming about. Indeed, part of the "new thing" is precisely the victory given to Cyrus.

(6) *There will be a new creation.* No prophet stresses the theme of creation so much as does Second Isaiah. God made all things and gave order to all things, as Genesis 1 expresses it so beautifully. All nations and all events are under the control of God's saving plan. A God this powerful has not forgotten Israel or fallen so low that he cannot use his power. The prophet also sees that this new salvation is really a re-creation. Important texts are found in Isaiah 40:12–31, 43:16–21, 45:7–9, 48:13–14, and 51:13–16. God has a plan and no one else knows it. It is on the basis that God alone is Creator that Second Isaiah bases all his lawsuits and trial speeches against the pagans and their idols. Not one of them can show what will happen next nor can they demonstrate any power to help their followers. This belongs to the Creator and only God, Yahweh.

Because of the great emphasis that the prophet gives to God as Creator and Lord of the whole world, commentators have long remarked that no book in the Old Testament puts greater stress on monotheism than does Second Isaiah. Israel is different from the other nations of the ancient world and their polytheism because of this conviction. It runs as a single thread that ties all of the message of revelation together from the patriarch Abraham down to the end of the Old Testament story. But no Old Testament book reaches a higher level of understanding of God's oneness than does Second Isaiah.

(7) *There is a role for all nations in God's plan.* Many scholars

have debated whether Second Isaiah is a narrow nationalist who sees salvation only for Israel, or the first universalist who envisions a rule of Yahweh over every nation. We must remember that his message is directed to Israelites in exile to give them hope, and so his message is first and foremost directed to those in covenant with Yahweh. But then it is all the more remarkable that so many passages indicate a concern for other nations as well. Yet the theology of one God and the stress of God as Creator really left the prophet no other choice. First of all, Cyrus and the Persians were divine means of salvation and blessed because of it. Secondly, Israel itself is not commanded to go forth and win over other nations, but there is a definite belief that the other nations will look to Israel and learn from its rescue from exile how good God is. They will come on their own to discover Yahweh in the restored Jerusalem. This is the message found in Isaiah 45:14-17, 45:22-25, and 55:1-5. It is found in a different and deeper way in the life of the servant, who will give witness by both teaching and suffering to the nations (see Is 42:4; 49:6; 53:11).

(8) *Yahweh will restore Zion.* One of the greatest sorrows of the exile was the knowledge that Jerusalem and the temple lay in ruins. We have seen the pain expressed in the Book of Lamentations. Now God will restore Zion and make it once again the center of the world. Chapters 49-55 shift toward dreaming of the restored city. The prophet counters the despairing complaint of the exiles that God has forgotten them altogether: "Zion says, 'Yahweh has forsaken me, my Lord has forgotten me.' Can a mother forget her infant, or have no compassion on the child of her womb? Even these may forget, but I will never forget you" (Is 49:14-15). He promises that the exiles shall return, "singing" as they come to Zion (Is 51:11). The city's watchmen will rejoice as they see Yahweh coming (Is 52:8). Zion will not only be a symbol of God's presence with Israel, but will be the seat of his kingly rule over the world. Many scholars have noted that Second Isaiah does not speak of the return of the Davidic king. He has no place for a covenant based on Israel's own power and independence. Instead, as Isaiah 55:1-5 makes clear, God will establish a covenant with the whole people and will rule over them and the nations directly from his throne in Zion. The return of Yahweh to Jerusalem is seen as a liturgical procession like those found in the temple services. Isaiah 49:17-21, 52:7-12 and 54:1-17 all describe the Lord's return in this manner, building on the descriptions of the new exodus and new creation to unite them all in one great vision.

The three themes of *creation, redemption* and the *universal rule of God* come together often in the prophet's thought. It is a "creative redemption" of the world. This is especially true in the prayer of chapter 51:

> Awake, awake, gird on strength,
>   O arm of the Lord;
> Awake as in the ancient days,
>   the ages long ago.
> Did you not cut Rahab in pieces.
>   and slay the dragon?
> Did you not dry up the sea,
>   the waters of the great abyss,
> And make the depths of the sea a road
>   for the redeemed to pass through? (Is 51:9-10).

In this poem, Second Isaiah combines the ancient pagan story of the battle of the gods against the chaotic ocean (in order to bring about ordered creation) with the traditions of the exodus to reveal that Yahweh alone is both Creator and Redeemer.

The Servant Songs

Second Isaiah frequently speaks about Israel (or Jacob) as "my servant" (Is 41:8-9; 42:19; 44:1-2; 45:4; 48:20, etc.). Israel as the servant is chosen by Yahweh, comforted by him, and given the spirit of Yahweh; yet the servant Israel is also called a worm, despised, rebellious, blind and deaf. The term "servant" has as many uses in Second Isaiah as Israel has roles to play. It sums up the people who sinned, suffered and now turn to God to be redeemed. It sums up God's loyalty and special relationship to them in turn.

But there are four passages which have always been seen differently. These are Isaiah 42:1-4, 49:1-6, 50:4-9 and 52:13-53:12. In these the servant is described as a single individual with enough personality to make the reader wonder if the prophet did not have someone particular in mind who actually played this role. True enough, in Isaiah 49:3, the text says outright that Israel is this servant, but most scholars believe this is a later comment that was added to the text by a reader who wanted to identify the mission of the servant with post-exilic Israel. It is difficult to see how Israel could be the servant when only three verses later, in Isaiah 49:6, the servant is to raise up Israel.

Most commentators have understood the servant either to be a real individual or a symbolic figure created to represent the best ideals of Israel. Before trying to choose one or the other, it is best to examine the texts themselves to get a picture of what the servant was like. The first servant song in Isaiah 42:1–4 describes a mission for the servant in which he will bring justice by means of gentle persuasion and quiet. The second song in Isaiah 49:1–6 suggests that speaking will again be part of the servant's mission, but even more he must show trust when he has no strength. By this he will not only convert Israel but become a witness to all nations. The third song in Isaiah 50:4–9 again describes the servant's role as speaking, but this time mixed with suffering and rejection. By accepting this, the servant will find that God supports his cause and he will emerge in victory. The fourth song in Isaiah 52:13–53:12 expresses in moving language how God uses the undeserved violence against his servant to save other guilty people. This is the famous "suffering servant" of Isaiah. It is a remarkable passage because it suggests more clearly than anywhere else in the Old Testament that God accepts one individual's suffering to atone for the sins of others. The scene is cast in the form of a dialogue between God and a chorus of voices to bring out the drama and the human involvement. But all is still in the hands of the powerful Creator and Redeemer to deliver the servant. Yet only God would value this broken and beaten servant who can no longer speak. This is another way of affirming that in the end Yahweh accepts the helpless in their helplessness and suffering even more than he does the strong.

Who is this servant who is chosen from the womb, speaks God's words, is abused and rejected and plotted against, and who finally manifests God's goodness before the nations of the earth? For those who believe the servant is just an image of Israel as a nation, the suffering servant is Israel past, while the servant vindicated and giving light to the nations is Israel restored and still to come.

This future dimension of the servant's role explains why the New Testament recognized Jesus as the true servant so readily. His crucifixion would lead to a new role in exaltation. Although Second Isaiah was thinking of the Babylonian exile and the return to Jerusalem, and saw with deep reverence that God used Israel's sufferings as a witness and light to the world, the New Testament authors tapped their faith in Jesus to see the same God acting to redeem all nations by his suffering in fulfillment of what Israel had already been asked to do in part. What Israel nourishes in its community, Christ did for still others outside.

But even for Israel, the personal and individual aspects of the suffering servant had deep meaning. No one could miss the image of the greatest of all prophets, Moses, whom Deuteronomy called repeatedly the "servant of Yahweh." What Moses taught as the Torah, the servant will teach anew. But he must bear the same rejection and rebellion that Moses bore in his mission. Nor could one miss the close connection between the servant in Second Isaiah and the picture of Jeremiah found in his life story. It is Jeremiah who remains faithful to the word of God even when they plot against his life. Still other examples have been proposed: King Jehoiachin in exile, Second Isaiah himself speaking autobiographically, Zerubbabel the first governor after the exile, and many others.

The most important line of thought brings out the kingly aspects of the servants. First of all, it was common for David and other kings to describe themselves as "your servant" when addressing Yahweh (see, e.g., 2 Sam 7:18–29). Secondly we know from ancient Near Eastern documents that kings often spoke of themselves as "called from the womb," "grasped by the hand of the God," "the servant of the God," and "giving light to those in prison." A well-known New Year's rite involved making a king strip off his clothes and crown and be beaten for the sins of his people before he was reinstalled in splendor for another year. This way he was the "scapegoat" for the whole nation over which he ruled.

All of this might lead us to consider that the servant figure combines in one person qualities of the king, Moses, and the prophet Jeremiah as an ideal Israelite. This would also permit us to see the servant representing the people Israel as well. Second Isaiah no longer waits for the king to be restored nor for the prophets to rise again. Instead, the people themselves must become invested with the royal and prophetic tasks ahead for the new Israel. We may never know all that Second Isaiah actually intended by his servant, but we must not rule out the possibility that he intended all the above suggestions. Hebrew thought often moved back and forth between the individual and the nation in describing God's covenant relationship. It is not too much to expect that the genius of this prophet was able to give shape to both an individual mission and a national one in the same prophetic word of hope.

For Christians, on the other hand, it is just as legitimate to see in the person of the servant, no matter what Second Isaiah intended, the key to understanding Christ's suffering, death and resurrection as redemption for all nations. God's hand that guides the faith

of Israel can easily prepare human understanding for a new and
unexpected follow-up in Christ's life and teaching. The faith to see
the connection was given to Jesus' disciples; it does not mean that
Second Isaiah saw such a coming event, nor that faithful Jews
reading Second Isaiah would see it. The Christian faith remains
faithful to its roots in the Old Testament and would be the first to
agree with the message of Second Isaiah that God acts always
"new." But faith in Christ is given not to all but to some only, and
does not lessen the beauty and faith present in the Jewish understanding of the servant passages.

STUDY QUESTIONS

1. Briefly describe the contents and characteristics of the Book of
    Lamentations. Why was it written?
2. Identify the following: Obadiah, Edom, Psalm 137, Amel-Mar-
    duk, Nabonidus.
3. Who was Cyrus the Persian? What significant role did he play in
    Hebrew history?
4. Who was "Second Isaiah"? What were the major themes in his
    prophecy?
5. Briefly describe the contents and characteristics of "Second
    Isaiah". When was this part of the Book of Isaiah written? What
    literary forms and devices are used?
6. How does Second Isaiah use the term "servant"? What is meant
    by the term "suffering servant"?

Chapter 21

THE STRUGGLE TO RESTORE
THE LAND (540–500 B.C.)

Suggested Scripture Readings:

Isaiah 60–63
Zechariah 1–4, 9–10

Persian Political Policy

Cyrus died fighting in Afghanistan about the year 530 B.C. He was succeeded by his son, Cambyses, whose eight year rule was notable for the conquest of Egypt. It was the first military campaign by any Persian army to the West, and it was probably only at this time that Persian control was made secure over the small states that had formerly been loyal to the Babylonians. Cambyses died suddenly on his way home from Egypt in 522, and a fierce struggle for power broke out. After two years of hard fighting, his brilliant general Darius was able to gain complete control over the empire. Darius reigned for thirty-six years and expanded the empire all the way to India in the east and to the borders of Greece in the west. He reorganized this vast kingdom into the famous system of satrapies. There were twenty in all, most as large as modern nations, and there were three leaders in each, so that no one person could gain too much power. The satrap was the chief political governor, but a general had independent control over the army units, and a special Persian noble, called "The Eyes and Ears of the King," was stationed in each satrapy to report directly back to the king in Susa or Persepolis. This system of checks and balances was designed to prevent rebellions or too much power in the hands of any one

431

person. It worked better than any earlier systems had for keeping the empire at peace during most of its two hundred year history.

The Persian government built an elaborate road system to link all parts of the empire with the capitals in Persia. A rapid courier network of horsemen was established that sped official news from post to post much as did the pony express in the western states after the Civil War. The Greek historian Herodotus praised these messengers in the words: "Neither snow, nor rain, nor heat, nor gloom of night stays these couriers from the swift completion of their appointed rounds." It has become the motto of the United States Post Office today.

Darius' success was marred by one major defeat—his attempt to invade Greece. His army was too large and unwieldy to fight a mountain war, and the Greeks under the leadership of Athens defeated the Persian hordes at Marathon in 490 B.C. Darius retreated home, but his son and successor, Xerxes, tried again ten years later. He overran the Greek armies at Thermopylae and burned the city of Athens to the ground. But the Athenian fleet had escaped, and, confident of victory, Xerxes decided to challenge them on the sea. The battle of Salamis led to a total destruction of the Persian navy in 480 B.C., and Xerxes was forced to return home as his father had done. Never again did the Persians attempt to take Greece by force.

Persian policy during the following one hundred and fifty years changed from military campaigns to simple bribery. They paid off a city-state in Greece or one of the Greek colonies on the coast of Turkey to attack another. Surprisingly, in the entire period, they never had any trouble winning over the Greeks by money. Despite most of our Western history books, Persia was by no means helpless and decaying after their failure to take Greece. Indeed, it was the Greek cities that proved to be greedy, unable to organize, constantly at war with one another and lacking in democratic government. Persia, on the contrary, represents the high point of the ancient world in tolerance for local customs, allowing a measure of self-rule, and skill in architecture and engineering. The ruins of their capital city of Persepolis still stand today as the most impressive monument from ancient times with its enormous complex of palaces, storerooms, columned halls, and wall carvings.

Because the empire was so large, there was usually trouble somewhere, but most wars were fought on a local level, and many parts of the empire could go a full century with no trouble at all. Judah, for example, was quiet during most or all of its two hundred

THE PERSIAN KINGS				
Cyrus the Great	556–530			
Cambyses	530–522			
Darius I	522–486	Temple rebuilt	516	
Xerxes	486–464	Battle of Marathon	490	
Artaxerxes I	464–423	Battle of Salamis	480	
Darius II	423–404	Ezra and Nehemiah	458, 445	
Artaxerxes II	404–360			
Artaxerxes III	360–338			
Arses	338–335			
Darius III	335–332			
Alexander the Great	332–321			

years of Persian rule, and as a result we know very little about life during this period, except what we find in Haggai, Zechariah, Malachi, Ezra, and Nehemiah, and nothing at all from the last hundred years, from 430 to 330. The discovery of coins in some Israelite cities with *yehud* inscribed on them does suggest that the Persians granted Judah enough local authority to mint money for itself.

Persian Religion: Zoroaster

The Persians were an Aryan people, i.e., they were not Semites like the peoples of Mesopotamia and Palestine, and had many links to other Aryan groups in northern India. Zoroaster lived sometime in the early sixth century B.C., in the northern part of Iran. He won a hearing for his religious views in the court of the king of the Medes and converted both the Medes and the Persians to his monotheistic faith. Zoroaster proclaimed one god who was lord of all: Ahura Mazda, creator of good and evil, the just and powerful one. But there were many lesser deities, spiritual powers, in the universe. One was a good spirit, Spenta Mainyu, and another was the evil spirit, Ahra Mainyu, or Ahriman. As chief of the devils, Ahriman produced an evil creation to match Ahura Mazda's good creation. Thus at the heart of Persian religious belief was a dualism between good and evil in the world.

Persian belief was filled with spirits or "angels," most of which represented abstract virtues such as "justice," "obedience," "good empire," and the like. These were the assistants of Ahura Mazda, but not gods with their own power. Zoroaster introduced the idea of a moral judgment for those who die and eternal reward and punishment in heaven or hell. Hell he described as a lake of fire, while the good entered into a paradise of all good things. At the end of time, there will be a cosmic judgment of all creation in which Ahura Mazda will finally triumph over the evil of Ahriman. Resurrection of the dead also plays a part in this final day of judgment. Many of these concepts would find their way into later biblical descriptions of God's judgment and victory over evil, and help give color to the growing belief in an afterlife that developed in later Judaism.

Zoroaster's religion also practiced a rite of fire-sacrifice, the non-burial of the dead, and eating the haoma-plant as a symbol of renewed life. These are still seen among the last followers of Zoroastrian faith today, the Parsees of Bombay in northern India. One aspect of an earlier Persian system of gods managed to continue on even after Zoroaster's reforms. That was the cult of the sun god Mithra. It became very popular among Roman soldiers who had served in the eastern lands during the early centuries of Christianity. Many shrines to Mithra can still be seen in Roman ruins, with their statues of the sun-hero slaying a bull. Another aspect that lived on despite Zoroaster's opposition was the office of magi. The Persian kings from Darius on changed Zoroaster's monotheism toward an elaborate religion of astrologers who could read the signs of the future, and the worship of Ahura Mazda was directed to the sacrifice of oxen. The magi were still flourishing in the first century as the Gospel stories of Christ's birth relate.

Biblical Sources for the Period after the Exile

Our knowledge of the exile came from a number of Old Testament books: parts of Jeremiah, especially chapters 26 to 45 and the prose sections, Ezekiel, 2 Kings 24–25, 2 Chronicles 36, Isaiah 40–55, Habakkuk, Lamentations, and Psalm 137, as well as from several non-Israelite documents: the *Babylonian Chronicles of Nebuchadnezzar* (ANET 305–308), the *Weidner Tablet* listing Jehoiachin's provisions, and the *Cyrus Cylinder* (ANET 315–316) with its account of victory over the Babylonians.

In a similar way, we can discover what life was like for those who came back from exile to their homeland by checking a wide range of biblical sources. For the twenty-five years immediately after Cyrus' decision to let Israel go back to Palestine in 538, we have the following books: Haggai, Zechariah, Isaiah 56–66 ("Third Isaiah"), Ezra 1–6, 2 Chronicles 36:22–23, and Psalms 85 and 126. For the following century, from 500 B.C. to 400 B.C., we have even more information available. From the Old Testament there is Ezra 7–10, 1 Esdras (an expanded Greek version of Ezra, with many additions), Nehemiah, Tobit, Esther, Joel, Jonah and Malachi. There are also some non-biblical accounts, such as the letters of the Jewish community that lived at Elephantine in Egypt, the traditions about Ezra the scribe found in the Jewish Talmud of the second to fifth centuries A.D., and the *Antiquities of the Jewish People* by Josephus, a first century A.D. Jewish historian. Josephus retold the story of Old Testament times by using the Bible itself as well as other traditions now lost.

Besides these works, there are a few other sources that definitely reflect the post-exilic times, but cannot be given an exact date. This is true for many psalms, but also for the Book of Job and parts of Proverbs, two wisdom books that combine both early and late reflections. Above all, it is true for the final editing of the Pentateuch by the priests and scribes who lived and worked in the Babylonian exile and in the period immediately after it. They brought together the Priestly sources with the earlier *J* and *E* materials, and arranged the entire tradition as we have it today in the first five books of the Bible. The combination of special themes in the *P* source with the outlook of the Priestly editing shows clearly that those who worked out the final shape of the Pentateuch did so to help Israel understand its older traditions in the light of the disaster of 586, the following exile, and the time of return.

The Return Gets Underway

Persian policy differed greatly from that of earlier Near Eastern empires. Cyrus respected the local gods and local self-rule as much as it was possible. He did for Israel what he did for all exiled groups—he issued a decree in 538 permitting them to return to their homeland. The Book of Ezra quotes a proclamation made by Cyrus which may actually be a Hebrew copy of the original decree:

> Thus says Cyrus, king of Persia. The Lord, the God of heaven, who has given me all the kingdoms of the earth,

has ordered me to build him a temple in Jerusalem of Judah. To all who are among his people: may God be with you and may each one go up to Jerusalem in Judah and help rebuild the temple of the Lord, the God of Israel, the God who dwells in Jerusalem (Ezr 1:2–4).

Ezra 6:2–12 quotes an Aramaic version of the decree which has even more detailed instruction about the right to sacrifice and a financial grant from the Persian treasury to help pay for the project. Cyrus also permitted the people of Judah to bring back the valuable gold and silver cups and plates which the Babylonians had taken when they destroyed the temple. Cyrus identifies Yahweh as his own God and makes a special point that his permission for the exiles to return to their homeland is to please Yahweh and to establish his worship in his own place. Naturally Yahweh (and all the worshipers) will be pleased with Cyrus, and the people will remain loyal to the Persian government and pray for blessing on the empire.

Despite this decree, however, not every Israelite jumped up and left for Palestine. As we have already seen in the last chapter, many prefered to stay on permanently in Babylon itself, and those who did go home did so in small groups. The first of these returned with one of the sons of King Jehoiachin, the prince Sheshbazzar. Ezra 1:5 lists "the heads of the paternal houses of Judah and Benjamin, the priests and levites, and all those whom the spirit of God stirred up to return for the rebuilding of the temple." Chapter 2 of Ezra records a second and larger group of people who returned under Zerubbabel, another royal prince, and the high priest Joshua. This group included people from all the tribes, more priests and levites, temple servants, and a large number of people who could not prove any longer exactly what their family or tribe was. Ezra 2:64 claims that there were 42,360 free people, 7,337 slaves and 200 singers in this group. This may be many more than actually made the journey itself, and may include the people already living in the Jerusalem area.

Little evidence of the actual post-exilic situation remains. The large cities had mostly been destroyed in the Babylonian attacks of 598 and 586, and a great number were never resettled at all. This suggests that the actual number of returnees was quite limited. Modern archaeological research on the walls of the city of Jerusalem also indicate that the area of population was quite a bit less than it had been in the pre-exilic period.

Opposition and Difficulties

From the accounts that have come down to us in the Book of Ezra and the prophets Haggai and Zechariah, the following picture of the return emerges. A first group departed for the holy land under Sheshbazzar sometime shortly after 538. They must have found conditions difficult, for although they made a start on rebuilding Jerusalem and the temple, they got no further than laying the foundations. Sometime later, perhaps twenty years, a second group of exiles under Zerubbabel, who may have been a nephew of Sheshbazzar, and Joshua, a priest, also came from Babylon. The Book of Ezra is confusing when it declares that the foundations of the temple were laid by both Zerubbabel (3:10) and earlier by Sheshbazzar (5:16). What is definitely stated by both accounts is that the people already in the land and the inhabitants of the old northern kingdom area of Samaria did not welcome these returning exiles and tried to block their building of a temple and of city walls for Jerusalem. This caused enough problems so that little was done between the first laying of the foundations about 538 and the year 520 when Zerubbabel and Joshua arrived on the scene.

In that year, the prophets Haggai and Zechariah began to preach warnings that God would not long stand for these delays and that the temple must be built. Zerubbabel and Joshua responded with an all-out effort, and the temple was finished by March or April of 516 B.C. In order to do this, Zerubbabel had to fight against the opposition of the governor of the neighboring Persian province of Samaria by obtaining a copy of Cyrus' decree ordering the rebuilding of the temple. After a long search, the scroll was finally located hidden in the archives of the Persian summer capital of Ecbatana. Interestingly, it was written in Aramaic and is the first real evidence that Aramaic had become the international language of the Persian empire. It would soon become the common language of the people of Palestine as well, and by the time of Christ Hebrew had faded into a language for scholars and synagogue leaders.

The strong resistance from the neighboring provinces and territories to a restored Judah indicates that Cyrus had left most of these local groups alone after his capture of the Babylonian empire. Only when the regional squabbles became so intense that they could not be ignored any longer did the governor of Beyond the River, the Persian satrapy that stretched from Mesopotamia to the Mediterranean Sea, actually intervene. He settled the dispute by appealing to the legal decree granted by the king. But despite the permission to go ahead given to Zerubbabel, the opponents did not give up their struggle to prevent Judah from regaining its old strength. The conflict broke out again only a half-century later in the days of Ezra and Nehemiah (see Chapter 22).

Our fullest picture of these difficult times comes from oracles found in Haggai, Zechariah and Third Isaiah (Is 56–66). However there is also a long description included in Josephus' *Antiquities.* Most of his material is simply copied out of Ezra, Haggai, and other Old Testament books. But Josephus also takes a large number of details from the Greek version of the Book of Ezra called First Esdras. He tells his readers that Cyrus ordered the rebuilding of the temple when he read the prophecies of Isaiah of Jerusalem spoken some two hundred years earlier. To prove his point, Josephus then cites Isaiah 44, the work of Second Isaiah during the exile, as though it were from First Isaiah:

> I say of Cyrus: He is my shepherd,
>   who will complete my commands,
> Saying of Jerusalem, "She is to be built,"
>   and of the temple, "Your foundations are to be laid" (Is
>   44:28).

This at least shows conclusively that by the first century A.D. Jewish tradition had forgotten the origins of the Book of Isaiah as a combination of several authors, and viewed the whole book as visions and predictions of the future by an eighth century prophet.

The Prophet Haggai

The major event of the first years after the return was the attempt to rebuild the temple. The effort had never gotten beyond laying the foundations when Haggai and Zechariah took up the cause with a series of oracles urging the people to renew their efforts.

Haggai is one of the shortest books among the Old Testament prophets—only two chapters, containing four oracles, all dated between August and December of 520 B.C. He addressed his oracles to Zerubbabel, the governor, and to Joshua, the high priest. His message was simple: The land is suffering from drought and hunger, poverty and failure, because the people think only of their own houses and fortunes, and have neglected the house of Yahweh. The land has been defiled and needs to be purified and consecrated by the presence of God in his temple. Until this is done, there would be no blessing in the new community. In this message Haggai stands in the tradition of Ezekiel, who foresaw a day coming when the land would be purified, a new temple would rise up and all the tribes would live in peace and order under the leadership of a prince and high priest (Ez 40–48).

The prophet combines a political program of rebuilding the temple with the demand for a people who will strive for holiness in their personal actions. For Haggai, as for Ezekiel and the entire line of prophetic voices back to Amos, a temple without individual fidelity will have no power to bring God's blessing on Israel. His prophecy had an effect:

> And the Lord stirred up the spirit of Zerubbabel, the son of Shealtiel, governor of Judah, and the spirit of Joshua, the son of Jehozadak, the high priest, and the spirit of all the remnant of the people. And they began to work on the house of the Lord of hosts, their God, on the twenty-fourth day of the sixth month (Hg 1:14–15).

But this first energy was not enough. The work slowed down and Haggai delivered three more warnings in the coming months. He encouraged the people's morale by pointing to Zerubbabel as God's appointed ruler and the one who would restore the family of David to the throne of Israel. After all, Zerubbabel was a grandson of Jehoiachin, the last of the Davidic kings (2 Kgs 24:8–17; 1 Chr 3:17), and the rightful successor to the throne of Judah. Besides, the Persian empire had been in turmoil for some years now, ever since Cambyses, the son of Cyrus, had committed suicide after a palace revolt had broken out. A Persian general, Darius, gradually gained power, but it took years of war against other hopeful leaders. Haggai's enthusiastic nationalism and hope for independence led him to extol Zerubbabel as the person God would use to bring blessing to the land:

> On that day, says the Lord of hosts, I will take you, Zerubbabel, son of Shealtiel, my servant, and wear you like a signet ring on my finger, says the Lord; for I have chosen you, says the Lord (Hg 2:23).

This kind of language was as good as treason in the eyes of a Persian king, and may have led to the removal of Zerubbabel from office. In any case, nothing ever came of the hopes of Haggai, and instead of a new Davidic Messiah, the high priest was given more and more authority by the Persian authorities in the years ahead. But if Haggai was wrong on that point, he did see the temple finished and dedicated within four years.

Haggai's Oracles

First oracle, 1:1–15   (August 520)
    Demand to build the temple if the land is to receive blessing

Second oracle, 2:1–9   (September–October 520)
    God will fill the land with riches if the temple is built

Third oracle, 2:10–19   (December 520)
    The land is cursed because the people sinned, but now blessing comes

Fourth oracle, 2:20–23   (December 520)
    God will overthrow the nations and establish Zerubbabel

The Prophet Zechariah

Zechariah preached in the same period as did Haggai. But the present Book of Zechariah combines Zechariah's own words in chapters 1–8 with a series of later oracles in chapters 9–14 which were delivered by an unknown prophet against the Greeks about one hundred and fifty years later. Just as most scholars now refer to a First Isaiah as well as a Second and Third Isaiah, they often speak of First Zechariah and Second Zechariah to describe these two parts.

Zechariah delivered his prophetic words between November 520 and November or December 518 B.C. These include at least three sets of oracles (Zec 1:1–6, 7:1–14, 8:1–23) and eight visions (Zec 1:7–6:15). He shares Haggai's concerns for rebuilding the temple, creating a purified community, and predicting the coming of a new messianic age centered on Zerubbabel. One of the differences between the two prophets is the greater attention to priestly matters in Zechariah. He is himself the son of a priest (Ezr 5:1), and he makes a special point of emphasizing the role of the high priest

Joshua beside that of Zerubbabel as prince. In chapter 4 he has a vision of a gold lampstand with two olive trees beside it. Zechariah asks what the two olive trees represent. An angel replies: "These are the two anointed who stand beside the Lord of the entire world" (Zec 4:14).

A second difference between Haggai and Zechariah is seen in the use of visions. Zechariah uses highly symbolic figures of horses of different colors (Zec 1:7–17), four horns (Zec 1:18–21), angels who explain the visions (chapters 3–5), a flying scroll (Zec 5:1–11), and flying chariots (Zec 6:1–8). Earlier prophets had also depended on visions in their preaching. Amos 7–8 contains a series of visions, and Ezekiel had a number of visions during his years of preaching, including the chariot of Yahweh (Ez 1), a scroll full of writing (Ez 2:8–10), and a valley full of dead bones (Ez 37:1–14). But Zechariah uses visions as the major point of his prophetic work, and his visions are much more mystical and symbolic than the rather clear metaphors of Ezekiel or Amos. Instead of making the message clearer, these colorful descriptions mask its real meaning to all except those who know what the prophet is talking about. Thus was born a prophetic code known to believers but hidden from pagans and outsiders. This use of an almost-secret language becomes more and more common in the last centuries of the Old Testament era, and reaches its fullest use in apocalyptic books such as Daniel or Revelation in the New Testament (see more on this in Chapter 24).

Despite this new way of expression, Zechariah stands within the tradition of Israel's prophets. He clearly follows the lead of Ezekiel in combining purification, moral uprightness and the divine blessings upon the people. He follows Ezekiel in hoping for a day of restoration when the land will have prosperity and peace. He matches the finest thought of the prophets who came before the exile when he says:

> Thus says the Lord of hosts: Do true justice, show compassion and mercy to your brother, do not oppress the widow, the orphan, the foreigner or the poor; and do not plan evil against one another in your hearts (Zec 7:9–10).

Second Zechariah

Second Zechariah in chapters 9–14 reveals an entirely different spirit. There are no visions, no concern for the temple, no further

---

COMPARISON OF FIRST AND SECOND ZECHARIAH

Zechariah 1–8 Outline		*Zechariah 9–14 Outline*	
1:1–6	Call to repentance	9:1–8	God as a divine warrior
1:7–17	Vision of four horsemen	9:9–10	The king as prince of peace
1:18–21	The four horns	9:11–17	The victorious exiles
2:1–5	Measuring the new Jerusalem	10:1–12	God gathers his exiles
2:6–13	A call to the exiles	11:1–3	The fall of pagan tyrants
3:1–10	Vision of Joshua the priest	11:4–17	The bad and good shepherds
4:1–14	Vision of the lampstand	12:1–9	The victory of Judah
5:1–4	Vision of a flying scroll	12:10–14	Jerusalem mourns
5:5–11	Woman in a bushel of grain	13:1–6	God cleanses her sin
6:1–8	Vision of four chariots	13:7–9	The shepherd's sword
6:9–15	Crowning of Joshua	14:1–21	The day of the Lord
7:1–14	Call to fast and repent		
8:1–23	God returns to Jerusalem		

Characteristics of First Zechariah	*Characteristics of Second Zechariah*
(1) Literary prose oracles	(1) All poetry
(2) Concern to rebuild temple	(2) No interest in the temple
(3) Exact dates of 520 to 518	(3) No dates mentioned
(4) Mostly vision oracles	(4) No visions
(5) Hope for new Davidic king	(5) Little concern with David
(6) Zerubbabel as the messiah	(6) No mention of Zerubbabel
(7) Jerusalem as the new center	(7) Judah as a whole is central
(8) Didactic purpose of oracles	(8) Traditional prophetic style

---

hopes for Zerubbabel, and no Davidic restoration dreams. It is poetry instead of prose, and stresses God as a divine warrior who will fight to deliver Jerusalem from the power of foreign nations. It especially develops several themes found in Ezekiel, especially those of God as the true shepherd of his people, and the coming day of the Lord.

Second Zechariah treats the theme of the shepherd in Zechariah 9:16–17, 11:1–17, and 13:7–9. In the final passage he proclaims that God will shepherd Israel:

> They will call on my name
>   and I will answer them.
> I will say, "They are my people,"
>   and they will say "The Lord is my God" (Zec 13:9).

Compare this with the great climax of Ezekiel's oracle on God as the good shepherd:

And they will know that I the Lord their God am with them, and that they, the house of Israel, are my people, says the Lord God. You are my flock, the sheep whom I pasture, and I am your God, says the Lord God (Ez 34:30–31).

He also intensifies the hopes of a great day of the Lord. God will not only restore Israel but transform the people and the land into a new paradise:

On that day there will be neither cold nor frost.
There will be only daylight and no longer night and day,
for even in the night there will be light (Zec 14:6–7).

There is a sense of a delayed coming of God in this passage. The hope that God will transform the whole world represents a new state of thought that developed in the centuries after Haggai and Zechariah. In the development of Israelite thought, they fall somewhere between the sixth century and the time of the Book of Daniel in the second century B.C.

Second Zechariah also continues many of the themes found in the original Zechariah, including the coming of a new age, the cleansing of all impurities from the holy land, the outpouring of the Spirit of Yahweh, and the place of Jerusalem as the center of God's restored land.

Isaiah 56–66

Another major source for our knowledge of conditions in the land of Palestine after the return from exile is the third and last part of the Book of Isaiah. Unlike Second Isaiah with its elevated poetry and long description of the coming salvation of Yahweh, chapters 56–66 are a mixture of prose and poetry, of hope and despair, at the same time. The viewpoint of the writer is no longer that of someone in Babylon, but of one already back in the promised land. Where Second Isaiah mocks foreign idols and believes they have no power over Israel, the prophet of this last section of the book berates Israel itself for falling into idolatry (Is 57:1–13). Where Isaiah 40–55 never accuses Israel of sin, but assures the people that their sins have been doubly forgiven, Isaiah 56–66 is full of condemnations of Israel's sin

(Is 58:1–9; 59:9–15; 65:1–7). For these reasons, scholars have identified Isaiah 56–66 as a completely separate collection of oracles by unknown prophets who spoke in the years immediately after the return from Babylon. This section is simply labeled Third Isaiah (or Trito-Isaiah).

Although quite different in many ways from the work of Second Isaiah, Third Isaiah does continue the major theme found in all parts of the Book of Isaiah: the love of "Holy One of Israel" for Jerusalem and Zion. And like Second Isaiah, he speaks to the people a word of comfort and hope that God will soon restore Jerusalem to its former glory and make a new home not only for the exiles but for all peoples. Indeed some chapters still sound like Second Isaiah at his most optimistic (especially chapters 60–62). But others express a deep pessimism and sense of disappointment. Where once the whole nation would enjoy divine glory, the authors of chapters 56, 57, 58 and 59 now single out only the righteous few who have been faithful. In these sections, there is a note of urgency as though most of the people were not listening to the prophet.

Third Isaiah places these opposite feelings side by side. The prophets have a vision, but the people fail to live up to it. The Lord wants justice not fasting (Is 58), he wants faithfulness to the covenant and not works of violence (Is 59), he wants repentance and a spirit of humility (Is 63–64). If the people will turn from their sinfulness, God will restore Jerusalem so that the just will live there in peace, and they will be the Lord's servants (Is 65). He will dwell in their midst as ruler and lord of all the world:

> Heaven is my throne
>   and the earth my footstool;
> What is this house that you would build me,
>   and what place am I to live in?
> My hand has created all these things
>   and so all these things belong to me, says the Lord (Is
>   66:1–2).

Probably chapters 56–66 contain some oracles by Second Isaiah after his return to the homeland, and still others by nameless prophets who lived at the same time. Together, they reflect the tensions between the *vision* of a renewed Israel and the plain, hard *reality* which the exiles found on their return. It was hard to convince this small but sturdy band who had to fight off their own countrymen, as well as combat the power plays of the governor of Samaria, that "the glory of the Lord has arisen upon you" (Is 60:1). They must have laughed at the prediction that the nations would stream to their light (Is 60:3), and that "all who despised you will bow down at your feet" (Is 60:14). It was too much to believe that they were all "priests of the Lord" (Is 61:6) or "a crown of beauty in the hand of the Lord" (Is 62:3). They were more aware of the fact that "the just person perishes and no one even cares" (Is 57:1) and that "we stumble at noon as though in the night, and among those who are strong and vigorous, we are like the dead" (Is 59:10). They must have asked often: "Why have we fasted and you did not see it? Why have we humbled ourselves and you did not even notice?" (Is 58:3).

Perhaps, too, Third Isaiah found it necessary to oppose the one-sided value given to the temple by other prophets such as Haggai and Zechariah. For Third Isaiah, Yahweh was more interested in true inner faithfulness than in external rites and forms. He reaches a high point in his concern for justice in chapter 58:

> Is this not the fast that I choose:
>   to break the chains of evil,
>   to untie the bonds of the yoke,
> And let the oppressed go free
>   and smash their yoke?
> Are you not to share your bread with the hungry,
>   and bring the homeless into your houses?
> When you see someone naked, should you not clothe him,
>   and not refuse to help your own relatives?
> Then light will burst upon you like the dawn,
>   and healing cover your wounds quickly (Is 58:6–8).

Jesus' own words about feeding the hungry and clothing the naked in his parable about the sheep and the goats (Mt 25:31–46) echo this passage of Third Isaiah.

Changes in Prophecy in the Exile and After

Under the pressure of the fall of Jerusalem and the exile, Israel's prophets had to face major changes in what they preached. No longer did it make sense to hold kings responsible for national evil, nor could one warn a people that they would lose their kingdom if they did not repent. The prophets from Jeremiah to Zechariah faced new situations never before dealt with by their predecessors, and they responded with new solutions. The result was a profound shift in the nature of prophecy in Israel. It now addressed the people in matters of daily living and worship that were much closer to the priestly concerns. At the same time, because Israel was no longer free to make its own political decisions, prophecy lost its sharp interest in the working of government and directed its attention more to rebuilding community life for the future. This made the prophetic message much more personal and inner-directed and less centered on judgment oracles against social injustices committed by the whole society. Naturally, the enduring prophetic concerns for fidelity to Yahweh, commitment to justice for the poor and oppressed, love for Zion, and confidence that Yahweh can and does punish as well as save are all maintained.

But in creating a new and deeper approach to God, prophecy put itself out of business. It had flourished in the tension between politics and loyalty to Yahweh. When only the area of worship was left to Israel's decision-making, prophecy gradually disappeared and was replaced by one of two options: by priestly instruction (the way of the Torah), or by visionary hope for the future expressed in apocalyptic forms (see Chapter 24).

Some of the major shifts in prophecy that took place as a result of 586 and after are:

(1) a stronger stress on individual responsibility and righteous behavior;

(2) a growing emphasis on monotheism in which God is the sole power that controls the actions of pagan nations as well as of Israel;

(3) a fuller sharing by the prophet in the suffering *of* his people, and frequent suffering *for* them as in the case of Jeremiah, Ezekiel and Second Isaiah;

(4) especially in the prophets of the Babylonian exile, a comparison to Moses as a mediator between God and the people is stressed;

(5) the beginning of hope by the prophets for a "new covenant" in which God will give people the power to live it rather than depend on the strength of Israel's own will power;

(6) more and more emphasis on the "law of Moses" or the "book of the law" as a written body of guides to life;

(7) the view of the "remnant" as not just those whom God allows to escape from his punishment and destruction, but as a faithful group of men and women who deserve to be saved;

(8) the belief that God will make Jerusalem and Zion the center of a renewed earth, and that Israel will be the leader of the world;

(9) especially in the post-exilic prophets, the belief that this will be followed by the conversion or conquest of the Gentiles and their submission to God in Zion;

(10) the belief that this time of glory may be long in coming, but that it will be a time marked by the fulfillment of God's promises to David.

One of the sharpest changes in the exile and after was the gradual loss of hope that Yahweh would restore the *kingship* to the house of David, and with it *independence* to the nation. Instead, the role of leadership was shifted to the priests and levites. Emphasis on (a) piety and worship, (b) the study of the law, (c) the right ordering of daily life, and (d) the universal rule of God over all aspects of life.

More importantly, the shock of total failure in the exile led to a major burst of creative rethinking of Israel's traditions. We have seen important responses to that challenge in Jeremiah and Eze-kiel, in the Deuteronomic history of Israel, and in Second Isaiah's theology of an entire nation consecrated as a priestly people. Still another significant effort was the completion of the Priestly docu-ment (P) to reorganize and represent the entire Pentateuchal mes-sage in a new way from that of the *J* and *E* documents. It added a great number of genealogies, cultic regulations (such as on the sabbath in Genesis 1 or on circumcision in Genesis 17), and law codes, which stressed aspects of daily life that would continue de-spite disasters and exiles. It gave directions for the community that were concrete and binding. In a real sense, by uniting the practical laws to the old traditions of God's saving and merciful actions in special moments of history, the Priestly authors were able to give the post-exilic community a "way of life."

STUDY QUESTIONS

1. Briefly describe Persian political policy. How did it change over the years?
2. What were the major characteristics of the Persian religion? Do you see any similarities with other religions?
3. What books describe the post-exilic period?
4. "Cyrus the Persian contributed greatly to the restoration of the Hebrew nation and people." Do you agree or disagree? Why? Give reasons and examples for your position.

5. Who was Haggai? What were the major themes and characteristics of his prophecy?
6. Briefly describe the contents of the Book of Zechariah. How do Haggai and Zechariah differ?
7. Who was "Third Isaiah"? What is characteristic of his prophecy? How does he differ from the previous two Isaiahs?
8. What are some major changes and shifts in emphases characteristic of prophecy during and after the exile?

Chapter 22

LIFE IN THE
POST-EXILIC COMMUNITY

Suggested Scripture Readings:

1 Chronicles 13–16
Ezra 7–10
Jonah 1–4

The Work of the Chroniclers

Our best knowledge of the post-exilic life of Israel comes from
the Books of 1 and 2 Chronicles, Ezra and Nehemiah. These four
books must be taken together, for they form a single continuing
view of how the small community in Judah adapted itself to a new
way of life that no longer depended on a king or national freedom
to survive. It was the beginning of a profound change that gradually
shaped Israel into what can be recognized as the beginnings of
modern Judaism. The Books of Chronicles stress the role of the cult,
prayer, worship and ritual purity as a way of life. Ezra the scribe
begins a shift toward separateness. Holy things are reserved to the
priests and levites, marriage with Gentiles is forbidden, and loyalty
to the Torah in its written form of the Pentateuch becomes manda-
tory. Nehemiah reinforces this sense of exclusive status by complet-
ing the walls of Jerusalem and forcing people to live within the city
and treat it as the center of the Jewish hopes.

Despite the work of Haggai, Zechariah, Zerubbabel and others
in getting the temple finished and rededicated in 516 B.C., the
fortunes of Judah did not change much for the better in the next
sixty years. Archaeological probes have shown that the population of

Jerusalem and its immediate neighborhood did double in area during this period, but the opposition of the governors of nearby provinces, such as Samaria, kept the people from finishing any walls around the city or gaining confidence in themselves. From the accounts in the Books of Ezra and Nehemiah, it appears that the people were losing their special sense of identity as a covenant people and slowly drifting into pagan marriages which cost many their faith. Radical surgery was called for, and it came in the form of two important developments: (1) the rewriting of Israel's historical

POST-EXILIC CHRONOLOGY

597/587	Babylonian Exile	call of Ezekiel
562	Death of Nebuchadrezzar	
556–539	Nabonidus & Belshezzar	
539	*Cyrus the Persian victory*	Second Isaiah
538	Decree of freedom	
520	Temple Rebuilt	Zechariah
		Haggai
500		Malachi, last prophet?
458	Ezra's mission	
445	Nehemiah arrives	
400		Joel (?)
332	*Alexander the Great*	
198	Seleucid control of Palestine	Sirach
168	Maccabean Revolt	I & II Maccabees
166	Hasmonean dynasty	
143+	Simon as king/priest	Qumran community (?)
100+		Book of Wisdom
63	Pompey conquest	
41	Herod the Great	
0		
30 A.D.	Death of Christ	
50		Pauline letters
		Mark
66–70	JEWISH REVOLT	
68	Death of Nero	
96	Domitian persecution	
90–100	Council of Jamnia	Normative Judaism
132–134	Bar Kochba Revolt	Rabbi Akiba: Halakah

traditions in 1 and 2 Chronicles, and (2) the mission of Ezra and Nehemiah, two important Jewish leaders in Persia sent by the king himself to do something about the sad conditions in Palestine.

The Books of Chronicles

Because of the changed world of Israel after the exile, the priestly leaders felt the need for an updated version of Israel's history. They took up and rewrote the great Deuteronomic history found in the Books of Samuel and Kings from their own perspective. No doubt one important reason to do this was to explain the proper role of the kings over Israel in the past now that they were gone for good. Another was to emphasize the temple for religious worship.

Chronicles often follows the Books of Samuel and Kings word for word through whole chapters. But we get a sense of its distinctive message when we compare the many places where it either leaves out matter found in Kings or adds to it new material. In the story of David, for example, it leaves out altogether his terrible sin with Bathsheba, or the revolt of his own son Absalom, and never mentions David's deathbed instructions to kill all his enemies. When Kings reports that David sinned in taking a census, Chronicles adds that it was Satan that tempted him. For the Chronicler, David was a holy and dedicated leader who followed Yahweh faithfully. All his faults are set aside or downplayed. Instead, the Chronicler praised David even more than Kings does. He stresses David's role in composing the psalms and establishing guilds of levites to serve the temple. And while David never built the temple itself, in Chronicles he gets everything ready and makes all the plans which Solomon only has to carry out (despite the fact that this clearly contradicts the view of the authors of Samuel and Kings that David was forbidden to plan a temple—see 2 Sam 7). In Chronicles David also prays a lot. In short, David is shown to be totally consumed with zeal for the right worship of Yahweh. He becomes a second lawgiver almost as great as Moses.

This picture of David as the founder of a community centered on the temple becomes the standard by which the Chronicler then judges the rest of Israel's history. For example, he explains the exile and destruction of the nation as the result of the people's failure to perform true worship. The main section of the Chronicler's history (from 1 Chronicles 10 through 2 Chronicles 34) was written soon

after the preaching of Haggai and Zechariah and the pitiful rebuilding of the temple in 516 B.C. It was intended as a blueprint for
struggling Judeans just back from exile. Past failures of the people
and the true example of David's faith both teach a lesson about how
urgent is the need to restore the temple liturgy to its proper ritual,
and perhaps even a search for a new king like David who would
dedicate his life not to political glory but to the glory of God's
worship.

The Chronicler had a second important reason for revising the
history of the nation. In the earlier traditions of Israel there was a
great deal of confusion about the role of the priests and the levites
in worship. There had been traditions of levites serving as priests at
important shrines such as Dan (Jgs 18), and Eli, who was not even a
levite, had been priest at Shiloh (1 Sam 1–4). David had named
priests from the family of Abiathar and from the family of Zadok (2
Sam 8:17). But Solomon had rejected the priests of Abiathar (1 Kgs
2:26). Ezekiel goes further and demands that the high priest come
only from the family of Zadok (Ez 44:10, 15). Deuteronomy makes a
special point that levitical priests, often without any place to live
and work, were active in many towns and cities (Dt 12:18–19; 18:1;
26:12–13), yet the Book of Numbers accepts only descendants of
Aaron as priests, and allows levites to be their helpers or assistants
(Num 3 and 18). In order to clear up this confusion and establish
temple worship on a firm basis with a clear description of the
different roles needed, the Chronicler goes into great detail about
the proper relationships between the priests and levites. He limits
those who could be priests to the family of Aaron, but assures the
levites an important and permanent place in the temple service by
explaining how David himself set up their jobs as singers, musicians,

---

OUTLINE OF CHRONICLES, EZRA AND NEHEMIAH

1 CHR 1–9	Genealogy lists from Adam to the post-exilic Judah
1 CHR 10–29	The history of David's reign
2 CHR 1–9	The history of Solomon's reign
2 CHR 10–36	The kings of Judah down to the end of the exile
EZR 1–6	The first exiles to return to Judah
EZR 7–10	The coming of Ezra and his reform
NEH 1–7	Memoirs of Nehemiah about rebuilding Jerusalem walls
NEH 8–10	Ezra's covenant renewal ceremony
NEH 11–13	Continuation of Nehemiah's memoirs

doorkeepers, sacristans and guardians of the temple alongside the role of the priests (1 Chr 23–26).

Other major theological concerns of the Books of Chronicles are the following:

(a) God often intervenes miraculously to save the people no matter what the odds (2 Chr 13, 14, 17, 25; 2 Chr 14, 16).

(b) Judah and Jerusalem are a holy kingdom or congregation— much more so than the northern Israelites (1 Chr 26:6–9; 28:4–7; 2 Chr 7:3–10; 13:8–12; 24:8–11).

(c) The high priest has authority even over the king (2 Chr 19:8–11; 26:16–21).

(d) The prophets support the cultic life of the people and do not oppose it as in earlier traditions (2 Chr 20:5–23).

(e) The law is now clearly the Pentateuch with its priestly regulations rather than the Deuteronomic law book in 2 Kgs 22 (1 Chr 6:48–49; 2 Chr 24:6–9).

All of these points are made by the Chronicler in order to achieve his purpose of giving hope to Jerusalem and Judah in a time of great depression. He extols all the works of God in history and he traces all the rules of life and worship back to the great heroes of Jewish history: Abraham, Moses, David. He especially wished to root the ministry of priests and levites in the all-important work of Moses and David. But he was not rewriting history simply to suit his own priestly leanings. He accepted almost all of the insights of the Deuteronomists by quoting most of his material from the Books of Kings. But where Deuteronomic theology had stressed the central place of prophecy, Chronicles stresses the *cultic* side of life.

St. Jerome gave us the title for these books when he said that they were "a chronicle of the whole of divine history." But unlike the prophets or the Books of Kings, they rarely use political explanations for events. Divine action works at all times in every situation to save and to punish. In short, Chronicles is intended as a series of lessons in the divine plan for history.

The Book of Ezra

Ezra can be divided into two major parts: chapters 1–6 and 7–10. Ezra 1–6 gives us some valuable information about the first two groups of returning exiles—those under Sheshbazzar, and those under Zerubbabel. Much of this was discussed in the previous chapter in relation to the work of Haggai and Zechariah. This first part of the Book of Ezra reaches a climax in the rebuilding of the temple in 516.

The scene shifts to many years later in chapters 7–10. Under the Persian king Artaxerxes, Ezra, a priest of the highest rank, a descendant of Aaron and Zadok, is sent from Babylon to restore the practice of Israelite faith according to the instructions in the "law of God" (see Ezr 7:10, 14, 25–26). Ezra faces two major problems. Many Israelites have married Gentiles, and this prevents them from keeping the law. Secondly, there was a general disregard for the regulations about sacrifice, worship, purity and special Jewish customs. He tackled both of these head-on. First, he acted forcefully to invalidate all marriages to pagans. This was not an easy task, for no doubt most of these marriages had been made in good faith and there were children to think of. Ezra called a great assembly of the people and they made public confession of their sins and faults. As a result, the men agreed to give up their foreign wives. They also agreed to observe the weekly sabbath day of rest and to support the temple with a yearly tax.

Ezra followed this policy because any religious reform, especially one which demanded that the people practice the unique requirements of their covenant law at home, would have been impossible if a large part of the people had different faiths and practices in their homes. There was the special stress not only on Israel's election by God as a chosen people, but on the need to be holy and set apart as a community to give witness to other nations. Unity of faith and practice was essential to achieve this goal.

The second problem was to re-establish the whole range of practices that most characterized Israel's special way of life. To this end, Ezra brought out the book of the law of God and had it read to the people in a second great assembly. Once again they celebrated a penance service and a renewal of the promise to obey the covenant in everything. As Ezra read the words, the people wept. At the same time, levites and priests helped to explain the meaning of each passage to the people. And Ezra himself took the priests and leaders aside and instructed them in the central points of the law. At the conclusion of this ceremony, the people celebrated the seven-day feast of Tabernacles in its pure form as the law had prescribed.

This whole scene is told not in the Book of Ezra but in chapters 8–9 of Nehemiah. It was put there to link Ezra's renewal of the covenant with Nehemiah's completion of the city walls to make Jerusalem a safe home for the temple. It seems almost certain that the law of God that Ezra read was an early version of the present five books of the Torah/Pentateuch. The events described in Nehemiah 8–9 fit very closely the Priestly source regulations on the priests, the feast-day observances, and the manner of accepting a covenant found in the Pentateuch, even though Ezra-Nehemiah never quote it directly.

Ezra's role was decisive. Every audience we have seen up to this time showed a Judah with little cohesion, having trouble getting itself together and with dashed hopes of a glorious new day after the exile. Ezra was able to restore the spirit of the people and set the underpinnings for the ideals of holiness, sense of election, and a worship-centered community of faith. He gave a new charter for a new Israel—the authentic traditions of the past were now written down forever in the Pentateuch as a normative guidebook for the future. And most important of all, the final priestly character of the Pentateuch showed a concrete way to put these traditions into daily practice for ordinary believers.

The Book of Nehemiah

Nehemiah began his work in the twentieth year of King Artaxerxes I, i.e., about 445 B.C. He was a high official in the court despite the lowly-sounding title he bore, "royal cupbearer." Nehemiah was a Jew, and had received a heartbreaking letter from his own brother in Palestine describing the terrible conditions that existed there. Since he was an advisor of the King, he had no difficulty in getting the king's ear. He persuaded Artaxerxes to make Judah an independent province, name him its governor, and allow him to rebuild the city walls of Jerusalem. He was skilled enough in political matters to foresee that he would face great obstacles from local officials who did not want any change in the power structure. Nehemiah quickly surveyed the situation and made preparations to start on the walls shortly after his arrival.

But as soon as the project became public, Sanballat, the governor of Samaria, Tobiah, the governor of Ammon, and Geshem, the governor of Edom and the Arab tribes sent troops to stop the fortifications. Nehemiah armed his own workers and finished the basic wall in a rapid fifty-two days. The speed with which he managed to get the work done shows how willing the people were to complete the project. He found, however, that the regulations of the law were being barely obeyed, and he was forced to take measures to re-establish the marriage laws and the sabbath observances. These were the same problems faced by Ezra, and it reveals how difficult was the task of making the reforms take hold permanently among the Jews.

Nehemiah was governor from 445 to 433. When his term ended, he returned to Susa, the capital of Persia. A year or two later he was reappointed and found that the law had again fallen into disuse. This time he took very strong action. He prevented people by force from doing business on the sabbath, broke up marriages with foreigners, arranged permanent sources for the support of the levites, and even threw out all the furniture of the Ammonite governor Tobiah from an apartment in the temple which the high priest, a relative, had let the governor use.

The Book of Nehemiah is built up around the memoirs of the governor in chapters 1–7 and 11–13. The nature of such an ancient "autobiography" was to leave a pious record of the leader's achievements. Thus we can expect a rather glowing account of his sense of duty and his success in carrying out his tasks. At the same time, it is an extremely valuable glimpse into the life and thought of a fifth century Jew. It does not tell us very much about the author's feelings, only his work, but it is perhaps the only first-person story that we actually find in the Old Testament.

Confusion between Ezra's and Nehemiah's Reforms

We know the dates for Nehemiah's terms as governor were 445–433 B.C. and 430 or 429 down to perhaps 417 at the most (that is, two twelve-year terms). But we are not sure about Ezra. If he had come before Nehemiah in 458, as has traditionally been believed, why did Nehemiah have to do the same reforms all over again? Many scholars solve this question by suggesting that Ezra really came after Nehemiah, in the year 398 B.C. They base this on the reference to the "seventh year of King Artaxerxes" in Ezra 7:7 for the beginning of Ezra's ministry in Jerusalem. But in fact there were two kings of Persia named Artaxerxes: Artaxerxes I ruled from 464 to 423, and Artaxerxes II from 404 to 358. Ezra 7:1 simply reads: "Now after this, Ezra . . . went up from Babylon in the reign of Artaxerxes, king of Persia." But which Artaxerxes is meant?

The traditional date for Ezra's arrival in Jerusalem has been 458

B.C., the seventh year of Artaxerxes I. He was followed some thirteen years later by Nehemiah, sent from Persia in 445 to govern the province of Judah and rebuild the walls of Jerusalem. Nehemiah served twelve years in that post and was recalled to Persia. But after a short period, he returned for a second term as governor. The biblical books seem to place Ezra and Nehemiah in Jerusalem at the same time working together on the reform of the people (Neh 8:9). But if so, then Ezra did very little for many years before Nehemiah's arrival—and this is just the opposite of the impression given by other references in the Book of Ezra which hint that Ezra got right to work.

The second solution places Ezra in the time of King Artaxerxes II, during Nehemiah's second term as governor. This would be 398 B.C., and it would mean that Nehemiah remained as governor for nearly fifty years, a most unlikely possibility. So neither answer really solves the question, but it seems most reasonable to presume that the two men did not work at the same time. They have probably been joined together by the editors, who either got the dates mixed up or wanted us to see that the accomplishments of Ezra and Nehemiah must be looked at as a single inspired work of restoring the faith of the people.

No matter what dates we give Ezra and Nehemiah, the problem remains of how the four books of 1 and 2 Chronicles, Ezra and Nehemiah fit together. They all share the same priestly outlook, but they often seem to overlap each other and sometimes to be at odds in their dates, as though written from different points of view. Yet almost all scholars agree that the four books were put together as a continuous story sometime after the events, and that they do not necessarily reflect the exact chronological order in which those events took place. The most common solution is to see that the stories and memoirs of Ezra and Nehemiah were originally separate books. Ezra was joined to the Books of Chronicles as a supplement, so that Chronicles gave a picture of Israel from Adam to the end of the exile and Ezra brought the story from the exile to the middle of the next century. The memoirs of Nehemiah were then added at a much later time to complete the picture with the re-establishment of Jerusalem as a city of glory and hope. In the process of all these combinings, some of the chapters about Nehemiah were added to the Book of Ezra, and some about Ezra were inserted into the last part of the Book of Nehemiah.

Ezra and the Beginning of the Old Testament Canon

Jewish tradition in the Talmud generally recognizes Ezra as the one who established which books in the Old Testament were sacred and therefore "canonical." On this basis, the rabbis argued against including the seven books in the Greek Bible (which have been accepted by Catholics) as too late in origin to qualify. Other passages in the Talmud, however, indicate that the decision was not made until the council of Jamnia, a gathering of the Pharisees about the years 90 to 100 A.D. Still other passages seem to suggest that the debate about certain books, such as the Song of Songs or Ecclesiastes, which gave scandal to many people, went on among the rabbis well into the second or third centuries A.D.

The book of the "law of God" which Ezra read to the people cannot be identified exactly from any remarks in the story (Neh 8–9). As pointed out above, though, it fits best the present Pentateuch with its five books. Thus the Pentateuch would have taken on a new status as *the* sacred book at that moment. This does not mean that a full idea of canon was yet in Ezra's mind so that every letter and mark was considered untouchable ever again. It is quite possible that later writers added lines and words even in the Pentateuch. And certainly the prophets were not yet a fixed body of sacred texts—some of the prophets may not even have been completed by the time of Ezra—for example, Malachi, Jonah, Joel, and Zechariah 9–14. And some other books, such as Daniel, would not be composed for at least another two hundred and fifty years.

Ezra is sometimes called the "father of Judaism." He deserves the title for his work of re-establishing the life and practice of Israel on a new basis. He did not rely on different interpretations of past practice and different versions of their past. He looked to a specific written source that became the guidebook and constitution of the people. Israel as it was known in the pre-exilic period disappeared and a new "people of the book" appeared. From the time of Ezra on, we normally no longer refer to the chosen people as the Israelites, but as Jews.

The Samaritans

One of the main opponents to the restoration of Jerusalem by Nehemiah was Sanballat, governor of Samaria, the territory of the former northern kingdom of Israel. This opposition has to be seen as something more than the ambition of one governor against another. The roots of tension between north and south existed from at least the death of Solomon, when the ten northern tribes separated from the house of David (1 Kgs 12:1-24). At that time it was a political decision that did not divide their religious convictions, but differing older traditions about the nature of the covenant probably already played some role in the separation. The northern tribes had a deep suspicion of the claims of David and his dynasty to a special relationship with Yahweh (2 Sam 7.)

The real break came when the northern kingdom fell to the Assyrian armies in 722–721 B.C., and the Assyrians deported the Israelites and brought in pagan peoples from "Babylon, Cuthah, Awwa, Hamath, and Seperwayim and settled them in the cities of Samaria" (2 Kgs 17:24). Although these new peoples agreed to worship Yahweh as the God of the land, they continued their old practices as well. 2 Kings 17 concludes that they tried to serve Yahweh *and* their graven images, "and their children, and their children's children—as their fathers did, so they do up to this very day" (2 Kgs 17:41). Josiah had brought this land back into the control of Judah for a short while in the late 600's, but when the Babylonians smashed Judah, Samaria was established as a separate province again. The evidence of the post-exilic books shows that a strong animosity grew up between the returning exiles in Judah and the so-called Jews of the north. Ezra 4:1-6 tells how the exiles refused to allow the Samaritans to help rebuild the temple, and Nehemiah 4 records how the Samaritans tried to prevent the rebuilding of the city walls.

The hatred was now too great to be healed, and slowly but

surely the two groups separated completely. The final break must have come sometime after the days of Ezra, for the Samaritans accepted the Pentateuch as sacred, but refused to allow any other biblical books into their canon. The story of the good Samaritan in the New Testament in Luke 10 and the meeting of Jesus with the Samaritan woman at the well in John 4 indicates that the Jews ordinarily refused to deal with a Samaritan in the first century (see esp. Jn 4:9). To this day, however, a small group of Samaritans has survived in the town of Nablus, the ancient site of Shechem, and still follow their faith completely. The five books of the Torah (Pentateuch) are held sacred, they sacrifice on the neighboring mountain of Gerizim, where they had placed a temple when the Jews refused to share worship in Jerusalem, and they still follow the Pentateuch's ritual laws. Because they were cut off from the main stream of Jewish thought so early, their religious practices still reflect the ways things were done in the first century—even to copying scrolls of the Torah in the ancient Hebrew script and praying in Aramaic.

The Jewish Colony at Elephantine

In 1893 a large number of ancient papyri were found in the desert around Aswan, the southern border of Egypt along the Nile River. These turned out to be written in Aramaic and recorded the activities of a Jewish military settlement that was stationed on the island of Elephantine, in the middle of the river. This colony had lived at the site since the time of Pharaoh Hophra about 585 B.C., if not earlier. However, the documents that were recovered all come from the last quarter of the fifth century during Persian rule. They list marriage contracts, sales of slaves, divorce settlements, and, most interestingly of all, letters to the high priests and governors back in Judah.

Many of their practices do not agree with the regulations of the Pentateuchal laws, especially Deuteronomy. Women, for instance, had the right to divorce, which is not found in the Bible. They also had a temple to Yahweh, a thing expressly forbidden by Deuteronomy's law that only Jerusalem was to have a temple. Some of the letters between the colony, which called itself Yeb in Aramaic, and the Palestinian officials dealt with the question of a temple to Yahweh that was destroyed by a mob of Egyptians in 411-410 B.C. Apparently the Persian forces were off somewhere, and the local

TWO LETTERS FROM ELEPHANTINE

The Jewish military colony at Elephantiné in southern Egypt was founded sometime in the 6th century. In 410 B.C., while the Persian governor was out of the country, local Egyptian pagans burned the Jewish temple to Yaho (Yahweh) on the island, and the Jews wrote to Bagoas, governor of Judea, asking him to persuade their own governor of Egypt, Arsames, to have the temple rebuilt. Following are two documents that deal with the rebuilding:

1. Memorandum of what Bagoas and Delaiah said to me: Let it be a memorandum to you in Egypt to say to Arsames concerning the altarhouse of the God of heaven, which was built in the fortress of Elephantiné long ago, before Cambyses, which that scoundrel Widgang destroyed in the 14th year of king Darius, that it be rebuilt in its place as it was before, and that meal-offering and incense be offered upon that altar as was formerly done.

2. Your servants Yedoniah, the son of G(emariah) by name, one, Ma'uzi, the son of Nathan, by name, one, Shemaiah, the son of Haggai, by name, one, Hosea the son of Yathom, by name, one, Hosea, the son of Nathun, by name, one: five persons in all, Syenians who (ow)n (proper)ty in the fortress of Elephantiné, say as follows: 'If your lordship is (favour)able and the temple of Yahu ou(r) God (is rebuilt) in the fortress of Elephàntiné as it was form(erly built), but sheep and oxen and goats are (no)t offered there, but incense and meal-offering . . . . and your lordship iss(ues) an edict (do this effect), we will pay to your lordship's house the sum of . . . in si(lver. . . .) a thou(sand) ardabs of barley.'

people rose up against the Jewish battalion that served on the island. The Jewish colonists wrote for permission to rebuild the temple both to Sanballat, governor of Samaria, and to Bagohi, governor of Judah, and also to Johanon, the high priest in Jerusalem. Sanballat at least answered and the temple was rebuilt. Since the colony could write to both governors in 410 for permission to do something against the Pentateuch's law, some experts have concluded that Ezra's reforms could not yet have been made by that date. They see it as proof that Ezra must have come after Nehemiah during the reign of the second King Artaxerxes. It is not a very strong piece of evidence, however, since we know so little about Jerusalem from these letters.

Strangely enough, alongside the name of Yahweh (usually spelled yeho or yahu), the letters mention other divine names: Eshem-Bethel, Herem-Bethel, Anath-Yahu, Anath-Bethel. Are these other gods worshiped beside Yahweh in this foreign temple? Or are they merely names for aspects of Yahweh's presence: "Name of the House of God" (Eshem-Bethel), "Sign of God's Presence" (Anath-Bethel), etc.? It is not easy, to be sure, but it is always possible that the Jews over the years had accepted many pagan practices into their faith, though there is no absolute evidence that this was so. The only hint of it is that one list mentions separate tax-support for Yahweh, Eshem-Bethel and Anath-Bethel. Another point of interest in these letters deals with the feast of Unleavened Bread. It seems clear that the Persian governor had a say in regulating its ceremonies. A letter dated 417 gives the decisions about the feast from the Persian official, Arsham.

While our information is only partial, the Elephantine papyri do give us a small glance into the daily life of Jewish settlers outside of the homeland of Palestine. It reveals that they were more liberal in their marriage laws and treatment of women, as well as a certain diversity in religious practice at the end of the fifth century indicating that Ezra's reforms had not yet spread out from Judah. It shows what a close grip the Persian government kept on all aspects of the religious decisions of subject peoples. But it also shows that Jews did look to Jerusalem for leadership even from so far away as southern Egypt.

The Book of Malachi

The prophet Malachi is the last book in the canon of the Old Testament. It is not dated, and the author is unknown. Its present title comes from the opening words of chapter 3, "My messenger" (in Hebrew, *malachi*). It is certainly post-exilic and may come from almost any period between the rebuilding of the temple in 516 B.C. and the end of the Persian period about 330 B.C. From its contents, it can probably be best placed just about the time of Ezra and Nehemiah. Malachi roundly condemns many abuses in Israel that Ezra worked to reform. The priests perform imperfect and careless service in this temple. The people are marrying pagans with ease and taking divorce lightly. They fail to pay the tithes and offerings which they owe to God. He warns them sternly that God will bring swift punishment on them if they do not change:

> Then I will approach you to give judgment;
>   I will be a speedy witness
> Against magicians, and adulterers, and those who make false
>   oaths,
>   and those who oppress the employee in wages,
> Who oppress the widow and orphan,
>   and who push aside the visiting strangers
> And who do not fear me,
>   says the Lord of hosts (Mal 3:5).

Malachi is a book of passion. The author obviously loves the temple and its worship, demands much of the priests in their office, and values religious instruction. He speaks of the covenant with deep respect. He fears that the sin of Israel is terribly serious because it breaks the covenant made with Yahweh. He goes behind the laws of the Pentateuch to ground God's will in the creation stories of Genesis (Mal 2:10). He roots his view of the enduring love of marriage in the covenant and even goes so far as to say "I hate divorce" and repeats twice the warning, "So take heed for yourselves and do not be unfaithful" (Mal 2:15-16). He even talks of a covenant made with Levi that demands fidelity of all priests to their ministry (Mal 2:4-6). He ends his book, as do all the later prophets, with a vision of the day of the Lord that will bring fire and punishment on the wicked but a glorious revival to the just.

Perhaps his most famous lines are the last in his book. They are both a powerful summary of Israel's foundations of faith and a firm statement of hope:

> Remember the law of my servant Moses,
>   the statutes and commandments
> That I gave him at Horeb for all Israel.
>   And behold, I will send to you Elijah the prophet
>   before the great and terrible day of the Lord comes.
> He will direct the hearts of fathers to their children
>   and the hearts of children to their fathers
>   so that I will not come to smite the land with a curse (Mal
>   3:23-24).

Because Malachi foresees the return of the prophet Elijah, this book was placed last in the canon of the Old Testament by the Greek translators of the Bible so that the whole of Scripture would look ahead to God's further action in the world.

Malachi is deeply in debt to Ezekiel and his vision of the future community of Israel. He also uses many of Ezekiel's methods of instruction. Where Ezekiel often begins an oracle with a proverb or quotation or colorful image, Malachi uses questions. Indeed, his whole style is question-and-answer, as though it were a child's catechism. There are six oracles in all, and each involves a question addressed to Israel or to God, and is answered by the prophet in God's name. In the answers we discover a mini-catechism of the covenant. Yahweh loves Jacob, is a father to Israel, is faithful to his word, and wants honesty in Israel's words, true worship, fidelity and trust in God's justice.

It seems clear that the full force of the Priestly law codes of the Pentateuch were not yet fully in force. Therefore Malachi probably lived and spoke sometime before Ezra and Nehemiah were able to overcome the indifference and loss of faith that had affected the people and their leaders alike.

The Book of Joel

The Book of Joel is a difficult book to classify. It seems to be as much a liturgy of penance as a collection of prophetic oracles. It has as many connections to the psalms as it does to Isaiah or Habakkuk or Jeremiah. It has no date and we know nothing of its author, so any attempt to place it somewhere in Israel's history must come from clues inside the book itself. Because it never mentions older political enemies like the Assyrians or Babylonians, and because it has high praise of the temple worship, and because it speaks of the land *once before* (the exile?) being totally destroyed (Jl 2:17-19, 27; 3:19), scholars generally place it in the post-exilic period after the rebuilding of the temple in 516 B.C.

In many ways the style of this book is very similar to a modern penitential liturgy for the sacrament of penance. The penitents lament their evil state and all their sins; the priests call for repentance and fasting; both together beg God to show mercy and forgiveness to them; finally, the penitents receive reassurance of God's forgiving love through the blessing of the priests. But the book is also much more than this alone. The theme of the day of the Lord weaves throughout, giving it a strong prophetic note of warning. Perhaps like Nahum and Habakkuk, Joel is a temple prophet who proclaims his message from God in the liturgical worship services. If people will only change their hearts and return to the Lord, the day of doom will become a day of blessing for them. But it must be sincere: "Rend your heart and not your garments; return to the Lord your God, for he is gracious and merciful, slow to anger, and rich in abiding love" (Jl 2:13).

The quotation of the covenant formula from Exodus 34:6-7 in this last passage is just one of numerous quotations from earlier books of the Bible. Joel describes the day of the Lord in the words of Amos 5:18-20 (Jl 2:2), and portrays the warriors who bring it about in the images of Nahum 2:1-5 and 3:1-3 (Jl 2:4-11); he reverses the metaphor of Isaiah 2:4 and Micah 4:3 in which swords shall be made into plowshares ("Beat your plowshares into swords"—Jl 3:10); he quotes the opening words of Amos 1:2 that God roars his judgment from Zion (Jl 3:16); he refers to the great vision of the river flowing from the side of the temple in Ezekiel 47:1-12 (Jl 3:18). Almost every verse has some reference to an earlier part of the Old Testament. It indicates perhaps that Joel was one of the very last of the prophetic books to be completed, and may suggest that he lived closer to the year 400 than 500 B.C.

The oracles of Joel open with a vision depicting a locust plague that has come over the land. It was a common horror in the Ancient Near East. Palestine is struck once in a while even today, and it seems that the African states below the Sahara are regularly devastated by locust hordes. These insects can move across a thousand miles of the Sudan and Ethiopia denuding all vegetation of its leaves. There still is no effective means of preventing the locusts from swarming when their numbers increase suddenly, and so it is not surprising that Joel would view this plague as a severe punishment from God that is beyond human control. But in true prophetic spirit, Joel saw far beyond the immediate evil of a locust attack. He saw it as nothing less than a precursor, a forewarning, of the coming of the Lord himself.

He mixes two other powerful ideas along with that of the grasshopper invasion. He describes an enemy army, the foe from the north sweeping down across the land, with the same clear eye as Jeremiah who had predicted the Babylonian invasion earlier. And he uses the imagery of the desert windstorm, the sirocco, that withers up all the plant life with its hot breath, as the symbol of God's anger against the land.

Locusts had come before and would come again, but there was to be a much greater moment when Yahweh made a definitive judgment between good and evil. Chapter 3 goes much further than the promise of relief from the plague and a restored harvest of plenty found in the end of chapter 2. In the final great poem that runs from Joel 2:28 to the end of the book, Joel pictures a new time in which the forces of nature itself will be changed into allies of the divine warrior, a time when he will come to vindicate Jerusalem and Mount Zion against all the pagan nations of the earth. This particular passage in Joel moves far beyond the hopes of earlier prophets that God would once again act in the days or years ahead to save his people. It uses images on a cosmic scale, including a great battle between God and the pagan nations in the Valley of Jehoshaphat somewhere near Jerusalem. This is the language of apocalyptic, a whole new development out of and away from classical prophecy. It no longer expects God to continue to act in ways that he has before, but looks forward to a new and decisive beginning in which the present world will be changed so much that one can honestly speak of an end of the present world and the creation of a new world. The apocalyptic approach becomes very common in the last centuries before Christ. It will be treated in more detail in Chapter 24 in the discussion on the Book of Daniel.

The strength of the Book of Joel lies in its confident hope that God does not forget his people or refuse to hear their prayers for help. It combines the traditions about Yahweh as divine warrior, the day of the Lord, the fidelity and mercy of the covenant relationship, the oracles against nations, the penitential psalms, and the promises of blessing into a renewed message of hope to the people of fifth century Judah.

The Book of Jonah

Jonah is found among the prophetic books, but it is totally unlike any other prophetic book. It contains no oracles at all, except the report of Jonah's words to Nineveh in Jonah 3:5. It is the story *about* a prophet, and right from the beginning we are warned to take this prophet with a grain of salt. The author has a great sense of literary style, full of abrupt changes of direction in thought, humor-

OUTLINE OF THE BOOK OF MALACHI

1:2–5	God's love for Israel over Edom
1:6–2:9	The sins of the priests in unworthy sacrifice
2:10–16	The people's sins through divorce
2:17–3:5	The coming of God's messenger in judgment
3:6–12	Call to repent and pay the tithes owed
3:13–4:6	The day of judgment will bless the just

OUTLINE OF THE BOOK OF JOEL

1:1–2:17	The locust plague as divine punishment
	1:2–20 Call to national mourning
	2:1–17 Repentance in the face of judgment
2:18–3:21	The coming day of blessing on the nation
	2:18–27 The restoration of fertility
	2:28–32 The day of the Lord
	3:1–15 Nations summoned to judgment
	3:16–21 God manifested in glory in Zion

OUTLINE OF THE BOOK OF JONAH

1:1–16	Jonah disobeys his call and is punished in the sea
1:17–2:10	Jonah is saved from the fish and praises God
3:1–10	Jonah obeys and Nineveh converts at his word
4:1–11	Jonah complains at God's mercy and is rebuked

ous touches, and unexpected twists in the plot. Verse 3 in chapter 1 must have made Israelites of the post-exilic period roar with laughter. The word of the Lord had come very solemnly to Jonah to go preach to Nineveh, but instead "he rose to flee to Tarshish"—i.e. in the exact opposite direction! We are next treated to a scene of great comedy despite the danger that it describes about the ship in peril. Jonah seems to be asleep in the midst of a huge storm, while the sailors implore their gods in vain. When they accuse him of the evil, he agrees to be a human sacrifice to calm the angry Yahweh. He is swallowed by a great fish and in its belly sings a grand hymn of thanksgiving to Yahweh. Since it took him three days before God released him, one wonders whether he repeated the hymn many times over.

The point to be made, of course, is that the author of the Book of Jonah knew that his audience would *enjoy* the story and not be forced to choose whether it could actually have happened or not, or whether the fish was a whale or a shark. Only in modern times have Christians forgotten the ability of the Bible to tell stories to make its points, and tried instead to explain everything "scientifically." Jonah is a rousing tale of a prophet gone off the deep end, so to speak. The author makes some important points about prophecy and the nature of God without ever losing his sense of humor while creating his outrageous tale and its several separate plots.

Its major literary style is that of irony. Jonah does everything a good prophet should not, from fleeing to refusing to speak to complaining that God does not fulfill all the threats of doom that he made Jonah preach. But it is also set up in a number of clever panels, so that the prayer in chapter 2 parallels exactly the dialogue found in chapter 4, although one is praise, the other complaint. The prophet takes action in chapters 1 and 3, but in one he refuses to act and in the other he does perform what God commands. The whole four chapters make a marvelous series of reverses:

Chapter 1:   the prophet is *disobedient* and refuses God,
Chapter 2:   so he *praises* God in the fish for his mercy;
Chapter 3:   the prophet *obeys* the word of God and preaches,
Chapter 4:   so he *complains* that God offers any mercy at all.

Even within single chapters, the literary style is very cleverly arranged to move in one direction and then go in reverse. Compare the structure of chapter 1:

vss.			
	4-5	The sailors fear while the sea is angry	A
	5	The sailors cry to their gods	B
	5-6	They attempt to save the ship	C
	6	Jonah is called on to get help from God	D
	7	The sailors seek the reasons	E
	7	The guilt is found in Jonah	F
	8	Jonah is told to explain the cause	G
	9-10	*Jonah fears Yahweh, who creates the sea*	H
	10	Jonah is told to explain this	G
	10	They know that Jonah was guilty	F
	11	The sailors seek Jonah to save them	E
	12	Jonah tells them how it will help	D
	13	They try to save the ship and fail	C
	14	The sailors now cry to Yahweh as God	B
	15-16	The sea calms and the sailors fear Yahweh	A

Several other interesting incidents stand out in the story of Jonah's mission to Nineveh. The fact that Nineveh was three days across in Jonah 3:3 has led to all kinds of guesses as to how large the city would have been, or whether the author might have meant a three-day walk around its edge since the ruins of the ancient city certainly were not large enough to take more than a few hours to cross. Also note that God saves Jonah from death despite his sin, yet Jonah will not let the Ninevites be saved from death even though they repent. The author also makes the very sharp point in the final verses that Jonah cared more for a leafy plant than for 120,000 human beings.

The hero of the story is himself a kind of ironic note. Jonah ben Amittai is mentioned in 2 Kings 14:25 as a prophet who predicts that King Jeroboam II will be able to expand his kingdom to take over the pagan nations. Here Jonah is summoned to preach the opposite—that God will bless these pagan nations. The book really addresses two major questions: (1) What is the relation of Israel and her God to other nations? (2) What is the meaning of divine justice? Jonah becomes a perfect character for the discussion of whether God can in fact use a prophet to bring good news to pagan nations. Certainly, the lesson is clear: God's mercy is more powerful than his judgments, and his plan will not be thwarted even by the negative "righteousness" of his prophet. Along the way the author makes use of several major prophetic stories from earlier books of the Bible. The prayer of Jonah in the belly of the fish resembles the prayer of King Hezekiah during his illness in Isaiah 38:10-20. Jonah's stay under the leafy plant is built on a similar incident from the life of

Elijah—only Elijah proved obedient (1 Kgs 19). Nineveh finds faith as a divine gift as Abraham did in Genesis 15:6. Above all, Jonah echoes expressions taken from Jeremiah, such as his use of "man and beast" to stand for everything that lives in the land (Jon 3:7-8), found in Jeremiah 7:20, 27:5, etc.

The reasons for reminding the reader of the entire history of prophecy from the beginning until the post-exilic days becomes clear in the final verses of the book. Does not God have greater pity and compassion on people, even pagans, than Jonah demands he have about a mere shrub? The book forcefully reminds Israel that prophecy had not simply been aimed at condemning all their enemies and making them feel important. Instead of claiming that their special place in God's covenant made them separate and better, they must recognize that God chose them to be witnesses to all peoples that God also loves them.

The message of course is more than just this one point. The story of Jonah has several lessons that work on many levels as we read it:

(1)   it presents the universal love of God even for Gentiles;
(2)   it shows God's control over all of nature and all peoples;
(3)   it ridicules some of the narrow nationalism in Judah;
(4)   it is a satire on the actions of many prophets;
(5)   it affirms that God is not merely "just" in his actions;
(6)   in fact, God acts in strange and sometimes humorous ways;
(7)   and we cannot figure God out according to our desires.

In short, Jonah is both entertainment and lesson, aimed at the community of Israel in the period after the exile. Nineveh is clearly a city from the distant past with a vague geography which has become a symbol for the author of the great capacity for both evil and good in all peoples. Second Isaiah had said that Israel must be a servant who would be a "light to the nations" (Is 42:6) in revealing Yahweh as the God of salvation. Unfortunately, in the eyes of the author of Jonah, the Jews had forgotten that their witness was above all to a God of forgiveness. Perhaps, too, there is a pointed message to the community around Jerusalem, the great city of God—if even Nineveh can turn to God in sackcloth and ashes, how much the more should Israel put on sackcloth and ashes and beg forgiveness!

Jonah brings us to the close of life in Judah under the Persians. It reminds us that the spirit of Israel had not died or been frozen by Ezra's reforms and the growing sense of stability centered on the priesthood, the temple and the book of the law. Post-exilic Judaism kept alive its sense of covenant and election as a gift of Yahweh to be shared with the world.

STUDY QUESTIONS

1. What does the Book of Chronicles attempt to do?
2. Describe what takes place in the Book of Ezra. What were Ezra's most significant contributions?
3. Who was Nehemiah? What did he do?
4. In attempting to date Ezra and Nehemiah, one encounters some problems and difficulties. What are they? How can they be resolved?
5. Identify the following: canonical, Jamnia, "Father of Judaism", Samaritans, Elephantine.
6. What is contained in the Book of Malachi? What is its significance?
7. What is narrated in the Book of Joel? What is the purpose of this book?
8. Briefly describe the Book of Jonah. What is its major literary style?

Chapter 23

THE CULTIVATION OF WISDOM

Suggested Scripture Readings:

Proverbs 1–3, 10–11
Job 1–7
Qoheleth 1–3

What Is a Wisdom Book?

The wisdom writings of the Old Testament include a wide variety of books that are often overlooked by modern readers but reflect a very important side of Israel's religious faith. The ancient respect for wisdom is well-illustrated by an incident recorded in 2 Samuel 15–16, in which David's son Absalom led a revolt against his father. David was dismayed to hear that his chief advisor and wise man, Ahitophel, had gone over to his son's side. David begged God to confuse Ahitophel's talents because "the counsel (wisdom) which Ahitophel gave in those days was as if one went to consult God. For that was how both David and Absalom considered the counsel of Ahitophel" (2 Sam 16:23).

The wisdom books differ among themselves in both style and subject matter, but they all have in common certain characteristics which set them off from other biblical books:

(1)   a minimum of interest in the great acts of divine salvation proclaimed by the Torah and the prophets;

(2)   little interest in Israel as a nation or in its history;

(3)   a questioning attitude about the problems of life: why

472

there is suffering, inequality and death, and why the wicked prosper;

(4) a search for how to master life and understand how humans should behave before God;

(5) a great interest in the universal human experiences that affect *all* people and not just believers in Yahweh;

(6) a joy in the contemplation of creation and God as Creator.

At times, wisdom seems decidedly secular in its outlook. Many of the sayings in the Book of Proverbs have no relation to faith in God at all. What atheist could not agree with Proverbs 10:4, "Lazy hands make a person poor, while active hands bring wealth." The same theme of secular optimism and confidence can be seen in the story of Joseph in Genesis 37–50. Indeed Joseph never receives any word of revelation from God. He judges and acts wisely, and in the events around him he perceives the plan and wisdom of God.

These qualities appear in some degree or other throughout the Old Testament. But a few books can be specifically labeled "wisdom" because they maintain a consistent focus on the intellectual reflection about life's problems, the quest for universal truth, the rules for life, and the nature of created reality before God. These books are:

(1) Proverbs
(2) Job
(3) Ecclesiastes (or more properly in Hebrew, Qoheleth)
(4) Ecclesiasticus (or, in Hebrew, Jesus ben Sira, or Sirach)
(5) The Wisdom of Solomon

To these should be added the Canticle of Canticles (Song of Songs). Although it lacks the questioning-type wisdom, it values the beauty of creation and expresses confidence in human life and capacity for happiness. Certain psalms also must be classified with the wisdom literature: Psalms 1, 19:8–15, 37, 49, 73, 111, 119, and perhaps others as well. Many scholars have pointed to strong wisdom elements in the prophetic books, especially Isaiah and Amos. Both prophets use typical wisdom expressions and are concerned with knowing God's counsel or plan, but only in a general sense. Besides these, there are echoes of wisdom thinking in such passages as the Garden of Eden story in Genesis 2–3, the life of Solomon in 1 Kings 3–11, the Joseph narrative of Genesis 37–50, and the Book of Daniel.

The International World of Wisdom

This special wisdom tradition is not unique to Israel. In fact, the evidence points to the opposite: Israel borrowed and learned its wisdom questions (but not its answers!) from other nations of the Ancient Near East. There are collections of proverbs from Sumeria and Babylon that date before 2000 B.C. Many sound like their counterparts in the Book of Proverbs. A Sumerian example says, "A chattering scribe—his guilt is great!" while Proverbs 18:13 reads, "He who answers before listening—that is folly and shame." Assyrian literature produced large collections of fables about trees and plants, and meditations on the sufferings of the just person and the meaning of God's justice. The most famous is the poem, "I Will Praise the Lord of Wisdom," in which a man tries to figure out why God has punished him with suffering:

> If I walk the street, fingers are pointed at me,
> My own town looks on me as an enemy;
> My friend has become a stranger,
> In his rage my comrade denounces me (ANET 596).

In these and other lines, the poem is so similar to the Book of Job that many refer to it simply as a "Babylonian Job." Another work is sometimes referred to as a "Babylonian Qoheleth," because it explores the question of *theodicy* (the problem of God's relation to the innocent person who suffers evil) so thoroughly. Since Babylonian wisdom was well-established long before Israel existed, we must conclude that many biblical authors borrowed common wisdom themes when writing their own books.

Egypt also provides a large body of wisdom writings. The favored style was a father's advice to his son on how to get ahead in life. The most famous is probably *The Instruction of the Vizier Ptah-Hotep*. In it, an aging prime minister passes on to his successor (his "son") the rules for success: "If thou art one of those sitting at the table of one greater than thyself, take what he may give when it is set before thy nose!" (ANET 412). Compare this to Proverbs 23:1, "When you sit to dine with a ruler, note well what is before you!" The much later *Instruction of Amen-em-opet* (eighth–seventh centuries B.C.) has many proverbs that are found in a similar form grouped as a unit in Proverbs 22:17–24:22. Proverbs 22:24 says, "Do not make friends with a hot-tempered man," while *Amenemopet* commands, "Do not associate to thyself the heated man" (ANET

THE WISDOM OF AMEN-EM-OPET AND PROVERBS 22—24

One of the closest parallels between Egyptian and Israelite Wisdom is found in the Instruction of Amen-em-opet and the collection of proverbs in Prov 22:17–24:22. Both date to the same period of history, sometime between 1000 and 600 B.C. Some of the closer parallels:

Amen-em-opet chap. 1
Give your ear and hear what is
    said,
Give your heart to understand it.
Putting them in your heart is
    worthwhile.

Proverbs 22:17–18
Bend your ear and hear the words
    of the wise;
apply your mind to my knowledge,
for it will be a delight
if you guard them within you.

Amen-em-opet, chap. 6
Better is bread when the heart
    is happy,
than riches with sorrow.

Proverbs 15:16
Better is little with Fear
    of the Lord,
than great wealth and trouble
    along with it.

Amen-em-opet, chap. 18
One thing are the words said by
    men,
Another thing is what the god
    does.

Proverbs 19:21
The plans in the mind of a
    man are many,
But it is God's purpose that
    will prevail.

423). While the exact relation between *Amenemopet* and Proverbs 22–24 is not known, it seems probable either that the biblical authors had the same collection, or else that both the Egyptian and biblical writers were copying from an earlier source they both knew.

This international sharing of wisdom helps explain why Israel's wise people gave so little attention to Israel's own beliefs and dogmas. They had joined the larger and more universal search for the meaning of human life.

The Origins of Wisdom in Israel

Two major sources for Israel's interest in wisdom have been suggested by scholars. One is the *family*. The lists of proverbs, in particular, often dwell on the relations of parents and children, education, and moral instruction of the young. Here and there we find special evidence that fathers passed on golden nuggets of experience to their children. Deuteronomy 32:7 has, "Ask your father and he will tell you, your elders and they will explain to you." Proverbs 4:3 tells us, "When I was a boy in my father's house, still tender and my mother's only child, he taught me and said, 'Take my words to heart!' "

A second source would be *formal education,* especially in the royal administration. No one doubts that some education took place at home, but a professional class of wise men (and women) would require formal schools. Both Sumerian and Babylonian societies had schools where young boys learned how to be scribes to prepare them for careers in the royal court or the temples. The Bible itself indicates that Israel had its professional scribes like other nations: 1 Chronicles 27:32–33, Proverbs 25:1, and Sirach 38:24–39:11. There are indications that there was even a special class of wise counselors that would be called on by the king (see 2 Sam 15:31; 16:15–17:23; 1 Kgs 12:6–7). In this, Israel followed the lead of other nations. The Bible often refers to the wise men of Edom and Egypt, Tyre and Assyria (e.g., Ez 28:3–4; Jer 49:7).

The king himself was considered to be the chief possessor of wisdom and judgment in the kingdom. David is called wise in 2 Samuel 14:20 and Solomon is famed for his wisdom. 1 Kings 3–11 describes his reign as the model of the royal wisdom. He first asks God for wisdom above wealth or power (1 Kgs 3) and then judges accurately and wisely in the case of two mothers claiming the same child (1 Kgs 3). His temple and its beauty are considered the product of his wisdom (1 Kgs 6–8), and the rulers of the far corners of the world, such as the queen of Sheba, come to hear his wisdom (1 Kgs 10). Even his government of the country is portrayed as wisely ordered (1 Kgs 4). The authors of his story have included a summary of Solomon's complete mastery of wisdom in 1 Kings: 4:29–34:

> God gave Solomon wisdom and understanding and insights as numerous as the sand on the seashore. Solomon's wisdom was greater than all the wisdom of the East and of the Egyptians. He was wiser than any other person—wiser than Ethan the Ezrahite, and Heman, Calcol and Darda, the sons of Mahol. And his fame spread among the surrounding nations. He composed three thousand proverbs and one thousand and five songs. He described plants from the cedar of Lebanon down to the hyssop that grows on the walls. He taught about animals, birds, insects and fish. And people came from all parts of the world, sent by the kings

of every nation who had heard of his wisdom, to listen to the wisdom of Solomon (In Hebrew, 1 Kgs 5:9–14).

There is no complete statement in the Old Testament that actually says someone made his living as a teacher of wisdom, but it is highly probable. A passing remark of Jeremiah places the wise on the same footing as priests and prophets:

> Then they said, "Come, let us plot against Jeremiah, for the teaching of the law will not disappear from the priest, nor counsel from the wise, nor the word from the prophet" (Jer 18:18).

Although it may be hard to prove exactly what a professional wise person did full-time, there are enough hints to put together a reasonable sketch. Wisdom sayings are directed to the educated, and education was usually restricted to the upper classes socially. The philosophy of life in wisdom books often reflects the concerns of people with money and those concerned with preserving political stability. The women mentioned in the Book of Proverbs seem to have the leisure time for study. And in general, the concern with good speech, skill in writing, proper manners, and career planning describes the ruling elite in Israel.

When David created an empire as large or larger than almost any other nation of his time, he had to find skilled diplomats, record-keepers and administrators quickly. This meant building a bureaucracy of scribes and political advisors from scratch. Under David and Solomon, a new burst of literary creativity took place, which included the first written story of Israel's faith, the J document. It also meant the founding of schools and the cultivation of wisdom as an art. In many early biblical passages, the word "wise" is used for *skilled* carpenters and craftsmen. From the time of the Davidic monarchy on, the real skill of the wise was in the field of education and statecraft.

The Way of the Wise

Wisdom literature uses many distinctive literary forms such as the proverb, the riddle, and fables. These are especially common in the Mesopotamian and Egyptian wisdom writings, but only the proverb is common in Hebrew. One or two fables occur in the Bible

(Jgs 9:8–15; Ez 19:10–14), and a single, complete riddle (Jgs 14:12–18), but none of these is in the Wisdom books. A few proverbs probably were recited as riddles, and most of these occur in a small collection of the "Sayings of Agur" in Proverbs 30. One example is:

> There are three things that are never satisfied,
> four things that never say, "Enough!":
> The grave, the barren womb,
> the land which never has enough water,
> and fire, which never says, "Enough!" (Prv 30:15–16).

One can imagine the teacher asking the question, and the students reciting the four answers, or even adding other possible variations.

The proverb was an important element in Israelite wisdom, as it was in other ancient nations, for it distilled the lessons of the past, of human experience that seemed to be always the same, and it did so in a practical and clever manner with a little bit of the sermon about it for teaching purposes. This was ideally suited to a society which learned by memory and had only a few educated professionals who actually read books. One of the best illustrations of how effectively a society can live by proverbs is found in James Michener's novel, *The Source.* In chapter 7, "In the Gymnasium," he has created a confrontation between a Jewish elder who seems to speak only in proverbs and the educated, reasonable Greek governor of the small town. The traditional values of Jewish faith are able to withstand the allure of Greek culture represented by the governor because they have been so deeply absorbed by means of the proverbs that fill the mind of the Jewish elder (see page 496 below).

The love for proverbs is a love for capturing the difficult problems of experience as well as the ordinariness of life in a new and interesting way. It helps to explain the other literary means adopted by the wise in Israel. They frequently used dialogue formats such as occur in the Book of Job, or question and answer exchanges, as in the Book of Ecclesiastes. Comparisons, allegories, and long images from nature are sometimes found, and the teachers always enjoyed rhetorical questions for dramatic effect. These are all means of *instruction.* Above all, theirs is an educational outlook. And when not using one of the clever literary forms, they fell back on the straightforward lesson plan. Proverbs 1–9 is almost entirely written in such a teaching style with twelve or thirteen separate lessons in all.

Because these proved to be such an effective method of educating people to both the traditional values and to moral reflection, the prophets often borrowed the techniques of the rhetorical question or the dialogue betweeen God and people (or prophet and people) to convey their messages. Some prophets, such as Ezekiel, used the metaphor and parable as their favored way of making a point (see Ez 16, 17, 18, 19, 29, 30, 31, 32). But the prophet spoke directly to the covenant demands of Yahweh, while the wise concentrated on the wider questions of human experience and the problems of life. Yet they shared a common concern for the place of justice in society, personal responsibility, and the proper human response to divine command. Wisdom, prophecy and law may have followed different ways, but they had similar goals in the real life of the Israelite.

The Book of Proverbs

Solomon's reputation for wisdom was so great that Israel considered him the founder of their wisdom tradition. On the basis of 1 Kings 4:29–34 quoted above, he was believed to have been the author of the Book of Proverbs as well as The Song of Songs and Ecclesiastes. Even the latest book of the Old Testament, The Wisdom of Solomon, is attributed to him. One charming legend in the Talmud guessed that Solomon had written the Song of Songs in his lusty youth, Proverbs in his mature middle age, and the skeptical Ecclesiastes as an old man.

The Book of Proverbs contains a great number of sayings whose message is as old as the civilization of the Sumerians in 3000 B.C., and there is no reason why many of these could not have been collected under Solomon's command and formed into a book. But the present book also has many later additions. One group of proverbs in chapters 25–29 are attributed to Solomon but were not written down until two centuries later in the time of King Hezekiah of Judah. Other small collections are labeled from other wise teachers and kings. Altogether, there are seven sections in the book:

(1) Chapters 1–9, labeled "The Proverbs of Solomon, Son of David."
(2) Chapters 10–22, labeled "Proverbs of Solomon."
(3) Chapters 22:17–24:22, labeled "The Sayings of the Wise."

(4)   Chapter 24:23–34, labeled "Also the Sayings of the Wise."
(5)   Chapters 25–29, labeled "More Proverbs of Solomon, Copied by the Men of Hezekiah, King of Judah."
(6)   Chapter 30, labeled "The Sayings of Agur, Son of Jakeh: An Oracle."
(7)   Chapter 31, labeled "The Sayings of King Lemuel: An Oracle."

The identity of Agur and Lemuel cannot be known, but the third section seems to be an adaptation of the Egyptian collection of Amenemopet, noted above. All the sections are primarily collections of individual proverbs with no absolutely clear order that governs their arrangement, except within the first section, Proverbs 1–9. This is a larger, planned whole with a mixture of short proverbs and long instructions. It forms a prologue to the rest of Proverbs and an explanation of wisdom as a way of life. Proverbs 1:7 declares the basic theme: at the heart of all wisdom stands fear of the Lord. And the author repeats it again at the end in Proverbs 9:10: "The fear of the Lord is the beginning of wisdom." This fear of the Lord is true reverence and worship, and suggests obedience to the law of Yahweh as the way to find wisdom. At the same time, the author or authors of Proverbs 1–9 have borrowed many early themes known from Canaanite religion, such as the woman, Dame Folly, who seduces the young searcher after wisdom, in order to illustrate their points, but the overall view is that of the post-exilic period stress on law and wisdom as one. Thus this prologue was probably added to many earlier collections only at the final stage of development of the book.

The older proverbs found in the remaining chapters can be divided between pragmatic, secular, often materialistic advice, and the specifically religious reflections on the role of Yahweh as God of Israel. This is to be expected since the wisdom teachers were eager to include the wisdom of all peoples within the vision of Israel's faith. The overall purpose of learning proverbs is to master life. And the way to life is praised endlessly: "The mouth of the just is a fountain of life" (Prv 10:11), and "He who takes correction has a path to life" (Prv 10:17). Other topics that dominate the proverbs are (1) the relationship of parents and children, especially in terms of respect for parents and discipline in education, (2) the contrast between the just and the wicked in their behavior, (3) the value of good friends and a loving wife, (4) the civic virtues of honesty, generosity, justice, and integrity, (5) personal mastery of passions and self-control, especially in sexual matters, (6) proper use of speech, including knowing when not to speak, (7) stewardship over wealth, prudence and hard work in planning for the future, (8) manners and proper behavior before superiors, and (9) the value of wisdom over foolish or careless behavior. These can be summed up in the words of a short maxim in Proverbs 13:20, "Walk with wise men and you will become wise, but the friends of fools will come to a bad end."

The nature of the proverb combines two somewhat opposed truths: it is *evident* to everyone as really so, but it is also *ambiguous*, and not always true in the same way in every case. Thus we can say, "Absence makes the heart grow fonder," and "Out of sight, out of mind," and mean both because different aspects of our experiences are brought out by each. So, too, Proverbs was not a boring book to our ancestors, but a treasure of practical wisdom which invited reflective thought and new discoveries of its meaning, especially in light of Yahweh's revelation of his word. It revealed the order of the world God had created and God's ultimate power over it: "Man plans his ways in his mind, but God controls his steps" (Prv 16:9).

The Book of Job

The dramatic dialogue between Job and his three friends about the relation of suffering to human behavior, and Job's impassioned assault on God himself, have made the Book of Job one of the all-time favorite classics of world literature. Many modern playwrights, including Archibald MacLeish (*J.B.*) and Neil Simon (*God's Favorite*), have used it as the basis of successful plays. Job itself is constructed like a dramatic play:

(1) Chapters 1–2   The scene is set with an old folktale about how God tested Job, who proved faithful in every case.

(2) Chapters 3–31   A dialogue between Job and three friends, Eliphaz, Bildad and Zophar, over the meaning of divine justice and Job's suffering, ending with Job demanding that God appear and defend himself if he is a just God.

(3)   Chapters 32–37   A sudden appearance of a fourth adversary, Elihu, who challenges both the friends and Job, and demands that they submit to the divine majesty and divine control of human events.

(4)   Chapters 38–41   God himself appears and recites the power and marvels beyond human understanding that show Job's demands for justice to be arrogant. Job submits twice.

(5)   Chapter 42:7–17   The final act of the old folktale in which God restores Job to his greatness and attacks the friends for accusing him.

The outline shows some of the inconsistency in the book from a modern logical point of view. The folktale in sections 1 and 5 has nothing bad to say about Job, but condemns the friends, while the dialogue sections present the friends as defenders of God and have God himself correct Job for his pride. As a result, we can detect two quite separate sources to the book. The prose folktale in chapters 1–2 and 42:7–17 was an older and quite legendary story of a wise man whom God tested and found faithful. A later author, unknown to us, composed the rich and profound exploration of human innocence and suffering, divine power versus a man's search for meaning, that creates the wisdom book as we now have it. Possibly a still later author inserted the remarks of Elihu in chapters 32–37 to prepare for God's speech in chapters 38–41.

The author had the courage to move beyond simple acceptance of God's will to ask hard questions of the traditional and overconfident wisdom so often found in Proverbs and sometimes in the prophets. If God does look after the just, and does always punish the wicked, as the friends claim, why does the opposite seem to be our real experience, in which evil people prosper from their deeds and the honest person never gets ahead (Jb 21:7–17)? In many ways the author is writing a parody of the smug prophets and wise teachers who assure people that everything will be all right. But the book explores a still deeper question of how one who is faithful ever comes to know God or understand his or her relationship with God. Most of Job's long speeches are concerned with either the silence of God or Job's desire for a "right" relationship with God based on justice and mutual terms. Ultimately, the harsh reply of God destroys this hope—no one relates to God on a basis of justice or equal rights. God gives himself by means of his law and his revelation that we are to obey. For this reason, the author inserted a special poem on wisdom in chapter 28 that breaks up the dialogues but makes the firm point that no one can find the way to wisdom; only God knows it and he has given it to humans through reverent worship: "Behold, the fear of the Lord is wisdom" (Jb 28:28). But worship is also the means of knowing God face-to-face. As Job finally admits, "I had only heard of you by word of mouth, but now my eye has seen you" (Jb 42:5).

Job was a well-known figure of wisdom, perhaps like Paul Bunyan in the legends of Minnesota. Ezekiel suggests that he was as famed for his justice as Noah (Ez 14:14, 20). Thus the use of the old folktale as an opening both establishes the agony of Job's situation and makes it clear that God controls what happens. This permits the author to put on Job's lips words and ideas that might shock many Israelites. The happy ending relieves the bad taste such attacks on divine goodness have created, and shows in the form of a drama how one man can grow and change his mind by learning wisdom. Other ancient peoples also explored these questions of suffering and faith. They even came up with roughly the same answer of faithful trust in the greatness of God. The Babylonian work, "I Will Praise the Lord of Wisdom," ends with the command, "Creatures endowed with breath . . . as many as there are, glorify Marduk!" (ANET 437). The author of Job has created a version that places these fundamental human questions within Israel's belief in Yahweh. The final form most resembles the great psalms of lament with (1) their threefold cry of human pain and lament, (2) their call for help to God, and (3) their promise to praise God forever. Ultimately from the midst of doubt and questioning, Job teaches us, comes trust.

The Book of Ecclesiastes

No one has ever challenged the Book of Ecclesiastes' right to the title of the most skeptical book in the Bible. Ecclesiastes, also called Qoheleth, has a unified approach to the value of wisdom: pessimism. While Proverbs sought to provide guidelines on what to do and not to do, and confidently summed up the way to wisdom as "fear of the Lord," Ecclesiastes has its doubts whether such confidence has any basis in human experience. The author's theme song is sounded at the beginning and again at the end of the book, "Vanity of vanities, all is vanity—and a striving after wind" (Eccl

1:2, 14; 12:8). Futility and emptiness result from the constant human search for the meaning of life. He is particularly aware of the useless attempts to understand the mystery of divine purpose behind the order of the world as it is, the tragic finality of death, the reasons for success and failure, and the justice of rewards and punishment for good and evil behavior. These are beyond our capabilities to discover.

The word Qoheleth is Hebrew for a "preacher," "head of the church assembly," or something similar, although no other example of the word exists in the Bible. The more traditional title of the book, Ecclesiastes, is nothing but a direct Greek translation of the Hebrew word. That the author was Solomon is implied by the first verse when it says Qoheleth was the son of David in Jerusalem, but cannot be taken as fact. The book shows the development of Israelite thought that comes after the exile, especially in its doubts about old answers and its attacks on the rational approaches of Greek thought that began to influence the Near East at that time.

The book has much in common with other wisdom literature, however. The author undertakes the investigation of experience at all levels, and asks questions about creation, justice, the wise versus the fool, just and unjust, and even quotes a large number of proverbs that he actually thinks will work in life. But certain things are clear to him that others have never allowed. While admitting that God does direct all things, he insists that we cannot know what God is doing or why, and so our proper human response is to enjoy what God gives us now and use it the best we can. As Ecclesiastes 5:17 puts it: "Here is what I understand as good: it is well if a person eat, drink and enjoy all the fruits of work under the sun during the limited days that God gives to one's life, for this is a person's lot." For Qoheleth, everything has its proper time: "a time to be born and a time to die ... a time to weep and a time to laugh" (Eccl 3:2–4), but the "why" is known only to God and not to us. His advice to enjoy life as it is may not seem very religious, but he tempers it with warnings "to fear God" (Eccl 5:6).

The Jewish rabbis fought a long time over whether the book was fit for the sacred canon of Scripture. The positive decision was made possible because Solomon was thought to be the author, and an editor added a pious afterword in Ecclesiastes 12:9–14 that summed up his message as "fear God and keep his commandments" (Eccl 12:13). It was fortunate that they recognized its inspired nature, for it teaches the great gulf between the transcendent God and our human striving to understand and so control him. In the end, Ecclesiastes' message is one with that of Job—trust and surrender yourself to God's loving care even if you cannot know where it will lead.

The Song of Songs (The Canticle of Canticles)

The third book attributed to Solomon is the Song of Songs, mainly because his name is mentioned in chapters 3 and 8. In both cases he seems more of a model to follow than an author, and we can safely say that the famous king did not write these songs. Like so many other wisdom books, The Song of Songs shows signs of being worked and reworked through many centuries. At the oldest level are love poems, perhaps wedding songs, many of which could go back to the time of Solomon. At the latest level are Persian and Greek phrases that indicate additions made after the exile. There seem to be hints of a dialogue between a young lover and his beloved (bride?), and perhaps even a chorus of the daughters of Jerusalem. At least the tradition of identifying different speakers goes back to the Greek translations before the time of Christ. But there is not enough unity among the different songs to say more than that it is a collection extolling the undying power of love between two people.

The close parallels between the language of The Song of Songs and Arab wedding songs from Syria were discovered in the late nineteenth century. The wedding customs included a dance with a sword by the bride on the day before her wedding in which she described her own beauty (Song 1:5; 2:1). For the week after the wedding, the couple is treated as a king and queen with much feasting and still more songs extolling the bride's beauty (Song 4:1–15; 5:10–16). Such village customs last over many centuries and can help us discover the original setting and use of the Song of Songs. The religious use of such love songs may even go back to hymns and ceremonies surrounding the sacred marriage rituals of the Canaanite followers of Baal. Certainly, Israel was not the only ancient nation to sing the beauties of the female body (and sometimes of the male). We have examples from both Babylon and Egypt (see ANET 467–69), and Psalm 45 is also a wedding psalm.

But the lusty nature of the songs gave scandal to many of the Jewish rabbis, and as late as the second century A.D. they still had not fully agreed that the book should be in the sacred canon. One of the deciding factors was the belief that it described allegorically the

THE SONG OF SONGS AS A WEDDING SONG COLLECTION

Researchers studied Arab village life in the late 19th century to find parallels to the ways of ancient Israel that might still be carried on almost unchanged through the intervening centuries. One remarkable parallel to the *Song of Songs* was the custom of singing a *wasf*, which was a wedding song about the beauty of a bride's or groom's body. Compare the following Syrian wedding song with Cant 7:1–4:

Syrian Wedding Song	Cant 7:1–4
Her teeth are like pearls,	Your thighs rounded like a jewel
Her neck like the neck of an antelope,	are the work of a master hand.
Her shoulders are firm,	Your navel is a rounded bowl
Her navel like a box of perfumes with all spices flowing from it;	that is always filled with wine.
Her body like strains of silk,	Your belly is a stack of wheat surrounded by lilies.
Her limbs like firm pillars.	Your breasts are like two fawns,
	the twins of a gazelle.
	Your neck is like an ivory tower.
	Your eyes like pools in Heshbon.

love of Yahweh for Israel as a beloved bride. The Christian Church accepted it quickly for the same reasons—it could easily describe in allegory the love of Christ for the Church, or for the soul of the believer. St. Bernard of Clairvaux in the twelfth century wrote a great number of sermons on the Song of Songs describing the love of Christ for the soul and the mystical union that came from this love. They have become the classic source of such a mystical spirituality. Other Christian writers of the Middle Ages saw an allegory of Christ's love for his Blessed Mother. In all of these cases, the later interpretations have gone far beyond the original Old Testament book with its rather graphic description of sexual love as a joyful and positive ideal. But they also underline the power of the book to lead people in all ages to discover that love, sexuality, and creation are gifts of God's goodness.

Sirach (Ecclesiasticus)

Sirach is the longest of the wisdom books with fifty-one chapters. It is a mixture of proverbs and lengthy essays on major themes within the wisdom tradition: use of speech, self-control, evil friends, the value of work, death, sickness, etc. Unlike Proverbs, it tends to group many sayings on the same topic close together: chapter 9 treats women, chapter 4 discusses the duties to parents, and chapter 19 deals with the proper use of speech. Between these discussions, Sirach has grouped reflections, hymns, poems and essays on (1) the value of wisdom and (2) how to obtain it. These are spaced throughout the book (chapters 1, 14, 24, etc.) but appear most dramatically at the end in a long recital of Israel's history which the author calls "In Praise of Famous Men." It stretches from chapters 44 through 50 and describes all the important Old Testament figures as wise men. At the same time, the author's interest in priestly matters and Torah is apparent from the large amount of space he gives to Aaron and priests after him.

The book can be divided into two major parts, chapters 1–24 and 25–50, with an appendix in chapter 51 that serves to summarize the book—it is a hymn in praise of wisdom. Other than the large groupings of sayings by certain themes, there is no real order to the book. The author identifies himself only at the end of chapter 50, but luckily his grandson translated the original into Greek and wrote a preface that gives us the one known date for a wisdom book. The youth arrived in Egypt in 132 B.C. and soon after translated his grandfather's book from Hebrew. That would place the writing of Sirach between 190 and 175 B.C. For many centuries it was thought to be only in Greek in the Septuagint. But a partial copy of the Hebrew original was found at the end of the last century hidden in a synagogue storeroom in Cairo, and another when archaeologists excavated Masada in Palestine in 1964. A few fragments also turned up at Qumran in 1947. Despite this evidence that first century Jews in Palestine used Sirach, it was never accepted into the Jewish canon because it was not from the time of Ezra or before. Its popular name in Church circles, Ecclesiasticus, "The Church Book," might also be a factor. The Christians liked it all too well in their catechetical instructions for Jews to be at ease with it.

Above all, Sirach stresses the ethical aspects of everyday life. He exalts the role of law and fear of the Lord as true wisdom. As a result, wisdom becomes tamed, and the wild questions of a Job and Qoheleth are no longer heard. But he does recognize a God of compassion, the ambiguity and uncertainty of human life, and the limits to human knowledge. Wisdom can be attained, but it is in the form of guidelines for human action, and not in speculation.

The Book of Wisdom

The Book of Wisdom is known only in Greek and may be the last book of the Old Testament to be written. It makes use of the philosophical arguments found in Philo of Alexandria and other Jewish writers in the Greek world of Alexandria, Egypt in the first century B.C., and employs many Greek oratorical devices of the same period. The book can be divided into the following major sections.

Chapters 1:1–6:21	Justice and wisdom under the eye of God brings victory and immortality to the just.
Chapters 6:22–11:1	Solomon's praise of wisdom for its unmatched value.
Chapters 11:2–19:5	A long review of the history of Israel up to the exodus as evidence of God's mercy on Israel.
Chapter 19:6–22	Concluding psalm in praise of wisdom.

The three major sections blend well together. The first ten chapters are quite conservative in seeing the goodness of wisdom in creation as a gift of God that has been specially revealed to Israel, and in accepting the attitude that God punishes evildoers and rewards the just. The author seems to have little or no interest in the problem of innocent suffering presented by Job, or in the understanding of what God wants raised by Qoheleth.

The main interest of the author is to reassure the Jewish community living in Egypt that keeping their faith is worthwhile despite the hardships in a pagan land. To achieve this, the author describes the mercy of God during the first exodus from Egypt as a symbol of hope for his own times. He even provides a long insert, or aside, in chapters 13–15, on the foolishness of pagan idolatry to show that it is not as profound as Jewish law. The book builds its case with much repetition and rhetorical overkill. The great events of the Old Testament become the object lessons of various *philosophical* approaches to wisdom. For example, the list of wisdom's attributes (Wis 7:22–30) tries to use deep philosophical terms but succeeds in making wisdom so abstract that it clashes with the Israelite tradition of wisdom as practical and concrete:

In her is an intelligent, holy, unique, many-sided, subtle, agile, clear, pure, certain keen . . . spirit. For wisdom is mobile beyond all motion. . . . She is an aura of the might of God and a pure effusion of the glory of the Almighty (Wis 7:22–25).

The Book of Wisdom stands out from previous wisdom writings in Israel by its intense concern with two themes: (1) salvation history as a lesson for learning wisdom, and (2) immortality as an explanation of how God rewards the sufferings of the just. If it is not the most profound of wisdom books, it does throw light on the struggles of Judaism in the Greek and Roman eras to preserve its heritage of faith in the midst of alien values and to fight pagan ideas by means of their own arguments.

The Achievement of Wisdom

Few readers give the wisdom books as much attention as they do the law or the prophets, but it must be remembered that wisdom lasted much longer than the prophetic movement as a central part of Israel's life. At the dawn of the national state with David and Solomon, wisdom already had a long tradition that could be taken over for structuring how Israel was governed. The prophets Amos, Hosea, Isaiah and Jeremiah frequently borrowed wisdom's insights for their messages. And in the post-exilic period when prophecy failed, wisdom reached its peak. Its international character allowed it to borrow from the best of other cultures and to adapt the most difficult questions of Israel's belief to new and deeper answers.

Some of wisdom's major achievements can best be listed rather than described at length:

(1) The importance of *order* for understanding God's creation and the role of humans within his plan. Order governs proper manners and ethical behavior and it explains the role and limits of everything known.

(2) The importance of *cause and effect*. Acts have consequences, and moral decisions for good or evil reap their rewards. Everything has its reason, and often what seems unexplainable can be explained by analogies to common experience.

(3) *Time* is important. Israel's sense of history was strongly oriented to the future, while most pagan nations were oriented toward the ideal first moment of creation in the past. Time moved on for Israel and God would always act again at his chosen moment.

Thus nothing was ever hopelessly lost because of the past. Indeed, Israel, could be labeled simply as a "people of hope."

(4) God is *revealed in creation.* The beauty and order of nature teach us lessons about God and give us confidence that we can trust our experience. God gives special knowledge of himself in the law, in the prophets and in historical events, but these must be measured against wisdom's discovery of order and meaning to show how reasonable Israel's faith is.

(5) Wisdom reveals that the transcendent mystery of God actually interacts in the world by its use of *personification.* Usually pictured as a woman, wisdom invites us to find her in the world through the life of worship and obedience to the law. Several major passages actually treat wisdom as an independent being, often called a *hypostasis* (in Greek), that stands by God's side, comes into the world, and speaks to humanity (Prv 1:20–33; Prv 8:22–31; Sir 24:1–31; Wis 9:9–11; Jb 28:1–28). While it is not likely that Israel thought of wisdom as a real divine being, its description as a person signified that God truly *communicated* himself and his plan to the world and that he could be heard and understood by humanity in personal relationship.

(6) *Suffering* has some meaning. It is either the consequence of evil done, disciplinary correction from God, or a testing of faith to deepen it. Based on experience, the wise affirmed that evil does not pay in the long run. Their answers to the mystery of why good people suffer were not adequate, yet neither are modern answers; but they did understand and teach that all things are in the hands of a good and merciful God.

(7) *Life is positive.* Creation is good because it is from God and it is orderly and under control. If misfortune happens, there is an explanation—and there is hope. We can rely on the lessons of experience to plan for the future, but above all we should enjoy what God gives in life.

(8) Humans are *responsible* for the world and are made co-creators with God (Gen 1) and his deputies over the earth (Gen 2). They must exercise this wisely and prudently according to God's plan.

(9) The divine plan is known by wisdom to be a *gift* beyond human control or total understanding. Fidelity to the revelation of the law is more true to wisdom than is human intelligence trying to figure it out. More than knowledge, wisdom is the person of God who asks us to imitate him (Lev 19) and be in his image and likeness

(Gen 1:26). Thus wisdom is above all ethical, and "fear of the Lord" requires honesty, humility, justice, etc.

(10) Finally, wisdom knows its *limits.* God's thoughts are beyond our understanding, and we must not challenge the basic structure of the universe and attempt to make God conform to our expectations. The basic virtue of the wise is *trust,* and on that trust is based our firm commitment to Yahweh for better or worse.

Wisdom does not stand opposed, therefore, to the teachings of the Pentateuch or the lessons of the prophets. It serves to unite teaching and reality, to integrate the ideals of faith into the practical experience of everyday doubt and uncertainty. And above all, it helped Israel understand that their faith in Yahweh spoke to the concerns of everyone in the world and had a universal message that was not to be kept hidden only in Judah.

STUDY QUESTIONS

1. How would one describe a Wisdom Book? How are Wisdom books different from other biblical books? What Old Testament books may be classified as Wisdom Books?
2. Is wisdom tradition unique only to Israel?
3. What are the origins of wisdom in Israel?
4. Describe some literary forms found in Wisdom literature.
5. What is contained in the Book of Proverbs?
6. What takes place in the Book of Job?
7. Describe the content and characteristics of the Book of Qoheleth (Ecclesiastes).
8. What is the Song of Songs? What are its distinctive features? Why does disagreement exist over whether this book should be included in the canon?
9. Briefly describe Sirach (Ecclesiasticus).
10. How could one describe the Wisdom of Solomon? What are its approach and major themes?
11. What are some major achievements of the Wisdom Books?

Chapter 24

FAITH CONFRONTING NEW CHALLENGES

Suggested Scripture Readings:

Daniel 1–3, 7–8
Ruth 1–4
1 Maccabees 1–4

A. JUDAISM IN THE WORLD OF THE GREEKS

Alexander the Great

Persia had twice tried to conquer Greece and failed—in 490 B.C. under Darius, and again ten years later in 480 under his son Xerxes. From that time on, the Persians learned that money could do more than armies in keeping the Greek city states under control. By offering bribes to one city against another, they kept the Greeks separated and at odds with each other. The well-run treasury and fabulous wealth of Persia contrasted sharply with the small states and cities of Greece and western Asia which were always starved for money. Greek unity achieved in the fight against Darius and Xerxes quickly disappeared, and soon Athens and Sparta, the two greatest states in Greece, were locked in a deadly civil war that lasted from 459 to 404 B.C. It left both cities crippled and weak.

During this same period, however, the cultural life of Athens reached its peak. The playwrights Aeschylus, Sophocles and Euripides wrote their great dramas, Aristophanes composed his comedies, Socrates, Plato and Aristotle taught their philosophy, Xenophon and

Herodotus recorded their histories, and Epicurus and Zeno the Stoic worked out their moral philosophies. Besides these written achievements, there was sculpture, painting, engineering and building of the highest quality. While Ezra and Nehemiah were restoring Jewish life in the fifth century, Sophocles and Socrates were at work in Athens; but in the fourth century, Judah slipped into the quiet backwater of culture while Plato, Aristophanes and Aristotle continued to make Athens the birthplace of new culture.

The Greeks were also great soldiers, and although they could not unite in a common cause for long, many served as mercenary troops for the Persians and other foreign powers. For the sake of appearances, the various Greek city states had formed a military league, but it was never much of a success until Philip, the king of the semi-barbaric land of Macedon just north of modern Greece, took over. He began to expand his military power and forced the Greeks to accept him as the head of their national league after he defeated them in battle in 338 B.C. Only two years later he was assassinated, and his young son Alexander, only twenty at the time, became king in his place. Alexander had been educated by his father as a Greek, and had the great Aristotle himself as his chief tutor. Alexander had a deep love for everything Greek and a dream to transform the East by means of Greek culture.

Alexander made his first move by putting down a revolt by the Greek city of Thebes with such harsh measures that it struck fear into other city states, and they agreed to accept him as their de facto leader. Alexander began his war against the Persian empire in 334 B.C. by liberating several Greek towns that lay inside Persian territory on the coast of Turkey. In a series of three major battles in three years, he totally defeated the huge Persian armies and sent them fleeing in panic. His father Philip had developed the phalanx, a military formation in which the infantry marched in an order like an arrowhead holding long spears in front of them. It was tightly organized, difficult to break apart and easily able to change direction at a moment's notice. In contrast, the very large battalions in the Persian forces came from different nations, had trouble speaking a common language to one another, were densely packed into space that did not allow for maneuvering, and were under commanders who had not worked together. Alexander's infantry, aided by daring cavalry charges, routed the Persians every time. The Persian king, Darius III, fled to the east, with the Greek army in pursuit, and was finally assassinated by local leaders hoping to make peace with Alexander.

THE LIFE OF ALEXANDER THE GREAT

356 B.C.	Alexander born in Macedon
338 B.C.	His father, Philip defeats the Greeks and rules Greece as well
336 B.C.	Philip is assassinated and Alexander becomes king
334 B.C.	Alexander wins the battle of Granicus in Turkey and rules western Turkey.
333 B.C.	Alexander wins the battle of Issus in Syria. All of the Near East up to the Euphrates is his.
331 B.C.	He establishes the city of Alexndria in Egypt. At the battle of Gaugamela, Alexander defeats Darius III completely, and gains control of the Persian empire.
326 B.C.	Alexander forced to turn home from India by his troops
323 B.C.	Alexander dies in Babylon of fever.

Alexander now controlled not only Greece and Macedonia, but also the entire Persian empire from Egypt to the borders of Afghanistan. He marched down the coastline of the Mediterranean, taking control of Palestine and founding a new city on the Egyptian coast named after himself, Alexandria. But having the largest empire the world had ever seen was not enough for Alexander. He desired to push his power farther east to India and beyond. He fought his way through Afghanistan and defeated several local armies in the plains of the Indus River in northern India. But by now his troops were exhausted, frightened of the strange lands and people, and wanted no more. They had even faced armor-covered elephants in battle. Weeping for the loss of his dream, Alexander was forced to return homeward. It was 326 B.C. A bare three years later, in 323, he died in Babylon from a combination of fever, the effects of old wounds and debauchery.

In a short life of thirty-three years he had become a folk hero to peoples in all the lands he conquered. But more importantly, he had set up an ideal that would change the Near East. He believed, often to the resentment of his Macedonian soldiers, that all people should be united in harmony. In Egypt he had himself declared the pharaoh with divine status; in Babylon he had accepted the title of king and worshiped the god Marduk; in Persia he had himself declared the successor of the Persian royal dynasty. He married several foreign wives, dressed in various native costumes, and generally identified himself with the peoples he ruled. He worked hard to establish the Greek language as the common means of communication in the whole Eastern world, built harbors and cities for commerce, settled his Greek soldiers in colonies all through the Near East, and even forced marriages between them and local girls. He replaced the Persian daric, a gold coin, with Greek money as the basic currency of his new empire. In all of this, he fulfilled his dream of bringing Greek ideas and Greek culture to the world.

Unfortunately, Alexander did not live long enough to achieve all these goals. At his death, his generals were forced to divide his world empire into four smaller kingdoms. Lysimachus got Thrace; Cassander got Macedon and Greece; Antigonus, followed shortly by Seleucus, got Syria and the east; Ptolemy got Egypt and Palestine. Because of the rivalry and conflicting aims between the Ptolemies and the Seleucid kings, both sides claimed Palestine and fought for control of its territories again and again. The Ptolemies managed to

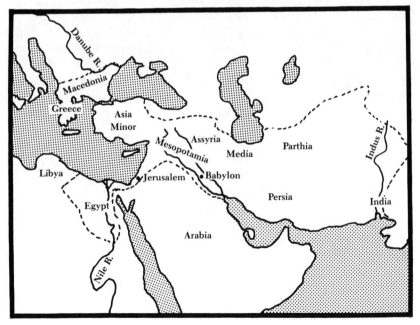

The Empire of Alexander the Great

hold it for more than a century, with several ups and downs, until the battle of Panion in 199/198 when it fell to Antiochus III and his Seleucid kingdom.

Hellenistic Culture

Love of things Greek is often called Hellenism after the name that the Greeks called themselves, Hellenes. But Greek influence in the other countries of the ancient world is usually referred to as Hellenistic, especially after the time of Alexander when the mixture of Greek and Near Eastern ideals produced a combined culture in most places. It should be noted that Judah and the rest of Palestine had already known much Greek influence before the time of Alexander. Attic pottery from the Athens area had reached Judah as early as the seventh century B.C., and Greek money was in common use after the fifth century. Greek styles in furniture and bronze were popular among the wealthy in the post-exilic period as a whole.

But the conquest of Alexander and the policies of the Ptolemy government after him established certain official practices aimed at turning the Jewish way of life more toward a Hellenistic culture. The Greek rulers set up a large number of new towns populated entirely by pagan Greeks and others; they organized taxation along Greek lines that would encourage tight-knit economies and foster trade with the Greeks in the West. The new cities had Greek temples, gymnasiums for leisure and sport, stadiums for horse racing, youth centers for the cultivation of health and education, and of course theaters. Knowledge of Greek became very important for anyone who dealt with government or traveled to other cities and regions. Greek education, with stress on scientific and philosophical knowledge, created a natural superiority complex over "barbarians" who held onto the older ways of Israelite life. This strong attraction for Greek ways and Greek education, however, only took hold among the upper classes in Judah. It created a great tension between those who believed in a future under Hellenistic culture and those who resisted it as pagan and unfaithful to Israelite religion.

James Michener captures the sense of those times in *The Source* in the chapter which describes the conflicts between a Greek governor and a Jewish elder who heads a small village and can barely understand Greek ways and seems to speak only in ancient proverbs. The power of Greek ideas over young Jews is brought out very well in Michener's story. Many young people enthusiastically adopted Greek fashions and customs. But along with the Greek education came a lifestyle that was often fixed on material pursuits, idleness for those with the money to afford it, and a sensual orientation that was foreign to Israelite ideals expressed in the prophets and the Book of Proverbs. There was also an ambitious greed in the Greek way that led to such behavior as that of the Tobiad family, a powerful clan that had made themselves wealthy collecting the taxes of Judah. It was this same tendency that had allowed the Persians to play off one Greek city against another in the past.

Jewish response in this period was complex and not fully known. We find both a *pious literature,* such as the Book of Ecclesiasticus or the Book of Tobit, and a *skeptical literature,* such as Ecclesiastes. Many scholars have thought that Ecclesiastes, in particular, was influenced by Greek thought, but this is not necessarily so—since there had always been a questioning and skeptical tradition in Ancient Near Eastern thought as well. But, certainly by the first century B.C., we find writings such as the Book of Wisdom, which use Greek words and ideas freely in presenting their message. On the other hand, the free movement in the Hellenistic world also allowed customs and ideas to flow the other way as well, and many Oriental beliefs from Persia and the East began to influence Jewish thought in the late Old Testament period. Apocalyptic language, concepts of heaven and hell, and a more positive view of the afterlife all enter biblical books in this period, probably mostly from the East. It was an age of syncretism, in which peoples took in new ways of thinking from both West and East.

The small island of Jews in Palestine could not keep out Greek influence even if they wanted to. Egypt and Syria were Greek states, and the Negev desert, Philistine territory, Galilee, the states across the Jordan, and Phoenicia were all filled with Greek cities. Even Samaria had become more a Greek city than Jewish. The Decapolis, the league of ten Greek cities in Galilee and Transjordan, which is mentioned in the New Testament, was already flourishing in the second century B.C. This early Greek period also gave rise to a number of Jewish writings in the style of short novels: Esther, Judith, Ruth, and Tobit.

The Book of Esther

The Book of Esther contains a thrilling tale of escape from mortal danger for the Jews. It is set in the Persian period under King Xerxes, who ruled from 486 to 465, and tells the story of a beautiful young Jewish maiden, Esther, who is chosen to be his queen when he becomes angry with his first queen and divorces her. Esther brings along her cousin and guardian, Mordecai, but soon he has enraged the Persian prime minister, Haman, by refusing him the proper signs of respect. In anger, Haman convinces the king that he should destroy all the Jews in a day of slaughter because they follow their own religion and do not worship as the Persians do. In this crisis, Mordecai convinces Esther to go before the king and change his mind. The king is won over when he realizes Haman's evil intentions, and he instead orders the prime minister to be slain while he gives the Jews permission to have their day of slaughter against their enemies. The book ends with the establishment of the feast of Purim, to be kept forever as a memorial of this great day of victory.

Thus one purpose of the book is to give the reason for the feast of Purim. But another reason is to show that the Jewish people must always keep themselves separated from the dangers of pagan governments and be prepared to defend their own faith when it is in danger. Interestingly, although every other book of the Old Testament has been found at Qumran among the famous Dead Sea Scrolls, no copy of Esther is known. The reason for this may well be in the wild nature of the feast of Purim at the time. The Jewish rabbis who wrote the Talmud noted that the two-day festival (one day to celebrate the slaughter of enemies in Persia, the second to celebrate the slaughter of those in the provinces) became so carried away with wine and rejoicing that some could not distinguish between "Blest be Mordecai" and "Cursed be Haman." For the sectarian Jews who lived a monastic life in the desert at Qumran, such levity was not tolerable.

But the Book of Esther was much appreciated in mainline Judaism. It became part of the Megilloth, the scroll of five short books that were to be read on feast days. Since the book was written to explain why a feast came to be, a real incident probably lies somewhere behind the present drama. Although the written story of Esther is played out on the level of the king and queen of Persia, it builds upon some local threat to the Jewish community that was averted by an unknown heroine. This small, original event became celebrated in prayer and story and from it the authors developed their final version. It is a difficult book to love since the spirit of vengeance seems to dominate the story. Moreover, it never mentions God or his direct help to his people. No one is sure why this is so, but it scandalized even the early Jewish translators of the Septuagint, who added to their translation prayers and petitions from Esther and Mordecai directly to God. The whole book must come from the latest Persian period or early Greek times. Its themes of divine help for persecuted Jews and the destruction of all their enemies are also found among other late books such as Judith and Daniel.

The Book of Judith

The Book of Judith tells the story of an heroic widow in a small hill town of Judah who saved the nation from the invasion of King Nebuchadnezzar and his army of Assyrians during the period after the exile. From what we have already seen of biblical history, every reader understands that this is an historically impossible and fantastic combination of the imagination. No doubt the authors intended it to be recognized as such immediately so that the reader or listener could enjoy the rousing story of how God rescued his faithful people in time of deepest danger. It has all the best ingredients of good fiction: a king famous for his total destruction of Jerusalem, a pagan people legendary for their cruelty, and a Judah helpless and poor after the exile. The story builds slowly to its climactic moment when Judith has fooled the general Holofernes into thinking she would sleep with him, made him drunk on wine, and finally beheaded him with his own sword.

Unlike many Old Testament books, this is a single dramatic tale from beginning to end. Nebuchadnezzar is angry at all of western Asia for its refusal to support him, and he sends his general across the land, taking state after state. No one can stop him as he comes up to Judah. He scorns the people's trust that Yahweh will protect them and begins his siege of Judith's hometown Bethulia. She fools him with God's help just as he is preparing the final death blow. With great humor the writer describes the panic and fear of the great army as it discovers that it is headless. The Israelites under Judith seize the moment and gain an overwhelming victory. The story contrasts from Nebuchadnezzar's side the blasphemies and threats that Yahweh is nothing with the humble contrite prayers of Judith and the people as they prepare for war. It ends with a long victory hymn of Judith and notes about her piety, blessedness and fame all her days.

The final hymn is modeled on the Song of Deborah in Judges 5, and the entire story seems to be inspired by the heroic work of Jael in killing the general Sisera in the same song. The overall message is very clear: God will give even unarmed women strength enough to defeat armies if the people only place their trust in him. It was probably composed to give hope in a period of difficulty or persecution. There is no special mention of anything Greek in the book, and the mention of Holofernes and Bagoas in the story suggests a late Persian period since both men are mentioned as officials of Artaxerxes III in the fourth century. But because of its theme of salvation from pagan threats against God, not typical of the Persians, it may have been written shortly after Alexander's generals took over the land of Palestine.

The Book of Ruth

The Book of Ruth appears in our Bibles right after the Book of Judges because its heroine is an ancestor of King David, whose story is told in the following Books of 1 and 2 Samuel. It tells of an Israelite woman, Naomi, who marries a Moabite man and goes to live in his country. They have two sons who marry local Moabite women. But soon Naomi loses her husband and both sons in death, and she decides to return home to Israel. One daughter-in-law, Ruth, although a Moabitess, decides to follow Naomi and serve her needs, even though she would be far from her own people. In this way Ruth gives a charming example of filial respect and care that eventually leads to her fortunate marriage with Boaz, the leading citizen of Naomi's hometown of Bethlehem. From their marriage will come the house of David.

The one thing that is certain about this book is that the story comes from a time long after the period of the judges. Like many children's fairy tales, it begins, "Once upon a time when there were judges . . ." It also has great interest in tracing the roots of David and ends with a little genealogy that goes from Boaz to David.

While the story is probably based on an old tale preserved in the folklore about King David and his family which goes back to the ninth or tenth century, it is written in its present form in the postexilic period, although a more exact date cannot be decided upon. The conflicts with the foreign wives may reflect the struggles over marriage in the days of Ezra and Nehemiah. And like the Book of Jonah, it has an outlook definitely favorable to foreigners. It prefers the pious person, no matter whether Jew or Gentile!

Ruth is a short story of very fine style. The characters all bear symbolic names that almost make it an allegory. Ruth means "companion," Boaz means "strength," and Orpah, the daughter-in-law who did not follow Naomi, means "disloyal." The book has a simple message about true faith in Yahweh. It is not blood or marriage that most matters, but faith. Ruth, although a Moabitess, is a perfect example of Israelite faithfulness at its best.

The Book of Tobit

The Book of Tobit shares the same short story style as do Esther, Judith and Ruth. It is a romance about how God bestowed merciful care upon two of his faithful adherents. One is Tobit, an exile from northern Israel after the fall of Samaria in 722 B.C., who was taken captive to Nineveh. The other is Sarah, the daughter of his relative Raguel. Both are examples of complete trust in Yahweh and fidelity to his law.

Tobit, at the risk of his life for disobeying the Assyrian rulers, continues to perform in exile acts of piety required by Jewish law: burying the dead, clothing the naked, giving alms to the poor, and avoiding all food offered to idols. But one day bird droppings fall into his eyes and blind him. He prays to Yahweh. Meanwhile, his relative's daughter, Sarah, has been seven times married, but each time on the wedding night an evil demon Asmodeus kills the new bridegroom out of jealous passion for her. She, too, prays to Yahweh. God is determined to answer their prayers, and sends an angel, Raphael ("the healer"), to guide their fates to a happy ending. At this moment Tobit suddenly recalls that a man owes him money in the land of the Medes very near Raguel's home. He decides to send his son Tobias to claim the money if a guide can be found. Raphael appears and offers to help. On the journey Raphael teaches Tobias how to use the organs and oil of a fish to heal blindness and ward off evil spirits. Soon they stop at Raguel's house, and Tobias falls madly in love with Sarah. They marry and prepare to go to bed. Meanwhile, Raguel, fearing the worst, is already digging a grave for Tobias, but the young hero remembers to use the fish oil and renders the demon powerless. They claim the money and return home to cure Tobit of his blindness. Raphael reveals who he really is and they all praise God. The story ends with a note on how Tobias and Sarah become the ideal Jewish couple, full of love, devotion and thanks to God all the days of their long and blessed lives.

This story has almost all of the elements we have seen in the preceding books. There is a dramatic buildup against great odds. The time and place are long ago and far away. The hero and heroine are models of piety and trust in God. God's eagerness to help those who are faithful is emphasized, as is the power of prayer and fasting. This colorful tale borrows heavily from earlier works, especially from a popular Assyrian and Aramaic story of the wise man Ahiqar. But it also draws from the wisdom in the Book of Proverbs and other Jewish sources, especially the legal sections of the Pentateuch. Its main purpose is to teach by way of example the model of an ideal Jewish way of life. Because of this characteristic, it can be dated to the same period as Judith, Esther or Ruth—i.e., somewhere in the post-exilic period, either near the end of the Persian rule or at the beginning of the Greek era.

The Book of Baruch and Letter of Jeremiah

The Book of Baruch claims to be from the hand of the famous secretary of Jeremiah who figures prominently in Jeremiah 36–45. This no doubt explains why it was treasured by the early Jewish community in Alexandria. It is known only in Greek, but it uses so many Hebrew expressions that it must have originally been written in Hebrew. While claiming to be from the time of the exile, it shows such poor knowledge of the times and events that it must instead be considered a book like that of Esther or Judith or Daniel—written later to encourage and console a discouraged or persecuted people.

It is made up of four parts:

Chapters 1:1–3:9	describes the celebration of a penitential rite among the exiles in Babylon that emphasizes the promises of God.
Chapters 3:9–4:5	exalts the observance of the law of Moses as the hope of Israel. Much like the Book of Sirach, it equates wisdom with the law.
Chapters 4:5–5:9	is a series of prophetic oracles of hope to the exiles and a call to trust in the Lord.
Chapter 6	is a letter of Jeremiah to the exiles. It is sometimes put separately in Bibles as an independent work. But like the rest of Baruch, it is modeled on the genuine book of Jeremiah, in this case his letter in Jeremiah 29 to the exiles. This author, however, attacks the useless worship of idols.

In short, the book shares so much with later Jewish piety that developed after Ezra set out the Torah as the norm for Israel that it must be dated between the third and first centuries B.C. as a work of encouragement to those Jews being forced to adopt Greek ways.

The Jewish Struggle for Freedom (175–160 B.C.)

Generally life in Judah was quiet and uneventful during the control of the Ptolemy family in Egypt. But in 200–199, Antiochus III ("the Great") of the Seleucid empire in Syria defeated his fellow Greek kingdom and took control of Palestine. This signaled a major change for the Jews. Antiochus soon lost a large part of his empire to Rome in a battle over territory in modern Turkey. This was followed by more disaster, for Antiochus III died in battle in 187, and his son Seleucus IV was a weakling who desperately needed more money. This led him to raid the Jerusalem temple for its treasures. Then he, too, was killed, this time by his own prime minister. Finally, in 175, the younger brother of Antiochus III got control of the throne under the name Antiochus IV Epiphanes ("the god made manifest").

Antiochus Epiphanes developed a two-pronged policy. He began to rebuild the military might of his empire, and he ordered the Hellenization of all his different ethnic peoples so that there would be unity. Both policies cost the Jews dearly. To finance his military campaigns against the Ptolemies, he twice stripped the temple of all its wealth, once in 169 B.C. and again in 168. At the same time he forbade the Jewish practices of circumcision, abstaining from pork, and sacrifice in the temple. He even went so far as to set up an altar to the Greek god Zeus in the sanctuary of the temple. The effect on the Jews was traumatic. Many of the faithful were already outraged by practices of the upper classes who neglected Jewish piety to imitate Greek customs, and this persecution was the last straw. In 167 a revolt broke out in the small Judean town of Modein under an old man named Mattathias, and it caught on rapidly all over the country.

This struggle of the Judean state for religious freedom and finally for political independence is related in two important sources, neither of them in the Hebrew canon of the Bible. One is in the Jewish historian Josephus, who wrote his *Antiquities of the Jews* about 100 A.D. The other is the two Books of Maccabees, which were written in Greek and make up part of the deuterocanonical books of the Catholic Bible. They tell the story of the fight for freedom in the years 168 to 160, and of the reigns as king of Mattathias and his three sons, Judas, Jonathan and Simon, down to the year 134 B.C. when Simon died. The two volumes are quite different in style. 1 Maccabees recounts the events of the entire period in good historical fashion, and since it was written down about the year 100 B.C. or so, is a much better source than Josephus. 2 Maccabees, on the other hand, does not continue this history, but gives an independent collection of heroic stories from the early period of persecution and struggle in battle. It is written more for edification than for historical record-keeping. Both books, however, are written from the viewpoint of very orthodox Jewish believers. They show a strong hatred of the Seleucids and have nothing but praise for those Jews who proved faithful.

The First Book of Maccabees

The First Book of Maccabees follows the battle for freedom through the eyes of Mattathias and his sons who led the struggle. It is therefore in some ways a "court history" of the royal family, who called themselves Hasmoneans after a long-dead ancestor. Mattathias died only a year after his revolt began, and was succeeded by his son Judas, who was given the nickname "Maccabeus," meaning "The Hammer." Judas was a great leader and an inspired general who put together a very mobile guerrilla army that snatched victory after victory from the Syrian armies sent by Antiochus IV. Judas attacked in narrow and difficult places where the large Seleucid forces could not operate. By 164 B.C. Judas had gained enough control of the country to purify and rededicate to Yahweh the temple in Jerusalem after its three years of defilement by the "Abomination of Desolation," the statue of Zeus and the pagan worship that went with it. Judas had not driven all the Syrian forces out of the capital city but had trapped them uselessly in their citadel.

The dedication ceremony was a highpoint that marked the people's commitment to Yahweh and his grace of victory to them. It is described in 1 Maccabees 4, but the decision to make it a feast to be observed by Jews for all ages is not mentioned until 2 Maccabees 1. It has become the feast of Hanukkah, the feast of Lights, celebrated very near the Christian feast of Christmas each year as a time of rejoicing. This same event is also described by Josephus in his *Antiquities,* and it is there that it first received the name Hanukkah.

Judas was able to fire up the enthusiasm of the whole people by this event and managed to extend the territory freed from Seleucid control down to the Negev desert in the south, out to the seacoast plain and up to Galilee. He even took territory across the Jordan River. In 160 he fell in battle trying to stop a major Syrian attack, and his brother Jonathan took over. For seventeen years Jonathan ruled over Judah and made many more gains by a combination of battles (when necessary) and playing off the competing rivals for the Seleucid throne (when possible). In 143 he was captured and died in a Syrian prison, but his brother Simon continued his policies and had even greater success during his nine years from 143 to 134. He, too, died a violent death at the hands of his own son-in-law.

1 Maccabees ends with the coronation of Simon's son, John Hyrcanus, in 134. A final note, however, implies that the book was not actually written down until after Hyrcanus himself died in 103 B.C. The importance of this book is the history it provides for the second century B.C. It revealed the tensions present between the ruling classes who were willing to accept Greek ways and the simpler faith of the people and the country priests who fought to preserve the older traditions and practices of the law. The lesson it taught was that fidelity to the law and trust in God always win through.

The Second Book of Maccabees

This volume was written sometime later than 1 Maccabees. It claims to be a condensed version of the five-volume history of the Maccabean period by one Jason of Cyrene. Jason's work is long lost so that there is no way of knowing how accurately the author of 2 Maccabees has followed his model. He does summarize the events from 170 to 160, but it is clearly a book of persuasion rather than a plain report of what happened.

The book can be divided into three parts. The first part (2 Mc 1:1–2:18) contains two letters to the Jews in Egypt giving directions about celebration of the feasts of Booths and Hanukkah. The second part (2 Mc 2:19–10:9) summarizes the account by Jason up to the dedication of the temple by Judas in 164. The third part (2 Mc 10:10–15:39) follows the remainder of Judas' life up to his great victory over the Syrian general Nicanor in 160. It does not mention his death which took place shortly afterward.

2 Maccabees has enjoyed great popularity in Christian circles

over the centuries because it includes so many stories of Jewish martyrs who died heroically in the persecution of Antiochus Epiphanes. It extols the courage of the mother who watched her seven sons killed as each professed total obedience to the law, and the bravery of the old man Eleazar who was broken on the rack. In praising their faith, the book describes an afterlife of happiness with God for the just person. The author also stresses that God was able to create the world out of nothing. These are new ideas in the second century, and they reflect the ability of Jewish tradition to broaden its own understanding when it comes into contact with the very culture of Greece that was trying to destroy it. Many of the incidents in 2 Maccabees do not agree with the accounts found in Josephus or even in 1 Maccabees. The author was not a careful historian perhaps, but he had a great gift for presenting moving stories of personal faith that would be of help to others in similar times of persecution and martyrdom.

B.   THE BOOK OF DANIEL AND APOCALYPTIC THOUGHT

The Book of Daniel

In English translations of the Bible, Daniel is always found as the fourth of the major prophets, standing immediately after Ezekiel and before the twelve minor prophets. This follows the Greek traditions of the Septuagint and it is easy to tell why they thought it should be among the more important prophets. The book is filled with dreams and visions that reveal coming events. But, in contrast, the Hebrew Bible always places Daniel among the last of the writings, and does not consider it to be prophecy at all. Indeed, it can be readily understood as edifying examples of trust in God not much different from the stories of Esther, Judith and Tobit. Some scholars consider it to be prophecy, others to be wisdom, and others to be a whole new kind of literature called apocalyptic, because it speaks about the overthrow of the whole world order.

But before deciding what *kind* of literature the Book of Daniel is, we must look at what it *contains*. It can be divided into two parts in the Hebrew, and three in the Greek (and modern Catholic) Bible:

Part 1 (chapters 1–6): six romantic stories, sometimes called "court tales," intended to edify and teach proper religious attitudes. They tell about a young hero who lived under great danger at the

OUTLINE OF THE BOOK OF DANIEL

I. *The Wise Daniel at the Babylonian Royal Court (Chaps. 1–6)*
1:1–21	The dietary law test of Daniel
2:1–49	Nebuchadnezzar's dream of the statue of four metals
3:1–24	The young men in the fiery furnace

(3:25–90 are only in the Septuagint. Hebrew Bibles begin v. 91)

3:25–45	The prayer of Azarias
3:46–90	The hymn of the three young men in the furnace
3:91–97	Nebuchadnezzar frees the young men
3:98–4:34	Nebuchadnezzar dreams of the great world tree
5:1–6:1	Belshazzar's feast and the writing on the wall
6:2–29	Daniel in the lion's den

II. *Daniel's Visions of the Future (Chaps. 7–12)*
7:1–28	The four beasts
8:1–27	The ram and the he-goat
9:1–27	The 70 weeks of years
10:1–12:13	The final revelation of war

III. *Appendix of Other Deeds of Daniel (Chaps. 13–14)*
13:1–64	Daniel rescues Susanna from false accusation
14:1–22	Daniel and the statue of Bel
14:23–42	Daniel and the dragon

courts of the king of Babylon, Nebuchadnezzar II (605–562 B.C.), and of the king of the Persians (about 539 to 485 B.C.).

Part 2 (chapters 7–12): four visions in which Daniel learns about coming occurrences either in a dream or through an angel. These all contain an explanation of past and future events that will culminate in the destruction of Israel's enemies and their wicked allies in a battle conducted from heaven itself.

Part 3 (chapters 13–14): these chapters contain three further stories about the hero Daniel but are found only in the Septuagint. The first shows Daniel's wisdom as he uncovers the lies of two elders against Susanna. The second and third tell of how Daniel refuses to worship a great statue of Baal and a dragon. He is thrown in the lions' den, but God delivers him from certain death, and the lions rip apart his accusers instead.

The entire book claims to take place in the sixth century B.C. and to report a series of visions that come to the boy Daniel, who is remarkable for his great wisdom and his ability to receive divine revelation about the future. Few scholars today, however, believe that this book originated in any way during the days of the Babylonian exile. And the ones who do usually have a very difficult time explaining the references to historical people and places which seem to be grossly wrong. Darius the Mede is called the son of Xerxes in 5:31 and 9:11, but both are wrong: Darius was not a Mede but a Persian and the father of Xerxes. Belshazzar is called the king of Babylon in chapter 7 and the son of Nebuchadnezzar in chapter 5. He was neither: he was only crown prince under his father Nabonidus. In chapter 6 Cyrus succeeds Darius as king of the Persians. This, too, has history backward, since Cyrus was the founder of the Persian dynasty. The author seems to be quite confused about his facts and either lived long afterward or else intended the giant bloopers to warn the audience that what follows is not intended as a history but a *story of faith*—similar to the approach of the Book of Judith.

The first part of the book is a collection of tales that originated during the Persian era from 529 to 333. They reflect many Persian court customs and interests, such as astrology and dream interpretation. But they are written from a very Jewish point of view using a legendary hero who was taken captive in the exile as a young boy and brought up in the court of the Babylonian king. This Daniel carefully observes all the Jewish dietary laws and yet stays healthier than his comrades (chapter 1); he interprets dreams that no one else can understand (chapters 2 and 4); he predicts the fall of Babylon (chapter 5), and is thrown into a lions' den for refusing to worship idols and yet is saved by God (chapter 6). These are all charming stories that make the point that God guards and blesses those who are faithful to him in following the law and in observing prayer. Because the stories are set in the moment of Israel's greatest persecution and disaster, they provide an example of how God delivers all who are faithful in their hour of greatest need.

The second part in chapters 7–12 with its four visions is also set during the Babylonian and early Persian years. Daniel is shown all the events of the centuries to come right down to the time of Antiochus IV Epiphanes and his persecution of the Jews. Chapter 7 opens with a vision of the four beasts representing Babylon, the Medes, Persia and Greece with ten horns (kings) and one little horn (Antiochus) in its midst. God gives judgment for its total destruction in a "time, two times and a half time" (= three and a half years). Chapter 8 pictures the victory of Alexander the Great over the

Persians in the image of a he-goat and ram battling. Chapter 9 describes how the angel Gabriel explains to Daniel the meaning of Jeremiah's seventy years of exile. And chapters 10–11 contain still another vision of the last times under the images of the four kingdoms. The book ends in the Hebrew at chapter 12 with final instructions from the angel Michael on keeping the message secret until those days shall arrive, and on how to know when that time has arrived.

The Special Purpose of Daniel

The clear purpose of these visions is to predict in a veiled fashion the end of the kingdom of Antiochus Epiphanes and his persecution. This makes it highly probable that the author of chapters 7–12 was living through this terrible time and wrote these visions to give strength to Jews suffering for their faith with the promise that God would end both the persecutor and his persecution shortly. The author actually predicts the death of Antiochus in a great battle with Egypt (Dn 11:40–45). But since this was not the way the king actually died—he perished defending his empire in the east—we can suggest that at least this part of the book was completed by 164, the year before he died.

Today the consensus of scholars understands the whole book to be put together by an author and editor who first collected traditional stories in chapters 1–6 about the boy-hero Daniel showing his courage during the persecutions of exile and then added to them the visions of chapters 7–12 that predicted the coming end of Antiochus Epiphanes and his persecution. This kind of writing is called a *vaticinium ex eventu,* a "prediction after the fact," in which an author creates a character of long ago and puts into his mouth as predictions all the important events that have already happened right up to the author's own time and place. The language is often coded with symbolic animals and colors and dates to protect its message from the persecuting authorities. And its focus is *not* predicting the *future,* but giving some meaning to *present* happenings by explaining the *past* events that led up to this terrible situation, and showing that all along God has permitted everything that takes place and is planning to act soon again to rescue his people.

To achieve such an important purpose, the authors mixed historical facts with older religious traditions and even pagan myths. Daniel is already known to the prophet Ezekiel during the exile (Ez

14) as an ancient figure of great holiness and wisdom, and not as a young captive of the Babylonians the way the stories portray him. Still earlier, a wise king, Daniel, forms part of *The Tale of Aqhat* in the Ugaritic literature of the thirteenth century B.C. (see ANET 149–155). Another religious theme accuses pagan kings of being arrogant and proud, rebelling against God. This echoes the oracles against nations found in the major prophets which often employ images of cosmic destruction or the motif of Yahweh as a divine warrior who comes to destroy Israel's enemies.

Although the Book of Daniel is not intended to be primarily an historical record, it does reflect the general course of events in the post-exilic period from the time of Nebuchadnezzar down to the Maccabees, a period of nearly four hundred years. Its whole purpose is to interpret that history without being wedded to the details. The authors were intensely interested in what was happening and what God would do about it. They were convinced that *God really does act at every moment even when it may seem that he has abandoned his people.* They also tried to answer why Israel suffered, and why God allowed people to be martyred for following his law. These were pressing problems at the time of the Maccabees, and the authors used all the skill at their command to create an answer, combining wisdom, prophecy and the new form of apocalyptic. They needed to convince a despairing people of the mercy of God and so they even left the court tales of chapters 2–7 in Aramaic, the language of the Babylonian court, for the sake of realism. Aside from a few chapters in Ezra, Daniel is the only Old Testament book with Aramaic in it.

The Lasting Significance of Daniel

The Book of Daniel is one of the latest books of the Old Testament and has played an important part in later interpretation of the Bible especially in Christian circles. Some of its more notable aspects can be listed:

(1) It has many connections to the wisdom tradition. Not only was the chief character based on a legendary wise man of old, but he acts with superb prudence and insight in every situation. Daniel's ability to interpret dreams and see through deceit expresses the Jewish concern for the wise practice of their religion over against the evil and stupid conduct of pagan nations who persecute them.

These concerns also explain why the model stories of Susanna, Bel and the dragon were added to the Hebrew original.

(2) Daniel and his friends frequently pray and fast, they show complete integrity and courage before the threat of death, and they study the law to learn right behavior. They are the ideal examples of good piety for the post-exilic period.

(3) The book contains the first explicit teaching about a divine promise that the just person will rise after death to a life of happiness with God (Dn 12:2). This teaching is echoed in the later book of 2 Maccabees and becomes a regular part of the faith of the Pharisee party in Judah at the time of Jesus.

(4) The book also projects a coming kingdom of God that will be brought about by a heavenly yet human figure, the Son of Man (chapter 7). It is not quite the same as the older idea of a messiah, an anointed king like the kings of old, which was to be found in Isaiah 7–11, Ezekiel 33–48 and Zechariah. But this Son of Man is clearly a messianic figure of salvation who will rule over Israel. Jesus himself used this term to describe his mission, and the early Church understood it to mean that Jesus was the eschatological Savior whose victory and the fulfillment of his mission would be known only after his own death and resurrectioin.

(5) Finally, Daniel reveals a new type of literary thought for Israel—especially in the four visions of chapers 7–12. Since prophets had ceased centuries earlier, apocalyptic continues the work of prophecy in a new form. It accents God as master of all events with a care and plan for the world that he reveals through special agents, such as angels, or through special visions or dreams. Unlike prophecy, however, the language is usually symbolic and often obscure, and it does not expect political changes or reform to come from human conversion but from a direct intervention in power from God on behalf of the good and upright.

More on Apocalyptic

The Greek word *apokalypsis* means "uncovering" or "revelation." To label a book as an apocalypse suggests that its chief characteristic is the revelation of some secret about the future. The word, however, covers a wide variety of books of Jewish (or Christian) origin, of which only two are part of the Bible itself: Daniel and the Revelation of John in the New Testament. There is evidence of some apocalyptic thought in Ezekiel 38–39, the famed battle between Gog of Magog and Yahweh, and in Zechariah 9–14, particularly in its vision of a paradisal age to come. The Gospel of Mark describes the end of Jerusalem in apocalyptic language in chapter 13. But the fullest examples of the apocalyptic genre are outside the Bible and are often collected among the Pseudepigrapha, Jewish religious writings that were never canonized:

(1) *The Book of Enoch.* There are several versions of this from the second century B.C. and after. The most famous is *First Enoch,* or *Ethiopian Enoch,* which tells of the coming Messiah, called the Son of Man, who foretells all the major events of the Old Testament and divides history into ten periods before a final judgment.

(2) *2 Baruch.* This is now known only in Syriac, but was originally in Hebrew or Aramaic. Jeremiah's scribe Baruch hears prophecies of everything from the time of the exile down to the coming of the Messiah, including the four kingdoms, the twelve woes, and the fourteen floods under which history is described. It was written sometime in the first century A.D.

(3) *4 Ezra.* This tells of the woes and miseries ahead for Israel until the Messiah comes as the Son of Man. There are four kingdoms and many signs of the approaching end. The book describes the last battle, a messianic kingdom of peace, the final judgment and a general resurrection of the dead. Although written late in the first century A.D., it became very popular with Christians.

(4) *The Assumption of Moses.* This claims to be the last words of Moses to Joshua and predicts the history of Israel from the conquest down to the coming of the Messiah. Part of this first century A.D. work is quoted in the Epistle of Jude, verses 9–10.

(5) *The Sibylline Oracles.* The Sybil was a famous Greek prophetess, but collections of Sibylline oracles are found among the Romans and Jews as well. The Jewish book has the pagan oracle-giver predict events of Jewish history and the coming of the Messiah. It is quite late, written perhaps in the second century A.D.

The majority of apocalyptic writings express the hopes and vision of minority groups within Judaism. We might call such groups "sects" because their ideals stood in contrast with the official Judaism upheld by the temple priests and the major teaching authorities, the Sadducees and Pharisees. The "official" view stressed living in the world according to the commands of the law of Moses, and adapting and dealing with the political powers of persecution and oppression as best one could. At times this might mean rebellion and war to achieve freedom and establish again the kingship of the

THE DEVELOPMENT OF APOCALYPTIC LITERATURE		
586–572	Ezekiel 38–39	Early vision of cosmic battle
520	Isaiah 56–66	Visionary hope for divine intervention
450's (?)	Isaiah 24–27	Cosmic images of final days
400 (?)	Zechariah 9–14	Developed images of world to come
168	Daniel	Cosmic battle, afterlife
165–100	I Enoch, Jubilees	Extensive speculation on world to come
40–1	Psalms of Solomon Assumption of Moses	Special revelations about the future from great figures of the past
50 A.D.	Mark 13	Imagery of final days of world and God's new inbreaking
66–70	Apocalypse of Moses	
70–132	Sibylline Oracles 4 Ezra Book of Revelation Apocalypse Baruch	Strong elements of secret revelations the end of the world

Davidic dynasty. In contrast, the apocalyptic believers, while they shared the hopes for an ideal Davidic state, despaired that it could be achieved against the forces of evil in the world. They were disenchanted with the power plays and compromises made by the leaders of Judaism and hoped instead for a dramatic divine intervention by God which would end the present unjust world and establish a new age, a glorious time of peace and justice for those who were faithful and upright.

Moreover, it can be seen from the nature of these books and their chief interests that they were written for a people who were suffering active persecution and needed some hope and consolation in facing the danger of death or imprisonment or loss of property. For this reason they use symbolic numbers, colors, and the like to mask their message from the persecuting powers and from those who do not share the group's beliefs. Thus for example, in Daniel 9, the angel Gabriel explains Jeremiah's "seventy years" of exile as seventy weeks of years, or four hundred and ninety years in all, roughly the time from Jeremiah to the Maccabees.

Some of the major elements of this type common to apocalyptic are:

(1) They use *famous names* from Israel's history to receive the revelations of what is to come. They are persons of real authority pitted against the claims of the present priestly leadership.

(2) The revelation is *secret* and must be kept secret until the events come to pass.

(3) The language is always highly *symbolic* and can be decoded only by the elect.

(4) It uses *prophetic prediction* to give authority to the words of revelation that are received.

(5) The real authors of these books are *anonymous* even though they often use the name of famous people of the past to lend weight to their books—figures such as Enoch, Moses, Ezra, Baruch, Isaiah, etc.

Besides these major characteristics, other elements appear regularly in one or more known apocalypses:

(1) *Pessimism* about the state of the world and human ability to change it.

(2) *Dualism* between the forces of good and evil and a final battle for world dominion.

(3) *Determinism* of a divine plan that is already preparing for the battle against evil and its final defeat.

(4) *Confidence in divine intervention* on behalf of the oppressed and the just who suffer.

(5) *Cosmic* viewpoint in which the struggle involves the whole universe.

(6) Use of *intermediary beings* such as angels and demons.

(7) An expectation that old *prophecies will be fulfilled* for the first time, or in a new way.

(8) Hope in the *resurrection of the dead* and victory of the just.

(9) Hope in a glorious *new kingdom* in heaven or on earth in which God will reign over the just while the wicked will perish.

The Value of Apocalyptic

There are already hints of an apocalyptic-type vision in some of the later prophets. Themes such as the day of the Lord as a day of total destruction, the killing of the chaos monster Leviathan, the great banquet for the just, and a glorious new paradise all play a role in Isaiah 24–27, Ezekiel 38–39, Zechariah 12–14, and Isaiah 60–62. But the key reason for apocalyptic's rise to popularity should be seen in the conflicts after the exile. Second Isaiah and those visionaries who shared his faith that God was about to act in wonderful new ways to deliver his people found in fact that the actual post-exilic community was based more on the priestly way of life proposed by

Ezekiel. In practice, Jewish practices had taken on a very narrow focus centered entirely on Judah. The visionaries did not see the Gentiles streaming to Jerusalem or a new creation taking shape around them. Once they realized that little would happen under the present system, they began to hope for a decisive new act on God's part that would match the miracle of the exodus or the glory of the original Garden of Eden. In many ways they were holding out for a God who was free to do remarkable things, and fighting against attempts to make God present only in day-to-day temple worship and ordinary events.

Some of this deep faith can still be appreciated today even though we have come for the most part to see people who make apocalyptic statements as a strange and radical fringe. Presumably, the Jewish leaders of the last centuries before Christ thought the same way about their apocalyptic fellow citizens. The following, however, are some of the lasting values basic to all apocalyptic thinking that Christians and Jews must never forget:

(1) God is *never indifferent* to his world, nor is he powerless to intervene for the sake of his name and to achieve justice.

(2) There are important moments in history when we can *expect God to act* in new ways and not in the same old ways.

(3) Belief decisively *rejects the power of evil* to control our lives and proclaims that death is not the final end for those who are faithful to Yahweh. Martyrdom will not be in vain.

(4) We must show a *strong trust in Yahweh* and reject human war and violence in favor of a pacificism. God will deliver us when he decides.

(5) The philosophy of apocalyptic writers stresses passionate devotion to the *Kingdom of God* and the urgency of being among the just rather than the wicked.

(6) Apocalyptic literature also brought the imagery of the *last judgment, heaven and hell* into Jewish and Christian thinking.

(7) Finally, it is to apocalyptic that we can attribute much of our present hope in the *resurrection of Jesus* as a source of life. The apocalypticists held the firm conviction that the just will rise to life because God is everlastingly faithful to his covenant promises.

Apocalyptic literature did not survive in Judaism and represents only a small part of the Bible, whether Old or New Testament. But it left a profound mark on the expression and perspective of both Christians and Jews, extending our horizon about the divine providence beyond the borders of our own times—and beyond the borders of death itself.

STUDY QUESTIONS

1. How did Alexander the Great and Hellenistic culture affect the Jewish way of life?
2. What is contained in the Book of Esther?
3. Identify the following: Purim, Megilloth, Nebuchadnezzar, Antiochus III, Antiochus Epiphanes, Judas Maccabeus, Hanukkah.
4. What does the Book of Judith narrate?
5. Briefly describe the Book of Ruth.
6. What is contained in the Book of Tobit?
7. What is characteristic about the Book of Baruch?
8. What are the purpose and significance of First and Second Maccabees?
9. What is distinctive about the Book of Daniel? What period of history does it cover? What is its purpose?
10. What is characteristic about apocalyptic writing? What is its significance?

Chapter 25

THE CLOSING
OF THE OLD TESTAMENT

Suggested Messianic Readings:

Psalms 2, 110
Isaiah 9, 11
Zechariah 9

Judaism at the Dawn of the Christian Era

As our study of the Old Testament comes to an end, it by no means suggests that Judaism was coming to an end. The framework of this study is determined by the historical times in which the individual books of the Old Testament were written, and both Jews and Christians recognize that this select body of literature was completed by the end of the first century B.C. Christians have often carelessly and all too narrowly assumed that the life of Jesus and the writing of the New Testament marked a break in history in which Jewish thought and culture began to wither and die because it had nothing more to say religiously. Although Christians do not rely on the authority of later Jewish writings, such as the Talmud, for determining their faith, they should be aware of the vitality of Judaism on into the centuries after the Old Testament comes to an end. Judaism was not dying in the first century; it was vigorous and thriving.

But there were many differences from the faith of the small kingdoms of Judah and Israel before the exile. In the post-exilic period, two major centers of Jewish settlement were well established outside of Palestine—one in Babylon, which continued to have major influence right into the Middle Ages, and the other in Alexandria, Egypt. Certainly this was one of the most profoundly important steps that Judaism took. When Alexander the Great captured Egypt in 332 B.C., he and his general Ptolemy built the most splendid Hellenistic city in the empire and named it after Alexander. A Jewish document of the second century B.C., the Letter of Aristeas, claims that Ptolemy brought one hundred thousand Jews from Palestine to live in the new city. Whether this is correct or not, it certainly reflects a true picture of strong Jewish presence in Alexandria. It may well have been the largest city in the ancient world, and fully one quarter of its population was Jewish, far more than lived in Jerusalem. Soon there were large Jewish colonies in Antioch, the largest city of Syria, and by the Roman era of the first century A.D. there were sizable Jewish groups in every major urban area. Some scholars estimate that eight percent of the Roman Empire was Jewish, and that only a quarter of these lived in Palestine. Acts 2:9–10 gives an impressive list of nations from which Jewish pilgrims came to visit Jerusalem for the annual feast days.

The Jews, however, faced great difficulties. Many times they did not receive full citizenship in the countries where they lived, were often confined to a special section of the city, and were regulated by special treaties and laws giving them exemptions from some pagan practices and some rights in commerce and trade. They looked to Jerusalem as their spiritual center and resisted many of the local customs and ways of their pagan neighbors because these would have made them go against the law of Moses. Naturally this made Jews unpopular with many pagan religious leaders and an easy scapegoat for political leaders who wanted someone to accuse for disasters or failures. They simply blamed the strange ways of the Jews for making the gods angry. On the other hand, the rapid spread of Christianity by apostles and missionaries was made possible by the presence of large Jewish populations throughout the Roman world. These became the seedbed of Christian community growth.

The End of Jewish Independence and the Rule of Rome

When Simon, the last of the Maccabees, died in 134 B.C., he was succeeded by his son John Hyrcanus who was in turn succeeded by his sons, Aristobulus I and Alexander Janneus (see chart of Hasmonean kings). But there was little peace in the land. Religious

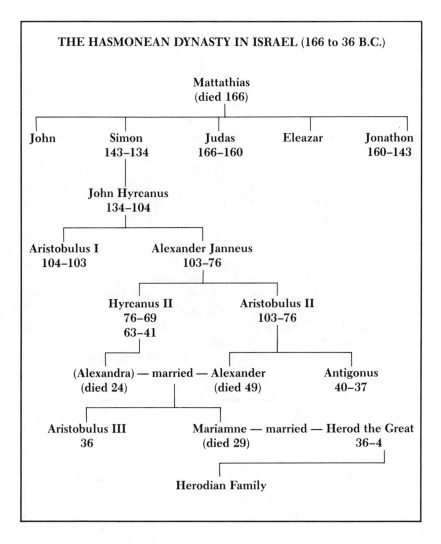

THE HASMONEAN DYNASTY IN ISRAEL (166 to 36 B.C.)

Mattathias
(died 166)

| John | Simon
143–134 | Judas
166–160 | Eleazar | Jonathon
160–143 |

John Hyrcanus
134–104

Aristobulus I
104–103

Alexander Janneus
103–76

Hyrcanus II
76–69
63–41

Aristobulus II
103–76

(Alexandra) — married — Alexander
(died 24)   (died 49)

Antigonus
40–37

Aristobulus III
36

Mariamne — married — Herod the Great
(died 29)   36–4

Herodian Family

leaders were divided between support and opposition to the Hasmonean rulers because they constantly named themselves or one of their sons to be high priests, even though they were not descendants of Aaron or the levites which the law required. Moreover, they constantly schemed against one another, brother against brother, in wars and plots that almost always involved help and interference from the Seleucid kings, the Arab rulers of Nabatea or the Roman generals to the west. Finally, in 63 B.C., the situation became stalemated when the two sons of Alexander Janneus both sought help from the Roman general Pompey in order to become king. Pompey moved into Jerusalem and, instead of supporting either, made Palestine into a Roman province subject to the governor in Syria whom he had just installed over the Seleucids.

Jewish independence was over, but for a number of years the Romans allowed Hyrcanus II, one of the two rivals, to function as high priest and have some political leadership as well. Rome itself was locked in one struggle for power after another in this period—soon Pompey was overthrown by Julius Caesar; then Caesar was assassinated in 44 B.C., and the conspirators, Cassius and Brutus, took over in the East; they were defeated by Mark Antony and his troops, and he was in turn defeated by Octavian in 31 B.C. Being now master of the entire Roman Empire, Octavian assumed the name Augustus, had himself declared emperor, and began the great period of prosperity and peace called the Pax Romana. He ruled for forty-five years (until 14 A.D.), during which time there were no internal civil wars. But during every upheaval in Rome before that, one party or another in Palestine fought to gain favor and power. Fighting and assassination were constant from 63 down to 37 B.C. In that year, Herod, the son of Antipater, the governor of Idumea, the southernmost province of Judah, managed to come out on top. Through a careful combination of plotting and making friends with Antony and Augustus, he had managed to get the Romans to name

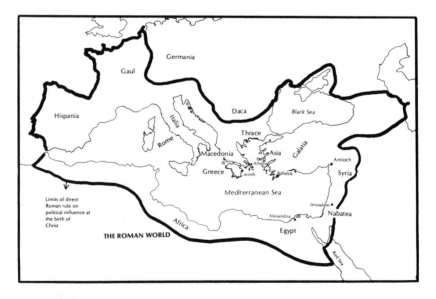

him king of Judea in 40 B.C. and proceeded to win his territory by means of a Roman army in 37 B.C.

Herod the Great (40 to 4 B.C.)

The recognition of Herod as king of Judea by the Romans put an end to the Hasmonean family and their claims. There was a new dynasty in power, and several of Herod's sons and grandsons played important roles in the political control of Palestine for the next three generations, right up to the ill-fated Jewish rebellion against Roman rule in 66 A.D. Most of his sons turned out to be poor rulers, and the Romans continually limited their power to ever smaller areas of the country. None of them ever had the energy or vision of their father. His iron control of the nation, and the vast number of cities and buildings that he constructed all over the country, have earned him the title "The Great." The one quality he lacked for this mark of achievement, however, was moral uprightness. Once he had gained power, he acted always to hold on to it, no matter what.

A period of great stability followed, although tensions were often high and violence was common. Herod ruthlessly murdered all possible rivals including most of the members of his own family and his wives; but once in solid control, he began great building projects and city renewal that made his Jewish state prosperous. He no longer even reported to the Roman legate in Syria, but had direct access to Augustus himself. Josephus, the Jewish historian, reports that Herod began his magnificent rebuilding of the temple in 20 B.C. Although he did all the major work immediately, parts were still being completed right up to 63 A.D., only seven years before the Romans destroyed it forever while putting down the Jewish revolt of 66–70. Herod died in 4 B.C., and the New Testament traditions place the birth of Jesus a year or two before his death (Mt 2:1–19; Lk 1:5).

The Religious Movements of the First Century B.C.

Judaism under the Hasmoneans and Romans developed a number of different movements or "schools" of thought. And, as in the political arena, all was not peace and harmony among them. The major parties that emerged in this period were (1) the Pharisees, (2) the Sadducees, and (3) the Essenes. Their particular viewpoints toward the faith were rooted in differences and tensions that had already begun in the Greek era of the Ptolemies when many of the upper classes had openly followed Greek ways and customs. But it came to the point of open splits among the Jews in the war for freedom under the Maccabees. Unfortunately our knowledge of the exact causes and time of origin of the three parties is limited. Most of our current understanding is derived from the following sources:

(1) The writings of Josephus, especially his *Antiquities* and *The Jewish War.*

(2) References in Philo of Alexandria, a Jewish philosopher in Egypt about the time of Christ.

(3) Mention made in the Talmud, Jewish pharisaical writings of the first to fourth centuries A.D.

(4) Hints and mentions found among the documents discovered at Qumran. These date to the first century B.C. and first century A.D. and seem to be from the Essenes.

(5) References made in the New Testament, especially the Gospels.

A. *The Pharisees*

There is no mention of a special group of especially rigorous followers of the law before the revolt of the Maccabees. But during that war, a group calling themselves *hasidim,* "the pious ones" or "devout ones," actively supported the Maccabees' cause against the Greek persecution (see 1 Mc 2:42, 7:12–25 and 2 Mc 14:6). They appear again about 140 B.C. in opposition to the claims of John Hyrcanus to be high priest. Now they are called Pharisees, the "separated ones." Hyrcanus persecuted them, as did his son Alexander Janneus, who murdered several hundred Pharisees for opposing him. But under the short rule of Alexander's widow, Salome Alexandra, from 76 to 65 B.C., they gained great power and prestige. They often opposed Herod the Great as well, but generally managed to keep as much out of political power as possible.

The chief characteristics of the Pharisees were: (1) they were not priests, but lay teachers and experts in the law; (2) they demanded strict obedience to all of the laws in the Pentateuch: 613 by their count; (3) they accepted not only the written Torah, but also an "oral law" built on the traditions and teachings of the great scribes and religious teachers since the days of Ezra; (4) they believed in doctrines not in the Pentateuch: the resurrection of the dead, reward and punishment in the life to come, angels; (5) they put a strong stress on human freedom under God's care and the ability to do good works of the law; (6) generally they also hoped for a coming "messiah" who would restore the freedom and glory of Israel.

Perhaps the most important element in Pharisaism is their belief in the "oral torah" which they called a "fence around the law." They developed a system for how each commandment in the Pentateuch must be observed, often far more demanding than the law itself. By keeping these strict interpretations, the believer would be protected from breaking one of God's commands by mistake or oversight. This outlook could create an attitude of pride and arrogance against others who did not keep all the laws. The Pharisees themselves looked down on the "people of the land," the farmers and lower classes who did not read and study and keep their laws. This led to the criticisms that Jesus levels in the New Testament against some Pharisaic positions. But at the same time, the Pharisees gave Judaism the means to adapt itself to changing times and new ways of fulfilling the law, and ultimately it was Pharisaism that survived the loss of Jewish freedom in Palestine and made possible the continuity of Israel's faith for the ages to come.

It was through the Pharisees and their love of learning and study of the Bible that the enduring system of synagogues in every local community arose. It was also through them that the Old Testament canon was completed and preserved.

B. *Sadducees*

The Pharisees were the liberals in Jewish life. They made room for lay people in the highest levels of religious life and were open to changing how the law should be interpreted, and yet strongly opposed any pagan influences. The Sadducees, on the other hand, represented almost entirely the priestly personnel and the wealthy families of Judah. The name "Sadducee" comes from the high priest under King David, Zadok, and stresses their legitimate claims to the priestly offices. This was no mass movement, but it contained Judah's most influential and powerful leadership, so that it played a major role in all national decisions. The Sadducees claimed to preserve the old traditions against innovations of the Pharisees, yet it was really among this group that the greatest deviations from older Jewish ways of thinking took place. It was they who embraced the Greek ways of dressing and speaking; it was they who meekly accepted the attempts of the Hasmoneans to make themselves the high priests, even though this would seem to be exactly counter to their own rights as priests. But for the sake of power, they usually went along with the kings and their policies.

On the more positive side, the Sadducees were primarily concerned for the traditions that protected the central role of the temple and its sacrifices and cult. It was for this reason that they were suspicious of the Pharisees and their "lay theology" that did not center itself on the temple ritual, and it was for the sake of the temple that they generally accepted Roman rule and sought to keep peace rather than fight it. Religiously, they insisted that only the Pentateuch, which stemmed from Moses, was binding law. All the rest, including the prophets, was of lesser value. Because of this limited stand, they also denied angels, the resurrection of the dead, and any afterlife with reward and punishment, since these were not affirmed in the Torah. They formed an important group in the Sanhedrin, the council of Jewish leaders that decided religious matters during the Roman period. But when the Jewish revolt of 66 A.D. brought total destruction on Jerusalem, most of the Sadducees finally sided against Rome and were killed in the attack on the city or executed later. They never appear again after this period.

C. *Essenes*

We know even less about the Essenes. The name means "pious ones," just like the *hasidim* of the Maccabees' day. One reference in the Roman historian Pliny the Elder lists them living at the northern end of the Dead Sea below Jericho. Josephus treats them briefly and also mentions their presence on the shore of the Dead Sea. He adds that they lived celibate lives there. This location could only refer to the ruins of Qumran which have been known since ancient times, but were not explored until 1947 after the discovery of a great number of ancient manuscripts in the caves surrounding the site. These scrolls are treated briefly in the next section. They include many biblical texts in Hebrew, making them the oldest copies known anywhere. But they also include a good number of commentaries on the prophets in Aramaic, and several special documents which belong to the Essene community's way of life. From these we can get some picture of their particular beliefs, which include: (1) community life with shared possessions; (2) loyalty to the teachings of the "Righteous Teacher," their founder who opposed the attempts of the "Wicked Priest" to allow as high priest those who were not qualified; (3) frequent use of water in rites for cleansing and admission to the group; (4) living of celibacy because the

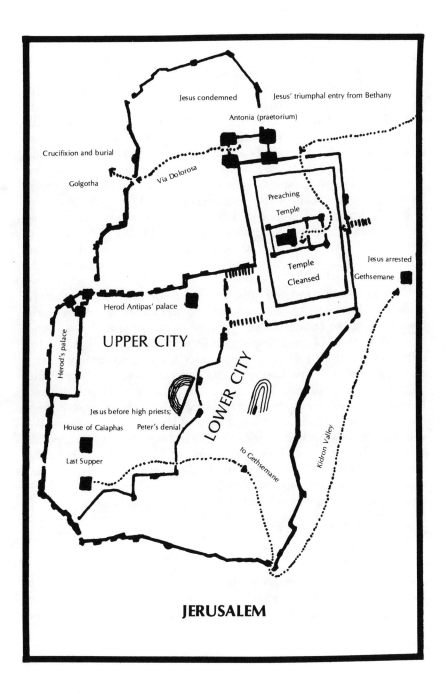

Jesus condemned

Jesus' triumphal entry from Bethany

Antonia (praetorium)

Crucifixion and burial

Golgotha

Via Dolorosa

Preaching

Temple

Temple

Cleansed

Jesus arrested

Gethsemane

Herod Antipas' palace

Herod's palace

UPPER CITY

LOWER CITY

Jesus before high priests;

House of Caiaphas

Peter's denial

Last Supper

to Gethsemane

Kidron Valley

JERUSALEM

final times are present; (5) the coming of two messiahs: the "Messiahs of Aaron and Israel," one a political ruler and the other a priest.

How did the Essenes originate? Like the Pharisees, they probably were once part of the *hasidim* movement. They broke with the Sadducees over the question of the Hasmoneans being high priests and with the Pharisees over the question of whether it was still legitimate to worship at the temple as a result of such sacrilege. This means that the "Righteous Teacher" may have lived as early as the time of Jonathan Maccabee (about 145 B.C.) or any of his successors. The site of Qumran shows evidence of the community's presence there by the last half of the second century B.C. Coins from the reign of John Hyrcanus (134–104 B.C.) were found among the ruins, and so a date (perhaps late) in his period would be a good guess for the origins of this desert monastery. The Essenes' separation from the Pharisees and Sadducees may have taken place some years earlier.

We would like to know much more about the Essenes than we presently do. Some of their practices resemble those of the early Jewish Christian communities reported in the Acts of the Apostles and the Letters of Paul. Examples include their use of water for initiation and purification, and of overseers for the community who act much as did the first bishops (the *episkopoi*) in St. Paul's churches. Many authors have also noted the similarities between Essene rigorism and the life and message of John the Baptist. But for now such connections are only clues to what might have been. We will have to wait until further finds give us more information on this group. However, the sudden appearance of the Essenes back on the stage of history in 1947 has warned all scholars who write on the Judaism of the first century that it was much more complex and diverse than it is presented in the New Testament.

The Dead Sea Scrolls

The scrolls and documents found in the caves around Qumran have become one of the most important archaeological discoveries of the twentieth century. A partial list of these scrolls gives us some idea of their interests:

(A)   *Biblical Texts*

Fragment pieces of all the books of the Old Testament except the Book of Esther have been found. The most popular were Deuteronomy, Isaiah and the Psalms. Only one is complete: the Isaiah scroll from Cave 1.

(B) *Biblical Commentaries*

Another large group of texts turned out to be commentaries on biblical books, especially on the prophets, although fragments on Genesis, 2 Samuel and Psalms 37 and 68 have also turned up. The largest surviving portion is on the Book of Habakkuk.

(C) *Apocrypha and Pseudepigrapha*

Small portions of the Book of Tobit, known up until now only in the Greek Septuagint, were found in both Hebrew and Aramaic. Fragments of non-biblical books were also present: First Enoch, The Book of Jubilees, the Testament of the Twelve Patriarchs, and some stories about Daniel that do not appear in the biblical text.

(D) *Essene Community Documents*

Several documents that were written especially for the Essenes and reflect their particular theological positions were among the other more generally known biblical books. Some of the more important of these are:

The Community Rule, also called the *Manual of Discipline;*

The *War Scroll* (sometimes titled "The War of the Sons of Light and the Sons of Darkness");

The *Thanksgiving Scroll* (a collection of hymns and psalms);

The *Zadokite Document* or *Damascus Document* (contains rules and reflections on the history of the group);

The *Genesis Apocryphon* (popular legends on the Noah and Abraham stories);

The *Temple Scroll* (legal observations and rules often quite different from those in Leviticus);

The *Copper Scroll* (claims to show where a treasure was hidden from invaders, but *whose* treasure is not clear; at first it was thought the temple wealth was meant).

Other Jewish Literature Outside the Bible

The term "apocrypha" is Greek for "hidden" or "secret" works. It may have been applied to certain Jewish religious writings that are not in the Bible because of statements like that of 4 Ezra

14:44–46 that claims Ezra did not reveal all that he was supposed to have dictated to his scribes:

> During forty days, ninety-four books were copied down. And at the end of the forty days, the Most High said to me, "Make public the first twenty-four books that you wrote, and both the worthy and unworthy are to read them; but keep the seventy that were dictated last in order to give them to your wise only."

Since many of the extra-biblical books were written for special groups and unorthodox sects, they were gradually excluded from consideration as inspired books, and sometimes even thought of as dangerous and heretical. Thus another possible origin of the term "apocrypha" comes from the rejection of such writings which were "hidden" from public reading or acceptance by the synagogues and churches. When the reformers of the sixteenth century began calling the deuterocanonical books of the Catholic Bibles "apocryphal" they invented the term "pseudepigrapha" ("false writings") for these books which had never been part of any canon of Scripture.

The last centuries before Christ and the first century after him produced large numbers of Jewish religious writings. Besides the apocalyptic works listed in the last chapter and the Qumran writings above, some of the more important books of this period include:

The *Book of Jubilees* (third or second century B.C.). It lists Priestly ideals based on Genesis and Exodus.

The *Testament of the Twelve Patriarchs* (about 100 B.C.). It contains farewell speeches of the twelve sons of Jacob who sound like members of the Qumran sect.

Psalms of Solomon (late first century B.C.). Eighteen psalms are included, all of which resemble the ethical practices of Qumran and the Essenes.

Letter of Aristeas (second century B.C.). This was written to explain the origin of the Septuagint as divinely inspired and reflects the Hellenistic Judaism of Alexandria.

3rd Maccabees (first century B.C.). This is a collection of legends from the Hellenistic period under the Ptolemy kings of Egypt (third century B.C.?).

4th Maccabees (first century A.D.). The stories collected here seem to be philosophical reflections on the pious legends found in 2 Maccabees.

Although not technically religious writers, two other important authors should be included in any survey of significant Jewish thought of the period: Philo of Alexandria and Josephus.

Philo of Alexandria (born about 25 B.C., died about 50 A.D.) left a library of philosophical-theological works on all aspects of Jewish life and law treated from a thoroughly Hellenistic Greek point of view. To achieve his explanation of Jewish law as completely reasonable to philosophy, Philo uses allegory freely.

Josephus (37 A.D. to about 100) was the first commander of Jewish rebels against Rome in Galilee in 66 A.D. When his forces faced defeaat, he turned himself over to the Romans and supported them. With his new Roman loyalty he wrote several important books that have increased our knowledge of Judaism of the post-exilic and first century period, including the *Antiquities of the Jews, The Jewish War* (66–70 A.D.), *Against Apion* (refuting anti-Jewish writer), and his own *Life*.

The Talmud

Basically the Talmud is a collection of post-biblical laws and teachings that originated with the rabbis who worked in either Babylon or Palestine in the first four Christian centuries. It consists of two types of material, *halakah* (legal material) and *haggadah* (narrative or story material) which is divided up under six major subject areas or "orders" that reflect the chief concerns of the Pentateuchal laws: (1) Agriculture ("Seeds"); (2) Festivals; (3) Women; (4) Damages and Injuries; (5) Holy Things; (6) Purity ("Clean Things").

The earliest part of the Talmud is the Mishnah, a collection of rules put together by Rabbi Judah the Prince about the year 200 A.D. It includes a few pre-Christian period references, but most of the opinions come from 1–200 A.D. A later addition of the opinions of rabbis from 200–500 A.D. is called the Gemara. Together they make up sixty-three treatises of the full Talmud—far longer than the Bible itself.

A discussion of the Talmud does not properly belong in a book on the Old Testament. But its origins lie rooted in a particular post-exilic development of Jewish legal interpretation that was, according to Jewish tradition, begun by Ezra himself. Much of this tradition is known only by legend and so is not very reliable. It

THE BABYLONIAN TALMUD

Made up of the **Mishnah** (systematic legal opinions about the laws of the Pentateuch) and the **Gemara** (supplementary opinions after 200 A.D.). The Talmud is arranged in 63 **Tractates** in 6 major *Orders:*

Seder ZERA'IM ("Seeds")

Berakoth ("Blessings")

Pe'ah ("Corner")
Lev 19, 23; Deut 24

Demai ("Doubtful cases")

Kilayim ("Two mixtures")
Lev 19; Deut 22

Sheb'ith ("Sabbath year")
Exod 23; Lev 25

Terumoth ("Wave Offering")
Num 18; Deut 18

ma'aseroth ("Tithes")
Num 18

Ma'aser sheni ("2nd Tithe")
Deut 14

Hallah ("Cakes")
Num 15

'Orlah ("Tree operations")
Lev 19

Bikkurim ("First Fruits")
Exod 23; Deut 26

Seder MO'ED ("Feasts")

Shabbath (Sabbath)
Exod 20, 23: Deut 5

Erubin (Mixtures)

Pesahim (Passovers)
Exod 12, 13; Num 28

Sheqalim (Shekels)
Exod 30

Yoma (Atonement Day)
Lev 16, 23

Sukkoth (Booths)
Lev 23; Num 29

Besah (Egg)

Rosh hashana (New Year)
Num 10, 28

Taanith (Fasts)

Megillah (Purim scroll)

Moeq qaton (Small feast)

Hagigah (Festivals)
Deut 16

Seder NASHIM ("Women")

Yebamoth (Sister-in-law)

Kethuboth (Wedding deal)

Nedarim (vows)
Num 30

Nazir (Nazirites)
Num 6

Gittin (Documents)
Deut 24

Sotah (Infidelity)
Num 5

Qiddushin (Sacred things)

Seder NEZIQIN ("Damages")

Baba qamma (Civil law)

Baba mesi (property)

Baba bathra (real estate)

Sanhedrin (Criminal law)

Makkoth (punishments)
Deut 25

Shebuoth (oaths)
Lev 5

Ediyyoth (testimony)

Abodah zera' (idolatry)

Pirqe Aboth (Father's Sayings)

Horayoth (Decisions)
Lev 4

Seder QODASHIM ("Holy Things")

Zebahim (Sacrifices)

Menohoth (Meat offering)
Lev 2, 6, 14

Hullin (Slaughtering)

Bekoroth (First born)
Exod 13; Lev 27

Arakin (Values)
Lev 25

Temurah (Exchange)
Lev 27

Keritoth (Ouster)

Me'ilah (Trespass)
Lev 5; Num 5

Tamid (Daily sacrifice)
Exod 29; Num 28

Middoth (measures)

Qinnim (Dove offering)
Lev 1, 5, 12

Seder TOHOROTH ("Purifications")

Kelim (Vessels)
Lev 11; Num 19

Ohaloth (Dead bodies)
Num 19

Nega'im (Diseases)
Lev 13, 14

Parah (Red Heifer)
Num 19

Teharoth (Impurities)

Miqwoth (Ritual baths)
Lev 14, 15; Num 31

Niddah (Female impurity)
Lev 15

Makshirin (Defilements)
Lev II

Zabim (Discharges)
Lev 15

Tebul Yom (Ritual bath)
Lev 15, 22

Yadayim (Hands)

Uqsin (Stems)

implies an unbroken line of rabbis, i.e., teachers learned in the law, who passed down official, or at least authoritative, decisions on the observance of the law going back to the time of Ezra. According to the oldest part of the Mishnah, the Pirke Aboth, the law was handed on as follows:

> Moses received Torah from Sinai and delivered it to Joshua, and Joshua to the elders, and the elders to the prophets, and the prophets to the men of the great synagogue. These (last) said three things: be deliberate in judging, and raise up many disciples, and make a fence for the Torah.

Ezra was the supposed founder of the Great Synagogue, and the last known member of it was Simeon the Just who lived about 270 B.C. At that time, a new system developed around the Sanhedrin, a kind of Supreme Court of religion. Its leaders were remembered in pairs—although it is not clear whether they represented a liberal versus conservative party or were merely the president and vice-president of the Sanhedrin. They passed on the "tradition." The last of these pairs were Hillel and Shammai, each of whom had a large following (or Academy). They lived about the time of Jesus. The Sanhedrin died in the revolt against Rome in 66–70 A.D., and its place was taken by a new academy founded by Rabbi Johanan ben Zakkai at Jamnia on the Palestine coast after Jerusalem was destroyed in 70 A.D. It was out of the debates of this Beth Din ("House of Judgment") that the Talmud was collected.

What is certain is that the Talmud reflects the Pharisees' view of Judaism, especially with its stress on the oral traditions of the fathers. The views of the Sadducees and Essenes were denied entrance into Judaism as we know it today.

Hope for a Messiah

At the time of Jesus, one of the strongest movements in Judaism was hope for a coming "Messiah." Evidence comes from the historian Josephus, the Talmud of the rabbis and, of course, the New Testament. Surprisingly, there is very little evidence for a messiah in the Old Testament itself, but part of the reason for that is the small number of books from the last three centuries B.C. This means that we can trace the development of ideas about a messiah in the

Hebrew Scriptures but cannot show that they actually led to any of the movements in the first century.

Literally, a "messiah" is one "anointed" (with oil). Such anointing was done for the high priest when he took office (Ex 29:7), and for the king when he was crowned (1 Kgs 1:39). It signified the consecrated status of the person before God that set him off from ordinary people. There is evidence that the Qumran community expected two messiahs, one a priest and one a king, to correspond to the two traditional anointed figures. Usually, however, "messiah" is reserved for an expected future king who will deliver the people from their present oppression or misfortune and restore the glory of David's kingdom. It would be a mistake to believe that Israel possessed a single, unified hope for such a savior-king. Many different concepts floated about and many of them did not even involve hopes for a new kingdom under a king. The idea of the "Son of Man," found in Daniel 7 and the Book of Enoch, involved a heavenly being who would bring about God's rule from heaven. Second Isaiah pictured the whole people Israel in the role of messiah and king, and described them as the "suffering servant in glory" (Is 53). Deuteronomy and the Deuteronomic History looked forward to a new Moses who would be a covenant mediator between the people and God.

But the most common theme of messiah in the Bible centers on the role of King David. It is this line that the New Testament accents about Jesus in discussions with the Jews, although the Gospels also identify Jesus as the coming Son of Man, and even as a new Elijah who was expected before God brought about his final judgment (see Mal 4:5–6). The concept of a royal messiah in the line of David underwent several stages of development in the Bible.

The first stage is found in the oracle of Nathan to David in 2 Samuel 7. The parallel account is found in 1 Chronicles 17, and is reflected in Psalms 89 and 132. Tradition remembers that God made a special covenant with David promising a dynasty ("house") that would be kept in power forever. The form of this promise was typical of the "royal grants" of ancient kings to their favorite servants in gratitude for work well done. God rewards David for his faithfulness in setting up the kingdom with a gift that has no strings attached. Only later does the Deuteronomic History add passages in 2 Samuel 7 and 1 Kings 9 and 11 that make the promise of a dynasty conditioned on obedience to the Sinai covenant.

The second stage is represented in the prophets up to the time of the exile. Isaiah in particular gives oracles that promise a better king will come through God's power. In chapters 7–9 and 11, he describes in glowing terms the greatness and majesty of this future messiah as Emmanuel (= "God with us"). This same shift from stage one's praise of the present Davidic king to the hope for a future and more obedient king can be seen in Micah 5:2–5, Jeremiah 23:2–6, and Ezekiel 34:23–24. The ideal king will have the spirit of God with him and his reign will be one of universal peace and prosperity.

The third stage takes place after the exile when the actual Davidic kings no longer exist. At first Haggai and Zechariah hold out hope for a descendant of the royal family, the local governor Zerubbabel, to be king. But this does not happen, and the prophets begin thinking toward some far-away future moment. Zechariah dreams of such a day: "Rejoice greatly, O daughter Zion; shout out, daughter Jerusalem. Behold, your king comes to you victorious and bringing salvation, meek and seated on a donkey" (Zec 9:9). As the years go by and Israel is ruled by one foreign power after another, many began to lose hope that the house of David could be restored. They turned instead to hope for a direct intervention of God himself to rule the world. This is reflected in the eschatological thinking of apocalyptic. Others took the pragmatic line that the promise was maintained by priestly service at the temple and the practice of the law.

Messianic hope can generally be distinguished from apocalyptic views because it expected the messiah-king to be an actual historical man who would restore some of the former glory and power and independence to Israel. Although not held by all groups, such messianic expectations were powerful enough to rouse several rebellions against the Romans in the time of the early Church (see Acts 5:36–37 for a list) and to lead to the total destruction of Jerusalem and Judah in the Great Jewish War of 66–70 A.D. Even Jesus was probably put to death on the charge he was a rebel inciting war against Rome when he claimed to be the Messiah (Mt 27:11; Lk 23:1–5).

The disciples of Jesus recognized him as the Messiah and as the Son of Man combined because they understood his kingship to be of a different kind altogether from political rule over Israel. Jesus' authority came from God from beyond the present world order (Son of Man), but demanded the total covenant loyalty and obedience to God that the Davidic king embodied on earth (Messiah). They also

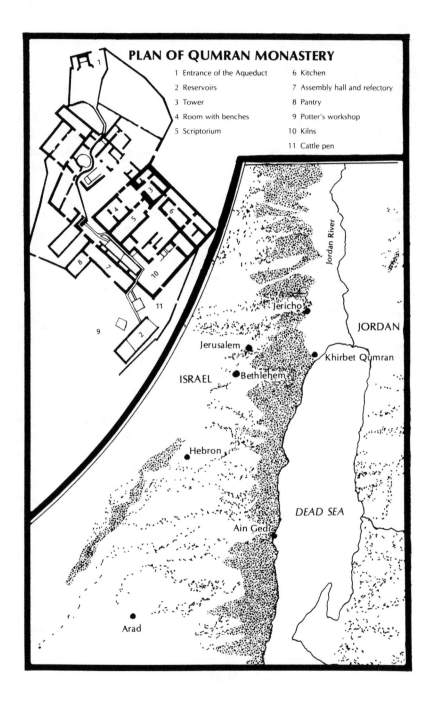

PLAN OF QUMRAN MONASTERY

1 Entrance of the Aqueduct   6 Kitchen
2 Reservoirs   7 Assembly hall and refectory
3 Tower   8 Pantry
4 Room with benches   9 Potter's workshop
5 Scriptorium   10 Kilns
   11 Cattle pen

Jordan River

Jericho

JORDAN

Jerusalem

Khirbet Qumran

ISRAEL   Bethlehem

Hebron

DEAD SEA

Ain Gedi

Arad

saw in Jesus both the prophet and the suffering servant of Isaiah. There is no other example of such claims anywhere in Jewish history.

Creating a Canon of Scripture

Chapter 1 discussed the problem of how many books make up the official canon of Scripture. In general, Christians accepted the decisions of Jewish leaders about which books belong to the Old Testament, but they added the seven books in Greek from the Septuagint. However, two questions still must be answered: (1) Why these books and not others? (2) What value has the Old Testament canon for Christians?

To the first question, the rabbis offered several reasons that are now found in various books of the Talmud. The most common was that a book was canonical only if written *before* the time of Ezra about 450 B.C. and thus before the promulgation of the Pentateuch as binding. Although we know that several books now included in the Hebrew Bible were in fact written after that time, they were thought to be earlier (e.g., Ecclesiastes claimed to be by Solomon). Other books that seemed to be early were rejected on the basis of their contents (thus the Song of Songs with its sexual imagery had such a hard time entering the canon). Josephus, the Jewish historian, defends the care that went into choosing the canon in his book, *Against Apion* (I:37–41):

> We do not possess myriads of inconsistent books, conflicting with each other. Our books, those which are justly accredited, are but *two and twenty*, and contain the record of all time.

Josephus goes on to divide the selected books into three categories: (1) the five books of Moses with law and the history of humanity down to Sinai; (2) the thirteen books of prophets which detail the history of their times; (3) the four books containing hymns to God and precepts for human life. He goes on to point out that the history from the time of the exile until his own day (first century A.D.) had also been written down but was not deemed sacred because of the failure of the line of prophets after the exile. Thus for Josephus the basic requirement of a book to be in the canon was that it revealed the prophetic word in history. To put it another way, Josephus

believed that the canon of Scripture was a "history of salvation" for
Israel, and its authority came from the inspired words of the prophets who had made known the divine actions in Israel's past. Without
prophets after the time of Ezra, no new books could be declared
sacred in the same sense.

The rabbis whose writings are contained in the Talmud almost
always combine the same two elements of *past history* and *prophetic message* in their description of the canon as did Josephus. But it
could not contain just any history, nor every prophetic word. The
key to why the Old Testament was a *sacred* body of literature was
inspiration. Thus all agreed that no book could be included in the
canon unless it had been written while the prophets still spoke
inspired words that interpreted the meaning of Israel's history. For
this reason, the *Baba Bathra,* one of the books in the Talmud
(usually referred to as one of the *tractates*), assigns every book in the
canon to one of the great leaders of the past, including Joshua,
Hezekiah, David and the "Men of the Great Assembly" (the *sanhedrin* of leaders founded by Ezra). Each could be called a prophet in
some way because each shared the inspired call of God.

The emphasis on the prophetic spirit was very strong in the
Jewish concept of Scripture, and they were very much aware and
pained that God had allowed prophecy to die out in Israel (see Mal
3:23–24; 1 Mc 4:46; 9:27; 14:41). But at the same time they maintained a strong sense of hope that God would again send prophets,
and they judged the central value of the inspired books of the Bible
to be the prophetic message they carried for the future. This point is
well illustrated by a passage in the same *Baba Bathra* (14b) that
discusses why the Hebrew order of the major prophets in the first
century placed the Book of Isaiah after Jeremiah and Ezekiel in the
canon even though he had clearly lived long before either of them:

> Isaiah was prior to Jeremiah and Ezekiel. Then why should
> not Isaiah be placed first? Because the Book of Kings ends
> with destruction, and Jeremiah speaks throughout of de-
> struction, and Ezekiel commences with destruction but
> ends with consolation, and Isaiah is full of consolation.

It was important in this early way of thinking that the message of
Scripture move from judgment and disaster to hope for the future.
Our Bibles do not follow this order because we have taken over the
coldly logical arrangement of the Greeks in the Septuagint who
tried to establish the proper historical sequence. Yet even the

Greeks were sensitive to the theological importance of hope for the future in their arrangement of the Old Testament. They achieved it by moving the whole collection of prophets to a place after the psalms and writings so that Scripture would end with the words of the prophets for the future. And it is this order that our Bibles follow to the present day.

From a Christian perspective, St. Paul captures the same insight on hope when he writes, "Whatever was written in the past was written for our instruction, so that by faithfulness and the encouragement of the Scriptures, we might have hope" (Rom 15:4).

The Value of the Old Testament for Christians

In coming to the end of a study of the Old Testament, Christian readers will naturally ask what relation God's revelation to Israel has for those who believe in Jesus Christ. The Catholic bishops of the Second Vatican Council echoed the tradition of twenty centuries of Christian belief when they said in the *Constitution on Divine Revelation:*

> The principal purpose to which the plan of the old covenant was directed was to prepare for the coming of Christ, the Redeemer of all and of the messianic kingdom, to announce this coming by prophecy (see Lk 24:44; Jn 5:39; 1 Pet 1:10), and to indicate its meaning through various types (see 1 Cor 10:12) (n. 15).

> For, though Christ established the new covenant in his blood, still the books of the Old Testament with all their parts, caught up into the proclamation of the Gospel, acquire and show forth their full meaning in the New Testament (see Mt 5:17; Lk 24:27; Rom 16:24–25; 2 Cor 14:16) and in turn shed light on it and explain it (n. 16).

These statements emphasize the Old Testament as *prophetic prediction* of Christ and as the bearer of a promise which is not complete until Jesus. They reflect the language of the New Testament itself. The first disciples and Christian writers were as strongly affected by the hope that prophecy would live again as were the Jewish rabbis discussed in the last section. Christians searched the Old Testament for passages that would throw light on the events of

Jesus' life, death and resurrection. Matthew's Gospel is a case in point. It is filled with quotations from the Old Testament to explain each major step in Jesus' life. Not every use of the Scriptures by Matthew can be considered an accurate interpretation of the original text. Matthew 2:15 quotes Hosea 11:1, "Out of Egypt I have called my son," which refers to the exodus event of Israel as a whole, but Matthew applies it to the story of Joseph's flight to Egypt with Mary and Jesus. Certainly Hosea never had such an idea in mind.

The Old Testament as *promise* and the New Testament as *fulfillment* was the dominant means of interpreting the Old Testament in the New Testament writings, in the Fathers of the Church and in the Middle Ages. This view is rooted in the fact that Jesus and his first followers were all Jews who naturally looked to the Bible for guidance in understanding God's plans for the world. Even Paul and the Church Fathers who spoke to non-Jewish peoples cited the Old Testament far more often than they did the Gospels, in order to explain who Christ was and what he had done. They had the conviction that God had always acted with a single unified plan for the world, and that the coming of Christ would be clearly visible in the pattern of divine revelation presented in the Hebrew Scriptures. If followed strictly, however, the *promise-fulfillment* relationship of the two Testaments would rob the Old Testament of any meaning in its own right as a history of God's actions for Israel as the chosen people. For this reason, few biblical teachers today favor this approach.

Other attempts to explain the relationship have been tried. Rudolf Bultmann basically saw *discontinuity* as the chief note. God had indeed given the promise and law to Israel in order to prepare for the coming of Christ. But Jesus showed that this was inadequate and instead revealed a new way of grace that replaced the law. Thus the Old Testament served mainly to show the need for Christ.

Gerhard von Rad and others have stressed *typology* as a means of continuity. They wish to avoid a strict promise and fulfillment connection, and instead speak of real events and real revelations in the Old Testament which serve as models by which to understand later historical realities and revelation in the New Testament. Thus, for example, the exodus from Egypt is a gift of free deliverance from evil and the formation of a new people in covenant with Yahweh. By understanding this truth, the Christian can understand the meaning of Christ's redeeming death and the formation of the Christian community as a new covenant. The key to the typology approach is that there is an historical continuity between Israel and the Church, and everything that God has revealed in history has its own value; but beyond that, earlier events of faith help us to understand later events more deeply.

Still another means of connecting the two Testaments is to see both as proclamation of faith in Yahweh the God of Israel who is also the Father proclaimed by Jesus. God is one, and both Jews and Christians share humble obedience and worship of the same God. Especially for Christians, then, the Old Testament properly becomes a necessary part of our own faith heritage in the lifelong search to know God better.

Themes of Continuity between the New and Old Testaments

Certainly faith in the basic revelation of the Old Testament must form the basis for New Testament claims that the same God spoke anew in his Son Jesus (Heb 1:1). Some of the most important themes that carry on the continuity between Israel and the Christian community can be listed briefly:

(1) *Monotheism.* The Christian concept of God as a compassionate Father is rooted in the biblical proclamation of Yahweh as the Holy One who offered himself in personal encounter and relationship with Israel and whose love endures forever despite human failings (cf. Ps 136).

(2) *Covenant.* The very name "New Testament" declares the Christian conviction that God's covenant must endure through all ages and can take new forms that will faithfully fulfill the heart of the first covenant's ideal of union with Yahweh. In this the Christians look especially to the new covenant passages of Jeremiah 31 and Ezekiel 36.

(3) *The Word of God.* We have seen above how Judaism considered the canon to be primarily God's sacred word. Following the same way of thinking, Christians declared Jesus to be the living word of God. John's Gospel frames the entire message of Jesus within its prologue on the Word (Jn 1).

(4) *The Spirit of God.* In the Old Testament, the *spirit* is never personal, but represents the *power* of God *acting*. The prophets, above all, can declare the spirit of God brings forth their oracles (see Ezekiel 37 as an example). Later prophecy looked forward to a time in which God's spirit would create a new age of fidelity and peace

(Is 42:1; Mic 3:8; Jl 2:18–3:21; Ez 39:29). Christians understood that all the lines of Old Testament hope came together in the outpouring of the Spirit in a personal manner through Jesus and in the new age of the Church.

(5) *The Kingdom of God.* Psalms 47, 93, 96 and 98 proclaim that Yahweh is king over the universe. He manifests his rule in the order of creation, in the power of judgment, and in the gift of freedom and restoration. Often these are very concretely connected with the blessing of Israel in the land of Palestine and the prosperous rule of the kings of Israel and Judah. The preaching of Jesus in the Gospels draws heavily on the Old Testament ideals of the Kingdom to help people understand the Father's claims on their lives.

(6) *Universal Salvation.* The love of God for the Gentiles does not find much room in the Old Testament message until the time of the exile. Second Isaiah's servant songs (Is 42, 49, 50, 53), the parable of Jonah, and the vision of Second Zechariah (Zech 9) begin to wrestle with this question, as does the beautiful poem on creation in Genesis 1. Jesus and the Christians make universal salvation the center of their new proclamation built upon the very nature of the merciful Creator confessed in the Old Testament.

(7) *The Suffering Servant.* In order to understand the positive value of why Jesus had to die for human salvation, Christians looked to the "suffering servant" texts of Isaiah 42:1–4, 50:4–9, and 52:13–53:12, and to the "confessions" of Jeremiah (chapters 12, 15, 17, 18, 20). The Christians went beyond any Jewish understanding of these texts to connect suffering with the very mission of the Messiah (see Jn 10:18; Acts 3:13, 26; 8:26–28). However, the idea was not entirely new—one non-biblical text, the *Testament of Benjamin,* spoke of a coming messiah from Ephraim and Joseph who would die for the godless.

Respecting the Old Testament Message

In some ways Christians are guilty of seeing too much connection between the Old and New Testaments. By seeing the Old Testament as primarily foreshadowing and preparing for Christ, mainly through prediction, they have often left little room for appreciating Israel's experiences of divine action as part of their own search to know God. Studying the wars of Joshua or the songs in honor of God's wrath in Nahum or Zephaniah may not have much to do with our idea of Jesus' message, but they will help us see how people three thousand years ago tried to understand God in their world. Even now, at the Passover seder meal, when Jews recite the story of the exodus, the youngest child asks in the name of all what these events mean for *today*. Christians must learn to ask that also.

Christians, faithful to their beliefs, must proclaim that Christ is the center and fulfillment of the Old Testament message and the highest expression of God's self-revelation for those who have the faith to see it; but they must not believe that God has rejected what he had earlier revealed, or withdrawn his covenant with Israel. In God's designs there is a mysterious purpose why he does not choose to have the whole world know Christ. Perhaps it is for the same reasons that in the days of Israel's monarchy Yahweh's people also remained only a small island of faith in one God amidst a sea of pagan polytheism. St. Paul struggled in his Letter to the Romans to express his conviction that God had a purpose in letting the covenant with Israel continue to the end of the world despite the existence of a new covenant with Christians (see Rom 9–11). It is our proper stance today to respect Jewish faith as it makes the revelation of the Old Testament alive in the twentieth century. We need to learn all that the word "covenant" implies before we can speak of a "new" covenant. If Christ is proclaimed as the fullness of Israel's faith, then God help us if there is no Israel to show us what that means.

The Old Testament is a great treasure chest in which a wealth of truth about God lies waiting for us to discover it. No Christian can fully understand the New Testament revelation of God if he or she has not seen a glimpse of that wealth. It is wonderfully expressed by the saying of Jesus, who asked his disciples if they understood his teaching about the Kingdom of God. When they answered "yes," he summed up the ideal disciple in the words, "Every scribe who has been trained for the Kingdom of heaven is like a homeowner who brings out of his storeroom both the new and the old" (Mt 13:52).

STUDY QUESTIONS

1. Briefly describe Judaism at the time immediately prior to the dawn of Christianity.
2. Identify the following: *Letter of Aristeas,* Pax Romana, Herod the Great, Pharisees, Sadducees, Essenes, Philo of Alexandria, Josephus.

3. What was found at Qumran?
4. Describe some of the extra-biblical books.
5. What is the Talmud?
6. Did Judaism have a singular and unified view of a Messiah? Explain.
7. What is the value of the Old Testament for Christians?
8. What are some themes of continuity between the New and Old Testaments?

Chapter 26

THEMES OF
OLD TESTAMENT THEOLOGY

Discovering the Central Focus of the Bible

The final chapter of an Old Testament Introduction has the task of pulling together many of the themes studied in the individual books of the Bible. The Old Testament is such a rich book, written over many centuries by many different authors, and containing such a wide variety of Israel's religious traditions, that readers often have difficulty finding any threads *to unify* it. The same reaction may have struck us as we read about the early books of the Pentateuch and then turned to the prophets or wisdom sections. In order to appreciate the whole Bible it is very important for us to be able to discover some unifying themes which make this a single Testament of faith *and* which enable us at the same time to treasure its many different voices expressing the breadth and beauty of the human experience of God over the ages.

The first question biblical theologians ask of the Old Testament is whether there is one *viewpoint* that characterizes all the books. Some have said that its central theme is *historical*—that is, the Bible tells the factual story of God's interventions into human history on behalf of the Israelites. This would not be ordinary history, but a special "salvation history" which concentrated attention on moments when God revealed himself in certain *events* or in the giving of divine words for human guidance through Moses or the prophets. Other scholars suggest that the major thrust is that of a "proclamation" or "confession" of God. It is Israel celebrating its relationship with God. This view especially takes account of how much of the Old Testament is not *historical* in nature, but rather *praise* and *questioning*—for example, the Book of Psalms or Job or Ecclesiastes.

543

If it is "confession," then we must ask a further question, "Does the Old Testament have a *single* central theme that is proclaimed?" Some possible ones might be God's *choice* of Israel above other peoples, or the lasting *covenant* that God made with Israel, or God's *holiness* manifest in the world, or the *promise* which runs through both Old and New Testaments.

Both those who emphasize the historical nature of Israel's traditions, and those who emphasize its proclamation of God's relationship, emphasize important truths, and to select one exclusively over the other would be to lose much of the power of the Scriptures. Israel was an intensely *historical* people; and more so than any of its neighbors, it was conscious of where it had come from and what had happened to it in different moments of its past. But it made that awareness of history alive by announcing the continual praises of God, and in living an established way of life that challenged every new generation.

The only fair candidate for a single dominant theme in the Old Testament would be the *person of God.* The implied questions— "Who is God?" "What does God do?" "Why does God do it?"—fill every page and every level of tradition in the Bible. Naturally, the Old Testament is also the story of the people Israel, for this one God interacted with them, and they began to understand God through their experience as a people. But it is not primarily the story of God and Israel *alone.* Although the people remembered what God had done for them, they also spoke about what God does for the *whole* world and all its nations. The Bible testifies to the universal greatness and love of God. Israel made no claim that God acted only on its behalf, nor did it insist that its knowledge of God was *entirely* special and revealed only to itself. In several passages of the Bible, Israel acknowledges the insights *other peoples* have had by borrowing their language and thoughts. One example is the flood story of Genesis 6–9, another is the description of God as Lord of the storm like Baal, found in Psalm 29.

Because Israel had a strong sense of God's special intervention into its history, it saw its duty both to *remember* the wonderful things God had done for it alone and to *proclaim* and affirm the truth about this God to the whole world.

The Only God

Thus the *first and most important* theological theme found in the Old Testament is that *God is one.* This may seem like a small statement, but it governs everything. Israel lived in a world with many competing gods and many debased ideas about divine power. The polytheism of its neighbors was based on an attempt to understand the forces of nature and the mysteries of life that faced humans every day. Why is there drought, sickness and death? How do we find blessing of good crops, children, security and peace? The common answer was to recognize different divine powers everywhere, often with competing aims and attitudes toward human beings. The means of relating to these gods was, in effect, to *manipulate* them into doing what we needed or wanted. Elaborate rituals and rites that *imitated* the force of storms or the generating acts of sex gradually led to an attitude toward divine beings as glorified humans complete with all our envies, pettiness, moods and self-interest. The world and its gods were nearly identical. In contrast, Israel insisted on a single divine being who ordered and controlled everything out of love for the goodness of creation. The creation story in Genesis 1 makes this clear. And God never acted from whims nor tolerated immoral behavior as part of worship—Genesis 2 and 3 make this clear. Nor were there to be any rivals nor struggles of other forces threatening to overwhelm God—the flood in Genesis 6 and the tower of Babel story in Genesis 11 make this clear. Above all, this God ruled human history and actively guided, protected, cared for and was involved in human affairs—the whole Bible tells this story. It affirms everywhere that God was never to be confused with the created things of the world. The Old Testament returns again and again to the themes that God is *holy,* God is *King.* God is *Shepherd* or *Father,* God is *Creator*—always to emphasize the transcendence of God. God is near the world but never of it. As Jeremiah 23:23 puts it, "Am I a God nearby, says the Lord, and not a God far away?" "Do I not fill heaven and earth?" Perhaps the highest point in Old Testament theology is reached in the famous prayer of Deuteronomy 6 on this very point: "Hear, O Israel, the Lord our God is one Lord, and you shall love the Lord your God with all your heart and with all your spirit and with all your power."

God Active in History

This brings us right to the heart of the *second important theological theme* in the Old Testament. God is an actor in history. Israel is literally created by the action of God. God reveals that history is not neutral, but is a stage for the discovery of the *self-revealing* God. Israel thus proclaims that pagan ideas of circular time, those unending repeating cycles of events in which nothing is every really new, must be discarded for good. History is *ever new,* it moves ahead, and we can grow better or worse in it, and we can certainly learn from it. This insight flows from the worship and adoration of a transcendent God. If God is not merely part of nature, tied to its ups and downs and its wet seasons and dry, God can act *upon* it. Some years ago, the term "salvation history" for the Old Testament was very popular. It expressed the sense that Israel remembered and learned from those moments when God acted in the events which were most crucial to its past existence. But theologians are now less willing to use that term, because it fails to call attention to the vital element of worship and philosophizing that makes up a large part of what the Bible says of itself. At the same time, we should not totally lose sight of this "salvation history" approach because it underscores Israel's breakthrough insight that God not only *cares about* humans but operates in a carefully *ordered* and loving way for the *good* of humans—and always has.

Above all, this insight into divine activity declares that God was a *Liberator and Savior.* He delivers the patriarchs Abraham, Isaac and Jacob; he saves Moses and the slaves at the Red Sea; he hears the cry of the poor and listens to them in the psalms; he frees his servant who gives witness through suffering in the Book of Isaiah; he pleads with Israel to return and change its heart and be liberated in Hosea and Jeremiah. There is perhaps no stronger theme anywhere in the biblical tradition than this one. It forms the background for understanding the New Testament proclamation of Jesus; it is the *central motif* of the later themes of *messiah* and *hope.* And it certainly has vital ramifications for our world today.

Personal Response and Prayer

The *third important theological theme,* which follows from the second about God as *actor* in *time,* asserts the necessity of *human response* to what God does. The Old Testament never accepts that a worship of God can be adequate which is grateful only for the preservation and daily working of nature. Ours is a personal God who demands from us a *personal* response of friendship, loyalty, obedience, and communication. In Scripture this truth takes many forms. It can be seen in the passages that recognize God's "glory" in the world, or in the temple in Jerusalem, and that lead Israel to awe and wonder. It takes shape in the spirit of trust and even complaints freely offered that form the fabric of the psalms. It makes possible the existence of the great prophets who not only speak in God's name but watch over and *insist upon* concrete replies by Israel in both deeds and words. The very creation of the Bible as a sacred book stems from the awareness that Israel must express itself fully before God—both in the telling of its story and in the constant praise of the living and present God in its midst, and even in the rather bold and daring questioning by wisdom writers who seek to understand their relationship with God more deeply.

Our *fourth theme* is really a concrete application of this human response—*prayer*—or the *praise of God*. The Bible is history and catechetics, speculative thought and poetry and entertaining tales and much more, but all of it is praise of God. Israel was a community that learned to place its purpose and hopes and self-understanding only in God. So when we read the Scriptures, we should not consider just the psalms as our prayer. *All of the biblical text* tells the glory of God. It is not always easy to see praise of a good God in the violence of Joshua or Judges, or in the doubts of a Job and an Ecclesiastes; but Israel saw God present in blessing even there, and could still pray in the midst of a very real sense of curse all around them. Today many people would like to blot out the harshness of human sin and divorce God from it, and demand of God an end to injustice before they give praise. Instead, the Bible teaches us something about our continual need to struggle for what is right while proclaiming that only God can accomplish it.

Covenant and Tradition

The *fifth theological theme* might be called *community* and *covenant*. The Old Testament came into existence as the remembering by an on-going community who received what had been the testimony of others and took responsibility for it. Above all, they clung stubbornly to a conviction that God had indeed entered into a special relationship of *covenant* with them—a covenant that established bonds of loyalty and responsibility between God and humanity in the person of Israel. Chapter 9 explained much about the nature of a covenant. It is our task now to recognize how this formed and preserved the true *inner bond* of Israel as a *community* which maintained a profound respect for the worth and love of the neighbor—as Leviticus 19:18 points out so strongly when it demands *love of neighbor* as much as of oneself.

A *sixth important theme* follows from the last one. Israel is above all a people of *tradition* and *institutions*. It is *torah*, "teaching" or, even better, "way of life." Israel does not shrink from including sacrifice laws and regulations about bodily ailments and sanitary practices right next to moral and ethical demands for justice and humility and caring. The Old Testament is a rather awkward collection of materials because it reflects *all* the different sides of life in community. We should keep in mind that the traditions come from a very long period of time, at least a thousand years, and probably much more. Anyone who has seen the musical "Fiddler on the Roof" knows the importance of tradition to keeping alive a sense of community in a difficult and often hostile world.

The greatness of biblical revelation is that it uses the structure of society to help a community function religiously, but at the same time moves beyond these structures. Thus Israel could demand of its kings a *fidelity* and *obedience* to God's law that no other Near Eastern monarch had to face. Or it could demand from individual tribes a cooperation and submission of their own purposes for the good of all Israel. When the Assyrians destroyed the northern kingdom of ten tribes, the rest could move on to a new understanding that God worked even when you did not have the promised land to live in; and when the temple and king were destroyed by the Babylonians, they moved on to perceive that these too could be dispensed with, and that God would now act in new ways. The Scriptures themselves are written so that Israel can be freed from any single human social structure or government or land and continue to meditate and proclaim the *enduring covenant* through time.

The Prophets and Justice

A *significant seventh theme* that follows from an honest wrestling with Israel's sense of concrete existence in the world is found in the *tension between God's will and our often sinful and selfish response.* Israel was no pollyanna that thought of human nature as always good and God as always forgiving of any and every fault. The Israelites never failed to proclaim God to be a God of mercy, as Exodus 34 expresses it, "slow to anger and rich in kindness," but they tempered it with a true awareness of *justice.* God does indeed make demands on the community, demands that they be *like* God. If the claim of Genesis 1:26 means anything when it says that humans are made in the image and likeness of God, it means that we too have moral choice and moral responsibility. Leviticus 19 insists over and over that Israel obey God's laws because God is *holy.* If God indeed faithfully treats the world in an ethical and right fashion, acting solely out of love and goodness, then the *proper* human response must be in kind.

This explains the central vitality of *prophecy* to the Old Testament tradition. The prophets are the *ethical watchdogs* par excellence. They should not be seen only as radical innovators or rebels against the laws and traditions. They recalled tradition to the people, showing them how God had acted in the past, and what the covenant had taught, and insisting that Israel not forget the freedom of God to act in new ways or the faithfulness of God that would not overlook repeated violations of the covenant. The prophetic word indeed stands in judgment on Israel's behavior only because Israel *forgets.* Ethics is therefore not divorced from the great sense of tradition but stands within it. There is no picture of God in the Hebrew Scriptures, unlike in many of the pagan myths and prayers, that ever *forgets* that he is a God of *action* who demands *actions* in return. God always acted rightly, and all Israel must act rightly because they remember as their sacred duty what God is. "Forgetting" negates the meaning of history and establishes evil practices because they seem helpful or useful for our present desires. Prophecy challenges these. As a result, prophecy has often been seen as the highlight of Old Testament revelation, and perhaps it is, but, if so, only because it roots itself forcefully in the covenant and narratives of the Pentateuchal revelation.

Hope and the Future

The office of the prophet as watchdog and critic and challenger of Israel's evil ways is balanced by the fact that the prophetic office also brings comfort and hope in times of trouble and loss. This is itself an *eighth theological* theme: *hope* and *optimism* about the future. Biblical theologians often speak about "eschatology" in the Bible and mean by it the dynamic expectation that God will act in the future. This is not just the natural assumption that he will work tomorrow as he did today, but the much greater confidence that God has all of time and human history under a plan and that there will be moments of profound change when he intervenes. This conviction took shape in any number of crisis moments facing Israel in the Old Testament—the rise of the kings in the tenth century, the loss of northern Israel and ten of 12 tribes in the eighth century, and the loss of land, temple, king and independence in the sixth century. Never in any of these crises did Israel come to the conclusion that God would *not act* again. They interpreted disasters as punishment for their own evil for the most part, and the prophets frequently warned the people that God had future punishment in mind if they would not *convert* their ways. But there always remained a conviction, even when the prophets used the most absolute and damning language condemning Israel, that God would *renew* or *restore* because above all God was faithful.

This led to the hope of a *messiah,* a figure sent by God, greater than any king of the past, who would bring about the full flowering of Israel. Such hopes were really quite late in the Old Testament period and are only mildly reflected in the actual books of the Bible—an example is Daniel—but were very common among other writings and in Jewish groups just before the time of Christ. As Christians think of the Old Testament's relation to the New, they must be careful not simply to say that Jesus *fulfilled* all the unfulfilled messianic words of the Hebrew Scriptures. Jesus acted differently than even the Old Testament expected and revealed what the Israelites always knew through the prophets—God *does not do* what you hope for; he acts in new and surprising ways. We cannot expect it, but we must know God well enough to *accept it.*

The sense of hope should be coupled with *another theme—the goodness of the world* and of the creation that God has made. Hope is rooted ultimately in the knowledge of a good God. Israel has many beautiful passages in its Scriptures that express this deep conviction of God's majestic power and blessing on all of creation. It can be found in the creation story of Genesis 1 and 2 in the blessing that God brings on the earth, and the fact that for each day of the creation story, God "saw that it was good." It can be seen in the blessing and promise themes to Noah, Abraham, Isaac and Jacob, in the wisdom poems of Job 28 or Proverbs 8 or Sirach 24, and in the overwhelming imagery of praise in the Book of Psalms.

Many scholars wondered why the Bible had so little to say of an *afterlife.* Only in one of the latest books of the Bible, Daniel, does such a belief emerge clearly. Perhaps Israel focused itself so strongly on the covenant with the *now-community* that it had little room for wondering how that bond could be continued after death. But eventually the radical belief that *God was good* without fail—from beginning to ultimate end—led to an equal assertion that God could raise the dead who had suffered unjustly—could preserve the faithful Israelite into the life to come. It remains a minor theme in the Hebrew Scriptures but takes a much more central place in light of the resurrection of Jesus.

The Mystery of God's Ways

Finally, we should conclude with a *last theme of importance:* the Bible is *wisdom.* Wisdom books are not just appendages but form a very important layer of tradition that affirms that God made humans *rational and free,* with divine powers of *searching* and *choosing* and behaving ethically. Wisdom writings boost the goodness of being human and seek to explore dimensions of God and the problem of relating to God that troubled everyone. Israel never developed philosophers like the Greeks who exalted human reason as a power that answers to nothing but itself. Israel maintained that the *search* for wisdom *must be done* in awe and fear of the Lord. Greeks were skeptical of how the gods could actually interact with the created world. Israel *never doubted* how active and directly present God was to the world. Israel's wisdom thinkers instead turned the believers' questions and difficult problems of suffering and inequalities among people toward the *mystery of existence.* God's ways were not our ways, and while we can see God at work we cannot understand with our insights the what or why. But covenant love for the one God demanded both proper reverence for divine transcendence and bountiful hope for divine nearness.

The legacy of the biblical traditions of Israel that have been brought together in the Scriptures is a *combination* of divine *nearness* and *distant* greatness, of intimate, individual love side by side with reasonable, orderly governance. These ten theological themes help bring this out about the God of Israel. Continued reading and study of the Old Testament will serve to nourish these truths more deeply and to open up innumerable *other aspects* of our relationship to God.

STUDY QUESTIONS

1. What would you describe as the central theme of the Old Testament? Is there one? Why?

2. Describe some important and major theological themes contained in the Old Testament. What does one learn about God by reading the Old Testament?
3. What is the special role of prophets?
4. What value and benefit do you see in reading and studying the Old Testament? Does it enhance your religious experience and understanding? How?

TABLE OF ABBREVIATIONS

ANE	The Ancient Near East: An Anthology of Texts and Pictures, edited by James Pritchard.
ANEP	The Ancient Near East in Pictures, edited by James Pritchard.
ANET	Ancient Near Eastern Texts relating to the Old Testament, edited by James Pritchard.
IDBS	Interpreter's Dictionary of the Bible, Supplement Volume.
JB	The Jerusalem Bible.
NAB	The New American Bible.
NEB	The New English Bible.
OT	Old Testament.
RSV	Revised Standard Version of the Bible.

READING LIST AND STUDY GUIDE

OLD TESTAMENT COMMENTARIES

Old Testament Message: A Biblical-Theological Commentary (Wilmington, Del.: Michael Glazier, 1982–1984). The best popular commentary series available today.

Collegeville Old Testament Commentary (Collegeville, Minn.: Liturgical Press, 1984). Handy, short commentaries on individual books.

The Anchor Bible (New York: Doubleday, 1964ff). A thorough and more advanced commentary series with much textual and critical information.

Old Testament Library (Philadelphia: Westminster Press). In this series are many individual commentaries on Old Testament books, many of them translations of the best European scholarship.

Jerome Biblical Commentary (Englewood Cliffs, N.J.: Prentice-Hall, 1968). A fine, one-volume commentary for general use, but now somewhat old. It has excellent articles on major biblical questions.

Toward Understanding the Old Testament (Mahwah, N.J.: Paulist Press, 1983). Audio tapes for study of the Old Testament book by book.

INTRODUCTIONS TO THE OLD TESTAMENT

Anderson, B.W., *Understanding the Old Testament* (4th revised edition; Englewood Cliffs, N.J.: Prentice Hall, 1985). Standard textbook used in many seminaries and colleges for introductory courses.

Barclay, William, *Introducing the Bible* (Nashville: Abingdon Press, 1972). A very readable start into study of the Bible.

Jensen, Joseph, O.S.B., *God's Word to Israel* (revised edition; Wilmington, Del.: Michael Glazier, 1982). The best Catholic introduction available today.

RESOURCE BOOKS

Pritchard, James, *Ancient Near Eastern Texts Relating to the Old Testament* (Princeton, N.J.: Princeton Univ. Press, 1969). The third edition has almost all ancient texts one could hope for in comparing Israel to the Ancient Near East culture.

Pritchard, James, *The Ancient Near East in Pictures* (Princeton, N.J.: Princeton Univ. Press, 1969). The revised edition has the photographs and charts to accompany the preceding volume.

Pritchard, James, *The Ancient Near East: An Anthology of Texts and Pictures* (Princeton, N.J.: Princeton Univ. Press, 1965). A two-volume paperback summary of the most important items from the two preceding volumes.

Interpreter's Dictionary of the Bible (Nashville: Abingdon Press, 1962). Edited by George Buttrick and others, this is a four volume work with a recent supplement that is the best available resource for biblical study.

McKenzie, John, *Dictionary of the Bible* (Milwaukee: Bruce, 1965). Excellent one-volume dictionary of all important words and ideas in the Old Testament.

Rad, Gerhard von, *Old Testament Theology* (New York: Harper and Row; 2 vols.: 1962 and 1965). Excellent theological treatment of Israel's faith and the development of its traditions.

History of Israel

Bright, John, *A History of Israel* (Philadelphia: Westminster Press, 1981; 3rd edition). Excellent treatment of the historical problems of the Old Testament.

Herrmann, Siegfried, *A History of Israel in Old Testament Times* (Philadelphia: Fortress Press, 1981). An excellent history from a German scholar's perspective.

ARCHAEOLOGY AND GEOGRAPHY OF THE BIBLE (CHAPTERS 2–3)

Aharoni, Yohanon, *The Archaeology of the Land of Israel* (Philadelphia: Westminster Press, 1982). Very readable presentation.

Aharoni, Y. and Avi-Yonah, M., *The Macmillan Bible Atlas* (New York: Macmillan, 1968). The best atlas for maps and explanations of historical problems.

Baly, Denis, *The Geography of the Bible* (Revised edition; New York: Harper and Row, 1974). Best in-depth treatment of the major geographical-historical questions of the Bible.

Cornfeld, Gaalyahu, *Archaeology of the Bible Book by Book* (New York: Harper and Row, 1976). Gives whatever archaeological finds help illuminate a passage—quite useful.

Hoppe, Leslie, O.F.M., *What Are They Saying About Biblical Archaeology?* (Mahwah, N.J.: Paulist Press; 1984). Illustrates the current problems of the Bible and archaeology with concrete cases.

Lance, H. Darrell, *The Old Testament and the Archaeologist* (Philadelphia: Fortress Press, 1981). A good treatment of the values and limits of archaeology in understanding the Bible.

BIBLICAL METHOD (CHAPTERS 4–5)

Alter, Robert, *The Art of Biblical Narrative* (New York: Basic Books; 1981). Good on the often-forgotten artistry of the Bible.

Brown, Raymond, S.S., *The Critical Meaning of the Bible* (Ramsey, N.J.: Paulist Press, 1981). The questions of interpretation that a Church believer must face in reading the Scriptures.

Cazelles, Henri, "Biblical Criticism of the Old Testament," *Interpreter's Dictionary of the Bible, Supplement* (hereafter *IDBS*), pp. 98–102. Survey of the modern problem is the best.

Habel, Norman, *Literary Criticism of the Old Testament* (Philadelphia: Fortress Press, 1971). This is the most helpful guide to understanding how source criticism is done.

Rast, Walter, *Tradition History and the Old Testament* (Philadelphia: Fortress Press, 1972). Companion to Habel for tradition criticism.

Tucker, Gene, *Form Criticism of the Old Testament* (Philadelphia: Fortress Press, 1971). Another guide similar to the previous two.

THE PENTATEUCH (CHAPTERS 6–9)

Brueggemann, W. and Wolff, W., *The Vitality of Old Testament Traditions* (Atlanta: John Knox Press, 1975). The very best summary of the four major Pentateuchal sources, J, E, P and D.

Bailey, Lloyd, *The Pentateuch* (Nashville: Abingdon Press, 1981). Readable and easy introduction to the Pentateuchal problems.

Clines, David, J.A., *The Theme of the Pentateuch* (Sheffield, England: Journal for the Study of the Old Testament Supplement series, 1978). An excellent search for the theological center of the Pentateuch.

Haran, M., "The Exodus," *IDBS,* pp. 304–310.

L'Heureux, Conrad, *In and Out of Paradise* (Mahwah, N.J.: Paulist Press, 1983). A very readable explanation of Genesis 1–11.

McCarthy, Dennis, S.J., *Old Testament Covenant: A Survey of Current Opinions* (Atlanta: John Knox Press, 1972). Good overview of the elements in ancient covenant thinking.

Newman, Murray, *The People of the Covenant* (Nashville: Abingdon Press, 1962). Treats how Israel became a nation after the exodus.

Vawter, Bruce, *On Genesis: A New Reading* (New York: Doubleday, 1977). A comprehensive treatment of the Book of Genesis.

THE HISTORICAL BOOKS AND RELIGION OF ISRAEL (CHAPTERS 10–13)

Albright, William Foxwell, *Yahweh and the Gods of Canaan* (New York: Doubleday, 1968). Excellent on Canaanite religion.

Craighie, Peter, *Ugarit and the Old Testament* (Grand Rapids: Eerdmans, 1983). A general survey of Ugaritic and Canaanite connections to the Bible.

Gottwald, Norman, *The Tribes of Yahweh* (New York: Orbis Books, 1979). Most thorough investigation of the period of the judges with arguments for internal revolution within Canaan.

Hayes, J. and Miller, J. Maxwell, *Israelite and Judean History* (Philadelphia: Westminster Press, 1977). A scholarly reconsideration of our historical knowledge of Israel.

Kraus, Hans-Joachim, *Worship in Israel* (Atlanta: John Knox Press, 1966). Very competent overview of Israel's religious practice.

McKenzie, John L., article on "Kingship" in *Dictionary of the Bible* (Milwaukee: Bruce, 1965). Very well done summary.

Ringgren, Helmer, *Israelite Religion* (Philadelphia: Fortress Press, 1966). Good treatment of religious practice in Israel.

Vaux, Roland de, *Ancient Israel* (New York: McGraw-Hill, 1961). A detailed treatment of all aspects of Israelite daily life.

THE PSALMS (CHAPTER 14)

Anderson, A.A., *The Book of Psalms* (London: Nelson, 1972). Two volumes of the New Century Bible—detailed yet readable.

Anderson, B.W., *Out of the Depths: The Psalms Speak for Us Today* (Philadelphia: Westminster Press, 1982, revised edition). A very meditative yet informative introduction to study of the Psalms.

Guthrie, Harvey, *Israel's Sacred Songs* (New York: Seabury Press, 1966). An introductory approach to study of the Psalms.

Stuhlmueller, Carroll, *Psalms 1, Psalms 2* (Wilmington, Del.: Michael Glazier, 1983). The most recent and update commentary from a theological perspective.

THE PROPHETS (CHAPTERS 15–18)

Blenkinsopp, Joseph, *A History of Prophecy in Israel* (Philadelphia: Westminster Press, 1983). A good, but higher-level introduction.

Boadt, Lawrence, *Jeremiah 1–25*, and *Jeremiah 26–52, Habakkuk, Zephaniah and Nahum* (Wilmington, Del.: Michael Glazier, 1982, 1983). A literary and theological explanation of the Book of Jeremiah and the crisis of the exile.

Buss, Martin J., "Prophecy in Ancient Israel," *IDBS*, pp. 894–897. A good survey of current thinking.

Freedman, David Noel, "Deuteronomic History," *IDBS*, pp. 226–228. An update on current scholarly research on the Deuteronomist.

Huffmon, H.B., "Prophecy in the Ancient Near East," *IDBS*, pp. 697–700. Summary of what is known of prophecy outside of Israel.

Koch, Klaus, *The Prophets* (2 vols.; Philadelphia: Fortress Press, 1982, 1983). Good on asking the whys and whats of prophecy.

Lindblom, Johannes, *Prophecy in Ancient Israel* (New York: Oxford University Press, 1962). Best sociological study of prophecy.

Lohfink, Norbert, "Deuteronomy," *IDBS*, pp. 229–232. Update on research into the Book of Deuteronomy.

Rad, Gerhard von, *The Message of the Prophets* (New York: Harper and Row, 1968). Excellent theological textbook on prophecy.

Scott, R.B.Y., *The Relevance of the Prophets* (New York: Macmillan, 1967). Older treatment but by far the most readable.

Winward, Stephen, *A Guide to the Prophets* (Atlanta: John Knox Press, 1976). A brief but thorough treatment of each prophet.

EXILIC AND POST-EXILIC PERIOD (CHAPTERS 19–22)

Ackroyd, Peter, *Exile and Restoration* (Philadelphia: Westminster Press, 1968). A very thorough treatment of the exile.

Clifford, Richard, S.J., *Fair-Spoken and Persuading* (Ramsey, N.J.: Paulist Press, 1984). Newest treatment of Second Isaiah with major attention to literary genius of the author.

Levine, Baruch, "Priestly Writers," *IDBS*, pp. 683–687. A good survey of current opinion on the role of the priestly writers on the formation of the Pentateuch and other books.

Muilenburg, James, "Isaiah 40–66," in the *Interpreter's Bible* (Vol. 5; Abingdon Press, 1956), pp. 381–773. The brilliant commentary of the master of understanding Hebrew literary art.

Raitt, Thomas, *A Theology of Exile* (Philadelphia: Fortress Press, 1977). Gives special attention to Jeremiah and the deuteronomic theology in the exile.

Zimmerli, Walther, *Ezechiel* (Philadelphia: Fortress Press, 1979, 1984). Two volumes in the Hermeneia commentary series. The most thorough study of Ezekiel ever done.

WISDOM LITERATURE (CHAPTER 23)

Boadt, Lawrence, *Wisdom Literature and Proverbs* (Collegeville, Minn.: Liturgical Press, 1986). Popular introduction to wisdom.

Crenshaw, James, *Old Testament Wisdom: An Introduction* (Atlanta: John Knox Press, 1981). General introduction to wisdom.

Gordis, Robert, *The Book of Job* (New York: Ktav Press, 1978). A very thorough and scholarly treatment of Job.

McKane, William, *Proverbs: A New Approach* (Philadelphia: Westminster Press, 1970). The most complete commentary on Proverbs available.

Rad, Gerhard von, *Wisdom in Israel* (Nashville: Abingdon Press, 1972). The classic theological treatment of wisdom.

Scott, R.B.Y., *The Way of Wisdom in the Old Testament* (New York: Macmillan, 1971). Getting old, but wearing well as a readable introduction to wisdom.

LATER DEVELOPMENTS AND APOCALYPTIC (CHAPTERS 24–26)

Charles, R.H., *The Apocrypha and Pseudepigrapha of the Old Testament in English* (2 vols; New York: Oxford University Press, 1913). The standard translation and notes on non-biblical books.

Charlesworth, James, editor, *The Old Testament Pseudepigrapha: Apocalyptic Literature and Testaments* (New York: Doubleday, 1983). A completely new and updated edition of the non-biblical materials of Jewish literature.

Rivkin, E., "Messiah: Jewish," *IDBS* pages 588–591. A good survey on current thinking about messianism in the Old Testament.

Russell, D.S., *Apocalyptic Ancient and Modern* (Philadelphia: Fortress Press, 1978). A very good explanation of apocalyptic literature.

Vermes, Geza, "The Dead Sea Scrolls," *IDBS*, pages 210–219. A survey of the present information on the scrolls and their importance.

INDEX OF MAPS,
CHARTS, ILLUSTRATIONS,
& SUPPLEMENTAL TEXTS

AUTHOR INDEX

Aharoni, Yohanon, 203
Albright, William Foxwell, 201
Alt, Albrecht, 203
Astruc, Jean, 81, 92–3

Botta, Emile, 59
Budde, Karl, 83
Bultmann, Rudolf, 538

Champollion, Jean-Francois, 53

Delitzsch, Franz, 53–4

Eliade, Mircea, 78–9

Gottwald, Norman, 203
Gunkel, Hermann, 84,106

Herodotus, 36, 432
Heschel, Abraham, 366

Jerome, 75, 92, 453

Josephus, 92, 435, 438, 503, 504,
    522, 524, 529, 535–6

Layard, Austen Henry, 59

Mendenhall, George, 203
Michener, James, 496–7

Noth, Martin, 203

Parrot, Andre, 62
Petrie, William Flinders, 58-9
Philo, 92, 522, 529
Pius XII, Pope, 13, 70, 87

Rawlinson, Henry, 53

Schliemann, Heinrich, 59
Simon, Richard, 92
Smith, George, 53

Von Rad, Gerhard, 538

Wellhausen, Julius, 82–3, 94–7,
    106, 107–8

Yadin, Yigael, 201

SUBJECT INDEX